W9-BDH-212

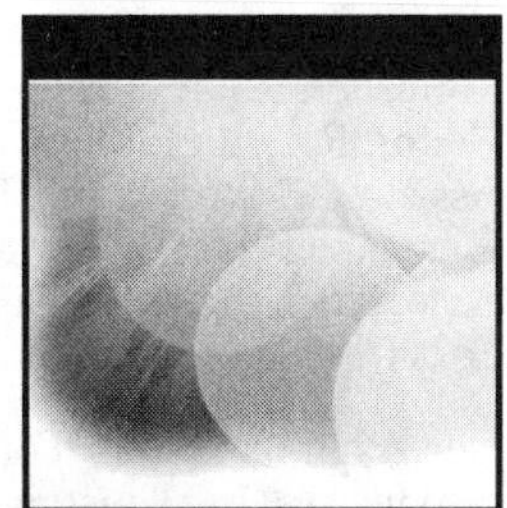

# Java Programming with CORBA

## Advanced Techniques for Building Distributed Applications

Gerald Brose
Andreas Vogel
Keith Duddy

**Third Edition**

**Wiley Computer Publishing**

**John Wiley & Sons, Inc.**

NEW YORK • CHICHESTER • WEINHEIM • BRISBANE • SINGAPORE • TORONTO

Publisher: Robert Ipsen
Editor: Robert M. Elliott
Assistant Editor: Emilie Herman
Managing Editor: John Atkins
Associate New Media Editor: Brian Snapp
Text Design & Composition: North Market Street Graphics

Designations used by companies to distinguish their products are often claimed as trademarks. In all instances where John Wiley & Sons, Inc., is aware of a claim, the product names appear in initial capital or ALL CAPITAL LETTERS. Readers, however, should contact the appropriate companies for more complete information regarding trademarks and registration.

Java and all Java-based trademarks and logos are trademarks or registered trademarks of Sun Microsystems, Inc. in the U.S. or other countries, and are used under license.

OMG marks and logos are trademarks or registered trademarks, service marks and/or certification marks of Object Management Group, Inc. registered in the United States.

This book is printed on acid-free paper. ♾

Copyright © 2001 by Gerald Brose, Andreas Vogel, Keith Duddy. All rights reserved.

Published by John Wiley & Sons, Inc.

Published simultaneously in Canada.

No part of this publication may be reproduced, stored in a retrieval system or transmitted in any form or by any means, electronic, mechanical, photocopying, recording, scanning, or otherwise, except as permitted under Sections 107 or 108 of the 1976 United States Copyright Act, without either the prior written permission of the Publisher, or authorization through payment of the appropriate per-copy fee to the Copyright Clearance Center, 222 Rosewood Drive, Danvers, MA 01923, (978) 750-8400, fax (978) 750-4744. Requests to the Publisher for permission should be addressed to the Permissions Department, John Wiley & Sons, Inc., 605 Third Avenue, New York, NY 10158-0012, (212) 850-6011, fax (212) 850-6008, E-Mail: PERMREQ@WILEY.COM.

This publication is designed to provide accurate and authoritative information in regard to the subject matter covered. It is sold with the understanding that the publisher is not engaged in professional services. If professional advice or other expert assistance is required, the services of a competent professional person should be sought.

***Library of Congress Cataloging-in-Publication Data:***

Brose, Gerald.
Java programming with CORBA : advanced techniques for building distributed applications / Gerald Brose, Andreas Vogel, Keith Duddy.
p. cm.
ISBN 0-471-37681-7 (paper/website)
1. Java (Computer program language) 2. CORBA (Computer architecture)
I. Vogel, Andreas, 1965– II. Duddy, Keith, 1967– III. Title.

QA76.73.J38 B77 2001
005.2'762—dc21 00-066246

Printed in the United States of America.

10 9 8 7 6 5 4 3 2 1

# Advance Praise for Java Programming with CORBA, Third Edition

I'm delighted that the authors have revised this influential text on using Java and CORBA together. This was one of the first books on exploiting the complimentary strengths of these two powerful technologies, and it remains one of the best. The CORBA and Java specifications have evolved and grown closer in the four years since the first edition, even as their use progressed from laboratory experiments to powering the servers of the New Economy. Today CORBA is included in every Java product, making this new revision even more relevant than before.

***Andrew Watson***
***Vice President and Technical Director***
***Object Management Group***

*Java Programming with CORBA, Third Edition*, is a comprehensive guide, providing readers with updated examples and detailed explanations of using Java with the latest CORBA specification. Changes inherent to CORBA 2.3 are examined and a number of valuable CORBA services are dealt with as well. This book will be invaluable for those who are serious about building distributed applications.

***Michael Cook***
***Executive Director***
***Advanced Network Architecture***
***Telcordia Technologies***

This book is a "must have" for anyone programming with both Java and CORBA. It provides a comprehensive coverage of virtually all features and issues programmers will need to deal with, and includes a large number of vendor-independent example programs. The authors are long-time experts in distributed systems, and that is reflected throughout the book. I certainly plan on using it in my distributed systems courses and CORBA tutorials.

***Dave Bakken***
***Assistant Professor***
***Washington State University***

# OMG Press Advisory Board

Karen D. Boucher
Executive Vice President
The Standish Group

Carol C. Burt
President and Chief Executive Officer
2AB, Inc.

Ian Foster
Business Director
PeerLogic, Inc.

Michael Gurevich
Chief Architect
Concorde Solutions, Inc.

V. "Juggy" Jagannathan, Ph.D.
Senior Vice President of Research and Development and Chief Technology Officer
CareFlow|Net, Inc.

Cris Kobryn
Chief Scientist and Senior Director
Inline Software

Nilo Mitra, Ph.D.
Principal System Engineer
Ericsson

Richard Mark Soley, Ph.D.
Chairman and Chief Executive Officer
Object Management Group, Inc.

Sheldon C. Sutton
Principal Information Systems Engineer
The MITRE Corporation

Andreas Vogel, Ph.D.
CTO
Inprise Corporation

# OMG Press Books in Print

(For complete information about current and upcoming titles, go to www.wiley.com/compbooks.)

- ***Building Business Objects*** by Peter Eeles and Oliver Sims, ISBN: 0471-191760.
- ***Business Component Factory: A Comprehensive Overview of Component-Based Development for the Enterprise*** by Peter Herzum and Oliver Sims, ISBN: 0471-327603.
- ***Business Modeling with UML: Business Patterns at Work*** by Hans-Erik Eriksson and Magnus Penker, ISBN: 0471-295515.
- ***CORBA 3 Fundamentals and Programming, 2nd Edition*** by Jon Siegel, ISBN: 0471-295183.
- ***CORBA Design Patterns*** by Thomas J. Mowbray and Raphael C. Malveau, ISBN: 0471-158828.
- ***Enterprise Application Integration with CORBA: Component and Web-Based Solutions*** by Ron Zahavi, ISBN: 0471-32704.
- ***Enterprise Java with UML*** by CT Arrington, ISBN: 0471-386804

- ***The Essential CORBA: Systems Integration Using Distributed Objects*** by Thomas J. Mowbray and Ron Zahavi, ISBN: 0471-106119.
- ***Instant CORBA*** by Robert Orfali, Dan Harkey and Jeri Edwards, ISBN: 0471-183334.
- ***Integrating CORBA and COM Applications*** by Michael Rosen and David Curtis, ISBN: 0471-198277.
- ***Java Programming with CORBA, Third Edition*** by Gerald Brose, Andreas Vogel, and Keith Duddy, ISBN: 0471-247650.
- ***The Object Technology Casebook: Lessons from Award-Winning Business Applications*** by Paul Harmon and William Morrisey, ISBN: 0471-147176.
- ***The Object Technology Revolution*** by Michael Guttman and Jason Matthews, ISBN: 0471-606790.
- ***Programming with Enterprise JavaBeans, JTS and OTS: Building Distributed Transactions with Java and C++*** by Andreas Vogel and Madhavan Rangarao, ISBN: 0471-319724.
- ***Programming with Java IDL*** by Geoffrey Lewis, Steven Barber and Ellen Siegel, ISBN: 0471-247979.
- ***UML Toolkit*** by Hans-Erik Eriksson and Magnus Penker, ISBN: 0471-191612.

# About the OMG

The Object Management Group (OMG) was chartered to create and foster a component-based software marketplace through the standardization and promotion of object-oriented software. To achieve this goal, the OMG specifies open standards for every aspect of distributed object computing from analysis and design, through infrastructure, to application objects and components.

The well-established CORBA (Common Object Request Broker Architecture) standardizes a platform- and programming-language independent distributed object computing environment. It is based on OMG/ISO Interface Definition Language (OMG IDL) and the Internet Inter-ORB Protocol (IIOP). Now recognized as a mature technology, CORBA is represented on the marketplace by well over 70 ORBs (Object Request Brokers) plus hundreds of other products. Although most of these ORBs are tuned for general use, others are specialized for real-time or embedded applications, or built into transaction-processing systems where they provide scalability, high throughput, and reliability. Of the thousands of live, mission-critical CORBA applications in use today around the world, over 300 are documented on the OMG's success-story Web pages at www.corba.org.

CORBA 3, the OMG's latest release, adds a Component Model, quality-of-service control, a messaging invocation model, and tightened integration with the Internet, Enterprise Java Beans and the Java programming language. Widely anticipated by the industry, CORBA 3 keeps this established architecture in the forefront of distributed computing, as will a new OMG specification integrating CORBA with XML. Well-known for its ability to integrate legacy systems into your network, along with the wide variety of heterogeneous hardware and software on the market today, CORBA enters the new millennium prepared to integrate the technologies on the horizon.

Augmenting this core infrastructure are the CORBAservices, which standardize naming and directory services, event handling, transaction processing, security, and other functions. Building on this firm foundation, OMG Domain Facilities standardize common objects throughout the supply and service chains in industries such as Telecommunications, Healthcare, Manufacturing, Transportation, Finance/Insurance, Electronic Commerce, Life Science, and Utilities.

The OMG standards extend beyond programming. OMG Specifications for analysis and design include the Unified Modeling Language (UML), the repository standard Meta-Object Facility (MOF), and XML-based Metadata Interchange (XMI). The UML is a result of fusing the concepts of the world's most prominent methodologists. Adopted as an OMG specification in 1997, it represents a collection of best engineering practices that have proven successful in the modeling of large and complex systems and is a well-defined, widely accepted response to these business needs. The MOF is OMG's standard for metamodeling and metadata repositories. Fully integrated with UML, it uses the UML notation to describe repository metamodels. Extending this work, the XMI standard enables the exchange of objects defined using UML and the MOF. XMI can generate XML Data Type Definitions for any service specification that includes a normative, MOF-based metamodel.

In summary, the OMG provides the computing industry with an open, vendor-neutral, proven process for establishing and promoting standards. OMG makes all of its specifications available without charge from its Web site, www.omg.org. With over a decade of standard-making and consensus-building experience, OMG now counts about 800 companies as members. Delegates from these companies convene at week-long meetings held five times each year at varying sites around the world, to advance OMG technologies. The OMG welcomes guests to their meetings; for an invitation, send your email request to info@omg.org.

Membership in the OMG is open to end users, government organizations, academia and technology vendors. For more information on the OMG, contact OMG headquarters by phone at +1-508-820 4300, by fax at +1-508-820 4303, by email at info@omg.org, or on the Web at www.omg.org.

*To Christine, Johannes, and Julius,*
*who patiently spent all those weekends alone.*

# Contents

# Foreword to the First Edition

The meteoric rise of the World Wide Web (dragging along with it the 25-year-old "overnight success" of the Internet) has managed, as I write this, to mask a pertinent fact: to wit, the Web is full of trash. Given the fantastic rate at which the Web continues to grow, it is truly impossible to estimate the average number of Web pages that have any intrinsic value, but any guess of that percentage above even my own inflated shoe size is likely to be too high.

Nevertheless, there is an amazing amount of value on the Web, from deep-space photographs to dictionaries, from world histories to cinematic masterpieces. Why the paradox? The reasons are simple: posting information (regardless of utility) is inexpensive, and the Web is still primarily static. Even Web pages that boast dynamic content tend to consist of lookup mechanisms onto static databases.

The next leap of the Internet will be the wide connection of the popular, simple Web browser–user interface to personal, corporate, national and international legacies not only of data, but of services as well. These services will mirror—in fact, they will be, in many instances—telecommunications services, and also other computerized services, from home electronics management to intercorporate data interchange to international flows of monetary instruments. The urge to standardize on a simple, single-user interface that can be taught to the beginning user—and that can yet be accessible to the power user—is impossible to ignore.

What technological leaps are holding us back from this dream? The primary reason is the poor programming model that underlies most Web services. The server-side Common Gateway Interface, and its logical mirror client-side Common Client Interface, rely on arcane bits of programming lore to be useful. Proprietary replacements exist but, unfortunately, lose the open, portable, interoperable nature of the rest of the Web structure.

Meanwhile, great strides have been made in the related distributed-object computing realm. Systems based on Object Management Architecture (OMA) and in particular CORBA, developed by the members of the Object Management Group, address enterprise integration issues, cross-platform portability and interoperability—but, interestingly enough, not user interfaces.

These two technologies, plus the exciting new programming language and virtual machine design named Java, provide a powerful potential solution to the elusive problem of simple interfaces to complex, distributed enterprise systems. This book presents the most comprehensive yet readable approach to understanding these three important technologies individually and in concert. Java-based CORBA extensions to Web browsers and servers—literally, the general communications devices of the future—are already in use at major banks, manufacturing companies, telecommunications utilities and health-care facilities. This important book brings us a vision of a heterogeneous, but integrated, future system based on these technologies.

***Richard Mark Soley, Ph.D.***
***Object Management Group, Inc.***
***Somewhere over the Atlantic Ocean***

# Foreword to the Second Edition

It takes a strong will and clever foresight to write a technical book about a technology in flux. Yet in the first edition of this book, the authors focused not only on CORBA specification—quite mature at six years old—but on using CORBA from the Java language. At that point, Java itself was only a toddler (even in Internet years), and Java mapping for CORBA was still being considered for standardization. The authors ignored these seemingly pertinent facts and muddled through. And what a glorious muddle! This justly well-received book enlighted tens of thousands on the obvious value of the CORBA/Java merger. In this second edition, they use the now-standardized Java mapping for CORBA, and have expanded their coverage of the integrated layered CORBAservices. They've managed, however, to find a new limb to walk out on, and in this tome cover the evolving worlds of component software and patterns based on Java and CORBA. Not only will readers new to this world enjoy this book, but readers of the first edition will find quite a lot of value as well.

Enjoy the journey!

***Richard Mark Soley, Ph.D.***
***Chairman and Chief Executive Officer***
***Object Management Group, Inc.***
***Lexington, Massachusetts, U.S.A.***

# Foreword to the Third Edition

When last I introduced this book, I focused on the changes that CORBA was undergoing just as the book was due to appear in the marketplace. Those changes were completed successfully, and the authors presciently calculated how such changes would reverberate through the standard. The result was a great step forward for those implementing tried-and-true interoperability solutions based on the CORBA standard.

The authors on this round have decided to take on an even tougher task: to explain the CORBA standard in a context in which the *context itself* is changing. As corporations turn to supporting their surf-in customers as well as their walk-in customers, merging their shiny new Web front-ends with their 40 years of accumulated computer systems technology, this book provides an invaluable guide to using the latest and greatest online technologies, letting CORBA itself provide the connecting role.

I applaud these brave souls, but even more so the reader who has chosen to take on the daunting integration task.

***Richard Mark Soley, Ph.D.***
***Chairman and Chief Executive Officer***
***Object Management Group, Inc.***
***Somewhere over the Pacific Ocean***

# Acknowledgments

In addition to the people mentioned below, we would like to thank those people who helped us in preparing the new edition of this book. First of all, to our editor at Wiley, Robert Elliott, and his assistant Emilie Herman.

Thanks to Gerald's employer, the Computer Science Department at Freie Universität Berlin, and especially his group leader Professor Peter Löhr, who has been very supportive. We want to thank Gerald's colleagues at Freie Universität. Richard Hall, Jürgen Quittek, Daniel Faensen, and Annika Hinze all helped to improve the presentation. Thanks also to Diego Sevilla Ruiz of Universidad de Murcia in Spain who commented on the Components chapter. Special thanks go to Reimo Tiedemann and Sebastian Staamann of Xtradyne Technologies AG for their advice and security expertise.

## Acknowledgments for the Second Edition

First of all, we want to thank those people who assisted us in writing this book. These are our editor at John Wiley & Sons, Robert Elliott, and his assistant Brian Calandra. Thanks also to Erin Singletary and the Wiley production team.

Thanks to Keith's employer, the Distributed Systems Technology Centre (DSTC) in Brisbane, Australia. DSTC's CEO David Barbagallo, Research Director Melfyn Lloyd, and Architecture Unit Leader Kerry Raymond have been very supportive. We owe David Jackson many thanks as he edited and proofread the whole book and very much improved its readability in terms of organization and English expression.

Andreas' colleagues at Visigenic Software have been very supportive. Special thanks go to Jonathan Weedon, George Scott, Wei Chen, Andre Srinivasan, and Dale Lampson.

Several DSTC people helped us resolve technical questions. Thanks for sharing your expertise. The CORBA experts are Kerry Raymond, Douglas Kosovic, Michi Henning, and Mark Fitzpatrick. The Java experts are Ted Phelps and Tim Mansfield. Thanks also to Michael Neville and Derek Thompson, the implementers of DSTC's CORBA Trading Service product.

Gerald Vogt, a student from the University of Stuttgart, spent the second half of 1996 at the DSTC working on his Masters thesis. He worked on the Universal CORBA Client and contributed substantially to Chapter 10. He has now completed his Masters.

We acknowledge the cooperation of the OMG, and in particular Richard Soley.

We would also like to thank the many and diverse participants of the Java ORB course from which the book evolved, our customers and all the many people who contribute to CORBA-related mailing lists and news groups. Their feedback has been very helpful and all their questions have improved the content of the book.

Dorit and Meta: I'm sorry for all the weekends I sat in front of the computer working on the book instead of spending them with you.

# Introduction

This book is about the combination of two of the most important technologies used in modern distributed computing: The Common Object Request Broker Architecture (CORBA) and Java. That this is in fact a powerful combination of technologies will become much clearer in the course of this book. If it wasn't, you would not be reading this book in its third edition now.

This book provides an in-depth presentation of the technology required to successfully use Java and CORBA. We also present some of the powerful high-level object services that you can use to build enterprise-scale distributed applications in Java. If you are a Java developer who wants to make most of CORBA, this book is for you.

## Overview of the Book and Technology

It has often been said that the success of the Java programming language and platform in the recent years is unprecedented. By now, Java as a language is fully established and implementations are available on almost any platform, from supercomputers to embedded devices. In addition to this wide availability, there are indeed a number of good technical reasons which make Java the language of choice in many settings. These include features such as Java's object-oriented concepts, downloadable code and dynamic binding, platform independence, automatic garbage collection, integrated thread support, exception handling, a wide range of libraries etc. One factor that sets it apart from any other language, however, is its unique support for Web-based applications in the form of Applets and Servlets.

CORBA has also been a very successful technology, even if it did not take the world over night. Since the first version of the specification was published by the Object Management Group (OMG) in 1991, CORBA has continuously matured and broadened in scope—and volume. Today, the OMG is the largest computer industry consortium in the world, and hundreds of mission-critical applications depend on CORBA technology.

CORBA is the middleware that provides the integration, standardization and interoperability necessary in today's heterogeneous world. Modern enterprise applications are typically distributed in heterogeneous environments that comprise different hardware platforms, operating systems, databases, and network protocols. They consist of components written in different programming languages and often need to integrate substantial legacy applications that it would be too expensive to rewrite or port. The only way of masking all these differences is by relying on standardized concepts. CORBA supports developing software for these environments by introducing a standard concept of distributed objects, and by clearly separating implementations of these objects from their interfaces through the use of a well-defined Interface Definition Language (IDL).

Java and CORBA are a powerful combination. Java, on the one hand, is an ideal match as an implementation language for CORBA objects because CORBA's object model is conceptually close to that of Java. Moreover, its Web support allows you to build Web-integrated CORBA applications in a convenient way. CORBA, on the other hand, offers highly scalable distributed objects and an extensive set of mature object services. These help to build sophisticated distributed applications that require persistence, transactions, event notifications, and security.

This book is about the marriage of Java and CORBA in the form of Java Object Request Brokers (Java ORBs). We explain both fundamental and advanced CORBA features and how to successfully use them in Java to make the best of this combination. For many CORBA concepts and features there are similar technologies in the Java world. For example, the Java platform defines the Java Naming and Directory Service (JNDI), the Java Message Service (JMS), and Enterprise Java Beans (EJB), which serve similar functions as CORBA's Naming and Notification Services and the CORBA Component Model. When describing CORBA technology, we always compare it with its counterparts in the Java world to provide a clear picture of the application area and the capabilities offered by the technology.

## What's New In the Third Edition

The third edition of this book is a complete revision and a significant extension over the popular second edition. Both the CORBA standard and the Java platform have seen considerable extensions since the second edition. By the time you read this, we expect CORBA 3 to be finally approved and published by the OMG. CORBA 3 is not just a new major version of the CORBA core specification but comprises a whole suite of documents that together make CORBA as a whole more flexible and usable. CORBA 3 combines specifications that address Internet integration, Quality of Service Control, and Components. With the exception of Quality of Service Control, we cover all these aspects and specifications in this book.

The version of the CORBA core that we cover is 2.3, which was the most recent version when this book went to press. It includes important CORBA core technology that was not presented or not covered in detail in the second edition, such as the Portable Object Adapter and Value Types. It also includes an updated version of the IDL/Java language mapping. Other important new technology not covered in the second edition includes Portable Interceptors, the Interoperable Naming Service, the Notification Service, the Persistent State Service, and the CORBA Component Model. All of these technologies are covered here.

## How This Book Is Organized

This book introduces Java ORBs to an audience familiar with the basic concepts of object-oriented programming and distributed systems. It contains chapters that fall into three categories: introduction and background, tutorial, and reference.

Chapter 1 gives the motivation for the use of Java ORBs and outlines the relationship between Java and CORBA in more detail. It explains what Java has to offer CORBA and what benefits CORBA has in store for Java developers.

Chapter 2 is an introduction to CORBA as a whole. It explains the organization of the Object Management Group (OMG) and outlines the specification process. Most importantly, it gives a thorough overview of the CORBA standard and summarizes CORBA 2.3.

Chapter 3 is a general introduction to Java and its object-oriented concepts. It also gives a more detailed overview of Java ORBs and explains the general architecture of Java CORBA applications.

Chapter 4 provides first examples that demonstrate the basic use of Java

ORBs. It explains in detail how a simple client-server program is developed in Java and which steps have to be followed.

A complete overview of the standard mapping from IDL to Java is given in Chapter 5. Chapter 6 documents the Java implementation of the pseudo-IDL interfaces ORB, Portable Object Adapter (POA), and Object.

Chapter 7 introduces two fundamental CORBA Services, the Naming and the Trading Service, which clients use to retrieve object references either by name or by properties. We present detailed examples that demonstrate their use.

Chapter 8 shows how to build applications with Java ORBs using a room booking system as a more comprehensive example. Advanced CORBA features are explained in Chapter 9. They include the Any type and TypeCodes, the Dynamic Invocation Interface (DII) and the Dynamic Skeleton Interface (DSI), the Tie approach for implementing objects, Portable Interceptors, and applet servers.

Chapter 10 is an in-depth tutorial on programming with the Portable Object Adapter (POA). It explains how the different POA policies combine and which POA usage patterns are appropriate in which applications. The chapter presents a complete example application comprising multiple servers to demonstrate POA capabilities.

In Chapter 11, we explain the CORBA Event and Notification Services and how they relate to Java event models, the JavaBeans InfoBus, and the Java Message Service (JMS) API. Event Service and Notification Service usage are demonstrated in detail.

Chapter 12 looks at security aspects of Java/CORBA applications, in particular in an Internet setting. It covers important issues as how to work with firewalls and gives an overview of the CORBA Security Service.

Chapter 13 explains how object state can be made persistent and introduces the new Persistent State Service. It presents the service architecture and the Persistent State Declaration Language (PSDL).

In Chapter 14, we introduce the new CORBA Component Model (CCM). CCM concepts are explained in detail and compared to their counterparts in Enterprise Java Beans (EJB).

Finally, design considerations for performance, scalability, and management of Java/CORBA applications are presented in Chapter 15.

Chapter 2 is a useful reference to the core CORBA specification, as are Chapters 5 and 6 for the Java language mapping and the Java portability interfaces. Chapter 8 is also somewhat of a reference chapter since it documents the interfaces of the CORBA Naming and Trading Services, but it also has tutorial character as it shows how to use these services. Chapters 11 to 14 provide both reference and background material on the services they present, but Chapter 11 again also has tutorial character.

Chapters 4 and 7 to 10 are mainly tutorials, but Chapter 10 is also a useful reference on POA policies.

## Who Should Read This Book

This book is written to be useful to both CORBA beginners and experts, but we assume a basic level of programming experience in an object-oriented programming language. We believe that this book will be most helpful to experienced Java developers who want to learn CORBA, and to CORBA developers who want background information and reference material about the newest CORBA technology.

We recommend to use this book for self-teaching as well as source material for training and university courses. It is highly recommended that users work through the examples provided.

Besides the default approach of reading the book front to back, we suggest the following paths through the book. Beginners should read the book from Chapter 1 to Chapter 4 and then continue with Chapter 7 to the end. Chapters 5 and 6 can be used as references as needed.

Advanced programmers will have experience with Java and CORBA. They can start reading at Chapter 3, but if they have already had some exposure to Java ORBs they can go straight to Chapter 7 and continue from there to Chapter 15.

We expect that experts will use this book as a reference only. They may also look up particular details of ORB implementations in Chapters 5 and 6 and details of POA policies in Chapter 10, and familiarize themselves with the CORBA services using Chapters 7, and 11 to 13. They will also find explanations of advanced features in Chapter 9 and scalability and performance patterns in Chapter 15.

## Tools You Will Need

To work with the examples in this book, you will need Sun Microsystems's Java Development Kit (JDK) version 1.2 or later. The JDK can be downloaded from Sun at http://java.sun.com. Additionally, you need a Java ORB. While a rudimentary Java ORB is part of the JDK, it is not sufficient for the examples in this book. To build the examples, we used both Visibroker 4.0 and JacORB 1.1, but we took care to avoid any proprietary code, so they will run on any compliant Java ORB. The companion Web site contains references to a number of Java ORBs.

Finally, the examples that explain CORBA services require service implementations. If these services are not included with your ORB you need to obtain separate implementations. For example, Visibroker does not come with a Trading Service, and neither Visibroker nor JacORB include implementations of the Notification Service.

An extensive list of CORBA service implementations for Visibroker is PrismTechnology's OpenFusion. We used the OpenFusion implementations for the Trading and Notification Service examples in Chapter 7 and Chapter 11. An evaluation license of OpenFusion can be downloaded from www.prismtechnologies.com/products/openfusion/. Again, the examples in this book do not depend on this particular vendor. Any other standard-compliant service implementation in Java should work just as well. In fact, CORBA interoperability allows you to use even those service implementations that were written in other languages than Java and run on non-Java ORBs. Please consult your ORB vendor to find out about available service implementations.

## What's on the Web Site

The Appendix on the companion Web site lists the complete source code (OMG IDL and Java) of all examples introduced throughout the book. The companion Web site for this book can be found at www.wiley.com/compbooks/brose. The source code on the Web site is organized according to chapters, and should be easy to navigate. In addition, the Web site contains references to Java ORBs.

## Summary

We hope that this book will help you to make the most of your Java/CORBA applications. You will find a detailed introduction to the CORBA world as well as comprehensive background and reference material. Reading through this book, you will learn how to successfully design your applications for performance and scalability, how to configure the POA, use advanced CORBA features such as Portable Interceptors, and make the best use of the object services provided in CORBA environments.

# About the Authors

**Gerald Brose** is a Research Scientist at Freie Universität Berlin, Germany, where he is a member of the Distributed Systems and Software Engineering Group. His research centers on distributed object and CORBA security issues. Gerald has been involved in teaching university courses and has published on distributed computing and security. He is the principal author and maintainer of the Open Source CORBA implementation JacORB.

Gerald completed a master's degree in English Literature and Computer Science in 1994. He is currently working to complete his Ph.D.

Gerald lives with his wife Christine and sons Johannes and Julius in Berlin. When not working or playing with the kids, he enjoys singing in choirs, good books, a glass of red wine, and a game of tennis now and then.

**Andreas Vogel** is founding CTO of mspect, where he uses CORBA and Java for implementing a management system for wireless data networks. Prior to his current engagement, he held a variety of executive, consulting, and research positions, including CTO and VP of development at TapCast Inc., Chief Scientist at Borland/Inprise, Principal Consultant at Visigenic, Principal Research Scientist at the DSTC, and researcher at the Université de Montreal.

He has co-authored *C++ Programming with CORBA* and *Programming with Enterprise JavaBeans, OTS and, JTS*. He also contributed to a number of OMG and ITU/ISO standards.

Andreas grew up and was educated in Germany. He holds a PhD and MSc in Computer Science from Humboldt University at Berlin. After having spent a few years living in Madrid, Montreal, and Brisbane, he now lives with wife Dorit and daughter Meta Hillmann in San Francisco's Mission district.

**Keith Duddy** is a Senior Research Scientist at the Distributed Systems Technology Centre (DSTC) in Brisbane, Australia. He is a project leader of the Pegamento project, which is investigating customizable generation of CORBA and workflow support for enterprise systems from high-level models. He has been involved in the submission of several standards to the OMG, including the Trading Service, Notification Service and Meta-Object Facility, and was the editor of the *UML Profile* for CORBA standard. He currently sits on the OMG's Architecture Board.

Keith completed an honors degree in Computer Science at the University of Queensland in 1989. He has worked in the Australian and European computer industries as a Unix operating systems and network programmer. He has been researching distributed systems at DSTC since 1995.

At night this mild-mannered computer scientist turns into DJ dud, playing eclectic dance music for a "gay and alternative" crowd at two weekly Brisbane dance and performance events organized by a www.lovemachinecorporation.com—the love machine corporation—of which he is one of three principal partners. He currently routes all his OMG standards travel through Sydney to spend time with his partner of 12 years, and fellow DSTC researcher, Tim Mansfield.

# Benefits of Java Programming with CORBA

This book brings together two of the major object models used in distributed computing: the *Common Object Request Broker Architecture* (CORBA) and Java. Each represents a different approach to distributed computing. On one hand, CORBA defines an abstract, inherently distributed object model and provides an infrastructure that enables invocations of operations on these objects as if they were local to the application using them. The implementations of objects can be located anywhere on a network and implemented in any programming language and on any operating system for which implementations of the CORBA infrastructure exist. The heterogeneity between the caller of the operation and its implementation is hidden by the CORBA infrastructure.

Java, on the other hand, is a regular, nondistributed, object-oriented programming language. Its main contribution to distributed computing is the introduction of platform-independent, low-level code that can be dynamically loaded and linked. When it is integrated with World Wide Web protocols and browsers, it results in what are known as *applets*. In this approach, instead of invoking a method on a remote object, the code for the class providing the method is transferred across the network and run locally, and then the method is invoked on a local object instance. Java has been extended with its own version of remote invocations also to support invocation-based distributed computing. This extension is known as Java Remote Method Invocation (RMI).

In 1999, Java was split into three different editions: the Java 2 Standard Edition (J2SE), the Java 2 Micro Edition (J2ME), and the Java 2 Enterprise Edition (J2EE). A subset of the CORBA standard, the basic IDL-based communications mechanism, is part of J2SE. Furthermore, the J2EE standard includes Enterprise JavaBeans (EJB). EJB is a component model for distributed Java programming. The EJB specification mandates RMI as the interface for communication between objects. The initial specification did not define a specific transfer protocol. For the 2.0 version of EJB, CORBA's Internet Inter-ORB Protocol (IIOP) has been selected as the protocol for ensuring interoperability. That makes EJB a component model on top of a Java/CORBA foundation.

Java and CORBA converge when a mapping is defined from CORBA's interface definition language, *OMG IDL*, to Java. When combined with a run-time system that supports this language mapping, the result is a *Java Object Request Broker* (Java ORB). For the remainder of this chapter we discuss this combination of the two paradigms. We explain the advantages of Java for CORBA users and the advantages of CORBA for Java users in sections 1.1 and 1.2. In section 1.3, we also explain the relationship between Java ORBs and RMI.

## 1.1 What Does Java Offer CORBA Programmers?

The main reasons for using a Java language mapping of OMG IDL can be broadly categorized into features unique to the Java programming language and features of Java as a development platform:

- Object-oriented language
- Portability across platforms
- Web integration
- Component model

### 1.1.1 Object-Oriented Programming Language

Java ORBs provide the same functionality as any other ORB. The main language bindings offered by current ORB products are C++, C, COBOL,

ADA, and Smalltalk. In our experience, Java provides a cleaner approach to object-oriented programming than C++, with fewer memory management responsibilities, no pointers, a less confusing syntax, and simpler method resolution rules. Moreover, its language syntax and its object model blend well with IDL. In other words, the IDL language mapping defined by the OMG is conceptually straightforward, so Java programmers are faced with only a moderate set of extensions when compared to other languages.

Additionally, Java provides features not available in C or C++, such as automatic garbage collection and integrated thread support. These features are generally desirable and particularly useful for distributed systems programming, as we shall see throughout this book.

### 1.1.2 Portability of Applications across Platforms

Java programs are highly portable due to the standardized byte-code representation generated by Java compilers. Wide industry support means that compilers and run-time systems for virtually any hardware platform and operating system are available, from smart cards to supercomputers. For improved support for this diversity of environments, Sun Microsystems provides three different editions of the Java 2 platform. The *Micro Edition* targets consumer devices such as pagers, PDAs, or even smart cards. The *Standard Edition* covers the traditional programming language features and JavaBeans, the Java component model. The *Enterprise Edition* provides a server-side component model and framework that together make up a Java Application Server.

The wide availability of the Java platform is a significant advantage over other programming languages because a single source code or compiled byte-code set will be usable on any platform without porting. This makes Java the ideal platform for component programming, as the deployment platform is not determined by hardware or operating systems; the Java platform *is* the deployment platform. Consequently, development and maintenance costs can be significantly reduced.

Java's portability also means that if your Java ORB is implemented entirely in Java, then it is automatically available on any system for which a Java platform exists. Many Java ORBs are indeed implemented entirely in Java. Another big plus of the Java platform is that it already contains a limited CORBA implementation: Java IDL is part of both the Standard and the Enterprise Edition of the Java 2 platform.

## 1.1.3 Web Integration

Java is often referred to as the programming language for the Internet. What does this mean? Basically, it means Java integrates well with both Web browsers and Web servers and thus provides excellent support for the development of Web-based applications. For CORBA applications that need to be integrated with Web infrastructure, Java is the natural choice.

The Java applet model allows the execution of Java code embedded in an HTML page, directly from a Web browser. Due to the varying support for Java in Web browsers and the bandwidth limitation of modem connections, applets have had only limited success in Internet applications. They do, however, play an important role for intranet applications. Typically, the complexity of enterprise applications is higher, requiring a more sophisticated GUI. Their requirements are usually better satisfied with applets than HTML/JavaScript pages. Furthermore, browser problems are overcome by standardization across a company for a specific Web browser product (and version), and bandwidth is not such a critical issue in a corporate LAN.

Furthermore, Java servlets and Java Server Pages (JSP) are becoming the most popular way of creating dynamic Web content. The architecture and design of Java servlets is superior to the Web server's traditional Common Gateway Interface (CGI) or other proprietary APIs. Servlets (JSPs are eventually compiled into servlets) can act as CORBA clients in a multitier architecture.

In the remainder of this subsection, we look at the advantages of using applets and servlets. To better understand the advantages of these technologies for integrating applications with the Web, however, we first sketch the problems of traditional CGI-based Web applications. When examining applets and servlets, we will also explain the final integration step for Web applications: interactive GUI capabilities combined with remote invocations.

### *1.1.3.1 Problems in Traditional Web Applications*

The interactivity of traditional HTML-based interfaces is provided mostly through the CGI. This enables the execution of programs on the server side. Unfortunately, the CGI has a number of limitations and drawbacks:

**Stateless clients.** A typical CGI-based application, as illustrated in Figure 1.1, works in a two-phase cycle. A client has some state that can be changed by data entered into a form or as a result of state changes in the server. The client in this case is a sequence of HTML pages where each page is created as the result of a CGI call. Hence, all client state information has to be passed to a program behind the CGI. The only way to do this is by encoding it into the URL or into cookies.

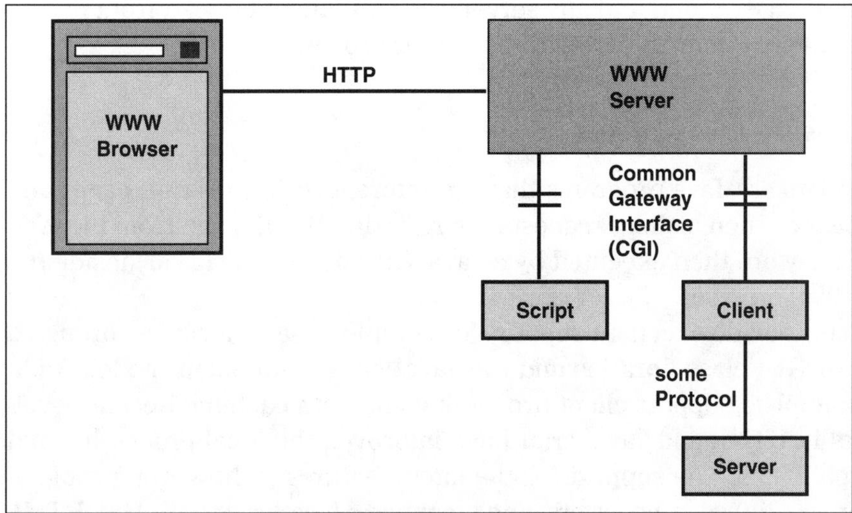


**Figure 1.1** CGI-based distributed applications.

**Non-type-safe interaction.** Writing a client as a sequence of HTML pages and URLs is an extremely tedious task and has great potential for errors. Data transferred from client to server must be encoded in the URL string, which must be parsed each time a new CGI call is received or pulled from client-side data-structures hidden in cookies.

**Notifications.** The Web programming model is a pull model that excludes communication mechanisms for delivering notifications to a user. Instead e-mail is used as poor substitute.

**Performance bottlenecks.** There are a number of performance bottlenecks in the CGI-based approach. Usually some scripting language program glues the application-specific program and the CGI together. As a result of an invocation a complete HTML page is returned to the client side (including all the hidden state and GUI information). These HTML documents contain a lot of repeated text and formatting data that remains unchanged since the last client action. The amount of unchanged HTML often outweighs the amount of actual data produced by the application program by an order of magnitude.

HTTP, the most popular protocol of the Web protocol suite, is not very efficient. The major performance bottleneck occurs because multiple connections can be created by loading a single URL, and the connection management creates a significant performance overhead. Furthermore, the CGI will start a new operating system process each time an application processes a user input, and any server-side state must be read from persistent storage or communicated from another process.

### 1.1.3.2 Using Java Applets

Java applets are Java programs that are referenced from HTML pages and downloaded when a client requests the referring HTML page from the Web server. They are then executed by a Java Virtual Machine (JVM) inside the client's Web browser.

Applets provide excellent support for complex user interfaces through a variety of GUI class libraries and the JavaBeans component model. Additionally, applets support client processing and data caching. Recent developments in HTML and JavaScript have improved the local processing and GUI capabilities. The support for the latest features is, however, problematic across different browsers and versions. JavaScript-enriched HTML pages have grown significantly and are coming close to the size of comparable applets. From a CORBA perspective, the main advantage of applets is that they can act as CORBA clients and can even host CORBA objects acting as remote callback objects. This allows you to provide notification-type features, as known from instant messaging applications.

#### Applets as Thin Clients

Because HTML-based clients are a sequence of stateless HTML pages downloaded every time from a server, they are considered to be *null clients.* At the other extreme is the case of an applet that executes in the browser without any outside communications or access to local data and contains all the application logic. In between there are a variety of options.

A *thin client* provides a complete GUI and keeps some state information; however, all the application logic and data is kept at the server. Thin clients overcome the limitations of null clients because they contain state and some application logic. They are relatively small and can be downloaded quickly over the network. Java applets can act as thin clients and overcome some of the problems of stateless clients by encapsulating the process of encoding state in URLs or HTTP POST requests. As long as they use the standard HTTP request/reply paradigm, however, they still appear as stateless clients to servers.

Thin clients can also overcome a major problem caused by software updates and their distribution. A typical distributed system could have a relatively small number of servers while the client front ends would number in the hundreds or thousands. When updating the software a new version of the client has to be shipped and installed on each of the client machines. This is a tedious, time-consuming, and high-cost task.

An applet client has the potential to overcome this problem. The shipping and installation process is automatically done by a Web browser. Today's caching mechanisms are rather simple, but it would be possible to implement one based on version numbers of applets. That would make the whole configuration process more effective because a client applet is downloaded only when the cached version is older than the one on the server. Similar means are available for Java applications, which can check with their (remote) code base to see if there have been any code changes. If so, the application will be updated automatically by downloading changes in the byte code.

#### Applets as CORBA Clients

Java ORBs overcome the statelessness problem by having continuously executing client and server programs that maintain their own state variables. CORBA's IDL provides typed interface specifications, overcoming the problem of untyped interaction. The performance problems are overcome by the ORB infrastructure, allowing the invocation of operations on remote objects, which communicate only the data they need for each interaction, and by using a much more efficient transport protocol. The ORB maintains a network connection between client and server, keeping a reasonable trade-off between lowering connection establishment overhead and freeing idle network resources.

In this light, applets are particularly attractive because the Java language binding allows applets to act as CORBA clients. This enables access to CORBA objects, and potentially to legacy applications wrapped into objects, using popular Web browsers. In an enterprise the same technology can be used in intranets because the same TCP/IP protocols are used. Although having applets that are only clients to CORBA objects is useful, applets can also implement CORBA objects. This approach is somewhat limited due to the applet sandbox model, which disables applets' access to resources on the machine where they execute. This means, for example, that those objects cannot be made persistent. Applets can provide callback interfaces so that they can respond to requests from other objects. Callback interfaces allow for CORBA-based push technology.

### *1.1.3.3 Java Servlets and JSP*

A servlet is a piece of Java code executed in response to HTTP requests that dynamically generates HTML pages as a reply, potentially performing complex computations or interacting with back-end systems in the course. Servlets are the Java replacement for CGI scripts and are managed by Java-enabled Web servers, which are also called servlet containers or engines. When the server receives HTTP requests to a URL that is associated with a servlet, it calls the servlet's method that is appropriate for the current request type, for example, `doGet()` if the HTTP request is GET.

Some of the problems of traditional Web applications are not as severe when Java servlets are used instead of the CGI. One of the main advantages of servlets over CGI is the multithreaded execution. While the CGI creates a new process for every request, a servlet's engine uses only a thread (typically from thread pool) for the execution of the request.

Writing servlets is generally much easier than writing CGI scripts, independent of the programming language used for the CGI script. Because servlet-enabled Web servers use a standard interface to invoke servlets, writing the code to access HTTP request data and to assemble the response is straightforward. The development of servlets is further supported by JSP technology. JSP essentially facilitates the integration of the HTML code that servlets must produce with the servlet's application code.

As with applets, servlets can use the entire range of Java APIs—such as the JDBC—to provide their application functionality. They can also make use of the IDL language mapping for Java and access remote resources using CORBA object invocations, for example, to contact back-end databases or legacy applications written in programming languages such as COBOL. Servlets can therefore be used to integrate CORBA applications with Web clients that use only standard HTTP and are thus not subject to the limitations for applets that we mentioned earlier. While the statelessness of clients and the inefficiency of HTTP communication are still the same with servlets as with the traditional CGI approach, they are better suited than applets to make CORBA applications accessible on the Internet.

## 1.1.4 Component Models

The term *component* is often used to describe reusable units of code that support the composition of applications. The main motivation for using components is the increase in developer productivity that can be achieved by enhancing code reuse and facilitating composition. Component technology is especially helpful in the context of distributed applications because of the inherent complexity of these applications.

Java provides two different component models, JavaBeans and Enterprise JavaBeans (EJB), with different application areas for each.

### *1.1.4.1 JavaBeans*

JavaBeans allow programmers to combine the functionality provided by a number of Java classes into a single component by defining a component interface that adheres to a few conventions, which are defined by the JavaBeans programming model. Components built this way can be easily put together to achieve new functionality. They can be regarded as a simple design pattern or implementation technique for more efficient development of reusable code modules. JavaBeans components are typically fine- to medium-grained and often are composed visually using developer tools that are part of integrated Java development environments.

#### *1.1.4.2 Enterprise JavaBeans*

JavaBeans are attractive because they make certain development tasks easier, but they do not address distributed computing in any way. *Enterprise JavaBeans* (EJB), however, is specifically designed for server applications. The name of this technology suggests similarities with JavaBeans, but it is important not to confuse these two technologies: JavaBeans facilitates the composition of functionality from existing components, whereas EJB provides the means to tackle the inherent complexity of multitiered, transaction-oriented, and security-critical server applications.

EJB addresses this complexity using the following approaches:

**Separation of concerns.** The EJB specification separates the development process into tasks that are assigned to specific roles. Responsibility for the development and deployment of applications is divided up between the Enterprise Bean Provider, the Application Assembler, the Deployer, and the System Administrator roles.

**Abstraction.** EJB incorporates a number of important design patterns for enterprise applications. These are called Stateless Session Bean, Stateful Session Bean, and Entity Bean. Developers can select from these and use code generation tools to automatically generate much of the required application code for using these patterns. They can thus concentrate on writing business logic rather than code for using the infrastructure.

**Configuring the infrastructure.** EJB defines high-level APIs for a number of services that are frequently used in enterprise applications, such as transactions, security, naming, and persistence. These service APIs are integrated in the run-time environment for components, the EJB Container. The container can be configured for the specific needs of particular applications and runs on top of the EJB Server, which provides the distribution platform.

**Enabling interoperability.** EJB implementations must support IIOP to enable interoperability between different vendors and with CORBA.

Some products, such as the Inprise Application Server, are built on top of full CORBA implementations. Applications may also use the reverse mapping from Java to IDL and RMI-IIOP, which means that CORBA is used only implicitly and is not visible to the application. RMI-IIOP is explained in section 1.3.

EJB implementations typically come with a host of visual development and deployment tools that are integrated in sophisticated development and run-time environments. Application servers also include implementations of the services mentioned previously. Still, the Enterprise JavaBeans specification is actually only a subset of its companion specification in the CORBA world, the CORBA Component Model (CCM).

The CCM provides more component design patterns and uses additional declarative languages to describe components and their interfaces. We explain the CCM in more detail in Chapter 14, "CORBA Components." If the additional features offered by the CCM are not required or if no suitable CCM implementation is available, EJB can be used to implement both CORBA servers and clients in Java. Because of the reverse mapping from Java to IDL and the required implementation of the CORBA transport protocol IIOP in EJB, this is possible without writing or compiling IDL specifications.

## 1.2 What Does CORBA Offer Java Programmers?

The Java programming language was not originally designed to support the development of distributed applications or systems. Before the advent of Java RMI, which we discuss in section 1.3, the only way to implement distributed applications that was directly supported in Java was to use the network library classes in the package `java.net`. Those classes provide an Application Programming Interface (API) for the handling of URLs and an API to sockets. Sockets are relatively low-level abstractions, providing access to transport protocols such as UDP/IP and TCP/IP. The socket API does not provide distribution transparency or connection management.

The URL API provides high-level access to Web resources. For example, it provides a mechanism to fetch the document specified in a URL using the protocol specifier in the URL. Hence, the API provides the same approach to distributed computing as a Web browser, that is, either fetching documents from a remote server or using the CGI to invoke a program at an HTTP server that creates an HTML document on the fly. The limitations and drawbacks of the CGI have already been explained in section 1.1 of this chapter.

The Java language binding for OMG IDL provides an application programmer with CORBA's high-level distributed object paradigm:

- Interfaces defined independently of implementations
- Access to objects implemented in other programming languages
- Access to objects regardless of their location (location transparency)
- Automatic code generation to deal with remote invocations
- Access to standard CORBA services and facilities

These advantages are discussed in detail in sections 1.2.1–1.2.6. Some of the functionality is also provided in Java RMI. We compare the two technologies in section 1.3 but also mention a few differences here.

## 1.2.1 OMG IDL Defined Interfaces

OMG IDL provides a means of separating interfaces from implementations for distributed object applications. This separation is particularly useful for software engineering processes. Systems designs based on object-oriented design methodologies and tools, such as the widely used Unified Modeling Language (UML), can be expressed in OMG IDL, although these high-level definitions will usually have to be revised for the actual design. Once interfaces are specified in IDL, different teams or individuals can independently implement different parts of the system.

The separation of interface from implementation is also useful for managing software component evolution. In particular, it allows access to multiple implementations conforming to the same interface specification. Additionally, interfaces can be extended by inheritance, where derived interfaces are substitutable for base interfaces.

Like IDL, Java also provides the option of separating interfaces from implementation. The OMG object model, though, is more general than Java's, and IDL offers language features useful for describing remote interfaces that are not found in Java, such as in, out, and inout parameters and oneway invocations. OMG IDL will be explained in detail in Chapter 2, "CORBA Overview."

## 1.2.2 Programming Language Independence

CORBA supports multiple language mappings for OMG IDL so that different parts of a system or application can be implemented in different programming languages. All interactions in an application happen through interfaces that are specified independently of the programming language in which they are implemented.

Previously, distributed applications were implemented in a particular programming language because of the availability of remote invocation libraries for that language. With CORBA the most appropriate programming language can be chosen for each object, based on the need for legacy integration, the prior experience of a development team, or the suitability of the language for implementing the object's semantics.

Wrapping legacy applications and hiding language and platform heterogeneity are two of the main application areas for CORBA. Through its wide availability on virtually any platform and by using the Java Native Interface (JNI) to the C programming language, it is in principle also possible to wrap legacy applications in Java. These wrapped applications can then be accessed using Java RMI or even IIOP. Whether this is an option in a given situation depends on a lot of factors, including the added run-time overhead of passing through the JNI. It is usually more efficient to use CORBA for wrapping if an ORB implementation is available in the required language.

## 1.2.3 Location Transparency and Server Activation

Socket- or URL-based distributed applications need to address a server by specifying a host name and a port number. In contrast, CORBA provides location transparency, which means that an object is identified independently of its physical location and can potentially change its location without breaking the application. The ORB provides the necessary mechanisms for this transparency.

In addition, CORBA provides great flexibility with regard to server configuration: CORBA's Portable Object Adapter (POA) lets developers select the most suitable combination of policies to control aspects of a server implementation's behavior. Examples for these policies include threading, object activation, object ID management, and object lifetime. Most CORBA implementations also provide a mechanism called Implementation Repository that can transparently start up servers on demand. Such a mechanism is useful if servers are to be transparently deactivated when they are unused so that resources can be reclaimed. Java RMI has a similar mechanism called Object Activation.

## 1.2.4 Automatic Stub and Skeleton Code Generation

Distributed systems traditionally required a number of lower-level and repetitious programming efforts including opening, controlling, and closing network connections; marshaling and unmarshaling of data (conversion of structured data into a programming language and architecture-independent format and back again); and setting up servers to listen for incoming requests on socket ports and forwarding them to object implementations. IDL compilers and ORB run-time systems free application programmers from these tasks. IDL compilers create representations of IDL-defined constructs such as constants, data types, and interfaces in a particular language binding, for example, C++ or Java. They also create the code to marshal and unmarshal the user-defined data types. Libraries are provided to support predefined CORBA types.

The generated code for the client side, that is, the code invoking an operation on an object, is known as stub code. The server-side generated code, which invokes the method on the implementation of that operation, is called skeleton code. The skeleton code, in conjunction with the ORB, provides a transparent run-time mechanism for handling incoming invocations and managing associated network connections.

## 1.2.5 Reuse of CORBA Services and Facilities

The ORB provides a means for the location-transparent invocation of methods on potentially remote objects. Typically, nontrivial distributed applications require additional functionality. Within the OMG these requirements have been analyzed and have led to the specification of corresponding fundamental services. These fundamental services are published with the brand CORBAservices. Examples are as follows:

- **Naming Service**—a white pages service for distributed objects
- **Trading Service**—a yellow pages service for distributed objects
- **Notification Service**—an asynchronous, subscription-based event notification service
- **Transaction Service**—transaction processing for distributed objects
- **Persistent State Service**—persistent storage of object state
- **Security Service**—a service that provides authentication, authorization, encryption, and other security features

There are specifications of higher-level application-oriented services that are known as CORBAfacilities. More details on CORBAservices and CORBAfacilities can be found in Chapter 2. The Java platform now provides similar service APIs for most of the CORBAservices. In general, however, it is fair to say that CORBAservices have richer interfaces and are more mature, while their Java counterparts are simpler and thus easier to use.

### 1.2.6 Vendor Independence through ORB Interoperability and Code Portability

CORBA 2.0 and later versions of the CORBA specification define the means by which objects implemented using different ORB implementations can interoperate. These include object addressing through interoperable object references (IORs) and a hierarchy of protocols—the General Inter-ORB Protocol (GIOP) and the TCP/IP-specific Internet Inter-ORB Protocol (IIOP). This interoperability allows a certain independence from ORB vendor products. Any application developed using an ORB that is compliant to CORBA 2.0 or later can integrate components developed using another interoperable ORB.

Another goal of the CORBA 2.0 specification was to provide portability of source code between ORB implementations from different vendors. Through the standardization of the ORB interface and the IDL language mappings, this portability was achieved for clients. The fact that the interface to the Basic Object Adapter (BOA) on the server side was underspecified, however, meant that vendors had to come up with proprietary interfaces. Consequently, server applications developed using vendor A's BOA interface were not portable to vendor B's ORB product without modifications.

The OMG finally deprecated the BOA in CORBA 2.2 and replaced it with the Portable Object Adapter (POA). Java applications are now truly portable between different ORB implementations if they are developed using the IDL-to-Java mapping revision 2.3 or later, which fixes the Java interfaces to the POA and ORB run time. We explain the POA in detail in Chapter 2 and Chapter 10, "Practical POA Programming." The Java Language Mapping is presented in Chapter 5, "OMG IDL to Java Mapping," and the ORB run-time interfaces are explained in Chapter 6. "ORB Run-Time System."

## 1.3 Java ORBs and Java RMI

Java's Remote Method Invocation (RMI) is an interface for remote method invocations on Java objects. Like CORBA, RMI is actually transfer protocol independent. Because the Java Remote Method Protocol (JRMP) is part of the Java environment, however, the close coupling between RMI and JRMP has created the perception that JRMP is the only transfer protocol for RMI. In this light, CORBA/IIOP and RMI/JRMP have been viewed and marketed as competing technologies. Does RMI make CORBA obsolete, then? Or does CORBA outperform RMI in every respect? This section tries to compare the two and outline where RMI is more appropriate and where CORBA should be used instead.

First, RMI is simpler and easier to use than CORBA. This ease of use is possible because RMI was not intended to be used for large-scale applications in heterogeneous environments and thus does not provide many of the more advanced features of CORBA, such as the POA, interceptors, and one-way invocations. It provides a feature called Object Serialization that allows objects to be passed by value, which was not possible in earlier CORBA versions.

Recently, however, CORBA and RMI have been converging. This convergence is mainly due to the following technologies, both released in mid-1999:

- Sun Microsystems defined RMI over IIOP (RMI-IIOP), an addition to RMI that allows the use of CORBA's Internet protocol, IIOP, as an alternative to its own proprietary protocol JRMP.
- The Object Management Group released version 2.3 of the CORBA specification, which contains three extensions significant for RMI-IIOP. IDL and IIOP have been extended to pass objects by value between remote machines in a way that is compatible with RMI. There is now a reverse mapping from Java to IDL supporting the RMI style of defining remote interfaces.

The significance of this development is that RMI developers can now write object implementations that are accessible from CORBA client programs. Java programmers need not define object interfaces in CORBA IDL. Rather, this description can be generated from Java interface specifications using a special compiler that realizes a reverse mapping from IDL to Java. We go into the details of mapping IDL to Java in Chapter 5 and also take a look at the OMG-defined reverse mapping there.

If IDL is thus generated from Java interfaces and made available to clients, CORBA clients of these interfaces can be written in any programming language for which CORBA implementations are available. When RMI-IIOP is used in this way, its run-time environment is actually that of a special Java ORB. It is also possible to access CORBA server objects using RMI-IIOP if their IDL definitions fall within the subset of IDL that can be handled by RMI-IIOP. Because this is not the general case, RMI-IIOP should be used mainly for developing server programs with interfaces defined in Java. The standard

Java run-time system, however, does not provide the scalability and flexibility in managing server objects that CORBA provides. For large-scale enterprise applications, the only adequate use for RMI-IIOP is within EJB.

In summary, these developments make Java programming with CORBA appear relatively similar to using RMI-IIOP. In some cases, the decision whether to use RMI or CORBA is now just a matter of style. The remaining distinctions between these two approaches to distributed computing are the following:

- Both RMI and RMI-IIOP are essentially Java-only solutions. They are generally easier to use but are not suitable for integrating legacy software into large-scale heterogeneous environments.
- CORBA provides much more flexibility and programmer control, for example, over the creation of object references and the management of the object life cycle. Large-scale, critical server applications should therefore be written in CORBA or by using an EJB implementation built on top of CORBA.

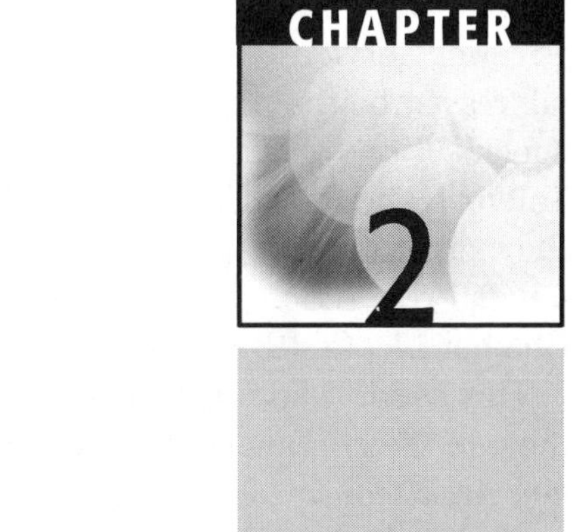


# CORBA Overview

This chapter contains detailed information, from a CORBA application developer's perspective, about the OMG and the architecture documents and specifications it has produced. Section 1 is an overview of the history, goals, organizational structure, and processes of the OMG. It provides descriptions of all the committees, task forces, and special interest groups within the consortium.

Section 2 is a detailed summary of the contents of the Object Management Architecture Guide, and it includes the changes made to the OMA since the third revision in mid-1995. There are two main topics in this section, the Core Object Model (section 2.2.2) and the OMA Reference Model (section 2.2.3).

The third, and longest, section summarizes the CORBA 2.3 specification, which is the foundation for CORBA 3. CORBA 3 is not a single specification but a whole suite of documents that all contribute to make CORBA more flexible and usable. In addition to the central specification of the Object Request Broker itself, CORBA 3 comprises specifications that address Internet integration, Quality of Service Control, and components. The specifications that address Internet integration are the OMG's Interoperable Naming

Service and Firewall specifications. These are covered in Chapter 7, "Discovering Services," and Chapter 12, "Security." Quality of Service Control is addressed by the Asynchronous Messaging and Quality of Service Control specifications as well as by the specifications for Minimum CORBA, Fault-Tolerant, and Real-Time CORBA. We don't cover any of these in this book as they target more specific requirements for distributed applications that are beyond our scope. The CORBA Component model, finally, is covered in Chapter 14, "CORBA Components."

This section attempts to balance conciseness and detail, and it covers most of the content of the central June 1999 *Common Object Request Broker: Architecture and Specification* document that is relevant to ORB users while briefly introducing the material relevant to ORB implementers. The major topics covered include the CORBA Object Model (section 2.3.2), The Object Request Broker Structure (section 2.3.3), OMG IDL (section 2.3.4), ORB and Object Interfaces (section 2.3.5), Portable Object Adapter (section 2.3.6), non-Java language mappings (section 2.3.7), Interoperability Architecture (section 2.3.8), TypeCode, Any, and Dynamic Any (section 2.3.9), Dynamic Invocation and Dynamic Skeleton Interfaces (section 2.3.10), and Interface Repository (section 2.3.11).

## 2.1 The Object Management Group

The Object Management Group (OMG) is the world's largest computer industry consortium, with over 800 members in 2000. It is a nonprofit organization that began in 1989 with eight members: 3Com, American Airlines, Canon, Data General, Hewlett-Packard, Philips Telecommunications N.V., Sun Microsystems, and Unisys. The organization remains fairly small, and it does not develop any technology or specifications itself. It provides a structure whereby its members specify technology and then produce commercial implementations that comply with those specifications. The OMG's processes emphasize cooperation, compromise, and agreement rather than choosing one member's solution over another's.

### 2.1.1 OMG's Goals

The goals of the OMG are promotion of the object-oriented approach to software engineering and development of a common architectural framework for writing distributed object-oriented applications based on interface specifications for the objects in the application.

## 2.1.2 The Organizational Structure of OMG

The OMG Board administers the organization and ratifies the activities of the other groups within the OMG. Most positions in the OMG are unpaid and are held by representatives of member companies.

The technical groups of the OMG are overseen by the Architecture Board (AB), whose members are experienced system architects. The AB is elected by the OMG membership. It reviews all technology proposals and specifications for consistency and conformance with the Object Management Architecture (OMA).

The structure of the committees, task forces, and other groups within the OMG reflect the structure of the OMA (see Figure 2.1). Two committees oversee the technology adoption of a number of task forces (TFs) and special interest groups (SIGs).

**Platform Technology Committee (PTC).** This committee is concerned with infrastructure issues: the Object Request Broker (ORB), Object Services, and the relationship of the OMA to object-oriented analysis and design.

**Domain Technology Committee (DTC).** This committee is concerned with technologies to support application development, in particular vertical markets such as manufacturing, electronic commerce, or health care.

Task forces may issue Requests for Proposals (RFPs). These are detailed statements of a problem that needs to be solved. Responses are solicited in the form of IDL specifications with object semantics explained in English. Two rounds of submissions are taken, usually three months apart, and then the most suitable specification is selected by a vote of members and presented to the task force's controlling committee.

Special interest groups may not issue RFPs directly or adopt technology specifications, but they may do so with the support of a task force. Usually special interest groups discuss areas of common interest and report their findings to their controlling committee via documents and presentations. Some special interest groups do not belong to either the PTC or the DTC. Instead they report directly to the Architecture Board.

### *2.1.2.1 PTC Task Forces and Special Interest Groups*

The following are the task forces and special interest groups that report to the Platform Technical Committee:

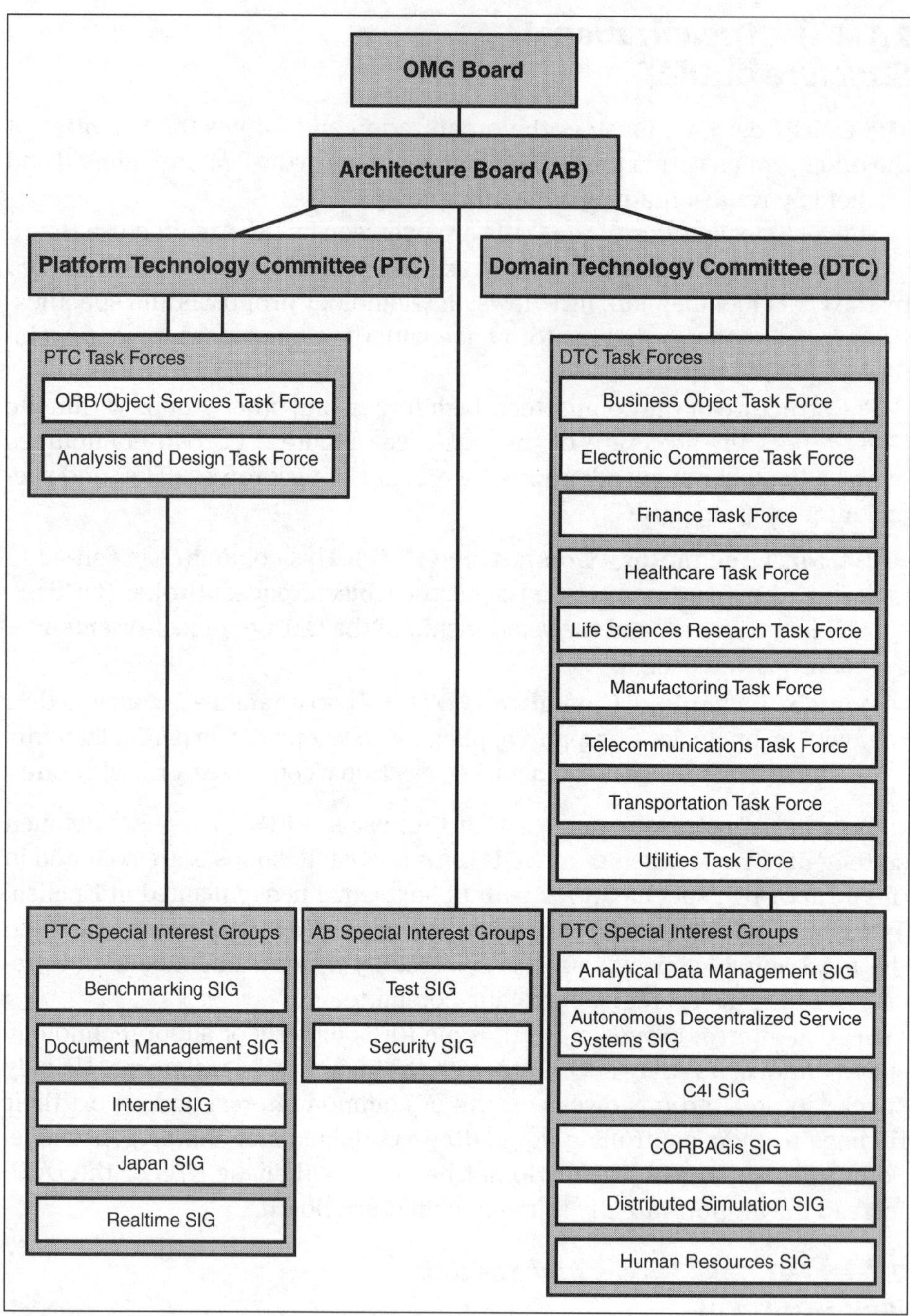


**Figure 2.1** Organization of the OMG.

**Analysis and Design Task Force (ADTF).** This task force is concerned with applying widely used object-oriented analysis and design methodologies to distributed object-oriented application development using CORBA. Its adopted specifications include the Meta-Object Facility (MOF) for meta-data and the Unified Modeling Language.

**ORB/Object Services Task Force (ORBOS).** This task force is responsible for specifying the ORB, which is published as the Common Object Request Broker Architecture and Specification (CORBA). The task force also specifies general-purpose Object Services (published as CORBAservices). This is the area that supports the basic infrastructure of object interaction. This task force has adopted the largest number of specifications.

**Benchmarking Special Interest Group (BSIG).** The Benchmark SIG discusses benchmarking and benchmarking-related issues such as what kinds of benchmark measurements are appropriate in a CORBA environment.

**Document Management Special Interest Group (DMSIG).** The DMSIG promotes the incorporation of document management services into OMA services.

**Internet Special Interest Group (ISIG).** The ISIG is concerned with the convergence between distributed objects and the Internet, both as a distribution mechanism and as a growing area of commercial activity.

**Japan Special Interest Group (JSIG).** The JSIG is a focus for Japanese developers of distributed objects and is particularly concerned with internationalization issues across the OMG.

**Real Time Special Interest Group (RTSIG).** The RTSIG is concerned with issues of guaranteed performance of requests to distributed objects, embedded systems, and fault tolerance.

### *2.1.2.2 DTC Task Forces and Special Interest Groups*

The following are the task forces and special interest groups that report to the Domain Technical Committee:

**Business Objects Task Force (BOTF).** The area covered by the Business Objects TF is broad: It includes any standard objects used in business processes. This covers such areas as workflow, document processing, and task scheduling. The first RFP issued by the BOTF was controversial in that it did not solicit a single well-focused specification, but rather invited submitters to specify anything that they consider to be a business object. In the end, work has been refocused on UML Profiles within the ADTF, known as the BOI or EDOC RFPs.

**Electronic Commerce Task Force.** The Electronic Commerce TF is interested in online commerce and electronic market systems.

**Finance Task Force.** This task force promotes the use of financial services and accounting software based on OMG standards. It is adopting specifications for standard interfaces to this kind of software.

**Healthcare Task Force (CORBAmed).** The CORBAmed task force is concerned with adopting specifications that meet the vertical domain requirements of the health care sector. It also promotes the use of object-oriented technology in the medical field.

**Life Sciences Research Task Force (LSR).** The LSR represents pharmaceutical companies, academic institutions, and software and hardware vendors to promote interoperability among computational resources in life sciences research.

**Manufacturing Task Force.** The Manufacturing TF promotes the use of CORBA technology in manufacturing industry computer systems and is adopting technology specifications tailored to that broad sector.

**Telecommunications Task Force (CORBAtel).** CORBAtel is working toward adoption of specifications that meet the needs of telecommunications providers. It also promotes the OMG and liaises with relevant telecommunications industry bodies.

**Transportation Task Force.** The Transportation TF examines the requirements of the transportation industry in the development of Distributed Object Applications.

**Utilities Task Force.** The Utilities TF develops object interface standards for the interoperation of electric, water, and gas utilities systems.

**Analytical Data Management Special Interest Group.** The ADM SIG works on tools, services, frameworks, and components in statistical data collection.

**Autonomous Decentralized Service System Special Interest Group.** This SIG gathers industry requirements and works on a system model for flexible and dependable Information Service Systems.

**Command, Control, Communications, Computers, and Intelligence Special Interest Group (C4I SIG).** The C4I SIG organizes and prioritizes military requirements for the OMG and supports commercial C4I systems implementation.

**Distributed Simulation Special Interest Group (SIM SIG).** The SIM SIG represents simulation tool vendors and works toward standards for interoperable, composable distributed simulation.

**Geospatial Information Systems (CORBAgis) Special Interest Group.** CORBAgis promotes the use of geospatial information in distributed object environments.

**Human Resources SIG.** This relatively new SIG's focus is interoperable Human Resources and Payroll domain software components.

#### *2.1.2.3 Architecture Board Special Interest Groups*

The following special interest groups report directly to the AB:

**Security Special Interest Group.** This SIG feeds the security requirements of end users into the OMG-wide technology adoption process.

**Test Special Interest Group (TSIG).** The TSIG is responsible for two distinct areas: conformance/compliance testing and end-user testing. It promotes the creation of guidelines that allow vendors to test their product's conformance and applications developers to perform appropriate testing of distributed applications.

### 2.1.3 OMG Technology Adoption Process

The process, in brief, is as follows:

- A task force offers a Request for Information (RFI) on a particular technology area. This is an optional step.
- If any RFI submissions are received, they are considered in the process of drawing up a Request for Proposals (RFP), which solicits submissions addressing its proposal from contributing members of the OMG. The task force then passes the draft on to its parent Technical Committee (TC).
- The TC submits the draft RFP to the OMG's Architecture Board (AB) for approval. After the AB approves and before the TC issues the RFP, the TC conducts a vote on the RFP.
- Any member company that wishes to respond to an RFP must submit a letter of intent (LOI) stating that they are willing to release a commercial implementation of their submitted specification within one year of its adoption, should it be chosen.

- A voting list is established from OMG members who express an interest in selecting from the submissions.
- A first submission takes place, usually about three months after the issue of the RFP. Typically there are three to six submissions.
- The task force session at one of the six annual OMG meetings will ask questions and provide feedback on the initial submissions.
- The submitters consider each other's specifications, and frequently some or all of them decide to produce a consensus merger of specifications that align fairly closely.
- Second submissions are made and evaluated by the task force, usually after another three months. This process is repeated until the task force decides to recommend submissions for adoption to its parent TC. If there is more than one submission the choice of which to recommend for adoption is put to a vote.
- The recommended specification is presented to a Technical Committee plenary session, and a yes/no vote to adopt the chosen submission is put to the entire OMG membership. The vote is usually begun at the meeting and completed electronically over the next few months. The recommended specification usually passes without problem.
- The Architecture Board then considers the broader implications of the new specification on the whole OMA. It may approve the specification unequivocally, suggest revisions, or simply reject the specification and advise the TC to issue a new RFP.
- Once the AB is happy with the specification it is ratified by the OMG Board based on a further vote by members.

The form of submissions to the OMG's task forces and technical committees is usually a form detailing the problem area that is being solved and proposing a number of interface definitions (in OMG IDL). The submission has to follow a predefined format strictly, and the IDL is accompanied by English text describing the semantics of the objects and the roles and relationships to other objects in the specification and outside of it. The interfaces are described in terms of the actions of their operations and not in terms of a particular underlying implementation.

## 2.2 The Object Management Architecture

This section introduces the OMA and provides a summary of the technical parts of the third edition of the OMG publication *Object Management*

*Architecture Guide*, which consists of two main parts: the Core Object Model (described in section 2.2.2) and the Reference Model (described in section 2.2.3).

## 2.2.1 Overview of the OMA

The OMA is the framework within which all OMG adopted technology fits. It provides two fundamental models on which CORBA and the other standard interfaces are based: the Core Object Model and the Reference Model.

The Core Object Model defines the concepts that allow distributed application development to be facilitated by an Object Request Broker (ORB). The Core Object Model is restricted to abstract definitions that do not constrain the syntax of object interfaces or the implementations of objects or ORBs. It then defines a framework for refining the model to a more concrete form. The model provides the basis for CORBA, but it is more relevant to ORB designers and implementers than to distributed object application developers.

The Reference Model places the ORB at the center of groupings of objects with standardized interfaces that provide support for application object developers. The groups identified are Object Services, which provide infrastructure; Domain Interfaces, which provide special support to applications from various industry domains; Common Facilities, which provide application-level services across domains; and Application Interfaces, which are the set of all other objects developed for specific applications. Since the disbanding of the Common Facilities Task Force, the OMA Reference Model has not been redefined, and a number of specifications still populate this space in the OMA.

The Reference Model is directly relevant to CORBA programmers because it provides the big picture from which components and frameworks can be drawn to support developers of distributed applications. The Reference Model also provides the framework for the OMG's technology adoption process. It does this by identifying logical groupings of interface specifications that are provided by the organizational groups (TFs and SIGs) that specify and adopt them.

## 2.2.2 Core Object Model

This section provides a detailed explanation of the theoretical underpinnings of CORBA. These specifics will not be of interest to everyone. We have tried to provide a readable summary of the contents of the OMG's *Object Management Architecture Guide*, but section 3 of this chapter on

CORBA is written without assuming that the reader is familiar with the details of the Core Object Model. This section will mostly be of interest to readers with a background in object-oriented theory, but it starts from first principles and so is readable by anyone with a somewhat broader interest than simply using CORBA as an application development platform.

### 2.2.2.1 Scope of the Core Object Model

The main goals of the Core Object Model are portability and interoperability. The most important aspect of portability to consider is *design portability*. This means knowledge of an object's interface and the ability to create applications whose components do not rely on the existence or location of a particular object implementation. The core does not define the syntax of interface descriptions, but it does describe the semantics of types and their relationships to one another.

Interoperability means being able to invoke operations on objects regardless of where they are located, on which platform they execute, or in what programming language they are implemented. This is achieved by the ORB, which relies on the semantics of objects and operations described in the Core Object Model. The ORB also requires some extensions to the core that provide specifications for specific communication protocols, an interface definition syntax, and basic services to object implementations. CORBA provides these extensions.

The Core Object Model is not a meta-model. This means that it cannot have many possible concrete instances of the basic concepts. It consists of an abstract set of concepts that allow understanding of objects and their interfaces. These concepts, however, cannot be redefined or replaced, only extended and made more concrete. The Core Object Model is specialized using components and profiles to provide a concrete architecture for an ORB.

### 2.2.2.2 Components and Profiles

A *component* is an extension to the abstract Core Object Model that provides a more concrete specialization of the concepts defined in the core. The core together with one or more components produces what is called a *profile*. CORBA is a profile that extends the core with several components that provide specializations such as a syntax for object interfaces and a protocol for interoperation between objects implemented using different ORBs.

Figure 2.2 shows how components and profiles are used to add to the Core Object Model.

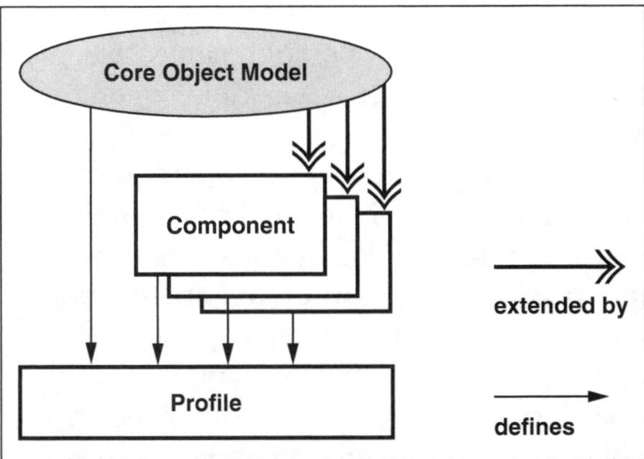


**Figure 2.2** Components and profiles.

### *2.2.2.3 Concept Definitions*

The Core Object Model is a classical object model. This means that actions in the system are performed by invoking operations on objects. The invocation will identify an operation and may contain parameters. The object will then execute the operation, and possibly return resulting values to the caller.

The concepts defined in the Core Object Model are the following:

- Objects
- Operations, including their signatures, parameters, and return values
- Nonobject types
- Interfaces
- Substitutability

**Objects.** Objects are defined simply as models of entities or concepts. For example, an object can model a document, a date, an employee, a subatomic particle, or a compiler. The important characteristic of an object is its identity, which is fixed for the life of the object and is independent of the object's properties or behavior. This identity is represented by an object reference.

**Operations, signatures, parameters, and return values.** An operation is a behavior offered by an object that is known to the outside world by its signature. The notion of sending a request to an object is equivalent to the notion of invoking an operation on an object.

An operation's signature has the following components: a name, a set of parameters, and a set of result types. Operation names are unique within a particular object. No syntax for describing operations and their types is provided.

When a request is sent to an object it nominates an operation and provides arguments matching the parameters in that operation's signature. The operation then performs some action on those arguments and will return zero or more results. It is important to note that object references may be returned as part of the result of an operation.

Operations may cause some side effects, usually manifested as changes in the encapsulated state of the object. When an object cannot process a request it will typically return an exception message, but exceptions are defined in a separate component that is part of CORBA, not in the Core Object Model.

The Core Object Model does not specify whether requests are accepted by an object in parallel or what the consequences of parallel execution would be if they were. An implementation of objects could choose to provide atomic operations or a sequence of operations for transaction management.

**Nonobject Types.** Unlike the object models of Smalltalk and Eiffel, there are types in the OMA core that are not object types. These are usually called data types. Object types and nonobject types make up the whole of the denotable values in the OMA.

While the Core Object Model does not specify a set of nonobject types, another component of CORBA does. Even though the OMA core is designed to be extensible into several profiles via different sets of components, the likelihood of an alternative profile to CORBA being specified in the OMA is almost nonexistent. This design decision has been made so that new components can be added to CORBA in a consistent manner, and so that new versions of CORBA can be defined in terms of the makeup of its components and their versions.

#### 2.2.2.4 Interfaces and Substitutability

An *interface* is a collection of operation signatures. Typically the interface to an object is the set of operations offered by that object, but this is left, once again, to CORBA to specify. Interfaces are related to one another by substitutability relationships. This means that an object offering an interface can be used in place of an object offering a "similar" interface. The Core Object Model simply defines substitutability as being able to use one interface in place of another without "interaction error." It is useful, however, to examine a more concrete definition.

The simplest form of substitutability occurs when two interfaces offer exactly the same operations. Generally, if an interface A offers a superset of the operations offered by another interface B, then A is substitutable for B. Substitutability is not symmetrical, except in the simple case where A and B offer the same operations; however, it is transitive. That is, if A is substitutable for B and B is substitutable for a third interface C, then A is also substitutable for C.

### 2.2.2.5 Inheritance

Because interfaces may offer operations with the same signatures that have different purposes and semantics, it is useful to have an assertion of compatibility between them. In order to ensure a semantic relationship, the model introduces inheritance. If interface A inherits from interface B, then A offers all of the operations of B and may also offer some additional operations. The set of operations of A is therefore a superset of the operations of B, and hence A is substitutable for B. However, because the relationship between A and B is explicit we can be certain that the operations they have in common serve the same purpose, and A and B don't merely coincidentally share signatures. Figure 2.3 shows this example in a graphical form.

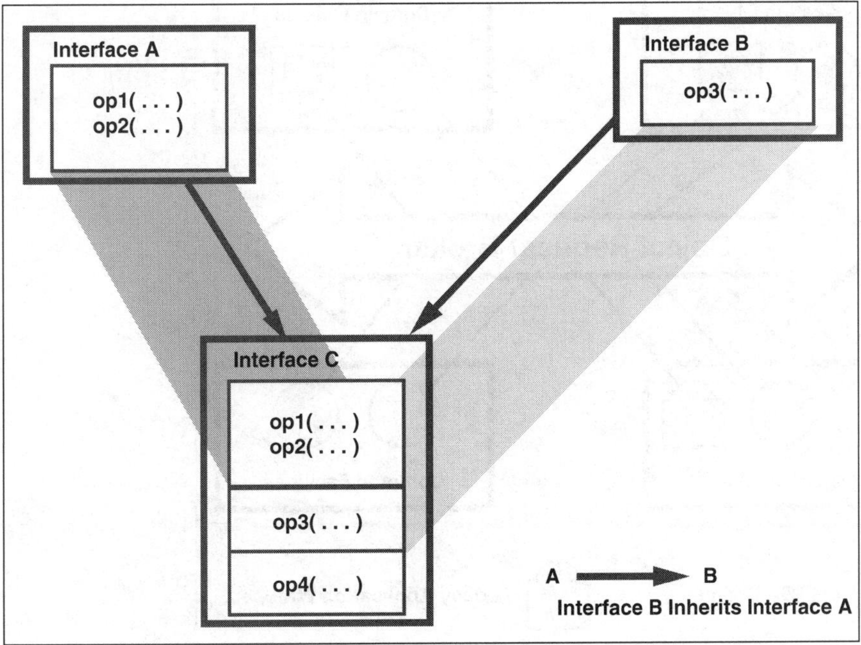


**Figure 2.3** Inheritance.

The Core Object Model defines *subtyping* as a form of substitutability dependent on inheritance of interfaces. That is, an interface A that inherits from an interface B is a subtype of B. We can also say that B is a supertype of A. In the Core Object Model, subtyping is the only acceptable form of substitutability.

The supertype of all objects in the Core Object Model is an abstract type *Object* that has an empty set of operations. The inheritance hierarchy places Object at the root and all other objects as its subtypes; it is also called the type graph.

## 2.2.3 The Reference Model

The OMA Reference Model is an architectural framework for the standardization of interfaces to infrastructure and services that applications can use. The object-oriented paradigm emphasizes reusability of components that perform small, well-defined parts of an application's functionality. The Reference Model allows users of components to understand what support they can expect in what areas from ORB vendors and third-party component providers.

The Reference Model is shown in Figure 2.4, which identifies five main components of the OMA:

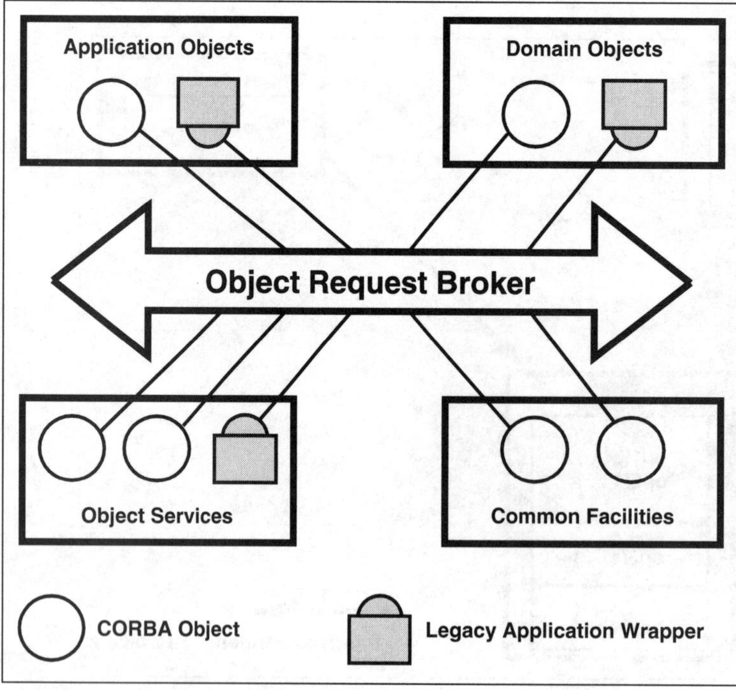


**Figure 2.4** The OMA Reference Model.

- Object Request Broker
- Object Services
- Common Facilities
- Domain interfaces
- Application interfaces

Only the last of these is not intended to have interfaces specified through OMG processes. Application objects are the project-specific part of an integrated application.

### 2.2.3.1 Object Request Broker (ORB)

The ORB is defined in the *Common Object Request Broker Architecture (CORBA) and Specification* document. CORBA builds on the OMA Core Object Model and provides the following:

- An extended CORBA core including a syntax and semantics for an Interface Definition Language (IDL)
- A framework for interoperability, including two specific protocol definitions
- A set of language mappings from IDL to implementation languages (C, C++, COBOL, Smalltalk, Ada'95, Java, Lisp, Python)

The ORB is situated at the conceptual (and graphical) center of the Reference Model. It acts as a message bus between objects that may be located on any machine in a network, implemented in any programming language, and executed on any hardware or operating system platform. The caller needs only an Object Reference and well-formed arguments in the language mapping of choice to invoke an operation as if it were a local function and receive results. This is called location and access transparency.

At the heart of CORBA is the Interface Definition Language (IDL), which is covered in detail in section 2.3.4. It provides a way of defining the interfaces of objects independently of the programming language in which they are implemented. It is a strongly typed declarative language with a rich set of data types for describing complex parameters. An IDL interface acts as a contract between developers of objects and the eventual users of their interfaces. It also allows the user of CORBA objects to compile the interface definitions into hidden code for the transmission of invocation requests across networks and machine architectures without knowledge of the network protocol, the target machine architecture, or even the location of the object being invoked.

### 2.2.3.2 Object Services

This set of interface specifications provides fundamental services that application developers may need in order to find and manage their objects and data, and to coordinate the execution of complex operations. Object Services are the building blocks from which other components of the OMA can be constructed and that application objects may require. The OMG brand name for these services is *CORBAservices*. The published services include the following:

- Naming
- Notification
- Life Cycle
- Persistent Object (deprecated, now superseded by the Persistent State Service)
- Relationships
- Externalization
- Transactions
- Concurrency Control
- Licensing
- Query
- Properties
- Security
- Time
- Collections
- Trading

Some of these are simply framework interfaces that will be inherited by the application or other objects, for example, the Life Cycle Service. Others represent low-level components on which higher-level application-oriented components can be built, for example, the Transaction Service. Others provide basic services used at all levels of applications, such as the Naming and Trading Services. These last two services provide a means of locating objects by name or by type and properties for late binding in an application. See Chapter 7, "Discovering Services," for a detailed description of these services.

### 2.2.3.3 Common Facilities

Common Facilities are those end-user-oriented interfaces that provide facilities across application domains. The first such specification adopted, published by the OMG as *CORBAfacilities*, is the Distributed Document Component Facility, based on OpenDoc. This specification is now a retired specification, which means that it is removed from the set of adopted specifications. Work has been completed on Internationalization and Time Facilities, Data Interchange and Mobile Agent Facilities, and a Printing Facility. A Meta-Object Facility, which is a way of defining repositories for IDL and non-IDL types, and a Systems Management Facility have also been adopted.

#### *2.2.3.4 Domain Interfaces*

The OMG contains a large number of special interest groups and task forces that focus on particular application domains such as telecommunications, Internet, business objects, manufacturing, and health care. This area of standardization was separated from the Common Facilities in early 1996 when it was called Vertical Facilities. Several Requests for Information (RFI) and Requests for Proposals (RFP) are in progress in the Domain task forces.

#### *2.2.3.5 Specification Adoption in the OMG*

Technology adoption in the OMG emphasizes the use of existing technologies and rapid market availability. To this end, submitters of specifications must vouch that an implementation of the specification exists and that, should their submission be adopted, they will make an implementation commercially available within a year of adoption. The adoption process is detailed in section 2.1.3.

## 2.3 Common Object Request Broker Architecture (CORBA)

This section provides a summary of the Common Object Request Broker: Architecture and Specification, version 2.3. The structure of the section is as follows:

- An overview of CORBA (section 2.3.1)
- The CORBA Object Model (section 2.3.2)
- The structure of the ORB (section 2.3.3)
- OMG Interface Definition Language (IDL) (section 2.3.4)
- The interfaces to the ORB and CORBA Object (section 2.3.5)
- The Portable Object Adapter (section 2.3.6)
- A brief description of other language mappings (section 2.3.7)

- The Interoperability Architecture (section 2.3.8)
- TypeCodes, Any, and DynAny (section 2.3.9)
- The Dynamic Invocation and Dynamic Skeleton interfaces (section 2.3.10)
- The Interface Repository (section 2.3.11)

## 2.3.1 Overview

CORBA is the specification of the functionality of the ORB, the crucial message bus that conveys operation invocation requests and their results to CORBA objects resident anywhere, however they are implemented. The CORBA specification provides certain interfaces to components of the ORB, but it leaves the interfaces to other components up to the ORB implementer.

The notion of transparency is at the center of CORBA. *Location transparency* is the ability to access and invoke operations on a CORBA object without needing to know where the object resides. The idea is that it should be equally easy to invoke an operation on an object residing on a remote machine as it is to invoke a method on an object in the same address space.

*Programming language transparency* provides the freedom to implement the functionality encapsulated in an object using the most appropriate language, whether because of the skills of the programmers, the appropriateness of the language to the task, or the choice of a third-party developer who provides off-the-shelf component objects. The key to this freedom is an implementation-neutral interface definition language, OMG IDL, that provides separation of interface and implementation.

IDL interface definitions inform clients of an object offering an interface exactly what operations an object supports, the types of their parameters, and what return types to expect. A client programmer needs only the IDL to write client code that is ready to invoke operations on a remote object. The client uses the data types defined in IDL through a *language mapping*. This mapping defines the programming language constructs (data types, classes, etc.) that will be generated by the IDL compiler supplied by an ORB vendor.

The IDL compiler also generates *stub code* that the client links to, and this translates, or *marshals*, the programming language data types into a wire format for transmission as a request message to an object implementation. The implementation of the object has linked to it similar marshaling code, called a *skeleton*, that *unmarshals* the request into programming language data types. The skeleton can be generated by a different IDL compiler with a different language mapping. In this way the object's method implementation can be invoked and the results returned by the same means. Figure 2.5 illustrates the use of stub, skeleton, and ORB to make a remote invocation.

IDL and IDL compilers allow programs providing and using object interfaces to agree on the form of their exchanges, even though they may be developed completely independently, in different languages, and on different ORB technologies. This means that objects offering the same interfaces are substitutable and that clients can decide which object to use at run time with the assurance that there will be no interaction mismatches. Because the implementation of a particular object offering an interface is hidden, there may be Quality of Service differences, or even differences in the semantics of operations. The Trading Service allows clients to find the most appropriate object that matches their particular performance, location, cost, or other criteria.

The interfaces to components of the ORB are all specified in IDL. This provides a language-neutral representation of the computational interface of the ORB. Certain parts of these definitions are designated as *pseudo-IDL (PIDL)*, which means that their implementations are not necessarily CORBA objects and data types. Any interface definition that is commented as pseudo-IDL may be implemented as a *pseudo-object*. This usually means that it is a library that is linked into the application using it. Although operations on pseudo-objects are invoked in the same way as operations on real CORBA objects, their references and pseudo-IDL data types cannot be passed as parameters to real CORBA objects.

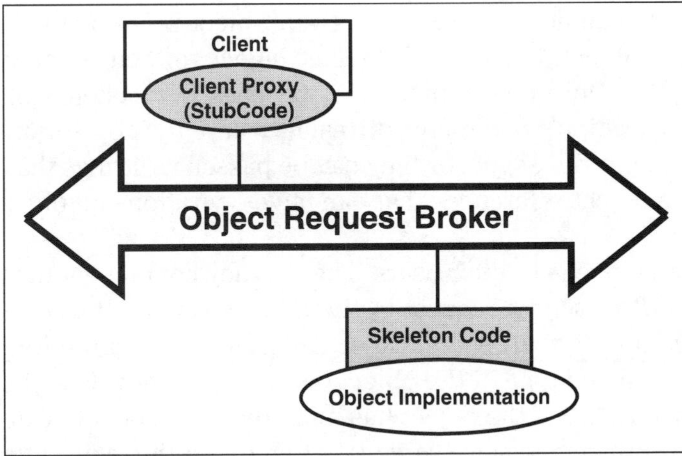


**Figure 2.5** Stub, ORB, and skeleton.

## 2.3.2 Object Model

The OMA Core Object Model provides some fundamental definitions of concepts that are extended by the CORBA specification. CORBA uses the same concepts as the OMA core, but it makes them more specific and concrete. The most precise specialization of the OMA model can be found in the chapter of the CORBA specification that describes the Portable Object Adapter, and these are the terms we use in the following. The definitions here refer to the way in which these concepts are declared, but they do not provide syntax for declarations. The syntax is provided by IDL (see section 2.3.4).

### *2.3.2.1 Servants and Object References*

It is necessary to distinguish between *servants* and *object references*. The former is a programming language entity containing code that implements the operations defined by an IDL interface definition, for example, a Java object. The latter is an object's identity and is used by clients to invoke operations on the object. It is important not to think of a servant as *being* the CORBA object because a CORBA object can be realized or *incarnated* by different servants over its lifetime.

A servant's code, the object implementation, is the part of a CORBA object that is provided by an application developer. Servants instantiated from it usually include some internal state, and they will often cause side effects on things that are not objects, such as a database, screen display, or telecommunications network element. The methods of this implementation may be accessed by any mechanism, but in practice most servants will be invoked via the skeleton code generated by an IDL compiler.

Object references are handles to objects. A given object reference will always denote a single object, but several distinct object references may denote the same object. Object references can be passed to clients of objects, either as an operation's parameter or result, where the IDL for an operation nominates an interface type, or they can be passed as strings that can be turned into live object references that can have operations invoked on them.

Object references are opaque to their users. That is, they contain enough information for the ORB to send a request to the correct servant, but this information is inaccessible to their users. Object references contain information about the location and type of the object denoted, but they do so in a sophisticated manner so that if the object has migrated or is not active at the time, the ORB can perform the necessary tasks to redirect the request to a new location or activate an object to receive the request.

Unless an object has been explicitly destroyed or the underlying network and operating system infrastructure is malfunctioning, the ORB should be able to convey an operation invocation to its target and return results. The ORB also supports operations that interpret the object reference and provide the client with some of the information it contains.

### 2.3.2.2 Types

Types are a concept for grouping entities that satisfy a common predicate associated with the type. Object types are related in an inheritance hierarchy, with the type *Object* at the root. An object type derived from another can be substituted for it. Object types may be specified as parameters and return types for operations, and they may be used as components in structured data types. A set of nonobject types are defined with specific properties in CORBA. These are represented by constructs in OMG IDL. The usual kind of basic numeric, string, and Boolean types are defined. A type called *Any* is also given as a basic type. It can store any legitimate value of a CORBA type in a self-describing manner. See Chapter 5, "OMG IDL to Java Mapping," for detailed descriptions of Anys and Chapter 9, "Advanced Features," for examples using Anys.

The basic types can be used as components for a rich set of structured types, including structures, arrays, variable length sequences, and discriminated unions. The syntax and specification of CORBA types are given in the OMG IDL description.

### 2.3.2.3 Interfaces

An *interface* is a description of the operations that are offered by an object; it can also contain structured type definitions used as parameters to those operations. Interfaces are specified in OMG IDL and are related in an inheritance hierarchy. In CORBA, interface types and object types have a one-to-one mapping. This is a restriction of the OMA Core Object Model, which implies that objects have single interfaces but does not state that this must be the case. The term *principal interface* is used to indicate the most specific (most derived) interface type that an object supports. The CORBA component model defines a new category of objects, components, with multiple interfaces.

### 2.3.2.4 Valuetypes and Abstract Interfaces

A *valuetype*, like an interface, is a description of a set of operations. Additionally, it can describe state that is accessible to a client. Instances of valuetypes are always guaranteed to be local implementations and, unlike objects, will be passed by value in operation invocations. Valuetypes can inherit from other valuetypes and, by providing the necessary operations, may support multiple interfaces. A valuetype may be abstract in the sense that it provides no state and may not have direct instances.

An abstract interface is a description of an entity that may be either an object or a valuetype instance at run time. Abstract interfaces are used in operation signatures to make parameter passing dependent on the run-time type of the operation's argument.

### 2.3.2.5 Operation Semantics

There are two kinds of operation execution semantics defined for static (stub code) invocations:

**At-Most-Once.** An operation is a named action for which a client can request an invocation. The invocation of an operation results in the ORB conveying the arguments to the object implementation and returning the results (if any) to the requester, which is blocked and waiting for a successful termination or an exception. The semantics of the invocation are "at-most-once." That is, the operation will execute exactly once if a successful completion takes place, or if an exception is raised it will have executed no more than once.

**Best-Effort.** If an operation is declared using the oneway keyword then the requester does not wait for the operation to complete and the semantics is "best-effort." Both these kinds of requests can be made using the generated stubs or using the Dynamic Invocation Interface (DII), but the DII also offers a third type of execution semantics—*deferred-synchronous.* This allows the requester to send the request without blocking and at some later time poll for the results.

### 2.3.2.6 Operation Signatures

Each operation has a signature, expressed in IDL, that contains the following mandatory components:

- An operation identifier (also called an operation name).
- The type of the value returned by the operation.
- A (possibly empty) list of parameters, each with a name, type, and direction indication. The direction will be one of in, out, or inout, stating that the parameter is being transmitted from the client to the

object, is being returned as a result from the operation, or is client data to be modified by the operation, respectively.

An operation signature may also have the following optional components:

- A raises clause that lists user-defined exceptions that the operation may raise. Any operation may raise system exceptions.
- A oneway keyword that indicates "best-effort" semantics. The signature must have a void return type and may not contain any out or inout parameters or a raises clause.
- A context clause that lists the names of operating system, user, or client program environment values that must be transmitted with the request. Contexts are transmitted as sets of string pairs and are not type safe. Contexts are intended to play a similar role to environment variables known from various operating systems.

#### 2.3.2.7 Attributes

An interface may contain *attributes.* These are declared as named types, with a possible readonly modifier. They are logically equivalent to a pair of operations. The first, an *accessor operation,* retrieves a value of the specified type. The second, a *modifier operation,* takes an argument of the specified type and sets that value. Read-only attributes will have only an accessor. Attributes cannot raise user-defined exceptions.

The execution semantics for attributes are the same as for operations. Attributes do not necessarily represent a state variable in an object, and executing the modifier operation with a particular argument does not guarantee that the same value will be returned by the next accessor execution. Section 2.3.4.6 contains a full syntax for operation and attribute declarations.

#### 2.3.2.8 Exceptions

An *exception* is a specialized nonobject type in OMG IDL. It is declared with the keyword exception and has a name and optional fields of named data values that provide further information about what caused the abnormal termination of an operation.

The standard IDL module, CORBA, contains declarations of 31 standard exceptions to address network, ORB, and operating system errors. These exceptions may be raised by any operation, either implicitly by the ORB or explicitly in the operation implementation. Each standard exception, also known as a system exception, has two pieces of data associated with it:

- A completion status, an enumerated type with three possible values—COMPLETED_YES, COMPLETED_NO, and COMPLETED_MAYBE—indicating that the operation implementation was executed in full, that the operation was not executed, or that this cannot be determined.
- A long integer minor code that can be set to some ORB-dependent value for more information.

Further user-defined exceptions may be declared in IDL and associated with operations in the raises clause of their signatures. An operation may raise only user exceptions that appear in its signature.

## 2.3.3 ORB Structure

As we have mentioned, OMG IDL provides the basis of agreement about what can be requested of an object implementation via the ORB. IDL, however, is not just a guide to clients of objects. IDL compilers use the interface definitions to create the means by which a client can invoke a local function and an invocation then happens, as if by magic, on an object on another machine. The code generated for the client to use is known as stub code, and the code generated for the object implementation is called skeleton code. Figure 2.6 shows the ORB core, stub and skeleton code, and the interfaces to the ORB.

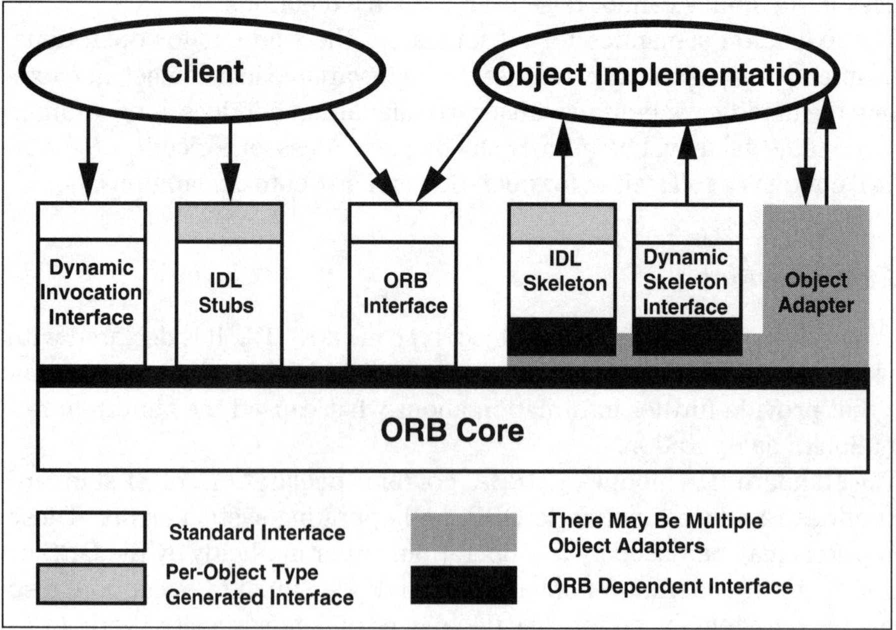


**Figure 2.6** ORB interfaces.

These two pieces of generated code are linked into the respective client and object implementations, and they interface with the ORB run-time system to convey requests and results for static invocations. Static means that the IDL is statically defined at compile time, and only operations on known interface types can be invoked.

The CORBA standard also defines an interface to allow requests to be built dynamically for any operation by a client. This is known as the *Dynamic Invocation Interface (DII)*. A symmetric interface is defined for responding to arbitrary requests, called the *Dynamic Skeleton Interface (DSI)*.

CORBA defines an interface for communicating with the ORB from either client or server. This interface deals mainly with ORB initialization and object reference manipulation.

Finally, object implementations need extra facilities for managing their interactions with the ORB. A component called an *Object Adapter* fills this role and is responsible for looking up and potentially activating implementations for executing operations.

### 2.3.3.1 Client Stubs

When a client wishes to invoke an IDL-defined operation on an object reference as if it were a local method or function call, it must link in stubs for the IDL interface that convey that invocation to the target object. In object-oriented implementation languages the stubs are instantiated as local proxy objects that delegate invocations on their methods to the remote implementation object. The stubs are generated from an IDL compiler for the language (and ORB environment) the client is using.

### 2.3.3.2 Dynamic Invocation Interface

A *Request* is a notional message that is sent to an object denoted by an object reference to request the invocation of a particular operation with particular arguments. The DII defines the form of such a message so that clients that know of an object by reference, and can determine its interface type, can build Requests without requiring an IDL compiler to generate stub code. A Request interface is defined in pseudo-IDL. It provides operations to set the target object for the invocation, name the operation to be invoked, and add arguments to send to it. It also provides operations to invoke the operation and retrieve any resulting values. As noted earlier, the implementation of pseudo-IDL is provided as a library and the operations map to local methods on a non-CORBA object.

The DII defines various types of execution semantics for operations invoked using Request pseudo-objects. The usual synchronous at-most-once semantics are available, as well as a deferred-synchronous option that sends the request and immediately returns to the client code to allow further processing while waiting for a response.

#### 2.3.3.3 Implementation Skeleton

Once a Request reaches a server that supports one or more objects, there must be a way for it to invoke the right method on the right implementation object. The translation from a wire format to in-memory data structures (unmarshaling) uses the language mapping to the implementation language. This is achieved by the skeleton code generated by an IDL compiler.

#### 2.3.3.4 Dynamic Skeleton Interface (DSI)

Implementation code may be written that deals with requests in a generic manner, looking at the requested operation and its arguments and interpreting the semantics dynamically. This is called the Dynamic Skeleton Interface and is realized by allowing the implementer access to the request in the form of a *ServerRequest* pseudo-object, which is the same as the DII Request except for the invocation operations.

An example use of the DSI is a minimal wrapper around some legacy command processing code that accepts each request it receives with a single string argument. It then parses the string for a numeric value and sets this in a register before passing the operation name to an interpreter. It then checks the contents of the register, and unless an error bit is set, encodes the rest of the register as a numeric string and passes it back as the result. Clients can then write IDL that matches the expected pattern and use the generated stubs in a type-safe way to invoke the server that was implemented before the IDL was written.

#### 2.3.3.5 Object Adapters

An Object Adapter is a component that connects servants with an ORB and that the ORB uses to manage the run-time environment of the object implementations. An adapter is used, rather than extending the interface to the ORB, so that different Object Adapters suitable for different implementations can be used for greater efficiency.

Currently CORBA defines one such interface, the Portable Object Adapter (POA). The Basic Object Adapter (BOA), which was defined in earlier versions of the CORBA specification, has been deprecated because it was underspecified. It is still supported by a number of ORBs to provide backward compatibility with code for their older products. The purpose of an Object Adapter is to generate and interpret object references and to activate and deactivate servants. The interface to the POA is described in detail in section 2.3.6.

## 2.3.4 OMG Interface Definition Language (IDL)

OMG IDL is a declarative language for defining the interfaces of CORBA objects. It is a language-independent way in which implementers and users of objects can be assured of type-safe invocation of operations, even though the only other information that needs to pass between them is an object reference.

IDL is used by ORB-specific IDL compilers to generate stub and/or skeleton code that converts in-memory data structures in one programming language into network streams and then unpacks them on another machine into equivalent data structures in another (or the same) language, makes a method call, and then transmits the results in the opposite direction.

The syntax of IDL is drawn from C++, but it contains different and unambiguous keywords. There are no programming statements, as its only purpose is to define interface signatures. To do this a number of constructs are supported:

- Constants—to assist with type declarations
- Data type declarations—to use for parameter typing
- Attributes—which get and set a value of a particular type
- Operations—which take parameters and return values
- Interfaces—which group data type, attribute, and operation declarations
- Valuetypes—which group data type, state, and operation declarations
- Modules—for name space separation

All of the declarations made in IDL can be made available through the Interface Repository (IR). This is part of the CORBA specification, and its interfaces are explained in section 2.3.11.

### *2.3.4.1 Lexical Analysis*

OMG IDL uses the ASCII character set except for string and character literals that may use the full ISO Latin-1 character set.

**Identifiers.** Identifiers must start with a letter and may be followed by zero or more letters, numbers, and underscores. The only strange feature of the lexical analysis of IDL is that identifiers are case sensitive but cannot coexist with other identifiers that differ only in case. To put it another way, to identify the same entity the identifier must use the same case in each instance, but another identifier with the same spelling and different case may not coexist with it. For example, short DisplayTerminal and interface displayTerminal denote different entities, but they may not both be declared in the same IDL. The reason for this is that language mappings to case-insensitive languages would not cope with both identifiers.

**Escaped Identifiers.** In the process of evolving IDL, a number of new keywords have been added to the language and thus become reserved words. To fix collisions with identifiers in existing IDL definitions, an escaping mechanism was defined. By prepending an underscore ('_') to an identifier, keyword checking for this identifier is turned off. The underscore will then be removed by the IDL compiler, so no identifiers with leading underscores will actually appear in the code generated by the compiler.

**Preprocessing.** The standard C++ preprocessing macros are the first thing to be dealt with in lexical analysis. They include #include, #define, #ifdef, and #pragma.

**Keywords.** Keywords are all in lowercase, and other identifiers may not differ only in case.

**Comments.** Both styles of C++ comments are used in IDL. The "/*" characters open a comment, and "*/" closes it. These comments cannot be nested. The characters "//" indicate that the rest of a line is a comment.

**Punctuation.** The curly brace is used to enclose naming scopes, and closing braces are always followed by a semicolon. Declarations are always followed by a semicolon. Lists of parameters are surrounded by parentheses with the parameters separated by commas.

#### 2.3.4.2 Modules and Interfaces

The purpose of IDL is to define interfaces and their operations. To avoid name clashes when using several IDL declarations together the *module* is used as a naming scope. Modules can contain any well-formed IDL, including nested modules. Interfaces also open a new naming scope and can contain constants, data type declarations, attributes, and operations.

```
// RoomBooking.idl
module RoomBooking {
  interface Room {};
};
```

Any interface name in the same scope can be used as a type name, and interfaces in other name scopes can be referred to by giving a scoped name that is separated in C++ style by double colons. For example, RoomBooking::Room is the name of the empty interface declared previously. This name can also be written ::RoomBooking::Room to explicitly show that it is relative to the global scope.

Modules may be nested inside other modules, and their contents may be named relative to the current naming scope. For example,

```
module outer {
  module inner { // nested module
    interface inside {};
  };
  interface outside { // can refer to inner as a local name
    inner::inside get_inside();
  };
};
```

The get_inside() operation returns an object reference of type ::outer::inner:inside, but it may use the relative form of the name due to its position in the same scope as the inner module.

Interfaces may be mutually referential. That is, declarations in each interface may use the name of the other as an object type. To avoid compilation errors an interface type must be forward declared before it is used. That is,

```
interface A; // forward declaration
interface B { // B can use forward-declared interfaces as type names
  A get_an_A();
};
interface A {
  B get_a_B();
};
```

The preceding example declares the existence of an interface with name A before defining interface B, which has an operation returning an object reference to an A. It then defines A, which has an operation returning an object reference to a B. Forward declaration of interfaces is often used for formatting and readability rather than mutual recursion.

When a declaration in a module needs some mutual reference to a declaration in another module, this is achieved by closing the first module and reopening it after some other declarations. This is shown in the following declaration:

```
module X {
  // forward declaration of A
  interface A;
}; // close the module to allow interfaces A needs to be declared
module Y {
  interface B { // B can use X::A as a type name
    X::A get_an_A();
  };
}
module X { // re-open module to define A
  interface C { // C can use A unqualified as it is in the same scope
    A get_an_A();
  };
  interface A { // A can use Y::B as a type name
    Y::B get_a_B();
  };
};
```

### 2.3.4.3 Inheritance

The set of operations offered by an interface can be extended by declaring a new interface that inherits from the existing one. The existing interface is called the *base interface*, and the new interface is called the *derived interface*. Inheritance is declared by using a colon after the new interface name, followed by a base interface name, as the following example shows:

```
module InheritanceExample {
  interface A {
    typedef unsigned short ushort;
      ushort op1();
  };
  interface B : A {
    boolean op2(ushort num);
  };
};
```

In this example, interface B extends interface A and offers operations op1() and op2(). The data type declarations are also inherited, allowing the use of ushort as a parameter type in op2(). All interfaces implicitly inherit from CORBA::Object. This becomes clear when looking at the language mapping. In Java, for example, interface A will map to a Java interface `A`, which extends a Java interface called `org.omg.CORBA.Object` provided by the ORB. In the same manner interface B will map to a Java interface `B` which extends `A`.

CORBA IDL allows any nonobject types declared in an interface to be redefined in a derived interface. We consider this to be an oversight, and it is not recommended that this feature ever be used. The beauty of inheritance is that it is a clean mechanism for determining subtyping and substitutability of interfaces. An object implementing interface B would be able to be used where an object of type A was required, as B is a subtype of A.

### 2.3.4.4 Multiple Inheritance

An interface may inherit from several other interfaces. The syntax is the same as single inheritance, and the base interfaces are separated by commas. For example,

```
interface C : A, B, VendorY::interfaceX {
  ...
};
```

The names of the operations in each of the inherited interfaces (including the operations they inherit from other interfaces) must be unique and may not be redeclared in the derived interface. The exception to this rule occurs when the operations are inherited into two or more interfaces from the same base interface. This is known as *diamond inheritance* (the inheritance graph is the shape of a diamond). For example,

```
module DiamondInheritanceExample {
  interface Base {
    string BaseOp();
  };
  interface Left:Base {
    short LeftOp(in string LeftParam);
  };
  interface Right:Base {
    any RightOp(in long RightParam);
  };
  interface Derived:Left,Right {
    octet DerivedOp(in float DerivedInParam,
        out unsigned long DerivedOutParam);
  };
};
```

Figure 2.7 shows the IDL in graphical form. Both interfaces Left and Right contain the operation BaseOp(), but they can both be inherited by Derived because BaseOp() comes from the same base interface. The rule that identifiers must be unique in an interface implies that it is not possible to overload operation names as in Java.

### *2.3.4.5 Types and Constants*

The name of any interface declared in IDL becomes an object type name that may be used as the type of any operation parameter or return value or as a member in a structured type declaration, for example, to declare the length of an array. The basic types are rich enough to represent numerics, strings, characters, and Booleans. The definitions of these are very precise to allow unambiguous marshaling. The structured types available in IDL are structures, discriminated unions, arrays, and sequences. Exceptions can be considered to be a special case of structures that are used only in raises clauses of operations.

The set of basic types provided by IDL and their required characteristics are as follows.

| Type Keyword | Description |
|---|---|
| [unsigned] short | Signed [unsigned] 16-bit 2's complement integer |
| [unsigned] long | Signed [unsigned] 32-bit 2's complement integer |
| [unsigned] long long | Signed [unsigned] 64-bit 2's complement integer |
| float | 16-bit IEEE floating-point number |
| double | 32-bit IEEE floating-point number |
| long double | 64-bit IEEE floating-point number |

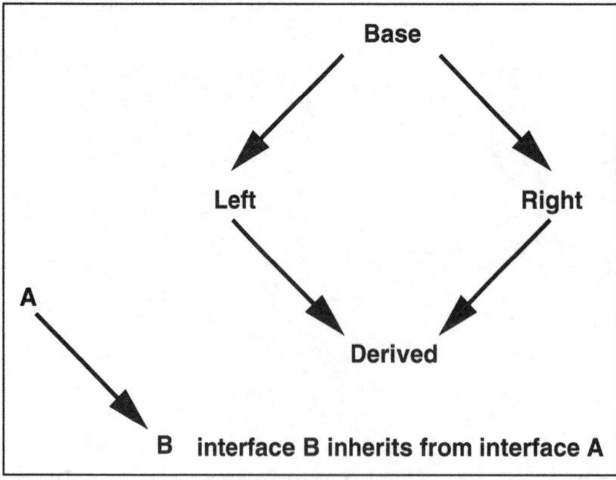


**Figure 2.7** Diamond inheritance.

| | |
|---|---|
| fixed | fixed-point decimal number of up to 31 digits |
| char | ISO Latin-1 character |
| wchar | character from other character sets to support internationalization. The size is implementation dependent |
| boolean | Boolean type taking values TRUE and FALSE |
| string | Variable-length string of characters whose length is available at run time |
| wstring | Variable-length string of wchar characters |
| octet | 8-bit uninterpreted type |
| enum | Enumerated type with named integer values |
| any | Can represent a value from any possible IDL type, basic or constructed, object or nonobject |
| native | Opaque type, representation specified by language mapping |

The keyword typedef allows aliases to be created for any legal type declaration. In the case of template types (types that require a parameter to determine their length or contents) a typedef is required before the type can be used in an operation or attribute declaration. See the following string example.

Strings may be bounded or unbounded. Bounded strings are a template type. That is, their declaration contains a maximum length parameter in angle brackets. For example,

```
interface StringProcessor {
    typedef octstring string <8>;
    typedef centastring string <100>;
    //...
    octstring MiddleEight(in string str);
    centastring PadOctString(in octstring ostr, char pad_char);
};
```

Fixed-point types are template types like strings and need to be introduced by a typedef. The template arguments are the number of decimal digits and the scale, which is expressed as a power of 10. The following IDL defines a fixed point with five digits and a scale of two. This means that the decimal point is positioned between the third and fourth digit from the right, as in “123.45.”

```
typedef fixed <5,2> three_point_two;
```

Enumerated types are declared with a name, which can be used as a valid type thereafter, and a comma-separated list of identifiers. The identifiers used in an enum declaration must be unique within the enclosing name space. Unlike structured types, enums do not open new name spaces themselves. For example,

```
enum glass_color {gc_clear, gc_red, gc_blue, gc_green};
```

**Any.** The Any type has an API defined in pseudo-IDL that describes how values are inserted and extracted from it and how the type of its contained value may be discovered. This is addressed in Chapter 6.

**Structures.** Structures are declared with the keyword struct, which must be followed by a name. This name is usable as a valid type name thereafter. This is followed by a semicolon-separated list of named type fields, as in C and C++. For example,

```
interface HardwareStore {
  struct window_spec {
    glass_color color;
    height  float;
    width   float;
};
```

**Discriminated unions.** Discriminated unions are declared with the keyword union, which must be followed by a name. The name, once again, becomes a valid type name for use in subsequent declarations. The keyword switch follows the type name, and it is parameterized by a scalar type (integer, char, Boolean, or enum) that will act as the discriminator. The body of the union is enclosed in braces and contains a number of case statements followed by named type declarations. For example,

```
enum fitting_kind {door_k, window_k, shelf_k, cupboard_k};
union fitting switch (fitting_kind) {
  case door_k,
       cupboard_k:  door_spec     door;
  case window_k:    window_spec win;
  default:          float         width;
};
```

The default case is optional, but it may not appear more than once. In each language mapping there is a means of accessing the discriminator value by name in order to determine which field of the union contains a value. The value of a union consists of the value of the discriminator and the value of the element that it nominates. If the discriminator is set to a value not mentioned in a case label, and there is no default case, then that part of the union's value is undefined.

**Sequences.** Sequences are template types. That means that their declarations nominate other types that will be contained within the sequence. A sequence is an ordered collection of items that can grow at run time. Its elements are accessed by index. Sequences may be bounded or unbounded. All sequences have two characteristics at run time, a maximum and a current length. The maximum length of bounded sequences is set at compile time. The advantage of sequences is that only the current number of elements is transmitted to a remote object when a sequence argument is passed.

Sequence declarations must be given a typedef alias in order to be used as types in operation parameters or return types. Here are some example sequences of hardware fittings used to convey orders to a hardware store:

```
// union type "fitting" declared above.
typedef sequence <fitting> HardwareOrderSeq;
typedef sequence <fitting, 10> LimitedHWQrderSeq;
typedef sequence <sequence <<fitting>, 3> ThreeStoreHWOrderSeq;
typedef sequence <sequence <fitting> > ManyStoreHWOrderSeq;
```

Sequence is the only unaliased complex type that may be used in angle brackets. All other types must be typedefed before sequences of them can be declared. Note that there is a space between the two closing angle brackets in the final declaration. If these were put side by side they would be parsed as the operator >>, which can be used when declaring integer constants. A better style would be to declare ThreeStoreHWOrderSeq as a sequence of HardwareOrderSeq.

**Arrays.** Arrays are also usually declared within a typedef, as they must be named before using them as operation parameter or return types. They may be declared as an element type of a union or member type of a struct.

Arrays at run time will have a fixed length. The entire array (regardless of useful content) will be marshaled and transmitted in a request if used in a parameter or return type. In contrast, sequences passed as arguments or returned as results will be transmitted only up to their length at the time of the invocation.

Arrays are declared by adding one or more square-bracketed dimensions containing an integer constant. For example,

```
typedef window WindowVec10[10];
typedef fitting FittingGrid[3][10];
struct bathroom {
   float      width;
   float      length;
   float      height;
   boolean has_toilet;
   fitting    fittings[6];
};
```

**Exceptions.** Exceptions are declared in exactly the same manner as structures, using the keyword exception in place of struct. A set of standard exceptions, also known as system exceptions, is declared in the CORBA module. Here are some examples of user-defined exceptions:

```
exception OrderTooLarge {
     long max_items;
     long num_items_submitted;
};
exception ColorMismatch {
   sequence <color> other_window_colors;
     color          color_submitted;
};
```

It is good style to include values of arguments that are relevant to the cause of a failure in an exception. That way exception handling can be done by a generic handler that does not know what arguments were given that may have caused the exception. The handler can determine the context of the operation that raised the exception from the values in the exception.

**Constants.** Constant values can be declared at global scope or within modules and interfaces. The declaration begins with the keyword const, followed by a Boolean, numeric, character, or string type name, an identifier, and then an equals sign and a value. Numeric values can be declared as expressions, with the full range of C++ bitwise, integer, and floating-point mathematical operators available. For example,

```
const short max_storage_bays = 200;
const short windows_per_bay = 45;
```

```
const long max_windows = max_storage_bays * windows_per_bay;
const string initial_quote = "fox in socks on knox on blocks";
const HardwareStore::CashAmount balance = (max_storage_bays – 3) / 1.45
```

### 2.3.4.6 Operations and Attributes

Operation declarations are similar to C++ function prototypes. They contain an operation name, a return type (or void to indicate that no value is expected), and a parameter list, which may be empty. In addition, an operation may have a raises clause, which specifies what user exceptions the operation may raise, and it may have a context clause, which gives a list of names of string properties from the caller's environment that need to be supplied to the operation implementation. Contexts are rarely used and should best be avoided.

Lists of parameters to operations are surrounded by parentheses, and the parameters are separated by commas. Each parameter must have a directional indicator so that it is clear in which direction the data travels. These are in, out, and inout, indicating client to object, return parameter, and client value modified by object and returned, respectively. These points are shown in the IDL that follows.

```
// interface HardwareStore cont..
typedef float CashAmount;
typedef sequence <window_spec> WindowSeq;
CashAmount OrderFittings(in HardwareOrderSeq order)
   raises (OrderTooLarge);
void OrderWindows(
      in WindowSeq        order,
      in CashAmount       willing_to_pay,
      out CashAmount      total_price,
      out short           order_number)
   raises (OrderTooLarge, ColorMismatch);
```

The parameter passing mode used to pass arguments is pass-by-value for basic types and for structure, union, and enumeration types. This means that their value is always copied, according to the direction indicated by in, out, and inout. Object type arguments, however, are always passed by reference, which means that the client of an operation and the receiving server can share objects. There are no pass-by-value semantics for regular object types. CORBA defines a hybrid data type, valuetypes, which can be passed by value. This is explained in the text that follows.

Operations can be declared oneway if it is desirable for the caller to send a noncritical message to an object. One-way operation invocations will use best-effort semantics. The caller will get an immediate return and cannot know for certain if the request has been invoked. For obvious reasons there can be no out or inout parameters declared on one-way operations. There must be no raises clause, and the operation must have a void return type. The following declaration illustrates this.

```
// interface HardwareStore cont . . .
oneway void requestAccountStatement(in short customer_id);
```

An attribute is logically equivalent to a pair of accessor functions—one to access the value, the other to modify it. Read-only attributes require only an accessor function.

Attributes are simpler to declare than operations. They consist of the keyword attribute followed by the type of the attribute(s) and then an attribute name list. The optional keyword readonly may precede the attribute declaration.

```
// interface HardwareStore cont . . .
readonly attribute CashAmount min_order, max_order;
readonly attribute FittingSeq new_fittings;
attribute string quote_of_the_day;
```

The previous attributes could be replaced by the following IDL:

```
CashAmount min_order();
CashAmount max_order();
FittingSeq new_fittings();
  string get_quote_of_the_day();
  void set_quote_of_the_day(in string quote);
```

As declared, the operations and attributes are equivalent. The actual names chosen for the methods in the object implementation are determined by the language mapping. Attributes and operations can both raise standard exceptions. Operations can be given raises clauses, allowing better handling of error conditions.

### 2.3.4.7 Valuetypes

Valuetypes are a special data type in IDL that were introduced to allow entities to pass by value rather than by reference in an operation invocation, so that accessing a value will always be a local operation.

Providing pass-by-value semantics for object references is only half of the contribution of valuetypes, however. The other half is providing sharing and "null" semantics for IDL values like structs and sequences. Using valuetypes, it is possible to pass an entire graph in an operation invocation in a way that preserves shared values in the graph. With ordinary IDL structured types, it is not possible to transmit a graph with sharing preserved. Another feature not present for base and structured IDL values is "null reference" semantics. For example, an IDL struct can be empty (that is, its values may not have been initialized), but it can never be null. Valuetypes allow this.

Valuetypes are a mixture of interfaces and structures and are declared using the keyword valuetype. A number of different kinds of valuetypes exist.

**Regular Valuetypes.** Regular or "stateful" valuetypes, like interfaces, can contain definitions of attributes, operations and local type declarations. Unlike interfaces, they can have state members and initializers.

```
interface Observer {
   void notify();
};

// sequence type HardwareOrderSeq defined above
valuetype ShoppingCart supports Observer {
   readonly attribute long current_value;
   private HardwareOrderSeq selected;
   void addToCart(in fitting item);
   factory init(in HardwareOrderSeq initial);
};
```

A valuetype's state members constitute the state that is marshaled and sent to the receiver. This is also the initial state of the value's copy in the receiving environment. State members can be declared public or private. Declaring a state member private does not keep it from being sent over the wire but determines that it should be accessible only to the implementation code of valuetype's operations and the marshaling code.

IDL compilers will generate standard marshaling code from definitions of valuetypes unless the modifier custom is used in the definition. Custom marshaling code must be supplied by the developer in a language-specific way.

```
custom valuetype MyCustomShoppingCart {
// ...
```

To create new instances, an initializer can be defined using the keyword factory. Like constructors in Java, initializers have no return type. Unlike Java constructors, an initializer's name need not be identical to the name of the type but can be freely chosen, subject only to the usual IDL operation name rules. The operation signatures for a valuetype need not be explicitly defined but can also be inherited from interfaces named after the keyword supports.

**Boxed Valuetypes.** These are a shorthand notation for valuetypes with no inheritance, no operations, and a single, unnamed state member. A boxed valuetype is best thought of as a simple container or "value box" and is useful mainly for turning sequences and strings into valuetypes so that they can be null or shared. Basically, boxed valuetypes are a simple means to pass null values where nonobject types would have to pass empty values.

```
valuetype ObserverSeq sequence <Observer>;
```

**Abstract Valuetypes.** Valuetypes can also be abstract, which means that they cannot be instantiated. Abstract valuetypes have no initializers or state members; only operation or data type definitions are possible.

```
abstract valuetype Cart supports Observer {
  void add(in Any item);
};
```

Note that a valuetype must be declared abstract to make it abstract; the mere absence of state members and initializers does not suffice.

**Valuetype inheritance**. Valuetypes, like interfaces, can inherit from each other. The general inheritance rules for name scoping are exactly analogous to interface inheritance and are not repeated here. Multiple inheritance is allowed only for inheriting from abstract valuetypes. As soon as a regular, stateful valuetype appears in an inheritance hierarchy, derived types may use only single inheritance.

Valuetypes may also support interfaces. This does not make any difference to their existence as a value rather than an object—valuetypes are not subtypes of CORBA::Object. A concrete implementation of a valuetype in a programming language, however, may also become a full CORBA object if it supports an interface and is registered with the ORB through an Object Adapter. The result of such an operation is a regular object reference, so passing the object as an argument in CORBA invocations will always have the usual by-reference semantics. Parameter-passing semantics is thus determined by the formal parameter type of an operation. If the formal parameter has an object type, parameters are passed by reference. If it has a valuetype, pass-by-value semantics applies.

Situations may arise where the receiver of a valuetype argument does not have an implementation of the actual argument's type. This may occur because the argument's type is a derived type, and its implementation simply was not known, or maybe did not even exist, at the time the receiver code was assembled. In this situation, the receiver should try to dynamically link an implementation of this type.

If no suitable implementation can be obtained, it may be possible to use the implementation of the formal argument type, which is higher up in the inheritance hierarchy. This may be done, however, only if it is semantically safe to assume that the derived type is substitutable for the base type. If it is, only those parts of the state that are inherited from the base type are sent to the receiver. This kind of widening operation is called truncating the argument value to its base type. If, however, the derived type has completely reinterpreted the state of its base for its own implementation, unpredictable behavior could result from truncation. To be able to determine whether it is safe to truncate a valuetype's state to its base type, a valuetype can be marked as being truncatable:

```
valuetype PersonRecord {
   private string name;
   private string address;
};
valuetype EmployeeRecord: truncatable PersonRecord {
   private string company_email;
};
valuetype ManagerRecord: truncatable EmployeeRecord {
   private unsigned long company_parking_lot_number;
}
```

Truncatability is a transitive property, so a ManagerRecord value can be truncated to a PersonRecord value.

**Abstract interfaces.** To allow operations to accept arguments that are either objects or values, another concept was added to IDL. Abstract interfaces can have derived types that are interfaces or valuetypes. For this reason, abstract interfaces do not implicitly inherit from CORBA::Object.

```
abstract interface MessageContainer {
   string getMessage();
};
```

```
interface Folder: MessageContainer {
   void merge(in MessageContainer a);
};

valuetype Envelope supports MessageContainer {
   private sequence<string> messages;
};
```

To determine which parameter-passing semantics applies to an argument with a formal parameter of an abstract interface type, the run-time type of the argument has to be consulted. If the argument of an operation like merge() is a CORBA object, for example, of type Folder, it will be passed by reference. If it has a valuetype, such as Envelope, it will be passed by value.

Valuetypes and abstract interfaces are relatively new concepts in the CORBA specification, and it is not certain whether they will be implemented by ORBs for languages other than Java and C++. The main motivation for the addition of valuetypes to CORBA was to allow for the reverse mapping from Java to IDL which in turn provides RMI developers with a smooth transition to CORBA—RMI-IIOP. Without valuetypes, existing RMI applications using Java object serialization would not be accessible via IIOP.

Also, valuetypes may be seen as structures with inheritance. The practical benefit of abstract interfaces, however, is not clear.

#### 2.3.4.8 Contexts

Contexts provide a way of passing string-to-string mappings from the computing environment of the client to the object implementation. The specification does not define the way in which an ORB populates contexts to pass to objects. Some ORBs treat contexts as equivalent to UNIX or DOS environment variables. Others require users to build context objects explicitly. The string literals within a context clause must start with a letter and may end with "*", the wild card matching character. The matching character will cause the ORB to find all context items with the leading characters in common.

Contexts are a powerful but low-level concept and should be avoided if possible. For example, the use of wild card pattern matching is especially dangerous, as the IDL author has no way at specification time of knowing what names will be defined in the context of all callers. A broad pattern match may cause many kilobytes of strings to be transmitted unnecessarily for an otherwise lightweight operation invocation. In general, contexts are a hole in an otherwise type-safe interface definition language.

## 2.3.5 ORB and Object Interfaces

The ORB interface is available directly to clients and object implementations for a few object management reasons. These include creating string representations of object references, and transforming them back again, copying and deleting object references, and comparing object references against the empty, or nil, object reference.

As already mentioned, there are a number of interfaces defined within the CORBA standard that use the IDL syntax for programming-language-neutral API definitions. They are interfaces to ORB components that are implemented as libraries or in whatever way ORB implementers see fit. The IDL is commented as pseudo-IDL.

### *2.3.5.1 Stringified Object References*

As object references are opaque, the only way to correctly store an object reference persistently is in its stringified form. A stringified object reference can be passed by means such as e-mail, Web sites, or pen and paper, and when supplied as an argument to the string_to_object() operation it will produce a valid object reference that can be invoked. In order to use generated stubs to do this, the returned object reference must be passed to the narrow ( ) method of the appropriate interface stub to cast the object reference into a reference to a more specific interface than Object.

```
module CORBA { //PIDL
  interface ORB {
    string object_to_string(in Object obj);
    Object string_to_object(in string obj);
    // several other operations are defined here but used in
    // other contexts, such as the ORB initialization and the DII
  };
};
```

The object_to_string() operation takes an object and produces a string. This string may be passed to the converse operation, string_to_object(), to generate a new object reference that can be invoked and will send its requests to the same object passed to object_to_string().

### *2.3.5.2 Managing Object References*

This subsection addresses the pseudo-IDL for the CORBA::Object interface. This is the base interface for all CORBA objects, and its operations can be invoked on any object reference. In most cases the functionality is implemented in the libraries provided by the ORB, and results are not obtained by sending a request to a servant.

```
module CORBA {
  interface Object { // PIDL
    InterfaceDef       get_interface();
    boolean            is_nil();
    Object             duplicate();
    void               release();
    boolean            is_a(in string logical_type_id);
    boolean            non_existent();
    boolean            is_equivalent(in Object other_object);
    unsigned long      hash(in unsigned long maximum);
    Policy             get_policy(in PolicyType policy_type);
    Object             set_policy_overrides(in PolicyList policies,
                                            in SetOverrideTyp set_add);
    DomainManagersList get_domain_managers();
    // the create_request operation used by the DII is defined here
  };
};
```

The get_interface() operation returns a standard interface from the Interface Repository. This allows a client to investigate the IDL definition of an interface via calls to objects that represent the IDL in the Interface Repository. This approach can be used to discover the operations available on an object reference when its type is unknown at compile time. The DII can then be used to invoke these operations.

The is_nil() operation returns TRUE if this object reference denotes no object. Object implementations that return object references as output parameters or return values may choose to return a nil object reference rather than raise an exception. Different language bindings implement object references differently, and an invocation on a nil object reference may result in a fatal error.

The duplicate() and release() operations are very important in programming languages where programmers do explicit memory management (such as C and C++). Luckily in Java this is done for us automatically. These operations ensure correct management of copies of an object reference. When an object reference is to be passed to another object, or thread of control, the opaque type that implements the object reference *must not* be copied by using features of the implementation language. The duplicate() operation must be used instead. The reason is that when a remote client uses an object reference, a proxy object is created locally for the client to invoke operations on directly. The proxy, in concert with the ORB, creates the request that ends up at the object implementation.

A proxy object keeps a counter of all object references that refer to it. This is called a reference count. If a copy of a reference to that proxy is created without the knowledge of the proxy, it cannot increase its reference count. When the counted references are released the proxy assumes that no other references to it exist, and it will deallocate its resources and delete itself. Now the reference copied without using duplicate() refers to a deleted proxy and invocations made on it will incur a run-time error. This is illustrated in Figure 2.8.

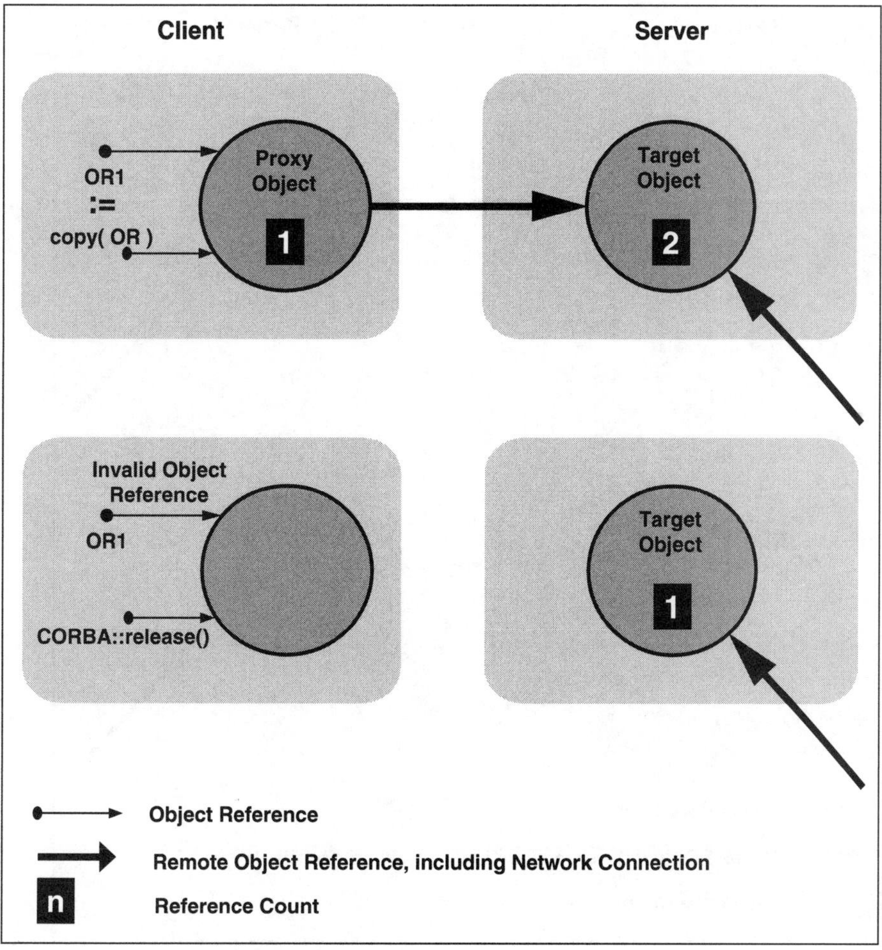


**Figure 2.8** Invalid object reference copy.

When duplicate() is called to obtain a new copy of the object reference, the proxy will increase its reference count and wait for all references to call release() before cleaning up and going away. This makes the importance of using release() equally clear. If the last reference to a proxy is deleted without calling release() the proxy will continue to consume memory, and probably network resources, until the process or task in which it executes dies. Figure 2.9 illustrates this case.

Figure 2.10 shows the correct use of duplicate() and release(), where the reference count in the proxy reflects the actual number of references to it.

Figure 2.11 shows what occurs when an object reference is duplicated for passing across machine boundaries. The figure does not show the tempo-

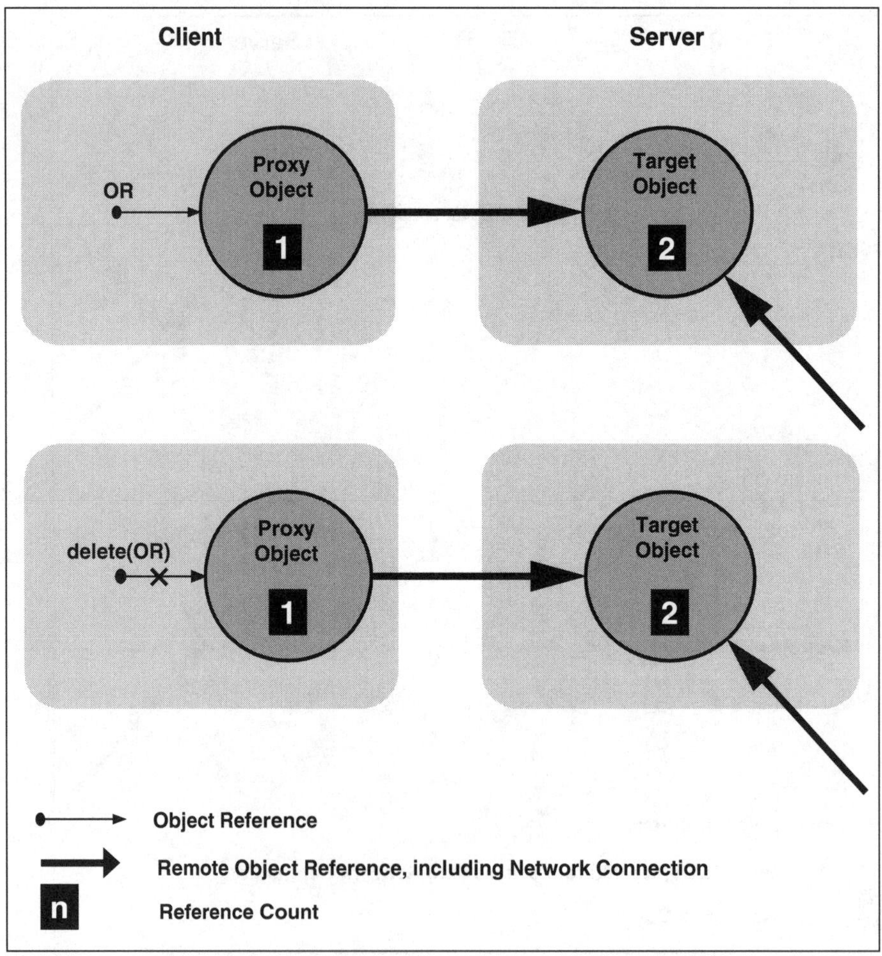


**Figure 2.9** Invalid object reference deletion.

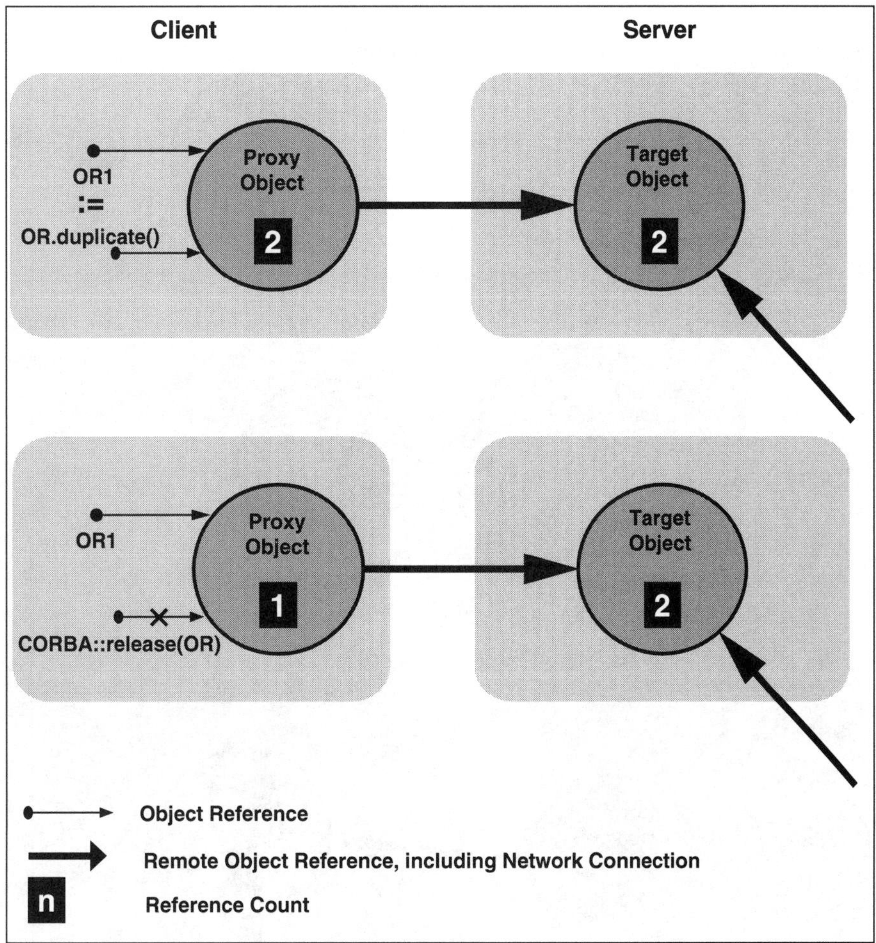


**Figure 2.10** Correct use of duplicate() and release().

rary increase in the reference count on proxy object B before the skeleton code does a release() when passing the reference back to the client.

The is_a() operation returns TRUE if the Interface Repository identifier passed to it refers to a type of which this object is a subtype. It is mainly used in dynamically typed languages that cannot support a narrow() method. We recommend the use of narrow(), which can be attempted for various object types. It will return a valid object reference if it is of a compatible type. Otherwise, it will return a nil object reference or raise an exception.

The non_existent() operation returns TRUE if the object implementation denoted by this reference has been destroyed. The ORB will return FALSE if the object exists or if it cannot determine the answer definitively.

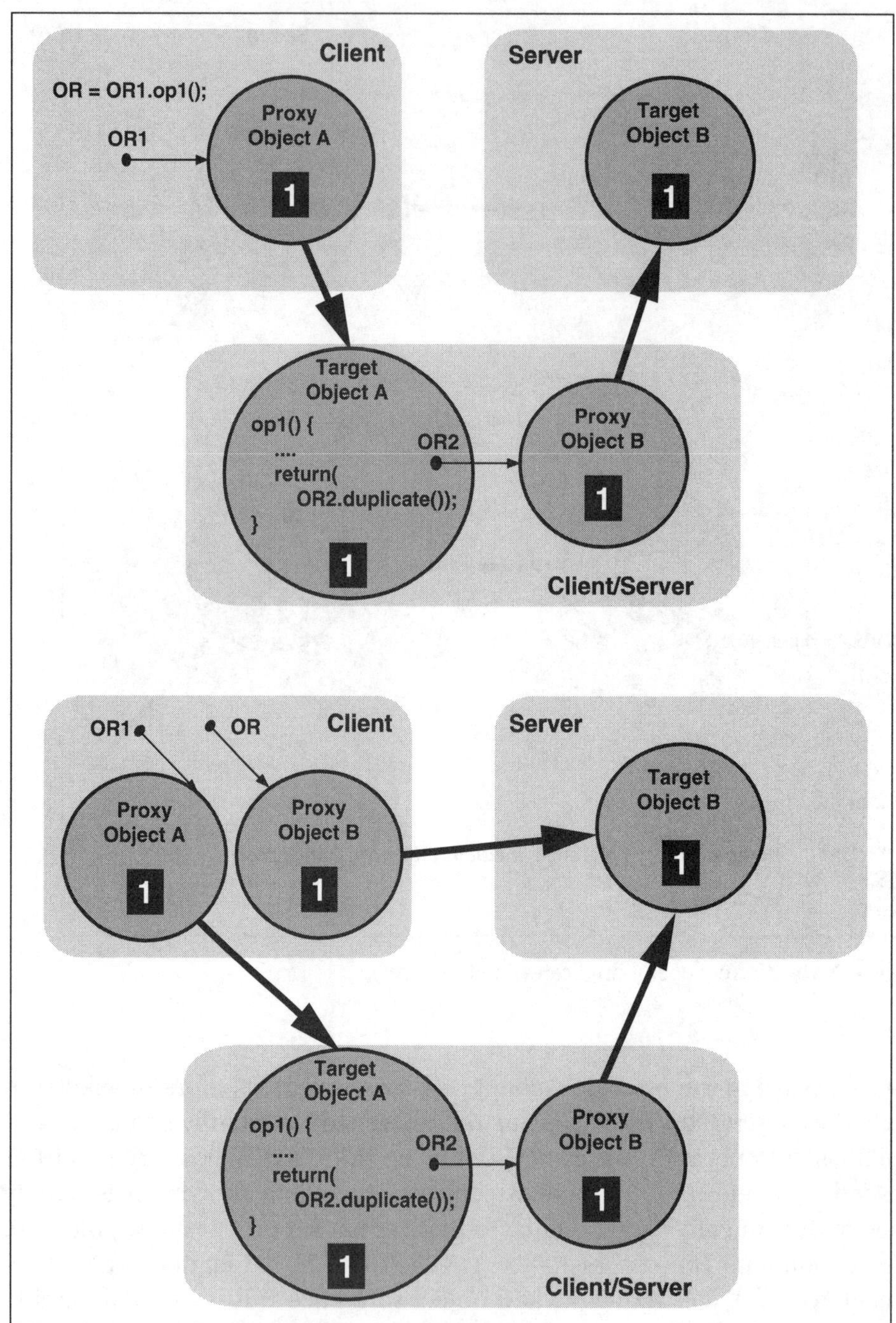


**Figure 2.11** Proxy creation when passing object references.

The is_equivalent() operation is the *only* way within CORBA of determining whether two object references denote the same object. All references that are created by calling duplicate() on a single object reference will be equivalent to the original reference and with each other. Even so, it is possible that two references that actually denote the same object may return a FALSE result from this operation. That is, a TRUE result guarantees that the object denoted is the same, but a FALSE result does not guarantee that two references denote different objects. String representations obtained from object_to_string() are ORB dependent and often are different every time they are generated. Hence, they do not offer a means of comparing references.

The hash() operation provides a way of searching for an equivalent object reference that is more efficient than comparing a reference against every object reference in a list. The same object reference will return the same hash value each time. This provides a way of selecting a small number of possibly identical references in a chained hash table, which can be compared pair-wise for a match. Most CORBA application programmers will never need to use is_equivalent() or hash().

The last three operations in the Object interface are related to managing policies that govern the life cycle and behavior of objects. The underlying management model is that of a policy domain. A policy domain is a set of objects to which a common policy applies. A domain is managed through the DomainManager interface that allows it to retrieve the policy object for the domain. An object may be a member of many different policy domains of different types (for example, one that has an security audit policy attached to it and another that has an access control policy object). These policies now govern aspects of the object's behavior, such as who may access its operations and which requests get logged in an audit log. An object's domain managers can be retrieved using the get_domain_managers() operation.

The get_policy() operation returns a policy object that applies to this object. The type of policy that is of interest here is specified in the operation argument. One such policy type defined in the CORBA core module itself is SecConstruction. This type of policy deals with mapping object references to domains at reference creation time. A number of other policies are introduced in the specification of the POA or the Security Service. The get_policy() operation returns the *effective* policy for the object. The effective policy is the one that would actually be used for an invocation on the object. It is a combination of client-side policies, which can be set using the set_policy_overrides() operation, and the policies associated with the object's domains.

### 2.3.5.3 Initialization

The CORBA module contains a pseudo-IDL operation ORB_init() for bootstrapping the ORB.

```
module CORBA { // PIDL
   typedef string ORBid;
   typedef sequence <string> arg_list;
   ORB ORB_init(inout arg_list argv, in ORBid orb_identifier);
};
```

ORB_init() is provided to obtain a reference to an ORB pseudo-object. Ordinarily operations must be associated with an interface, but ORB_init() is freestanding. ORB_init() takes the command-line arguments from a UNIX shell-style process launch and removes any that are intended for the ORB. It also takes the name of the ORB to be initialized in the form of a string.

The ORB interface supports some further operations to allow any ORB user to get access to fundamental object services and/or facilities by name. The declarations that follow allow the ORB user to find out which basic services and facilities the ORB supports and obtain references to their objects. This mechanism is also used to obtain a POA reference. The list_initial_services() operation provides a list of the strings that identify the services and facilities, and the resolve_initial_references() operation takes these strings as an argument and returns an object reference.

```
   interface ORB { // PIDL
   typedef string ObjectId;
   typedef sequence <ObjectId> ObjectIdList;
   exception InvalidName {};
   ObjectIdList list_initial_services();
   Object resolve_initial_references (in ObjectId identifier)
      raises (InvalidName);
 }; // interface ORB
}; // module CORBA
```

The resolve_initial_references() operation is a bootstrap to get object references to the POA, the DynAnyFactory, and CORBAservices, such as the Naming Service, Interface Repository, and Trading Service. The argument is a string specified in each CORBA service specification, for example, "NameService" for the Naming Service and "TradingService" for the Trader.

The type of interface expected as a return type is well known, and the object reference returned can be narrowed to the correct object type: CosNaming::NamingContext for the Naming Service and CosTrading::Lookup for the Trader. See Chapter 7 for a full explanation of how to obtain these references using the Java language binding and how to use them to obtain references to application objects.

## 2.3.6 The Portable Object Adapter

The first Object Adapter to be specified for CORBA was the Basic Object Adapter (BOA). The semantics of the BOA specification were left intentionally vague because it was not clear which features would be required on various platforms or how implementations would be achieved. As a result, different vendors implemented different parts of the BOA with differences in their semantics. This implementation experience was used as the basis for the specification of the Portable Object Adapter (POA), which eliminates these inconsistencies and standardizes some of the proprietary features that have emerged to fill the gaps in the BOA specification. The BOA has been deprecated since version 2.2 of the CORBA specification, but it is still supported by many ORB implementations for backward compatibility. We do not cover the BOA here because it is no longer part of the standard and because the POA offers developers much more flexibility. Also, actual BOA implementations vary a lot.

### *2.3.6.1 POA Overview*

The POA provides a comprehensive set of interfaces for managing object references and servants. The code written using the POA interfaces is now portable across ORB implementations and has the same semantics in every ORB that is compliant to CORBA 2.2 or above.

The POA defines standard interfaces to do the following:

- Map an object reference to a servant that implements that object
- Allow transparent activation of objects
- Associate policy information with objects
- Make a CORBA object persistent over several server process lifetimes

In the POA specification, the use of pseudo-IDL has been deprecated in favor of an approach that uses ordinary IDL, which is mapped into programming languages using the standard language mappings, but which is *locality constrained.* This means that references to objects of these types may not be passed outside of a server's address space. The POA interface itself is one example of a locality-constrained interface. One addition has been made to IDL: the native keyword. Parts of the specification tagged as native may be mapped to programming languages in a manner different from the standard language mappings.

The rest of this section will explain the architecture of the POA and give an overview of the important interfaces it provides as well as the object activation policies that the interfaces may administer. Detailed examples of making use of the flexibility provided by the POA will be given in Chapter 10.

### 2.3.6.2 POA Architecture

First it is useful to provide definitions of some key concepts used in the POA specification:

**Servant.** An implementation object that provides the run-time semantics of one or more CORBA objects.

**Object ID.** An identifier, unique with respect to a POA, that the POA uses to identify an abstract CORBA object.

**Active Object Map.** A table of associations between Object IDs and servants kept by a POA to allow it to dispatch incoming requests.

**Incarnate.** The action of providing a running servant to serve requests associated with a particular Object ID. A POA will keep this association in its active object map if the respective policy is set.

**Etherealize.** The action of destroying the association between a servant and an Object ID.

**Default Servant.** An object to which all incoming requests for Object IDs not in the Active Object Map are dispatched.

The purpose of a POA is to dispatch incoming invocation requests to the correct servant. It does so based on policies determined by the programmer of the CORBA server. This allows a range of behaviors from automatic generation of unique Object IDs, which are kept with servant references in the Active Object Map, to the use of programmer-supplied servant manager objects, which interpret Object IDs and return appropriate servants for invocations.

There can be more than one POA active in a particular server; however, there is always a root POA from which all of the other POAs are created. Each POA has a name relative to the POA in which it was created, and a find operation is defined to allow POAs to be located (and activated) by their parents. POAs themselves have manager objects that activate them and may change their processing state to allow them to suspend processing of requests or even to discard requests for some period (see Figure 2.12).

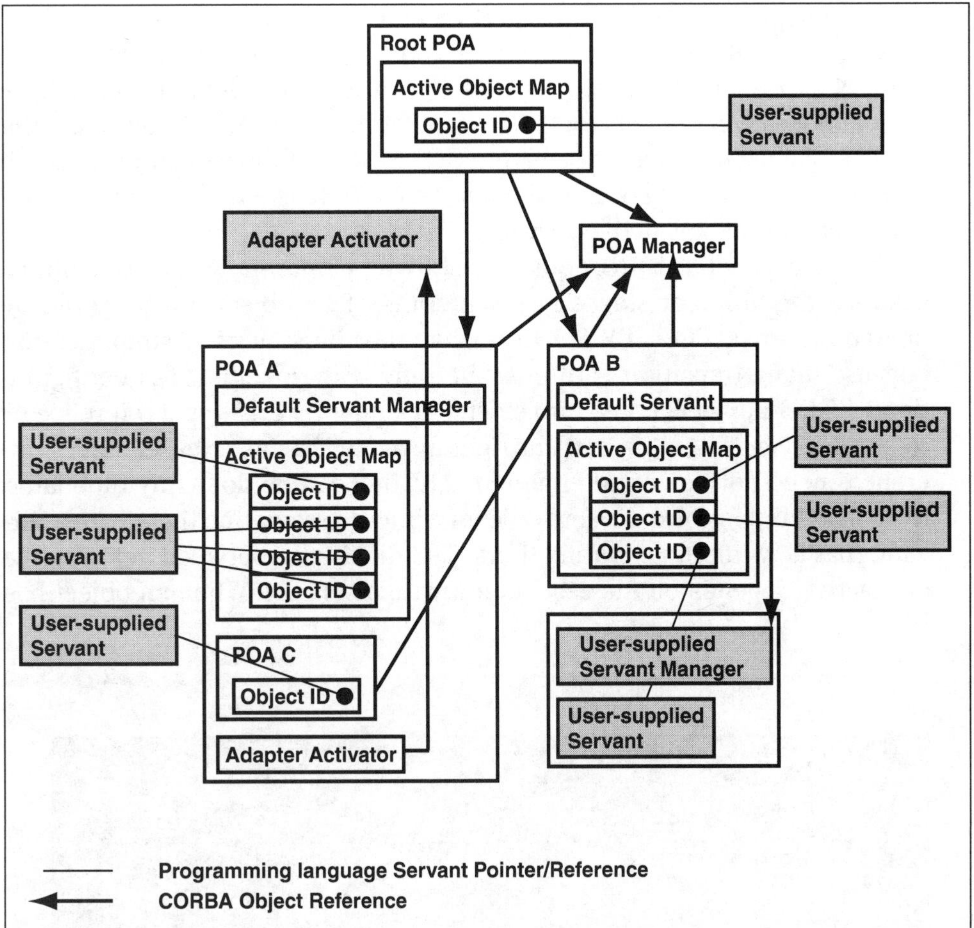


**Figure 2.12** POA architecture.

Each POA is associated with a specific combination of policy values that cannot be modified after the POA is created. From a management point of view, POA instances may thus also be viewed as policy domains: All objects managed by a POA are subject to the same policy combination. The reason for allowing multiple POAs in a single server is simply to allow a server to host objects with different policy combinations. The standard policies that can be associated with a POA are explained in the text that follows.

### 2.3.6.3 Object and Servant Lifetimes

It is important to understand that the POA is the component in the CORBA architecture that maps the abstract concept of a CORBA object onto concrete concepts provided by a particular programming language. Many aspects of this mapping can be configured very flexibly using a number of policies explained in the text that follows. It is especially important to be clear about the relationship between the lifetime of a CORBA object and the lifetime of a servant that implements CORBA operation semantics at some point. These lifetimes are not identical, so a CORBA object can and often will exist without any active servant.

The life cycle of a CORBA object is shown in Figure 2.13. The transitions between the different stages in the lifetime of an object are triggered by operations on a POA. Please note that the diagram is a simplification because many transitions are possible only with specific POA configurations. CORBA objects come into existence either by creating a reference or by explicitly *activating* a servant right away. In this latter case, object references need not be created immediately; this can be done any time later. Note that it is possible to create objects without associating them with a servant, that is, without activating them. The difference between being active or inactive depends on the association with a servant. When an object has

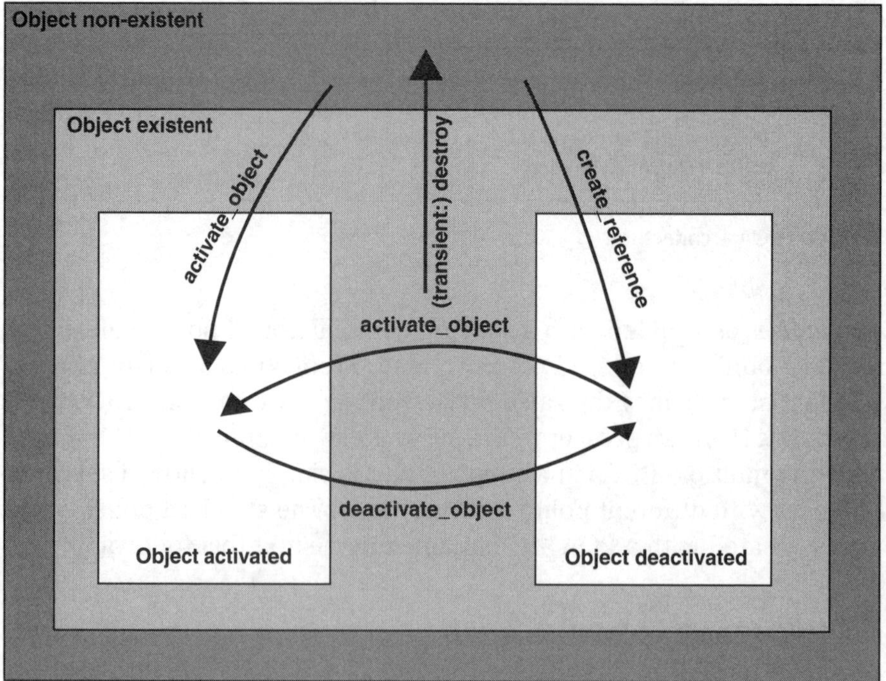


**Figure 2.13** Object life cycle.

been activated, its associated servant is *incarnating* the object. Deactivating an object means breaking the association with a servant. From a servant's point of view, this process is called *etherealization.*

In the case of ordinary, transient objects an object's lifetime is bounded by the lifetime of its POA: If the POA is destroyed, the object ceases to exist and can never be re-created under its previous identity. While references to the object may, of course, still exist, no invocations using these references are possible.

Figure 2.13 does not show any servants. The reason for this is that there is actually no relationship between the lifetime of a servant and that of an object beyond the simple fact that a servant must exist at the time the object is activated. The servant may have been created before the object activation or even before the object reference creation. Also, it may exist beyond the time the CORBA object is active or even exists—a servant's lifetime is not bound by that of the object's POA. The only limitation for the lifetime of the servant is the lifetime of the server process in which it is contained. If the CORBA object has been created by a POA with a persistent lifetime, it can outlive its POA and server process and thus also any servants that might have been associated with it. While this very loose coupling between objects and servants may appear a little confusing at first sight, it provides developers with the utmost flexibility. In Chapter 10, we will make use of these features.

### 2.3.6.4 POA Policies

The policies used by POAs are divided into several interacting categories:

**ID Uniqueness.** Determines whether more than one Object ID may refer to the same servant object. The names of the policies are UNIQUE_ID and MULTIPLE_ID.

**ID Assignment.** Determines whether the POA or the programmer assigns Object IDs. The names of the policies are USER_ID and SYSTEM_ID.

**Lifespan.** Determines whether objects are transient or persistent. That is, whether the CORBA object is available to clients after its POA is destroyed or whether it returns the OBJECT_NOT_EXIST exception when the POA is created anew. The names of the policies are TRANSIENT and PERSISTENT.

**Servant Retention.** Determines whether the POA keeps Object ID/servant associations in its Active Object Map or relies on default servants or servant locators to find servants for each request. The names of the policies are RETAIN and NON_RETAIN.

**Request Processing.** Determines whether the POA uses only the Active Object Map, only the default servant, only a servant locator, or some combination of these to locate the correct servant for incoming requests. The POA also relies on the value of the servant retention policy to determine its request processing behavior. The names of the policies are USE_ACTIVE_OBJECT_MAP_ONLY, USE_DEFAULT_SERVANT, and USE_SERVANT_MANAGER. Because this is one of the more complex policies, we will examine it more closely here. An important concept introduced for this policy is that of a Servant Manager. A Servant Manager is a programmer-supplied object that manages servants. There are two subtypes of this abstract interface: activators and locators.

**Servant Activator.** An object that a POA uses to incarnate servants for continual use and then to etherealize them when their life cycle is complete.

**Servant Locator.** An object that a POA uses to obtain a servant to invoke a single operation on an object identified by an Object ID. A POA will not place this association in its Active Object Map.

**Thread Policy.** Determines whether single threading is used so that safe deletion of servants may be achieved and implementations that are not MT-safe can be used safely. The names of the policies are ORB_CTRL_MODEL and SINGLE_THREAD_MODEL.

**Implicit Activation Policy.** Determines whether the POA can implicitly activate a servant when a reference or ObjectID is created for a servant. The names of the policies are IMPLICIT_ACTIVATION and NO_IMPLICIT_ACTIVATION.

Policies are specified as IDL interfaces in the PortableServer module. They all derive from a base interface called CORBA::Policy. The values that the policy objects represent are specified as read-only enum attributes. There are factory operations defined in the POA interface for creating these objects. For example, the LifespanPolicy object is specified as follows:

```
enum LifespanPolicy Value {
  TRANSIENT,
  PERSISTENT
};
interface LifespanPolicy {
  readonly attribute LifespanPolicyValue value;
};
```

with the following operation defined in the POA interface to create the object:

```
LifespanPolicy create_lifespan_policy(in LifespanPolicyValue value);
```

The way in which a new POA is created and initialized is by using the root POA (or one of its extant children) to create policy objects that are then passed in a sequence to the create_POA() operation.

#### Useful Policy Combinations for Child POAs

USE_ACTIVE_OBJECT_MAP_ONLY. This relies on servers to explicitly activate new objects. No mechanisms for dynamically providing servants are used, so static knowledge about servant code is necessary. Note that USE_ACTIVE_OBJECT_MAP_ONLY must be used in conjunction with RETAIN.

USE_SERVANT_MANAGER. This uses user-supplied code to provide servants. Using Servant Managers is generally useful if the number of objects that will be activated in this POA is large and not known in advance so hard-coding object activations is either impossible or tedious. It is also useful when context information is needed to map requests to servants.

If RETAIN is used in conjunction with this policy, the POA uses the ServantActivator when an object is not found in the Active Object Map. Each ServantActivator supports the operation incarnate(), which takes an Object ID and returns the servant that implements the object identified. A frequently used policy combination is to use the PERSISTENT life span and USER_ID id assignment policies. If ObjectIDs are assigned to contain, for example, database keys, the ServantActivator can fetch persistent object state from a database and incarnate the servant with this state.

The NON_RETAIN policy is used when a POA wishes to be in control of mapping each incoming invocation request to the appropriate servant. The servant manager used in this situation is a ServantLocator, which the POA calls using operations called preinvoke(), which obtains the servant that will service the request, and postinvoke(), which allows the server to clean up afterward. This is the most flexible request processing policy. It allows the ServantLocator to provide different servants for different invocations of the same operation on the same object. This might be useful, for example, for load balancing purposes. The NON_RETAIN policy might, however, also be used for scalability reasons: If the expected number of objects in this POA is very high, the Active Object Map might simply grow too large to be kept in memory.

USE_DEFAULT_SERVANT. When used in conjunction with RETAIN, the POA assumes that objects not found in the Active Object Map are to be implemented by a generic servant object (probably using the DSI), which is registered with the POA as its default servant. The POA will raise the OBJECT_ADAPTER system exception if no default servant has been registered. If NON_RETAIN is used, no Active Object Map is kept, meaning that all requests are sent to the default servant.

#### 2.3.6.5 POA Life Cycle

A reference to the root POA is always available from the ORB. Its name is RootPOA and is obtained using the ORB::resolve_initial_references() operation. It has a predetermined set of policies, which can be summarized by saying that all object references are transient, mapping a single servant to an Object ID that is set by the POA and retained in the Active Object Map. When a server is being initialized it is responsible for setting up any other (descendant) POAs that it requires to support its objects.

**Creating POAs Manually**

In order to create other POAs, the createPOA() operation must be invoked on the root POA. A hierarchy of POAs can be created by subsequently calling createPOA() on the resulting child. When a POA is no longer required its destroy() operation must be invoked. The other operation used in relation to children of a POA is find_POA(), which allows a relative name to be resolved and returns the POA with the given name.

```
interface POA {
   create_POA(in string adapter_name,
      in POAManager a_POAManager,
      in CORBA::PolicyList policies)
    raises (AdapterAlreadyExists, InvalidPolicy);
```

The create_POA() operation takes a name parameter and a POAManager parameter, which is usually a nil object reference, indicating that the ORB should assign a manager to the POA. It also requires a list of consistent policies, such as the combinations given previously.

```
find_POA (in string adapter_name, in boolean activate_it)
   raises (AdapterNonExistent);
```

The find_POA() operation may find child POAs that have been activated by create_POA(), or they may be used to activate a POA using a preregistered adapter activator.

Adapter activators are associated with POAs at the time of their first creation and allow them to be made persistent when their objects are not being used and reactivated when required. The adapter activator for a POA is registered by setting the POA attribute called the_activator.

Adapter activators have a single operation:

```
interface AdapterActivator {
  boolean unknown_adapter(in POA parent, in string name);
};
```

This operation is called when find_POA() is invoked with the activate_it argument set to TRUE or when an invocation request is received nominating a POA that is not active. In this case the activators are called in succession from the one closest to the root to the furthest descendant. The parent parameter passes the reference of the parent POA to the activator. A typical activator implementation retrieves any stored information about the child and uses the parent POA's policy operations to create the correct policies. It then uses its create_POA() operation to instantiate the child. If it can successfully create the child, the activator returns TRUE from the unknown_adapter() call. The ORB can then call unknown_adapter() on the adapter activator of the new child to activate the next POA in the chain. For example, if the currently instantiated POA hierarchy consists only of the root POA and its child A, an incoming request for an object controlled by a POA identified as "<root>/A/B/C" will result in the following calls (in pseudo-code):

```
if (A.the_activator.unknown_adapter (A, "B"))
      then B.the_activator.unknown_adapter(B, "C")
```

### POA References to Other Objects

Certain POA policies require the assistance of other objects, such as managers, and the POA interface provides operations to set and get references to these objects. References to other objects are implicit in the POA's position in the hierarchy or are derived from the arguments provided to its parent at creation.

There are a number of attributes that POAs support:

```
// interface POA contd.
readonly attribute string the_name;
readonly attribute POA the_parent;
readonly attribute POAManager the_manager;
attribute AdapterActivator the_activator;
```

The read-only attributes allow users of the POA (ORB and server implementers) to access the name of the POA with respect to its parent, the POA's parent, and its manager. The writable attribute the_activator must be set if this POA is not always created by the server initialization code.

If the USE_DEFAULT_SERVANT policy is set, a servant must be nominated as the default using:

```
void set_servant(in Servant p_servant) raises(WrongPolicy)
```

The default servant can be retrieved using:

```
Servant get_servant() raises (NoServant, WrongPolicy);
```

The WrongPolicy exception is raised by both operations if the USE_DEFAULT_SERVANT policy is not set. NoServant is raised by get_servant() when set_servant() has not yet provided a default servant.

If the USE_SERVANT_MANAGER policy is set then the following operations are used in the same manner as set/get_servant() to initialize the ServantManager to be used by the POA:

```
void set_servant_manager(in ServantManager imgr)
    raises(WrongPolicy);
ServantManager get_servant_manager()
    raises(WrongPolicy);
```

### POA Processing State

Between a POA's creation and configuration and eventual destruction when the server exits, it need not always be active. POAs can also be in a holding state, a discarding state, or even inactive. Because it was expected that POAs would be managed per server process (rather than individually) the operations to set a POA holding, discarding, or inactive are not defined in the interface of the POA itself but in the POAManager interface. A POA's state is thus controlled by and actually even identical to its associated manager's state. A POA's POAManager is configured using the the_manager attribute. If the set_discarding() operation of a POAManager is called, it will set all its associated POAs to the discarding state.

A POA that has been created using create_POA() is not active but *holding*. If a POA is in the holding state, it still accepts incoming requests. These requests, however, are not dispatched but only buffered. Request processing can be resumed by setting the POA to the *active* state again. A POA can be set holding for reconfiguration operations, such as changing default servants, or to temporarily protect it against request flooding.

A POA in the *discarding* state also does not deliver requests. Moreover, it does not even buffer them but rejects them altogether. Clients will receive a TRANSIENT system exception for every invocation on an object in a discarding POA. This can also be used as a kind of flow control for requests. Clients prepared to handle TRANSIENT exceptions may now be able to use alternatives to calling objects in this POA. A POA might automatically be set from holding to discarding if its internal resource limits are reached so that no further request buffering is possible.

Prior to destruction, a POA can enter the *inactive* state. This is a final state used only for shutting POAs down. It is not possible to reactivate an inactive POA or to set it to any of the other states.

### 2.3.6.6 Using the POA to Create Object References

The other operations of the POA interface are for mapping Object IDs to servants and for activating servants that already have Object IDs, thereby creating usable object references that can be handed to clients. If the USER_ID policy is set, servers can allocate their own Object IDs and map them to servants using the following operation:

```
void activate_object_with_id(in ObjectId id, in Servant p_servant)
    raises (ServantAlreadyActive, ObjectAlreadyActive, WrongPolicy);
```

The ServantAlreadyActive exception is raised if the servant is already mapped and the UNIQUE_ID policy is set. The ObjectAlreadyActive exception is raised when this Object ID is already in use. The operation requires the RETAIN policy. If this policy is not set, the WrongPolicy exception is thrown.

When the SYSTEM_ID policy is set then activate_object_with_id() will raise the WrongPolicy exception. Explicit server activation with the SYSTEM_ID policy is done using:

```
ObjectId activate_object(in Servant p_servant)
    raises (ServantAlreadyActive, WrongPolicy);
```

The return value is the POA's allocated Object ID for the new servant. This operation requires both the SYSTEM_ID policy and the RETAIN policy.

One more step is required (under the USER_ID policy) to make a usable object reference. The create_reference_with_id() operation is used to associate an object reference with an Object ID.

```
Object create_reference_with_id(in ObjectId oid, in CORBA::RepositoryId intf);
```

The Object ID becomes associated with an object reference and conforms to the type specified in the Interface Repository using the RepositoryId provided as the intf argument. Note that this operation does not perform any activation by itself. The object is only active if the Object ID has been passed as an argument to activate_object_with_id() or returned by activate_object().

The association between Object IDs and object references can also be made by the POA when the policy is SYSTEM_ID:

```
Object create_reference(in CORBA::RepositoryId intf)
    raises(WrongPolicy);
```

Once the object is no longer required, its Object ID is deallocated and the mapping is removed from the Active Object Map using:

```
void deactivate_object(in ObjectId oid)
    raises(ObjectNotActive, WrongPolicy);
```

This operation requires the RETAIN policy.

### *2.3.6.7 Discovering the Mappings in a POA*

If the Active Object Map is being used (RETAIN policy is set) the following operations allow its mappings between Object ID, object reference, and servant to be interrogated:

```
ObjectId reference_to_id(in Object reference)
    raises (WrongAdapter, WrongPolicy);
Object id_to_reference(in ObjectId oid)
    raises (ObjectNotActive, WrongPolicy);
Servant reference_to_servant(in Object reference)
    raises (ObjectNotActive, WrongAdapter, WrongPolicy);
Servant id_to_servant(in ObjectId oid)
    raises (ObjectNotActive, WrongPolicy);
```

The mappings from servant to Object ID and reference can also be obtained if the UNIQUE_ID policy is set:

```
  ObjectId servant_to_id(in Servant p_servant)
    raises(ServantNotActive, WrongPolicy);
  Object servant_to_reference(in Servant p_servant)
    raises(ServantNotActive, WrongPolicy);
}; // POA
```

These last two operations can also perform implicit activation of objects if the IMPLICIT_ACTIVATION policy is set and the servants are not already active. If they are and the MULTIPLE_ID policy is set, they will be activated with a POA-generated Object ID; otherwise, a WrongPolicy exception is raised. This is usually the most convenient way to create object references and activate servants as it requires only a single operation and thus saves the extra call to activate_object().

### *2.3.6.8 The Current Interface*

When a servant implements methods for more than one Object ID it often needs to know which CORBA identity is associated with the request that has been dispatched to it. For this purpose an interface is defined that allows the servant to acquire information about its POA and its Object ID in that POA. The CORBA::Current interface is inherited by the PortableServer::Current interface, which adds the following operations:

```
interface Current: CORBA ::Current {
  exception NoContext { }
  POA get_POA() raises(NoContext);
```

This operation allows the servant to determine which POA processed the request and to examine the policies of that POA.

```
ObjectId get_object_id() raises (NoContext);
}; //Current
```

This operation allows the Object ID relative to that POA to be discovered, and the servant can use this identity to access the correct state for the CORBA object it is serving for the current invocation.

## 2.3.7 Language Mappings

The OMG has standardized eight language bindings and has RFPs issued to standardize several more. The current adopted specifications are C, C++, Smalltalk, Ada '95, COBOL, Lisp, Python, and Java. In addition, a number of unofficial mappings exist, for example, for PERL. From a developer's perspective, the difference between a standardized and a nonstandardized language mapping is not the quality of the document but the fact that using a standard mapping ensures source code portability across ORB implementations.

### 2.3.7.1 C

The C mapping was published along with the CORBA 1.1 specification. It provides an example of how to implement CORBA clients and servers in a nonobject-oriented language. Operation and interface names are concatenated to provide function names, and object references are passed explicitly as parameters.

### 2.3.7.2 C++

The C++ language mapping is the most widely supported language mapping at the moment. Its syntactic resemblance to IDL provides class definitions that very closely mirror IDL interface definitions. The generated stub code can be incorporated by inheritance into object implementation classes or can delegate to them. The major drawback of this mapping is that implementers of clients and servers must pay very close attention to memory management responsibilities. The rules for allocation and deallocation of data memory are just as complex as old-style Remote Procedure Call (RPC) programming. Some helper classes are defined that can deallocate memory when they go out of scope, but these must be declared and used with care because they might deallocate memory that is still being used by another object.

### 2.3.7.3 Smalltalk

Smalltalk is a dynamically typed, single-inheritance object-oriented language in which all types are first-class objects. The data type mappings use existing Smalltalk classes, and operations map to methods on classes. The way in which IDL interfaces map to Smalltalk objects is unconstrained. Explicit protocol mappings are made for some IDL types, such as unions and Anys, which provide a standard way of accessing their discriminators and TypeCodes, respectively. Implicit mappings may be used by programmers.

### 2.3.7.4 COBOL

The IDL/COBOL mapping was adopted in 1997. As COBOL is not object-oriented, the mapping is not as natural as, for example, those for C++ or Java. In particular, IDL concepts such as name scopes, interfaces, and inheritance require complex mapping rules. The data type mapping is based on the optional COBOL typedef construct. Older COBOL compilers may not provide typedefs, in which case the mapping has to use COBOL copy files as an alternative.

### 2.3.7.5 Lisp

The Lisp language mapping is a recent addition to the CORBA standard and was adopted in late 1999. Lisp is a hybrid language that combines features from a number of programming paradigms, among others from functional programming. The Lisp language mapping is the first standardized mapping for a basically nonimperative language.

### 2.3.7.6 Python

Like the Lisp language mapping, the Python language mapping is a very recent addition to the list of standardized mappings. Python is a popular object-oriented scripting language.

## 2.3.8 Interoperability

The CORBA specification has a section called Interoperability. It specifies an architecture for interoperability, as well as an out-of-the-box interoperability protocol, running over TCP/IP, and a second, optional protocol that uses the DCE RPC transport.

The specification contains a lot of technical detail about the protocols specified and about bridging between proprietary protocols. Here we will give an overview of the framework within which the two specified protocols exist and of the mandatory Internet Inter-ORB Protocol (IIOP). The rest of the standard applies to ORB implementers and will not be covered.

### *2.3.8.1 The ORB Interoperability Architecture*

The architecture contains definitions of ORB domains, bridges, and interoperable object references (IORs). It defines domains as islands within which objects are accessible because they use the same communication protocols, the same security, and the same way of identifying objects. In order to establish interoperability between domains, one of these elements must be replaced with a common element, or a bridge must be set up to facilitate translation of the protocol, identity, or authority between domains.

The approach of the architecture is to identify the things that can be used as common representations (canonical forms) between domains and then suggest ways in which ORB domains can create half-bridges that communicate using the common representation. The first step, a common object reference format, is defined as part of the architecture. An IOR contains the same information as a single domain object reference, but it adds a list of protocol profiles indicating in which communication protocols the domain of origin can accept requests. The protocol interoperability problem is addressed in a separate component called the General Inter-ORB Protocol (GIOP). Allowance is also made for the introduction of third-party protocols called Environment-Specific Inter-ORB Protocols (ESIOPs) within this framework. Figure 2.14 illustrates the relationships between these protocols.

### *2.3.8.2 General Inter-ORB Protocol*

The GIOP defines a linear format for the transmission of CORBA requests and replies without requiring a particular network transport protocol.

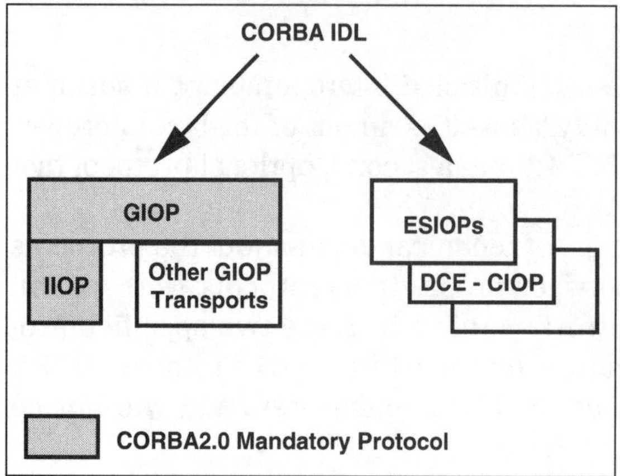


**Figure 2.14** ORB protocols.

### *2.3.8.3 Internet Inter-ORB Protocol*

The IIOP is a specialization of the GIOP that specifies the use of TCP/IP (the Internet Protocol). It defines some primitives to assist in the establishment of TCP connections. This protocol is required for compliance to CORBA 2.0 and is intended to provide a base-level interoperability between all ORB vendors' products, even though some vendors will continue to support proprietary protocols. Java ORBs are all implemented using IIOP.

### *2.3.8.4 Other Approaches*

As can be seen in Figure 2.14, the interoperability architecture allows for the specification of ESIOPs that will provide "islands of interoperability," but that should be able to be bridged to other ORBs using IIOP. The first adopted ESIOP is the DCE Common Inter-ORB Protocol (DCE-CIOP), which was already used by a number of ORBs before the introduction of GIOP/IIOP.

Before the CORBA 2.0 specification was introduced, each ORB vendor had to choose or invent a protocol for the transmission of invocation requests and responses. Most vendors had a customer base with extant objects that used a certain protocol, and so it was in their interest to continue to support old protocols alongside IIOP. Leading ORB products now support IIOP as their native protocol.

## 2.3.9 TypeCode, Any, and Dynamic Any

This section gives details about the interfaces to the generic container type Any and its supporting type, the TypeCode, which it uses to identify its contents. The ORB Portability Specification adopted by the OMG in 1997 extends the functionality available from Anys by adding a new interface called DynAny, which allows programmers to navigate the contents of Anys and access constituent parts without requiring compiled stub code with which to extract the entire contents of an Any.

#### 2.3.9.1 Any

The Any type is a basic type in IDL. It designates a container that can contain a value of any IDL type and identifies the type of its contents for type-safe extraction of the value. The pseudo-IDL type TypeCode is used to identify the type of a value in an Any and can be used outside of the context of Anys to identify IDL types in general. TypeCodes are not IDL basic types, but they may be declared as parameters to operations and members of structured types.

As the keyword any in IDL is a basic type and does not have a signature represented in PIDL, it is left to each language mapping to define the mechanism for inserting and extracting values from Anys and defining the TypeCodes that identify the values they contain.

#### 2.3.9.2 Language Mapping for Any

The mapping for Anys in Java is given in Chapter 6 and provides methods on an Any class that allow the insertion and extraction of all basic types, as well as additional methods on Helper classes for IDL-defined types that produce Anys. To provide us with a very basic notion of what an Any is, let us have a look at the C mapping:

```
typedef struct CORBA_any {
      CORBA_TypeCode _type;
      void * _value;
} CORBA_any;
```

There are no helper functions defined in the mapping, and programmers are responsible (as is usual in C) for ensuring that the `_value` structure member is cast in a type-safe manner. To do this the programmer must compare the `_type` member against TypeCode constants that correspond to known IDL types and then cast the `_value` member to the mapped C type for that IDL.

#### 2.3.9.3 TypeCode

The ORB specification defines a pseudo-IDL interface to a type called TypeCode, which is used to describe any IDL type. TypeCodes are one of only two PIDL types that can be used in IDL definitions as components of structured types or as parameter and return types of operations or attribute values. The other is Principal, which is used for Security but has been deprecated in favor of a more comprehensive approach to security. The PIDL for TypeCodes is given in the Interface Repository (IR) section of the CORBA 2.3 document. They are implemented as a combination of library and IDL compiler-generated code and are available to CORBA programmers independent of the IR.

In concept, a TypeCode consists of a *kind* field and a set of parameters that provide more information about that kind of TypeCode. For example, a TypeCode for a struct will give the name of the struct and the names and types (using recursive TypeCodes) of the members of that struct. The PIDL for TypeCode provides operations to allow the programmer access to the parameters, as well as an operation to compare TypeCodes for equality. All of the following PIDL is situated in the CORBA module.

**TypeCode Kinds.** The kinds of types in IDL are given as an enumeration.

```
enum TCKind {
    tk_null, tk_void,
    tk_short, tk_long, tk_ushort, tk_ulong,
    tk_float, tk_double, tk_boolean, tk_char,
    tk_octet, tk_any, tk_TypeCode, tk_Principal, tk_objref,
    tk_struct, tk_union, tk_enum, tk_string,
    tk_sequence, tk_array, tk_alias, tk_except,
    tk_longlong, tk_ulonglong, tk_longdouble,
    tk_wchar, tk_wstring, tk_fixed,
    tk_value, tk_value_box,
    tk_native, tk_abstract_interface
};
```

**TypeCode Operations.** The TypeCode interface provides two equality operators with slightly different semantics:

```
interface TypeCode { // PIDL
  boolean      equal (in TypeCode tc);
  boolean      equivalent (in TypeCode tc);
  TypeCode     get_compact_typecode();
```

The equal() operator uses the following strong definition of equality: Two TypeCodes are considered equal only if the set of legal operations for them is equal and all operations return identical results. To satisfy this definition, both TypeCodes must be of the same kind and, if applicable, have the same name and RepositoryId. Moreover, all of their constituents, if any, have to be identical. Under this definition, a type and its typedefed alias are not equal.

Note that the semantics of equal was underspecified in CORBA 2.2. Also, RepositoryIds for TypeCodes other than tk_objref and tk_except were optional in the CORBA transport protocol prior to CORBA 2.3. It is therefore possible that ORBs conforming to earlier CORBA versions than 2.3 do not transmit these RepositoryIds to save network bandwidth. The outcome of comparing two TypeCodes using equal() thus not only is dependent on the CORBA version number of the ORB the comparison is performed on, but also depends on the version of the CORBA transport protocol a TypeCode value was marshaled with.

A weaker form of equality, which is used by the ORB when determining type equivalence for values in Anys, can be tested using the equivalent() operation. Before comparing two TypeCodes, type aliases are replaced by their type definitions. To be considered equivalent, TypeCodes must, of course, have the same kind. If RepositoryIds are present, they must be equal. If one or both of the TypeCodes has an empty RepositoryId, the operation continues to compare the two TypeCodes structurally by examining their constituents and ignoring any differences in the results of the name() and member_name() operations. In a similar spirit, the get_compact_typecode() operation returns a representation of a TypeCode with all optional names and member names stripped off, but leaves RepositoryIds and type aliases untouched.

Making an analysis of a TypeCode begins with determining its kind with the kind() operation, so that other appropriate operations may then be chosen to find out more information about the type.

```
TCKind        kind();
```

Most types also have definitions stored in the Interface Repository, which can be used as an alternative source of type information. The id() operation returns the RepositoryId for any nonbasic type. Basic types are not stored in the IR, and if the TypeCode's kind is inappropriate, a BadKind exception is raised. This exception is raised whenever an operation inappropriate to a TypeCode's kind is invoked.

```
exception     BadKind {};
RepositoryId  id() raises (BadKind);
```

Object references and structured types except for sequences always have an interface or tag name. These are returned using the name() operation:

```
Identifier    name() raises (BadKind);
```

Structs, unions, enums, nonboxed valuetypes, and exceptions contain named member fields. The number and names of these members are discovered using the following operations. The exception Bounds is raised by indexed operations when the index parameter exceeds the number of elements.

```
exception       Bounds {};
unsigned long   member_count () raises (BadKind);
Identifier      member_name (in unsigned long index)
                    raises (BadKind, Bounds);
```

The members of structs, unions, and exceptions (but not enums) each have a type as well. These are returned as nested TypeCodes, which can be interpreted in the same way as their parent TypeCode.

```
TypeCode        member_type(in unsigned long index)
                    raises (BadKind, Bounds);
```

Unions also have a discriminator type and label values of that type for each member, as well as an optional default case. The member_label() operation will return the value for each case. It returns an Any containing a zero octet for the default case, if it exists. The discriminator_type() operation returns the TypeCode of the ordinal type in the switch clause of the union, and the default_index() operation returns the index of the member that corresponds to the default case or zero if it does not exist.

```
any             member_label(in unsigned long index)
                    raises (BadKind, Bounds);
TypeCode        discriminator_type() raises (BadKind);
long            default_index() raises (BadKind);
```

Sequences and strings may be bounded to a certain length, and arrays are always of a fixed length. The return value from the length() operation is zero for unbounded sequences and strings.

```
unsigned long   length() raises (BadKind);
```

Arrays and sequences contain elements of a particular type, and typedef aliases also refer to a previously declared type. The content_type() operation returns a TypeCode that can be interrogated to find out what type they contain.

```
TypeCode        content_type() raises (BadKind);
```

**Standard TypeCode Instances.** The CORBA module defines TypeCode constants for all basic IDL types. For example, the constant tc_long represents the TypeCode for longs.

IDL compilers usually generate TypeCode instances to correspond to all types in an IDL definition. They are named according to the language mapping. If no stubs are available for a particular type, however, the ORB interface defines operations to create TypeCodes from relevant parameters and an Interface RepositoryId to nominate the IDL in which the type belongs. These are seldom used in user code, and we will give only an example here:

```
TypeCode create_union_tc (
    in RepositoryId id,
    in Identifier name,
    in UnionMemberSeq members
);
```

The UnionMemberSeq type is defined in the Interface Repository specification.

### 2.3.9.4 DynAny

The ability to access the contents of an arbitrary Any had not been specified in CORBA until the adoption of the ORB Portability specification, and very few ORB implementations provided the ability to do so without access to compiled stub code. The implementation of Object Services and other interfaces that use the type Any to pass arbitrary values for storage or transmission often requires some access to these values in order to perform their specified semantics. DynAny provides an interface to do this in a standard way. It is defined in the DynamicAny module.

**Creating DynAnys.** An Any must first be inserted into a DynAny before its values can be accessed. DynAnys are created by invoking operations on other DynAnys or by using the DynAnyFactory interface:

```
module DynamicAny {
  interface DynAnyFactory {
    exception InconsistentTypeCode {};
    DynAny create_dyn_any(in any value)
      raises(InconsistentTypeCode);
    DynAny create_dyn_any_from_type_code(in CORBA::TypeCode type)
      raises(InconsistentTypeCode);
  };
```

The create_dyn_any() operation creates a new DynAny object and associates a copy of an Any value with it. The create_dyn_any_from_type_code()

operation creates a new DynAny object associated with a newly created Any. The DynAny is initialized with appropriate default values for its type. The DynAnyFactory object can be obtained from the ORB by calling ORB::resolve_initial_references("DynAnyFactory").

A DynAny cannot be used as an operation parameter directly, and so a conversion back to an Any is also required. This functionality is provided as follows:

```
interface DynAny {
    exception InvalidValue {};
    exception TypeMismatch {};
    void from_any (in any value) raises (InvalidValue, TypeMismatch);
    any to_any ();
```

Assignment of one DynAny to another, production of a new copy of an existing DynAny, and the destruction of DynAnys are achieved using the following operations:

```
void assign (in DynAny dyn_any) raises (TypeMismatch);
DynAny copy();
void destroy();
```

The DynAny interface also supports operations for the insertion and extraction of all the IDL basic types. These take the form of a pair of operations per basic type:

```
void insert_basic_type (in basic_type value) raises (TypeMismatch, InvalidValue);
basic_type get_basic_type() raises (TypeMismatch, InvalidValue);
```

It is easy enough to insert and extract basic types from Anys, so DynAny extends this functionality by adding operations to traverse structured types. These return new DynAnys that refer to individual components of a structured type, which can be recursively traversed. The model is that of a cursor pointing to a current element.

```
    DynAny current_component() raises (TypeMismatch);
    boolean next();
    unsigned long component_count();
    boolean seek(in long index);
    void rewind();
    //...
};//interface DynAny
```

The Boolean return values are set to TRUE if there is a component at the index to which they move the cursor. The components of structured types depend on the type. For example, the components of structures are their members, and the components of arrays and sequences are their elements. The specification then defines a number of interfaces that inherit from DynAny to provide more specific access to the components of particular structured types. We will look at a number of significant examples.

**Accessing Structs.** The interface DynStruct provides a way of getting the names of structure members and getting and setting their values. Values can be retrieved or set as either anys or DynAnys:

```
typedef string FieldName;
struct NameValuePair {
    FieldName id;
    any value;
};
typedef sequence<NameValuePair> NameValuePairSeq;
struct NameDynAnyPair {
    FieldName id;
    DynAny value;
};
typedef sequence<NameDynAnyPair> NameDynAnyPairSeq;
interface DynStruct : DynAny {
    FieldName current_member_name()
        raises (TypeMismatch, InvalidValue);
    TCKind current_member_kind()
        raises (TypeMismatch, InvalidValue);
    NameValuePairSeq get_members();
    void set_members(in NameValuePairSeq value)
        raises (TypeMismatch, InvalidValue);
    NameDynAnyPairSeq get_members_as_dyn_any();
    void set_members_as_dyn_any(in NameDynAnyPairSeq value)
        raises (TypeMismatch, InvalidValue);
};
```

The operations inherited from DynAny are used to move the current cursor, and the new operations access the value at the cursor.

**Accessing Enums.** The type DynEnum provides attributes that allow access to and change of the value of an enum as either a string tag name or an unsigned long integer value:

```
interface DynEnum : DynAny {
    string get_as_string();
    void set_as_string(in string value) raises (InvalidValue);
    unsigned long get_as_ulong();
    void set_as_ulong(in unsigned long value) raises (InvalidValue);
};
```

## 2.3.10 Dynamic Invocation and Dynamic Skeleton Interfaces

This section describes the interfaces to the symmetrical pair of ORB components: the Dynamic Invocation Interface (DII) on the client side and the Dynamic Skeleton Interface (DSI) on the server side. The DII enables a client to invoke operations on an interface for which it has no compiled stub code. It also allows a client to invoke an operation in deferred synchronous mode. That is, it can send the request, do some further processing, and then check for a response. This is useful regardless of whether the interface type is known at compile time, as it is not available via a static, or stub-based, invocation.

The DSI is used to accept a request for any operation, regardless of whether it has been defined in IDL. The mechanism allows servers to implement a class of generic operations of which it knows the form but not the exact syntax. It helps in writing client code that uses compiled IDL stubs based on an abstract IDL template. The client can then invoke operations on a compiled proxy stub in a type-safe manner.

### *2.3.10.1 Requests (DII)*

The heart of the DII is the Request interface. A Request has an object reference and a target operation name associated with it, as well as operations to add arguments. Once the Request has the correct arguments it is invoked using the invoke() operation, and this blocks in the same way as a stub invocation until the response (or an exception) is returned. The Request interface is defined in PIDL in the CORBA module as follows:

```
module CORBA {
  typedef string Identifier;
  typedef unsigned long Flags;
  native OpaqueValue;
  pseudo interface Request {
    void add_arg(in Identifier       name,
                 in TypeCode        arg_type,
                 in OpaqueValue value,
                 in long             len,
                 in Flags            arg_flags);
    void invoke(in Flags             invoke_flags);
    void delete();
    void send(in Flags               invoke_flags);
    void get_response() raises (WrongTransaction);
    boolean poll_response();
  };
}; // CORBA
```

### 2.3.10.2 Deferred Synchronous Invocation

The send() operation provides the means for a deferred synchronous invocation. This returns to the caller immediately and allows the client to perform some processing while the request is being transmitted and executed. The get_response() operation, when called in this situation, will either block until the request has returned its response or, if a flag is set, will return a status value indicating whether the request has completed. Operations are also provided, but not specified in PIDL, for sending the requests to multiple objects and getting the responses from these invocations.

The PIDL in the CORBA document does not specify the types of all the parameters and return values of the operations on a Request, and so we provide the details of these operations in Chapter 6, "ORB Run-Time System." The use of the DII in Java is demonstrated in Chapter 9, "Advanced Features."

### 2.3.10.3 ServerRequests (DSI)

In a particular object adapter implementation, an object reference is usually associated with an object implementation of the equivalent type in a particular language binding. An implementation that can deal with requests of several object types, called a Dynamic Implementation Routine (DIR), could be associated with an object reference instead. In this case, the object adapter does not look up a particular method and make an up-call by passing it the arguments in a request. Instead it creates a ServerRequest pseudo-object and passes this to the DIR. This is the definition of the ServerRequest interface:

```
module CORBA {
  pseudo interface ServerRequest {
    readonly attribute Identifier  operation;
    Context   ctx();
    void      arguments(inout NVList params);
    void      set_result(in any val);
    void      set_exception(in any val);
  };
};
```

The DIR can check the interface on which the request was made and look up its details using the Interface Repository. It could also be expecting requests of a known form and not require any IDL details. It can use the preceding interface to check the operation name, unpack the arguments, and find a location in which to place the result. The Java language mapping for the DSI is explained in Chapter 6.

### 2.3.10.4 Named Value Lists and Contexts

The PIDL for the Request and ServerRequest interfaces uses the PIDL type NVList to represent the values in an argument list. It is a type that is defined in each individual language mapping for the best implementation. It is logically equivalent to the following PIDL definition:

```
struct NamedValue {
  Identifier  name;
  any         argument;
  long        len; //length/count of argument value
  Flags       arg_modes; //in, out, or inout
};
typedef sequence <NamedValue> NVList;
```

The other type that is used in Requests is the Context. This is another construct that is more concretely defined in particular language bindings, but it is hardly ever used. Its PIDL may not be directly translated using the language mapping. The PIDL is not given here but is explained in full in Chapter 6.

## 2.3.11 Interface Repository

The IR is a fundamental service in CORBA that provides run-time type information about the interface types of objects supported in a particular ORB installation. It can be thought of as a set of objects that encapsulate the IDL definitions of all CORBA types available in a particular domain.

The Interface Repository specification defines a set of interfaces that correspond to each construct in IDL: module, interface, operation, sequence, constant, and so on. It also uses the idea of a containment hierarchy to relate objects of these types to one another. The Container interface is inherited by all IDL construct description interfaces that contain other constructs, and the Contained interface is inherited by all the interfaces that describe IDL constructs contained in others. For example, an interface can be contained in a module and can contain an attribute.

The term *abstract interface* is used informally to indicate that an interface is meant to be inherited only into other interfaces. No objects of an abstract interface type will ever be instantiated. This is not the same as if these interfaces were declared abstract using the corresponding IDL keyword that means that subtypes can be both interface and valuetypes. The term *concrete interface* is used to indicate that objects of this interface type will be instantiated.

All of the interfaces shown here are defined in the CORBA module. There are two mechanisms for finding out the properties of virtually all IDL constructs:

- The interfaces named *idl-construct*Def provide attributes and operations that explain the construct's properties and relationship to other IDL constructs. For example, SequenceDef is an interface definition with an attribute, bound, that gives the upper bound of a bounded sequence or zero for an unbounded sequence. It has another attribute to return the type of the elements of the sequence it is describing.
- The Contained interface has a describe() operation that returns an enumerate value of type DefinitionKind, as explained in the text that follows, to identify the kind of IDL construct, and a value of type Any that contains a structure dependent on that kind. The CORBA module defines a structure corresponding to each IDL construct named *idl-construct*Description. The structure contains the name, the repository identifier, the container where this construct is defined, its version, and some other members depending on the kind. For example, InterfaceDescription contains a list of base interfaces of the interface it describes.

This design has received a good deal of criticism. Some of the problems that have been observed with the current specification are the following:

- It contains a large amount of redundancy.
- Often operations return RepositoryIds, which then need to be resolved at the Repository interface, rather than object references to the *idl-construct*Def objects denoted by the IDs.
- Values are returned in a generic manner by base interfaces (e.g., in an Any) and then need to be interpreted based on an enumerated type. This functionality should have been pushed down to well-typed operations in the derived interfaces.

We recommend that you use Figure 2.15 as a basis for understanding the relationships between interfaces because the IR specification can get rather confusing.

### 2.3.11.1 The Abstract Base Interfaces

The interfaces to various syntactic constructs in IDL share common properties inherited from a number of abstract base interfaces that provide the common properties of these groups.

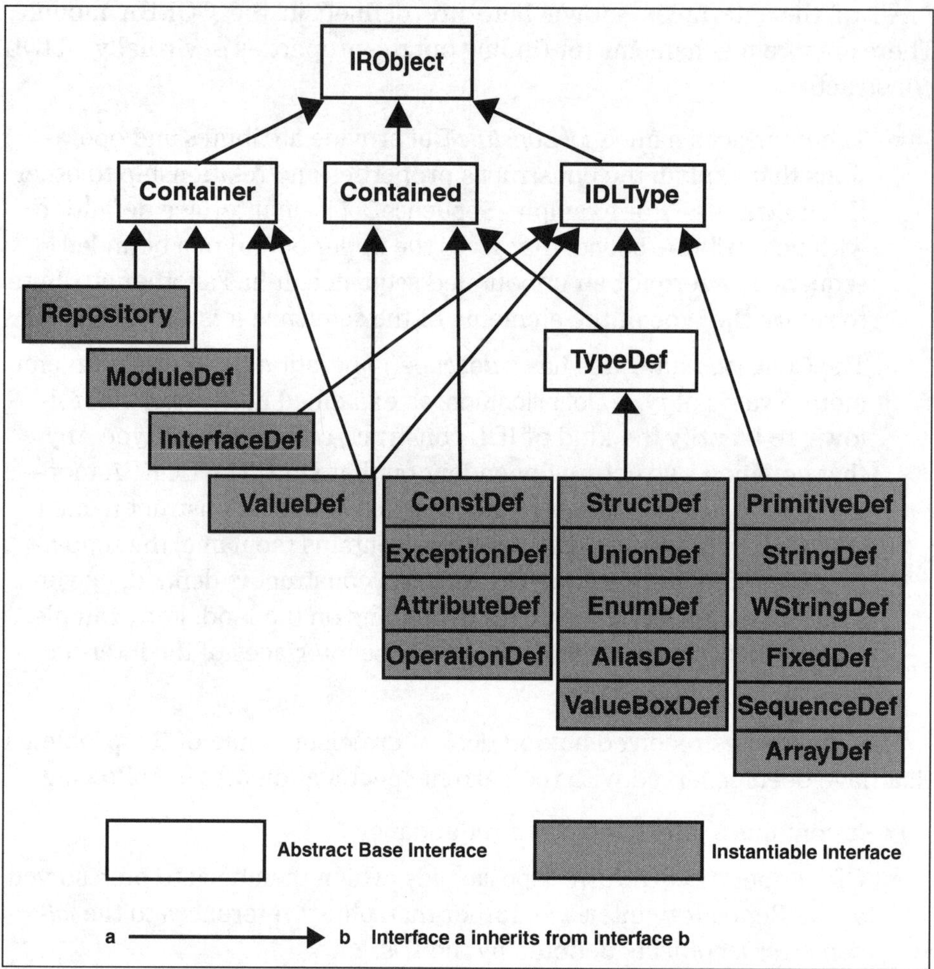


**Figure 2.15** Structure of the Interface Repository.

- The IRObject interface provides an attribute returning a value from an enumerated type that distinguishes between all IDL syntactic constructs. This attribute is available on all object references in the IR and allows the user to determine to what kind of IDL construct description object they have a reference.
- The Contained interface is inherited by all interfaces representing user-defined IDL constructs, and it offers attributes to discover the name of the construct and to obtain a structure that describes it.
- The Container interface is inherited by the Repository, ModuleDef, InterfaceDef, and ValueDef interfaces of the IR and contains operations

to look up and describe the contents of these containers. It also contains operations to create all the objects that inherit from Contained. These creation operations establish a containment relationship between the Container and the object that its operations create.

- The IDLType interface is inherited by all the interfaces that represent data types, including all the basic type interfaces and user-defined data type interfaces. It is also inherited by InterfaceDef and ValueDef because interface types can be used wherever data types are used in IDL. IDLType offers a single attribute that returns the TypeCode of the construct it describes.
- The TypedefDef interface is inherited by all the user-defined type interfaces that are given a type name: structs, unions, enums, boxed valuetypes, and typedef aliases. It offers a single operation that describes the type.

#### *2.3.11.2 Nondata-type Interfaces*

There is an interface for each IDL construct that forms part of an interface:

- Repository. Top-level naming scope. Can contain constants, typedefs, exceptions, interface definitions, and modules.
- ModuleDef. A logical grouping of interfaces. Can contain constants, typedefs, exceptions, interface definitions, and other modules.
- InterfaceDef. Can contain constants, typedefs, exceptions, operations, and attributes.
- AttributeDef. Represents an attribute definition.
- OperationDef. Consists of a list of parameters and raised exceptions.
- ExceptionDef. Can contain named members.
- ConstantDef. A constant value.

#### *2.3.11.3 Data Type Interfaces*

The following objects are used to represent the data types that IDL offers:

- InterfaceDef.
- StructDef.
- UnionDef.
- EnumDef.
- ValueBoxDef.

- AliasDef. Typedefs that rename a defined type.
- PrimitiveDef. CORBA-defined types that cannot be changed by users.
- StringDef.
- WStringDef.
- FixedDef.
- SequenceDef.
- ArrayDef.

### 2.3.11.4 IDL Definitions of the IR Interfaces

The IDL for the IR separates the functionality of the operations and attributes into *read* and *write* sections. The implementations of the IR that we have seen implement only the read part of the specification. The repository is usually populated by the IDL compiler using proprietary means. The purpose of this section is to allow users to investigate the functionality of an interface at run time, so we will ignore the write interface.

#### The IRObject Interface

This base interface offers only a read-only attribute that indicates what kind of IDL object you have.

```
enum DefinitionKind {
  dk_none, dk_all,
  dk_Attribute, dk_Constant, dk_Exception, dk_Interface,
  dk_Module, dk_Operation, dk_Typedef,
  dk_Alias, dk_Struct, dk_Union, dk_Enum,
  dk_Primitive, dk_String, dk_Sequence, dk_Array,
  dk_Repository,
  dk_Wstring, dk_Fixed,
  dk_Value, dk_ValueBox, dk_ValueMember,
  dk_Native
};
interface IRObject {
  readonly attribute DefinitionKind def_kind;
};
```

#### The Contained Interface

The Contained interface is inherited by all Interface Repository objects that represent IDL definitions are contained within other definitions.

```
typedef string VersionSpec;
interface Contained: IRObject {
```

```
  attribute RepositoryId id;
  attribute Identifier name;
  attribute VersionSpec version;
```

The read/write attributes are a global ID, a simple name, and a version (default set to 1.0).

```
readonly attribute Container defined_in;
readonly attribute ScopedName absolute_name;
readonly attribute Repository containing_repository;
```

The read-only attributes are the module, interface, or repository where the text of this construct is defined; the scoped name of this instance of the construct; and the repository object where this construct definition object is kept.

```
struct Description {
  DefinitionKind kind;
  any value;
};
Description describe ();
}; // Contained
```

The describe() operation returns a Description structure containing a kind and a value. The value returned depends on the kind. We will see what values correspond to each kind when we reach the concrete interfaces. The type name for the value will be of the form idl-constructDescription, for example, InterfaceDescription for interfaces.

### The Container Interface

The Container interface is used to look up or enumerate nested IDL elements starting from their containing IDL definition.

```
typedef sequence <Contained> ContainedSeq;
interface Container: IRObject {
    Contained lookup (in ScopedName search_name);
```

The lookup() operation finds an object with a scoped name relative to this container. If the scoped name begins with '::' then the name is found from the enclosing Repository.

```
    ContainedSeq contents (
      in DefinitionKind limit_type
      in boolean exclude_inherited
    );
```

The contents() operation returns a sequence of the objects in this container. The list may be limited to a certain type and may exclude inherited objects.

```
    ContainedSeq lookup_name (
      in Identifier search_name
      in long levels_to_search
      in DefinitionKind limit_type
      in boolean exclude_inherited
    );
};
```

The lookup_name() operation performs a recursive search down the containment hierarchy for a simple name. Restrictions can be placed on the number of levels to search, the types searched for, and whether to look at inherited objects.

### The IDLType Interface

```
interface IDLType: IRObject {
  readonly attribute TypeCode type;
};
```

This interface is inherited by built-in types like sequences and arrays, and it offers only the TypeCode of the object.

### The TypedefDef Interface

```
interface TypedefDef: Contained, IDLType {};
struct TypeDescription {
  Identifier name;
  RepositoryId id;
  RepositoryId defined_in;
  VersionSpec version;
  TypeCode type;
};
```

This interface combines the functions of the Contained and IDLType interfaces. As it is the base interface for all user-defined data type description objects and a derived interface of Contained, it has a description structure that is returned by the describe() operation that it inherits. The TypeDescription structure has a similar form to the other idl-constructDescription structures. It serves for all interfaces derived from TypedefDef, as its type member can describe any CORBA type.

#### The Repository Interface

This interface is the outer shell of the containment hierarchy, and it is where all the definitions for the base or primitive types are contained. It is also the starting point for browsing and allows users to find definitions using their RepositoryIds.

```
enum PrimitiveKind {
  pk_null, pk_void, pk_short, pk_long, pk_ushort, pk_ulong,
  pk_float, pk_double, pk_boolean, pk_char, pk_octet,
  pk_any, pk_TypeCode, pk_Principal, pk_string, pk_objref,
  pk_longlong, pk_ulonglong, pk_longdouble,
  pk_wchar, pk_wstring, pk_value_base
};
interface Repository: Container {
  Contained lookup_id (in RepositoryId search_id);
  PrimitiveDef get_primitive (in PrimitiveKind kind);
};
```

The lookup_id() operation finds an object with a certain identifier in this repository. The get_primitive() operation returns a primitive definition object contained in this repository.

### 2.3.11.5 The Multiply Derived Interfaces

Figure 2.15 shows that ModuleDef, InterfaceDef, and ValueDef are the only concrete interfaces in this specification that inherit directly from more than one abstract interface.

#### The ModuleDef Interface

```
interface ModuleDef: Container, Contained {};
struct ModuleDescription {
  Identifier name;
  RepositoryId Id;
  RepositoryId defined_In;
  VersionSpec version;
};
```

ModuleDef offers the operations from Container and Contained and a structure that allows them to be described in terms of name, ID, and version. This will be the value in the Any returned from Contained::describe() for modules.

### The InterfaceDef Interface

The InterfaceDef interface inherits operations from all three of the second-level base interfaces.

```
interface InterfaceDef: Container, Contained, IDLType {
  attribute InterfaceDefSeq base_interfaces;
  boolean Is_a (in RepositoryId interface_id);
```

The base_interfaces attribute allows us to find all the interfaces that this interface directly inherits. Is_a() returns TRUE if this interface has the identifier passed as an argument and FALSE otherwise.

```
struct FullInterfaceDescription {
    Identifier name;
    RepositoryId Id;
    RepositoryId defined_in;
    VersionSpec version;
    OpDescriptionSeq operations;
    AttrDescriptionSeq attributes;
    RepositoryIdSeq base_interfaces;
    TypeCode type;
  };
  FullInterfaceDescription describe_interface();
}; //InterfaceDef
struct InterfaceDescription {
  Identifier name;
  RepositoryId Id;
  RepositoryId defined_in;
  VersionSpec version;
  RepositoryIdSeq base_interfaces;
};
```

The describe_interface() operation returns a FullInterfaceDescription structure that contains all the information about an interface's contents in a number of sequences that contain other idl-constructDescription structures. A FullInterfaceDescription contains all the information needed to construct a Request to invoke an operation on an object of this interface type using the DII. No further, potentially expensive remote operations on the IR are necessary to retrieve information about an interface's type. See the DII section in Chapter 10 for an example of its use.

InterfaceDescription is the structure contained in the Any returned by the describe() operation inherited from Contained.

### The ValueDef Interface

Like the InterfaceDef interface, the ValueDef interface inherits operations from Container, Contained, and IDLType.

```
struct Initializer {
   StructMemberSeq  members;
   Identifier           name;
}
typedef sequence<Initializer> InitializerSeq;
interface ValueDef: Container, Contained, IDLType {
   attribute InterfaceDefSeq  supported_interfaces;
   attribute InitializerSeq     initializers;
   attribute ValueDef            base_value;
   attribute ValueDefSeq       abstract_base_values;
   attribute boolean             is_abstract;
   attribute boolean             is_custom;
   attribute boolean             is_truncatable;
   boolean is_a(in RepositoryId id);
```

The attributes supported_interfaces, base_value, and abstract_base_values indicate the interfaces this valuetype directly supports, the base valuetype this valuetype is derived from, and the abstract valuetypes that are inherited. The attribute initializers lists the initializers for this valuetype. The remaining Boolean attributes determine whether this valuetype is an abstract valuetype, uses custom marshaling, and is truncatable to one of its base valuetypes. The operation is_a() has the same functionality as in the InterfaceDef interface.

```
   struct FullValueDescription {
      Identifier                  name;
      RepositoryId               id;
      boolean                     is_abstract;
      boolean                     is_custom;
      RepositoryId               defined_in;
      VersionSpec                version;
      OpDescriptionSeq         operations;
      AttrDescriptionSeq       attributes;
      ValueMemberSeq          members;
      InitializerSeq             initializers;
      RepositoryIdSeq          base_interfaces;
      RepositoryIdSeq          abstract_base_values;
      boolean                     is_truncatable;
      RepositoryId               base_value;
      TypeCode                   type;
   };
   FullValueDescription describe_value();
}; // ValueDef
struct ValueDescription {
      Identifier                  name;
      RepositoryId               id;
```

```
        boolean               is_abstract;
        boolean               is_custom;
        RepositoryId          defined_in;
        VersionSpec           version;
        RepositoryIdSeq       base_interfaces;
        RepositoryIdSeq       abstract_base_values;
        boolean               is_truncatable;
        RepositoryId          base_value;
};
```

Like the describe_interface() in InterfaceDef, the describe_value() operation returns a structure that contains all the information about a valuetype's contents in a number of sequences that contain other idl-constructDescription structures. The type of this structure is FullValueDescription. Another descriptive structure of type ValueDescription is contained in the Any returned by the describe() operation inherited from Contained.

### 2.3.11.6 Interfaces Derived from TypedefDef

The TypedefDef abstract interface is derived from Contained and IDLType. TypedefDef adds a TypeCode attribute. All the interfaces derived from it are structured types that must be user defined.

#### StructDef

```
struct StructMember {
  Identifier name;
  TypeCode type;
  IDLType type_def;
};
typedef sequence < StructMember > StructMemberSeq;
interface StructDef: TypedefDef {
  attribute StructMemberSeq members;
};
```

A StructDef describes its members by name and type, giving both a TypeCode and a reference to the object that describes that type.

#### UnionDef

```
struct UnionMember {
   Identifier name;
   any label;
   TypeCode type;
   IDLType type_def;
};
```

```
typedef sequence < UnionMember > UnionMemberSeq;
interface UnionDef: TypedefDef {
   readonly attribute TypeCode discriminator_type;
   attribute IDLType discriminator_type_def;
   attribute UnionMemberSeq members;
};
```

A UnionDef describes its discriminator type with a TypeCode and by reference to the object describing that type with discriminator_type and discriminator_type_def, respectively. Its members are accessed in a similar manner to those of a structure, but they contain a label value in addition to the name and type.

#### EnumDef

```
typedef sequence < identifier > EnumMemberSeq;
interface EnumDef: TypedefDef {
   attribute EnumMemberSeq members;
};
```

The only information an enumerated type definition requires over that inherited from TypedefDef is the list of names used for its values.

#### AliasDef

```
interface AliasDef: TypedefDef {
   attribute IDLType original_type_def;
};
```

Aliases are typedefs that simply provide a new name for an existing type. The AliasDef interface has an attribute that refers to the object that describes the original type.

#### ValueBoxDef

```
interface ValueBoxDef: TypedefDef {
   attribute IDLType original_type_def;
};
```

A ValueBoxDef interface identifies the IDL type the values of which may be contained in values of this boxed valuetype.

### 2.3.11.7 Interfaces Derived from IDLType

These objects represent the primitives and system-defined types.

#### PrimitiveDef

```
interface PrimitiveDef: IDLType {
```

```
    readonly attribute PrimitiveKind kind;
};
```

The kind attribute returns an enumerated value identifying the basic type that this object represents.

### StringDef and WStringDef

```
interface StringDef: IDLType {
    attribute unsigned long bound;
};
interface WStringDef: IDLType {
    attribute unsigned long bound;
};
```

A bound value of 0 means that the string or wstring type represented by this interface is unbounded.

### FixedDef

```
interface FixedDef: IDLType {
    attribute unsigned short digits;
    attribute short scale;
};
```

The number of decimal digits specified by the digits attribute must be in the range from 1 to 31. The scale attribute specifies the position of the decimal point.

### SequenceDef

```
interface SequenceDef: IDLType {
   attribute unsigned long bound;
   readonly attribute TypeCode element_type;
   attribute IDLType element_type_def;
};
```

A bound of 0 means that the sequence is unbounded. The other two attributes identify the type contained in the sequence by TypeCode and object reference.

### ArrayDef

```
interface ArrayDef: IDLType {
   attribute unsigned long length;
   readonly attribute TypeCode element_type;
   attribute IDLType element_type_def;
};
```

Multidimensional arrays are created by having another array as the element, described by element_type and identified by element_type_def.

### 2.3.11.8 Interfaces Derived Directly from Contained

A number of interfaces represent definitions that are contained within others and thus inherit from Contained. These interfaces are explained in the text that follows.

#### ConstantDef

```
interface ConstantDef: Contained {
  readonly attribute TypeCode type;
  attribute IDLType type_def;
  attribute any value;
};
struct ConstantDescription {
  Identifier name;
  RepositoryId id;
  RepositoryId defined_in;
  VersionSpec version;
  TypeCode type;
  any value;
};
```

A constant has a type described by type and referenced as another IR object in type_def. It also has a value. The ConstantDescription structure is returned as the value of the Any returned by the describe() operation inherited from Contained.

#### ExceptionDef

```
interface ExceptionDef: Contained {
  readonly attribute TypeCode type;
  attribute StructMemberSeq members;
};
struct ExceptionDescription {
  Identifier name;
  RepositoryId id;
  RepositoryId defined_in;
  VersionSpec version;
  TypeCode type;
};
```

An exception, like a structure, has a list of members that return more specific information about the exception. The inherited describe() operation returns an ExceptionDescription structure in an Any.

### AttributeDef

```
enum AttributeMode {ATTR_NORMAL, ATTR_READONLY};
interface AttributeDef: Contained {
  readonly attribute TypeCode type;
  attribute IDLType type_def;
  attribute AttributeMode mode;
};
struct AttributeDescription {
  Identifier name;
  RepositoryId id;
  RepositoryId defined_in;
  VersionSpec version;
  TypeCode type;
  AttributeMode mode;
};
```

AttributeDef supplies information about an attribute's type, as well as a reference to the object in which that type is defined. The mode attribute indicates whether this is a read-only attribute. The inherited describe() operation returns an AttributeDescription structure in an Any.

### OperationDef

Operations are perhaps the most complex entities that the IR describes. They contain parameters and return types and may also raise exceptions and carry context. Parameters are represented by structures, whereas definitions of exceptions are objects.

Here are the types required for the OperationDef interface and the OperationDescription structure:

```
enum OperationMode {OP_NORMAL, OP_ONEWAY};
enum ParameterMode {PARAM_IN, PARAM_OUT, PARAM_INOUT};
struct ParameterDescription {
  Identifier name;
  TypeCode type;
  IDLType type_def;
  ParameterMode mode;
};
typedef sequence < ParameterDescription > ParDescriptionSeq;
typedef Identifier ContextIdentifier;
typedef sequence < ContextIdentifier > ContextIdSeq;
```

```
typedef sequence < ExceptionDef > ExceptionDefSeq;
typedef sequence < ExceptionDescription > ExcDescriptionSeq;
```

This is the IDL for the interface that describes operations and the structure returned by the describe() operation inherited from Contained.

```
interface OperationDef: Contained {
  readonly attribute TypeCode result;
  attribute IDLType result_def;
  attribute ParDescriptionSeq params;
  attribute OperationMode mode;
  attribute ContextIdSeq contexts;
  attribute ExceptionDefSeq exceptions;
};
struct OperationDescription {
  Identifier name;
  RepositoryId id;
  RepositoryId defined_in;
  VersionSpec version;
  TypeCode result;
  OperationMode mode;
  ContextIdSeq contexts;
  ParDescriptionSeq parameters;
  ExcDescriptionSeq exceptions;
};
```

The params attribute of OperationDef is a list of ParameterDescription structures. The contexts attribute gives a list of scoped names of context objects that apply to the operation.

### *2.3.11.9 RepositoryIds*

Repository identifiers are strings that name individual entries in the repository and can be used to retrieve these entries. These identifiers should not be confused with IDL scoped names. The format of a scoped name is fixed, and its structure is always determined by the position of an IDL construct's definition within enclosing name scopes. Repository identifiers can have different formats and can be manipulated using special IDL compiler directives. Thus, they need not reflect the name space structure in an IDL file.

There are four forms of repository identifiers currently defined by the OMG:

**IDL format.** The string starts with "IDL:" and then uses the scoped name followed by a major and minor version number to globally identify an object. Objects with the same major number are assumed to be derived from one another. The identifier with the larger minor number is assumed to be a subtype of the one with the smaller minor number.

**RMI hashed format.** The string starts with "RMI:" and is followed by a Java class name, a colon, and a hash code that was computed from a class definition. Using this hash code, it can be determined whether, for a given class name, the sender's and receiver's version of a class are equivalent. If a class definition was changed, this can be detected by comparing hash codes. Optionally, the string is ended with a colon and a serialization UID. This format was introduced to allow transmission of Java RMI values mapped to IDL using the Java/IDL reverse mapping.

**DCE UUID format.** The string starts with "DCE:" and is followed by a UUID, a colon, and then a minor version number.

**LOCAL format.** The string starts with "LOCAL:" and is followed by an arbitrary string. This format is for use with a single repository that does not communicate with ORBs outside its domain.

# CHAPTER 3

# Overview of Java and Java ORBs

Java is both a programming platform and an object-oriented programming language using principles similar to those of other object-oriented languages. The first part of this chapter discusses the principles of the Java programming language; correspondences to CORBA concepts are also noted, but we mostly ignore Java platform issues. This is not a detailed Java tutorial, however. There are plenty of well-written books on Java. The topics we cover include interfaces, classes, and objects, inheritance, methods and exceptions, packages and name scoping, objects at run time, Java applets, and JavaBeans. We close our Java introduction with a Hello World example. Although it is rather simple, it shows the principles of building Java applications, servlets, and applets. In Chapter 4, "A First Java ORB Application," we distribute this example using CORBA.

The second part of this chapter introduces the architecture of Java ORB applications. After reviewing some necessary terminology, we discuss the requirements for Java applications and applets to communicate with CORBA objects. Specifically we cover the following topics:

- Java applications as clients and servers
- Java applets as clients and servers

- Clients and servers implemented using other programming languages
- Standardization and productization of Java ORBs

## 3.1 Interface, Class, and Object

Java's three major object-oriented constructs are as follows:

**Interface.** The Java design concept. An interface defines an abstract data type by introducing a type name plus method (action) signatures, but it does not contain executable statements. It may also introduce constant fields.

**Class.** The Java implementation construct. Classes implement the actions that objects perform and define variable fields. A class can implement methods declared in an interface, or it can declare and implement methods of its own.

**Object.** A run-time entity, created as an instance of a class. It encapsulates state that is defined by the values of the fields that are defined in this object's class. The state of the object can be altered by directly modifying the value of public variables or by invoking methods on the object.

Figure 3.1 illustrates the relationship between Java interfaces, classes, and objects. Interfaces define the signature. A class implements the methods defined in the class or in an interface that it implements. Objects are run-time instances of a class executed on a virtual machine. Objects contain state.

The Java interface closely resembles CORBA IDL's interface. Java interfaces must be implemented by Java classes, while IDL interfaces can be implemented by constructs from various programming languages, including Java classes.

## 3.2 Inheritance

Java distinguishes between the inheritance of interfaces and the inheritance of implementations. Java allows multiple inheritance for interfaces, but only single inheritance for classes. In Figure 3.1, this is denoted by the cardinality of the associations representing inheritance.

### 3.2.1 Classes

The inheritance relationship is declared with the keyword `extends`. For example, a class `Derived` inheriting from class `Base` is declared as

```
class Derived extends Base { ... }
```

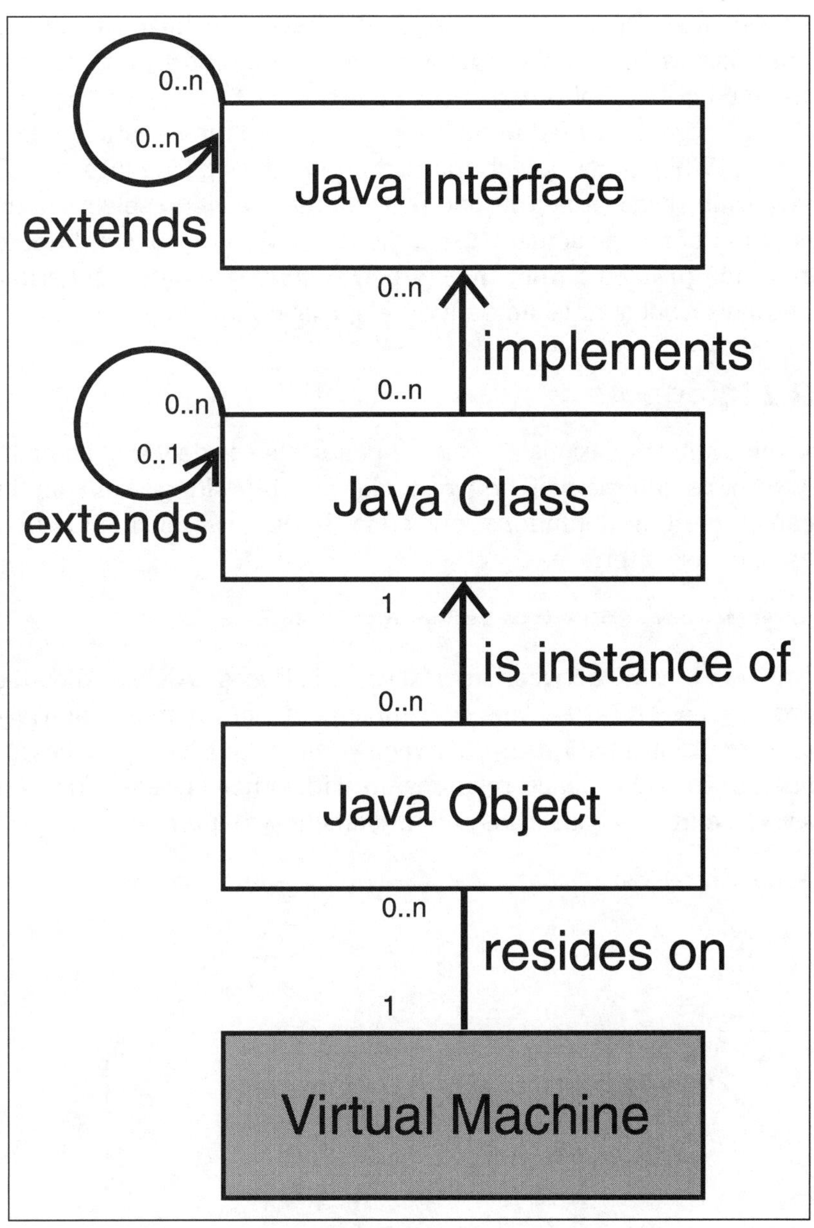


**Figure 3.1** Relationship between interface, class, and object.

The motivation to disallow multiple inheritance of classes is to avoid inconsistencies in the derived class. A typical example of such an inconsistency occurs in the case of diamond inheritance, as illustrated in Figure 3.2. If both classes `Left` and `Right` implement a method `m()`, then it is unclear if the method `m()` of the class `Derived` is `Left.m()` or `Right.m()`. If `m()` is also implemented in the `Base` class then the situation is even more complex. While other object-oriented programming languages like Eiffel or C++ permit these situations and provide the means to select which implementation of `m()` is actually used, the restriction to single inheritance prevents such problems from the start. Disallowing multiple inheritance has saved Java a substantial amount of language complexity.

## 3.2.2 Interfaces

The inheritance relationship between interfaces is declared using the same keyword as inheritance between classes. Inheriting from an interface means inheriting definitions, not code. Interfaces can inherit from more than one base interface:

```
interface Derived extends Left, Right { ... }
```

The relationship between interfaces and classes is declared with the keyword `implements`. A class can implement one or more interfaces. The implementation relationship between a class and its interfaces does not constrain the inheritance relationship with other classes. For example, a class can extend a base class and implement two interfaces:

```
class Car extends Vehicle implements Observable, Derived {
    // ....
}
```

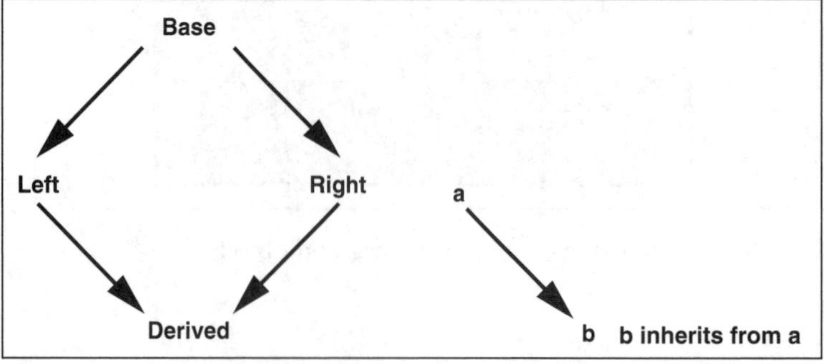


**Figure 3.2** Diamond inheritance.

Because interfaces declare only signatures and not implementations, multiple inheritance is not problematic. Naming conflicts when using multiple inheritance are handled by a set of clearly defined rules. Let's assume a diamond inheritance case, in which the interfaces `Left` and `Right` both declare a method `m()`. Then the following cases can occur:

- The two signatures differ in number, order, or type of arguments. Therefore, the two methods are distinguishable. The methods need to be separately implemented in a class that implements the interface `Derived`.
- The two signatures have the same number and order of arguments, and corresponding arguments are of the same type, but the methods have different result types. Therefore, the two methods would not be distinguishable when invoked. The interface `Derived` is considered illegal in this case.
- The two signatures have the same number and order of arguments, and corresponding arguments are of the same type. The methods have the same result type. There are two subcases:
  - The methods throw the same set of exceptions. The methods are identical, and there is only one implementation of the two declarations.
  - The methods throw different sets of exceptions. There is one implementation of the method declaration that can throw exceptions only from the common subset, even if this is the empty set. A common implementation for both method declarations that throws exceptions defined in only one signature is not allowed.

OMG IDL defines multiple inheritance of IDL interfaces. IDL allows no operation overloading and so has an even simpler way of determining the signature of derived interfaces. IDL interfaces correspond well to Java interfaces, and inheritance relationships can be mapped to Java naturally.

## 3.3 Methods and Exceptions

An object has methods that can be declared in an interface and are implemented by a class. Method declarations have parameters with a name and a type. The parameter-passing semantics are *call-by-value*. This means that at run time an argument has a value when the method is invoked, which is passed to the implementation of the method. Once the method returns from the invocation the parameter still has the original value because the implementation can operate only on a local copy. Results of a method can be passed to the invoking context in two ways:

- As the method's result
- As values in fields (members) of an exception in the signature of the method

In addition to these two kinds of regular and irregular results, methods may also produce effects on parameters even though they cannot modify them. If a method parameter is a reference to an object, the value passed to the method is a copy of the reference that denotes the same object as the original, so the method cannot change the reference. It can use the reference, however, to change the state of the object. Any state changes effected on this object are visible after the method returns.

Exceptions are instances of classes derived from the predefined class `java.lang.Exception`. Before an exception can be included in the signature of a method, a corresponding exception class, and in particular its constructor, must be defined. For example, we can define:

```
class MyException extends Exception {

    // public member
    public int value;

    //constructor
    MyException( int i ) {
        value = i;
    }
}
```

A method signature can contain multiple exceptions that are declared with the keyword `throws`.

```
int myMethod( boolean flag ) throws MyException {

    if( flag )
        throw new MyException( 1 );
    else
        return 1;
}
```

For example, the method `myMethod()` can return a value as a result or as a variable in an exception object. Exceptions are a powerful concept for signaling abnormal conditions but should not be used to return regular results. When an exception is thrown, it need not be received by the immediate caller. If the calling code does not provide a `catch` clause to receive and handle the exception, it is propagated until it is handled at some outer nesting level. If no suitable handler is found it will lead to abnormal program termination.

OMG IDL defines operations that are an equivalent concept to Java methods. Operations can raise exceptions, which are equivalent to methods throwing exceptions. In CORBA there are system exceptions and user-defined exceptions. User-defined exceptions do not support inheritance as they do in Java.

## 3.4 Packages

Packages are Java's name-scoping mechanism. Name scopes achieve the following results:

- They group related classes and interfaces together.
- They allow the same names to be used inside different scopes and to be distinguished by qualifying them using the scope name.

Packages are declared by using the `package` keyword. There is a convention that the name of a package reflects the name of the directory in which the Java source code file is located. Package scopes can be nested within other scopes, and subpackages are usually kept in subdirectories. Names are constructed by using dot notation. By convention, package names should begin with a lowercase letter, whereas class names should begin with a capital letter.

Here is a package example:

```
// outerPackage/MyClass.java:
package outerPackage;
public class MyClass {
}

// outerPackage/innerPackage/MyClass.java:
package outerPackage.innerPackage;
public class MyClass {

    public outerPackage.MyClass my_object1;
    public MyClass my_object2;
}

// outerPackage/innerPackage/MyOtherClass.java:
package outerPackage.innerPackage;
public class MyOtherClass {

    public MyClass my_other_object1;
    public outerPackage.innerPackage.MyClass my_other_object2;
}
```

In the previous example the types of my_object1 and my_object2 are different (the latter is a recursive declaration), and the types of my_other_object1 and my_other_object2 are the same. Java packages also provide access control to the interfaces and classes defined in the package by use of the public keyword. If no such modifier is applied to, for example, the definition of the field MyOtherClass. my_other_object1, code from outside the package is not allowed to access this field.

In addition to packages, Java provides another construct that can be used to scope names. It is possible to nest a class or interface definition in another:

```
package outerPackage.innerPackage;
public class Outer {
    public static class Inner { ... }
}
```

The class Inner is called an *inner class* and its qualified name is outerPackage.innerPackage.Outer.Inner. Inner classes are an advanced language construct and not only useful for partitioning name spaces into distinct scopes.

Modules are OMG IDL's principal name-scoping construct. They provide grouping and qualified naming, but no usage restrictions. Qualified names in IDL are separated with a double colon "::", and names defined from the global scope can be preceded by a double colon.

## 3.5 Objects

Objects are run-time instances of classes. An object always resides on a Java Virtual Machine. The virtual machine allocates the memory for an object to keep its state and executes the Java byte code that represents the object's behavior.

A virtual machine can host one or more objects. The machine can be implemented in hardware or run as an operating system process. Java does not handle invocations of methods across virtual machine boundaries. This has to be done through network APIs. Java's RMI API and Java ORBs provide high-level facilities to realize such invocations.

Within a Java virtual machine, an object can be represented simply by a piece of memory keeping its state and the byte code of the class representing its functionality. The program execution follows the method invocations and returns in a sequential, or single-threaded, manner (see Figure 3.3).

Alternatively, Java enables objects to have their own thread of execution.

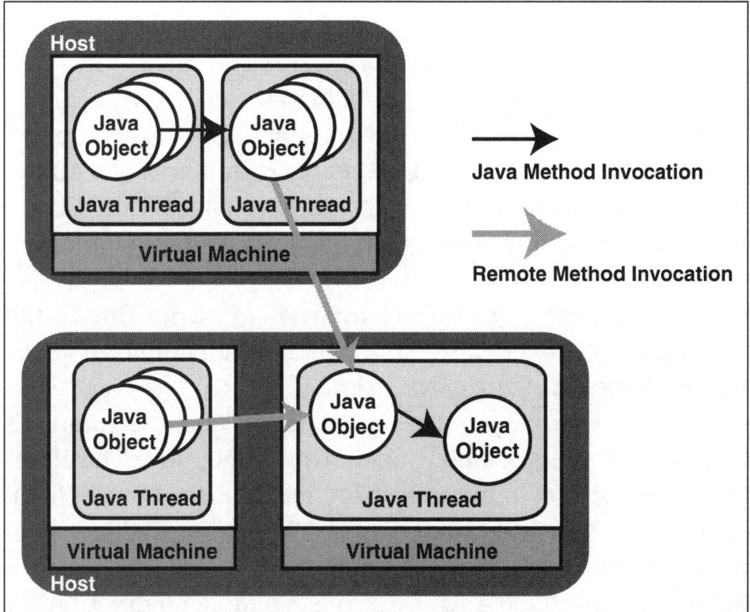


**Figure 3.3** Java threading and remote invocation.

This is provided by the core package of the language, `java.lang`, in the class `Thread`. This package also provides a predefined interface, `Runnable`, to objects whose behaviors are associated with a thread. The interface defines a single method:

```
public void run();
```

Classes can implement this method to define their particular run-time behavior—for example, the scheduling of the thread with respect to other threads, the synchronization between threads, or the interruption of other threads.

CORBA does not prescribe how to configure the run-time behavior of objects implementing IDL interfaces. Because threads help to solve many problems typical of distributed systems and because Java provides a convenient way of handling threads, Java ORBs are typically multithreaded. Because not every piece of application code might have been designed to allow the concurrent activity of multiple threads, the POA thread policy explained in Chapter 2, "CORBA Overview," allows developers to configure the POA such that only a single thread will be active in a servant method at any given time.

## 3.6 Java Applets

Applets are objects instantiated from subclasses of `java.applet.Applet`. This class and other interfaces in the package `java.applet` allow applet code to be executed in Web browsers and similar tools. Applet code is anchored in documents that are usually marked up in HTML. Figure 3.4 illustrates the interfaces and classes of the package and their relationships to other interfaces and classes.

All applet classes extend the class `java.applet.Applet`. Due to the inheritance structure of the Applet class, an applet contains the basis for a GUI through the inherited class `java.awt.Panel`.

The interface `AppletContext` provides information about the applet's environment, for example, the document anchoring the applet. The interface `AppletStub` provides a communication mechanism between an applet and the browser in which it is executing. The stub, an object conforming to this interface, is attached to the applet using the applet's `setStub()` method. The interface `AudioClip` is a simple abstraction for playing an audio clip.

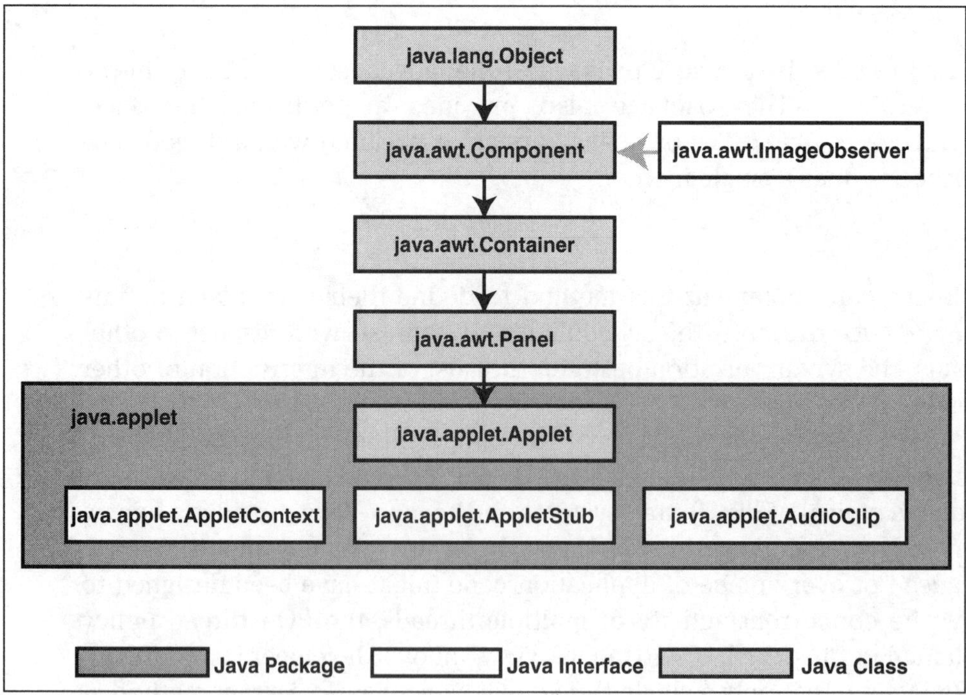


**Figure 3.4** Package java.applet.

Applets are executed by the Java virtual machine in a Web browser or similar tool. These virtual machines enforce a number of security restrictions that the Java Virtual Machine does not. This is known as *applet sandboxing.*

First, applets are not allowed to access local resources, such as the file system, on the machine where the browser executes. They also cannot execute native code on that machine, without explicit permission from the user. The motivation for these restrictions is to prevent applets acting as viruses, for example, by executing commands to remove or alter local files. On the other hand, these restrictions disable a number of useful features, even some that would increase security. For example, it is not possible for an applet to access a smart card reader on a host machine to authenticate a user.

The second major restriction regards networking. Applets are allowed only to open socket connections to the host from which they were downloaded (the check is based on IP numbers). Enforcing this restriction has a major impact on distributed applications involving applets, in particular for CORBA-based applications. CORBA provides the concept of location transparency, that is, one can invoke an operation on an object regardless of its location. In section 3.12 of this chapter and Chapter 12, "Security," we explain approaches to achieving location transparency despite this restriction.

## 3.7 Java Servlets

Java servlets are the server-side equivalent of applets. A servlet class is a piece of Java code that is executed in the Web server rather than downloaded to the user's browser. Servlets are executed in response to HTTP requests. You can think of servlets as the Java replacement for CGI scripts.

Servlets are instances of implementations of `javax.servlet.Servlet`, which is part of the Java 2 Enterprise Edition. The Servlet API can also be installed in a separate Servlet Development Kit. Servlets are managed by Java-enabled Web servers. When the server receives HTTP requests to a URL that points to a servlet, it calls one of the servlet's methods that is appropriate for the current request, for example, `doGet()` if the HTTP request is GET.

As parameters of its request handling methods, a servlet receives an object of type `javax.servlet.http.HttpServletRequest` and one of type `javax.servlet.http.HttpServletResponse`. The servlet uses the first argument to retrieve information about the request, such as request parameters. The second argument, `HttpServletResponse`, is used to set response headers and to create a response body. In the normal case, a servlet uses this argument to retrieve an output stream and simply prints out the contents of the HTML page that clients of the servlet will see in their browser when they enter a URL pointing to the servlet. We provide a simple example of a servlet in the next section.

## 3.8 Hello World Example

We will now introduce a simple Java example, a Hello World program. We show the optional definition of a Java interface and its implementation in a Java class. We then explain how to build both a Java application and an applet. In both cases an object of the implementation class is created and a method is invoked on the object. We return to the same example in Chapter 4, "A First Java ORB Application," where we distribute the components using a Java ORB.

The Hello World example contains an object of a class `GoodDay` that provides a method `hello()`. This method returns a string containing the message "Hello World from *location*," where *location* is the name of a geographical location, for example, Brisbane.

### 3.8.1 Interface Specification

A Java interface defines the signature of an object, that is, its types, fields, and methods. Hence, it allows various substitutable implementations. For our example we define the interface `GoodDay`, which has one method, `hello()`.

```
package com.wiley.compbooks.brose.chapter3.HelloWorld;
interface GoodDay {
    // method
    public String hello();
}
```

### 3.8.2 Implementation

An interface is implemented by a class. For our example we have implemented the class `GoodDayImpl`. The keyword `implements` defines the relationship between the interface and its implementing class.

```
package com.wiley.compbooks.brose.chapter3.HelloWorld;
class GoodDayImpl implements GoodDay {

    private String location;
```

```
    // constructor
    GoodDayImpl( String location ) {
        this.location = location;
    }

    // method
    public String hello() {
        return "Hello World, from " + location;
    }
}
```

Java does not prescribe the use of interfaces. Classes can both define a signature and implement methods. If a programmer chooses not to define an interface, this class declaration would change to

```
class GoodDayImpl {...}
```

The remainder of the class would be the same.

### 3.8.3 Application

The application that makes use of the class `GoodDayImpl` is also implemented as a class. We call this class `Application` and implement only its `main()` method.

```
package com.wiley.compbooks.brose.chapter3.HelloWorld;
import java.io.*;

public class Application {

    public static void main(String args[]) {

        // create object of class GoodDayImpl
        GoodDayImpl goodDay = new GoodDayImpl( "Brisbane" );
        // invoke method hello() and print result
        System.out.println( goodDay.hello() );
    }
}
```

Within the implementation of the method `main()` we create an object `goodDay` of the class `GoodDayImpl`. We invoke the method `hello()` on this object and print the result to standard output.

To run our application we have to compile the Java code:

```
> javac Application.java
```

We then start the Java run-time system with the application class. When we execute the application it prints the expected message:

```
> java com.wiley.compbooks.brose.chapter3.HelloWorld.Application
Hello World, from Brisbane.
```

### 3.8.4 Applet

Applet code differs from an application in that it is executable only in the environment of a Web browser or similar tool. An applet needs to be anchored in an HTML document to be loaded by a browser. For our example we have written the following HTML file:

```
<html>
<header>
<! — JavaHelloWorldApplet.html —>
<title>
Simple Hello World Example
</title>
<BODY BGCOLOR=15085A TEXT=FFD700 LINK==FFFFFF VLINK=FFFFFF ALINK=FFFFFF>
<center>
<pre>
</pre>
<h1>
Simple Hello World Example
</h1>
</center>
<pre>
</pre>
<center>
<applet
code=com/wiley/compbooks/brose/chapter3/simple/HelloWorld/Applet.class
width=400 height=80>
</applet>
</center>
</body>
</html>
```

The HTML tag `<applet>` anchors the file containing our applet class, `Applet.class`.

An applet class always extends the Java Applet class, `java.applet.Applet`. Our applet implementation uses the JDK event model and hence implements the interface `ActionListener`. When implementing our applet we override the method `init()` of the Applet class. This method initializes the applet. Applets require a GUI, so we initialize such an interface within the `init()` method. We create two graphical elements, a button object `hello_world_button` of the class `java.awt.Button` and a text field object `text_field` of the class `java.awt.TextField`. The button object is used to cause the invocation of the `hello()` method. We register the button with the applet so that the button sends events to the applet. The results of the invocation are displayed in the text field. The two objects are displayed on the applet's panel using a simple layout manager, `java.awt.GridLayout`.

```
package com.wiley.compbooks.brose.chapter3.HelloWorld;

import java.awt.*;
import java.awt.event.*;
import java.io.*;

public class Applet
    extends java.applet.Applet
    implements ActionListener {

    private GoodDay goodDay;
    private Button helloWorldButton;
    private TextField textField;

    public void init() {

        helloWorldButton = new Button("Invoke local method");
        helloWorldButton.setFont(new Font("Helvetica",
            Font.BOLD, 20));
        helloWorldButton.setActionCommand("invoke");
        helloWorldButton.addActionListener( (ActionListener)this );

        textField = new TextField();
        textField.setEditable(false);
        textField.setFont(new Font("Helvetica", Font.BOLD, 14));

        setLayout( new GridLayout(2,1));
        add( helloWorldButton );
        add( textField );

        // create object
        goodDay = new GoodDayImpl("Brisbane");
    }
```

To catch and process events we implement the method `actionPerformed()` of the interface `ActionListener`. We check if the command that caused the event is `"invoke"`, and if so we invoke the `hello()` method on the `goodDay` object. We display the result of the invocation in the text field object using its method `setText()`.

```
    public void actionPerformed( ActionEvent e ) {
        if( e.getActionCommand().equals("invoke") ) {
            // invoke the operation
```

```
            textField.setText( goodDay.hello() );
        }
    }
}
```

When the applet is loaded into a Web browser it appears as shown in Figure 3.5. Figure 3.6 shows the applet after the button has been clicked, the `hello()` method has been invoked, and its result displayed.

## 3.8.5 Servlet

Like applets, servlets are executed in a specific container environment. For applets, this environment is a user's browser that downloads and starts an applet. Servlets are managed by Java-enabled Web servers and respond to HTTP requests. A servlet class must implement the interface `javax.servlet.Servlet`. For usual HTTP-style communication, servlets generally inherit from `javax.servlet.http.HttpServlet`, which implements `javax.servlet.Servlet`.

```
package com.wiley.compbooks.brose.chapter3.HelloWorld;

import javax.servlet.*;
import javax.servlet.http.*;
import java.io.*;

public class Servlet
    extends javax.servlet.http.HttpServlet {

    private GoodDay goodDay;

    public void init(ServletConfig config)
        throws ServletException {
```

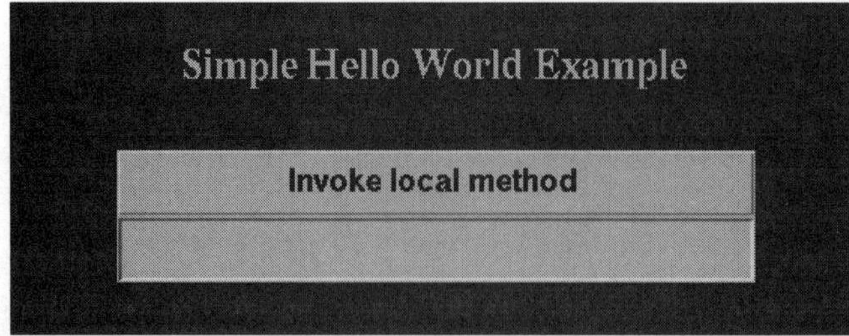


**Figure 3.5** Applet in initial state.

**Figure 3.6** Applet after method invocation.

```
        super.init(config);
        goodDay = new GoodDayImpl("Berlin");
    }

    public String getServletInfo() {
        return "A HelloWorld Servlet";
    }
```

The life cycle of a servlet is managed by its container, that is, the Web server. When the server finds that a servlet of a particular class is needed, it loads this class and creates an instance. It then calls `init()` to initialize the servlet. In the implementation of the `init()` method, we create an instance of `GoodDayImpl` on which we can later call `hello()`. The `getServlet Info()` method is used to return a descriptive string about the servlet.

The servlet code can override a number of methods from its superclass to respond to particular HTTP requests. The example servlet handles standard HTTP GET requests, so it overrides `doGet()`. In the implementation of this method, we simply set the type of the response to `"text/html"` to indicate an HTML response and then print the body of the response to a `PrintWriter` object obtained from the second argument of `doGet()`, an `HttpServletResponse`. The method implementation writes HTML tags and the hello message from the `goodDay` object to the `PrintWriter`. Finally, it closes the `PrintWriter` and returns.

```
    protected synchronized void doGet (HttpServletRequest req,
                                       HttpServletResponse resp)
        throws ServletException, IOException {

        // set header field first
        resp.setContentType("text/html");

        // then get the writer and write the response data
        PrintWriter out = resp.getWriter();
```

```
        out.println("<HTML><HEAD><TITLE>Hello World Servlet</TITLE></HEAD>");
        out.println("<BODY bgcolor=1585A text=FFD700>");
        out.println("<h1>" + goodDay.hello() + "<h1>");
        out.println("</BODY>");
        out.println("</HTML>");
        out.close();
    }
}
```

To have this servlet executed in a Web server, the servlet class must be installed such that the Web server can map a URL to the servlet. Figure 3.7 shows the HTML page generated by the servlet in response to the HTTP GET request that the browser issues when we type in the URL for the servlet.

## 3.9 JavaBeans

Beans are Java's component model. The JavaBeans specification defines a Java bean as a reusable software component that can be manipulated visually in a builder tool. There is no beans base class that all beans extend. Instead, a bean is a Java object that supports certain interfaces and follows certain conventions. Various beans can look quite different, but usually they support the following features that distinguish them from other Java objects. Figure 3.8 illustrates the features of JavaBeans.

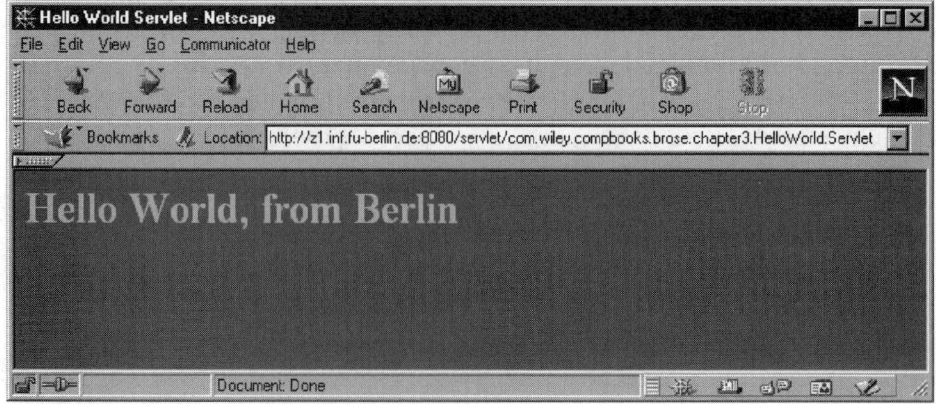


**Figure 3.7** Output of the Hello World servlet.

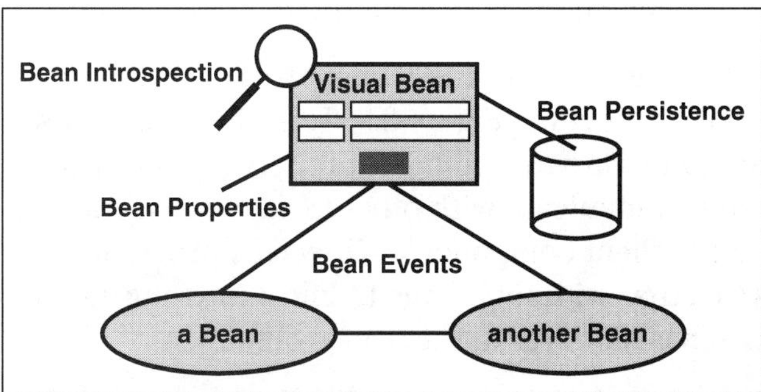


**Figure 3.8** JavaBeans.

**Introspection.** Introspection lets third-party objects, for example, builder tools, discover the interface of the bean. There is a general low-level mechanism, called *reflection,* to discover the signature of an interface. The reflection API is available by default to all objects implemented with JDK 1.1 or higher. Additionally the bean's specification introduces naming conventions to aid in understanding the semantics of the methods in the signature. The most widely used conventions are for methods related to setting and getting properties and to sending and receiving events. A bean can also be explicitly described by a corresponding `BeanInfo` class.

**Properties and customization.** The appearance and behavior of a bean can be modified directly by changing its properties. It can be modified indirectly by calling methods on a `Customizer` object that belongs to the bean. Properties allow a scripting language environment to control a bean.

**Events.** Beans events allow communication between beans through the predefined Java event interfaces. Since JDK 1.1, the package `java.util` contains classes dealing with events. The details are explained in Chapter 11, "Events." There are also naming conventions for derived event classes and their methods.

**Persistence.** JavaBeans' persistence allows a customized bean to be stored for future use by using Java Object Serialization or Externalization.

JavaBeans can be categorized as visible beans or invisible beans. Visible beans provide some kind of GUI, while invisible beans do not. The invisible beans implement non-GUI interfaces and provide some or all of the features described here.

In the context of CORBA, beans might be used in the following areas:

**Client side.** Visible CORBA client bean. A GUI client to a CORBA server can be made into a bean, as shown in Figure 3.9. The GUI characteristics and the CORBA attributes are described as properties. The visible CORBA client bean can communicate with other local components via bean events. Such CORBA client components allow GUI programmers to put new interfaces together without having to know anything about CORBA and the CORBA-based server in the background.

**Invisible CORBA client bean.** A simple client-side stub class (client-proxy) as generated by the IDL compiler can be extended to create a bean, as illustrated in Figure 3.10. Its introspection interface will allow a component to understand the proxy's interface and hence the target CORBA object's interface. The bean could also have properties that describe nonfunctional characteristics of the target object. Other beans can interact with these proxy beans via bean events, as shown in Figure 3.8.

**Server side.** Object implementation as a bean. A CORBA object implementation can be extended to become a bean. Besides providing introspection, the bean could have properties to describe related components or databases.

**Server as a bean.** A server can be extended to become a bean. This bean's properties could describe characteristics of the ORB and object adapter initialization, such as naming domain or security domain. Other properties could describe the objects that are hosted

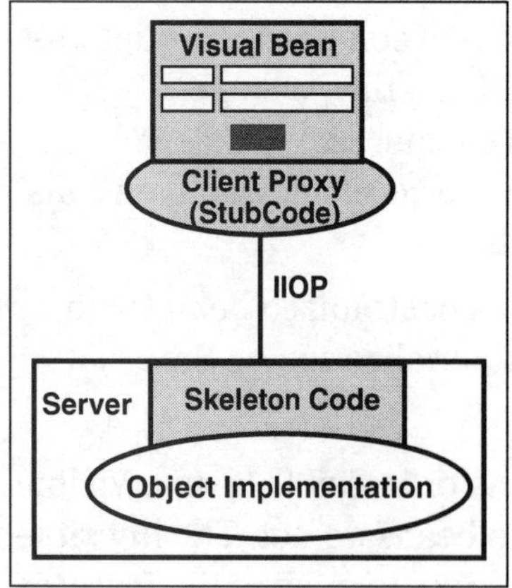


**Figure 3.9** Visible CORBA client bean.

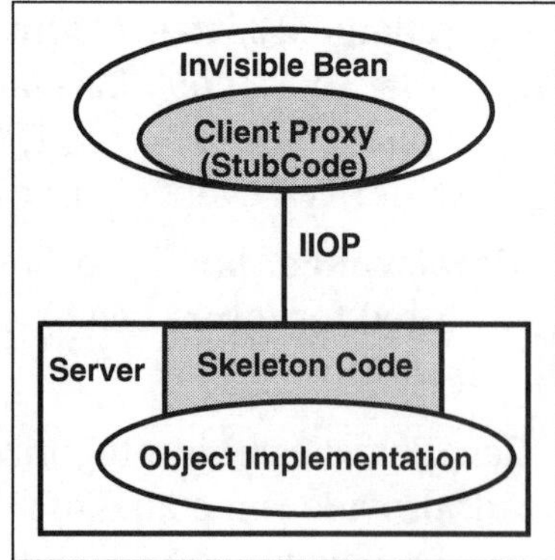


**Figure 3.10** Invisible CORBA client bean.

by the server. Properties can also give policy information required for graceful shutdown, load balancing, or fault tolerance.

We expect to see the combination of beans and CORBA used mostly on the client side to provide benefits to application/GUI programmers. Details of the JavaBeans Event Model and its relationship to CORBA and the CORBA Notification Service are given in Chapter 11.

While JavaBeans provide for convenient reuse and assembly of components, they do not especially target distributed computing. This is where Enterprise JavaBeans come into play. We will cover this kind of server-side component technology in greater detail in Chapter 14, "CORBA Components," and explain its relation to its companion technology in the CORBA world, CORBA components.

## 3.10 Java ORB Terminology

In this chapter and throughout the rest of the book, we use a number of terms that have specific technical meanings. Because both CORBA and Java are object-oriented and have similar object models at the interface level, some terms will apply to both. Most of the time, though, we use different language to refer to concepts in each domain. Here is the way in which we differentiate:

**Object.** The term *object* refers to a run-time entity with a well-defined interface. We usually refer specifically to CORBA objects, whose interfaces are represented in OMG IDL, and Java objects, whose interfaces are represented by Java declarations. CORBA objects have two parts:

- A *reference*: The part that allows the object's operations to be invoked from any location and using any programming language. The way this is implemented will become clear through the rest of this chapter.
- An *implementation*: The part that implements the operations in the interface. This is referred to as the object implementation or servant code. In the ORBs that we are interested in, the object implementation will be a Java class.

**Operation.** A behavior offered at an interface. Both CORBA and Java objects are targets of operation invocations.

**Method.** A Java implementation of an operation. Invoking an operation on a Java object causes the execution of a method as defined in the object's class (or one of its superclasses). When a Java object acts as a servant, its methods are executed in response to operation invocations on the CORBA object it incarnates.

**Servant.** A role played by a Java object when it incarnates a CORBA object. A servant's class is an implementation of a CORBA interface.

**Client.** A role played by a program when it invokes a CORBA object operation.

**Server.** A role played by a program when it makes an object implementation available to a client. Many programs that are servers are also clients to other servers. We use the term *CORBA server* to refer to a program that performs specified interactions with an ORB to make known the existence of the CORBA objects that it hosts.

## 3.11 Clients and Servers as Java Applications

Figure 3.11 illustrates the simplest scenario involving Java ORBs: a client interacting with a server. Client and server are both implemented in Java. Figure 3.11 is an abstract representation of the client/server model in Java ORBs. We see five components in the figure. Two of these are Java virtual machines (JVMs) that allow the execution of the client and server programs. The other three are the client and server programs and the ORB. The client communicates with the ORB in order to convey a request for an operation invocation to the server, which then sends results via the ORB back to the client. The interfaces these components use are defined by the CORBA standard and by the application-specific IDL definitions that the object at the server supports.

Figure 3.12 shows a more concrete view of how the ORB performs the task of conveying an invocation from client to server. The lightly shaded objects in the diagram are all provided by the ORB (compare with Figure 2.5 in Chapter 2). The following subsections describe the functionality of each of these components.

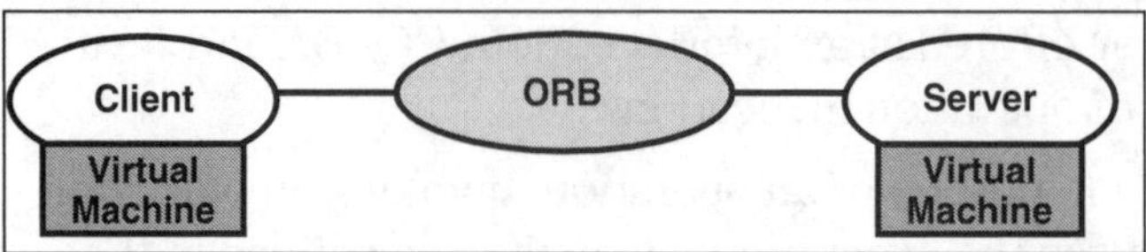


**Figure 3.11** Client/server model with Java ORBs: abstract view.

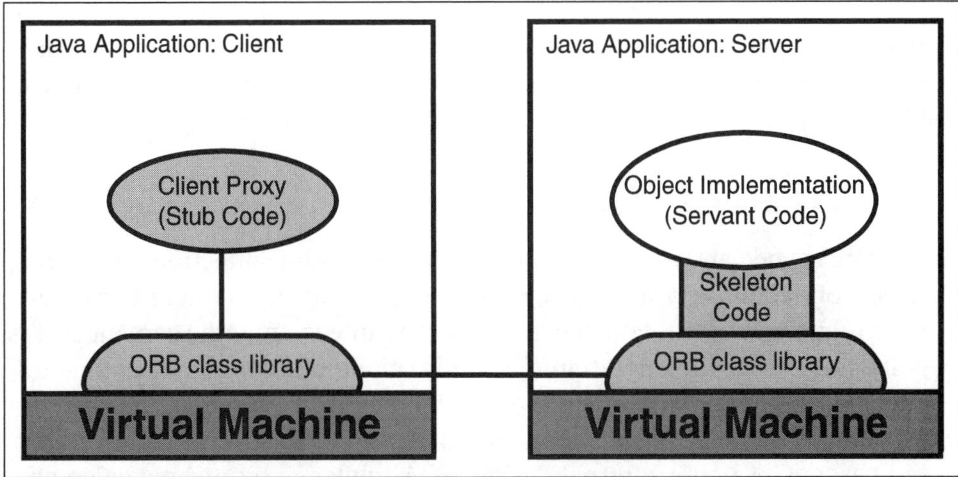


**Figure 3.12** Client/server model with Java ORBs: concrete view.

## 3.11.1 Stub and Skeleton Code

The IDL compiler generates a number of Java classes known as stub classes for the client and skeleton classes for the server. The role of the stub class is to provide code for proxy objects on which clients can invoke operations. The proxy object method implementations invoke operations on the servant, which may be located remotely. If the servant is at a remote location the proxy object marshals and transmits the invocation request. That is, it takes the operation name and the types and values of its arguments from language-dependent data structures and places them into a linear representation suitable for transmitting across a network. The code to marshal programmer-defined data types is an essential part of the stub code generated by the IDL compiler. The resulting marshaled form of the request is sent to the servant using the particular ORB's infrastructure. This infrastructure involves a network transport mechanism and additional mechanisms to locate the servant, and perhaps to activate the CORBA server program that hosts the servant.

The skeleton code provides the glue between an object implementation, a CORBA server, and the ORB, in particular the object adapter. The CORBA specification leaves many of the interfaces between the ORB core, object adapter, and server program partially or totally unspecified. For this reason different ORBs have different mechanisms to activate servers and for use by object adapters to inform the ORB that their objects are ready to receive invocation requests.

The skeleton class implements the mechanisms by which invocation requests coming into a server can be unmarshaled and directed to the right method of a servant. The implementation of those methods is the responsibility of the application programmer who provides the servant class.

## 3.11.2 ORB and Object Adapter

The ORB sends and receives requests over network connections. Managing these connections is one of the central tasks of the ORB code. After receiving a request, the ORB consults the object adapter to find the servant that is going to execute the operation. The ORB can do this through the standardized POA interface and finally uses the marshaling routines of the skeleton to unpack the request arguments and make the invocation on the servant. For reasons of better internal design, POA implementations may also provide a private interface to the ORB that is not standardized in CORBA. Design issues like these are, of course, entirely up to individual CORBA implementations. What this means, however, is that generally the object adapter functionality is implemented as part of the same code as the ORB, usually in libraries.

The ORB and object adapter code sometimes also communicate with an ORB run-time daemon that knows which servers host which objects and can locate and/or activate servers when requests are made to them. The information about how objects and servers are associated with running processes or how processes can be started up on demand is stored in the Implementation Repository. The Implementation Repository is an optional component of CORBA. Its interface is not specified and is different in each ORB. Some implementations don't even provide Implementation Repositories. In the simplest case, objects are created by a server program and the objects exist as long as the server process or JVM does. For these situations, no Implementation Repository is needed, and all the information required to locate the server host and process is contained in the object reference. In more sophisticated cases, however, objects have persistent lifetimes and outlive their server processes. The Implementation Repository is then used to activate both servers and their objects on demand.

If the server hosting the target of a request is not running, the request is received by the ORB daemon, which checks whether it can start the appropriate server process using information from the Implementation Repository. If it succeeds and the server is up, the ORB daemon tells the client's ORB run time to reissue the request directly to the new server process. This mechanism is transparent to the client application. When the request reaches the server but the target object is not yet active, the server's POA must be able to activate the object. Depending on the POA configuration, this might involve calling a servant manager. The servant manager might now, for example, retrieve the object's state from a database. We will see how to use the POA to this effect later in Chapter 10, "Practical POA Programming."

## 3.12 Clients as Java Applets

A Java applet can also be a CORBA client, as shown in Figure 3.13. For CORBA there is no difference between a Java application and an applet invoking CORBA objects. *Applet sandboxing*, however, introduces limitations. Applet sandboxing is a term used to describe the security restrictions imposed on applets. A JVM in a Web browser limits an untrusted applet's functionality to prevent it from causing damage to the local machine. The limitations prevent access to local resources such as the file system, devices, and networking. Network calls are limited to using connections with the host from which the applet has been downloaded.

Java applet sandboxing is in conflict with CORBA location transparency. Location transparency means that clients can invoke operations in the same way on objects regardless of their physical location. An applet client is restricted to invoking operations on objects that are local or reside on its host of origin.

The problem is overcome by IIOP forwarders or gateways. The idea is that a client's stub code sends all its remote requests to an IIOP gateway, which forwards them to the target object, wherever it may be. The target object sends the response back to the client via the IIOP gateway. This mechanism is illustrated in Figure 3.14.

Typically the IIOP gateway also acts as a safe portal through the firewall on the server side. It may also help the applet to bootstrap, that is, to obtain initial object references to services that it needs. We explain IIOP gateways in greater detail in Chapter 12.

## 3.13 Clients as Servlets

It is also possible to write servlets that act as CORBA clients. Any interaction with the servlet is via HTTP, so users can use standard browsers without any IIOP capabilities. The servlet executed in the Web server receives HTTP requests and reacts by initiating IIOP requests to remote objects. When it receives IIOP results it returns these as HTTP responses to the client.

A further advantage of this mechanism is that this communication style is usually not restricted by security measures. Even if the HTTP client is an

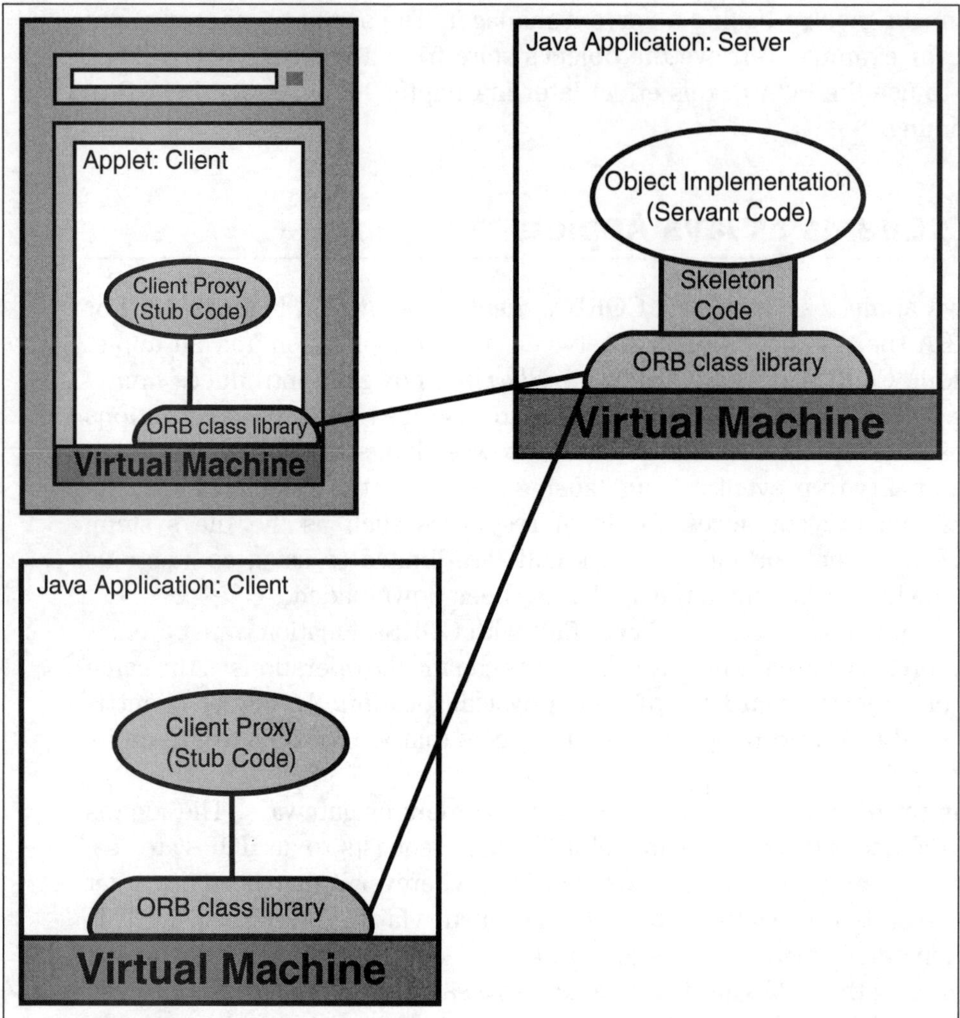


**Figure 3.13** Client as Java applets.

applet, no applet restrictions apply because the communication is with the applet's Web server. Moroever, HTTP requests are allowed to pass through many firewalls. Effectively, the servlet acts as an IIOP gateway. Figure 3.15 illustrates this configuration.

## 3.14 Servers as Java Applets

A server can also be implemented as an applet. Again we face a restriction of CORBA functionality imposed by applet sandboxing. Because applets are

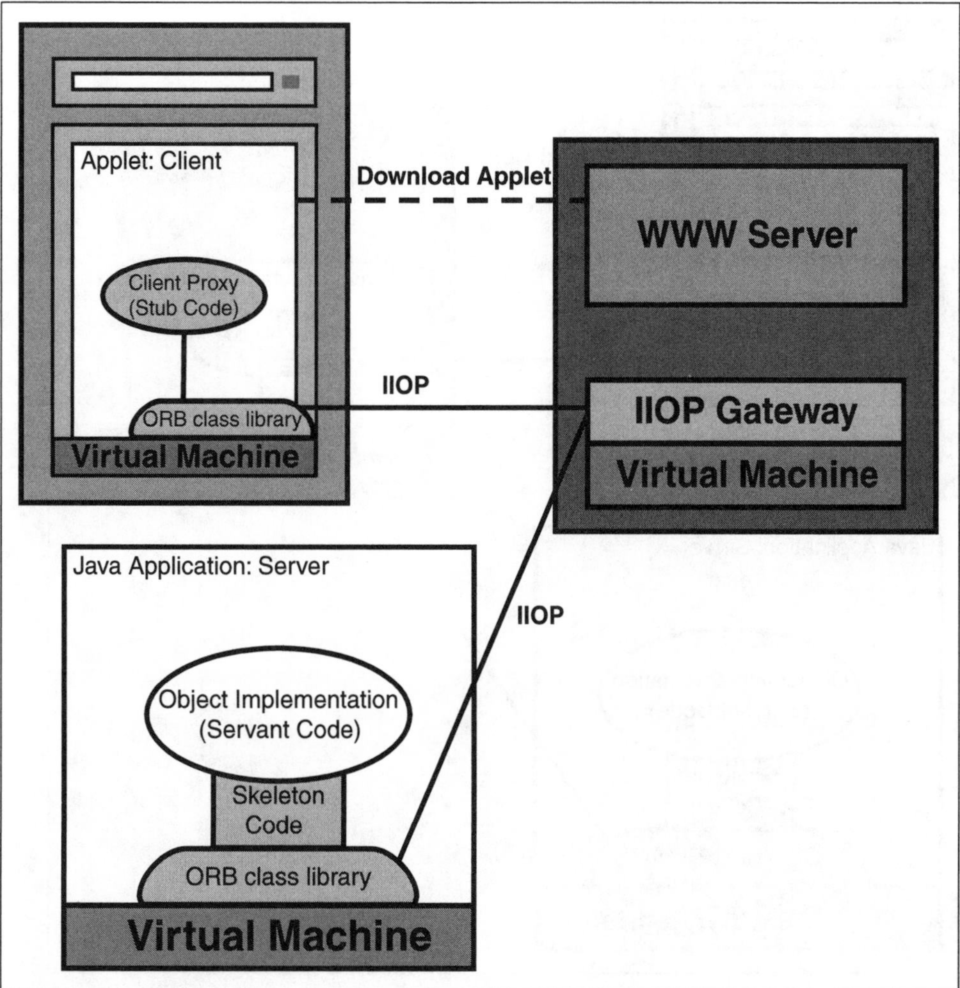


**Figure 3.14** IIOP gateway.

not allowed to access resources on the host machine, object implementations cannot be made persistent, nor can they make any data persistent. Typically objects that are hosted by applets have transient object references, which means that they are valid only for the lifetime of the applet. In all other respects, applets initialize the ORB and an object adapter and create objects in the same way that normal servers do. Clients to these objects have to communicate through an IIOP gateway unless they are located on the machine from which the applet was downloaded. Figure 3.16 shows a typical scenario.

You will find that objects hosted by applets are mostly used for implementing various kinds of objects for servers to call back. Another example

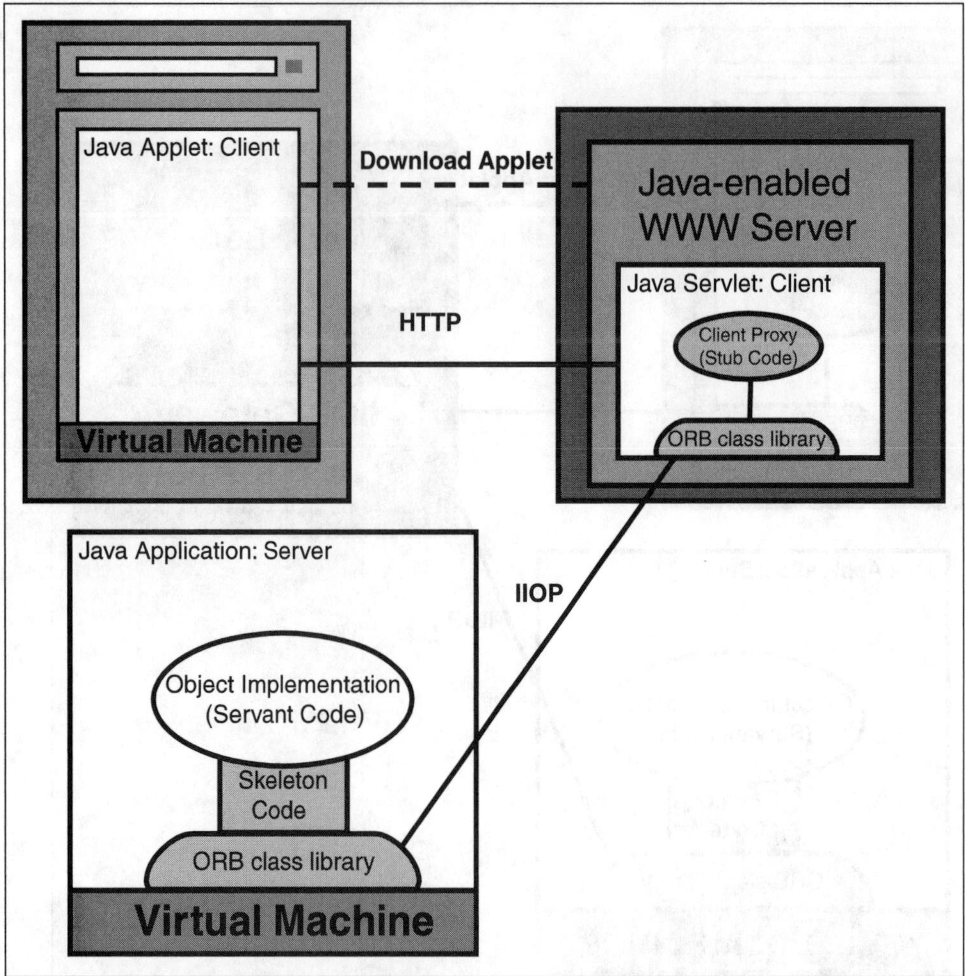


**Figure 3.15** Client as servlet.

of applet servers is explained in Chapter 9, "Advanced Features," in which objects communicate from applet to applet. In Chapter 15, "Performance, Scalability, and Management," we provide various design patterns involving callback mechanisms that are also applicable to applets.

Applets acting as servers need to handle two event loops: one to deal with incoming CORBA requests and the other to deal with applet events such as those caused at the GUI. This is a nontrivial issue in C and C++ ORBs, but Java threads handle this problem elegantly.

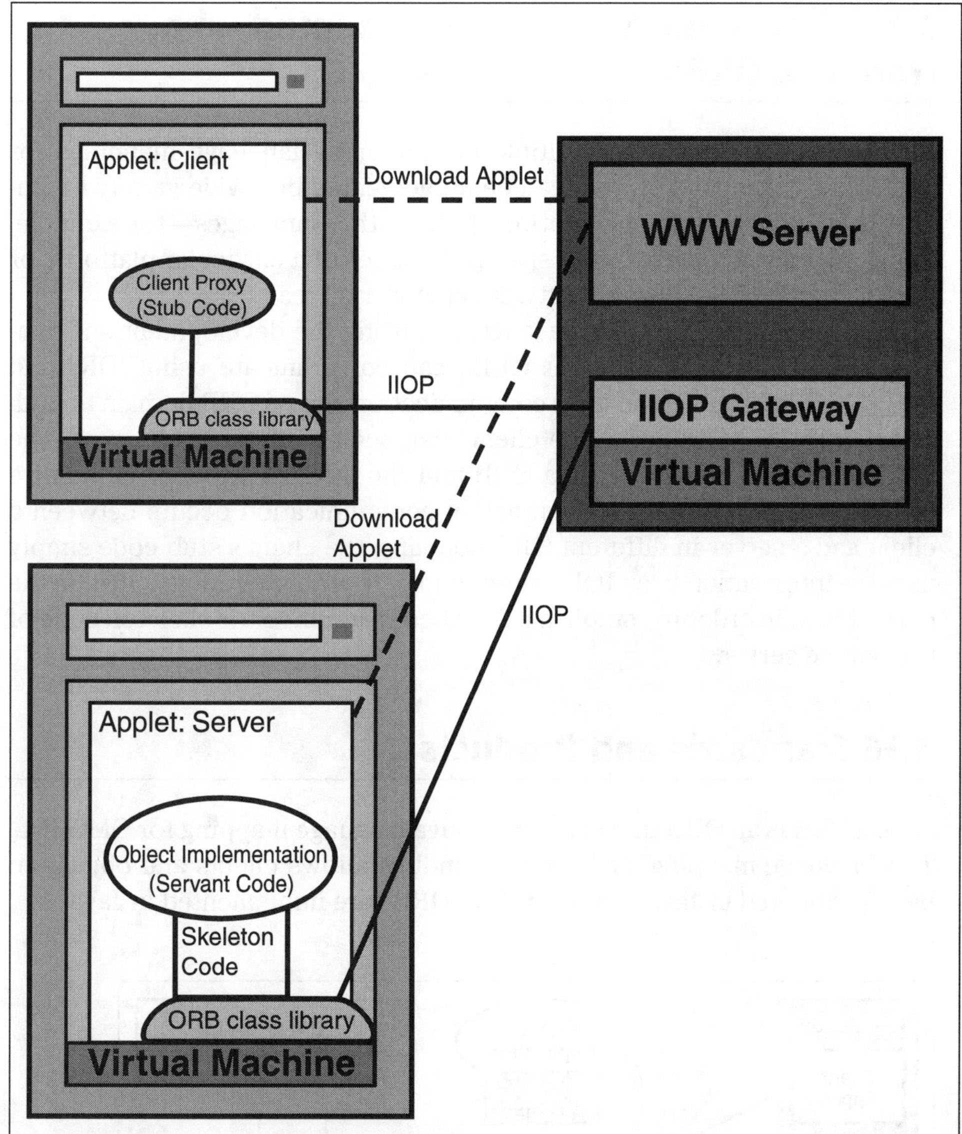


**Figure 3.16** Applet as a CORBA server.

Signed applets have the same capabilities as Java applications as long as the browser user applies the necessary settings. Hence, signed applets can potentially open IIOP connections to servers on arbitrary hosts and have access to local resources.

## 3.15 Clients and Servers Implemented with Non-Java ORBs

Because CORBA provides multiple programming language mappings for OMG IDL, clients and servers can be implemented in a wide variety of languages. There are many motivations to use other languages—for example, to integrate legacy code, to use specific features of a particular platform, or to exploit specific skills of a software engineering team.

Implementations in different languages using the development and runtime environments of different ORBs can communicate using IORs and IIOP. This is often referred to as communication across ORB domain boundaries. In Figure 3.17 any of the clients can access any of the servers. The IIOP channel between the Java ORB and the other ORB is symbolic of a bridging of ORB domains. When actual communication occurs between a client and a server in different ORB domains, the client's stub code simply uses the information in an IOR to communicate with the foreign ORB on the correct host in order to establish a direct connection to the skeleton code of the remote server.

## 3.16 Standards and Products

A Java ORB is an ORB that supports a Java language mapping for OMG IDL. This language mapping, or language binding, allows clients and objects to be implemented in Java. Typically Java ORBs are implemented in Java.

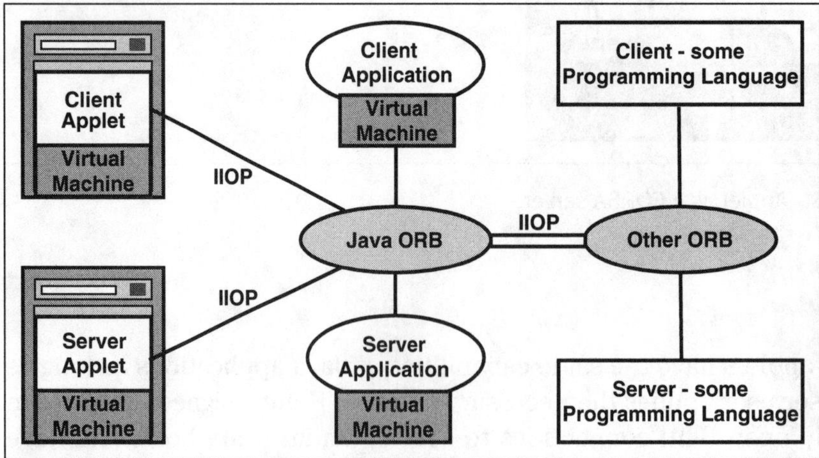


**Figure 3.17** Interoperability.

OMG's Platform Technical Committee voted in favor of the final and unified IDL-to-Java mapping specification in April 1997. The specification was officially adopted a few months later by approval from the Architecture Board and the OMG Board. This first version of the language mapping has undergone a number of revisions since its initial adoption to align it with the evolving POA and Objects-by-Value specifications. In its current form, the Java language mapping is part of CORBA 2.3, which was officially adopted in June 1999. Details of the IDL/Java mapping are explained in Chapter 5 and Chapter 6, "ORB Run-Time System."

Java ORBs are implemented and distributed by a large number of organizations. There are industrial-strength implementations available, including services such as Security, Transactions, Naming, and Events. Lightweight Java ORBs are included as part of JDK 1.2 and the Netscape browser. Java ORBs are also available in Java development environments such as Inprise's JBuilder.

These commercial implementations usually don't come with source code. A number of Open Source ORB implementations, however, also distribute the source code and, depending on the software licensing scheme, even permit modification and redistribution. Access to source code can be useful in many respects. It allows us to learn about the ORB design and the implementation quality, to work around limitations, and to customize the ORB in ways not foreseen by its original ORB designers.

From a customer perspective, the diversity of Java ORBs is, of course, both a curse and a blessing. While it does offer alternatives, it requires thorough evaluation of the available products. There are too many implementations to list and compare in this book.

# A First Java ORB Application

In this chapter we will use two Hello World examples to introduce the principles of building distributed applications with Java ORBs. Those examples expand the Hello World example introduced in Chapter 3, "Overview of Java and Java ORBs." We will implement a client that is a Java application, a client that is a Java applet, and a server hosting an object implementation. Figure 4.1 illustrates the components of our examples.

All code is available in electronic form from the companion Web site for this book at www.wiley.com/compbooks/brose. The examples use only standard CORBA features so the ORB you choose to run this code does not matter—as long as it complies to CORBA version 2.3. Various ORB products that conform to the CORBA specification differentiate themselves with implementation details that have an impact on performance and scalability. Most also have extensions to the CORBA core.

This chapter starts with a summary of the development process for CORBA applications in Java (section 4.1). We give detailed explanations of the development of a simple example application (sections 4.2 through 4.8) and then extend this to include more features (section 4.9). In Chapter 9, "Advanced Features," we return to application development with a substantial example.

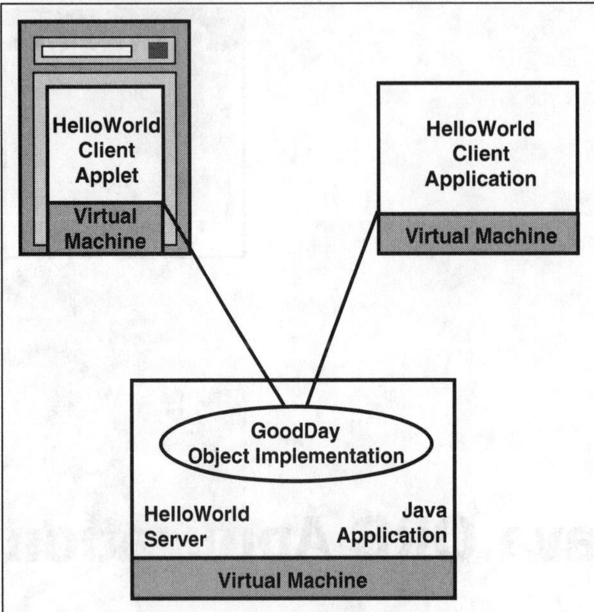


**Figure 4.1** Hello World application.

## 4.1 Summary of the CORBA Development Process

The examples presented in this chapter follow roughly the same steps:

- Write some IDL that describes the interfaces to the object or objects that will be used or implemented.
- Compile the IDL file. This produces the stub and skeleton code that provides location transparency. That is, it will cooperate with the ORB library to convert an object reference into a network connection to a remote server and then marshal the arguments we provide to an operation on the object reference, convey them to the correct method in the object denoted by our object reference, execute the method, and return the results.
- Identify the IDL compiler-generated interfaces and classes that we need to use or specialize in order to invoke or implement operations.
- Write code to initialize the ORB and inform it of any CORBA objects that we have created.

- Compile all the generated code and our application code with a Java compiler.
- Run the distributed application.

Figure 4.2 shows the use of IDL and the IDL compiler when building the application.

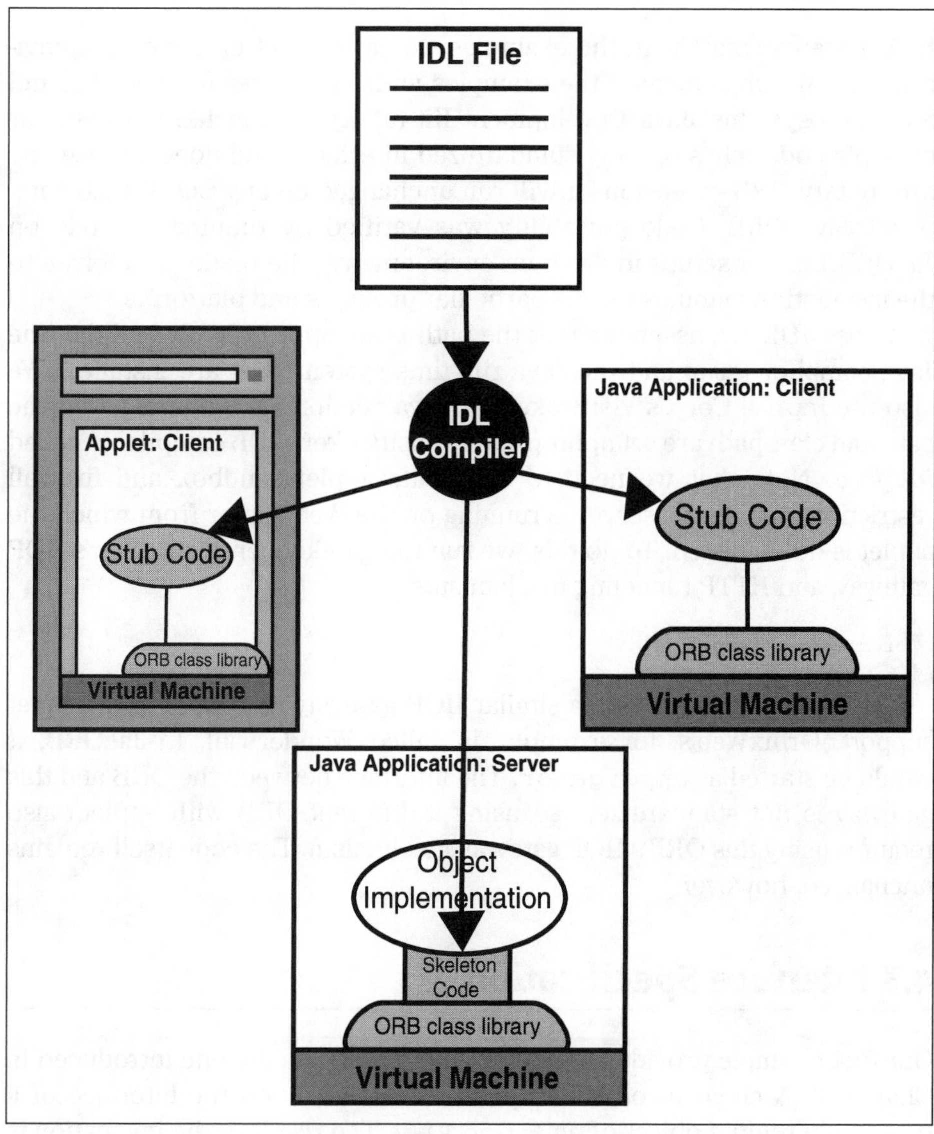


**Figure 4.2** Building the Hello World application.

When you execute the IDL compiler for the Java ORB you have installed, it will generate two sets of Java code files: stub code to create proxy objects that a client can use for making invocations on object references of the interface types defined in the IDL file and skeleton code for access to objects that support those interfaces.

## 4.2 Environment Setup

Before we can start with the examples we have to set up a working environment. We implemented the examples with VisiBroker for Java 4.1, and Sun Microsystems' Java Development Kit (JDK) version 1.2. Because our example code relies on only standardized interfaces and does not use any proprietary ORB extensions it will run unchanged on any CORBA 2.3 compliant Java ORB. Code portability was verified by running all code on JacORB 1.2. For setups in different environments, the reader is referred to the installation manuals for the particular products and platforms.

We use JDK 1.2, assuming that the path is set appropriately and that the Java compiler *javac* and the Java run-time system *java* are installed. We also use Inprise Corp.'s VisiBroker for Java version 4.1, assuming that the path and classpath are set appropriately. VisiBroker's IDL compiler is called *idl2java*. Note that we need to overcome applet sandbox and firewall restrictions unless the server is running on the Web server from which the applet is downloaded. To do this, we run the gatekeeper, VisiBroker's IIOP gateway, and HTTP tunneling mechanisms:

```
prompt> gatekeeper &
```

Many Java ORBs provide a similar IIOP gateway as part of their applet support. OrbixWeb's, for example, is called Wonderwall. In JacORB, it would be started as `appligator`. The interface between the ORB and this gateway is not standardized, so using a different ORB with applets also requires using this ORB's IIOP gateway mechanism. The code itself remains unchanged, however.

## 4.3 Interface Specification

Our first example provides the same functionality as the one introduced in Chapter 3. A client invokes an operation `hello()` on the interface of a potentially remote object of type `GoodDay`. The result of the invocation is a message that is printed by the client.

For any CORBA application we must write an IDL specification that defines data types and interfaces, including attributes and operations. For our example, we defined an IDL interface called HelloWorld that resembles the Java interface of the Hello World example from Chapter 3. We place the IDL file HelloWorld.idl, containing this definition, in a directory that represents its location in the book: com/wiley/compbooks/brose/chapter4/simple.

```
// HelloWorld.idl
module com {
module wiley {
module compbooks {
module brose {
module chapter 4 {
module simple {
module helloWorld {
  interface GoodDay {
    string hello();
  };
};};};};};};};
```

The file contains the specification of a hierarchy of modules. It is good specification style to use modules to create a separate name space for an application or its major components and to follow the same naming conventions that have been introduced for Java packages. To align with Java coding conventions, we recommend using module names that begin with lowercase letters and interface names beginning with capital letters.

Within the module helloWorld we define one interface: GoodDay. The interface is not in any inheritance relationship. It provides one operation, hello(). This operation does not have any parameters and returns a result of type string.

As we will see in the implementation, the object returns a string describing its locality as part of the result of the operation hello(). The operation returns a message saying: "Hello World, from *location*."

## 4.4 Compiling the IDL

The next step in the application development is to compile the IDL to generate the stub and skeleton code. The compile command in VisiBroker for Java is

```
prompt> idl2java -strict -root_dir generated HelloWorld.idl
```

The IDL compiler maps each module to a Java package and uses Java conventions for putting packages in directories. Both directory and package are named after the IDL module. The Java package contains Java interfaces and classes implementing stub, skeleton, and other code to support your distributed application. To distinguish between generated code and handwritten code, we direct the compiler to place its output in a different directory tree by supplying it with the name of root directory for the generated code. This directory is called `generated`. The `-strict` switch tells the compiler that it must not include any proprietary extensions in the generated code but abide by the letter of the specification, in particular the Java ORB Portability Interfaces, which we explain in Chapter 5, "OMG IDL to Java Mapping." These interfaces ensure the portability of code from one ORB to another.

While the names of compiler switches depend on which vendor's compiler is used, the files generated by any compliant IDL compiler are always the same. These are:

```
GoodDay.java
GoodDayHolder.java          GoodDayHelper.java
GoodDayStub.java            GoodDayPOA.java
GoodDayOperations.java      GoodDayPOATie.java
```

The IDL interface GoodDay is mapped to a Java interface of the same name in the file `GoodDay.java`. The class `GoodDayHolder` provides support to handle IDL inout and out parameters, as you will see toward the end of this chapter. The class `GoodDayHelper` contains miscellaneous static methods, most importantly the `narrow()` method. In Chapter 5 we explain the complete mapping from OMG IDL to Java and also the meaning of the generated Java classes and interfaces.

The remaining files that are generated by the IDL compiler contain classes that have general functionality. The class `_GoodDayStub` contains the stub code that allows us to create a client-side proxy for the object implementation. The class `GoodDayPOA` contains the skeleton code that is used with the POA. The interface `GoodDayOperations` and the class `GoodDayPOATie` are used for the Tie mechanism on the server side. This is explained in Chapter 5 and demonstrated by an example in Chapter 9.

## 4.5 A Client as a Java Application

When implementing a client as a Java application, we don't have to worry about the restrictions that exist for applets, and so we can explain CORBA programming in its usual form. A client implementation follows these steps:

- Initialize the CORBA environment; that is, obtain a reference to the ORB.
- Obtain an object reference for the object on which to invoke operations.
- Invoke operations and process the results.

## 4.5.1 Generated Java Interface

The Java interface that corresponds to the interface defined in IDL is an empty interface. It extends two base classes for CORBA Objects and IDL entities and the Java interface `GoodDayOperations`, which contains the actual operation signatures:

```
// generated Java - GoodDay.java
package com.wiley.compbooks.brose.chapter4.simple.helloWorld;

public interface GoodDay extends GoodDayOperations,
                                 org.omg.CORBA.Object,
                                 org.omg.CORBA.portable.IDLEntity
{
}
```

The `GoodDayOperations` interface defines a Java method `hello()` that returns a Java string. The reason for this division of labor between `GoodDay` and `GoodDayOperations` is that in some cases it is necessary to use an operations interface that does not extend `org.omg.CORBA.Object`. This will be explained in more detail in Chapter 6, "ORB Run-Time System."

```
// generated Java - GoodDayOperations.java
package com.wiley.compbooks.brose.chapter4.simple.helloWorld;

public interface GoodDayOperations {
    public java.lang.String hello();
}
```

## 4.5.2 Initializing the ORB

We define a Java class `Client` in our implementation package and define the `main()` method for this class. Initializing an ORB means obtaining a reference to the ORB pseudo-object. The ORB is called a pseudo-object because its methods will be provided by a library in communication with the run-time system, and its pseudo-object reference cannot be passed as a parameter to CORBA interface operations. Excluding that restriction, however, a reference to an ORB looks like any other object reference.

```
package com.wiley.compbooks.brose.chapter4.simple.helloWorld;

import java.io.*;
import org.omg.CORBA.*;

public class Client {
    public static void main(String args[]) {
        try {
            // initialize the ORB
            ORB orb = ORB.init (args, null);
```

After we have declared the package to which our client class belongs, imported the appropriate classes, and declared the class and the main method, we initialize the ORB. The static method `init()` on the class `org.omg.CORBA.ORB` returns an instance of an ORB.

## 4.5.3 Obtaining an Object Reference

References to objects can be obtained by various means, as explained in Chapter 7, "Discovering Services." Here we use a rather unsophisticated method. Object references are opaque data structures; however, an object reference can be converted into a string (as we show when explaining the server). This is known as *stringifying* an object reference. The resulting string is called a *stringified object reference.* Stringified object references are reconvertible into "live" object references. This is done using the two corresponding operations, object_to_string() and string_to_object(), defined on the CORBA::ORB interface. Stringified interoperable object references can be converted into working object references by any CORBA-compliant ORB.

```
            // get object reference from command-line argument
            org.omg.CORBA.Object obj = orb.string_to_object( args[0] );
```

For this example client we assume that a stringified object reference is provided as the first argument to the client program. It is then provided as the argument to the method `string_to_object()`, which is invoked on the ORB pseudo-object. The method returns an object reference of type CORBA::Object, the base type of all CORBA objects, which is mapped to the interface `org.omg.CORBA.Object`. You have to use the fully qualified name to avoid confusion with `java.lang.Object`. To make use of the object it needs to be narrowed to the appropriate type. Narrowing is equivalent to down-casting in some object-oriented programming languages. The narrow operation is type-safe because it returns a null object reference if the object reference passed to it is not of a correct type. If it successfully returns a nonnull reference then we can be sure that the reference is valid and of the correct type. It can also raise the exception CORBA::BAD_PARAM.

The narrow method is defined in the class GoodDayHelper.

```
        GoodDay goodDay = GoodDayHelper.narrow( obj );
        if( goodDay == null ) {
            System.err.println(
                "stringified object reference is of wrong type");
            System.exit( -1 );
        }
```

Note that you should always use a narrow() operation when you have to down-cast a CORBA object and never the Java casting mechanism.

## 4.5.4 Invoking the Operation

Once the ORB is initialized and an object reference is obtained, CORBA programming looks very much like standard object-oriented programming. Invoking methods on objects looks exactly the same for remote and local objects.

```
        System.out.println( goodDay.hello() );
```

Our simple client invokes the method hello() on the object goodDay, and the result is printed to standard output.

The last thing to consider is handling exceptions that might occur. Because there are no user exceptions raised by the hello() operation, we only have to catch and process CORBA system exceptions, which can be thrown by any CORBA-related method including the initialization of the ORB, the narrow call, and the hello() method.

```
        }
        catch(SystemException ex) {
            System.err.println(ex);
        }
    }
}
```

Note that the SystemException class is defined in the package org.omg.CORBA.

## 4.5.5 Compiling and Executing the Client

To make the client program executable by a Java virtual machine it needs to be compiled. This is done by calling the Java compiler.

```
prompt> javac Client.java
```

We execute the client by calling the Java run-time system with two arguments: the name of the client class and a stringified object reference. You will see how to generate this string when we consider the server implementation.

```
prompt> java com.wiley.compbooks.brose.chapter4.helloWorld.Client
IOR:000000000000002149444c3a53696d706c6548656c6c6f576f726c642f476f6f6444
61793a312e300000000000000001000000000000004c000100000000000e3133302e3130
322e3137362e3900fc7d0000003000504d43000000010000001a53696d706c6548656c6c
6f576f726c643a3a476f6f644461790000000000000002febddb22
```

The client then prints the expected message.

```
Hello World, from Brisbane
```

## 4.6 A Client as an Applet

When writing a client as an applet you have to follow the same steps as for the application client. You also have to make the following additions and alterations:

- Anchor the applet in an HTML page to make it addressable and loadable.
- Provide a GUI to enable interaction through a Web browser.
- Extend the Java applet class and override some of its methods.
- Use a different ORB initialization.

### 4.6.1 Anchoring the Applet into HTML

To make an applet accessible over the Web it needs to be anchored in an HTML page. When a browser downloads such a document, the Java byte code representing the anchored applet will also be received and executed by the Java Virtual Machine in the browser. Here is an example HTML file:

```
<html>
<header>
<title>
Hello World Example
</title>
<body>
<center><h1>
```

```
Hello World Example
</center>
<center>
<applet code=com/wiley/compbooks/brose/chapter4/simple/helloWorld/
Applet.class
    width=400 height=80>
</applet>
</center>
</body></html>
```

For our simple applet we have an HTML file `HelloWorldApplet.html` that contains only a header and a reference to our applet class `com.wiley.compbooks.brose.chapter4.helloWorld.Applet`. There may be a need for parameter tags in the applet tag. These are very ORB and browser dependent, and you should look up details in the relevant reference manuals.

## 4.6.2 Initializing the Applet

We define our applet as a class `Applet` that extends the Java applet class `java.applet.Applet`. Within the class we declare a number of private variables:

- `goodDay`—to hold the object reference of the remote object
- `helloWorldButton`—a button to enable users to invoke the method
- `textField`—a text field to display the result of the method

Then we override the method `init()` inherited from the applet base class. First, we initialize the GUI components, that is, we create a Button and a TextField object and set some properties of these objects. Then we define the layout of the user interface using the Java layout manager `GridLayout` and add the two GUI components to the layout. We also register the applet as an event listener at our Hello World button according to the Java event model and set the action command to "invoke."

```
package com.wiley.compbooks.brose.chapter4.simple.helloWorld;

import java.io.*;
import java.net.*;
import java.awt.*;
import java.awt.event.*;
import org.omg.CORBA.*;
```

```
public class Applet
    extends java.applet.Applet
    implements ActionListener {

    private ORB orb;
    private GoodDay goodDay;
    private Button helloWorldButton;
    private TextField textField;

    public void init() {
        helloWorldButton = new Button("Invoke remote method");
        helloWorldButton.setFont( new Font( "Helvetica",
            Font.BOLD, 20));
        helloWorldButton.setActionCommand( "invoke" );
        helloWorldButton.addActionListener( (ActionListener)this );
        textField = new TextField();
        textField.setEditable( false );
        textField.setFont( new Font( "Helvetica", Font.BOLD, 14));
        setLayout( new GridLayout( 2,1 ));
        add( helloWorldButton );
        add( textField );
```

## 4.6.3 Locating Objects

In the next step we locate an object implementation. In the application client we did this using a stringified object reference. Because stringified IORs are rather inconvenient to use in applet parameters, we use the following convention to access initial IORs. We expect that a file containing the target IOR is supplied in the same directory where the HTML page containing the applet was found on the Web server. Details on how to locate an object more flexibly are provided in Chapter 7.

To initialize the ORB we again call the method `init()`, this time with the applet object itself as the first argument (using the Java keyword `this` to do so). This initialization changes the behavior of the stub. As part of its bootstrap code the stub will establish a connection to an instance of the IIOP gateway, which it expects to be running on the machine from which the applet has been downloaded. Details of the problems related to IIOP gateways and their solutions are discussed in Chapter 12, "Security." If your ORB does not provide an IIOP gateway, you must make sure that the server that hosts the remote object is running on the machine from which the applet was downloaded; otherwise, it won't be reachable from within the applet.

To obtain a reference to the remote object we use the following method `readIOR()`. This method constructs a URL for the location where the IOR file is expected. It then opens a connection to this resource and reads a line of text that is assumed to contain the stringified object reference. Because applets are allowed to connect to their Web server this operation will succeed if the IOR has been properly provided.

```
    private String readIOR() {
        try {
            URL iorURL = new URL( getCodeBase().toString()+"ior");
            BufferedReader in = new BufferedReader(
                new InputStreamReader( iorURL.openStream() ));
            String line = in.readLine();
            in.close();
            return line;
        } catch( Exception ex ) {
            System.err.println(ex);
        }
        return null;
    }
```

Applet initialization is finished with the catching and processing of exceptions.

```
    try {
        // initialize the ORB (using this applet)
        orb = ORB.init( this, null );
        org.omg.CORBA.Object obj =
            orb.string_to_object( readIOR());
        goodDay = GoodDayHelper.narrow( obj );
    }
    catch( SystemException ex ) {
        System.err.println( "ORB is not initialized" );
        System.err.println( ex );
    }
}
```

## 4.6.4 Handling Applet Events

To handle events from the graphical user interface, in our case from the Hello World button, we implement the method `actionPerformed()` of the interface `java.applet.awt.event.ActionListener`. This method handles GUI events of type `ActionEvent`. In this case we have to deal with only one event, which is fired when the Hello World button is pressed. This event is associated with the command "invoke."

```
    public void actionPerformed( ActionEvent e ) {
        if( e.getActionCommand().equals("invoke") ) {
            // invoke the operation
```

```
            try {
                textField.setText( goodDay.hello() );
            }
            // catch CORBA system exceptions
            catch(SystemException ex) {
                System.err.println(ex);
            }
        }
    }
```

We check if the action command of the event was "invoke." If not, we do nothing. Otherwise, we invoke the method `hello()` on the object `goodDay`. We display the result of the invocation in the text field. Again, we watch for possible CORBA system exceptions and print them if they occur.

## 4.6.5 Compiling and Executing the Applet

To make the applet executable it needs to be compiled. This is done by calling the Java compiler.

```
prompt> javac Applet.java
```

To execute the applet we have to point a Java-enabled Web browser to the URL of the HTML document that anchors our applet. Figure 4.3 shows the initial state of the applet's execution in the browser.

Once the button has been clicked, the result of the operation invocation is displayed in the text field, as shown in Figure 4.4.

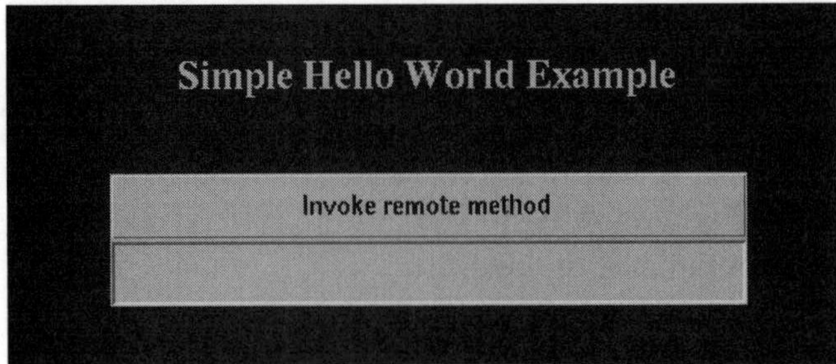


**Figure 4.3** Hello World applet—initial state.

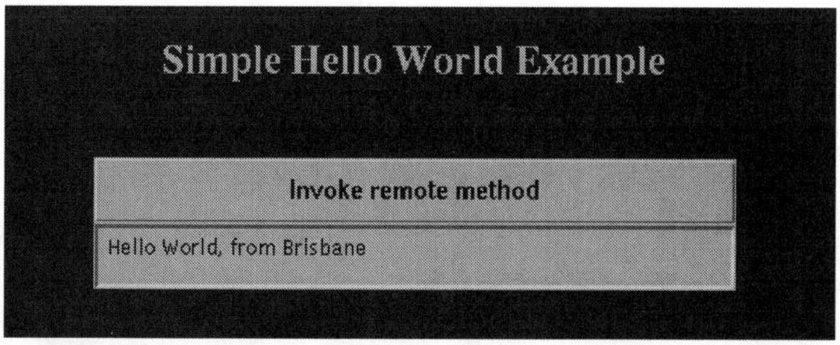

Simple Hello World Example

Invoke remote method

Hello World, from Brisbane

**Figure 4.4** Hello World applet–invoked method.

## 4.7 An Object Implementation

Now we turn to the implementation of the object whose interface has been specified in IDL. This implementation is also known as the *servant class*. The IDL/Java mapping specification defines a *servant base class* that is named after the IDL interface: *InterfaceName*POA. This base class is a skeleton generated by the IDL compiler. There are alternatives to this implementation style. The two main ways of associating object implementation classes with a skeleton class are by *inheritance* or *delegation*.

The inheritance approach involves a Java implementation class extending the servant base class. The servant base class is an abstract implementation of the Java interface that corresponds to the IDL interface. The object implementation is an extension of the base class and implements the methods. The delegation approach is also known as the Tie method. This is done by providing the skeleton with a reference to an implementation object. This is explained in detail in Chapter 9.

In our example we have an implementation class `GoodDayImpl` that extends the servant base class `GoodDayPOA`. As in the implementation of the `GoodDayImpl` class shown in Chapter 3, we declare a private variable, `location`, that will hold a string identifying the location of the service. Here we mean the geographical location, as shown in the previous client examples.

We also have to implement the constructor of the class. The constructor has one parameter that it assigns to the private variable `location`.

```
package com.wiley.compbooks.brose.chapter4.simple.helloWorld;
import org.omg.CORBA.*;

public class GoodDayImpl extends GoodDayPOA {
    private String location;

    // constructor
```

```
    GoodDayImpl( String location ) {
        // initialize location
        this.location = location;
    }

    // method
    public String hello() {
        return "Hello World, from " + location;
    }
}
```

We implement the method `hello()`, which returns a string composed of the message "Hello World, from" and the value of the variable `location`.

Again we have to compile the Java source into byte code:

```
prompt> javac GoodDayImpl.java
```

## 4.8 A Server

Now we have to implement a server class. This class initializes the environment, creates the implementation object, makes it available to clients, and listens for events. The server class for our example is called `Server`. We only implement the `main()` method in this class. We check for the right number of arguments, one of which indicates the location of the server. A server is responsible for initializing the ORB, creating the object, and making the object accessible.

We initialize the ORB in the same way we did on the client side by calling `ORB.init()`, which returns a reference to the ORB pseudo-object. We then create an instance of the servant class `goodDayImpl` by calling Java's `new` operator and supply one argument to the constructor that we copy from the command-line argument.

```
package com.wiley.compbooks.brose.chapter4.simple.helloWorld;

import java.io.*;
import org.omg.CORBA.*;
import org.omg.PortableServer.*;

public class Server {
    public static void main(String[] args) {
        if( args.length != 1 ) {
            System.out.println("Usage: java
com.wiley.compbooks.brose.chapter4.simple.helloWorld <location> ");
            System.exit( 1 );
        }
        try {
```

```
            //init ORB
            ORB orb = ORB.init ( args, null );
            // create a GoodDay object
            GoodDayImpl goodDayImpl = new GoodDayImpl( args[0] );
```

At this stage we have only a Java object. To make it incarnate a CORBA object we must enable the object to act as a servant and to receive CORBA operation invocations. This is done via an object adapter. To create a CORBA object reference that we can later export, we first need to obtain a reference to an instance of a POA and initialize it. We do not need any advanced object adapter features here, so it is sufficient to use the ORB's root POA, which can be obtained by calling `resolve_initial_references("RootPOA")` on the ORB. After narrowing the result to type POA we need to activate the object adapter because, as explained in Chapter 2, "CORBA Overview," object adapters are initially in a holding state and do not process incoming requests.

```
            //init POA
            POA poa = POAHelper.narrow(
                orb.resolve_initial_references("RootPOA") );
);
            poa.the_POAManager().activate();
```

Now that we have set up the POA we can create an object reference from our `goodDayImpl` servant. Note that the servant incarnates a transient CORBA object. The object reference of a transient object is valid only for the lifetime of a particular instance of its POA. We explain and compare transient and persistent object references in detail in Chapter 5. Creating an object reference from a servant object is done by calling `servant_to_reference()` on the POA, supplying the servant object as an argument.

```
            // create the object reference
            org.omg.CORBA.Object obj =
                poa.servant_to_reference( goodDayImpl );

            // print stringified object reference
            System.out.println( orb.object_to_string( obj ) );
);

            // wait for requests
            orb.run();
        }
        catch(InvalidName e) {
            System.err.println(e);
        }
        // POA exceptions WrongPolicy and ServantNotActive
        catch(UserException e) {
```

```
            System.err.println(e);
        }
        catch(SystemException e) {
            System.err.println(e);
        }
    }
}
```

After creating the object reference, we print its stringified reference to the standard output. Note that we have implicitly activated the new CORBA object with the call to `servant_to_reference()`, so it is ready to receive requests now. Finally, we call `run()` on the ORB that blocks the server's main thread waiting for incoming requests.

Again we catch possible exceptions. Two more exceptions can occur here. The first of these is `InvalidName`, which can be thrown by `resolve_initial_references()` if an invalid string argument is supplied. The other kind of possible exceptions are two `UserExceptions` defined for the POA's `servant_to_reference()` method. We handle both of them by defining a catch clause for `UserExceptions`. The exact types of these exceptions are `WrongPolicy` and `ServantNotActive`, and they are both declared in the `org.omg.PortableServer` package.

### 4.8.1 Compiling and Starting the Server

We have to compile the Java source into byte code:

```
prompt> javac Server.java
```

We now start the server:

```
prompt> java com.wiley.compbooks.brose.chapter4.simple.helloWorld.Server
Brisbane
```

This prints out a stringified IOR which looks like this:

```
IOR:000000000000002149444c3a53696d706c6548656c6c6f576f726c642f476f6f6444
61793a312e30000000000000000100000000000000004c000100000000000e3133302e3130
322e3137362e3900fc7d0000003000504d430000000010000001a53696d706c6548656c6c
6f576f726c643a3a476f6f6444617900000000000000002febddb22
```

It's probably a good idea to redirect standard output to a file. In our example we call this file `shw.ior`:

```
prompt> java com.wiley.compbooks.brose.chapter4.simple.helloWorld.Server
Brisbane > shw.ior
```

Now we can really run our clients as we have shown earlier. A client can be conveniently started using the IOR file:

```
prompt> java com.wiley.compbooks.brose.chapter4.simple.helloWorld.Client
`cat shw.ior`
```

## 4.9 Extending the Hello World Example

In this section we will modify the simple Hello World example to introduce another feature. In this example the server will return not only a message but also the current time at the server's location. We will look at some new aspects of application development and revisit some of the issues discussed in the earlier version of this example application. Specifically we deal with the following:

- Further aspects of the specification of interfaces
- Parameter mapping and the semantics of parameter passing
- The development of a client
- Applet implementations
- The implementation of an object

### 4.9.1 Interface Specification

We again specify an interface GoodDay with an operation hello(). The module is again called helloWorld. To avoid name clashes with the previous example, all code will be developed in the package `com.wiley.compbooks.brose.chapter4.extended`.

The signature of the operation is different. Its result is still a string, but this time the operation has parameters, and it returns the description of the server's location. The parameters are tagged as out, meaning that their values will be supplied by the invoked object. They are both of type short, and their intended meaning is that they hold the current time at the server's location: hour holds the hour and minute the minute.

```
module com {
module wiley {
...
module extended {
module helloWorld {
  interface GoodDay {
    string hello(
```

```
        out short hour,
        out short minute );
    };
};...};
```

### 4.9.2 Parameter Mapping

An out parameter in an IDL operation has pass-by-result semantics. This means that a value for this parameter will be supplied by the invoked object. The value will be available to the client after the invocation is completed.

The parameters in Java operations have pass-by-value semantics, meaning that a value is passed from the caller to the invoked object. There is a mismatch in the semantics of parameter passing between IDL and Java for IDL's out and inout parameters. The solution is provided by *Holder objects*. Instead of passing an argument itself, an object is used as an argument to the Java method. The Holder object contains a variable `value` of the type of the IDL parameter. This way the Java object's reference passed need not change, but contents may change as a result of the invocation (see Figure 4.5).

Holder classes for predefined IDL types are provided in the package `org.omg.CORBA`, as listed in Chapter 5. The IDL compiler generates Holder classes *`TypeName`*`Holder` for user-defined types. In our examples we use the predefined Holder class `org.omg.CORBA.ShortHolder`.

### 4.9.3 A Client

The main difference to the previous example is that we create two objects, `minute` and `hour`, of the class `org.omg.CORBA.ShortHolder` for the out parameters of the `hello()` operation.

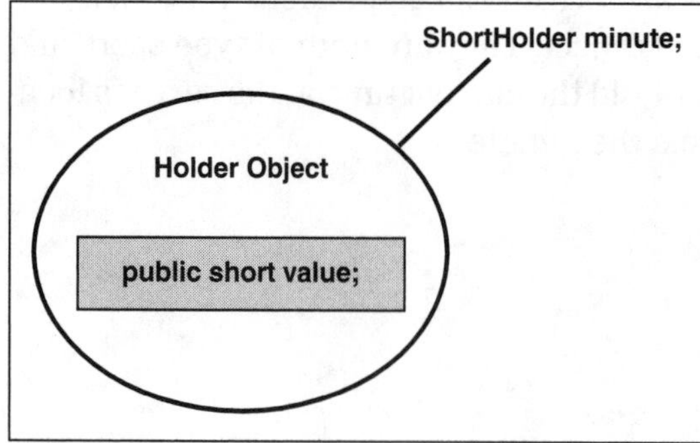


**Figure 4.5** Holder objects.

```
package com.wiley.compbooks.brose.chapter4.extended.helloWorld;

import java.io.*;
import org.omg.CORBA.*;

public class Client {
    public static void main(String args[]) {

        // create Holder objects for out parameters
        ShortHolder minute = new ShortHolder();
        ShortHolder hour = new ShortHolder();
        try {
            // initialize the ORB
            ORB orb = ORB.init(args, null);
            // get object reference from command-line argument
            org.omg.CORBA.Object obj =
                orb.string_to_object( args[0] );
            // and narrow it to GoodDay
            GoodDay goodDay = GoodDayHelper.narrow( obj );
            if( goodDay == null ) {
                System.err.println(
                   "stringified object reference is of wrong type");
                System.exit( -1 );
            }
```

#### 4.9.3.1 Invoking the Operation

After we initialize the ORB and obtain a narrowed object reference, we invoke the operation. We assign the result of the operation to a string `location`. After the successful return of the invocation, the variables named `value` in the two holder objects will carry values set by the invoked object.

```
            // invoke the operation
            String location = goodDay.hello( hour, minute );
            // print results to stdout
            System.out.println("Hello World!");
            if( minute.value < 10 )
               System.out.println("The local time in " + location +
                  " is " + hour.value + ":0" + minute.value + "." );
            else
               System.out.println("The local time in " + location +
                  " is " + hour.value + ":" + minute.value + "." );
        }
        // catch exceptions
        catch(SystemException ex) {
            System.err.println(ex);
        }
```

```
    }
}
```

When we print out the results we obtain the time at the remote location from the variable `value` of the holder objects `hour.value` and `minute.value`. We compile the client as before and execute it. The stringified object reference must refer to an object that provides the extended Hello World interface. The following is a typical result:

```
prompt> java com.wiley.compbooks.brose.chapter4.extended.helloWorld.Client
IOR:000000000000001b49444c3a48656c6c6f576f726c642f476f6f644461793a312e30000
0000000010000000000000004c00010000000000e3133302e3130322e313762e39008384000
0003000504d4300000000000000001448656c6c6f576f726c643a3a476f6f644461790000000
0c476f6f64446179496d706c00
Hello World!
The local time in Brisbane is 16:42.
```

## 4.9.4 An Applet

The applet implementation does not add much new. We have the same structure as in the simple example, and we make additions and modifications as in the aforementioned client. We add two private variable declarations to the class and create the corresponding objects within the method `init()`.

```
package com.wiley.compbooks.brose.chapter4.extended.helloWorld;

import java.io.*;
import java.net.*;
import java.awt.*;
import java.awt.event.*;
import org.omg.CORBA.*;

public class Applet
    extends java.applet.Applet
    implements ActionListener {

    private ShortHolder minute;
    private ShortHolder hour;
    private GoodDay goodDay;
    private String text;
    private String locality;
    private Button helloWorldButton;
    private TextField textField;

    public void init() {
```

```
        minute = new ShortHolder();
        hour = new ShortHolder();
        helloWorldButton = new Button("Invoke remote method");
        helloWorldButton.setFont(
            new Font( "Helvetica", Font.BOLD, 20 ));
        helloWorldButton.setActionCommand("invoke");
        helloWorldButton.addActionListener( (ActionListener)this );
        textField = new TextField();
        textField.setEditable(false);
        textField.setFont(new Font("Helvetica", Font.BOLD, 14));
        setLayout( new GridLayout(2,1);
        add( helloWorldButton );
    }
```

#### 4.9.4.1 Invoke the Operation

In the method `actionPerformed()`, we invoke the operation and display the result in the text field.

```
    public void actionPerformed( ActionEvent e ) {
        if( e.getActionCommand().equals("invoke") ) {
            // invoke the operation
            try {
                locality = new String(goodDay.hello(hour, minute ));
            }
            // catch exceptions
            catch(SystemException ex) {
                System.err.println(ex);
            }
            if( minute.value < 10 )
                text = new String("The local time in " + locality +
                    " is " + hour.value + ":0" +
                    minute.value + "." );
            else
                text = new String("The local time in " + locality +
                   " is " + hour.value + ":" + minute.value + "." );
            textField.setText( text );
        }
    }
}
```

When the applet is compiled and loaded into a browser via an HTML page, we see a user interface, as shown in Figure 4.3. When the button is clicked and the operation invoked we see the following text in the display.

```
Hello World! The local time in Brisbane is 16:44.
```

## 4.9.5 Object Implementation

The variable declarations and the constructor are as in the class GoodDay-Impl of the first example, but the signature of the method hello() has changed. There are now two short holder objects as parameters.

We create an object date that holds the time information of the system. The corresponding class is defined in java.util.Date. We retrieve the hour and the minute by invoking the methods getHours() and getMinutes() on the object. We assign the values to the corresponding value variables of the container objects. We return the locality as in the earlier example.

```
package com.wiley.compbooks.brose.chapter4.extended.helloWorld;

import java.util.Date;
import org.omg.CORBA.*;

public class GoodDayImpl extends GoodDayPOA {
    private String location;

    // constructor
    GoodDayImpl( String location ) {
        this.location = location;
    }

    // method
    public String hello( ShortHolder hour, ShortHolder minute ) {
        // get local time of the server
        Date date = new Date();
        hour.value = (short) date.getHours();
        minute.value = (short) date.getMinutes();
        return location;
    }
}
```

The server implementation in the class Server again uses the POA. Once the ORB is initialized, we obtain a reference to the root POA instance by calling resolve_initial_references("RootPOA") on the ORB pseudo-object, activate the POA, and create an instance of the servant as before. To make it a CORBA object, we call the method servant_to_reference() on the POA. This again creates an object reference and implicitly activates the CORBA object; that is, it associates it with the servant goodDayImpl. The new object is now accessible by CORBA clients. Again we print out the stringified object reference. Finally we call run() on the ORB which puts the server in an infinite loop waiting for incoming calls.

```
package com.wiley.compbooks.brose.chapter4.extended.helloWorld;

import org.omg.CORBA.*;
import org.omg.CORBA.ORBPackage.*;
import org.omg.PortableServer.*;

public class Server {

    public static void main(String[] args) {

        try {
            //init orb
            ORB orb = ORB.init( args, null );

            //init basic object adapter
            POA poa = POAHelper.narrow(
               orb.resolve_initial_references("RootPOA"));
            poa.the_POAManager().activate();

            // create a GoodDay object
            GoodDayImpl goodDayImpl = new GoodDayImpl( args[0] );

            // export the object reference
            org.omg.CORBA.Object obj =
                poa.servant_to_reference( goodDayImpl );
            System.out.println( orb.object_to_string( obj ) );

            // wait for requests
            orb.run();
        }
        catch(InvalidName e) {
            System.err.println(e);
        }
        // POA exceptions WrongPolicy and ServantNotActive
        catch(UserException e) {
            System.err.println(e);
        }
        catch(SystemException e) {
            System.err.println(e);
        }
    }
}
```

In this chapter, you have seen all the basics of programming with Java ORBs and are now ready to start with experiments of your own. We have explained the basic steps that you need to follow, and how the various development stages fit together. You will see that we go through these steps even in the more advanced examples later in this book.

# OMG IDL to Java Mapping

This chapter explains the mapping from OMG IDL to Java as defined by the OMG IDL/Java Mapping standard (document formal/99-07-53). The chapter should be seen mainly as a reference.

The mapping begins with the basic IDL data types, then presents the structured data types. Later sections detail the mappings for operations and attributes, valuetype interfaces and their inheritance relationships, and modules.

## 5.1 Reserved Names

A number of names and name patterns are reserved by the mapping and should not be used by programmers. For each user-defined IDL type called *IDLType* and each primitive Java type *JavaType* the following names are reserved: *IDLType*Helper, *IDLType*Holder, *JavaType*Helper, and *JavaType*Holder.

For each IDL interface *IDLInterface*, the names *IDLInterface*Operations, *IDLInterface*POA, *IDLInterface*POATie, and *IDLInterface*Package are also reserved. All keywords of the Java language are also reserved. If a programmer uses one of the Java keywords in IDL, it will be mapped to the name with a leading '_', for example, class in IDL will be mapped to `_class` in Java.

## 5.2 Basic Data Types

The mapping for basic data types is straightforward due to the similarity between the IDL basic types and Java primitive types. (See Table 5.1.)

### 5.2.1 Boolean

The IDL type boolean is mapped to the Java type `boolean`. The IDL constants TRUE and FALSE are mapped to the Java constants `true` and `false`.

### 5.2.2 Char and Wide Char

The IDL type char is mapped to the Java type `char`. The IDL char is an 8-bit type using the ISO 8859.1 character set, and the Java char is a 16-bit type using the UNICODE character set. When a value of type `char` is outside the range defined for the IDL type char, the exception CORBA::DATA_CONVERSION is raised. The IDL type wchar is a 16-bit type that corresponds exactly to the Java `char` but can also be used to hold characters from other character sets than Java's native Unicode set.

**Table 5.1** Basic Data Type Mappings

| IDL TYPE | JAVA |
|---|---|
| boolean | `boolean` |
| char/wchar | `char` |
| string/wstring | `java.lang.String` |
| octet | `byte` |
| short/unsigned short | `short` |
| long/unsigned long | `int` |
| long long/unsigned long long | `long` |
| float | `float` |
| double | `double` |
| fixed | `java.math.BigDecimal` |

## 5.2.3 Octet

The IDL type octet is mapped to the Java type `byte`.

## 5.2.4 Integer Types

There is a difference between OMG IDL and Java with respect to the various IDL integer types. OMG IDL defines short and unsigned short (16-bit), long and unsigned long (32-bit), and long long and unsigned long long (64-bit). Java has the types `short` (16-bit), `int` (32-bit), and `long` (64-bit), which are all signed.

Obviously there is a mismatch between unsigned integer types in IDL and the signed integer types in Java. For example, the `int` type in Java is capable of representing all the values for the signed IDL type long, but not all of the values of the IDL type unsigned long because values from $2^{31} - 1$ to $2^{32} - 1$ cannot be represented. Nonetheless, both signed and unsigned short in IDL map to `short` in Java, the IDL signed and unsigned long types both map to Java `int`, and the IDL signed and unsigned long long types both map to Java `long`.

## 5.2.5 Floating-Point Types

The IDL floating-point types, float and double, are mapped to the corresponding Java floating-point types `float` and `double`. Both languages have adopted the IEEE Standard for Binary Floating-Point Arithmetic (ANSI/IEEE Std. 754-1985).

## 5.2.6 Fixed-Point

The IDL type fixed is mapped to the Java class `java.math.BigDecimal`. Range checking is performed at run time. If values fall outside the defined range, the exception CORBA::DATA_CONVERSION is raised.

## 5.2.7 String Types

OMG IDL defines strings and wide strings that can be either bounded or unbounded. All IDL strings and wide strings are mapped to a Java object of the class `java.lang.String`.

Because the upper bound of a bounded string or wide string is not mapped, an application programmer has to be aware of this bound when creating the corresponding Java `String` object. The stub code generated from the IDL checks the correctness of the string bound at run time and raises the exception CORBA::MARSHAL if it is exceeded. If the range in a character of the string is violated, the exception CORBA::DATA_CONVERSION is raised.

## 5.3 Holder Classes

To accommodate the passing of inout and out parameters in Java, which can pass arguments only by value, there are holder classes for IDL predefined and user-defined types. Holder classes for user-defined types are generated by the IDL compiler. Holder classes for IDL predefined types are provided as part of the CORBA class library and reside in the package `org.omg.CORBA`.

Holder classes implement the interface `org.omg.CORBA.portable.Streamable` to support the Java Portability Interface, which will be explained in section 5.14 of this chapter. All holder classes, both generated and predefined, follow the same basic pattern. As an example, we give the definition of the predefined holder class `org.omg.CORBA.ShortHolder`:

```
package org.omg.CORBA;

final public class ShortHolder
    implements org.omg.CORBA.portable.Streamable {

    public short value;

    public ShortHolder() {}
    public ShortHolder( short initial ) {
        value = initial;
    }

    public void _read(org.omg.CORBA.portable.InputStream is) {
        value = is.read_short();
    }
    public void _write(org.omg.CORBA.portable.OutputStream os) {
        os.write_short(value);
    }
    public org.omg.CORBA.TypeCode _type() {
        return org.omg.CORBA.ORB.init().get_primitive_tc(
            TCKind.tk_short);
    }
}
```

The `value` field allows a value to be inserted into and extracted from the holder. There are constructors to create empty and initialized holders. The `_read()` and `_write()` methods are used by marshaling code. The `_type()` method provides an easy way to access the TypeCode of a type.

The same pattern is used for user-defined types. For a user-defined type *Type* the IDL compiler would generate a holder class like the following:

```
final public class TypeHolder
    implements org.omg.CORBA.portable.Streamable {

    public Type value;
    public TypeHolder() {}
    public TypeHolder( Type initial ) {}

    public void _read(org.omg.CORBA.portable.InputStream i )
    { ... }
    public void _write(org.omg.CORBA.portable.OuputStream o )
    { ... }
    public org.omg.CORBA.TypeCode _type()
    { ... }
}
```

## 5.4 Helper Classes

For all IDL type definitions, the IDL compiler also generates a Java Helper class that has the same name as the IDL type with an additional "Helper" suffix. A helper class is a collection of static methods for a number of type-specific operations. These include narrowing object references to the correct interface type, inserting values into and extracting values from Anys, and marshaling and unmarshaling values to and from streams. In addition, helper classes provide information about the type such as its RepositoryId and TypeCode.

The general pattern for generating helper classes for an IDL type *Type* is the following:

```
abstract public class TypeHelper {

    // any insertion/extraction
    public static void insert(org.omg.CORBA.Any a, Type t) {...}
    public static Type extract(org.omg.CORBA.Any a) {...}

    // type information
    public static org.omg.TypeCode type() {...}
    public static String id() {...}

    // portable marshaling interface
    public static Type read(org.omg.CORBA.portable.InputStream in)
    {...}
    public static void write(org.omg.CORBA.portable.OutputStream out,
Type value)
```

```
        {...}

        // narrowing object references to the correct type
        public static Type narrow(org.omg.CORBA.Object obj) {...}
    }
```

Note that the `narrow()` operation is present only in helper classes generated from IDL interface definitions. Also, if the IDL type is an abstract interface, the parameter to `narrow()` is of type `java.lang.Object` rather than `org.omg.CORBA.Object`. You will see concrete examples of helper classes later in this chapter.

## 5.5 Enums

An IDL enum type is mapped to a generated Java final class with the same name as the enum. This class implements the portability interface `org.omg.CORBA.portable.IDLEntity` and defines a pair of static data members for each enum member, one of type `final int` and the other of the type of the generated class. The `int` version is used in switch statements or as an index type, for example, to access an array member, and the class constructor version is used for strongly typed parameter passing.

There are also two public methods, `value()` and method `from_int()`. The constructor for the enum class is protected because the class must ensure that there is only one instance for every member. It is called only from the initializer of the static fields for each enum member. This restriction ensures that equality tests using enum references will work correctly.

The mapping follows the template:

```
public final public class enum_name
    implements org.omg.CORBA.portable.IDLEntity {

    // static data members for each enum member
    public static final int _enum_member = <value>;
    public static final enum_name = new enum_name(_enum_member );

    public int value() { ... }

    public static enum_name from_int ( int value );

    //constructor
    protected enum_name( int ) { ... }
}
```

Here is an example enum in IDL:

```
enum Slot { am9, am10, am11, pm };
```

which is mapped to the following Java class:

```
public final class Slot implements org.omg.CORBA.portable.IDLEntity
{
    private int _value;

    public static final int _am9 = 0;
    public static final int _am10 = 1;
    public static final int _am11 = 2;
    public static final int _pm = 3;

    public static final Slot am9 = new Slot(_am9);
    public static final Slot am10 = new Slot(_am10);
    public static final Slot am11 = new Slot(_am11);
    public static final Slot pm = new Slot(_pm);

    protected Slot (final int value) {
        this._value = value;
    }

    public int value () {
        return _value;
    }

    public static Slot from_int (final int value) {
        switch (value) {
            case 0: return am9;
            case 1: return am10;
            case 2: return am11;
            case 3: return pm;
            default: throw new org.omg.CORBA.BAD_PARAM();
        }
    }
}
```

A holder class is also generated for each enum type. The class is named after the IDL enum with the suffix `Holder`. The holder class follows the pattern we just explained. The following holder class is generated for the previous example:

```
final public class SlotHolder
    implements org.omg.CORBA.portable.Streamable {

    public Slot value;
    public SlotHolder() {}

    public SlotHolder(Slot value) {
        this.value = value;
    }
```

```
        public void _read(org.omg.CORBA.portable.InputStream input) {
            value = SlotHelper.read(input);
        }
        public void _write(org.omg.CORBA.portable.OutputStream out) {
            SlotHelper.write(out, value);
        }
        public org.omg.CORBA.TypeCode _type() {
           return SlotHelper.type();
        }
    }
```

## 5.6 Struct

An IDL struct is mapped to a Java final class that provides fields for the members of the struct and some constructors. The class is named after the struct and, like mapped enum classes, implements the `IDLEntity` interface. There is a constructor that has a parameter for each member of the struct and initializes the object properly. A second constructor, the null constructor, creates only the object; the values of the structure members have to be filled in later. A holder and a helper class are also generated.

Here is an example IDL struct:

```
struct TestStruct{
        short a_short;
        long a_long;
};
```

which is mapped to the Java class:

```
public final class TestStruct
    implements org.omg.CORBA.portable.IDLEntity {

    public short a_short;
    public int a_long;
    public TestStruct(){}
    public TestStruct(short a_short, int a_long){
        this.a_short = a_short;
        this.a_long = a_long;
    }
}
```

## 5.7 Unions

An IDL union is mapped to a Java final class that provides a constructor, an accessor method for the discriminator, accessor methods for each of the branches, and various modifier methods. The constructor is a null constructor, which means that values for the discriminator and the corresponding branch must be set explicitly by using a modifier method.

The accessor method for the discriminator `discriminator()` returns a value of the type defined in the IDL switch expression. The accessor method for a branch is named after the branch. The accessor has no parameters and returns a value of the type corresponding to the branch.

There are modifier methods for each of the cases including the default case. If there is more than one case label per branch, the modifier sets the discriminant to the value of the first case label of that branch. Additional modifier methods are generated that take an explicit discriminator parameter.

Note that it is illegal to specify a default case when the explicitly defined cases already cover the whole range of the discriminator type. The IDL compiler should detect this error. Helpers and holders are generated as usual.

Here is an example union for which Java code is generated:

```
enum Slot { am9, am10, am11, pm };

union TestUnion switch( Slot ) {
    case am9: boolean boolean_flag;
    case am10:
    case am11: char char_flag;
    default: short short_flag;
};
```

```
// Java
public final class TestUnion
    implements org.omg.CORBA.portable.IDLEntity {

    private java.lang.Object _object;
    private Slot _disc;
    boolean _defaultState = true;

    public TestUnion() {
    }
    public Slot _discriminator() {
        return _disc;
    }
    public boolean boolean_flag() {
        if (_disc == Slot.am9) {
          return ((java.lang.Boolean)_object).booleanValue();
        }
        throw new org.omg.CORBA.BAD_OPERATION("boolean_flag");
    }
    public void boolean_flag(boolean _vis_value) {
        _disc = Slot.am9;
```

```
            _object = new java.lang.Boolean(_vis_value);
            _defaultState = false;
        }
        public char char_flag() {
            if (_disc == Slot.am10 ||
                _disc == Slot.am11) {
              return ((java.lang.Character)_object).charValue();
            }
            throw new org.omg.CORBA.BAD_OPERATION("char_flag");
        }
        public void char_flag(char _vis_value) {
            _disc = Slot.am10;
            _object = new java.lang.Character(_vis_value);
            _defaultState = false;
        }
        public void char_flag(Slot disc, char _vis_value) {
            _disc = disc;
            _object = new java.lang.Character(_vis_value);
            _defaultState = false;
        }
        public short short_flag() {
            if (_defaultState) {
              return ((java.lang.Short)_object).shortValue();
            }
            throw new org.omg.CORBA.BAD_OPERATION("short_flag");
        }
        public void short_flag(short _vis_value) {
            _disc = Slot.pm;
            _object = new java.lang.Short(_vis_value);
            _defaultState = true;
        }
        public void short_flag( Slot disc, short _vis_value) {
            _disc = disc;
            _object = new java.lang.Short(_vis_value);
            _defaultState = true;
        }
    }
```

## 5.8 Typedef

Java has no aliasing for types, unlike IDL, which uses the typedef for aliases. Consequently, IDL typedefs are ignored, except when they give names to anonymous sequences, arrays, or bounded strings. This means that the base type has to be used where the typedef name is expected in the Java implementation. Also, the original type's holder class is used for inout or out parameters, so no holder classes are generated, with the exception of IDL array and sequence typedefs. Helper classes are generated for each typedef. Examples will be shown in the sections on sequence and array types.

## 5.9 Exception Type

The mapping for exception type definitions is explained in this section.The raises clause for IDL operations, which makes use of exceptions, is explained with the mapping for operations. The mapping for exceptions is similar to that for structs. A user-defined IDL exception is mapped to a generated Java class that provides instance variables for the fields of the exception and some constructors. The class is named after the exception. CORBA system exceptions are also provided by the ORB library.

### 5.9.1 User-Defined Exceptions

User-defined exceptions are part of an exception hierarchy, as shown in Figure 5.1. It is useful to distinguish between user-defined and system exceptions because user-defined exceptions are thrown by user code and may signal application-specific exceptions. System exceptions, on the other hand, are thrown transparently to the application, such as when a connection is dropped. As a rule of thumb, user-defined exceptions should be meaningful enough so that the caller of an operation and receiver of an exception can potentially handle the exception and continue.

For this reason, user-defined exceptions are mapped to "checked" exceptions. Checked exceptions are those exceptions in Java that are subclasses of `java.lang.Exception`. The Java compiler will check that all declared checked exceptions are handled somewhere in the code. Unchecked exceptions are subclasses of `java.lang.RuntimeException` and need not be explicitly handled. The CORBA exception base class `org.omg.CORBA.UserException` is a checked exception.

Here is the code of `org.omg.CORBA.UserException`:

```
package org.omg.CORBA;

abstract public class UserException
    extends java.lang.Exception
    implements org.omg.CORBA.portable.IDLEntity {

    public UserException() {
        super();
    }
    public UserException(String value) {
        super(value);
    }
}
```

The generated classes are declared final and extend the class `org.omg.CORBA.UserException`. A generated class has a data member for each of

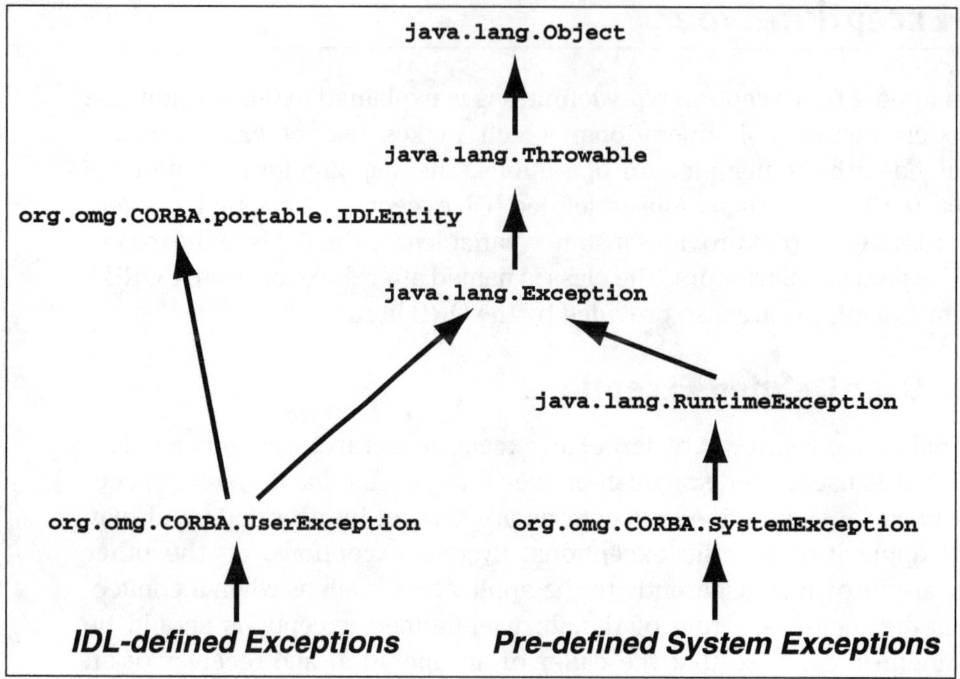


**Figure 5.1** Exception hierarchy.

the exception declaration's members. Additionally it has three constructors, one of which is the null constructor, and creates only the object, leaving the values of the fields to be filled in later. It does, however, call the constructor of `UserException`, passing the exception's RepositoryId `"IDL:SomethingWrong:1.0"` for the example shown next as a string argument and thus transitively initializing the reason string in `java.lang.Exception`. The second constructor has a parameter for each field of the class and initializes the object properly. It also passes the exception ID to the superclass constructor. The third or "full" constructor takes an additional string argument that it appends to the exception ID before passing it on to the superclass constructor. As usual, helper and holder class are generated.

Here is an example exception declaration in IDL:

```
exception SomethingWrong {
   long id;
};
```

```
// Java
public final class SomethingWrong
    extends org.omg.CORBA.UserException {
```

```
    public int id;

    public SomethingWrong() {
        super( SomethingWrongHelper.id() );
    }

    public SomethingWrong( int id) {
        this();
        this.id = id;
    }

    public SomethingWrong( java.lang.String _reason, int id ) {
        super( SomethingWrongHelper.id() + " " + _reason );
        this.id = id;
    }
}
```

Because `UserException` is abstract, the ORB cannot create instances of it when it receives user exceptions it does not recognize. This may happen as a result of sending a request using the DII. In this case, it wraps the exception in an instance of `UnknownUserException`:

```
package org.omg.CORBA;

final public class UnknownUserException
    extends UserException {

    public Any except;
    public UnknownUserException () {
        super();
    }
    public UserException(Any value) {
        super();
        except = value;
    }
}
```

### 5.9.2 CORBA System Exceptions

Table 5.2 lists all CORBA system exceptions and their mapping to Java exceptions.

## 5.10 Arrays

IDL arrays are mapped to Java arrays. That means there is no particular Java data type or class generated. An application programmer just defines a

**TABLE 5.2** CORBA System Exceptions in Java

| CORBA EXCEPTIONS | CORBA EXCEPTIONS IN JAVA |
|---|---|
| CORBA::BAD_CONTEXT | org.omg.CORBA.BAD_CONTEXT |
| CORBA::BAD_INV_ORDER | org.omg.CORBA.BAD_INV_ORDER |
| CORBA::BAD_OPERATION | org.omg.CORBA.BAD_OPERATION |
| CORBA::BAD_PARAM | org.omg.CORBA.BAD_PARAM |
| CORBA::BAD_TYPECODE | org.omg.CORBA.BAD_TYPECODE |
| CORBA::CODESET_INCOMPATIBLE | org.omg.CORBA.CODESET_INCOMPATIBLE |
| CORBA::COMM_FAILURE | org.omg.CORBA.COMM_FAILURE |
| CORBA::CTX_RESTRICT_SCOPE | org.omg.CORBA.CTX_RESTRICT_SCOPE |
| CORBA::DATA_CONVERSION | org.omg.CORBA.DATA_CONVERSION |
| CORBA::FREE_MEM | org.omg.CORBA.FREE_MEM |
| CORBA::IMP_LIMIT | org.omg.CORBA.IMP_LIMIT |
| CORBA::INITIALIZE | org.omg.CORBA.INITIALIZE |
| CORBA::INTERNAL | org.omg.CORBA.INTERNAL |
| CORBA::INTF_REPOS | org.omg.CORBA.INTF_REPOS |
| CORBA::INV_FLAG | org.omg.CORBA.INV_FLAG |
| CORBA::INV_IDENT | org.omg.CORBA.INV_IDENT |
| CORBA::INV_OBJREF | org.omg.CORBA.INV_OBJREF |
| CORBA::INV_POLICY | org.omg.CORBA.INV_POLICY |
| CORBA::INVALID_TRANSACTION | org.omg.CORBA. INVALID_TRANSACTION |
| CORBA::MARSHAL | org.omg.CORBA.MARSHAL |
| CORBA::NO_IMPLEMENT | org.omg.CORBA.NO_IMPLEMENT |
| CORBA::NO_MEMORY | org.omg.CORBA.NO_MEMORY |
| CORBA::NO_PERMISSION | org.omg.CORBA.NO_PERMISSION |
| CORBA::NO_RESOURCES | org.omg.CORBA.NO_RESOURCES |
| CORBA::NO_RESPONSE | org.omg.CORBA.NO_RESPONSE |
| CORBA::OBJECT_NOT_EXIST | org.omg.CORBA.OBJECT_NOT_EXIST |
| CORBA::PERSIST_STORE | org.omg.CORBA.PERSIST_STORE |
| CORBA::TRANSACTION_REQUIRED | org.omg.CORBA.TRANSACTION_REQUIRED |
| CORBA:: TRANSACTION_ROLLEDBACK | org.omg.CORBA. TRANSACTION_ROLLEDBACK |
| CORBA::TRANSIENT | org.omg.CORBA.TRANSIENT |
| CORBA::UNKNOWN | org.omg.CORBA.UNKNOWN |

Java array of the mapped base type of the IDL array. For example, to create an instance of the following IDL array in a Java application:

```
typedef long long_array[10][5];
```

a programmer has to declare and allocate the array in the Java application code:

```
int[][] a_long_array;
a_long_array = new int[10][5];
```

The IDL compiler generates a holder class for the array typedef.

```
final public class long_arrayHolder
    implements org.omg.CORBA.portable.Streamable {

    public int[][] value;

    public long_arrayHolder() {}
    public long_arrayHolder( int[][] value ) {
        this.value = value;
    }

    public void _read( org.omg.CORBA.portable.InputStream input) {
        value = long_arrayHelper.read(input);
    }

    public void _write(
        org.omg.CORBA.portable.OutputStream output
    ) {
        long_arrayHelper.write(output, value);
    }

    public org.omg.CORBA.TypeCode _type() {
        return long_arrayHelper.type();
    }
}
```

The checking of array bounds is done in the marshaling code generated into the array's helper class. The helper class generated for this array example looks as follows:

```
public final class long_arrayHelper {

    private static org.omg.CORBA.TypeCode _type;

    public static int[][] read(
        org.omg.CORBA.portable.InputStream in
    ) {
```

```
        int[][] result;
        result = new int[10][];
        for (int i = 0; i < 10; i++) {
            result[i] = new int[5];
            for (int j = 0; j < 5; j++) {
                result[i][j] = input.read_long();
            }
        }
        return result;
    }

    public static void write(
        org.omg.CORBA.portable.OutputStream out,
        int[][] value
    ) {
        if (value.length != 10) {
            throw new org.omg.CORBA.BAD_PARAM("Inv. array length");
        }
        for (int i = 0;  i < 10; i++) {
            if (value[i].length != 5) {
                throw new org.omg.CORBA.BAD_PARAM(
                    "Invalid array length");
            }
            for (int j = 0; j < 5; j++) {
                output.write_long((int)value[i][j]);
            }
        }
    }

    public static void insert(org.omg.CORBA.Any any, int[][] value)
    {...}
    public static int[][] extract(org.omg.CORBA.Any any) {...}
    public static org.omg.CORBA.TypeCode type () {...}

    public static java.lang.String id () {
        return "IDL:long_array:1.0";
    }
}
```

## 5.11 Sequences

Sequences are similarly mapped to arrays. That is, no data type or class is generated. The bound of a bounded sequence is checked at run time, and the exception BAD_PARAM is raised if it is violated.

Here are some example sequences in IDL:

```
typedef sequence< long, 10 > bounded_10_seq;
typedef sequence< long > unbounded_seq;
```

As with arrays, it is the application programmer's responsibility to declare and create a Java array of the corresponding member type. For our example we would declare

```
// Java
int[] a_bounded_sequence;
int[] an_unbounded_sequence;
a_bounded_sequence = new int[10];
an_unbounded_sequence = new int[20];
```

The corresponding holder classes are

```
final public class bounded_10_seqHolder
    implements org.omg.CORBA.portable.Streamable {

    public int[] value;

    public bounded_10_seqHolder() {}

    public bounded_10_seqHolder(int[] value) {
        this.value = value;
    }

    public void _read(org.omg.CORBA.portable.InputStream input) {
        value = bounded_10_seqHelper.read(input);
    }

    public void _write(
        org.omg.CORBA.portable.OutputStream output
    ) {
        bounded_10_seqHelper.write(output, value);
    }

    public org.omg.CORBA.TypeCode _type() {
        return bounded_10_seqHelper.type();
    }
}

final public class unbounded_seqHolder
    implements org.omg.CORBA.portable.Streamable {

    public int[] value;

    public unbounded_seqHolder() {}

    public unbounded_seqHolder(int[] value) {
        this.value = value;
    }

    public void _read(org.omg.CORBA.portable.InputStream input) {
        value = unbounded_seqHelper.read(input);
    }
```

```
    public void _write(
        org.omg.CORBA.portable.OutputStream output
    ) {
        unbounded_seqHelper.write(output, value);
    }

    public org.omg.CORBA.TypeCode _type() {
        return unbounded_seqHelper.type();
    }
}
```

## 5.12 The Any Type

The IDL Any type is a predefined, self-describing type that can hold values of an arbitrary IDL type (including another Any). It describes the type information about the contained value using a TypeCode, which is explained in Chapter 6, "ORB Run-Time System."

The IDL Any is mapped to the predefined class `org.omg.CORBA.Any`. This class provides methods to store values in and retrieve values from an Any object. These methods deal with only predefined IDL types. The Helper classes that are generated for user-defined types contain methods to insert values into and extract values from Anys. An instance of the Any class can be obtained from the ORB, by calling its method `create_any()`, as explained in Chapter 6.

### 5.12.1 General Methods on the Class Any

The type of an Any object can be obtained and modified with the methods

```
org.omg.CORBA.TypeCode type();
void type(org.omg.CORBA.TypeCode a_type);
```

If you change the type of an Any that is already initialized with a value, the value is discarded. If you try to extract the value of an Any where only the type has been set, but no value was supplied, the exception CORBA::BAD _OPERATION is raised. You should not use the type modifier method unless you intend to use this Any as an out parameter. Additionally there are methods to supply the value of an Any in the form of a CORBA input stream and to extract the value as an CORBA output stream:

```
abstract public void read_value(
    org.omg.CORBA.portable.InputStream input,
    org.omg.CORBA.TypeCode type_code
```

```
)
     throws org.omg.CORBA.MARSHAL;

abstract public void write_value(
    org.omg.CORBA.portable.OutputStream out)
```

The read method throws an exception if the value of the input stream does not match the supplied type code. You can use these two methods if you want to create Any objects dynamically (as shown in Chapter 9, "Advanced Features"). They are also used for inserting and extracting arbitrary values for user-defined types. The main motivation for a stream interface, however, is to create a portability API for use by the IDL compiler when generating marshaling code. If this API is used, then stubs and skeletons generated by an IDL compiler can use the CORBA class libraries of any compliant ORB.

## 5.12.2 IDL Predefined Types

There is a pair of methods for inserting and extracting each predefined IDL type *type*. These methods follow the pattern:

```
abstract public void insert_type(type value)
    throws org.omg.CORBA.BAD_OPERATION;

abstract public type extract_type()
    throws org.omg.CORBA.BAD_OPERATION;
```

Table 5.3 lists the complete set of insert and extract methods.

## 5.12.3 User-Defined Types

The specification cannot prescribe any particular methods for inserting user-defined values into the Any class, but Anys have generic methods to insert input streams and extract output streams. This means that methods can be generated in helper classes by the IDL compiler that use these ORB implementation constructs.

A user-defined IDL type, *usertype*, will have the following methods in its helper class `usertypeHelper`:

```
public static void insert(Any a, usertype t) {...}
public static usertype extract(Any a) {...}
```

The `insert()` method is implemented by creating a stream that is inserted into the Any. The `extract()` method uses the output stream from an Any to get its value and create a user-defined type.

**Table 5.3** Insert and Extract Methods

```
abstract public class org.omg.CORBA.Any
    implements org.omg.CORBA.portable.IDLEntity {

    public abstract org.omg.CORBA.TypeCode type();
    public abstract void type(org.omg.CORBA.TypeCode);

    public abstract void read_value(
        org.omg.CORBA.portable.InputStream input,
        org.omg.CORBA.TypeCode type);
    public abstract void write_value(
        org.omg.CORBA.portable.OutputStream output);

    public abstract org.omg.CORBA.portable.OutputStream
        create_output_stream();
    public abstract org.omg.CORBA.portable.InputStream
        create_input_stream();

    public abstract boolean equal(org.omg.CORBA.Any a);

    public abstract short extract_short();
    public abstract void insert_short(short s);

    public abstract int extract_long();
    public abstract void insert_long(int i);

    public abstract long extract_longlong();
    public abstract void insert_longlong(long l);

    public abstract short extract_ushort();
    public abstract void insert_ushort(short s);

    public abstract int extract_ulong();
    public abstract void insert_ulong(int i);

    public abstract long extract_ulonglong();
    public abstract void insert_ulonglong(long l);

    public abstract float extract_float();
    public abstract void insert_float(float f);

    public abstract double extract_double();
    public abstract void insert_double(double d);

    public abstract java.math.BigDecimal extract_fixed();
    public abstract void insert_fixed(java.math.BigDecimal f);
    public abstract void insert_fixed(java.math.BigDecimal f,
                                  org.omg.CORBA.TypeCode t);
```

**Table 5.3** *(Continued)*

```
    public abstract boolean extract_boolean();
    public abstract void insert_boolean(boolean b);

    public abstract char extract_char();
    public abstract void insert_char(char c);

    public abstract char extract_wchar();
    public abstract void insert_wchar(char c);

    public abstract byte extract_octet();
    public abstract void insert_octet(byte b);

    public abstract org.omg.CORBA.Any extract_any();
    public abstract void insert_any(org.omg.CORBA.Any a);

    public abstract org.omg.CORBA.TypeCode extract_TypeCode();
    public abstract void insert_TypeCode(org.omg.CORBA.TypeCode t);

    public abstract org.omg.CORBA.Object extract_Object();
    public abstract void insert_Object(org.omg.CORBA.Object o);
    public abstract void insert_Object(org.omg.CORBA.Object o,
                                       org.omg.CORBA.TypeCode t);

    public abstract java.io.Serializable extract_Value();
    public abstract void insert_Value(java.io.Serializable v )
    public abstract void insert_Value(java.io.Serializable v,
                                      org.omg.CORBA.TypeCode t);

    public abstract java.lang.String extract_string();
    public abstract void insert_string(java.lang.String s);

    public abstract java.lang.String extract_wstring();
    public abstract void insert_wstring(java.lang.String s);

    public abstract org.omg.CORBA.TypeCode extract_ TypeCode();
    public abstract void insert_TypeCode(org.omg.CORBA.TypeCode t);


    public abstract void insert_Streamable(
                           org.omg.CORBA.portable.Streamable s);
    public abstract org.omg.CORBA.portable.Streamable
                           extract_Streamable();
}
```

In Chapter 9 we explain how to use the Any type and illustrate the method with several examples.

## 5.13 Valuetypes

Valuetypes have different mappings depending on the kind of the valuetype definition. We will first look at regular or stateful valuetypes, then examine the mapping for abstract valuetypes and look at inheritance. Finally, we'll explain how value box types map to Java.

### 5.13.1 Stateful Valuetypes

A stateful IDL valuetype is mapped to an abstract Java class with the same name. This mapped class contains a field for any state member of the valuetype, mapping public state members to `public` fields and private members to `protected` fields. It implements `org.omg.CORBA.portable.CustomValue` if the valuetype has been declared to use custom marshaling, and `org.omg.CORBA.portable.StreamableValue` otherwise. Through these interfaces all valuetypes indirectly implement the base interface `org.omg.CORBA.portable.ValueBase`:

```
package org.omg.CORBA.portable;

public interface ValueBase extends IDLEntity {
    String [] _truncatable_ids();
}
```

The mapped Java class contains an implementation for the method `_truncatable_ids()` declared in `org.omg.CORBA.portable.ValueBase`, which returns the RepositoryIds of all base types to which values of this type may safely be truncated. Consider the following IDL definition:

```
valuetype Node {
    private any value;
    any getValue();
    void setValue(in any val);
    factory createNode(in any val);
};
```

The IDL compiler generates the following mapped Java class for this valuetype:

```
public abstract class Node
    implements org.omg.CORBA.portable.StreamableValue  {
```

```
    protected org.omg.CORBA.Any value;

    abstract public org.omg.CORBA.Any getValue ();
    abstract public void setValue (org.omg.CORBA.Any val);

    public org.omg.CORBA.TypeCode _type () {
        return NodeHelper.type();
    }

    public void _read (org.omg.CORBA.portable.InputStream in){
        value = in.read_any();
    }

    public void _write (org.omg.CORBA.portable.OutputStream out) {
        out.write_any((org.omg.CORBA.Any)value);
    }

    private static java.lang.String[] _truncatable_ids = {
        "IDL:Node:1.0"
    };

    public java.lang.String[] _truncatable_ids () {
        return _truncatable_ids;
    }
}
```

In addition to the mapped Java class, the IDL compiler generates a Java factory interface, a helper class, and a holder class for a valuetype definition. The mapped factory interface extends `org.omg.CORBA.portable.ValueFactory` and contains one method for each factory declared in IDL. If no factory operations have been declared for a valuetype, the Java factory interface is not generated. The factory interface for the example is:

```
public interface NodeValueFactory
    extends org.omg.CORBA.portable.ValueFactory {

    public Node createNode (org.omg.CORBA.Any val);
}
```

The implementation of this factory interface has to be provided by the developer and must be registered with the ORB to be accessible at run time.

The holder class is generated according to the usual pattern. The helper class for a valuetype is similarly generated according to the standard pattern. It has one additional static method for each factory declaration. These factory methods have the same name and take the same arguments as the IDL factory. They also take an additional argument of type `org.omg.CORBA.ORB`. The ORB argument is used to look up an implementation of the factory interface for this valuetype, using the ORB run-time interface, as explained in Chapter 6. The helper's factory method will then delegate the call to the corresponding method in the factory implementation and pass on its own arguments.

```
public final class NodeHelper {
    private static org.omg.CORBA.TypeCode _type;
    private static boolean _initializing = false;

    // ...
    private static NodeValueFactory getValueFactory(
        org.omg.CORBA.ORB orb
    ) {

        if ( !(orb instanceof org.omg.CORBA_2_3.ORB) ) {
           throw new org.omg.CORBA.BAD_PARAM();
        }

        org.omg.CORBA.portable.ValueFactory factory =
           ((org.omg.CORBA_2_3.ORB)orb).lookup_value_factory(id());

        if (factory instanceof NodeValueFactory) {
           return (NodeValueFactory)factory;
        }
        throw new org.omg.CORBA.BAD_PARAM();
    }

    public static Node createNode (
        org.omg.CORBA.ORB orb,
        org.omg.CORBA.Any val
    ) {
        return getValueFactory( orb ).createNode( val );
    }
}
```

## 5.13.2 Abstract Valuetypes

An abstract valuetype is one that cannot instantiated; only derived concrete valuetypes can be instantiated. The definition of an abstract valuetype is mapped to a single Java interface that extends `org.omg.CORBA.portable.ValueBase`. It contains method definitions for all operations specified in IDL, mapped according to the rules explained for mapping IDL operations to Java in section 5.17. Helpers and holders are also generated.

## 5.13.3 Valuetype Inheritance

Valuetypes may inherit definitions from other valuetypes, both abstract and stateful. Consider the following example:

```
abstract valuetype NodeBase {
        any getValue();
        void setValue(in any val);
};

valuetype Node : NodeBase {
        private any value;
        factory createNode(in any val);
};

valuetype BinaryTree: Node {
        public BinaryTree leftChild;
        public BinaryTree rightChild;
factory createBinaryTree(in any val, in BinaryTree left, in BinaryTree right);
};
```

Valuetype Node inherits from NodeBase, which defines basic operations on nodes. The mapped Java class `Node` then implements the mapped Java interface `NodeBase` generated for the abstract valuetype. In the case of BinaryTree, which inherits from a stateful, nonabstract valuetype, the mapped Java class `BinaryTree` extends the mapped Java class `Node`.

If a valuetype, both abstract and stateful, supports one or more IDL interfaces, then the generated Java class implements the operations interfaces of all the IDL interfaces that it supports.

## 5.13.4 Value Box Types

A value box type definition is treated differently for boxed primitive types than for boxed types that are mapped to Java classes. For primitive types, the valuetype maps to a Java class with the same name as the valuetype and that implements the base interface `org.omg.CORBA.portable.ValueBase`. This class has a single public field of the mapped Java type for the boxed IDL type. For example, the IDL definition

```
valuetype SharableInteger long;
```

would map to this Java class:

```
public class SharableInteger
    implements org.omg.CORBA.portable.ValueBase {

    public int value;

    public SharableInteger (int value) {
        this.value = value;
    }
}
```

If the boxed type maps to a Java class, no class is generated for the valuetype itself. Rather, the original type's mapped Java class has to be used everywhere the valuetype is expected. In this respect, a value box type definition is similar to an IDL typedef. The marshaling code dealing with the values of these types, however, passes values according to valuetype semantics rather than the original semantics.

Holders and helpers are generated for all value box types, with the generated holders following the usual pattern. The generated helper classes all implement the base interface `org.omg.CORBA.portable.BoxedValueHelper`. In addition to the usual helper methods they contain two methods inherited from this interface, `read_value()` and `write_value()`:

```
public final class SharableIntegerHelper
    implements org.omg.CORBA.portable.BoxedValueHelper {

    private static final SharableIntegerHelper _instance =
        new SharableIntegerHelper();

    public java.io.Serializable read_value (
        org.omg.CORBA.portable.InputStream in
    ) {
        final int result;
        result = in.read_long();
        return new SharableInteger(result);
    }

    public void write_value (
        org.omg.CORBA.portable.OutputStream out,
        java.io.Serializable value
    ) {
        if (!(value instanceof SharableInteger)) {
            throw new org.omg.CORBA.MARSHAL();
        }
        SharableInteger valueType = (SharableInteger)value;
         out.write_long((int) valueType.value );
    }
    // ...
}
```

## 5.14 Interfaces

Nonabstract IDL interfaces are mapped to two public Java interfaces. On of these, the *signature* interface, is implemented on the client side by the generated stub code. On the server side, the *operations* interface is implemented by the generated skeleton code and the programmer-provided servant class. There are also helper classes and holder classes for each IDL interface type.

Let's assume we have defined an IDL interface called *InterfaceName*. The following Java interface and helper and holder classes are generated by the IDL compiler. Additional interfaces and classes are generated for the client and server side, which we explain in separate sections.

`InterfaceNameOperations`

The Java interface *`InterfaceName`*`Operations` contains the mappings of IDL type and exception definitions within the IDL interface, as explained in the previous sections. It also contains mappings of IDL constants, attributes, and operations defined within the IDL interface, which are explained in the following sections.

`InterfaceName`

This Java interface is the *signature* interface and extends *`InterfaceName`*`Operations`, thus inheriting the mapped definitions contained in the operations interface. In addition, it extends the CORBA object base class, `org.omg.CORBA.Object`, and the IDL base interface `org.omg.CORBA.portable.IDLEntity`:

```
public interface InterfaceName
    extends InterfaceNameOperations,
            org.omg.CORBA.Object,
            org.omg.CORBA.portable.IDLEntity {
... }
```

Clients obtain references to objects that implement this interface, so we could informally call it the *reference* interface.

`InterfaceNameHelper`

The class *`InterfaceName`*`Helper` contains the same methods for use with Anys as all other user-defined types (see section 5.12.3) as well as a static `narrow()` method:

```
abstract public class InterfaceNameHelper {
  public static InterfaceName narrow (org.omg.CORBA.Object object) {
      ...
  }
  ...
}
```

This method allows objects of type `org.omg.CORBA.Object` or other interfaces that are less specific than *`InterfaceName`* to be narrowed to the more specific interface type *`InterfaceName`*.

```
InterfaceNameHolder
```

The class *`InterfaceName`*`Holder` is the usual holder class for inout and out parameters. It also provides methods to deal with input and output streams, and the method `_type()` to obtain the TypeCode of the interface. This method actually uses code from the helper class to return the correct TypeCode:

```
final public class InterfaceNameHolder
  implements org.omg.CORBA.portable.Streamable {
  public InterfaceName value;
  public InterfaceNameHolder () { ... }
  public InterfaceNameHolder (InterfaceName value) { ... }
  public void _read(org.omg.CORBA.portable.InputStream input) {
... }
  public void _write(org.omg.CORBA.portable.OutputStream output) { ... }
  public org.omg.CORBA.TypeCode _type() {
     return InterfaceNameHelper.type();
  }
}
```

Abstract IDL interfaces map to just a single Java interface with the same name as the type. This interface serves as both the operations and the signature interface and contains all mapped definitions from the IDL interface. Also, it extends org.omg.CORBA.portable.IDLEntity. Helpers and holders are generated according to the usual rules. The only difference is the argument type for the `narrow()` method in the generated helper class. For abstract interfaces, `narrow` accepts arguments of type `java.lang.Object`, as it must be able to handle both interface and valuetypes.

## 5.14.1 Portability Issues

Possibly the most important characteristic of Java is the portability of Java programs in byte-code format. As a consequence, Java applets can be executed in Web browsers on almost any platform, and Java programs can be run on JKD implementation on any operating system. The IDL/Java mapping aims to provide a similar level of portability with the ORB.

The CORBA specification, and conformant ORB implementations, provide interoperability between applications developed with products from different vendors. The portability of CORBA applications from one ORB to another, however, remains an unsolved problem. Restricting applications to use only standard CORBA features, and the decoupling of CORBA-specific parts from application-specific parts, can ease the porting process but does not automate it. This does not match the expectations of the Java community. For example, it is expected that you should be able to develop a CORBA-enabled applet with one vendor's ORB and run the applet with another vendor's ORB in the same way as you can run an applet on any vendor's JVM.

The problem is that the CORBA specification does not address issues below the interface specification level, and so it does not ensure portability. There are two separate problems, one on the client side, the other at the server involving both the object implementation and the object adapter.

Client operation invocations on object references are well defined in the various IDL/programming language mappings, including the one for Java. This means that the application is portable from one ORB to another. The problem is that there is no OMG specification for the stub code, which means that the IDL must be recompiled and the new stubs linked into the client. That seems to be reasonable for porting applications in a traditional computing environment. However, for a Java and browser-based environment, it is hardly acceptable. When a Java class is loaded into a remote browser that provides a Java ORB run-time environment, it should just function. Providing many sets of stub code to match different ORB environments is not acceptable.

At the server side there are two portability problems. One is similar to what we have just discussed for the client side. To run objects in a browser, a single skeleton class must function regardless of the browser's ORB run-time environment. These problems have been addressed in the IDL/Java mapping specification by the introduction of Portability Interfaces, which we explain in detail in the next section.

The other problem is accessing and configuring the run-time environment for object implementations, the Object Adapter. In CORBA versions before 2.2, the only specified Object Adapter was the Basic Object Adapter, and this adapter was actually underspecified. To make their ORBs work, the various ORB implementers had to make extensions to the CORBA specification. The OMG reacted to this situation by issuing an RFP called "ORB Portability Enhancement." The core of the resulting specification (OMG document orbos/97-04-14) is the definition of a Portable Object Adapter (POA), which solved the server-side portability problem. We introduced the POA in Chapter 2, "CORBA Overview," and we discuss its Java mapping in more detail in Chapter 6. In this section, we show the portability interface for implementation code on the server side and how it relates to the generated skeleton code.

## 5.14.2 Java ORB Portability Interfaces

Note that this section describes portable stubs and skeletons as background information for the interested reader only. You don't have to know how these things are implemented when writing a Java/CORBA application.

The Java ORB Portability Interfaces address the portability of stub and skeleton classes generated by IDL-to-Java compilers. The basic idea is that stubs and skeletons must use a standardized interface to the ORB run time. CORBA defines one such interface, the Dynamic Invocation Interface (DII) and the Dynamic Skeleton Interface (DSI), respectively. The DII and the DSI are fully specified in the CORBA specification and hence provide a portability layer consisting of common interfaces across CORBA-compliant ORB implementations (see Figure 5.2). Alternatively, the Java Portability Interfaces define a stream-based ORB interface that in most cases provides better performance because using the DII/DSI involves wrapping all values in Anys, which can become quite costly. A CORBA 2.3-compliant ORB run time must provide both the DII/DSI and the stream-based interface. An IDL compiler may thus generate stubs and skeletons for either of these interfaces. In addition, a vendor-independent implementation of the interface `org.omg.CORBA.Object` has been defined.

The Java ORB Portability Interfaces consist of the following interfaces and classes defined in the Portability Packages `org.omg.CORBA .portable` and `org.omg.PortableServer`:

- The class `org.omg.CORBA.portable.ObjectImpl`, which implements the interface `org.omg.CORBA.Object` in a standard way

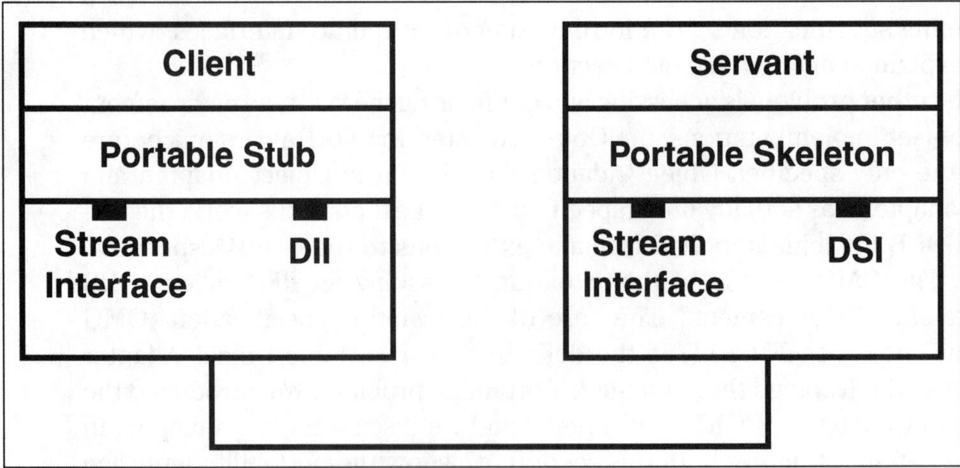

**Figure 5.2** ORB portability architecture.

(using the interface `org.omg.CORBA.portable.Delegate` to hide the ORB-specific implementation).

- The interfaces and classes that deal with streaming, that is, the transformation of IDL type instances into streams and vice versa. Streams are used for marshaling operation parameters and results, and for the insertion of complex data types into and their extraction from Any objects. The interfaces involved are `org.omg.CORBA.portable.Streamable`, `org.omg.CORBA.portable.InputStream`, and `org.omg.CORBA.portable.OutputStream`.
- The class `org.omg.PortableServer.Servant`, which is the base class for all POA-based server implementations and, similar to `org.omg.CORBA.portable.ObjectImpl`, hides ORB-specific features by delegating to `org.omg.PortableServer.portable.Delegate`.

Details of these classes and interfaces are explained in the following sections.

#### *5.14.2.1 A Portable CORBA Object Implementation*

The class `org.omg.CORBA.portable.ObjectImpl` is a proxy implementation of the interface `org.omg.CORBA.Object` because it delegates all method invocations to an implementation of the interface `org.omg.CORBA.portable.Delegate`. ORB vendors can implement this interface in any way they choose.

Figure 5.3 shows the class `org.omg.CORBA.portable.ObjectImpl`. Most noticeable is the declaration of a delegate `_delegate` and the methods to set and get the delegate. The remainder is a straightforward implementation of the interface `org.omg.CORBA.Object`, which calls the delegate.

Figure 5.4 shows the declaration of the interface `org.omg.CORBA.portable.Delegate`. It is very similar to the interface `org.omg.CORBA.Object`. The only difference is the extra parameter in each of the operations that refers to the object on which the operation was originally invoked.

#### *5.14.2.2 Portable Streams*

Portable streams are used for marshaling of operation parameters and results and for the insertion into and extraction of values from Any objects.

```
package org.omg.CORBA.portable;

abstract public class ObjectImpl implements org.omg.CORBA.Object {

    private transient Delegate __delegate;

    public Delegate _get_delegate() {
        if (__delegate == null)
          throw new org.omg.CORBA.BAD_OPERATION();
        return __delegate;
    }
    public void _set_delegate(Delegate delegate) {
        __delegate = delegate;
    }

    public boolean _is_a(String repository_id) {
        return _get_delegate().is_a(this, repository_id);
    }

    // and so on for all other operations defined in the
    // interface org.omg.CORBA.Object
}
```

**Figure 5.3** Portable CORBA object implementation.

There are two kinds of streams, input and output, defined in the classes `org.omg.CORBA.portable.InputStream` and `org.omg.CORBA.portable.OutputStream`, which are shown in Figures 5.5 and 5.6, respectively.

Input streams provide methods to read values from a linear representation, and output streams provide methods to write values to this form. These methods can be provided only for predefined IDL types. Methods for user-defined types will be generated by the IDL compiler and placed in Holder classes. The signatures for the Holder class methods are defined in the interface `org.omg.CORBA.portable.Streamable`:

```
public interface Streamable {
    void _read(org.omg.CORBA.portable.InputStream istream);
    void _write(org.omg.CORBA.portable.InputStream ostream);
    org.omg.CORBA.TypeCode _type();
}
```

The ORB serves as a factory for output streams by providing the method `create_output_stream()`. Input streams are created from output streams by their method `create_input_stream()` (see Figure 5.6).

```
package org.omg.CORBA.portable;

public abstract class Delegate {

    public org.omg.CORBA.Object get_interface_def(
        org.omg.CORBA.Object self
    ) {
        throw new org.omg.CORBA.NO_IMPLEMENT();
    }

    public abstract org.omg.CORBA.Object duplicate(
        org.omg.CORBA.Object self );

    public abstract void release(
        org.omg.CORBA.Object self );

    public abstract boolean is_a(
        org.omg.CORBA.Object self,
        String repository_id );

    public abstract boolean non_existent(
        org.omg.CORBA.Object self );

    public abstract boolean is_equivalent(
        org.omg.CORBA.Object self,
        org.omg.CORBA.Object rhs );

    public abstract int hash(
        org.omg.CORBA.Object self,
        int max );

    public abstract org.omg.CORBA.Request create_request(
        org.omg.CORBA.Object self,
        org.omg.CORBA.Context ctx,
        String operation,
        org.omg.CORBA.NVList arg_list,
        org.omg.CORBA.NamedValue result );

    public abstract org.omg.CORBA.Request create_request(
        org.omg.CORBA.Object self,
        org.omg.CORBA.Context ctx,
        String operation,
        org.omg.CORBA.NVList arg_list,
        org.omg.CORBA.NamedValue result,
        org.omg.CORBA.ExceptionList exclist,
        org.omg.CORBA.ContextList ctxlist );
```

*continues*

**Figure 5.4** Portable delegate interface.

```
public abstract org.omg.CORBA.Request request(
    org.omg.CORBA.Object self,
    String operation );

public org.omg.CORBA.portable.OutputStream request(
    org.omg.CORBA.Object self,
    String operation,
    boolean responseExpected
) {
    throw new org.omg.CORBA.NO_IMPLEMENT();
}

public org.omg.CORBA.portable.InputStream invoke(
    org.omg.CORBA.Object self,
    org.omg.CORBA.portable.OutputStream os)
    throws ApplicationException, RemarshalException {
    throw new org.omg.CORBA.NO_IMPLEMENT();
}

public void releaseReply(org.omg.CORBA.Object self,
    org.omg.CORBA.portable.InputStream is
) {
    throw new org.omg.CORBA.NO_IMPLEMENT();
}

public org.omg.CORBA.Policy get_policy(
    org.omg.CORBA.Object self,
    int policy_type
) {
    throw new org.omg.CORBA.NO_IMPLEMENT();
}

public org.omg.CORBA.DomainManager[] get_domain_managers(
    org.omg.CORBA.Object self
) {
    throw new org.omg.CORBA.NO_IMPLEMENT();
}

public org.omg.CORBA.Object set_policy_override(
    org.omg.CORBA.Object self,
    org.omg.CORBA.Policy[] policies,
    org.omg.CORBA.SetOverrideType set_add
) {
    throw new org.omg.CORBA.NO_IMPLEMENT();
}

public org.omg.CORBA.ORB orb(org.omg.CORBA.Object self) {
```

**Figure 5.4** *(Continued)*

```
            throw new org.omg.CORBA.NO_IMPLEMENT();
        }

        public boolean is_local(org.omg.CORBA.Object self) {
            return false;
        }

        public ServantObject servant_preinvoke(
            org.omg.CORBA.Object self,
            String operation, Class expectedType
        ) {
           return null;
        }

        public void servant_postinvoke(
            org.omg.CORBA.Object self,
            ServantObject servant
        ) {
        }

        public String toString( org.omg.CORBA.Object self ) {
            return self.getClass().getName() + ":" + this.toString();
        }

        public int hashCode(org.omg.CORBA.Object self) {
            return System.identityHashCode(self);
        }

        public boolean equals(
            org.omg.CORBA.Object self,
            java.lang.Object obj
        ) {
            return (self == obj);
        }
    }
```

**Figure 5.4** *(Continued)*

## 5.14.3 Client-Side Mapping

After all this background information on the Java ORB Portability Interfaces, we return to the mapping of an IDL interface to Java and how it is used on the client side. A client obtains an object reference in the usual way, for example, via `string_to_object()`, from a Naming or Trading Service, or from a third-party object. Regardless of the mechanism used to obtain an object reference, a client-side proxy object is created. The client-

```
package org.omg.CORBA.portable;

public abstract class InputStream extends java.io.InputStream {

    public int read() throws java.io.IOException {
        throw new org.omg.CORBA.NO_IMPLEMENT();
    }

    public org.omg.CORBA.ORB orb() {
        throw new org.omg.CORBA.NO_IMPLEMENT();
    }

    public abstract boolean        read_boolean();
    public abstract char           read_char();
    public abstract char           read_wchar();
    public abstract byte           read_octet();
    public abstract short          read_short();
    public abstract short          read_ushort();
    public abstract int            read_long();
    public abstract int            read_ulong();
    public abstract long           read_longlong();
    public abstract long           read_ulonglong();
    public abstract float          read_float();
    public abstract double         read_double();
    public abstract String         read_string();
    public abstract String         read_wstring();

    public abstract void read_boolean_array(
            boolean[] value, int offset, int length);
    public abstract void read_char_array(
            char[] value, int offset, int length);
    public abstract void read_wchar_array(
            char[] value, int offset, int length);
    public abstract void read_octet_array(
            byte[] value, int offset, int length);
    public abstract void read_short_array(
            short[] value, int offset, int length);
    public abstract void read_ushort_array(
            short[] value, int offset, int length);
    public abstract void read_long_array(
            int[] value, int offset, int length);
    public abstract void read_ulong_array(
            int[] value, int offset, int length);
    public abstract void read_longlong_array(
            long[] value, int offset, int length);
    public abstract void read_ulonglong_array(
            long[] value, int offset, int length);
```

**Figure 5.5** Input stream.

```
    public abstract void read_float_array(
            float[] value, int offset, int length);
    public abstract void read_double_array(
            double[] value, int offset, int length);

    public abstract org.omg.CORBA.Object read_Object();
    public org.omg.CORBA.Object read_Object(java.lang.Class clz) {
        throw new org.omg.CORBA.NO_IMPLEMENT();
    }

    public abstract org.omg.CORBA.TypeCode read_TypeCode();
    public abstract org.omg.CORBA.Any read_any();

    public org.omg.CORBA.Context read_Context() {
        throw new org.omg.CORBA.NO_IMPLEMENT();
    }

    public java.math.BigDecimal read_fixed() {
        throw new org.omg.CORBA.NO_IMPLEMENT();
    }
}
```

**Figure 5.5** *(Continued)*

side proxy is an instantiation of the stub class, which is an implementation of the Java signature interface corresponding to the IDL interface.

The stub class is an ORB-specific layer that sits between the defined Java interface and the portability layer we discussed in the previous section. The IDL/Java mapping prescribes only that the stub class must be implemented by using either the DII or the stream-based interface. Figure 5.7 illustrates how the various interfaces and classes fit together on the client side.

A CORBA-compliant IDL compiler creates a portable stub class called `_`*`InterfaceName`*`Stub`. Some compilers let you choose between stream-based or DII-based stub generation. For example, the VisiBroker 4.0 IDL compiler produces stream-based stubs and skeletons by default but will generate DII/DSI-based ones when the compiler switch `-dynamic_marshal` is set. In a client program, you need only declare an object reference of the Java interface type, such as

```
InterfaceName myTester;
```

and assign a value to the variable, for example,

```
CORBA.Object obj = orb.string_to_object( iorString );
myTester = InterfaceNameHelper.narrow( obj );
```

```
package org.omg.CORBA.portable;

public abstract class OutputStream extends java.io.OutputStream {

    public void write(int b) throws java.io.IOException {
        throw new org.omg.CORBA.NO_IMPLEMENT();
    }

    public org.omg.CORBA.ORB orb() {
        throw new org.omg.CORBA.NO_IMPLEMENT();
    }

    public abstract InputStream create_input_stream();

    public abstract void write_boolean    (boolean        value);
    public abstract void write_char       (char           value);
    public abstract void write_wchar      (char           value);
    public abstract void write_octet      (byte           value);
    public abstract void write_short      (short          value);
    public abstract void write_ushort     (short          value);
    public abstract void write_long       (int            value);
    public abstract void write_ulong      (int            value);
    public abstract void write_longlong   (long           value);
    public abstract void write_ulonglong  (long           value);
    public abstract void write_float      (float          value);
    public abstract void write_double     (double         value);
    public abstract void write_string     (String         value);
    public abstract void write_wstring    (String         value);


    public abstract void write_boolean_array(
            boolean[] value, int offset, int length);
    public abstract void write_char_array(
            char[] value, int offset, int length);
    public abstract void write_wchar_array(
            char[] value, int offset, int length);
    public abstract void write_octet_array(
            byte[] value, int offset, int length);
    public abstract void write_short_array(
            short[] value, int offset, int length);
    public abstract void write_ushort_array(
            short[] value, int offset, int length);
    public abstract void write_long_array(
            int[] value, int offset, int length);
    public abstract void write_ulong_array(
            int[] value, int offset, int length);
    public abstract void write_longlong_array(
```

**Figure 5.6** Output stream.

```
            long[] value, int offset, int length);
    public abstract void write_ulonglong_array(
            long[] value, int offset, int length);
    public abstract void write_float_array(
            float[] value, int offset, int length);
    public abstract void write_double_array(
            double[] value, int offset, int length);

    public abstract void write_Object(org.omg.CORBA.Object value);
    public abstract void write_TypeCode(org.omg.CORBA.TypeCode value);
    public abstract void write_any(org.omg.CORBA.Any value);

    public void write_Context(org.omg.CORBA.Context ctx,
                        org.omg.CORBA.ContextList contexts) {
        throw new org.omg.CORBA.NO_IMPLEMENT();
    }
    public void write_fixed(java.math.BigDecimal value) {
        throw new org.omg.CORBA.NO_IMPLEMENT();
    }
}
```

**Figure 5.6** *(Continued)*

The client program can now invoke methods on this object in the usual Java manner. The difference is in the execution of the method. The proxy object forwards the call to the implementation object by calling the DII, which in turn calls the portable ORB library to send the call to the remote object via the CORBA transport protocol, IIOP.

## 5.14.4 Server-Side Mapping

An object implementation has to implement the Java operations interface that has been generated from the IDL interface. There is a class called the *servant base class* that implements the Java operations interface and provides the skeleton code for a portable transient object implementation. The servant base class is generated by the IDL compiler and follows this naming scheme:

```
public class InterfaceNamePOA implements InterfaceNameOperations {
    ...
}
```

Like stub classes, skeleton classes either can be based on the DSI or can use the ORB's stream interface. Figure 5.8 shows the structure of the classes

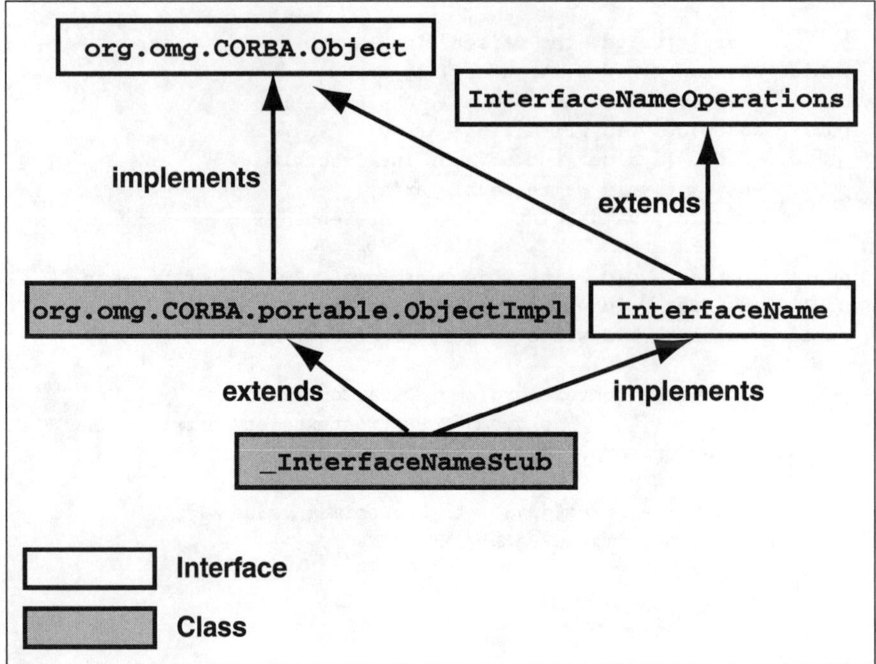


**Figure 5.7** Portable stub classes.

and interfaces on the server side. Note that a DSI-based skeleton extends just `org.omg.PortableServer.DynamicImplementation` whereas a stream-based skeleton has to implement `org.omg.CORBA.portable.InvokeHandler` and directly extends `org.omg.PortableServer.Servant`.

On the server side, the only standardized object adapter is the POA, which defines how the object is accessed when a client makes an operation invocation. Portable skeleton code generated by the IDL compiler is tailored to the POA, which is why the names of generated skeletons end in "`POA`" or "`POATie`." These two different skeleton classes correspond to the two approaches that are available to make your object implementation accessible with the POA: the Inheritance approach and the Tie approach. These two options are also outlined in Figure 5.8.

### *5.14.4.1 Inheritance versus Tie Approach*

To implement the Java operations interface and provide the application semantics of the operations using the inheritance approach, your implementation class (conventionally called *`InterfaceName`*Impl) is attached to the skeleton by extending the implementation base class:

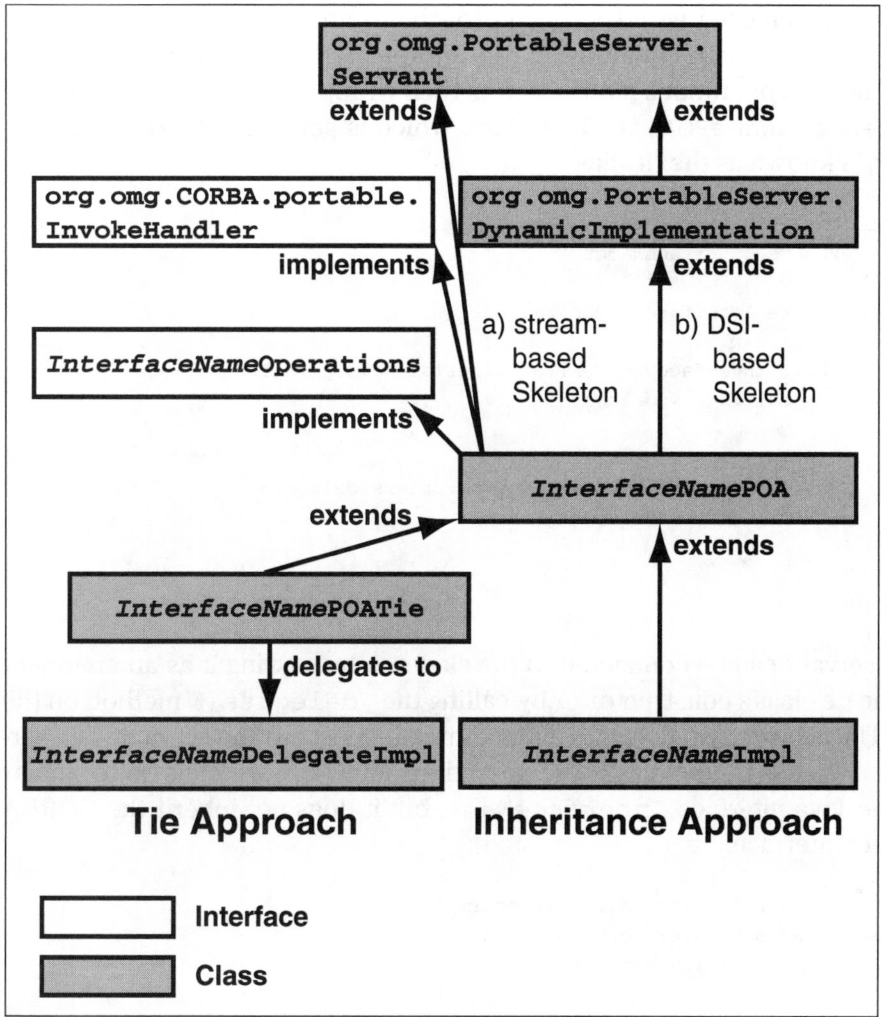


**Figure 5.8** Server-side portability.

```
public class InterfaceNameImpl extends InterfaceNamePOA {
    ...
}
```

Using this approach, your implementation class has to inherit from the skeleton or servant base class. While this is both straightforward and convenient, it might not be possible in cases where design dictates that implementation classes must inherit from other classes. Because Java provides only single inheritance of implementations, it must be possible to provide operation implementations without having to inherit from the servant base class.

This is achieved with the tie approach. To attach your implementation class to the skeleton code using this approach, the implementation has to use the Java operations interface. It is then wrapped in a Java object of type *InterfaceName*POATie. This class, which is generated by the IDL compiler, is known as the tie class.

```
public class InterfaceNamePOATie
    extends InterfaceNamePOA {

    private InterfaceNameOperations _delegate;

    public InterfaceNamePOATie (InterfaceNameOperations delegate) {
        _delegate = delegate;
    }

    public void _delegate(GoodDayOperations delegate) {
        _delegate = delegate;
    }
    // ...
}
```

A servant can be connected to the skeleton by passing it as an argument to the tie class's constructor or by calling the `_delegate()` method on the tie. The tie will then delegate all incoming requests to the servant. The servant class has to implement the operations interface, which is quite similar to the Java interface *InterfaceName*, but it does not inherit the CORBA Object interface.

```
public class InterfaceNameDelegateImpl
    implements InterfaceNameOperations {
    // implementing methods
}
```

An example of using the Tie mechanism is given in Chapter 9.

### 5.14.4.2 Object Lifetime and Threading

CORBA object references can be transient or persistent. A transient object reference is valid only for the lifetime of a particular object adapter. A persistent object reference can survive several adapter lifetimes. Its implementation can also be activated and deactivated in a server. For example, you may not create an instance of the implementation when starting the server, but it will be created when a client uses its reference. The instance may move to a different JVM or host. If the original instance disappears a replica may be used instead. Obviously the ORB and the object adapter have to provide far more sophisticated functionality for persistent objects than for transient ones. Persistent object references and persistent object state are covered in detail in Chapter 10, "Practical POA Programming," and Chapter 13, "The Persistent State Service."

Another thing that is controlled by an object adapter is the threading model. There are many variations of threading models, but the most common ones are these:

- Single-threaded servers. All incoming invocations are sequential and queued if necessary.
- Multithreaded—one thread per client. For each client, which typically means each connection to the server, a thread will be provided.
- Multithreaded—one thread per request. Each incoming request gets its own thread (up to a maximum number of threads in a pool). When the request is completed the thread is returned to the pool.

So far, threading policies have not been addressed by the OMG prior to specifying the POA, and ORB implementers provide control of the threading models in different ways. Even the POA acknowledges only that threads exist and are controlled by the ORB; it does not specify complex threads policies. The POA threading policy simply helps ensure that implementations that are not thread-safe are called only sequentially. Thus, you can avoid potential inconsistencies or deadlocks in the implementation that might arise when multiple threads are active at the same time.

In general, you should try to carefully design your implementations to be thread-safe because this usually results in higher request throughput. For optimal performance, however, you need to resort to ORB-specific configuration mechanisms for thread parameters because the specification does not standardize the more sophisticated threading models that allow fine-tuned threading to application behavior.

For a thread pool model, for example, typical configuration parameters are the maximum and minimum size of the thread pool. Typically, a large minimum size of the pool means that an incoming request can be immediately serviced by a waiting thread, but a large number of waiting threads may lock up too many resources in some cases. If no waiting threads are found in the pool, a new thread needs to be created if the maximum pool size is not yet reached. Creating threads is an expensive operation, however. The maximum pool size puts an upper limit of how many resources a server process may consume. The optimal values for these thread pool parameters depend on the interaction behavior of the application.

## 5.15 Constants

Following the Java conventions for constants, IDL constants are generally mapped to a static final variable that has the value of the constant. The attributes of the variable ensure the semantics of an IDL constant: `static` ensures that instances of that class have the same value, and `final` ensures that the value cannot be overridden. IDL constants, however, are mapped differently depending on where they are defined in the IDL specification. The two cases that are distinguished are constant declarations within and outside of an interface.

### 5.15.1 Constants within Interfaces

A constant that is defined within an interface is mapped to a final public static field of the Java interface, which is generated for the IDL interface containing the constant. The field is named after the IDL constant. The type of the field corresponds to the mapped IDL type of the constant. The field is initialized as defined in the IDL definition. The following example illustrates the mapping. The IDL constant MaxSlots

```
interface Tester {
    const short MaxSlots = 8;
};
```

is mapped to the field `MaxSlots` in the Java signature interface `Tester`:

```
public interface Tester
    extends TesterOperations,
            org.omg.CORBA.Object,
            org.omg.CORBA.portable.IDLEntity {

    final public static short MaxSlots = (short) 8;
    ...
}
```

### 5.15.2 Constants outside Interfaces

IDL constants that are defined outside interfaces are mapped to a public interface named after the IDL constant. This interface contains a public final static variable that is always called `value`. This variable is initialized to the value of the constant.

Declaring the same IDL constant as above, but outside an interface

```
const short MaxSlots = 8;
```

leads to the following Java mapping:

```
public interface MaxSlots {
    final public static short value = (short) 8;
}
```

## 5.16 Attributes

IDL attributes are mapped to Java methods: an accessor method, and, if the attribute is not declared readonly, a modifier method. Both methods have the same name as the IDL attribute, but they differ in their signatures. The accessor method does not have parameters, and it returns a value of the attribute type (mapped to Java). The modifier method return type is `void` and has one parameter of the attribute type.

Here are two example attributes in an IDL interface:

```
interface Tester {
  attribute string name;
  readonly attribute long id;
}
```

These attributes map to the following Java methods, defined in the Java interface `TesterOperations`:

```
public interface TesterOperations {
    public void name(java.lang.String name);
    public java.lang.String name();
    public int id();
}
```

## 5.17 Operations

IDL operations are mapped to methods in the generated Java operations interface. This interface is then inherited by the reference interface. The type of the operation result is mapped to Java according to the mapping for data types previously described. The mapping of the parameter types depends on their direction tag.

### 5.17.1 Parameter Semantics

IDL defines three different parameter-passing modes, indicated by the tags in, inout, and out. The tag in defines pass-by-value semantics: A client supplies a value that is left unchanged during the time of the invocation. The tag out defines pass-by-result semantics: The server supplies a value that will be available to the client after the invocation returns. The tag inout defines a combined semantics: The client supplies a value that is subject to change by the server. The modified value is available to the client after the invocation returns.

Java defines only pass-by-value semantics for method parameters. This matches the semantics for in parameters only. To map inout and out parameters, additional mechanisms are needed.

When a Java client invokes a method and supplies a Java object reference as an argument, the invoked object can modify the state of the object that was referenced by the parameter. After the invocation, the client still has the same reference to the object, but the object itself has been modified.

This mechanism is used to handle inout and out parameters in Java. Java objects called holder objects are used as containers for these parameters. References to the holder objects are passed instead of the parameters themselves. This mechanism is illustrated in Figure 5.9.

As we have already seen in the mappings of the various data types, holder classes follow the same pattern: They have a public instance variable called `value` that holds the actual value of the parameter. These classes also provide a couple of constructors. One is a null constructor (intended for `out` parameters); the other is a constructor that has a parameter of the contained type (intended for `inout` parameters).

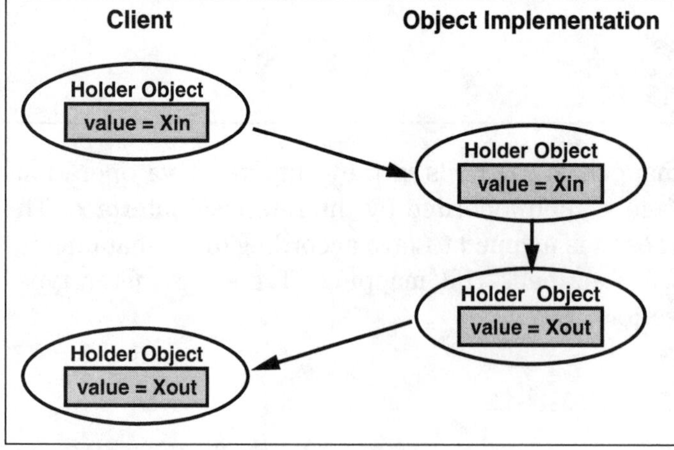


**Figure 5.9** Holder classes.

## 5.17.2 Mapping from Operations to Methods

IDL operations are mapped to Java methods of the same name. An operation's result type is mapped according to mapping for data types. The IDL void return type is mapped to Java `void`. IDL in parameters are also mapped according the mapping for IDL types. IDL inout and out parameters are mapped to the Holder classes that are generated for their IDL type.

IDL operations can explicitly raise one or more user-defined exceptions and can also implicitly raise system exceptions. Java methods that map IDL operations may always throw CORBA system exceptions that extend `java.lang.RuntimeException`. We have already seen that IDL exceptions map naturally to Java exceptions and that all mappings of user exception types are extensions of the Java class `org.omg.CORBA.UserException`, which itself extends `java.lang.Exception`. The raises clause of an IDL operation is mapped to a `throws` clause on the equivalent Java method. As an example, we use an operation that has parameters with all the different tags and raises a user-defined exception.

```
exception SomethingWrong {
    long id;
};

interface Tester {
    boolean test( in string name, inout boolean flag, out long id )
      raises( SomethingWrong );
};
```

The operation is mapped to a method whose out and inout parameters are Holder objects.

```
public interface TesterOperations {
    public boolean test (
        java.lang.String name,
        org.omg.CORBA.BooleanHolder flag,
        org.omg.CORBA.IntHolder id
    ) throws SomethingWrong;
}
```

## 5.17.3 Portable Stub Implementation

In this section we want to examine the implementation of portable stubs using the Java ORB Portability Interfaces. As we explained earlier, portable stubs can use either the DII or the stream interface to invoke operations. We choose to look at stream-based skeletons as generated by the VisiBroker IDL compiler. This section once again provides extra information for the interested reader, but it is not needed to write Java ORB applications. We will use the IDL from the previous section as an example and mention a few more details on parameter passing.

The class `_TesterStub` extends the portability layer represented by the class `org.omg.CORBA.portable.ObjectImpl` and implements the Java interface `Tester`. The body of the class implements the method `test()`. For our example, the following portable stub class is generated:

```
public class _TesterStub
    extends org.omg.CORBA.portable.ObjectImpl implements Tester {
    // ...

    public boolean test (
        java.lang.String name,
        org.omg.CORBA.BooleanHolder flag,
        org.omg.CORBA.IntHolder id
    ) throws SomethingWrong {

    while (true) {
        if (!_is_local()) {
            org.omg.CORBA.portable.OutputStream _output = null;
            org.omg.CORBA.portable.InputStream  _input  = null;
            boolean _result;
            try {
                // create an output stream for operation "test"
                _output = this._request("test", true);

                // marshal arguments
                _output.write_string((java.lang.String)name);
                _output.write_boolean((boolean)flag.value);
```

After the request has been written to the output stream, the method `_invoke()` inherited from `org.omg.CORBA.portable.ObjectImpl` is called, passing the request output stream as an argument. As a result, an `InputStream` object is returned from which we read the operation result and the values for the in and inout parameters. These are assigned to the appropriate holder fields, and the result is returned:

```
                // create an input stream as
                // a result of the invocation
                _input = this._invoke(_output);

                // read operation result
                _result = _input.read_boolean();
```

```
            // read values of out and inout parameters
            flag.value = _input.read_boolean();
            id.value = _input.read_long();
            return _result;
        }
```

If an exception has occurred, the `_invoke()` method will throw an `ApplicationException`. The stub code is prepared to handle this exception, extract exception information from the InputStream provided by the `ApplicationException`, and throw the appropriate Java exception:

```
        catch(org.omg.CORBA.portable.ApplicationException _ex){

            // create an input stream to
            // read exception information
            final org.omg.CORBA.portable.InputStream in =
                _ex.getInputStream();

            // read exception id
            java.lang.String _except_id = _ex.getId();

            // throw the appropriate Java exception object
            if (_except_id.equals(SomethingWrongHelper.id())) {
                throw SomethingWrongHelper.read(
                    _ex.getInputStream() );
            }
            // if we did not get the exception
            // we are prepared for:
            throw new org.omg.CORBA.UNKNOWN(
                "Unexpected User Exception: " + _excep_id);
        }
        // ...
    }
  }
}
```

## 5.17.4 Portable Skeleton Implementation

A portable skeleton class is also generated by the IDL compiler. This time, we let the computer-generated code that uses the DSI rather than the stream interface. For our example the class `TesterPOA` is generated.

```
public abstract class TesterPOA
    extends org.omg.PortableServer.DynamicImplementation
    implements TesterOperations {
...
```

All DSI-based object implementations must implement the interface `org.omg.PortableServer.DynamicImplementation`. Its single method `invoke()` has one parameter, which is a ServerRequest object. The ServerRequest interface is explained in detail in Chapter 6.

```
public void invoke (org.omg.CORBA.ServerRequest _request) {

    TesterOperations _self = this;
    java.lang.Object _method = _methods.get(_request.op_name());
    if(_method == null) {
        throw new org.omg.CORBA.BAD_OPERATION(_request.op_name());
    }
    int _method_id = ((java.lang.Integer) _method).intValue();

    switch(_method_id) {
        case 0: {
```

If the `test()` method is selected, its invocation follows these steps. First, a parameter list containing NamedValue objects for each of the parameters we expect from test() is created. The NamedValues are given only a TypeCode and a flag and are added to the parameter list. Then the parameter list is given to the ServerRequest, which places the incoming argument values into it.

```
            try {
                org.omg.CORBA.NVList _params =
                    _orb().create_list(0);

                org.omg.CORBA.Any __param_name =
                    _orb().create_any();
                __param_name.type(
                    _orb().get_primitive_tc(
                        org.omg.CORBA.TCKind.tk_string )
                );
                _params.add_value("name",
                                  __param_name,
                                  org.omg.CORBA.ARG_IN.value);

                org.omg.CORBA.Any __param_flag =
                    _orb().create_any();
                __param_flag.type(
                    _orb().get_primitive_tc(
                        org.omg.CORBA.TCKind.tk_boolean )
                );
                _params.add_value("flag",
                                  __param_flag,
                                  org.omg.CORBA.ARG_INOUT.value);
```

```
org.omg.CORBA.Any __param_id = _orb().create_any();
__param_id.type(
    _orb().get_primitive_tc(
        org.omg.CORBA.TCKind.tk_long )
);
_params.add_value( "id",
                   __param_id,

org.omg.CORBA.ARG_OUT.value );
_request.params(_params);
```

Now variables are declared for each parameter to the method implementation and initialized from the `_params` NVList object that the ServerRequest has now populated. The method on the implementation object (`_this`) is invoked.

```
java.lang.String name;
name = __param_name.extract_string();
org.omg.CORBA.BooleanHolder flag =
    new org.omg.CORBA.BooleanHolder();

flag.value = __param_flag.extract_boolean();
org.omg.CORBA.IntHolder id =
    new org.omg.CORBA.IntHolder();
boolean _result = _self.test(name, flag, id);
```

The values of the inout and out parameters are then inserted into the Any objects owned by the ServerRequest's parameter list `_param`, so that they can be returned to the caller. There is also an Any object created for the result in which the method's return value is inserted. Now the ServerRequest object contains all the values produced by the implementation ready to be sent back to the client.

```
    org.omg.CORBA.Any _resultAny = _orb().create_any();
    _resultAny.insert_boolean((boolean)_result);
    _request.result(_resultAny);

    __param_flag.insert_boolean((boolean)flag.value);
    __param_id.insert_long((int)id.value);
}
```

If the method implementation raised an exception, it must be placed into the Any object set in the `except()` method on the ServerRequest.

```
catch (wiley.SomethingWrong _exception) {
    org.omg.CORBA.Any _exceptionAny =
        _orb().create_any();
    SomethingWrongHelper.insert(_exceptionAny,
```

```
                                        _exception);
                _request.except(_exceptionAny);
            }
            return ;
        } // case
    }
}
```

### 5.17.5 Parameter Management

Table 5.4 summarizes the responsibilities of the invoking client and the object implementation for the declaration, creation, and initialization of parameters and operation result.

## 5.18 Inheritance

OMG IDL allows multiple inheritance for interfaces, that is, an IDL interface can inherit from any number of interfaces. Java allows only single inheritance for classes, that is, a class can extend only one superclass (see Chapter 3, "Overview of Java and Java ORBs"). The Java language designers deliberately made this decision to avoid semantic problems and language complications caused by the inheritance of implementations. Java interfaces consist only of signatures. This means that multiple inheritance for interfaces does not imply implementation inheritance, and so it is allowed in Java.

**Table 5.4** Parameter Management Responsibilities

| | INVOKING CLIENT | OBJECT IMPLEMENTATION |
|---|---|---|
| Operation result | Declares variable of return type and assigns result. | Declares variable, creates and initializes instance, and returns instance. |
| in parameters | Declares variable, creates and initializes instance, and passes to invocation. | Declares parameter and uses value passed. |
| inout parameters | Declares variable, creates Holder object, initializes with a value, and passes to invocation. | Declares Holder parameter, modifies `value` field of Holder parameter. |
| out parameters | Declares variable, creates Holder object, and passes to invocation. | Declares Holder parameter, initializes `value` field of Holder parameter. |

Because IDL interfaces are mapped to Java interfaces, the mapping of inheritance is straightforward. A Java interface representing a derived IDL interface, D, extends all the Java interfaces representing the base interfaces of D. The following example illustrates inheritance by using a diamond inheritance structure (see Figure 5.10).

```
interface Base {
    void baseOp();
};
interface Left:Base {
    void leftOp();
};
interface Right:Base {
    void rightOp();
};

interface Derived: Left, Right { };
```

When we look at the generated code we see the same pattern mirrored by the Java interfaces:

```
public interface Base extends org.omg.CORBA.Object { ... }
public interface Left extends Base { ... }
public interface Right extends Base { ... }
public interface Derived extends Left, Right { ... }
```

It is interesting to examine the generated stub and skeleton classes because Java classes do not support multiple inheritance. As can be seen, there is no problem with the skeleton classes because they directly or indirectly extend only the class `org.omg.PortableServer.Servant` and implement the corresponding Java operations interface.

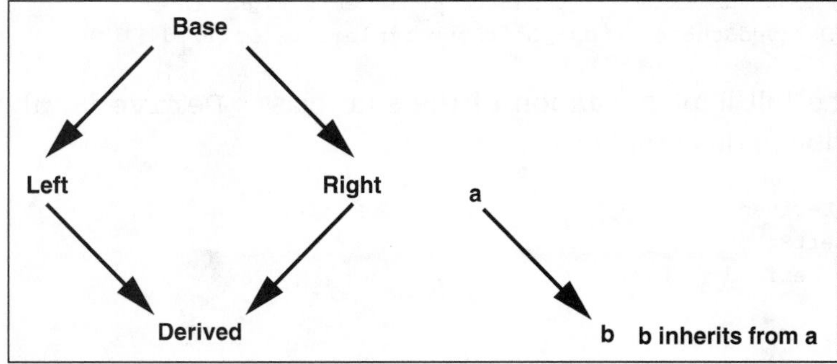


**Figure 5.10** Diamond inheritance.

```
abstract public class BasePOA
    extends org.omg.PortableServer.Servant
    implements org.omg.CORBA.portable.InvokeHandler, BaseOperations
{...}

abstract public class LeftPOA
    extends org.omg.PortableServer.Servant
    implements org.omg.CORBA.portable.InvokeHandler, LeftOperations
{...}

abstract public class RightPOA
    extends org.omg.PortableServer.Servant
    implements org.omg.CORBA.portable.InvokeHandler,RightOperations
{...}

abstract public class DerivedPOA
    extends org.omg.PortableServer.Servant
    implements org.omg.CORBA.portable.InvokeHandler,
               DerivedOperations
{...}
```

The situation, though, is different for the stub classes. Note that multiple inheritance need not be a problem as it could simply be avoided altogether: The stub generated for the interface Derived could simply implement all methods from `DerivedOperations` and all operations interfaces of Derived's base interfaces. That means that stub code for operations in superclasses is generated multiple times, increasing the overall size of generated code.

To avoid generating unnecessary code, stub classes can extend the base stub class corresponding to a base IDL interface. But when there is more than one base interface, as with our interface Derived, the class has to choose which base type to extend.

```
public class _BaseStub
    extends org.omg.CORBA.portable.ObjectImpl implements Base {
public class _LeftStub extends _BaseStub implements Left {
public class _RightStub extends _BaseStub implements Right {
public class _DerivedStub extends _LeftStub implements Derived {
```

A look into the full implementation of the stub class `_DerivedStub` reveals the solution to this problem.

```
public class _DerivedStub
    extends _LeftStub
    implements Derived {

    // ...

    public Right _Right;
```

```
    // ...
    public void rightOp() {
        this._Right.rightOp( );
    }
}
```

The stub class declares an instance of a proxy class for the interface Right and explicitly implements the method `rightOp()`, which calls the object `_Right`.

A related problem is how to deal with the inheritance structure in implementation classes. This problem is addressed in the same way by the Tie, or delegation, approach and is explained by an example in Chapter 9.

## 5.19 Modules and Name-Scoping Rules

Modules provide a name scope for identifiers in IDL specifications to prevent clashes with identifiers used in other specifications. Java provides packages for scoping identifiers. IDL modules are mapped to Java packages of the same name, where each package corresponds to a directory in the file system. The IDL compiler creates a subdirectory named after the IDL module. All generated files containing mapped interfaces and classes for the contents of a module are put into this directory. The files created contain a corresponding package declaration.

Modules can be nested, that is, one can define modules within modules. Nested module definitions result in a corresponding nesting of subpackages and subdirectories.

Additional packages are created for data-type definitions within the scope of an interface. These packages are named after the interface with a suffix `Package`. They are nested in the package corresponding to the module in which the interface is defined. Figure 5.11 illustrates these mapping rules.

The following IDL provides an example of the scoping rules discussed previously. It also illustrates an important IDL feature, namely, that modules can be reopened, which allows for complex cross-module dependencies. You should be aware that not all C and C++ ORBs implement this feature due to the lack of appropriate support in the programming language. Although C++ has name spaces to provide name scoping, they are still not implemented by all C++ compilers and run-time systems. So if you plan to use C or C++ to implement part of your system you should check whether your C/C++ ORB supports this feature.

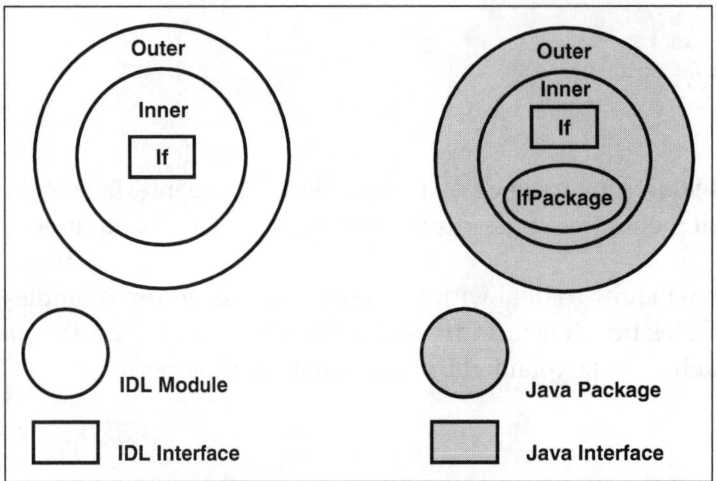


**Figure 5.11** Name scoping.

```
module a {
    exception ModuleException{};
};
module b {
    interface B1 {};
    module c {
        interface C1{};
    };
};
module a {
    interface A1: b::B1, b::c::C1 {
        attribute string name;
        exception InterfaceException{};
        boolean test( in string name, inout boolean flag, out long id)
          raises( ModuleException, InterfaceException );
    };
};
module b {
    interface B2: a::A1 {};
};
```

When the IDL is compiled, the following package structure is created:

- Package a
  Exception `ModuleException` and its helper and holder classes
  Interfaces `A1Operations` and `A1`, its skeleton and stub classes and interfaces, and helper and holder classes

Package `A1Package`
Exception `InterfaceException` and its helper and holder classes

- Package b
  Interfaces `B1Operations` and `B1`, its skeleton and stub classes and interfaces, and helper and holder classes
- Package b.c
  Interfaces `C1Operations` and `C1`, its skeleton and stub classes and interfaces, and helper and holder classes
  Interfaces `B2Operations` and `B2`, its skeleton and stub classes and interfaces, and helper and holder classes

## 5.20 Mapping from Java to IDL

So far, we have explained how IDL compilers realize the standardized mapping from OMG IDL to Java. This mapping is necessary to implement interfaces and data types in Java that were defined in an implementation-independent way in IDL, Java being just one out of potentially many implementation language choices.

The relation between OMG IDL and Java is not, however, limited to this one-way mapping. The OMG has also defined a reverse mapping from Java to IDL (OMG document ptc/99-03-09), which makes it possible to generate IDL definitions from existing Java programs that use RMI as their distribution platform. This applies mainly to EJB applications that are to be integrated with CORBA. To allow Java server components not only to access CORBA objects but also to be accessed using CORBA interfaces, Sun Microsystems designed a CORBA 2.3-compliant ORB run time into RMI. This variant of RMI uses IIOP as its transport protocol rather than the original Java Remote Method Protocol (JRMP) and is known as RMI over IIOP (RMI-IIOP).

Providing transport-level support for accessing RMI objects is not sufficient, however, to fully integrate Java with CORBA. At this level, IDL definitions would have to be manually reverse-engineered so that these could be used to generate stub code to access Java resources over IIOP. Especially for applications that make heavy use of Java's object serialization features, this is a tricky task that is easy to get wrong. One prerequisite for the reverse mapping is obviously that CORBA support RMI-style serialization semantics, which was achieved with the introduction of valuetypes to IDL and the corresponding extensions in the CORBA transport protocol GIOP.

Using a standardized reverse mapping and an automated tool, integrating

Java/RMI applications with CORBA is becoming feasible. RMI-IIOP as delivered by Sun provides the reverse mapping as an additional functionality of RMI's stub generator tool `rmic`. To generate IIOP stubs rather than JRMP stubs from a Java class, `rmic` must be invoked with the `-iiop` option. To generate IDL definitions from an existing Java class, you have to use the `-idl` switch.

Java and CORBA are now very close in a number of concepts central to distributed computing. A few mismatches between the two object models still exist that are either hard or impossible to come by. In the remainder of this section, we briefly look at the restrictions to Java/RMI that developers must observe to allow the reverse-mapping to IDL. We do not provide any programming examples here, however.

## 5.20.1 The RMI/IDL Subset of Java

A number of platform issues must be addressed when trying to convert a regular Java/RMI program into one that uses RMI-IIOP. The most prominent change is that remote interfaces now must implement `javax.rmi.PortableObject` rather than `java.rmi.server.UnicastRemoteObject`. Also, programs must not use the RMI registry but a CORBA Naming Service instead. In Java, the CORBA Naming Service can be accessed using the Java Naming and Directory Interface (JNDI), which is available in the package `javax.naming`. The name server can be started with the `tnameserv` command.

In addition, a number of language restrictions must be observed. We will examine some of these here. First, possible name clashes with OMG-defined identifiers must be avoided by escaping names with a leading underscore, so a Java name `factory` would be mapped to _factory in IDL. Also, Java names that already have leading underscores like `_counter` have to be dealt with, because leading underscores are treated as escapes by IDL compilers and would be removed when the IDL is processed. Leading underscores are therefore prefixed with a capital letter "J", so `counter` becomes J_counter. Overloaded method names must be mangled as IDL does not allow method overloading. Methods like

```
string foo();
string foo(int x);
string foo(java.lang.Object o)
```

would be named apart like this:

```
CORBA::WstringValue foo__();
CORBA::WstringValue foo__long(in long x);
CORBA::WstringValue foo__java_lang_Object(in ::java::lang::_Object o);
```

**Table 5.5** Summary of Standard Classes Mapped to IDL

| JAVA | OMG IDL |
|---|---|
| `java.lang.Object` | ::java::lang::_Object |
| `java.lang.String` | ::CORBA::WstringValue<br>wstring (for `String` constants) |
| `java.lang.Class` | ::javax::rmi::CORBA::ClassDesc |
| `java.io.Serializable` | ::java::io::Serializable |
| `java.io.Externalizable` | ::java::io::Externalizable |
| `java.rmi.Remote` | ::java::io::Remote |
| `org.omg.CORBA.Object` | Object |

This example also shows that some Java standard library types are given special treatment. Table 5.5 summarizes how Java standard classes and interfaces are mapped to IDL scoped names.

The class `java.lang.String` is mapped differently when used in string constants than when it is used as a normal parameter, result, or data field type. In this latter case, it must be mapped to the value box type WStringValue to preserve its null and sharing semantics. This type is defined in the CORBA module. Constant strings are mapped to the IDL base type wstring. Like Java strings, arrays are reference types in Java and are therefore mapped onto IDL value box types to preserve their semantics.

In Java/RMI, references to remote objects could be simply cast to the desired type because RMI stubs could be dynamically downloaded. Using RMI-IIOP, narrowing has to be done by calling the static method `narrow` provided by `javax.rmi.PortableRemoteObject`:

```
OtherType obj = getObject();
Server server = (Server)javax.rmi.PortableRemoteObject.narrow(
                                                   obj,Server.class);
```

Using RMI-IIOP is different from using plain RMI, as these examples from the reverse-mapping specification show. Converting existing programs is generally not possible without adapting them to the RMI/IDL subset of Java and the RMI-IIOP run-time API.

# ORB Run-Time System

The CORBA 2.3 specification defines the ORB run-time system in the form of the pseudo-objects ORB and Object and the locality-constrained object POA. Other pseudo-objects assist in dynamic invocations, dynamic server responses, TypeCode creation, and name/value pair manipulation. Pseudo-objects provide interfaces like normal CORBA objects, but they do not inherit from CORBA::Object, and operations on those interfaces are implemented in libraries and do not result in remote invocations. Also, these interfaces are generally not mapped using the standard mapping rules but require language-specific modifications, even if the Java mapping of pseudo-IDL follows the mapping for all other IDL very closely. Moreover, pseudo-objects cannot be used as arguments to regular CORBA operations, the one notable exception being TypeCodes.

The definition of pseudo-objects, which are simply marked "PIDL" in IDL comments, poses a number of problems because of the broad meaning of "pseudo" as used in different OMG documents. It covers purely local implementations, singleton objects, library objects with their own memory management rules, and interfaces with operations that take non-IDL arguments. In newer documents, the OMG accepts no PIDL definitions. Instead, locality-constrained objects such as the POA are defined. Marking an interface as locality-constrained means that the interface is mapped according to normal language mapping rules, but that references to objects may not be externalized, either by stringifying them or passing them in remote invocations: The object can be used only within the local process.

In this chapter we explain the language mapping of those interfaces that make up the ORB run-time system as specified in the IDL/Java Language Mapping standard. There are a few omissions from the standard, notably missing raises clauses in some operation declarations. Where these are actually required, we have included them in the pseudo-IDL and the corresponding throws clause of the mapped method. This chapter contains mappings for the following interfaces:

- Object (section 6.1)
- ORB (section 6.2)
- POA (section 6.3)
- TypeCode (section 6.4)
- Types used for dynamic invocations (section 6.5)
- Dynamic Invocation Interface (section 6.6)
- Dynamic Skeleton Interface (section 6.7)
- Registration of Valuetype factories (section 6.8)

## 6.1 Object Interface

All CORBA objects, that is, objects that have been specified in OMG IDL and implemented in a CORBA environment, are extensions of the interface CORBA::Object. This interface defines operations that are applicable to any object. These operations are implemented by the ORB local to the client that has a reference to the object instead of being passed to the (possibly remote) object implementation.

In this section we will discuss the mapping of the IDL operations into Java. The mapping of the interface type itself is

IDL Interface interface CORBA::Object { // PIDL;

Java interface
```
package org.omg.CORBA;
  public interface Object {...};
```

The following sections each explain an operation in the Object interface.

### 6.1.1 get_interface()

The Interface Repository contains type information about IDL-defined types. The type information for a CORBA object's interface type is represented by objects with the IDL interface CORBA::InterfaceDef. Operations on this interface allow clients to query the Interface Repository about the details of the data types, operations, and attributes supported by the object. The operation get_interface() returns an InterfaceDef object reference that represents the interface type of the object it was called on.

IDL operation InterfaceDef get_interface();

Java method `org.omg.CORBA.Object_get_interface_def();`

The mapped Java method `_get_interface_def()` returns a result of type `org.omg.CORBA.Object` rather than of the mapped Java class `org.omg.CORBA.InterfaceDef`, but the returned result can be narrowed to this type. The reason why `org.omg.CORBA.InterfaceDef` is not returned directly is that it allows delivery of a smaller set of `org.omg` classes with the CORBA implementation in JDK 2, which does not provide an Interface Repository. Otherwise, the JDK would have to contain the complete set of mapped classes for all the definitions related to the Interface Repository.

The use of this method is demonstrated in Chapter 9, "Advanced Features."

### 6.1.2 is_nil()

An object reference can be tested to see if it is nil (denotes no object) by the operation is_nil(). Java uses the null type as a nil object reference. Therefore, a test like `if( obj == null )` is used in place of is_nil().

### 6.1.3 duplicate() and release()

There is no need to map the operations duplicate() and release() because Java provides memory management for object references, as it does for any other object or data type. The mapping does provide these operations for completeness:

IDL operation Object duplicate();

Java method `org.omg.CORBA.Object _duplicate();`

IDL operation void release();

Java method `void _release();`

## 6.1.4 is_a()

The operation is_a() tests if an object is of the interface type supplied as an argument. The string argument is interpreted as a RepositoryId. Chapter 2 explains the format of these identifiers.

| | |
|---|---|
| IDL operation | boolean is_a( in string logical_type_id); |
| Java method | `boolean _is_a(String Identifier);` |

The `_is_a()` method returns TRUE if the object is of the type identified. This means either that the object's type and the identified type are the same or that the identified type is a base type of the object's type. Calling this method may require the ORB to contact a remote Interface Repository. In case this fails, an exception is raised so that a caller can distinguish between TRUE, FALSE, and indeterminate results.

## 6.1.5 non_existent()

The operation non_existent() can be used to test if an object has been destroyed. It returns TRUE if the ORB can authoritatively determine that the referenced object does not exist. Otherwise, it returns FALSE. Like is_a(), this operation may require the ORB to contact the remote location, which may result in an exception. Note that a FALSE return value may not mean that the object still exists at the time the call returns.

| | |
|---|---|
| IDL operation | boolean non_existent(); |
| Java method | `boolean _non_existent();` |

## 6.1.6 is_equivalent()

The operation is_equivalent() determines if two object references are equivalent, that is, are identical or refer to the same object. The operation returns TRUE if the object reference on which the operation was called and the reference other_object are known to be equivalent; otherwise, it returns FALSE. Note that a FALSE return value does not mean that the object could not possibly be the same.

| | |
|---|---|
| IDL operation | boolean is_equivalent( in Object other_object); |
| Java method | `boolean _is_equivalent(Object that);` |

## 6.1.7 hash()

The operation hash() is used to effectively manage large numbers of object references. It generates a hash value for the object reference on which the operation is called. The hash value relates to an ORB-internal identifier. As usual with hash functions, different object references can result in the same hash value, and further operations such as is_equivalent() need to be called to determine whether two objects are equivalent.

| | |
|---|---|
| IDL operation | unsigned long hash( in unsigned long maximum ); |
| Java method | `int _hash(int maximum);` |

## 6.1.8 get_policy()

The get_policy() operation returns the *effective* policy of a given type for the object. It raises the CORBA::INV_POLICY exception if no policy of that type exists or if the policy type is not supported by the ORB.

The effective policy is the one that would be used for an invocation on the object. It is a combination of client-side policies, which can be set using the set_policy_overrides() operation explained in the text that follows, and the policies associated with the object's reference. The main examples for policies that get implicitly associated with object references are security policies such as those determining the quality of protection used when transmitting requests.

| | |
|---|---|
| IDL operation | Policy get_policy(in PolicyType policy_type); |
| Java method | `Policy _get_policy(int policy_type);` |

## 6.1.9 get_domain_managers()

The operation get_domain_managers() returns a list of DomainManager objects for the domains to which the object immediately belongs. The DomainManager interface, in turn, allows retrieval of policy objects for the domain that governs object behavior, such as access control policies. Calling this operation might involve contacting the remote ORB to which the target object is connected.

| | |
|---|---|
| IDL operation | DomainManagersList get_domain_managers(); |
| Java method | `DomainManager[] _get_domain_managers();` |

### 6.1.10 set_policy_overrides

The set_policy_overrides() operation is used to associate new policies with an object reference by either adding to or overriding existing policies. If successful, it returns a copy of the object reference with an updated list of policies. The operation may raise the CORBA::NO_PERMISSION exception if overriding an existing policy is not allowed.

IDL operation enum SetOverrideType { SET_OVERRIDE, ADD_OVERRIDE };
Object set_policy_overrides(in PolicyList policies, in SetOverrideType set_add);

Java method
```
org.omg.CORBA.Object _set_policy_overrides(
Policy[] policies,
 SetOverrideType set_add );
```

## 6.2 ORB Interface

The ORB interface provides operations to bootstrap a CORBA application. This includes the conversion of object references into strings, and vice versa, and the resolution of initial references. One of these initial references is the reference to the POA that is needed to allow objects to be made available for invocations. We will introduce these in section 6.2.3.

Other operations are defined on the ORB pseudo-interface that are concerned with TypeCodes (see section 6.4), Contexts (section 6.5), the Dynamic Invocation Interface (section 6.6), the Dynamic Skeleton Interface (section 6.7), and the registration of factories for instances of valuetypes (section 6.8). The mappings for those operations are explained in the appropriate sections.

The ORB interface is mapped as follows:

IDL Interface pseudo interface ORB {

Java class
```
package org.omg.CORBA;
   public abstract class ORB {...}
```

### 6.2.1 ORB Initialization

Before an application can use the operations on the ORB interface it needs a reference to an ORB pseudo-object. ORBs in Java applets require different initializations to Java applications to overcome applet security restrictions. This initialization is performed by calling static methods in the ORB class.

### *Initialization for Java Applications*

| | |
|---|---|
| IDL operation | ORB ORB_init( inout arg_list argv, in ORBid orb_identifier ); |
| Java default method | `public static ORB init();` |
| Java method for applications | `public static ORB init (String[] args, Properties props);` |
| Java method for applets | `public static ORB init (Applet app, Properties props);` |

The default `init()` method returns a reference to a "singleton" ORB, which acts only as an Any and TypeCode factory (see section 6.4). All other operations called from an applet on this ORB object will raise a system exception.

The other two standard methods are designed specifically for use by Java applications and applets, respectively. The application version of `init()` can take arguments that were given to the application at start-up, as well as a list of Java properties. The applet version must be passed a pointer to the applet, and it may also take a list of properties. The ORB will know how to interpret two standard properties; however, particular ORB products may recognize other proprietary properties.

The standard properties are as follows:

- `org.omg.CORBA.ORBClass`—which contains the name of an ORB implementation class
- `org.omg.CORBA.ORBSingletonClass`—which contains the name of the "singleton" ORB implementation that acts only as a TypeCode factory

## 6.2.2 Converting Object References into Strings and Vice Versa

Object references can be externalized by converting them into strings. A stringified object reference can be conveniently stored in a file or passed around by means other than CORBA, for example, by e-mail. A stringified object reference is reconvertible into a real object reference, which refers to the same object as the original one.

There are two operations at the ORB interface that stringify and destringify object references. The object_to_string() operation converts an IOR into a string.

IDL operation string object_to_string(in CORBA::Object obj);

Java method
```
String object_to_string(org.omg.
    CORBA.Object obj);
```

The operation string_to_object() converts a stringified object reference back into an IOR.

IDL operation Object string_to_object( in string obj);

Java method
```
org.omg.CORBA.Object string_to_object(
    String str);
```

It is guaranteed that a stringified IOR produced by object_to_string() is reconvertible by string_to_object() regardless of on which ORB the operations are invoked. Note that the result of string_to_object() is of type CORBA::Object and must be narrowed to the object type expected.

## 6.2.3 Obtaining a POA Reference

The ORB offers an operation to retrieve references to initial references, that is, references that are needed to bootstrap. This operation is also used to obtain a reference to the root POA, which is needed to make objects available for remote invocations.

IDL operation CORBA::Object resolve_initial_references(in string name);

Java method
```
public abstract org.omg.CORBA.Object
    resolve_initial_references (String name);
```

The `resolve_initial_references` operation takes a string argument used to indicate which out of a number of available bootstrap references is required. Assuming that the ORB pseudo-object has been properly initialized, a reference to the root POA can be obtained like this:

```
org.omg.CORBA.Object obj =
    orb.resolve_initial_references("RootPOA");
org.omg.PortableServer.POA rootPOA =
    org.omg.PortableServer.POAHelper.narrow(obj);
```

Note that the root POA, like any newly created POA, is initially in a holding state and will not process incoming requests. To enable request processing, it is necessary to call `activate()` on the POA's POAManager. POAManagers are explained in more detail in Chapter 2; suffice it to say here that code like the following is necessary eventually:

```
rootPOA.the_Manager().activate();
```

## 6.3 Portable Object Adapter Interface

To create object references and to make these objects available for remote invocations, the interface to the POA is used. We just explained how to obtain an initial reference to the root POA in the previous section. In this section, we will look at the generation of new object references, the implicit activation and deactivation of objects, and the creation of child POAs with different policies.

The POA's locality-constrained interface is defined in the module PortableServer and is mapped according to the regular language mapping rules. The mapped Java interfaces and classes are in the `org.omg.PortableServer` package:

IDL Interface
```
module PortableServer {
    interface POA { // locality-constrained;
```

Java class
```
package org.omg.PortableServer;
    public interface POA {...}
```

### 6.3.1 Reference Creation

The POA interface has two operations to explicitly create new object references, as explained in Chapter 2:

IDL operations
```
Object create_reference( in RepositoryID intf );
Object create_reference_with_id( in ObjectId oid,
    in RepositoryID intf );
```

Java method
```
org.omg.CORBA.Object create_reference(
    String intf );
org.omg.CORBA.Object create_reference
    _with_id( byte [] oid,
    String intf);
```

In both cases, the type of the object must be specified in the form of a RepositoryID. If no user-defined object ID is required, create_reference() is used. Note that the newly created references are not associated with any servant yet, which means they are not activated. While the abstract object exists now and its reference can be exported using object_to_string() or via a name service, it is still necessary to associate the object with a servant.

### 6.3.2 Implicit Activation and Deactivation

In many cases where no specialized POA configuration is used and the POA allows implicit activation of servants, the most convenient way of creating an object reference is to activate it at the same time the reference is created, rather than calling one of the create_reference operations and then explicitly activating the object by calling activate_object() or activate_object_with id().

IDL operation Object servant_to_reference(in Servant servant);

Java method
```
org.omg.CORBA.Object servant_to_reference(
        Servant s);
```

Using this operation, a single call suffices:

```
MyServerImpl servant = new MyServerImpl();
org.omg.CORBA.Object obj = poa.servant_to_reference(servant);
```

The servant_to_reference() operation can create a reference from a Java servant object and simultaneously activate the object, which means it can associate the object with the servant and make an entry in its Active Object Map. This is called an implicit activation and requires both the IMPLICIT_ACTIVATION and RETAIN policies. Also, the specified servant must either not be currently active or the POA must also have the MULTIPLE_ID policy set. Note that for the POA to be able to assign an object ID for a new object reference, the ID assignment policy must have a value of SYSTEM_ID.

With the root POA, the servant_to_reference operation can be used to conveniently create object references from servants because the root POA has all the required policies. If we were using a different POA that had its activation policy set to NO_IMPLICIT_ACTIVATION, the servant_to_reference() operation could not create any new references. In cases like this, the operation can be used to find out which CORBA object an active servant is currently incarnating. We have to distinguish between two possible situations here:

- The servant_to_reference operation can be invoked from within an operation executing in the specified servant. Within the context of an operation execution, the POA knows about the association between the active servant and the object it is incarnating because otherwise the operation execution could not have started in the first place. Thus, it does not matter whether the servant is incarnating multiple objects or whether the association between the servant and the object is kept in the Active Object Map, that is, whether the POA has the RETAIN and UNIQUE_ID policies set. At any one instant, the servant can be executing this code on behalf of only a single CORBA object.
- If the servant_to_reference operation is invoked for another servant than the one that is currently executing an operation, or not from an

operation execution context at all, then the POA in question must have both the RETAIN and UNIQUE_ID policies set. Otherwise, it would not be able to determine which CORBA object the servant in question is incarnating, if any.

The Java mapping prescribes that the generated POA skeleton code contain a shortcut for invoking servant_to_reference: the method `_this()`. If `_this()` is used to implicitly activate the servant, the POA responsible for realizing this behavior is determined by calling `_default_POA()`, which will return the ORB's root POA. It is possible to override this method, however, so the servant code can set up any POA configuration that is required and make sure it is used for implicit activation of this code. If `_this()` is called to find out which object a servant is incarnating, the POA responsible for the execution context is determined.

After a server program has initialized its ORB, obtained a reference to the root POA, and activated its objects, the server's main thread of control usually hands over to the ORB to let it wait for incoming requests and do the request processing. This is done by calling the ORB's `run()` method.

IDL operation void run(); // ORB interface

Java method `void run();`

A simple example server might thus look like this:

```
public class Server {

    public static void main( String[] args ) {

        // initialize the ORB
        org.omg.CORBA.ORB orb = org.omg.CORBA.ORB.init(args, null);
        try {
            // get the root POA
            org.omg.PortableServer.POA poa =
                org.omg.PortableServer.POAHelper.narrow(
                  orb.resolve_initial_references("RootPOA"));

            // activate the POA
            poa.the_POAManager().activate();

            // implicitly activate an object
            org.omg.CORBA.Object o =
                poa.servant_to_reference( new myImpl() );

            // wait for requests
            orb.run();
        } catch ( Exception e ) {
            e.printStackTrace();
```

```
            }
        }
    }
```

Objects can be deactivated explicitly by calling `deactivate_object()` if the POA has the RETAIN policy. Objects are deactivated implicitly in a number of ways: by destroying their POA with the POA's `destroy()` operation, by deactivating their POA through its POAManager's `deactivate()` operation, or by shutting down the ORB. In the simplest possible case, where objects are transient and no clean-up or explicit resource freeing is necessary, the object might simply disappear together with its server process. Any references held by clients are no longer usable at this stage. You will see examples of deactivating objects and, for example, saving object state to persistent storage, in Chapter 10, "Practical POA Programming." We will briefly explain how the ORB can be shut down so that resources can be reclaimed. The ORB interface provides two related operations for this task:

IDL operation
```
void shutdown (in boolean wait_for_completion); // ORB
void destroy();
```

Java method
```
void shutdown(boolean wait_for_
    completion);
    void destroy();
```

Calling `shutdown()` on an ORB pseudo-object causes the ORB to stop processing requests and to prepare for destruction. It also destroys all its object adapters. The Boolean parameter indicates whether this operation is to return immediately or only when the shutdown is complete. Destroying the ORB's root POA and all its descendent POAs results in the deactivation and etherealization of all objects. After the ORB is shut down, the only methods that may be called are object reference management operations.

The `destroy()` method releases all resources of an ORB. If the ORB has not shut down when `destroy()` is called, this method will start the shutdown.

## 6.3.3 Child POAs

Whenever you want to create objects that require policies other than those provided by the root POA, a new POA with the desired combination of policies must be created. The only factory for a POA is another POA, the only exception being the root POA, which is retrieved from the ORB. Consequently, all POAs are direct or indirect children of the root POA. To create a new POA with a different set of policies, the `create_POA()` operation is used.

IDL operation POA create_POA(
in string adapter_name,
in POAManager a_manager,
in CORBA::PolicyList policies);

Java method `org.omg.PortableServer.POA create_POA(`
`java.lang.String adapter_name,`
`org.omg.PortableServer.POAManager`
`a_POAManager,`
`org.omg.CORBA.Policy[] policies)`

The create_POA() operation requires a name argument that is not already used by another child of the current POA. If the a_manager argument is null, a new manager will be created for the child POA. The policies passed as the third argument to this call express differences from the standard set of policies. If no policies are passed, these standard policies are applied to the new POA. Policies are not inherited from the parent POA. The standard policies are: TRANSIENT lifetime, SYSTEM_ID ID assignment, NO_IMPLICIT_ACTIVATION activation, RETAIN servant retention, USE_ACTIVE_OBJECT_MAP_ONLY request processing, UNIQUE_ID ID uniqueness, and ORB_CTRL_MODEL threading. Note that the root POA has all these policies with one exception: The root POA allows IMPLICIT_ACTIVATION. To create a POA with persistent object lifetime and user-defined object IDs that uses a servant manager and its parent POA's POAManager, the following code would be used:

```
org.omg.CORBA.Policy [] policies = new org.omg.CORBA.Policy[3];

policies[0] = rootPOA.create_id_assignment_policy(
    IdAssignmentPolicyValue.USER_ID );

policies[1] = rootPOA.create_lifespan_policy(
    LifespanPolicyValue.PERSISTENT );

policies[2] = rootPOA.create_request_processing_policy(
    RequestProcessingPolicyValue.USE_SERVANT_MANAGER );

POA myPOA = rootPOA.create_POA("ChildPOA",
                               rootPOA.the_POAManager(),
                               policies );
```

This policy configuration is typically used when object state is kept persistent in files or a database and when user-defined code to access this state is used in the form of a servant manager. State for individual objects would be looked up using the user-defined object ID, which could be used as a file name or primary database key. We will present a more complete application example using these policies in Chapter 10.

## 6.4 TypeCode Interface

TypeCodes can represent type information about any IDL type. Many IDL data types are structured and contain other types within them. These are represented as nested TypeCodes. In this section we look at how TypeCodes are identified and compared (section 6.4.1), navigated to discover their component parts (section 6.4.2), and created without use of IDL stub code (section 6.4.3). The TypeCode pseudo-interface is mapped to an abstract Java class in the package `org.omg.CORBA`.

IDL interface pseudo interface CORBA::TypeCode { ... };

Java interface `public abstract class TypeCode {...}`

The following sections explain the mapping of the operations in the TypeCode interface to Java methods in the corresponding class. The use of TypeCode is illustrated by an example in Chapter 9 in the context of the type Any and by the example Trader code in Chapter 7, "Discovering Services."

### 6.4.1 Types Used by TypeCodes

The CORBA module defines a pseudo-IDL definition of an enum, TCKind. This enum defines constants to distinguish between various "kinds" of TypeCodes. Different operations are allowed on different kinds of TypeCodes.

IDL type enum TCKind {tk_null, tk_void, tk_short, tk_long,....}; // PIDL

Java class
```
public final class TCKind {
    public static final int _tk_null = 0;
    public static final
    TCKind tk_null = new TCKind(_tk_null);
        ...
    }
```

This is the same as the mapping for any other IDL enumeration, except that no holder and helper classes are defined, as this type will never be used in making remote invocations. The complete definition of the `TCKind` class follows:

```
package org.omg.CORBA;
public final class TCKind
   implements org.omg.CORBA.portable.IDLEntity {
   private int value = -1;
   public static final int _tk_null = 0;
   public static final TCKind tk_null = new TCKind(_tk_null);
   public static final int _tk_void = 1;
   public static final TCKind tk_void = new TCKind(_tk_void);
   public static final int _tk_short = 2;
   public static final TCKind tk_short = new TCKind(_tk_short);
   public static final int _tk_long = 3;
   public static final TCKind tk_long = new TCKind(_tk_long);
   public static final int _tk_ushort = 4;
   public static final TCKind tk_ushort = new TCKind(_tk_ushort);
   public static final int _tk_ulong = 5;
   public static final TCKind tk_ulong = new TCKind(_tk_ulong);
   public static final int _tk_float = 6;
   public static final TCKind tk_float = new TCKind(_tk_float);
   public static final int _tk_double = 7;
   public static final TCKind tk_double = new TCKind(_tk_double);
   public static final int _tk_boolean = 8;
   public static final TCKind tk_boolean = new TCKind(_tk_boolean);
   public static final int _tk_char = 9;
   public static final TCKind tk_char = new TCKind(_tk_char);
   public static final int _tk_octet = 10;
   public static final TCKind tk_octet = new TCKind(_tk_octet);
   public static final int _tk_any = 11;
   public static final TCKind tk_any = new TCKind(_tk_any);
   public static final int _tk_TypeCode = 12;
   public static final TCKind tk_TypeCode = new TCKind(_tk_TypeCode);
   public static final int _tk_Principal = 13;
   public static final TCKind tk_Principal = new TCKind(_tk_Principal);
   public static final int _tk_objref = 14;
   public static final TCKind tk_objref = new TCKind(_tk_objref);
   public static final int _tk_struct = 15;
   public static final TCKind tk_struct = new TCKind(_tk_struct);
   public static final int _tk_union = 16;
   public static final TCKind tk_union = new TCKind(_tk_union);
   public static final int _tk_enum = 17;
   public static final TCKind tk_enum = new TCKind(_tk_enum);
   public static final int _tk_string = 18;
   public static final TCKind tk_string = new TCKind(_tk_string);
   public static final int _tk_sequence = 19;
   public static final TCKind tk_sequence = new TCKind(_tk_sequence);
   public static final int _tk_array = 20;
   public static final TCKind tk_array = new TCKind(_tk_array);
   public static final int _tk_alias = 21;
   public static final TCKind tk_alias = new TCKind(_tk_alias);
   public static final int _tk_except = 22;
   public static final TCKind tk_except = new TCKind(_tk_except);
```

```
    public static final int _tk_longlong = 23;
    public static final TCKind tk_longlong = new TCKind(_tk_longlong);
    public static final int _tk_ulonglong = 24;
    public static final TCKind tk_ulonglong = new TCKind(_tk_ulonglong);
    public static final int _tk_longdouble = 25;
    public static final TCKind tk_longdouble = new TCKind(_tk_longdouble);
    public static final int _tk_wchar = 26;
    public static final TCKind tk_wchar = new TCKind(_tk_wchar);
    public static final int _tk_wstring = 27;
    public static final TCKind tk_wstring = new TCKind(_tk_wstring);
    public static final int _tk_fixed = 28;
    public static final TCKind tk_fixed = new TCKind(_tk_fixed);
    public static final int _tk_value = 29;
    public static final TCKind tk_value = new TCKind(_tk_value);
    public static final int _tk_value_box = 30;
    public static final TCKind tk_value_box = new TCKind(_tk_value_box);
    public static final int _tk_native = 31;
    public static final TCKind tk_native = new TCKind(_tk_native);
    public static final int _tk_abstract_interface = 32;
    public static final TCKind tk_abstract_interface =
       new TCKind(_tk_abstract_interface);

    public int value() {
        throw new org.omg.CORBA.NO_IMPLEMENT();
    }
    public static TCKind from_int(int value){
       switch (value) {
          case // ...
          default: throw new org.omg.CORBA.BAD_PARAM();
       }
    }
    protected TCKind(int i){
       throw new org.omg.CORBA.NO_IMPLEMENT();
    }
}
```

Two exceptions defined in the CORBA specification may be raised when a query on a TypeCode is invalid. These are:

```
exception Bounds {};
exception BadKind {};
```

Bounds is usually raised when an indexed query parameter exceeds the length of the list being queried, for example, when asking for the fourth member of a struct with only two members. BadKind is raised when an inappropriate query is made for the kind of TypeCode, for example, asking for the discriminator type of a string. They are mapped in the usual way to exceptions in the package `org.omg.CORBA.TypeCodePackage`.

## 6.4.2 Identifying and Comparing TypeCodes

The operation equal() returns TRUE only if the sets of legal operations on the TypeCode and its argument `tc` are equal and all operations return identical results. Otherwise, it returns FALSE.

IDL operation boolean equal(in TypeCode tc);

Java method `public abstract boolean equal(TypeCode tc);`

The operation `equivalent()` is a less strict check and certifies equivalence also in the presence of type aliases. A detailed explanation of these two operations was given in Chapter 2.

IDL operation boolean equivalent(in TypeCode tc);

Java method
```
public abstract boolean equivalent
         (TypeCode tc);
```

The operation get_compact_typecode() returns a representation of a TypeCode with all optional names and member names stripped off, but it leaves RepositoryIds and type aliases untouched.

IDL operation TypeCode get_compact_typecode();

Java method
```
public abstract TypeCode get_compact_type
         code();
```

The operation kind() returns an enum of type `TCKind`, indicating the kind of TypeCode—for example, `tk_union` when it defines a union type, or `tk_alias` when it defines a typedef.

IDL operation TCKind kind();

Java method `public abstract TCKind kind();`

The operation id() returns a RepositoryId (which is a string) for a type in the Interface Repository (see Chapter 2).

IDL operation RepositoryId id() raises (BadKind);

Java method
```
public abstract String id()
         throws BadKind;
```

The operation name() returns the unscoped name of the type as specified in IDL. This is valid only for `tk_objref`, `tk_struct`, `tk_union`, `tk_enum`, `tk_alias`, `tk_except`, `tk_value`, `tk_value_box`, `tk_native`, and `tk_abstract_interface`.

IDL operation Identifier name() raises (BadKind);

Java method
```
public abstract String name()
    throws BadKind;
```

## 6.4.3 Navigating TypeCodes

Once the TCKind of a TypeCode is identified, we can determine what other sorts of information a TypeCode will contain. For example, if the kind is `tk_struct`, we can expect it to have a list of named members, each of which will have a name and a TypeCode of its own. If the kind is `tk_string`, we can expect to find out only what its bound is or if it is an unbounded string.

### *6.4.3.1 Methods for Structured Types*

The operation member_count() returns the number of members in the type description. It is valid for only the following TypeCode kinds: `tk_struct`, `tk_union`, `tk_enum`, `tk_value`, and `tk_except`.

IDL operation unsigned long member_count()
raises (BadKind);

Java method
```
public abstract int member_count()
    throws BadKind;
```

The operation member_name() returns the name of the indexed member. It is valid for the same set of TypeCode kinds as the member_name() operation:

IDL operation Identifier member_name( in unsigned long index )
raises (BadKind, Bounds);

Java method
```
public abstract String member_name(
    int index)
    throws BadKind, Bounds;
```

The operation member_type() returns the type of the indexed member. It is valid only for the following TypeCode kinds: `tk_struct`, `tk_value`, `tk_union`, and `tk_except`.

IDL operation TypeCode member_type( in unsigned long index )
raises (BadKind, Bounds);

Java method
```
public abstract TypeCode member_type(
    int index)
    throws BadKind, Bounds;
```

### 6.4.3.2 Methods for Unions

The following three operations are for discovering more information about union definitions. They will raise the BadKind exception if called on a TypeCode that is not of kind `tk_union`.

The operation member_label() returns the label value of a case statement for the member at the index provided.

IDL operation any member_label( in unsigned long index )
raises (BadKind, Bounds);

Java method
```
public abstract Any member_label(int index)
    throws BadKind, Bounds;
```

The operation discriminator_type() returns the type of the union discriminator.

IDL operation TypeCode discriminator_type()
raises (BadKind);

Java method
```
public abstract TypeCode discriminator_type()
    throws BadKind;
```

The operation default_index() returns the member index of the default case of the union, if one is declared. Otherwise, it returns -1.

IDL operation long default_index()
raises (BadKind);

Java method
```
public abstract int default_index()
    throws BadKind
```

### 6.4.3.3 Methods for Template Types

The operation length() returns the number of elements contained by the type. It returns zero for unbounded strings and sequences. It is valid only for the following TypeCode kinds: `tk_string`, `tk_sequence`, and `tk_array`.

IDL operation unsigned long length()
raises (BadKind);

Java method
```
public abstract int length()
    throws BadKind
```

The operation content_type() returns the base type of the template types (`tk_sequence`, `tk_array`) or the aliased type (`tk_alias`). It is also applicable to value box types (`tk_value_box`).

IDL operation
```
TypeCode content_type()
    raises (BadKind);
```

Java method
```
public abstract TypeCode content_type ()
    throws BadKind
```

#### 6.4.3.4 Methods for Fixed Point Types

The methods in this subsection are valid only for the TypeCode `tk_fixed`.

The operation fixed_digits() returns the number of decimal digits for this type.

IDL operation
```
unsigned short fixed_digits()
    raises (BadKind);
```

Java method
```
public abstract short fixed_digits()
    throws BadKind;
```

The operation fixed_scale() returns the scale used by this fixed point type.

IDL operation
```
short fixed_scale()
    raises (BadKind);
```

Java method
```
public abstract short fixed_scale()
    throws BadKind;
```

#### 6.4.3.5 Methods for Valuetypes

The following operations are valid only for the TypeCode kind tk_value. The operation member_visibility() returns the visibility for a given valuetype member, which can be either private or public.

IDL operation
```
typedef short Visibility;
    const Visibility PRIVATE_MEMBER = 0;
    const Visibility PUBLIC_MEMBER = 1;
    Visibility member_visibility(in unsigned long index)
    raises (BadKind, Bounds);
```

Java method
```
public abstract short member_visibility
    (int index)
    throws BadKind, Bounds;
```

The operation type_modifier() returns a value indicating whether the valuetype is abstract, uses custom marshaling, or is truncatable.

IDL operation
```
typedef short ValueModifier;
    const ValueModifier VM_NONE = 0;
```

```
const ValueModifier VM_CUSTOM = 1;
const ValueModifier VM_ABSTRACT = 2;
const ValueModifier VM_TRUNCATABLE = 3;
ValueModifier type_modifier()
raises (BadKind);
```

Java method

```
public abstract short type_modifier()
  throws BadKind;
```

The operation concrete_base_type(), finally, returns the TypeCode of this valuetype's concrete base type if one exists. Otherwise, a nil TypeCode reference is returned.

IDL operation

```
TypeCode concrete_base_type()
  raises (BadKind);
```

Java method

```
public abstract TypeCode
  concrete_base_type()
  throws BadKind;
```

## 6.4.4 Creating TypeCodes

TypeCodes are created using operations in the CORBA::ORB interface. All the TypeCode creation methods follow a similar pattern. The result of each method is the newly created TypeCode object. These methods must be recursively applied for TypeCodes of nested types.

### *6.4.4.1 Structured Types, Aliases, Valuetypes, and Interfaces*

The methods to create TypeCodes for structured types, that is, structs, unions, enums, exceptions, and those for creating TypeCodes for aliases, valuetypes, and interfaces have the same first two parameters:

- The first parameter is a RepositoryId specifying the unique identifier used in the Interface Repository to identify the type in its IDL context. These are usually of the form `"IDL:modulename/interface-name/typename:1.0"`; see Chapter 2 for details about RepositoryIds.
- The second parameter is the unscoped type name of the type, which corresponds to the last component of an IDL RepositoryId before the version number.

Further parameters provide specific type information depending on the kind of TypeCode.

The method `create_struct_tc()` creates a TypeCode describing an IDL struct. The parameter `members` provides a sequence of name/type/type definition tuples defining the members of the struct.

```
package org.omg.CORBA;

public final class StructMember
    implements org.omg.CORBA.portable.IDLEntity {

    public java.lang.String name;
    public org.omg.CORBA.TypeCode type;
    public org.omg.CORBA.IDLType type_def;
}

// ORB interface
public abstract TypeCode create_struct_tc(
    String id,
    String name,
    StructMember members[] );
```

The method `create_union_tc()` creates a TypeCode describing an IDL union. The parameter `discriminator_type` gives the type of the discriminator, that is, the type used in the switch statement. The parameter `members` provides a sequence of tuples defining the members of the union.

```
package org.omg.CORBA;

public final class UnionMember
    implements org.omg.CORBA.portable.IDLEntity {

    public java.lang.String name;
    public org.omg.CORBA.Any label;
    public org.omg.CORBA.TypeCode type;
    public org.omg.CORBA.IDLType type_def;
}

// ORB interface
public abstract TypeCode create_union_tc(
    String id,
    String name,
    TypeCode discriminator_type,
    UnionMember members[] );
```

The method `create_enum_tc()` creates a TypeCode describing an IDL enum. The parameter `members` provides an array of strings defining the members of the enum.

```
public abstract TypeCode create_enum_tc(
    String id,
```

```
    String name,
    String members[] );
```

The method `create_alias_tc()` creates a TypeCode describing an IDL typedef alias. The parameter `original_type` is the TypeCode for the aliased type.

```
public abstract TypeCode create_alias_tc(
    String id,
    String name,
    TypeCode original_type);
```

The method `create_exception_tc()` creates a TypeCode describing an IDL exception. The parameter `members` provides a sequence of name/type pairs defining the members of the exception. Note that exceptions are created using the same parameters as structs, but they have a different TCKind.

```
public abstract TypeCode create_exception_tc(
   String id,
   String name,
   StructMember[] members]);
```

The method `create_interface_tc()` creates a TypeCode describing an IDL interface.

```
public abstract TypeCode create_interface_tc(
   String id,
   String name);
```

The method `create_value_tc()` creates a TypeCode describing an IDL valuetype. The parameter `type_modifier` is a constant indicating whether the type is abstract, truncatable, or uses custom marshaling. The parameter `concrete_base` is the TypeCode for the new type's concrete base type or nil if it has no base type. The `members` parameter provides a sequence of structs describing the members of the valuetype. These member descriptions are instances of the mapped Java class `ValueMember`, which is defined as follows:

```
package org.omg.CORBA;
public final class ValueMember
    implements org.omg.CORBA.portable.IDLEntity {

    public java.lang.String name;
    public java.lang.String id;
    public java.lang.String defined_in;
    public java.lang.String version;
    public org.omg.CORBA.TypeCode type;
```

```
    public org.omg.CORBA.IDLType type_def;
    public short access;
}
```

The id and defined_in members of this class are RepositoryIds for the type of the member and the enclosing valuetype. The access member holds a constant that describes whether the valuetype member is public or protected.

```
// ORB interface
public TypeCode create_value_tc(
    String id,
    String name,
    short type_modifier,
    TypeCode concrete_base,
    ValueMember[] members ) {...}
```

The method create_value_box_tc() creates a TypeCode describing an IDL value box type. The boxed_type parameter provides the TypeCode of the boxed type.

```
public TypeCode create_value_box_tc(
    String id,
    String name,
    TypeCode boxed_type) {...}
```

The method create_native_tc creates a TypeCode for a native type. It has no additional parameters.

```
public TypeCode create_native_tc(
    String id,
    String name) {...}
```

The method create_abstract_interface_tc creates a TypeCode for an abstract IDL interface.

```
public TypeCode create_abstract_interface_tc(
    String id,
    String name) {...}
```

### 6.4.4.2 Template Types

The methods to create TypeCodes for template types, that is, strings, sequences, and arrays, have the same first parameter, length. This parameter specifies the length of bounded types. A zero value specifies an unbounded type.

The method `create_string_tc()` creates a TypeCode describing an IDL string.

```
public abstract TypeCode create_string_tc( int length );
```

The method `create_wstring_tc()` creates a TypeCode describing an IDL wstring.

```
public abstract TypeCode create_wstring_tc( int length );
```

The method `create_sequence_tc()` creates a TypeCode describing an IDL sequence. The parameter `element_type` is the type of the elements contained by the sequence.

```
public abstract TypeCode create_sequence_tc(
    int length,
    TypeCode element_type );
```

The method `create_array_tc()` creates a TypeCode describing an IDL array. The parameter `element_type` determines the type of the elements contained in the array.

```
public abstract TypeCode create_array_tc(
    int length,
    TypeCode element_type );
```

TypeCodes for multidimensional arrays can be created by first creating an array TypeCodes for the right-most array dimension and then passing this TypeCode in the `element_type` argument of the `create_array_tc()` method for the next dimension of the array.

### 6.4.4.3 Types Containing Recursion

The method `create_recursive_tc()` creates a TypeCode that serves as a placeholder when constructing TypeCodes that contain recursion. For example,

```
struct binary_tree {
    element short;
    branch sequence <binary_tree, 2>;
};
```

which defines a binary tree of short values.

```
public TypeCode create_recursive_tc(String id) {...}
```

The parameter `id` is the RepositoryId of the type that is represented by the placeholder. In our example the ID would be `"IDL:binary_tree:1.0"`.

## 6.5 Types Used for Dynamic Invocations

A number of common types are used to represent parameters and return values in the DII and DSI. In this section we introduce the following:

- Flags—which indicate the direction of operation parameters (section 6.5.1)
- NamedValues—used to describe parameters and results of operations (section 6.5.2)
- NamedValue Lists—used to describe the parameter list of an operation (section 6.5.3)
- Environment—which is used to check whether an invocation returned successfully or raised an exception (section 6.5.4)

### 6.5.1 Flags

When constructing lists of arguments for operation invocations the programmer must specify whether the argument will be in, out, or inout. Pseudo-IDL constants are defined for this purpose:

```
typedef unsigned long Flags;
const Flags ARG_IN = 1;
const Flags ARG_OUT = 2;
const Flags ARG_INOUT = 3;
```

These are mapped in the same way as ordinary IDL constants, and they become interfaces in the package `org.omg.CORBA`.

```
public interface ARG_IN {
   public static final int value = 1;
}
public interface ARG_OUT {
   public static final int value = 2;
}
public interface ARG_INOUT {
   public static final int value = 3;
}
```

## 6.5.2 NamedValues

A NamedValue was originally specified in CORBA 2.0 as a struct, but its definition has changed to a more appropriate pseudo-interface:

```
typedef string identifier;
pseudo interface NamedValue {
    readonly attribute identifier name;
    readonly attribute any value;
    readonly attribute Flags flags;
};
```

The attribute name determines the name of a parameter. The attribute value carries the type and value of a parameter, encapsulated in an Any. The flags attribute determines if a parameter is in, inout, or out. The type Named Value is mapped as follows:

```
public abstract class NamedValue {
    public abstract String name();
    public abstract Any value();
    public abstract int flags();
}
```

As you can see, this class allows access only to the contents of a NamedValue that is already initialized. NamedValues must be created using the following method on the `ORB` object:

```
NamedValue create_named_value (String name,
                               Any value,
                               int flags);
```

The value part of the NamedValue can be modified by using the `value()` method to obtain a reference to its Any component, which supports methods for updating its contents. In the same way, the name part of the NamedValue can be modified using the `String` object returned by the `name()` method.

## 6.5.3 NamedValue Lists

The interface NVList represents a list of NamedValues. It was defined in pseudo-IDL in the CORBA 2.0 specification, but its definition has also been updated to a pseudo-interface for the Java mapping:

```
pseudo interface NVList{
    readonly attribute unsigned long count;
```

```
    NamedValue add(in Flags flags);
    NamedValue add_item(in identifier item_name, in Flags flags);
    NamedValue add_value(in identifier item_name,
                         in any val,
                         in Flags flags);
    NamedValue item( in unsigned long index ) raises (CORBA::Bounds);
    void remove( in unsigned long index ) raises (CORBA::Bounds);
};
```

This interface is mapped to the Java class `public abstract class NVList`. These operations and their mappings to methods in the `NVList` class are explained in the following section.

### 6.5.3.1 Adding Elements to NVLists

Three operations add new NamedValues to the NVList. Each of them initializes an additional part of the NamedValue.

The add() operation creates a new NamedValue that contains only a flag and adds it to the list.

IDL operation NamedValue add(in Flags flags);

Java method `public abstract void add(int flags);`

The name and value of the `NamedValue` created can be added later by obtaining a reference to the `NamedValue` object using the `item()` method.

The operation add_item() is used to create a new NamedValue that has a name and a flag and to add it to the list. This is most suitable for adding out parameters, which have the flag CORBA::ARG_OUT and a parameter name, but no initial value. A value can be added as explained in section 6.5.2.

IDL operation NamedValue add_item(in identifier item_name,
in Flags flags);

Java method

```
public abstract void add_item(
        String item_name,
        int flags
        );
```

The operation add_value() creates a fully initialized NamedValue and adds it to the list. This is usually used to add in or inout parameters, which have the flag CORBA::ARG_IN or CORBA::ARG_INOUT, as well as a name for the parameter and a value for the argument being supplied by the caller.

IDL operation NamedValue add_value( in identifier item_name,
in any val,
in Flags flags );

Java method
```
public abstract void add_value(
      String item_name,
      Any val,
      int flags
);
```

### 6.5.3.2 List Management

The NVList pseudo-interface provides the operation count(), which returns the total number of items in the list. This is mapped to an accessor method of the same name in Java.

IDL attribute readonly attribute unsigned long count;

Java method `public abstract int count();`

The item() operation returns the indexed element from the list. It will raise a Bounds exception if the index is larger than the list length. In Java the `Bounds` exception is defined in the `CORBA` package as well as in `TypeCodePackage`.

IDL operation NamedValue item(in unsigned long index)
raises (CORBA::Bounds);

Java method
```
public abstract NamedValue item(int index)
   throws org.omg.CORBA.Bounds;
```

The NamedValue returned from the `item()` method is owned by the NVList, and modifications to its name or value will update the list.

The remove() operation removes the indexed element from the list. It also raises Bounds if the index is greater than the list length.

IDL operation void remove(in unsigned long index)
raises (CORBA::Bounds);

Java method
```
public abstract void remove(int index)
   throws org.omg.CORBA.Bounds;
```

## 6.5.4 Environment

The Environment pseudo-object stores the exceptions that may be raised during an invocation. It is not represented in IDL because exceptions cannot be used as attributes or operation parameters. The CORBA 2.0 specification defines C and C++ programming language APIs to the environment, and the IDL/Java Mapping specification defines the following mapping:

```
package org.omg.CORBA;
public abstract class Environment {
    void exception(java.lang.Exception except);
    java.lang.Exception exception();
    void clear();
}
```

The set method `exception()` allows an exception to be raised by a server. The caller provides an argument of a derived type of `java.lang.Exception`, which is the base class of all CORBA exceptions in Java. The accessor method of the same name allows this exception to be retrieved by the client once the call is completed. We will see how this class is used in sections 6.6 and 6.7.

## 6.5.5 Context Interface

A context object contains a list of properties, which are pairs of names and values. Contexts are rarely used and are treated here for completeness only. CORBA restricts values to type string. The intended role of context objects is similar to that of environment variables in various operating systems, which can determine a user's or an application's preferences. They could be defined for a system, for a user, or for an application. Context objects can be manipulated by concatenating their property lists or by arranging them into context trees.

Operations can be declared with a context by adding a context clause after the raises expression. A context is made available to the server by an additional argument to the stub and skeleton interfaces. When an operation with a context is invoked through either the stub or the DII, the ORB will insert the values of the properties of the specified context.

### *6.5.5.1 Creating a Context Object*

Contexts are organized into trees. Each context has an internal reference to its parent context. The root context is the global default context. The pseudo-interface Context is mapped to a Java abstract class in the package `org.omg.CORBA`.

| | |
|---|---|
| IDL interface | pseudo interface Context; |
| Java class | `public abstract class Context {...}` |

The ORB pseudo-interface provides the operation get_default_context() to obtain the root context. The equivalent method is provided by the Java class `org.omg.CORBA.ORB`.

IDL operation Context get_default_context();

Java method
```
public abstract Context get_default_
  context();
```

### 6.5.5.2 Manipulating a Context Object

The pseudo-interface Context provides operations to add values to a context object. The operation set_one_value() sets the value of a named property.

IDL operation
```
void set_one_value(
    in Identifier propname,
    in any propvalue
    );
```

Java method
```
public abstract void set_one_value (
  String propname,
  Any propvalue
  );
```

The value is supplied as an Any rather than a string, although the value contained must be a string. This is for compatibility with NamedValues, which have values of type Any.

The operation set_values() sets the values of those properties named in the values parameter.

IDL operation void set_values(in NVList values );

Java method
```
public abstract void set_values(
  NVList values);
```

Note that the flags of the items of the `NVList` must be 0 and that the TypeCode field of the values of the items must represent a string. Values can be read with the operation get_values().

IDL operation
```
NVList get_values(
    in Identifier start_scope,
    in Flags op_flags,
    in Identifier pattern
    );
```

Java method
```
NVList get_values (
  String start_scope,
```

```
        int op_flags,
        String pattern
    );
```

The pattern parameter specifies the name of the returned properties. A string can specify multiple property names by using a naming convention with a wildcard "*" similar to the notations used in various operating system shells. The parameter start_scope determines the scope of this query within the context hierarchy. The naming of scopes is implementation dependent. The op_flags parameter can have the value CORBA::CTX_RESTRICT_SCOPE, which limits the scope to the specified start_scope. A zero flag uses the whole context tree.

The operation delete_values() deletes the named property from the context object. If `propname` contains a wildcard then multiple properties may be deleted.

IDL operation void delete_values( in Identifier propname );

Java method
```
public abstract void delete_values
    (String propname);
```

There is a read-only attribute that allows the name of the current Context to be discovered. The attribute is mapped to an accessor method in Java.

IDL attribute readonly attribute Identifier context_name;

Java method `public abstract String context_name();`

The name of a context is determined when it is created, as we will see in the following section.

#### 6.5.5.3 Manipulating the Context Object Tree

There are additional operations on the context object to manipulate the context tree. The operation create_child() creates a new context object that is a child of the object on which the operation is invoked.

IDL operation Context create_child( in Identifier child_ctx_name);

Java method
```
public abstract Context
    create_child(String child_ctx_name);
```

The tree may be navigated to its root using the attribute parent.

IDL attribute readonly attribute Context parent;

Java method `public abstract Context parent();`

The `parent()` method returns `null` if the context is the global default context.

## 6.6 Dynamic Invocation Interface

The Dynamic Invocation Interface (DII) enables clients to invoke operations on objects without compile-time knowledge of their IDL type, that is, without the stub code generated by the IDL compiler. A client creates a *Request*, which is the dynamic equivalent to an operation. A Request contains an object reference, an operation name, and type information and values of the arguments that are supplied by the client. Once initialized with all these parameters a Request can be invoked, which has the same semantics as invoking the operation using stub code.

Request is a pseudo-IDL interface that provides the operations to initialize an operation invocation request and then dynamically invoke an operation on an object. Requests are created by the ORB.

### 6.6.1 Creating a Request

In Java a `Request` object is created by calling methods on object references (Java objects of type `org.omg.CORBA.Object`). The IDL pseudo-operation shown next, however, is found in the ORB interface.

IDL operation

```
Status create_request( // in interface ORB
    in Context ctx,
    in Identifier operation,
    in NVList arg_list,
    inout NamedValue result,
    out Request request,
    in Flags req_flags
    );
```

Java methods

```
Request _create_request(
    Context ctx,
    String operation,
    NVList arg_list,
    NamedValue result
    );

    Request _create_request(
    Context ctx,
```

```
                         String operation,
                         NVList arg_list,
                         NamedValue result,
                         ExceptionList exclist,
                         ContextList ctxlist
                    );
```

The two methods are identical except that the second version adds some extra type information, as explained by the following parameter descriptions. The flags parameter to the IDL operation is used for memory management for some programming languages, and it is not mapped in Java.

- `ctx`—specifies the execution context of the Request (see section 6.5.5)
- `operation`—determines the name of the operation to be invoked
- `arg_list`—provides the arguments to that operation
- `result`—a NamedValue with its value initialized to contain only the type expected as the result from the operation
- `exclist`—a list of TypeCodes that indicates the user exceptions that are declared in the operation's raises clause
- `ctxlist`—a list of strings that corresponds to the names in the context clause of an operation declaration

The newly created `Request` object is returned as the result of the Java method. There is an additional operation to create partially initialized `Request` objects:

```
Request _request (String operation)
    throws SystemException
```

All the parameters provided to `_create_request()` must be set using the resulting object's interface, as described later.

## 6.6.2 Request Interface

The pseudo-IDL for Request was originally defined in the CORBA 2.0 specification. It has also been redefined in the IDL/Java Mapping. The first part of the interface definition, which defines read-only attributes (and one read/write attribute) to access the contents of the Request, is as follows:

```
pseudo interface Request {
    readonly attribute Object target;
```

```
        readonly attribute Identifier operation;
        readonly attribute NVList arguments;
        readonly attribute NamedValue result;
        readonly attribute Environment env;
        readonly attribute ExceptionList exceptions;
        readonly attribute ContextList contexts;
        attribute Context ctx;
        // operations follow
        ...
};
```

The target attribute is the object reference from which the Request was obtained. The operation, result, arguments, and ctx attributes are the same as the arguments supplied to the first version of the `_create_request()` method defined previously. The exceptions and contexts attributes are the same as the additional arguments supplied to the second version of the `_create_request()` method. These additional attributes can be used to check that the operation is of the type expected because the exceptions and context strings will be the same as in the Interface Repository.

The Request pseudo-interface is mapped to the Java abstract class `org.omg.CORBA.Request.` The attributes map according to the standard language mapping, into equivalent accessor methods (and a set method for ctx):

```
abstract public class Request {
    public abstract Object target();
    public abstract String operation();
    public abstract NVList arguments();
    public abstract NamedValue result();
    public abstract Environment env();
    public abstract ExceptionList exceptions();
    public abstract ContextList contexts();
    public abstract Context ctx();
    public abstract void ctx(Context c);
    ...
}
```

### 6.6.2.1 Initializing a Request

Operations are defined for adding arguments when a Request has not been initialized with an argument list, for example, when it was created with the `_request()` method. The following operations each create a new NamedValue in the Request's arguments NVList. Each operation sets the appropriate flag in the NamedValue, and some also set the name.

```
any add_in_arg();
any add_named_in_arg(in string name);
any add_inout_arg();
any add_named_inout_arg(in string name);
any add_out_arg();
any add_named_out_arg(in string name);
```

In Java these operations are mapped to equivalent methods:

```
public abstract Any add_in_arg();
public abstract Any add_named_in_arg(String name);
public abstract Any add_inout_arg();
public abstract Any add_named_inout_arg(String name);
public abstract Any add_out_arg();
public abstract Any add_named_out_arg(String name);
```

If a value is required in an argument, as in the case of in and inout parameters, you can then set the value using the interface to the returned Any. This Any is owned by the NamedValue created by the operation.

Unless the Request was fully initialized by creating it with `create_request()`, one further initialization is required to set up a Request for invocation: The return type must be set. This is done with the following operation/method:

| | |
|---|---|
| IDL operation | void set_return_type(in TypeCode tc); |
| Java method | `public abstract void set_return_type( TypeCode tc);` |

### 6.6.2.2 Invoking a Request Synchronously

When the Request is correctly initialized it can be invoked by calling several different operations. The simplest of these is the invoke() operation/method:

| | |
|---|---|
| IDL operation | void invoke(); |
| Java method | `public abstract void invoke();` |

The `invoke()` method is a blocking synchronous call, and when it returns the invocation has completed. The Environment attribute env must then be checked for its status because the operation may have raised an exception. If an exception has been raised it can be accessed by calling the `exception()` accessor method on the Environment returned from the `env()` method of the Request. If the result is null, then the operation has completed successfully.

If the operation has returned successfully, its result is set in the result attribute of the Request, and the inout and out parameters have been modified in the Request's arguments attribute by the object implementation. These are accessed via the `result()` and `arguments()` methods, respectively.

#### 6.6.2.3 Invoking a Request Asynchronously

The operation send_deferred() allows an asynchronous invocation to be made. The semantics are that the operation returns without waiting for the target object to complete the invocation.

| | |
|---|---|
| IDL operation | void send_deferred(); |
| Java methods | `public abstract void send_deferred();` |

It is paired with the operations get_response() and poll_response(), which allow the caller to check for results at a later time.

| | |
|---|---|
| IDL operation | void get_response(); |
| Java methods | `public abstract void get_response();` |

The operation result and any inout or out parameters won't be valid until `get_response()` has been called and has returned. The method `get_response()` blocks until the result as well as inout and out parameters from an operation invocation initiated by the `send_deferred()` method are returned.

The operation poll_response() has a Boolean return value. It will return TRUE if the invocation is complete and the result and the inout and out parameters are ready for inspection. If it returns FALSE then the invocation is not complete and the attributes that contain the results will have undefined values. Once a TRUE result is returned, the get_response() method must be called.

| | |
|---|---|
| IDL operation | boolean poll_response(); |
| Java method | `public abstract boolean poll_response();` |

#### 6.6.2.4 Invoking a One-way Operation Request

The operation send_oneway() is for sending oneway operation invocation requests. These invocations have no return values, and so no further calls to the Request are required.

| | |
|---|---|
| IDL operation | void send_oneway(); |
| Java method | `void send_oneway();` |

### 6.6.2.5 Invoking Multiple Requests

The CORBA specification provides operations for making multiple requests. These operations are defined on the ORB pseudo-interface:

```
void send_multiple_requests_oneway(in RequestSeq req);
void send_multiple_requests_deferred(in RequestSeq req);
boolean poll_next_response();
Request get_next_response();
```

These are mapped in the standard way to methods in the `ORB` class:

```
public abstract void send_multiple_requests_oneway(
    Request[] req );
public abstract void send_multiple_requests_deferred(
    Request[] req );
boolean poll_next_response();
Request get_next_response();
```

The method `send_multiple_requests_oneway()` takes a list of initialized Request objects and sends them all. No further action is needed because one-way operations do not return.

The method `send_multiple_requests_deferred()` takes a list of initialized Requests and invokes them asynchronously. When they return, the completed Requests are given back to the user one at a time using the `get_next_response()` method. The `get_next_response()` method will block if there are no completed Request invocations, until one returns. It returns null if all outstanding responses have been returned. The caller may use the `poll_next_response()` method to check if any Requests have completed before calling `get_next_response()`. A return value of TRUE indicates that a Request has completed, and FALSE indicates that none is yet ready.

## 6.7 Dynamic Skeleton Interface

The DII provides a mechanism to invoke operations from a client without compile-time knowledge about the interface. The Dynamic Skeleton Interface (DSI) provides a similar mechanism for the other side. It allows the ORB to invoke an object implementation without compile-time knowledge about the interface, that is, without a skeleton class. For an object implementation, calls via a compiler-generated skeleton and the DSI are not distinguishable.

The idea behind the DSI is to invoke all object implementations via the same general operation. This is specified in an abstract class `DynamicImplementation` that contains an operation, called by the ORB, to convey the original request to the server. This class presents a pseudo-object of type ServerRequest to the server to allow it access to information about the operation being invoked and its arguments. It also uses references to the contents of this object to return the results of the invocation.

## 6.7.1 ServerRequest Interface

The pseudo-IDL specification of ServerRequest in the CORBA 2.0 specification provides operations that are rewritten in a pseudo-interface shown in the Java Mapping Specification. The Java Mapping provides one additional operation that allows the setting of exceptions. As with the Request pseudo-object, ServerRequest is mapped to a public abstract class in the `org.omg.CORBA` package.

IDL interface pseudo interface Server Request;

Java class `public abstract class ServerRequest {...}`

The operation operation() returns the name of the operation that was invoked.

IDL operation readonly attribute Identifier operation();

Java method `public abstract String operation();`

The operation ctx() provides the invocation Context of the operation.

IDL operation Context ctx();

Java method `public abstract Context ctx();`

The arguments() operation takes an NVList as an argument. This list must contain the names and parameter direction flags of the arguments expected by the server for the operation given by operation(). When the arguments() operation returns the ORB will have inserted the values of incoming arguments into the NVList for use by the server. This NVList will also be used to return the new values for inout and out parameters once the server has finished processing.

IDL operation void arguments (in NVList params);

Java method `public abstract void arguments(NVList params);`

The set_result() operation has an Any parameter for the result of the invocation.

IDL operation void set_result( in any res );

Java method `public abstract void set_result (Any a);`

The last operation provided by Request is set_exception(). This operation allows the invocation to return an exception instead of a result.

IDL operation void set_exception( in any ex );

Java method
```
public abstract void set_exception(
    Any a);
```

### 6.7.2 DynamicImplementation Class

Servers that wish to use the DSI must implement the abstract class `DynamicImplementation`, which extends the base class `Servant` used for all object implementations:

```
package org.omg.PortableServer;

public abstract class DynamicImplementation
   extends Servant {

   public abstract void invoke(
       org.omg.CORBA.ServerRequest request);
}
```

Servers then use the `ServerRequest` argument of the `invoke()` method in the manner just described to access the operation name and its arguments and to set the results of executing this operation.

## 6.8 Registering Valuetype Factories

When valuetypes are received and unmarshaled, the receiving ORB must be able to create a new instance of the valuetype. To do this, it looks up a factory for this valuetype and calls the `read_value()` operation. All value factories implement the interface CORBA::ValueFactory, which is a native type in CORBA 2.3 and requires language-specific mappings. The Java Language Mapping defines the following base interface for value factories as a mapping for CORBA::ValueFactory:

```
package org.omg.CORBA.portable;

public interface ValueFactory {

    java.io.Serializable read_value(
```

```
        org.omg.CORBA_2_3.portable.InputStream is);
}
```

Note that the argument is of type `org.omg.CORBA_2_3.portable.InputStream` and not just `org.omg.CORBA.portable.InputStream`. The package `org.omg.CORBA_2_3` contains definitions that extend the standard CORBA interfaces with operations for managing valuetypes.

For the ORB to be able to find the correct value factory for a valuetype, the factory must be either explicitly registered with the ORB for the valuetype's RepositoryId, or the Java class implementing the factory interface must have a name that ends in `DefaultFactory`. This kind of implicit or default registration is possible, however, only if the Java class name and the valuetype's RepositoryId have the same structure, that is, if the Repository has not been modified by IDL compiler pragmas such as `#pragma prefix`. In this latter case, the factory implementation class must be registered explicitly because it cannot be found using the simple method to locate default factories. To look up a default factory, the ORB strips off `"IDL:"` and `":1.0"` from the RepositoryID and appends "DefaultFactory" to the resulting string.

The operations offered by the ORB to register, unregister, and look up factory classes are declared in the interface `org.omg.CORBA_2_3.ORB`:

```
package org.omg.CORBA_2_3;

public abstract class ORB extends org.omg.CORBA.ORB {

   public org.omg.CORBA.Object get_value_def( String repid )
       throws org.omg.CORBA.BAD_PARAM {
       throw new org.omg.CORBA.NO_IMPLEMENT();
   }

   public org.omg.CORBA.portable.ValueFactory
   register_value_factory(
       String id,
       org.omg.CORBA.portable.ValueFactory factory
   ) {
       throw new org.omg.CORBA.NO_IMPLEMENT();
   }

   public void unregister_value_factory( String id ) {
       throw new org.omg.CORBA.NO_IMPLEMENT();
   }

   public org.omg.CORBA.portable.ValueFactory
   lookup_value_factory( String id ){
       throw new org.omg.CORBA.NO_IMPLEMENT();
```

```
    }
    // ...
}
```

The `register_value_factory()` method is used to register a valuetype explicitly. The string argument `id` provides the RepositoryId for which the second argument `factory` is to be registered. The ORB uses this ID to look up the factory when unmarshaling values of this type. Factories can be unregistered again with `unregister_value_factory()`. The factory currently registered for a given RepositoryId can be looked up with the method `lookup_value_factory()`.

The base type for all valuetypes is CORBA::ValueBase:

```
valuetype ValueBase {
   ValueDef get_value_def();
};
```

The get_value_def() operation is used to retrieve type information from the Interface Repository and corresponds to the get_interface() operation in CORBA::Object. Because ValueBase maps to `java.io.Serializable` in Java, this operation had to go to the ORB interface.

# Discovering Services

This chapter provides an overview of mechanisms for discovering CORBA objects. We explain the two most important CORBAservices for locating objects: the Naming Service (section 7.1), which finds objects by name, and the Trading Service (section 7.2), which finds objects by type and properties. These CORBAservices are often compared to a white pages service and a yellow pages service. The Naming Service, on one hand, works like a phone book and lets you retrieve a single reference using an identifier that functions as a key. The Trading Service, on the other hand, lets you retrieve a set of references that match your search criteria, much like the yellow pages.

There is still the question of how to find initial references to instances of those services. In section 7.3, we explain the operations on the ORB pseudo-interface that can be used for bootstrapping.

## 7.1 The CORBA Naming Service

The Naming Service allows object implementations to be identified by name and is thus a fundamental service for distributed object systems. This section is organized as follows:

- We give an overview and explain how to use the Naming Service (section 7.1.1).
- We explain the interface specification in detail (section 7.1.2).
- We provide an example (section 7.1.3).
- We explain the relationship between the Naming Service and the Java Naming and Directory Interface (section 7.1.4).

### 7.1.1 Overview of the Naming Service

The Naming Service provides a mapping between a name and an object reference. Storing such a mapping in the Naming Service is known as *binding an object to a name*, and removing this entry is called *unbinding* the name. Obtaining an object reference that is bound to a name is known as *resolving the name.*

Names can be hierarchically structured by using contexts. Contexts are similar to directories in file systems, and they can contain name bindings as well as subcontexts.

The use of object references alone to identify objects has two problems for human users. First, object references are opaque data types, and second, their string form is a long sequence of numbers. When a server is restarted, its objects typically have new object references. In most cases, however, clients want to use the server repeatedly without needing to be aware that the server has been restarted.

The Naming Service solves these problems by providing an extra layer of abstraction for the identification of objects. It provides readable object identifiers for the human user; users can assign names that look like structured file names, a persistent identification mechanism, and objects that can bind themselves under the same name regardless of their object reference.

The Naming Service uses an IDL-defined name structure to represent names, but it also defines a standard string format for names and conversion operations between the internal and the external name format. Thus names, like object references, can be stringified and exported. The receiver of such a name string can turn the string into a name again and then contact the Naming Service and try to resolve the name. The first Naming Service specification did not define a standard string format, so stringified names could reliably be used only with a single implementation of the service.

The typical use of the Naming Service involves object implementations binding their objects to names in the Naming Service when they come into existence and unbinding them before they terminate. Clients resolve names to objects, on which they subsequently invoke operations. Figure 7.1 illustrates this typical usage scenario.

## 7.1.2 Interface Specification

The central interface is called NamingContext, and it contains operations to bind names to object references and to create subcontexts. Names are sequences of NameComponents. NamingContexts can resolve a name with a single component and return an object reference. The effect of resolving names with more than one component is the same as resolving the first component to a subcontext and passing the remainder of a name to that subcontext for resolution.

### *7.1.2.1 The Name Type*

The CosNaming module provides type definitions used to identify objects by names:

```
module CosNaming {
    typedef string Istring;
    struct NameComponent {
        Istring id;
        Istring kind;
    };
    typedef sequence <NameComponent> Name;
```

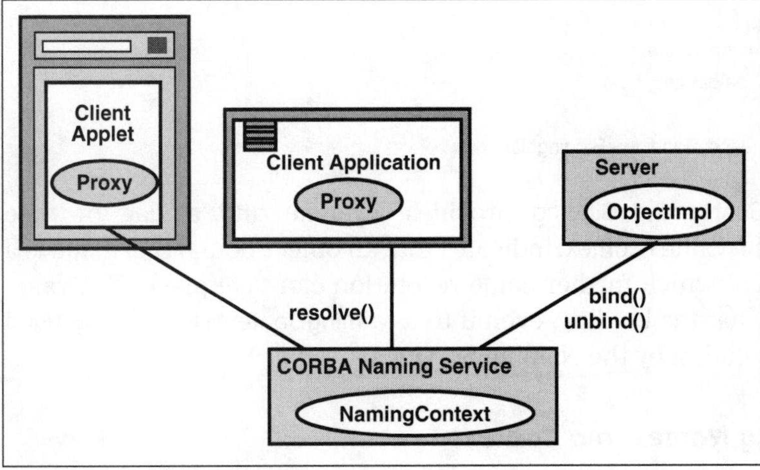


**Figure 7.1** Typical use of the CORBA Naming Service.

The type Istring was used to define the Name type for an intended future compatibility with internationalized strings. Even in the second version of the specification, this type is still defined to be string, however. A NameComponent has two fields: id contains the string that will actually be matched when a name is resolved; kind is available for application-specific purposes. Both fields are interpreted by the Naming Service, so names with identical id fields, but different values in kind fields are regarded as distinct.

The Name type is a sequence of component, or atomic, names. The syntax for the textual representation of names uses the separator character "/" to separate components when printing names for users. The id and kind fields are separated using a single dot ("."). Stringified names such as "outercontext .ctx/innercontext.ctx/MyServer.service" thus strongly resemble file names. It should be noted that it is possible to use name components in the name resolution process with either or both fields left empty. The second component of the name "here/./.we/go" has an empty id field and an empty kind field. This is represented by a single dot. The third component has an empty id field, and both the first and the last components have empty kind fields.

To use the characters "/" and "." within an id or kind field, they must be escaped using the backslash character "\". We strongly discourage using these characters within name components, however.

### 7.1.2.2 Bindings

The Binding type provides information about the bindings in a context:

```
// module CosNaming
    enum BindingType {nobject, ncontext};
    struct Binding {
        Name binding_name;
        BindingType binding_type;
    };
    typedef sequence <Binding> BindingList;
```

The type CosNaming::Binding provides a name and a flag of type BindingType. The value ncontext indicates that an object bound to a name is a NamingContext at which further name resolution can take place. The value nobject means that the binding, even if to a NamingContext, will not be used for further resolution by the Naming Service.

### 7.1.2.3 Adding Names to a Context

There are two operations for binding an object to a name in a context, and two for binding another context to a name.

```
// module CosNaming
    interface NamingContext {
        // we elide the exceptions declared here
        void bind( in Name n, in Object obj )
            raises( NotFound, CannotProceed, InvalidName, AlreadyBound );
        void rebind( in Name n, in Object obj )
            raises( NotFound, CannotProceed, InvalidName );
        void bind_context( in Name n, in NamingContext nc )
            raises( NotFound, CannotProceed, InvalidName, AlreadyBound );
        void rebind_context( in Name n, in NamingContext nc)
            raises( NotFound, CannotProceed, InvalidName );
```

The bind() and bind_context() operations associate a new name with an object. In the case of bind_context() the object must be of type NamingContext. We will see how to create new contexts in the following section. If the name used has more than one component, the NamingContext will expect that all but the last component refers to an existing nested context, and it will make the binding in the context resolved by the first part of the name. For example, consider Figure 7.2.

In our example we invoke the bind() operation on the NamingContext object we have called "Context1" with the parameters "Context2/Context5/MyName" and some object reference. This results in a new atomic name, "MyName," being bound to the object in the "Context5" context (see Figure 7.3). The BindingType of the resulting binding will be nobject.

If we invoked bind_context with the same parameters (although the object reference must be to a NamingContext) then the same situation would result. The BindingType would be ncontext, and the "Context5" context would then be able to resolve names like "MyName/x/y/z" by passing the remainder, "x/y/z," to the new "MyName" context.

The rebind() and rebind_context() operations work the same as bind() and bind_context(), but rather than raising an exception if the name already exists, they simply replace the existing object reference.

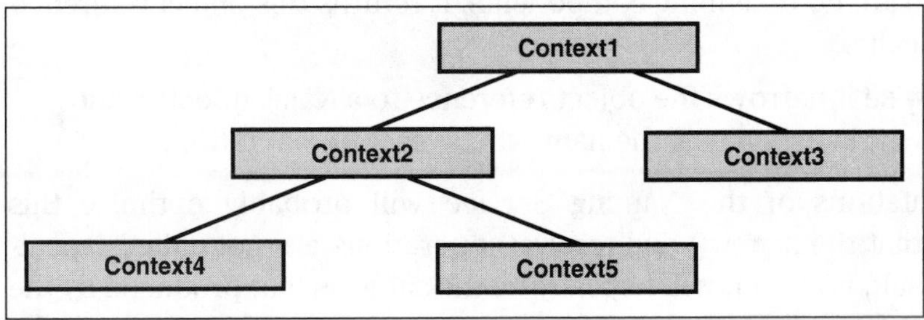


**Figure 7.2** Naming context structure—before binding.

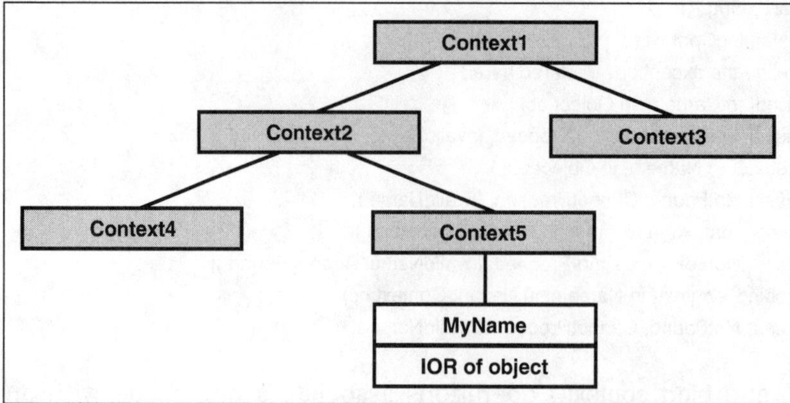


**Figure 7.3** Naming context structure–after binding.

### 7.1.2.4 Removing Names from a Context

The operation unbind() will remove a name and its associated object reference from a context or one of its subcontexts.

```
void unbind(in Name n)
  raises(NotFound, CannotProceed, InvalidName);
```

### 7.1.2.5 Name Resolution

The resolve() operation returns an object reference bound to a name supplied as its argument.

```
Object resolve (in Name n)
  raises(NotFound, CannotProceed, InvalidName);
```

The resolve() operation behaves as follows:

- It resolves the first component of the name, n, to an object reference.
- If there are no remaining components, it returns this object reference to the caller.
- Otherwise it narrows the object reference to a NamingContext and passes the remainder of the name to its resolve() operation.

Implementations of the Naming Service will probably optimize this process so that the narrow() and resolve() operations are not called repeatedly. The result, however, will logically be the same as that produced by the previous algorithm.

### 7.1.2.6 Exceptions

Here are the exceptions omitted in the preceding text:

```
// interface NamingContext
enum NotFoundReason { missing_node, not_context, not_object };
exception NotFound {
    NotFoundReason why;
    Name rest_of_name;
};
exception CannotProceed {
    NamingContext cxt;
    Name rest_of_name;
};
exception InvalidName {};
exception AlreadyBound {};
exception NotEmpty{};
```

The NotFound exception indicates that the name does not identify a binding. It may be raised by any operation that takes a name as an argument. The Naming Service specification defines the meaning of the why member of this exception in relation to the rest of the name. In any of the following situations, the rest_of_name member returns the rest of the sequence from the unresolvable name onward:

- missing_node: The first NameComponent returned in rest_of_name does not denote a binding within its parent context.
- not_context: The first NameComponent in rest_of_name is bound to an object with a binding type of nobject rather than ncontext.
- not_object: The first NameComponent in rest_of_name denotes a context where an object reference was expected.

The CannotProceed exception returns a NamingContext object reference and a part of the original name. It indicates that the resolve() operation has given up, for example, for security or efficiency reasons. The client may be able to continue at the returned context. The rest_of_name member returns the part of the name that should be passed to the returned context ctx for resolution.

The InvalidName exception indicates that the name is syntactically invalid. For example, it might contain a zero-length NameComponent. The names acceptable to different Naming Services may be further restricted by the implementation.

The AlreadyBound exception may be raised by bind operations. It informs the caller that a name is already used and cannot be overridden without using a rebind operation.

NotEmpty is an exception raised by the destroy() operation defined later. Contexts that still contain bindings cannot be destroyed.

#### 7.1.2.7 Context Creation

There are operations to create new contexts defined in the NamingContext interface.

```
// interface NamingContext
NamingContext new_context();
NamingContext bind_new_context(in Name n)
    raises(NotFound, AlreadyBound, CannotProceed, InvalidName);
```

New NamingContexts may be created and later used alone or bound into other contexts using bind_context(). They can also be created with a particular name and bound in a single operation. new_context() produces an empty NamingContext that can be used anywhere. bind_new_context() also creates a new context but binds it as a subcontext of the context on which the operation is invoked. It can raise the usual exceptions for an operation that takes a name as an argument.

#### 7.1.2.8 Context Destruction

When a context is no longer used, and all the bindings it contained have been unbound, it can be destroyed.

```
// interface NamingContext
void destroy()
    raises(NotEmpty);
```

The destroy() operation will delete a context as long as it contains no bindings. Be sure at the same time to remove any bindings that may refer to this context.

#### 7.1.2.9 Browsing Contexts

A NamingContext supports browsing of its contents by use of the list() operation.

```
// interface NamingContext
void list ( in unsigned long how_many,
```

```
                out BindingList bl,
                out BindingIterator bi); // BindingIterator was forward declared
    }; // end of interface NamingContext
```

The parameters of the list() operation allow the caller to specify how many bindings to return in a BindingList sequence. The rest will be returned through an iterator object (whose interface is explained in the following section) referred to by the bi parameter, which will be a nil object reference if there are no further bindings. The sequence may contain fewer bindings than allowed by how_many. If the how_many parameter is zero, only an iterator will be returned.

### *7.1.2.10 Binding Iterators*

A BindingIterator object will be returned if the number of bindings in a context exceeds the how_many argument value of the list() operation invoked on the context.

```
// module CosNaming
    interface BindingIterator {
        boolean next_one(out Binding b);
        boolean next_n(in unsigned long how_many,
                        out BindingList bl);
        void destroy();
    };
}; //end of module CosNaming
```

If there are remaining bindings, the next_one() operation returns TRUE and places a Binding in its `out` parameter. If the next_one() operation returns FALSE the value of the out parameter is indeterminate.

The next_n() operation returns a sequence of at most how_many bindings in the `out` parameter bl. It also returns FALSE if there are no further bindings to be iterated over. In this case, the out parameter will be a zero-length sequence.

The destroy() operation allows the iterator to deallocate its resources, and it will render the object reference invalid. Iterators may sometimes be implemented so that they time out or are deleted on demand for resource recovery. It is legal for a Naming Service implementation to reclaim resources and destroy iterators at any time, so clients should be prepared to handle OBJECT_NOT_EXIST exceptions when trying to invoke iterator operations.

### 7.1.2.11 Converting Names

Names can be converted into different types of string representations. One of these is the stringified name format presented at the beginning of this section; the other one is a URL format for names. The conversion operations are defined in the NamingContextExt interface. This interface is a subtype of the NamingContext interface. When the name conversion operations were added to the existing Naming Service specification, the NamingContextExt interface was introduced so the NamingContext interface could be left unchanged for backward compatibility.

Here is the NamingContextExt interface:

```
// module CosNaming
interface NamingContextExt : NamingContext {
    typedef string StringName;
    typedef string Address;
    typedef string URLString;

    StringName to_string(in Name n)
        raises (InvalidName);
    Name to_name(in StringName sn)
        raises (InvalidName);

    exception InvalidAddress {};

    URLString to_url(in Address addrkey, in StringName sn)
        raises (InvalidAddress, InvalidName);

    Object resolve_str(in StringName sn)
        raises(NotFound, CannotProceed, InvalidName);
};
```

The to_string() and to_name() operations convert between names and their stringified form. The operation to_url() is used to convert a stringified name into the URL format. This format uses two URL schemes, `corbaloc` and `corbaname`, which we describe in the text that follows. It is constructed from an address and key string as its first parameter and a stringified name supplied in its second parameter. Note that the NamingContextExt interface provides no operation to turn a URL reference back into a name or an object. This conversion is handled by the string_to_object() operation in the ORB interface.

The reason for introducing URL schemes for object references is to allow for a more convenient way of exchanging and constructing references than is possible with stringified IORs. Without such a scheme, contacting a service is not possible even if both its network address and port are known because it is not possible to create usable object references in an ad hoc way. As we shall see in section 7.3, this is especially useful for configuring initial references. Stringified IORs do not help because they are too cumbersome to construct directly.

The `corbaloc` URL scheme can be seen as a simplification of a regular IOR. It provides the minimum information necessary to contact a remote object. To understand how `corbaloc` URLs can be constructed, let's look at the syntax for these URLs:

```
<corbaloc>          = "corbaloc:" <obj_addr_list>["/"<key_string]
<key_string>        = <string> | empty_string
<obj_addr_list>     = [<obj_addr> ","]* <obj_addr>
```

Following the scheme identifier `corbaloc` is a comma-separated list of object addresses and the object key. The object key itself comprises the POA name and an object ID. If the object key contains nonprintable characters, these must be escaped. A character outside the ASCII character set is represented by its hexadecimal value prefixed by a "%" sign. The object key is separated from addressing information with a single forward slash.

```
<obj_addr>          = <prot_addr> | <future_prot_addr>
<prot_addr>         = "rir:" | <iiop_prot_addr>
```

Object addresses each begin with a protocol identifier. Currently, the only supported protocols are `iiop` and `rir`. The latter is short for `resolve_initial_references` and tells the receiver to use the `object_key` part of the URL as the string argument to the ORB's resolve_initial_references operation. If no protocol is specified, `iiop` is assumed. The structure of the IIOP protocol information in the URL is the following:

```
<iiop_prot_addr>    = <iiop_id> | <iiop_addr>
<iiop_id>           = ":" | "iiop:"
<iiop_addr>         = <version> <host> [ ":" <port>]
<host>              = DNS-style Hostname | ip_address
<version>           = <major> "." <minor> "@" | empty_string
```

For `iiop`, it is possible to specify the protocol version before the host address, using `@` as the separator character. The host address can be either a DNS host name or a plain IP address. The host address is optionally followed by a port number, which is assumed to be 2809 by default. The protocol and address information is followed by the object key, which may need to be escaped as described earlier.

Now that we have examined the structure or corbaloc URLs, let's look at some examples:

```
corbaloc::myhost.mycompany.com/Test/object_a
corbaloc:iiop:1.1@myhost.mycompany.com:4711/Development/object_b
corbaloc:rir:/TradingService
```

The first example omits the protocol specifier, so `iiop` is assumed. It also omits the protocol version number, which means that 1.0 is used. The host name is given in DNS style, but no port number is given, so we again have to use the default value, which is 2809. The object key, finally, is `"Test/object_a"`. The second example explicitly specifies that the object supports IIOP 1.1 and also gives a specific port number, 4711. The object key is `"4711/Development/object_b"`. The third example URL does not rely on IIOP but refers to the object that is the result of calling `resolve_initial_references("TradingService")` on the local ORB object.

Let's return to the explanation of the operations in the NamingContextExt interface. Together, the addressing information and the object key string can be supplied as the first argument to the to_url operation of the `NamingServiceExt` interface. The second argument, a stringified name, may be empty. The naming service will then construct a `corbaloc` URL in the obvious way by prefixing the argument string with `corbaloc`. It is not legal to pass an empty string in the first argument.

If a stringified name is supplied, however, a `corbaname` URL is constructed instead. A `corbaname` URL is simply a concatenation of a `corbaloc` URL and a stringified name. The two parts are separated using the "#" character. In this case, the object referenced by the `corbaloc` part is interpreted as a naming context that is used for resolving the stringified name. An example for a `corbaname` URL is:

```
corbaname::serverhost.mycompany.com:8001/NamePOA/Context1#public/FunServ
ice
```

This URL denotes the object bound to the name `public/FunService` in a naming context with object ID `Context1` in POA `NamePOA`. The naming context server is reachable on port 8001 of host `serverhost.mycompany.com`.

## 7.1.3 Using the Naming Service from a Java Client

This subsection contains some of the methods for a `ContextLister` class that can be used to print all bindings in a NamingContext to a Java stream.

First let's look at the declaration of the class, its private fields, and constructors. There are two constructors, one of which obtains a root context via the ORB, the other of which uses a stringified object reference for bootstrapping.

```
package com.wiley.compbooks.brose.chapter7.naming;

import org.omg.CosNaming.*;
import org.omg.CosNaming.NamingContextPackage.*;
import java.io.*;
import java.util.*;

public class ContextLister {
    private NamingContextExt root_context;
    private Hashtable contexts = new Hashtable();

    public ContextLister(org.omg.CORBA.ORB orb) {
        // initialise Naming Service via ORB
        try {
            System.out.println("Initial services: " );
            String[] services = orb.list_initial_services();

            if( services.length == 0 )
                System.out.println("No services available");

            for( int i = 0; i < services.length; i++ )
                System.out.println( services[i] );

            org.omg.CORBA.Object obj =
                orb.resolve_initial_references("NameService");
            root_context = NamingContextExtHelper.narrow( obj );
        }
        catch( org.omg.CORBA.ORBPackage.InvalidName inex ) {
            inex.printStackTrace();
        }
        catch(org.omg.CORBA.SystemException corba_exception) {
            System.err.println(corba_exception);
        }
        if( root_context == null ) {
            System.err.println("No Naming Context, giving up ...");
            System.exit( 1 );
        }
    }
```

We first list all available initial services by calling `list_initial_services()`. This is not needed to initialize the object, but we use the opportunity to demonstrate the use of the ORB bootstrap operation. We then try to obtain a reference to a root context of the Naming Service by calling `resolve_initial_references()` on the ORB. We obtain an object reference of the type CORBA::Object, which we narrow to a NamingContext. If the root_context is null, the obtained object is of the wrong type or not available and we give up.

Alternatively, there is a constructor that initializes the ContextLister object with a stringified object reference for a root context. This constructor can be used for cross-ORB bootstrapping.

```
public ContextLister( org.omg.CORBA.ORB orb, String str ) {
    // initialise Naming Service via stringified IOR
    try {
        org.omg.CORBA.Object obj = orb.string_to_object( str );
        root_context = NamingContextExtHelper.narrow( obj );
    }
    catch( org.omg.CORBA.SystemException corba_exception ) {
        System.err.println(corba_exception);
    }

    if( root_context == null ) {
        System.err.println("No Naming Context, giving up ...");
        System.exit( 1 );
    }
}
```

Both constructors will create an object with a properly initialized root_context private field. We can now look at the methods provided by the ContextLister class.

A method called list() takes a Java PrintStream argument on which it will print the list of bindings in the root context:

```
public void list(java.io.PrintStream ps ){
    list( root_context, "    ", ps );
}
```

This method simply calls another, private list() method that can be used for recursive calls on nested naming contexts. The string argument is used for indenting bindings in nested contexts. The implementation of this method looks like this:

```
private void list( NamingContext n,
                   String indent,
                   PrintStream ps ) {

    if( isMarked( n ) ) {
        return;
    }
    mark(n);
```

```
        try {
            BindingListHolder blsoh =
                new BindingListHolder(new Binding[0]);
            BindingIteratorHolder bioh =
                new BindingIteratorHolder();
            n.list( 0, blsoh, bioh );

            BindingHolder bh = new BindingHolder();

            if( bioh.value == null )
                return;

            while( bioh.value.next_one( bh )) {
                String stringName =
                    root_context.to_string(bh.value.binding_name);
                ps.print( indent + stringName );
                if( bh.value.binding_type.value() ==
                    BindingType._ncontext ){

                    String _indent = indent + "\t";
                    ps.println("/");

                    NameComponent [] name =
                       root_context.to_name(stringName);
                    NamingContext sub_context =
                       NamingContextHelper.narrow(n.resolve(name));
                    list(sub_context, _indent, ps);
            }
            else
                System.out.println();
        }
    }
    catch ( Exception e ) {
        e.printStackTrace();
    }
}
```

A naming graph constructed by binding names need not be a tree. To avoid running into infinite loops for naming graphs with cycles, we have to check whether a naming context has already been listed. We use a method `mark()` to mark a naming context as listed and another method `isMarked()` for the check. The remainder of `list()` gives an example of using a `BindingIterator`. The iterator is passed as an out parameter of the list() operation on NamingContext objects. Passing 0 as the first argument in this call means that we do not want any bindings returned in the second out parameter, a sequence of bindings. Rather, we iterate over all bindings in the context using the `BindingIterator`. For every binding we print the binding's name to the `PrintStream`. For bindings of type `ncontext`, we append a trailing slash as an indicator and call our `ContextLister`'s `list()` method recursively.

As an example, here is the output for the naming graph of Figure 7.2 with `Context1` as root context:

```
Context2.context/
   Context4.context/
   Context5.context/
Context3.context/
```

The complete implementation of `ContextLister` is shown on the companion Web site at www.wiley.com/compbooks/brose. You will see more examples of using the Naming Service throughout this book.

## 7.1.4 The Java Naming and Directory Interface

The CORBA Naming Service is, in fact, a special case of a more general kind of service, namely, a directory service. Directory Services, like the Naming Service, provide named objects, and they typically also support structured names that can span multiple name spaces. Some of the most widely used directory services today are the Domain Name Service (DNS), the Network Information System (NIS), and the Lightweight Directory Access Protocol (LDAP), which is a streamlined version of the complex OSI X.500 directory. Because of the popularity of these services, Sun Microsystems has specified a general API to access directory services, the Java Naming and Directory Interface (JNDI). Individual service implementations function as *providers* for the JNDI.

Directory Services are often used as a kind of lightweight distributed database that allows grouping network-wide information and gives meaningful structure to its contents through the use of names. The information in the directory is represented as attributes (name/value pairs) in directory objects. Directory objects also behave as naming contexts and can thus be organized hierarchically and accessed using structured names. A typical directory might have directory objects representing user-related information such as e-mail addresses and a password, or it might give names to network resources like printers. Typically, directory services also offer search facilities that support content-based lookup of directory objects using attributes.

A CORBA NamingContext is thus just a special case of a directory object that acts as a context only and has no attributes. In fact, the JNDI is designed specifically to allow the Naming Service to act as one provider so that Java applications can access the Naming Service using the uniform API. Other potential providers are the RMI registry and LDAP, which is currently one of the most widely used directory services. If an LDAP server is installed at your site and you also have access to an LDAP client that supports the JNDI Service Provider Interface (SPI), Java programs can conveniently make use of all its functionality.

A different option is to use LDAP as a mechanism for implementing the Naming Service because LDAP already provides all the functionality that a NamingService would need to support. This could even be done using the JNDI so that such an implementation would be just a simple Java wrapper around the JNDI LDAP interfaces provided by LDAP clients. The resulting implementation would benefit from the efficiency and scalability of existing LDAP implementations.

## 7.2 Trading Service

The Trading Service has its basis in the ISO Open Distributed Processing (ODP) standards. The trader work in this group had reached a Draft International Standard (DIS) level within ISO when responses were due for OMG's Object Services RFP 5. The submitters to the RFP were mostly people who had been working on the ODP standard, which enabled the convergence of the Trading standards from both groups. Even though ODP uses OMG IDL as an interface specification language, implementations of ODP standards may use any technology. The common underlying semantics of the two efforts greatly enhances the prospects for future cross-platform interworking.

In this section, we first provide an overview of Trading (section 7.2.1) and the interfaces in the Trader specification (section 7.2.2). Sections 7.2.3 and 7.2.4 show how services can be offered and found using a Trader.

### 7.2.1 Overview of Trading

Traders are repositories of object references that are described by an interface type and a set of property values. Such a description of an interface is known as a *service offer*. Each service offer has a *service type*, which is a combination of the interface type of the object being advertised and a list of properties for which a service offer of this service type should provide values.

An *exporter* is a service or some third party acting as an agent for the service that places a service offer into a trader. That service offer can then be matched by the trader to some client's criteria.

A client that queries a trader to discover a service is called an *importer*. An importer provides the trader with a specification of a service type and a constraint expression over the properties of offers of that type. The constraint expression describes the importer's requirements. A typical use of the Trading Service is illustrated in Figure 7.4. A server—the exporter—may register a service using the Trading Service's Register interface. Clients, which can be either applets or applications, can act as importers and find out about services using the Lookup interface.

A long-standing example of a trading scenario is that of printing services. Currently system administrators configure new printers in a network by providing a unique name for a new device and then notify potential users by e-mail, news, or notice board. Then each user must remember the printer's name and type it into a dialog box in an application. A better way to discover new printers is to allow applications or users to provide their requirements to the application, which then sends the print job to the most appropriate printer.

This is achieved as follows:

- We assume that new printers are provided with an implementation of a standard printing interface, specified in IDL. For example,

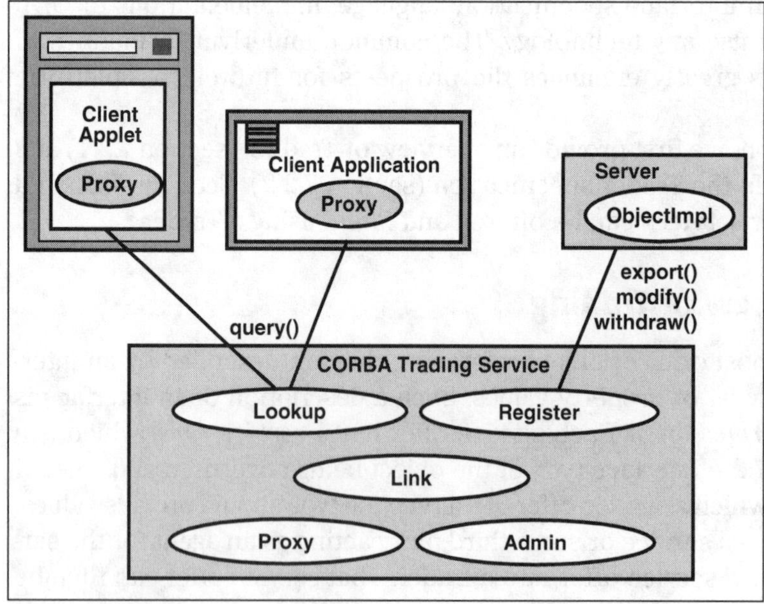


**Figure 7.4** Typical use of a CORBA Trading Service.

```
module com {
...
module chapter7 {
    module printing{
        interface Printer {
            typedef string filename;
            exception PrinterOffLine {};
            void print_file(in filename fn)
                raises(PrinterOffLine);
            short queue_length()
                raises(PrinterOffLine);
        };
    };
};};};};
```

- Then we define a service type that nominates the Printer interface and a number of property names and types; for example, the printer's location, its language (ASCII, PostScript, HP PCL, etc.), its resolution in DPI, its color properties, its print queue length, and its name.
- Each printer is then advertised by exporting a service offer to the trader. For convenience we will refer to the following example printers by their "name" property. Table 7.1 lists example printers and their properties
- Applications configure print requests based on user preferences, from a user's environment, a dialog box, or a text query. This results in a constraint expression that can be passed to the trader in an import query. For example,

```
building == "A Block" && floor <= 5 && language == "postscript"
```

- This query would result in matching two printers ("12ps" and "monster"). The query can ask for the resulting service offers to be ordered according to a *preference expression.* This provides the matched service offers in order based on some minimal, maximal, or Boolean expression. For example, a preference to give us the highest resolution printers first would be expressed as

```
max resolution
```

The `queue_len` property is a *dynamic property,* which means that its value is not stored but looked up each time a query is made. So we would probably have a default preference criterion of `min queue_len`. This would sort the printers that are returned so that we print to the one that matches the constraint expression *and* has the shortest queue.

**Table 7.1** Printer Properties

| PROPERTY | VALUE |
|---|---|
| building | "A Block" |
| floor | 2 |
| language | PostScript |
| resolution | 300 |
| color | black |
| queue_len | —-> [PrinterObjectRef]->queue_length() |
| name | "12ps" |
| **PROPERTY** | **VALUE** |
| building | "A Block" |
| floor | 3 |
| language | PostScript |
| resolution | 600 |
| color | black |
| queue_len | —->[PrinterObjectRef]->queue_length() |
| name | "monster" |
| **PROPERTY** | **VALUE** |
| building | "A Block" |
| floor | 7 |
| language | PostScript |
| resolution | 600 |
| color | 256color |
| queue_len | —->[PrinterObjectRef]->queue_length() |
| name | "rib" |

Let's imagine that a new color printer is installed in Block A and that it is higher in resolution than the "rib" printer. All users who want high resolution will have this maximized in their preferences, and when they next require a color printer the new printer is automatically selected when their application does an import. If, on the other hand, a new printer is installed on floor 1 of the building, then people who used to walk upstairs to collect printouts will have their ordinary black-and-white PostScript print jobs directed to the new printer on their floor, without having to change their environment or even knowing the name of the printer. In this way they will be informed of a new device as soon as they trade for a printer and the new one meets their requirements.

Of course, it is hard to set requirements and preferences when you don't know what is available. Some applications that regularly use the Printer interface will have browsers built in to allow users to see all available printers and their properties by querying the trader with a simple constraint such as:

```
building == "A Block".
```

#### 7.2.1.1 Service Types and Service Offers

Service types are templates from which service offers are created. They ensure that groups of services that offer the same interface and have the same nonfunctional considerations are grouped together. This allows efficient searching and matching of service offers in the trader. Most importantly, it allows exporters and importers to use the same terminology (property names) to describe a common set of features so that expressions written in terms of those properties will always be evaluated correctly.

#### 7.2.1.2 Export and Lookup of Service Offers

Any program may export a service offer to a trader if it has an object reference to some application object and knowledge of the implementation behind the reference so that it can describe the properties of that object. Often services will advertise themselves by exporting a service offer.

Any client that is compiled using a set of IDL stubs for a particular interface may assign any valid object reference to a variable at run time and execute operations on that object. As new implementations of servers become available, a client may wish to select objects based on some proximity, Quality of Service, or other characteristics. To do this it formulates a constraint expression in terms of the property names of a service type. This expression determines which service offers of that type match the client's requirements.

A client may also ask a trader to sort the matching service offers based on some preference expression that emphasizes the values of particular properties. The trader will return a sorted list of matching service offers, and the client will then use the object reference extracted from one of these.

#### *7.2.1.3 Trader Federation*

Each trader contains a database of service offers it searches when it receives an import request. It may also store a number of *links* to other traders to which it can pass on queries to reach a larger set of service offers. Links are named within a trader and consist of an object reference to the Lookup interface of another trader, as well as some rules to determine when to use the link to satisfy an importer's request. Traders that are linked in this manner are said to be interworking, or *federated.*

*Federated queries* are import requests passed from one trader via its links to other traders, and perhaps by them to other traders and so forth. These queries can be constrained by policies passed in by the initial importer, by the policies of each trader, and by the rules stored in the links themselves.

### 7.2.2 Overview of the Trading Service Interfaces

In this section we give an overview of the specification of the CORBA Trading Service. The specification includes the following interface definitions:

- Service Type Repository
- Trader Components
- Lookup
- Iterators
- Register
- Link
- Admin
- Proxy
- Dynamic properties

We will look at each of these in separate subsections next.

#### *7.2.2.1 Service Type Repository*

We have seen the importance of service types in the scenario presented in section 7.3.1. If a service offer does not provide an object reference of a known type then it is impossible for an importer to invoke operations on the object references it gets back. In the same way, service types are important for writing constraint expressions. If a service offer's property names and types vary then the constraint and preference expressions that express the requirements of an importer will fail to match relevant service offers. For example, if one service offer for a Printer described its floor via the property ("Floor", "ground"), and another as the property ("level", 4), then it would be impossible to compare them for proximity.

Service types are stored in the Service Type Repository. A service type consists of a name, an interface type, and a set of property specifications. A property specification gives the name and TypeCode of properties that will occur in service offers of this type. Properties are also given modes that allow them to be specified as read-only and/or mandatory. Read-only properties may not be modified after export. Mandatory properties must be included in a service offer to be accepted as an instance of this service type.

The data types and operations for the Service Type Repository are contained in the CosTradingRepos::ServiceTypeRepository interface. Most traders will implement a compiler for a service type language (for which there is no standard syntax) and browsing tools to enable importers to compose queries to a trader without needing to write clients to the Service Type Repository. The only type needed when importing via a trader is ServiceTypeName, which is a string.

```
module CosTradingRepos {
    interface ServiceTypeRepository {
        typedef sequence <CosTrading::ServiceTypeName> ServiceTypeNameSeq;

        enum PropertyMode {
          PROP_NORMAL, PROP_READONLY,
          PROP_MANDATORY, PROP_MANDATORY_READONLY
        };

        struct PropStruct {
          CosTrading::PropertyName name;
          CORBA::TypeCode value_type;
          PropertyMode mode;
        };

        typedef sequence <PropStruct> PropStructSeq;
        typedef CosTrading::Istring Identifier; // IR::Identifier

        struct IncarnationNumber {
          unsigned long high;
          unsigned long low;
        };

        struct TypeStruct {
          Identifier if_name;
```

```
            PropStructSeq props;
            ServiceTypeNameSeq super_types;
            boolean masked;
            IncarnationNumber incarnation;
        };
    };
};
```

### Substitutability of Service Types

Service types, like IDL interfaces, are substitutable via an inheritance relationship. For IDL interfaces this simply means that all the attributes and operations defined in the base interface become part of the derived interface. In service types, however, there are three aspects to substitutability:

- The interface type of a derived service type may be a subtype of the interface type in the base service type.
- The property set may be extended in a derived service type with new property names (and their associated type and mode specifications).
- Inherited properties may be strengthened. That is, nonmandatory properties may be made mandatory, and modifiable properties may be made read-only. The data type of an inherited property, however, must remain the same.

When an importer queries the trader it may receive service offers of a subtype of the requested service type, in the same way that object references to subtypes of a required interface type may be passed where a base type is required.

The masked member of the TypeStruct allows service types to be declared as abstract base service types. The incarnation member is assigned an increasing index so that queries on service type definitions can be restricted to those that were defined after some other service type that has a lower incarnation number.

### Creating and Deleting Service Types

Exporters and trader administrators will often want to write code to define a new service type. This is done by populating a PropStructSeq and then calling the add_type() operation.

```
IncarnationNumber add_type (
    in CosTrading::ServiceTypeName name,
    in Identifier if name,
    in PropStructSeq props,
    in ServiceTypeNameSeq super type,
```

```
) raises (
    CosTrading::IllegalServiceType,
    CosTrading::UnknownServiceType,
    ServiceTypeExists,
    InterfaceTypeMismatch,
    CosTrading::IllegalPropertyName,
    CosTrading::DuplicatePropertyName,
    ValueTypeRedefinition,
    DuplicateServiceTypeName
);
```

The name parameter is the name of the service type, which is used by importers to nominate the types of service offers they wish to search over. The if_name parameter is a RepositoryId that identifies the type of the object to be advertised by service offers of this type. If the name argument does not conform to the syntax for service type names, this operation will raise an IllegalServiceType exception. The UnknownServiceType exception is raised when any of the service type's supertypes are not defined in the service type repository. You will encounter these two exceptions in almost any operation signature that takes ServiceTypeName arguments.

The properties expected in service offers of this type are given in the props parameter. The final parameter specifies a list of existing service types that are being subtyped by the new service type. The rules for inheritance of service types were explained previously. The exceptions are mostly self-explanatory, and many of them relate to conditions in which the properties added or modified in a subtype do not follow the compatibility rules.

Service types should not be removed from a repository unless no service offers of this type are currently exported to the trader. Even in this case it is probably better to mask service types (see the text that follows) than delete them, as this avoids the reuse of old service type names, which can lead to confusion. On the rare occasions when a service type should be deleted, the operation remove_type() performs this action.

```
void remove_type (
    in CosTrading::ServiceTypeName name
) raises (
    CosTrading::IllegalServiceType,
    CosTrading::UnknownServiceType,
    HasSubTypes
);
```

A known service type cannot be removed if it has subtypes, and the exception HasSubTypes is raised in these circumstances.

### Obtaining Service Type Information

The repository has operations to list the service types it holds. It can also describe them, either in terms of their supertypes and additional or modified properties, or in terms of the properties that must go into a service offer to conform to this type.

The operation list_types() returns all the service type names in the repository. The parameter can be used to select whether only the subset of service types should be returned that was defined after a given incarnation number.

```
ServiceTypeNameSeq list_types (
    in SpecifiedServiceTypes which_types
);
```

The operation describe_type() returns a TypeStruct that contains the service type's definition as it was added to the repository. It does not include any properties inherited from its supertypes.

```
TypeStruct describe_type (
    in CosTrading::ServiceTypeName name
) raises (
    CosTrading::IllegalServiceType,
    CosTrading::UnknownServiceType
);
```

The fully_describe_type() operation, on the other hand, gives a full list of properties derived from all of a type's supertypes. This operation would usually be called by importers and exporters who want to know what properties to expect in a service offer of this type.

```
TypeStruct fully_describe_type (
    in CosTrading::ServiceTypeName name
) raises (
    CosTrading::IllegalServiceType,
    CosTrading::UnknownServiceType
);
```

### Masking Types

Masking a service type is used to either deprecate an existing service type, for which there are already offers in the trader, or to declare an abstract base service type that must be subtyped before service offer instances will be accepted by the trader. As a service type becomes widely used, people think of additional properties of a service that they wish to describe. Rather than simply adding nonstandard extra properties to their service offers they create a new service type that subtypes the existing type. If the new properties become important or widely accepted, then the old type can be masked to prevent new service offers from being created without the extra properties.

The operation mask_type() indicates that this type is no longer used, at least in its base form:

```
void mask_type (
    in CosTrading::ServiceTypeName name
) raises (
    CosTrading::IllegalServiceType,
    CosTrading::UnknownServiceType,
    AlreadyMasked
);
```

The unmask_type() operation reverses this masking, and the trader will once again accept offers of this type. The Trading Service authors think that this operation will seldom be used.

```
void unmask_type (
    in CosTrading::ServiceTypeName name
) raises (
    CosTrading::IllegalServiceType,
    CosTrading::UnknownServiceType,
    NotMasked
);
```

#### *7.2.2.2 TraderComponents–Finding the Right Interface*

The trader defines five separate interfaces:

- Lookup, where importers make queries
- Register, where exporters advertise new service offers
- Link, where links to federated traders are administered
- Admin, where policies of the trader are administered
- Proxy, where legacy mechanisms for advertising services are added so that they look like service offers

A single interface, TraderComponents, is inherited by all the interfaces listed here. This allows users to locate the other interfaces supported by a particular trader implementation.

```
interface TraderComponents {
    readonly attribute Lookup lookup_if;
    readonly attribute Register register_if;
```

```
    readonly attribute Link link_if;
    readonly attribute Proxy proxy_if;
    readonly attribute Admin admin_if;
};
```

### 7.2.2.3 Lookup

The Lookup interface is used by importers to find service offers that meet their needs. It offers a single operation, query(), that requires a specification of the service type and matching constraint expression and returns a list of service offers. The signature for query() is significantly more complex than this simple explanation would indicate:

```
void query (
  in ServiceTypeName type,
  in Constraint constr,
  in Preference pref,
  in PolicySeq policies,
  in SpecifiedProps desired_props,
  in unsigned long how_many,
  out OfferSeq offers,
  out OfferIterator offer_itr,
  out PolicyNameSeq limits_applied
) raises (
  IllegalServiceType,
  UnknownServiceType,
  IllegalConstraint,
  IllegalPreference,
  IllegalPolicyName,
  PolicyTypeMismatch,
  InvalidPolicyValue,
  IllegalPropertyName,
  DuplicatePropertyName,
  DuplicatePolicyName
);
```

The third parameter, pref, is a minimizing, maximizing, or boolean sorting expression that tells the trader which matched offers to return first. The policies parameter allows the importer to influence the way in which the trader searches its service offers and the way in which it propagates the query to other traders. Often query invocations will be given an empty PolicySeq since the trader administrator will configure the trader to allow a trade-off between search space and resource usage that will deliver appropriate services to users.

Many aspects of trader behavior can be modified by policies. Policies are name/value pairs and are defined in module CosTrading:

```
module CosTrading {
    // ...
    typedef string PolicyName;
    typedef sequence<PolicyName>;
    typedef any PolicyValue;
    struct Policy {
        PolicyName name;
        PolicyValue value;
    };
```

Policies can be classified according to whether they scope the extent of a search or whether they determine the functionality that the trader applies to an operation. An example for a scoping policy is return_card, which sets an upper bound on the number of offers that are returned from a query. An example of a policy that modifies operation functionality is use _dynamic_properties, which instructs the trader to ignore offers with dynamic properties if set to false. Dynamic properties are explained in section 7.2.2.8. Trader administrators will configure a number of default policies, so even when you do not supply policies in query operations, the trader usually will not do an exhaustive search of its entire search space. You will see examples of creating and using policies in section 7.2.4.

A desired_props argument must be provided so that the trader knows whether to return properties of the service offers that matched together with the object reference or just the object references to the services. The SpecifiedProps type is defined as follows:

```
enum HowManyProps { none, some, all};
union SpecifiedProps switch ( HowManyProps ) {
    case some: PropertyNameSeq prop_names;
};
```

Sometimes a service type will contain many properties that do not interest a particular importer. In this case, the importer will need to specify in the prop_names field of the desired_props which property values to return. In many cases, the choice to ignore the property values or to require all the values is sufficient.

The how_many parameter specifies that the importer wishes to receive a certain number of offers back in the form of a sequence (in the offers out parameter). The rest of the offers will be obtained through an iterator, whose object reference is returned in the offer_itr out parameter (see section 7.2.2.4). Typically, importers are interested in the following:

- Getting back a small number of offers so that they can ensure that one service is actually available at the time
- Examining a large number of service offers for direct comparison outside the trader

In the first case, an importer may save the trader the time and resources of creating an iterator by specifying a policy called return_card. This policy instructs the trader to return only the number of matching service offers specified by the policy. Making its value the same as the how_many argument will prevent the creation of an iterator.

#### 7.2.2.4 Iterators

An iterator is an object that controls a logical list of objects or data items and can return them to a client a few at a time. We use the term *logical list* because the object supporting the iterator may produce new items for the list as they are required. This is a common style used in many OMG specifications. We have already seen an example of using iterators in section 7.1 when iterating over the bindings in a naming context. In the trader two iterators are specified:

- OfferIterator is used when a large number of service offers are returned from the Lookup::query operation.
- OfferIdIterator is used to return all of the OfferIds held in a particular trader from the Admin::list_offers operation.

They have essentially the same interface, so we will look at only one of them here.

```
interface OfferIterator {
    unsigned long max_left ()
      raises (UnknownMaxLeft);

    boolean next_n (
      in unsigned long n,
      out OfferSeq offers
    );
    void destroy ();
};
```

The max_left() operation provides an upper bound on the number of offers that the iterator contains. If the offers are being constructed a few at a time, then the upper bound may not be easily calculated, so the UnknownMaxLeft exception will be raised. The next_n() operation will return up to $n$ offers in the offers out parameter, and a return value of FALSE indicates that no other offers are contained in the iterator.

Although the trader may clean up iterators from time to time to reclaim resources, responsible clients will call destroy() on iterators as soon as they have extracted enough offers.

### *7.2.2.5 Register*

The Register interface provides operations for advertisers of services. The most important operations are the following:

- export()—advertises a service offer in the trader and returns an identifier for it
- withdraw()—removes an identified service offer from the trader
- describe()—returns the properties of an identified service offer
- modify()—allows an exporter to change the values of nonread-only properties of a service offer

Other operations allow exporters to withdraw all service offers matching a particular query and to obtain the Register interface of a linked trader by name.

```
OfferId export (
    in Object reference,
    in ServiceTypeName type,
    in PropertySeq properties
) raises (
    InvalidObjectRef,
    IllegalServiceType,
    UnknownServiceType,
    InterfaceTypeMismatch,
    IllegalPropertyName, // e.g., prop_name = "<foo-bar"
    PropertyTypeMismatch,
    ReadonlyDynamicProperty,
    MissingMandatoryProperty,
    DuplicatePropertyName
);
```

The export() operation takes three parameters that describe a service and places that service offer in the trader's database for return as a result of an importer's query. The reference parameter must contain an object reference of the type specified in the service type named by the second parameter, type. The properties parameter must contain a value for each mandatory property in the service type and may contain values for other properties. All values provided for property names specified in the service type must be of the property type specified, and additional properties of any other name and type may also be included. Any nonread-only property value may be replaced by a structure of the following type:

```
struct DynamicProp {
    DynamicPropEval eval_if;
    TypeCode returned_type;
    any extra_info;
};
```

This will cause the property's value to be determined at import time, which means that the constraint will be evaluated on up-to-date information. The previous printer example has a property that reflects the length of the current print queue. The eval_if member is an object reference to a standard interface that has a single operation that returns an Any. The returned_type member is the type of the value expected in that Any, and it must match the type specified for this property in the service type.

The exceptions that may be returned are mostly self-explanatory. The ReadonlyDynamicProperty exception indicates that it is illegal for a read-only property to change after export.

The withdraw() operation passes the trader an OfferId returned from a previous export(), and the trader will remove the corresponding service offer from its database.

```
void withdraw (
   in OfferId id
) raises (
   IllegalOfferId,
   UnknownOfferId,
   ProxyOfferId
);
```

The other withdraw operation, withdraw_using_constraint(), will remove all service offers that match a particular constraint expression. This should generally be used only by the administrator.

The describe() operation returns an OfferInfo structure corresponding to the id parameter. OfferInfo contains exactly the same information as the three parameters to export(): an object reference, a service type, and a sequence of properties.

```
struct OfferInfo {
    Object reference;
    ServiceTypeName type;
    PropertySeq properties;
};
OfferInfo describe (
    in OfferId id
) raises (
    IllegalOfferId,
    UnknownOfferId,
    ProxyOfferId
);
```

The modify() operation allows exporters to change the properties contained in a particular service offer. Some traders do not allow the modification of service offers and will raise the NotImplemented exception. Traders that implement this operation must succeed on all modifications or fail on all. Properties listed in the del_list parameter will be deleted if possible, and property values in modify_list will replace current values in the identified service offer, if this is allowed. The reasons the operation may fail are reflected in its long raises clause. In short, the two list parameters may be inconsistent, or the caller may be trying to modify something read-only or delete something mandatory.

```
void modify (
    in OfferId id,
    in PropertyNameSeq del_list,
    in PropertySeq modify_list
) raises (
    NotImplemented,
    IllegalOfferId,
    UnknownOfferId,
    ProxyOfferId,
    IllegalPropertyName,
    UnknownPropertyName,
    PropertyTypeMismatch,
    ReadonlyDynamicProperty,
    MandatoryProperty,
    ReadonlyProperty,
    DuplicatePropertyName
);
```

The resolve() operation is for obtaining a reference to the Register interface of another trader, to which this trader has a named link. This is how one exports service offers to and withdraws them from federated traders.

```
Register resolve (
    in TraderName name
) raises (
    IllegalTraderName,
    UnknownTraderName,
    RegisterNotSupported
);
```

#### 7.2.2.6 Link

Links can be considered a specialization of service offers. They advertise other traders that can be used to perform federated queries. The Link interface therefore looks much the same as the Register interface, with operations to add and remove, as well as describe and modify links. Each link has four associated pieces of information: its name, its object reference (to a Lookup interface), and two policies on link following. Most users of traders do not need to know what links a trader has or how they are followed. The trader administrator sets up link policies and trader defaults.

#### 7.2.2.7 Admin

The Admin interface contains a large number of operations to set the policies of a trader and operations to list the OfferIds of service offers contained in the trader. Ordinary trader users can query the attributes of the other interfaces to determine the current policies of a trader, but they will never need to use the Admin interface. Some traders will not even offer this interface because all policy will be determined by the implementation.

#### 7.2.2.8 Proxies and Dynamic Properties

Proxies are objects that sit alongside service offers but hide some legacy mechanism of service creation or discovery. Most traders will not support the Proxy interface. Traders that do return identical results from a proxy as from a normal service offer.

Dynamic properties are a mechanism to allow a service to provide a property value at import time that reflects the current state of the service. We have seen in the explanation of the export operation that the value of a non-read-only property may be replaced by a DynamicProp structure. This will cause the trader to call back to an interface supported by the service (or some associated server) to obtain the property value when the constraint expression of a query is being evaluated. The object reference provided in that structure must be of the following interface type:

```
interface DynamicPropEval {
    any evalDP (
        in CosTrading::PropertyName name,
        in TypeCode returned_type,
        in any extra_info
    ) raises (
        DPEvalFailure
    );
};
```

When evaluating a dynamic property, the trader invokes the evalDP() operation of the eval_if member of the DynamicProp, passing the property name and the returned_type and extra_info members of the structure. It receives an appropriate value in return.

The evaluation of a query that involves calling back to several services to determine the dynamic value of a property can be very costly, and some traders will not support dynamic properties, as indicated by the SupportAttributes::supports_dynamic_properties Boolean attribute. For some services, though, the information is invaluable for determining their suitability for a purpose. For example, a printer that is one floor up from me and has a zero-length queue is much more useful than one in the same room that has 30 jobs queued or is out of toner.

## 7.2.3 Exporting a Service Offer

In this section we provide an example implementation of the Printer interface introduced in section 7.2.1. The server that supports objects of this type will export service offers describing the printer objects to the trader. In this way, printer clients can choose printers using an expression of their requirements, rather than the usual method of choosing the name of a printer they know.

The Printer interface is very simple, and it emulates the kind of command-line interface provided by UNIX print commands such as `lpr`. The purpose of this implementation is to show how a minimal wrapper of this kind of service, which describes printer attributes in service offers, can allow users more flexibility. They can not only choose a printer based on some capability that it has, such as high resolution, but they can also choose it based on its current state, such as the length of its print queue. In addition, users can discover new printers that they were previously unaware of.

The environment in which we implemented this server is one in which many different operating systems run on different machines. Although they all have access to the same file systems via NFS, it is too complex to integrate all the different printing services, and printing is available on only some machines. One way of extending printer availability is to install this server on one of the printing machines, using a CORBA client on the other machines that passes the name of the file to be printed.

The implementation of the printer server has the usual steps. The first of these, specifying the interface of a CORBA object, has already been done in section 7.2.1, although we will extend this IDL to facilitate the evaluation of dynamic properties. The second is to compile the IDL, and following that we need to implement the TradingPrinter interface and write a server that creates instances of the implementation class. Our server will also create service offers for the printers it creates and export these to the trader.

### 7.2.3.1 Implementing the Printer Interface

We intend to allow the trader to use its dynamic property evaluation to get the printer queue length at query time, so that clients of the trader can sort their returned printer service offers according to the length of the queue. In order to do this we need to implement the interface CosTradingDynamic::DynamicPropEval so that the trader can call its evalDP() operation to get the `queue_len` property of each printer service offer. The best way to do this is to create a new interface that multiply inherits from the printer and the dynamic property evaluation interfaces. We reopen the Printing module and define a new interface as follows:

```
module com {
...
module chapter7 {
module printing {
    interface TradingPrinter : Printer,
        CosTradingDynamic::DynamicPropEval {};
    };
};};};};
```

The IDL compiler generates the following classes and interfaces:

```
Printer.java
PrinterHelper.java                PrinterHolder.java
PrinterOperations.java            _PrinterStub.java
PrinterPOA.java                   PrinterPOATie.java
TradingPrinter.java
TradingPrinterHelper.java         TradingPrinterHolder.java
TradingPrinterOperations.java _TradingPrinterStub.java
TradingPrinterPOA.java            TradingPrinterPOATie.java
```

```
PrinterPackage/PrinterOffLine.java
PrinterPackage PrinterOffLine/Helper.java
PrinterPackage/PrinterOffLineHolder.java
PrinterPackage/filenameHelper.java PrinterPackage/filenameHolder.java
```

Our implementation of the TradingPrinter interface is done in the class `PrinterImpl`, which extends the default skeleton class `TradingPrinterPOA`. We define the package, which corresponds to the module structure, and import the classes in the `org.omg.CORBA` package, as well as those for our generated IDL and the generated classes for the CosDynamicTrading IDL module. We also need to import the `java.io` package that will be used in the implementation.

```
package com.wiley.compbooks.brose.chapter7.printing;

import org.omg.CORBA.*;
import com.wiley.compbooks.brose.chapter7.Printing.PrinterPackage.*;
import org.omg.CosTradingDynamic.*;
import java.io.*;

class PrinterImpl extends TradingPrinterPOA {
```

Because the printer interface is so simple, we need only `PrinterImpl` to know the command we will use to find the queue length, the command to print files, and the name of the printer to which it will send them. Therefore we define three private string array members to store the commands and the name and a constructor that accepts three corresponding string arguments. These arrays will constitute the command lines for starting command processes. The additional member `ret_type` is for the dynamic property evaluation return type.

```
    private String[] print_command;
    private String[] queue_command;
    private String printer_name;
    private TypeCode ret_type;

    // constructor
    PrinterImpl (String p_command,
                 String q_command,
                 String name,
                 TypeCode dp_eval_ret_type) {

        print_command = new String[3];
        print_command[0] = p_command;
        print_command[1] = "-P" + name;
        queue_command = new String[2];
        queue_command[0] = q_command;
```

```
        queue_command[1] = name;
        printer_name = name;
        ret_type = dp_eval_ret_type;
    }
```

We could have chosen to initialize printer objects with all the characteristics we will export in their service offers, but because we don't define any attributes or operations to retrieve these properties, there is no point in doing so. Instead we make the server aware of these characteristics and it exports service offers with corresponding property values on the objects' behalf.

The remainder of the implementation consists of the methods mapped from the IDL operations. The first of these is `print_file()`:

```
public void print file (String fn)
    throws PrinterOffLine {

    try {
        Process p;
        Runtime run = Runtime.getRuntime();
        print_command[2] = fn;
        p = run.exec(print_command);
    } catch (java.io.IOException ioe) {
        System.err.println(ioe);
        throw new PrinterOffLine();
    }
}
```

The method is implemented very simply by concatenating the print command, the printer name, and the file name and executing it via the `Runtime` object's `exec()` method. The `queue_len()` method is also implemented by making a call to an executable. We assume that this executable returns the length of the printer queue. While there is no such command on either standard UNIX or DOS, it is easy to write a script that outputs the contents of the printer queue and then counts the number of lines.

```
public short queue_length()
    throws PrinterOffLine {

    try {
        short len;
        Process p;
        Runtime run = Runtime.getRuntime();
        p = run.exec(queue_command);
        String cmd_output =
            (new BufferedReader( new InputStreamReader(
                p.getInputStream()))).readLine();
```

```
            len = Short.parseShort( cmd_output );
            System.out.println("Printer " + printer_name +
                                  " queue_len:" + len);
            return len;
        } catch (java.io.IOException ioe) {
            System.err.println(ioe);
            throw new PrinterOffLine();
        }
    }
```

The other method that must be implemented is for the dynamic property evaluation operation evalDP(). Its parameters are extracted from the value of any dynamic property in a service offer. This value will always be of type

```
struct DynamicProp {
    DynamicPropEval eval if;
    TypeCode returned type;
    any extra info;
};
```

The eval_if member of this struct will be a reference to our PrinterImpl object, and the other two parameters will be passed to the evalDP() operation on that interface. This is what we implement here:

```
    public Any evalDP (
        String name,
        TypeCode returned_type,
        Any extra_info )
    throws DPEvalFailure {

        if ( !name.equals("queue_len") ) {
            throw new DPEvalFailure();
        }

        if (! returned_type.equal(ret_type)) {
            throw new DPEvalFailure();
        }

        Any ret_val = _orb().create_any();
        try {
            ret_val.insert_short(this.queue_length());
        } catch (PrinterOffLine pol) {
            throw new DPEvalFailure();
        }
        return ret_val;
    }
}
```

The name argument to the evalDP() method is the name of the property in the service offer being evaluated. We are expecting only one such name, queue_len, and if we receive any other, we will throw the DPEvalFailure exception. The result of the evaluation must be an Any with the TypeCode passed in the returned_type argument. If the TypeCode expected is not the one passed by the server to our constructor then we also raise an exception. We are not expecting any extra information (such as arguments to supply to a method call), so we then create an Any object and place the result of the call to queue_length() into it and return the Any. The last failure condition may occur when the printer is offline and cannot return a queue length value. In this case we also throw the DPEvalFailure exception.

### *7.2.3.2 Implementing the Printer Server*

Now that we have an implementation of a PrinterImpl class that satisfies the requirements of printer clients and the trader, we will implement a server that creates printer objects and service offers that represent their characteristics and then exports them to the trader. We have used the JacORB Trader implementation for testing.

Our server will take the following command-line arguments:

- A command to send a file to the printer that takes the printer name and a file name
- A command to check the printer queue length that takes a printer name
- The characteristics of one or more printers including each printer's name, resolution in DPI, building location, and floor number

The PrinterServer class is in the same package as the PrinterImpl class, and it needs to import the CORBA classes, the printer IDL classes, and the trader IDL classes:

```
package com.wiley.compbooks.brose.chapter7.printing;

import org.omg.CORBA.*;
import org.omg.PortableServer.*;
import com.wiley.compbooks.brose.chapter7.Printing.PrinterPackage.*;

import org.omg.CosTrading.*;
import org.omg.CosTrading.Register.*;
import org.omg.CosTrading.RegisterPackage.*;
import org.omg.CosTradingRepos.*;
import org.omg.CosTradingRepos.ServiceTypeRepositoryPackage.*;
import org.omg.CosTradingDynamic.*;
```

```
public class PrinterServer {
   // constants for array access
   static final int NAME = 0;
   static final int BUILDING = 1;
   static final int FLOOR = 2;
   static final int RESOLUTION = 3;
   static final int QUEUE_LEN = 4;
   static final int COLOR = 5;
   static final int LANGUAGE = 6;

   public static void main (String[] args) {
      int num_printers;
      PrinterImpl [] printers;
      String printer_name;

      if( args.length < 4 || args.length % 4 != 2) {
         System.out.println("Usage: vbj Printing.PrintServer print_
command queue_len_command name resolution building floor [ name res
build floor ... ]");
         System.exit (1);
      }
```

An array is declared for storing references to the printers. Various ORB and trader variables are declared, and then the usual ORB initialization is carried out.

```
      // allocate an array to store Printer Implementation Objects
      num_printers = (args.length - 2) / 4;
      printers = new PrinterImpl[num_printers];

      int i;
      try {
         //initialize the ORB and POA
         ORB orb = ORB.init(args, null);
         POA poa = POAHelper.narrow(
                        orb.resolve_initial_references("RootPOA"));
         poa.the_POAManager().activate();

         // Trader object reference declarations
         Lookup lookup;
         Register register;
         ServiceTypeRepository st_repos;

         // get the trader reference and initialise the
         // ServiceTypeRepository and Register interface
         // references from the initial Lookup interface

         org.omg.CORBA.Object obj =
                  orb.resolve_initial_references("TradingService");
```

```
lookup = LookupHelper.narrow(obj);
if (lookup == null) {
   System.err.println("Lookup narrowed incorrectly");
   System.exit(1);
}

register = lookup.register_if();
obj = register.type_repos();
st_repos = ServiceTypeRepositoryHelper.narrow(obj);
if (st_repos == null) {
   System.err.println("ServiceTypeRepository narrowed
                       incorrectly");
   System.exit(1);
}
```

The trader's reference is obtained using the ORB's bootstrap operation resolve_initial_references(). The first reference for a trader is to a Lookup interface, from which we obtain references to its Register interface and the service type repository. The service type repository reference returned from the attribute type_repos is specified as type Object in the standard, in anticipation of the interface ServiceTypeRepository being replaced by a repository specified by the Meta-Object Facility, which was adopted by the OMG in September 1997. This is why the returned reference must be narrowed.

The next thing we need to do is to check if the service type that we want to use is already defined in the service type repository. We do this by checking the result of a call to the describe_type() operation, which will raise the UnknownServiceType exception if it is not yet created.

```
// check for Service Type existence
boolean type_exists = false;
String repos_id = "IDL:com/wiley/compbooks/brose/chapter7/
                   Printing/Printer:1.0";
String serv_type_name = "Printer";
IncarnationNumber incarn_num;
TypeStruct type_desc;

try {
   type_desc = st_repos.describe_type(serv_type_name);
   System.out.println("called describe_type - returned
                       typedesc");
   type_exists = true;
}
catch (UnknownServiceType ust) {
   System.out.println("called describe_type - raised
                       UnknownServiceType");
   type_exists = false;
}
catch (IllegalServiceType ist) {
```

```
      System.err.println(ist);
      System.exit (1);
   }
   catch (SystemException se) {
      System.err.println(se);
      System.exit (1);
   }
```

If the service type is not present then we must create it. We will use the same properties as shown when we introduced the printing example in section 7.2.1. We make all the properties mandatory so that we can be sure that a query using any property name in the service type will be evaluated on all service offers of this type.

```
   if (! type_exists) {
      System.out.println("service type does not exist");
      // we will create a new service type

      // create a prop stuct list with the property names
      // for a printer service type

      PropStruct[] st_props = new PropStruct[7];
      st_props[NAME] = new PropStruct( "name",
                                    orb.create_string_tc(0),
                                    PropertyMode.PROP_MANDATORY);

      st_props[BUILDING] = new PropStruct( "building",
                                    orb.create_string_tc(0),
                                    PropertyMode.PROP_MANDATORY);

      st_props[FLOOR] = new PropStruct("floor",
                            orb.get_primitive_tc(TCKind.tk_short),
                                    PropertyMode.PROP_MANDATORY);

      st_props[RESOLUTION] = new PropStruct("resolution",
                            orb.get_primitive_tc(TCKind.tk_short),
                                    PropertyMode.PROP_MANDATORY);

      st_props[QUEUE_LEN] = new PropStruct( "queue_len",
                           orb.get_primitive_tc(TCKind.tk_short),
                                    PropertyMode.PROP_MANDATORY);

      st_props[COLOR] = new PropStruct("color",
                                    orb.create_string_tc(0),
                                    PropertyMode.PROP_MANDATORY);

      st_props[LANGUAGE] = new PropStruct( "language",
                                    orb.create_string_tc(0),
                                    PropertyMode.PROP_MANDATORY);
```

The other arguments required by the repository's add_type() operation are a service type name, an interface's RepositoryId, and a list of supertypes. We are not using any supertypes here.

```
        // create an empty super type list
        String[] super_types = new String[0];

        // add the new Service Type
        System.out.println("about to add_type");
        incarn_num = st_repos.add_type( serv_type_name,
                                        repos_id,
                                        st_props,
                                        super_types);
        System.out.println("Created Service Type:" +
                                              serv_type_name);
        System.out.println("Incarnation Number: high=" +
                                            incarn_num.high);
        System.out.println("                       low=" +
                                          incarn_num.low);
    }
```

Now we are ready to create a template service offer, which we can reuse for all the printers that we will export. This server is going to support only printers that are black and white and use PostScript, so we can set the values for the `color` and `language` properties now. The other property that will share a value for all service offers is `queue_len`, which will contain a `DynamicProp`. It will be initialized with the type expected from the dynamic evaluation, but the actual object reference will be added once the printer object is created.

```
    // create Service Offer Property Seq to use for export
    Property[] so_props = new Property[7];

    // create a Dynamic Property for queue length evaluation
    DynamicProp queue_prop = new DynamicProp(null,
                    orb.get_primitive_tc(TCKind.tk_short),
                    orb.create_any());

    // The first 5 properties will be different for each
    // printer, so we initialize them in the loop below

    so_props[NAME] = new Property("name",orb.create_any());
    so_props[BUILDING] = new Property("building",
                                        orb.create_any());
    so_props[FLOOR] = new Property("floor", orb.create_any());
    so_props[RESOLUTION] = new Property("resolution",
                                        orb.create_any());
    so_props[QUEUE_LEN] = new Property("queue_len",
                                        orb.create_any());
```

```
// the last two properties' values are assumed by this
// server so we initialize them for all printers

so_props[COLOR] = new Property("color", orb.create_any());
so_props[COLOR].value.insert_string("black");
so_props[LANGUAGE] = new Property("language",
                                          orb.create_any());
so_props[LANGUAGE].value.insert_string("postscript");
```

The next step is to process the command-line arguments and create printers with the corresponding characteristics. We do this in a loop, creating the `PrinterImpl` objects, making them available to the ORB, and then updating the template service offer to advertise them.

```
for (i = 0; i < num_printers; i++) {
   // create a Printer object and register it with the POA
   printers[i] = new PrinterImpl(
                 args[0],
                 args[1],
                 args[i*4 + 2],
                 orb.get_primitive_tc(TCKind.tk_short));
   // implicitly activate the servant
   org.omg.CORBA.Object printerObject =
                poa.servant_to_reference( printers[i] );

   System.out.println("Created printer: " + args[i*4 +2]);
   // initialize the properties we get from the command line
   // name
   so_props[NAME].value.insert_string(args[i*4 + 2]);
   // resolution
   so_props[RESOLUTION].value.insert_short(
                      Short.parseShort(args[i*4 + 3]));
   // building
   so_props[BUILDING].value.insert_string(args[i*4 + 4]);
   // floor
   so_props[FLOOR].value.insert_short(
                      Short.parseShort(args[i*4 + 5]));

   // update the dynamic prop struct and insert into
   // the queue_len property of the service offer
   queue_prop.eval_if = DynamicPropEvalHelper.narrow(
                                       printerObject );
   DynamicPropHelper.insert(so_props[QUEUE_LEN].value,
                         queue_prop);

   // export the service offer
   register.export(printerObject,
                serv_type_name,
                so_props);
```

```
            System.out.println("Exported printer: " +args[i*4 +2]);
         } // end for loop
```

Once the printers are all created and their offers exported, we call `orb.run()` to allow the server to accept incoming requests. We also have to catch the various CORBA user and system exceptions that can be raised, as well as the `NumberFormatException` that can be thrown when parsing `short` arguments.

```
         // take requests for our printers
         orb.run();
      }
      catch (PropertyTypeMismatch pm) {
         System.err.println(pm);
         System.err.println(pm.type);
         System.err.println(pm.prop.name);
         System.err.println(pm.prop.value);
      }
      catch (NumberFormatException ne) {
         System.err.println("Badly formatted numeric argument");
         System.err.println(ne);
         System.exit (1);
      }
      catch (UserException ue) {
         System.err.println("User exception caught");
         ue.printStackTrace();
         System.exit (1);
      }
      catch (SystemException se) {
         System.err.println("System exception caught");
         se.printStackTrace();
         System.err.println(se);
         System.exit (1);
      }
   }
}
```

## 7.2.4 Finding an Object Using a Trader

In this section we implement a simple Java application client that trades for a suitable Printer object to which it can send its print job. The application is implemented as a class `PrintClient`, in which we implement a single method, `main()`. The application expects a mandatory and two optional arguments:

- The name of the file we wish to print
- A constraint expression to select suitable printers
- A preference expression to order the printer service offers returned

The structure of the application is as follows:

- The class usage is checked for the appropriate number of arguments.
- We obtain a reference to a Lookup object.
- The command-line arguments to the application are processed.
- Some basic policies for a trader query are established.
- The query is made.
- The returned Printer objects are tried in order until one successfully prints the file.

Let's look at the code starting with the package declaration, the imported classes, the PrintClient class definition, and the command-line argument check:

```
package com.wiley.compbooks.brose.chapter7.printing;

import org.omg.CORBA.*;
import com.wiley.compbooks.brose.chapter7.printing.PrinterPackage.*;

import org.omg.CosTrading.*;
import org.omg.CosTrading.Lookup.*;
import org.omg.CosTrading.LookupPackage.*;
import org.omg.CosTrading.Register.*;
import org.omg.CosTrading.RegisterPackage.*;
import org.omg.CosTradingRepos.*;
import org.omg.CosTradingRepos.ServiceTypeRepositoryPackage.*;
import org.omg.CosTradingDynamic.*;

public class PrintClient {
   public static void main(String args[]) {
      if( args.length < 1 || args.length > 3 ) {
         System.out.println("usage: PrintClient printfile
                             [constraint [preference]]");
         System.exit( 1 );
      }
```

The application exits if it has not been run with the mandatory file name argument.

The next piece of code declares some variables and then initializes the ORB and obtains a reference to the trader's Lookup interface.

```
      try {
         //initilize the ORB and POA
         ORB orb = ORB.init( args, null );
         org.omg.CORBA.Object obj;

         // get reference to trader lookup interface
         Lookup lookup = null;
```

```
try {
   obj = orb.resolve_initial_references("TradingService");
   lookup = LookupHelper.narrow( obj );
}
catch( org.omg.CORBA.ORBPackage.InvalidName in ) {}

if (lookup == null) {
   System.err.println("Null Trader Reference");
   System.exit(1);
}
```

As in the PrinterServer, we obtain a reference to the Trading Service and then narrow the reference to the Lookup type. The next step is to prepare the query for a printer. We use any constraint and preference strings received from the command line and provide suitable defaults when they are not provided.

```
// determine the constraint
String constr;
if( args.length > 1 ) {
   constr = args[1];
} else {
   constr = "";
}

// determine the prefs
String prefs;
if (args.length > 2 )
   prefs = args[2];
else
   // if no preference, compare the offers for shortest queue
   prefs = "min queue_len";
```

An empty constraint string will match all service offers of the right type. If the user does not supply a preference, then we use a default that orders the returned printers by shortest queue length. Now we set parameter values and policies to ensure that we get a reasonable result.

```
// set some basic policies
org.omg.CosTrading.Policy[] query_pols =
                         new org.omg.CosTrading.Policy[2];

//declare variables needed in the query()
int num_offers = 3;
String serv_type_name ="Printer";

SpecifiedProps desired_props;
OfferSeqHolder return_offers = new OfferSeqHolder();
OfferIteratorHolder iter = new OfferIteratorHolder();
PolicyNameSeqHolder limits = new PolicyNameSeqHolder();
```

We will ask for at most three offers back, as this provides a reasonable likelihood of one printer being operational. We initialize a short variable num_offers to the value 3. This is used in the policy return_card, which specifies the maximum number of service offers to return from a query. If we then pass the same value to the query() operation's how_many parameter, we can ensure that all of the results will come back in the offers out parameter, and we will not have to process an iterator.

```
// we want at most 3 offers back
Any card_policy_any = orb.create_any();
card_policy_any.insert_ulong( num_offers );
query_pols[0] = new org.omg.CosTrading.Policy(
                                        "return_card",
                                        card_policy_any);
```

The other policy we will pass to the trader is use_dynamic_properties, which tells the trader to evaluate the queue_len property dynamically so that the value used is up to date.

```
// we want to use dynamic props to find printer queue length
Any dynamic_policy_any = orb.create_any();
dynamic_policy_any.insert_boolean(true);
query_pols[1] = new org.omg.CosTrading.Policy(
                                "use_dynamic_properties",
                                dynamic_policy_any);
```

The desired_props parameter to query() lists the property names whose values we want returned with the query result. For easy processing, in this example we will ask for only the printer name, which assumes that users of our application know their printers by name so that they can go and pick up a printout from the right location. Remember that by using the trader we can discover new printers that only the system administrator knows about. A more advanced printing application would probably ask for all the properties and provide the user with information on the location of printers, which would enable newly discovered printers to be found by location.

```
// we want back only the name property
String[] desired_prop_names = new String[1];
desired_prop_names[0] = "name";
desired_props = new SpecifiedProps();
desired_props.prop_names(desired_prop_names);
```

The SpecifiedProps type is a union, so we must initialize its value and discriminator. Java mapping specifies that a method corresponding to a union branch name will set the discriminator for us. We use the method prop_names() to set the value of the only branch.

Having created objects or variables for each of the parameters to the query() method, we can now invoke it:

```
// make a query
try {
    lookup.query( serv_type_name,
                  constr,
                  prefs,
                  query_pols,
                  desired_props,
                  num_offers,
                  return_offers,
                  iter,
                  limits);
}
```

Because we have set the value in policy return_card to the value of num_offers (the size of the sequence we are prepared to accept back into our return_offers object) we can ignore the iterator. We also ignore the feedback from the trader about what policy restrictions it applied to our query, which are returned in the limits object. This time we must catch the user exceptions as well as any system exceptions. Rather than catching each of the 10 possible user exceptions that the query() operation could raise, we will catch the base class of all of these, CORBA.UserException.

```
// catch exceptions
catch (UserException ue) {
    System.err.println("Query failed - User Exception: "
                       + ue);
    System.exit(1);
}
catch (SystemException se) {
    System.err.println("Query failed: "+ se);
   System.exit(1);
}
```

Having received a response from the trader we will now attempt to use the service offers to print the file. We do this by entering a loop that exits once the print_file() operation has been invoked successfully on one of the objects returned in a service offer. First we declare and initialize some variables, including a string and an Any to extract the printer's name from the single returned property in each service offer.

```
// send job to printer
int i = 0;
boolean printed = false;
String pname = "";
Any return any = orb.create_any();
```

Then we enter the loop.

```
// we'll try all the returned printers until one works
while (i < return_offers.value.length && !printed) {
   try {
      return_any =
               return_offers.value[i].properties[0].value;
      pname = return_any.extract_string();
      Printer printer = PrinterHelper.narrow(
                          return_offers.value[i].reference);
      if (printer == null) {
         System.out.println("Printer " + pname +
                              " not found");
         i++;
         continue;
      }
      printer.print_file( args[0] );
      printed = true;
      System.out.println("File " + args[0] +
                            " sent to printer " + pname);
}
```

If the string extraction from `return_any` and the narrow of the reference work, then we attempt to print the file named in the second command-line argument. If the `print_file()` call works, the termination variable is set to true, a message is printed, and the loop will exit. Other possibilities are that the printer is offline or that the invocation fails for some other reason.

```
catch (PrinterOffLine pol) {
   System.out.println("Printer " + pname + " offline!");
}
catch (SystemException se) {
   System.out.println("Printer " + pname +
                         " raised: " + se);
}
i++;
}
```

Finally, we catch any system exceptions that are raised during ORB initialization.

```
      }
      catch (SystemException se) {
         System.out.println(se);
      }
   }
}
```

Any failures to print are notified to the user, and the next printer is tried. This is an example of how we might run the application:

```
.../Print> java com.wiley.compbooks.brose.chapter7.printing.PrintClient
myfile.ps \
    'language == "postscript" && floor < 4'
```

Our constraint expression expresses our need for a PostScript printer somewhere on the lower floors of our building. We do not specify a preference, as the default preference for the shortest print queue length is suitable. The execution may result in the following output:

```
Printer 12ps offline!
File myfile.ps sent to printer monster
```

### 7.2.4.1 Possible Enhancements to the Print Client

The example exercises the query() operation, demonstrates how to pass policies and how to specify the properties we want back, and shows how to extract the returned property values. It does not deal with the situation where no service offers match the constraint expression.

A more sophisticated printer query might look up the user's default printer constraint expression and preferences from a file if none was supplied on the command line. It could also check that at least one working printer offer is returned, and if not, it could make a less specific query with an empty constraint string to match all available offers of the service type.

In the case where the first attempt fails, it could query for all printers and ask for all of their properties to be returned, then display a list and allow the user to select an appropriate printer. This would require that the `return_card` policy not be set and that an iterator be used because the number of offers returned would be unpredictable. When making a query that might match a large number of offers, it is often best to set the how_many argument to zero and have a single loop process the iterator, as shown in the Naming Service example. This avoids having to have two loops, one for the returned sequence of offers and the other to invoke the next_n() operation on the returned iterator reference.

## 7.3 Bootstrapping

As demonstrated in this chapter, CORBA solves the bootstrapping problem by providing a pair of operations on the ORB pseudo-interface:

- list_initial_services()—lists the names of initial services that are available from the ORB.
- resolve_initial_references()—returns an initial object reference to a named service. For example, a naming context is returned when a Naming Service reference is requested.

We introduced these operations in Chapter 2, "CORBA Overview," and explained their Java mapping in Chapter 6, "ORB Run-Time System." Until now, we have used only the identifiers `"NameService"`, `"TradingService"`, and `"RootPOA"` in calls to resolve_initial_references(). Other reserved identifiers that can be used as arguments are `"POACurrent"`, `"InterfaceRepository"`, `"SecurityCurrent"`, `"TransactionCurrent"`, `"DynAnyFactory"`, `"CodecFactory"`, and `"PICurrent"`. Your particular ORB implementation may provide additional references using other identifiers.

These two operations provide a very basic name service as a bootstrapping mechanism for services. This support alone is not sufficient, however: It is not clear which object instance will be returned when several are available.

CORBA does not define an association between the ORB and services, and there is also no such thing as *the* ORB. When you obtain an ORB pseudo-object by calling `org.omg.ORB.init()`, a local instance of the class `org.omg.ORB` is created that implements the operations defined in the pseudo-interface CORBA::ORB. Furthermore, novice users sometimes assume that an ORB is associated with an IP subnet—this is not the case! Whenever your ORB is initialized locally and obtains a reference to an object, you can invoke operations on that object.

As you can see, the ORB does not solve our problem. What we want is something that allows us to share the same instances of initial services among a set of objects and clients. We call this a *domain*. There are multiple kinds of domains. In this context we have a naming domain and a trading domain, that is, a set of objects and clients that share the same Naming Service or Trading Service, respectively.

In the case of the Naming Service we face an additional problem. The Naming Service specification does not define a structure for the relationships between naming context objects. Even though you organize your naming contexts as a tree, the Naming Service does not know this and does not have a predefined root. Hence, any context may be returned by resolve_initial_references().

So a domain is specific to a service and identifies which initial object instance provided by such a service is returned. All members of a domain will obtain the same initial object. For the Naming Service, this means that all clients and objects that belong to the same naming domain obtain the same context object when calling `orb.resolve_initial_references("NameService")`.

CORBA provides only a minimal interface for choosing service domains such as naming and trading domains. To achieve this, we have to use the parameters that can be used to initialize the ORB object. The Java language binding defines the following alternatives of the ORB's `init()` operation:

```
ORB init();
ORB init( Applet applet, Properties props );
ORB init( String[] args, Properties pros );
```

Using these parameters, we can pass command-line arguments to initialize the local ORB object so that it belongs to a certain naming and/or trading domain. Alternatively, Java properties can be used for this purpose.

In previous versions of the CORBA specification it was left to the individual ORB implementations how the ORB could be configured to return specific references. The updated Naming Service specification, however, has introduced standard arguments that all compliant ORBs must recognize. It has also defined a default algorithm for determining initial references.

To set up the list of initial references for an ORB instance, the standard ORB option `-ORBInitRef` can be used. For example, to configure the ORB to provide a specific naming context object as the result of `orb.resolve_initial_references("NameService")`, we can pass the option `-ORBInitRef NameService=IOR:000001234...` on the command line. As you would expect, it is also possible to provide `corbaloc` or `corbaname` URLs instead of using the IOR URL scheme. When resolving initial references the ORB always looks for references specified in this way first. With VisiBroker 4.0, the command line could also use Java properties and would thus look like this:

```
vbj -DORBInitRef=NameService=IOR:.... mypackage.MyProgram
```

A second option for configuring initial references is `-ORBDefaultInitRef`. This option requires a base URL that can be extended with the required object identifier to yield a complete URL. If we pass `-ORBDefaultInitRef corbaloc::myserver.mycompany.com:4711` to the ORB, it would look for the initial Trading Service using the URL `corbaloc::myserver.mycompany.com:4711/TradingService`. The ORB will use this URL only if no `-ORBInitRef` option has been set for the Trading Service, however. If none of these options was used, the ORB may fall back to using a vendor-specific configuration mechanism.

# Building Applications

In this chapter we explain how to build applications using Java ORBs. We have selected a simple room booking system as an example. Because we want to demonstrate CORBA features rather than prove that we can implement a sophisticated booking system, we have kept the application-specific semantics simple. But, as will be seen in the IDL specification, we have chosen a very fine-grain object model that allows the creation of many CORBA objects and the demonstration of invocations between them. We will also demonstrate the use of the CORBA Naming Service. We will substantially extend this example in Chapter 10, "Practical POA Programming," and discuss various design approaches and patterns in Chapter 15, "Performance, Scalability, and Management," where we revisit the room booking application. This chapter covers the development of an entire application including interface specification (section 8.1), implementing objects (section 8.2), implementing a server (section 8.3), implementing a factory (section 8.4), starting servers (section 8.5), and clients as applications and applets (section 8.6). We mention possible extensions to the example application in section 8.7.

## 8.1 Application Specification

The room booking system allows the booking of rooms and the cancellation of such bookings. It operates over one-hour time slots from 9 A.M. to 4 P.M. To keep things simple, we do not consider time notions other than these slots, so there are no days or weeks. The rooms available to the booking system are not fixed; the number and the names of rooms can change. When booking a room, a purpose and the name of the person making the booking should be given. All objects presented here are transient and do not keep persistent state. We will extend the example in the next chapter and show how persistent references can be created. We do not consider security issues, and anyone can cancel any booking.

The following key design decisions were made:

- Rooms and meetings are CORBA objects.
- A Meeting object defines a purpose and the person responsible for the meeting.
- A Meeting Factory creates meeting objects.
- A Room stores Meetings indexed by time slots.
- Rooms have a name and register themselves under this name with the Naming Service.

Figure 8.1 illustrates a typical configuration of the room booking system. There are three Room servers, which all have one Room object implementation. There is also a Meeting Factory server that has created a Meeting Factory object. The Meeting Factory has created several Meeting objects that are in the same process space, which corresponds to a JVM in the Java case. There is also a Naming Service that has various Naming Context objects forming a context tree. The Room and the Meeting Factory object implementations are registered with the Naming Service.

### 8.1.1 IDL Specification

The IDL specification of the room booking system is contained in a hierarchy of modules as described in Chapter 4, "A First Java ORB Application." It contains a number of interface specifications: Meeting, MeetingFactory, and Room.

The interface Meeting has two attributes: purpose and participants, which are both of type string and readonly. The attributes describe the semantics of a meeting. The interface also has a one-way operation destroy() to complete its life cycle.

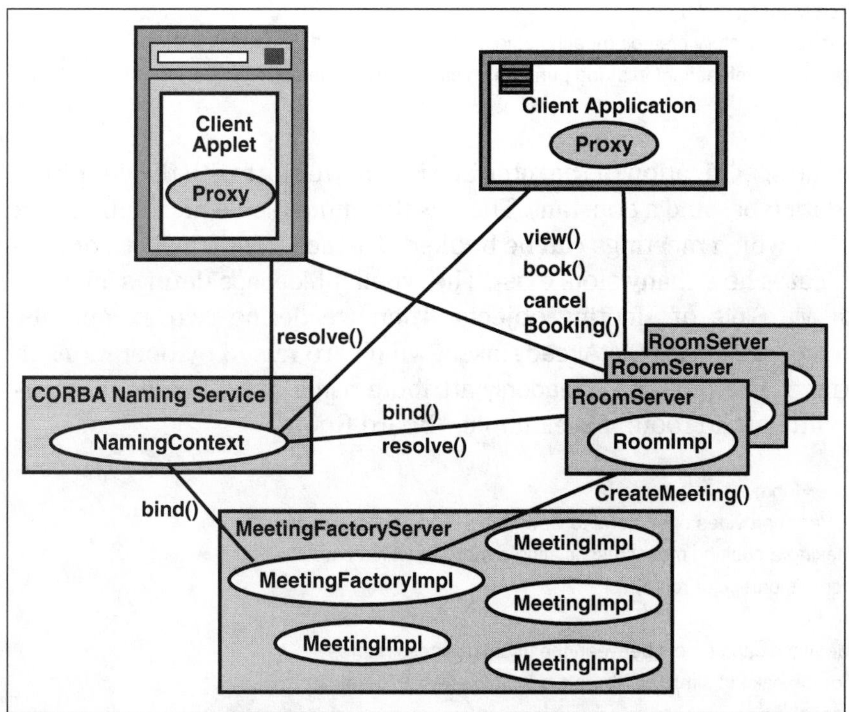


**Figure 8.1** Room booking system—a typical configuration.

Meeting objects are created at run time by a Meeting Factory, which is specified in the interface MeetingFactory. It provides a single operation createMeeting(), which has parameters corresponding to the attributes of the Meeting object and returns an object reference to the newly created Meeting object.

```
module com {
module wiley {
...
module chapter8 {
module roomBooking {

  interface Meeting {
     // A meeting has two read-only attributes that describe
     // the purpose and the participants of that meeting.

     readonly attribute string purpose;
     readonly attribute string participants;

     oneway void destroy();
  };
```

```
interface MeetingFactory {
   // A meeting factory creates meeting objects.
   Meeting createMeeting( in string purpose, in string participants);
};
```

Within the specification of the interface Room, we start with the definition of some data types and a constant. There is the enum Slot, which defines the time slots in which meetings can be booked. The constant MaxSlots, of type short, indicates how many slots exist. The typedef Meetings defines an array of length MaxSlots of Meeting objects. Then we define two exceptions, NoMeetingInThisSlot and SlotAlreadyTaken, which are raised by operations in the interface. There is also a readonly attribute name of type string that carries the name of the room, for example, "Board Room."

```
interface Room {
   // A Room provides operations to view, make, and cancel bookings.
   // Making a booking means associating a meeting with a time-slot
   // (for this particular room).

   // Meetings can be held between the usual business hours.
   // For the sake of simplicity there are 8 slots at which meetings
   // can take place.

   enum Slot { am9, am10, am11, pm12, pm1, pm2, pm3, pm4 };

   // since IDL does not provide means to determine the cardinality
   // of an enum, a corresponding constant MaxSlots is defined.

   const short MaxSlots = 8;

   // Meetings associates all meetings (of a day) with time slots
   // for a room.

   typedef Meeting Meetings[ MaxSlots ];

   exception NoMeetingInThisSlot {};
   exception SlotAlreadyTaken {};

   // The attribute name names a room.

   readonly attribute string name;

   // view returns the bookings of a room.
   // For simplicity, the implementation handles bookings
   // for only one day.
```

```
    Meetings view ();

    void book( in Slot a_slot, in Meeting  a_meeting )
      raises(SlotAlreadyTaken);

    void cancelBooking( in Slot  a_slot )
      raises(NoMeetingInThisSlot);
  };
}; ... };
```

There are three operations defined in the interface Room. The operation view() returns Meetings, the previously defined array of Meeting objects. The meaning is that a Meeting object reference indicates that this Meeting is booked into the indexed slot. A nil object reference means that the indexed slot is free.

The operation book() books the meeting a_meeting in the slot a_slot of the Room object on which the operation is invoked. The operation raises the SlotAlreadyTaken exception if there is already a meeting booked into the specified slot.

The operation cancelBooking() removes the meeting at the slot a_slot. It raises the NoMeetingInThisSlot exception if there is no meeting in the slot.

## 8.1.2 Compiling the IDL Specification

When we compile the IDL specification with an IDL compiler, the compiler generates different Java interfaces and classes depending on the compiler flags chosen. Here we show the files we use in our implementation.

There are Java signature and operation interfaces for each of the IDL interfaces:

```
MeetingFactory.java MeetingFactoryOperations.java
Meeting.java        MeetingOperation.java
Room.java           RoomOperations.java
```

Holder classes are also generated, but we do not use out or inout parameters in this chapter. Among other methods, the helper classes contain the `narrow()` methods for each interface:

```
MeetingFactoryHelper.java MeetingHelper.java RoomHelper.java
```

The stub and skeleton classes are generated for each interface. We use the following classes:

```
MeetingFactoryPOA.java _MeetingFactoryStub.java
MeetingPOA.java        _MeetingStub.java
RoomPOA.java           _RoomStub.java
```

Additionally, there are classes for the data types, and exceptions are defined within the IDL interface Room that are in the Java package `RoomPackage`:

```
MeetingsHelper.java       MeetingsHolder.java
Slot.java                 SlotHolder.java           SlotHelper.java
SlotAlreadyTaken          SlotAlreadyTakenHolder    SlotAlreadyTakenHelper
  .java                    .java                      .java
NoMeetingInThisSlot.java NoMeetingInThisSlotHolder.java
NoMeetingInThisSlotHelper.java
```

# 8.2 Implementing Objects

The classes we have to implement are for the IDL interfaces Meeting and Room. We do this by extending the generated POA skeleton classes.

## 8.2.1 Implementing the Meeting Object

We implement the Meeting object in a class `MeetingImpl` that extends the implementation base class `MeetingPOA`. We define two private variables, `purpose` and `participants`, that correspond to the attributes with the same names. The constructor has two parameters that are used to initialize the two private variables.

```
package com.wiley.compbooks.brose.chapter8.roomBooking;

import org.omg.CORBA.*;
class MeetingImpl
    extends MeetingPOA {

    private String purpose;
    private String participants;

    /** constructor */
    MeetingImpl( String purpose, String participants){

        // initialize private variables
        this.purpose = purpose;
        this.participants = participants;
    }
```

IDL attributes are mapped to Java methods. These consist of an accessor method and a modifier method if the attribute is not read-only. Because the attributes of the interface Meeting are readonly we have to implement only the accessors. Their implementation is straightforward; they just return the value of the corresponding private variable.

```
    // attributes
    public String purpose() {
        return purpose;
    }

    public String participants() {
        return participants;
    }
```

We also implement the `destroy()` method by deactivating the object in its object adapter, so that it can be garbage-collected once all other references to it are released.

```
    /** deactivates the object */
    public void destroy(){
    try {
        _poa().deactivate_object( _poa().servant_to_id(this));
    }
    catch( Exception e ){
        // ignore
    }
}
```

The method `_poa()` is inherited from the skeleton base class `org.omg.PortableServer.Servant`, which our implementation extends indirectly. It retrieves the POA instance from the current execution context that is responsible for this CORBA object.

## 8.2.2 Implementing the Room Object

The Room object is implemented in the class `RoomImpl`, extending the corresponding skeleton class, `RoomPOA`. We declare two private variables: `name` to hold the name of the Room object and `meetings` to hold the array of booked meetings. Within the constructor we assign the only argument, determining the name of the room to be created, to our private variable `room`.

```
package com.wiley.compbooks.brose.chapter8.roomBooking;

import org.omg.CORBA.*;
import com.wiley.compbooks.brose.chapter8.roomBooking.RoomPackage.*;

public class RoomImpl
    extends RoomPOA {
```

```
    private String name;
    private Meeting[] meetings;

    /** constructor */
    public RoomImpl( String name ) {
        this.name = name;
        meetings = new Meeting[ Room.MaxSlots ];
    }
```

As introduced in Chapter 5, "OMG IDL to Java Mapping," IDL bounded arrays are mapped to Java arrays; however, it is the application programmer's responsibility to initialize the array to the length declared in the IDL. The ORB provides only a run-time check to ensure that the specified boundaries hold. Our variable `meetings` is such a bounded array. We use the constructor to initialize it appropriately. The length of the array is defined in the specification of the interface Room as a constant MaxSlots. This constant is mapped by a generated class variable `MaxSlots` in the interface `Room`:

```
package com.wiley.compbooks.brose.chapter8.roomBooking;

public interface Room
    extends RoomOperations,
            org.omg.CORBA.Object,
            org.omg.CORBA.portable.IDLEntity
{
    public final static short MaxSlots = (short)8;
}
```

The attribute name is read-only and hence only the accessor method needs to be implemented. It returns the value of the corresponding private variable.

```
public String name() {
    return name;
}
```

The operations of IDL interfaces are mapped to Java methods. The implementation of the method `view()` is rather straightforward. It returns the array `meetings`, which holds the object references to the currently booked meetings.

```
public Meeting[] view() {
    return meetings;
}
```

The method `book()` has two parameters: One determines the slot in which a meeting should be booked, and the other identifies the meeting object. We check if the slot is empty, that is, if the object reference indexed by the slot is nil. Although the CORBA pseudo-interface CORBA::Object provides a corresponding operation is_nil(), the IDL/Java mapping shortcuts this by defining a nil CORBA object reference as a Java null. Hence, we check if the indexed slot is `null`. If the slot is empty we assign the meeting to the slot; otherwise, we raise the exception `SlotAlreadyTaken`. The class for the exception is defined in the package `RoomPackage` because the corresponding IDL exception was defined in the interface Room.

```
public void book( Slot slot, Meeting meeting )
    throws SlotAlreadyTaken {
    if( meetings[slot.value()] == null ) {
            meetings[slot.value()] = meeting;
    }
    else {
        throw new SlotAlreadyTaken();
    }
    return;
}
```

The method `cancelBooking()` is implemented similarly. We check if the slot is occupied, and if so we assign a null object to the slot. To allow the object adapter to reclaim resources associated with a meeting, we must deactivate it. This is done by calling the method `destroy()` on the Meeting object. In the case where there is no meeting object in the indexed slot, we throw the exception `NoMeetingInThisSlot`.

```
    public void cancelBooking( Slot slot )
        throws NoMeetingInThisSlot {
        if( meetings[slot.value()] != null ) {
           meetings[slot.value()].destroy();
           meetings[slot.value()] = null;
        }
        else {
            throw new NoMeetingInThisSlot();
        }
    }
}
```

## 8.3 Building Servers

To instantiate the object implementations and to make them available to clients we have to implement a server. This is code that at run time executes as an operating system process or task. In the Java case it is a Java virtual machine in which object instances run. There can be one server per object, or a server can handle multiple objects. A server has four fundamental tasks:

- Initialize the environment, that is, get references to the pseudo-objects for the ORB and the POA
- Create servants
- Make objects accessible to the outside world
- Execute a dispatch loop to wait for invocations

Additional server tasks can include the registration of the objects with the Naming Service or the Trading Service.

The server `RoomServer` carries out these four fundamental tasks and registers the newly created room with the Naming Service. This is achieved by defining a class `RoomServer` and implementing its method `main()`. We define two strings that are used when registering the Room object with the Naming Service. Then we check that the number of arguments is correct and exit the program if it is not. We expect one argument determining the name of the Room object.

To use the Naming Service successfully, objects that want to share information via the Naming Service have to agree on a naming convention. For this example we use the following convention, which is illustrated in Figure 8.2: Under a root context we have a context "Building Applications" that contains a context called "Rooms." We bind Room objects into the context "Rooms" and the Meeting Factory object into the context "Building Applications." Following this convention will ensure that clients can locate the appropriate objects. Note that the Trading Service provides a more formal approach to categorization based on service types (see Chapter 7, "Discovering Services").

According to this naming convention we initialize the variable `context_name` with a corresponding string version of the Room context name.

```
package com.wiley.compbooks.brose.chapter8.roomBooking;

import java.io.*;
import org.omg.CORBA.*;
import org.omg.PortableServer.*;
import org.omg.CosNaming.*;
import org.omg.CosNaming.NamingContextPackage.*;

public class RoomServer {

    public static void main(String[] args) {
        String context_name, str_name;

        if( args.length != 1 ) {
            System.out.println("Usage: vbj
```

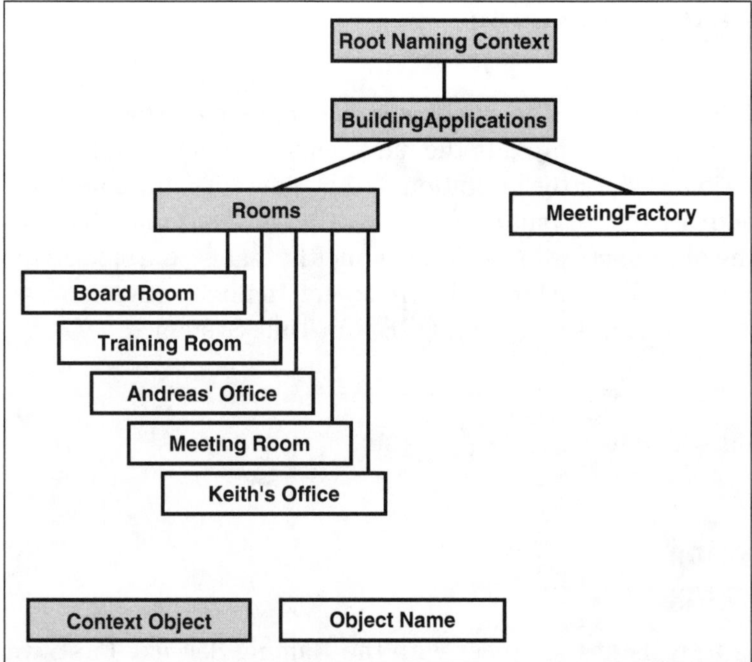


**Figure 8.2** Naming convention.

```
com.wiley.compbooks.brose.chapter8.roomBookingImpl.RoomServer
room_name");
              System.exit( 1 );
        }

        context_name = "BuildingApplications/Rooms";
```

## 8.3.1 Initializing the ORB

The first task is to initialize the ORB and obtain a reference to the POA. To get a reference to the ORB we call the class method `init()` on the class `CORBA.ORB`. We call `resolve_initial_references("RootPOA")` on the ORB pseudo-object `orb`. This returns a reference to a POA object. We then activate the POA via its POAManager.

```
        try {
            //init
            ORB orb = ORB.init( args, null );
            POA poa = POAHelper.narrow(
                        orb.resolve_initial_references("RootPOA"));
            poa.the_POAManager().activate();
```

## 8.3.2 Creating and Activating a Servant

The second task is to create the Room object. We create an instance of the servant class RoomImpl and provide the name as a parameter to the constructor (see section 8.2.2 for the definition of that class). Then we perform the third task: activate the servant as an incarnation of the Room object at the RootPOA. The object activation is done implicitly, that is, as a side effect of creating the object reference for the Room object. Implicit activation was explained in section 6.3.2 of Chapter 6, "ORB Run-Time System."

```
// create the Room object and export the
// object reference
org.omg.CORBA.Object room_obj =
   poa.servant_to_reference( new RoomImpl( args[0] ) );
```

## 8.3.3 Registering with the Naming Service

The next step is to register the object with the Naming Service. First, we obtain a reference to an initial context of a Naming Service via the ORB's bootstrap mechanisms. The Naming Service handles simple names including contexts in a notation similar to the notation of file names in various operating systems:

```
/<context1>/<context2>/.../<contextn>/<name>
```

It parses strings in this format and creates Naming Service names of type CosNaming::Name, which maps to CosNaming.NameComponent[] in Java.

We initialize such a string in the variable str_name, for example, with a value "/BuildingApplications/Rooms/Board Room." Before binding our Room object to a name, however, we had better make sure that the "Rooms" context actually exists at this stage. If this server is the first to run, we will receive a NotFound exception from the Naming Service (unless the context has been set up by administrative action outside our application). If the context already exists, we will get an AlreadyBound exception, but we can safely ignore it. Finally, we bind the Room object to a name by calling bind() on the root Naming Context. The argument to bind() is a name created from the string str_name.

```
// register with naming service
str_name = context_name + "/" + args[0];

NamingContextExt root = NamingContextExtHelper.narrow(
     orb.resolve_initial_references( "NameService" ));
```

```
            try {
                // make sure the "rooms" context is bound
                root.bind_new_context(root.to_name(context_name));
            }
            catch( AlreadyBound ab ) {
                // does not matter .
            }
            root.bind( root.to_name( str_name ), room_obj );
```

## 8.3.4 Entering the Dispatch Loop

The fourth task of the server is to enter a dispatch loop by calling `run()` on the ORB to wait for incoming invocations.

Finally, we catch exceptions. If an exception of type `AlreadyBound` is raised, we realize that a room with our room's name is already registered with the Naming Service. We handle any exception that is raised by printing the exception's string representation and exiting.

```
            // wait for requests
            orb.run();
        }
        catch( AlreadyBound already_bound ) {
            System.err.println("Room " + context_name + args[0] +
                                   " already bound.");
            System.err.println("exiting ...");
        }
        catch(UserException ue) {
            System.err.println(ue);
            System.err.println("Room " + context_name + args[0] +
                                   " already bound.");
        }
        catch(SystemException se) {
            System.err.println(se);
        }
    }
}
```

# 8.4 Building Factories

A factory is an object implementation with a particular design pattern. The difference from ordinary objects is that factories provide methods to dynamically create new objects. They perform the same initialization of new objects as a server's `main()` method; that is, they create objects and make them invokable. The process of building factories contains the same steps as building any other server: implementing the object and implementing the server.

## 8.4.1 Meeting Factory Object Implementation

The Meeting Factory implementation, the class `MeetingFactoryImpl`, is an extension of the corresponding skeleton class `MeetingFactoryPOA`.

```
package com.wiley.compbooks.brose.chapter8.roomBooking;
import org.omg.CORBA.*;

class MeetingFactoryImpl
    extends MeetingFactoryPOA
{
```

The only method of the Meeting Factory, `createMeeting()`, is shown next. Its parameters correspond to those of the Meeting object constructor, `MeetingImpl()`. We pass the parameters to the `MeetingImpl` constructor, which creates a new instance of a Meeting servant. We store the reference to this object in the variable `newMeeting`. Once the servant is created we create an object reference from it and thereby implicitly activate it at the same POA that is responsible for the Meeting Factory object. The new Meeting object is now invokable via this reference, which we then return to the caller.

```
    public Meeting createMeeting(String purpose,
                                 String participants ){
        MeetingImpl meetingImpl =
             new MeetingImpl(purpose, participants);
        try {
            org.omg.CORBA.Object obj =
                _poa().servant_to_reference(meetingImpl);
            Meeting meeting = MeetingHelper.narrow(obj);
            return meeting;
        }
        catch( Exception se ){
            System.err.println(se);
        }
        return null;
    }
}
```

## 8.4.2 Meeting Factory Server

The Meeting Factory server follows the same pattern as the Room server. We initialize the ORB and the POA, create the Meeting Factory object, and activate it.

```
package com.wiley.compbooks.brose.chapter8.roomBooking;

import java.io.*;
import org.omg.CORBA.*;
import org.omg.PortableServer.*;
import org.omg.CosNaming.*;
import org.omg.CosNaming.NamingContextPackage.*;

public class MeetingFactoryServer {

    public static void main(String[] args) {
        String str_name, context_name;

        if( args.length != 0 ) {
            System.out.println("Usage: java MeetingFactoryServer");
            System.exit( 1 );
        }

        // the stringified names we want to use
        context_name = "BuildingApplications";
        str_name = context_name + "/MeetingFactory";

        try {
            //initialize ORB
            ORB orb = ORB.init( args, null );

            // initialize and activate POA
            POA poa = POAHelper.narrow(
                        orb.resolve_initial_references("RootPOA"));
            poa.the_POAManager().activate();

            // create the MeetingFactory object
            MeetingFactoryImpl meeting_factory =
                                            new MeetingFactoryImpl();

            // export the object reference
            org.omg.CORBA.Object meeting_factory_obj =
                        poa.servant_to_reference(meeting_factory);
```

Like the Room server, the Meeting Factory first checks that the naming context it wants to use exists. We then try to bind the Meeting Factory object to the name defined previously. If the name is already bound, we override the old binding and rebind the name to our new Meeting Factory. Note that we use rebind only to demonstrate another feature of the Naming Service; the rebind semantics are not implied by the Meeting Factory.

```
            // register with the CORBA Naming Service
            NamingContextExt root = NamingContextExtHelper.narrow(
                    orb.resolve_initial_references("NameService"));
```

```
            try {
                // make sure our context exists
                root.bind_new_context( root.to_name( context_name ));
            } catch( AlreadyBound ab ) {
                // ok, we ignore that
            }

            // bind our new meeting factory
            try {
                root.bind( root.to_name( str_name ),
                           meeting_factory_obj);
            }
            catch( AlreadyBound ab ) {
                root.rebind( root.to_name( str_name ),
                             meeting_factory_obj);
            }
```

We finish by calling `orb.run()` to wait for incoming invocations and then catch exceptions.

```
            // enter event loop
            orb.run();
        }
        catch(Exception e) {
            System.err.println(e);
        }
    }
}
```

## 8.5 Starting Servers

Starting the servers requires the following steps. As explained in Chapter 7, we use a `corbaloc:` URL to define the initial reference to the Naming Service.

Start VisiBroker Naming Service on host `z1`, port 4711:

```
> nameserv -J-Dvbroker.se.iiop_tp.scm.iiop_tp.listener.port=4711 &
```

Start Meeting Factory server:

```
> vbj -DORBInitRef=CosNaming=corbaloc:iiop:z1:4711/NameService
  com.wiley.compbooks.brose.chapter8.RoomBookingImpl.
  MeetingFactoryServer &
```

Start Room servers:

```
> vbj -DORBInitRef=CosNaming=corbaloc:iiop:z1:4711/NameService
com.wiley.compbooks.brose.chapter8.RoomBookingImpl.
  RoomServer "Board Room" &
> vbj -DORBInitRef=CosNaming=corbaloc:iiop:z1:4711/NameService
com.wiley.compbooks.brose.chapter8.RoomBookingImpl.
  RoomServer "Training Room" &
> vbj -DORBInitRef=CosNaming=corbaloc:iiop:z1:4711/NameService
  com.wiley.compbooks.brose.chapter8.RoomBookingImpl.
  RoomServer "Meeting Room" &
> vbj -DORBInitRef=CosNaming=corbaloc:iiop:z1:4711/NameService
  com.wiley.compbooks.brose.chapter8.RoomBookingImpl.
  RoomServer "Andreas' Office" &
> vbj -DORBInitRef=CosNaming=corbaloc:iiop:z1:4711/NameService
com.wiley.compbooks.brose.chapter8.RoomBookingImpl.
  RoomServer "Keith's Office" &
```

## 8.6 Building Clients

Clients can be implemented as Java applications or applets. The differences between the two kinds of client are as follows:

**Different initialization of graphical user interface.** When using Java's AWT classes to build a GUI, the class `java.awt.Component` is the base class from which any GUI class is derived. The Applet class `java.applet.Applet` is an extension of the Component class and can be used directly to create a user interface. The GUI for an application is based on the class `java.awt.Frame`, which is also an extension of the Component class.

**Different initialization of the ORB.** The main difference here is applet sandboxing, which we discussed in Chapter 3, "Overview of Java and Java ORBs." This constrains the establishment of network connections to the host from which the applet was loaded. Another issue is client-side firewalls, which also stop network connections to arbitrary ports. These factors make applets quite different from ordinary Java applications. Java ORBs respond to this situation by providing different mechanisms for initializing the ORB depending on whether the program is an applet or an application.

**Access of the classes.** An application accesses CORBA and application-specific classes from the local file system, for example, as specified by the environment variable `CLASSPATH`. Applets and the CORBA classes they require are loaded into a Web browser via a network or from the file system. Netscape browsers (4.0 and later) have CORBA classes (VisiBroker for Java) built in.

Figures 8.3 to 8.6 illustrate our graphical user interfaces for both applet and application clients in various stages of their use. They aid understanding of the code in the following subsections.

Figure 8.3 shows the initial state of a client that is viewing a booking system containing four bookings made previously by other clients. This figure shows the applet client.

Figure 8.4 shows the action that takes place after the user has clicked a button labeled "Book" for the Training Room's 9 A.M. time slot. The user has entered the relevant data into the text fields. This is a view of the Java application version of the client.

Figure 8.5 shows the application after the booking is made.

Figure 8.6 shows the form produced by clicking the "View" button for the same meeting slot.

We have separated the parts of a client that are independent of the kind of client into a class `RoomBookingClient` which is implemented in section 8.6.3. That leaves the tasks of creating an object of the class `RoomBookingClient` and catching and processing user events in the applet or application class. In section 8.6.1 we look at the applet class, and in section 8.6.2 we look at the Java application class.

Room Booking Applet

Room Booking System

| Rooms | AM 9 | 10 | 11 | 12 | PM 1 | 2 | 3 | 4 |
|---|---|---|---|---|---|---|---|---|
| Board Room | Book | View | Book | Book | Book | Book | Book | Book |
| Meeting Room | Book | Book | Book | Book | Book | View | Book | Book |
| Keith's Office | Book | Book | View | Book | Book | Book | Book | Book |
| Andreas' Office | Book | Book | Book | Book | Book | Book | Book | Book |
| Training Room | Book | Book | Book | Book | View | Book | Book | Book |

**Figure 8.3** Applet–initial state.

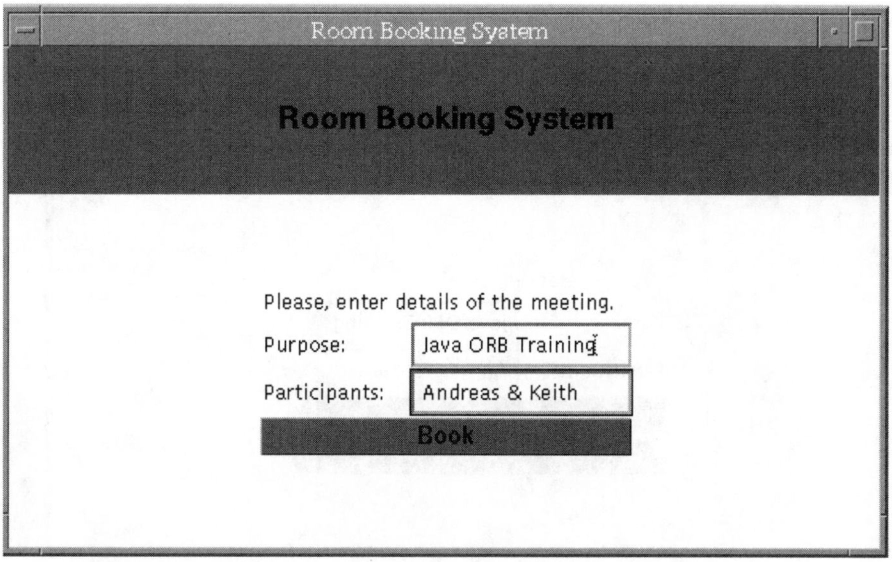

**Figure 8.4** Application—booking form.

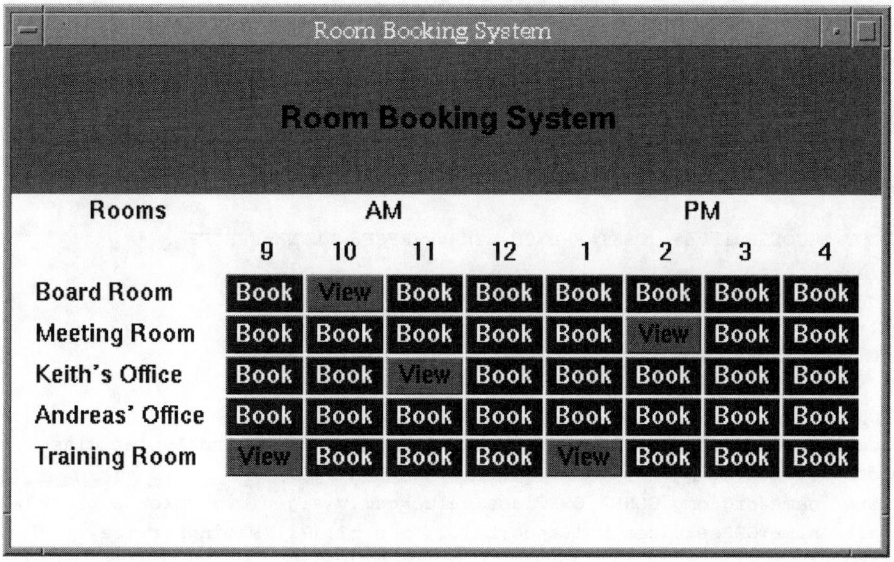

**Figure 8.5** Application—view after booking.

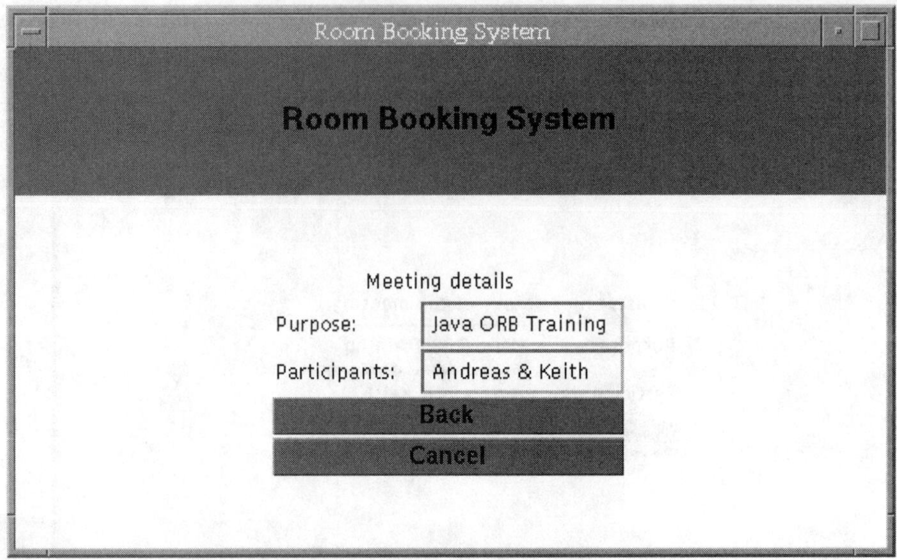


**Figure 8.6** Application–cancel form.

## 8.6.1 Client as Applet

The first thing we have to do to develop the applet is to write an HTML page that anchors it. We give the page a title and a header and put the applet in the middle of the page. The applet class is `RoomBookingApplet`, and we reserve a display area of 600 by 300.

```
<html><header>
<title>
Room Booking Applet
</title>
<BODY BGCOLOR=15085A TEXT=FFD700 LINK==FFFFFF VLINK=FFFFFF
ALINK=FFFFFF>
<center>
<h1>
Room Booking Applet
<h1>
<applet
code=com/wiley/compbooks/brose/chapter8/roomBooking/ClientApplet.class
width=600 height=300>
<param name=org.omg.CORBA.ORBClass value=com.visigenic.vbroker.orb.ORB >
<param name=ORBservices value=corbaloc:iiop:z1:4711/NamingService>
</applet>
</center>
</body></html>
```

The structure of an applet is based on the structure of its base class, `java.applet.Applet`. We override the method `init()` of the applet base class. We declare a variable as a reference to an object of the class `RoomBookingClient`. Then we create the object within the method `init()`. We have two constructors for the class `RoomBookingClient` that are similar to the two kinds of constructors for the ORB: one to be used by applets, the other by applications. As you will see later on, these constructors use the appropriate ORB constructor and get a root context of the Naming Service, which we introduced in Chapter 7.

We initialize the GUI with method `init_GUI()` on the object `client` of class `RoomBookingClient`. To do this we have to provide an object of class `java.awt.Container`. The Applet class extends the Container class.

We start by calling the method `init_from_ns()` on the `client` object, which obtains the Meeting Factory and Room naming context references from the Naming Service. Then we invoke the method `view()`, which obtains the available rooms from the Naming Service and invokes the operation view() on each of these Room objects.

```
package com.wiley.compbooks.brose.chapter8.roomBooking;
import java.awt.*;
import org.omg.CORBA.*;
import com.wiley.compbooks.brose.chapter8.roomBooking.RoomPackage.*;
public class ClientApplet
    extends java.applet.Applet {

    private RoomBookingClient client;
    // override init method of Class Applet
    public void init() {
        // create a RoomBookingClient client -
        // using the applet constructor
        client = new RoomBookingClient( this );
        // initialize the GUI
        client.init_GUI( this );
        // initialize the Naming Service
        client.init_from_ns();
        // view existing bookings
        client.view();
    }
}
```

## 8.6.2 Client as Application

To make the room booking system client a Java application we implement a class `ClientApplication`. This class extends `java.awt.Frame`, a specialization of the class java.awt.Component. The application class also implements the Java interface java.awt.WindowListener.

The implementation of the constructor of the ClientApplication class invokes the constructor of the superclass (java.awt.Frame). Its only parameter sets the title of the corresponding window. We pass the string "Room Booking System" to the constructor (see Figure 8.4).

```
package com.wiley.compbooks.brose.chapter8.roomBooking;

import java.awt.*;
import java.awt.event.*;
import org.omg.CORBA.*;
import com.wiley.compbooks.brose.chapter8.roomBooking.RoomPackage.*;

public class ClientApplication
    extends Frame
    implements WindowListener {

    private static RoomBookingClient client;

    /** constructor */
    ClientApplication() {
        super( "Room Booking System" );
    }
```

We also implement the main() method of the class, which is similar to the init() method of the applet class. The main() method must create an object of the application class itself. We call this object gui because it plays the role of our graphical user interface. We again create an object of the class RoomBookingClient. Here we use a different constructor that is suitable for applications rather than applets. Then we again initialize the GUI and obtain some object references from the Naming Service by calling init_from_ns() on the client object. Then we invoke the method view() to get the booking information from each Room.

```
    public static void main(String args[]) {
        // create an object of its own class
        ClientApplication gui = new ClientApplication();

        // create a RoomBookingClient object -
        // using the application constructor
        client = new RoomBookingClient();

        // initialize the GUI
        client.init_GUI( gui );

        // initialize the Naming Service
        client.init_from_ns();
```

```
        // view existing bookings
        client.view();
    }
}
```

## 8.6.3 Client-Type Independent Code

In this subsection we explain the client code that is independent of the applet or application details, that is, the client code that makes calls to the various object implementations. This code is encapsulated in a class `RoomBookingClient`. The code of the class is rather voluminous, mainly due to the necessity of managing the graphical user interface. We will partition the code to aid understanding.

### *8.6.3.1 Overview of Methods*

The class `RoomBookingClient` implements the following methods:

```
public void init_GUI( java.awt.Container gui )
```

This method initializes the graphical user interface.

```
public void init_from_ns()
```

This method gets the room context from the root context and obtains a reference to the Meeting Factory by resolving it from a predefined name.

```
public boolean view()
```

This method queries all rooms and displays the result at the user interface.

```
public boolean cancel()
```

This method cancels a selected booking.

```
public boolean process_slot(int selected_room, int selected_slot)
```

This method processes the event of clicking a button to book or view a meeting. It decides if the room is free and a booking can be made or if the booking details should be displayed.

```
public boolean meeting_details()
```

This method queries and displays the details of a meeting. The method deals mainly with GUI programming; the code is available on the companion Web site at www.wiley.com/compbooks/brose.

```
public void booking_form()
```

This method produces a booking form for a user to enter meeting details. As this is pure GUI programming, we have omitted its explanation in the following text. Again, the complete code is on the companion Web site.

```
public boolean book()
```

This method creates a meeting and books it into a selected slot.

```
public boolean actionPerformed()
```

This method catches and processes user events.

### 8.6.3.2 Variable Declarations

We start the implementation of the class with a number of local variables. The buttons are defined as `public` because they are used by the applet and application objects.

```
package com.wiley.compbooks.brose.chapter8.roomBooking;

import java.util.*;
import java.awt.*;
import java.awt.event.*;
import org.omg.CORBA.*;
import org.omg.CosNaming.*;
import com.wiley.compbooks.brose.chapter8.roomBooking.RoomPackage.*;

public class RoomBookingClient
    implements ActionListener {

    public Button viewButton;
    public Button bookButton;
    public Button cancelButton;
    public Button exitButton;
    public Button[][] slotButton;

    private TextField participants_tf;
    private TextField purpose_tf;

    private Panel mainPanel;
    private Panel titlePanel;

    private boolean[][] booked;

    private int selected_room;
    private int selected_slot;
```

```
private ORB orb;
private NamingContextExt root_context;
private NamingContextExt room_context;

private MeetingFactory meeting_factory;
private Room[] rooms;
private Meeting[] meetings;

private String ior;
private boolean is_application = true;

Color green = new Color( 0, 94, 86 );
Color red = new Color( 255, 61, 61 );
```

### *8.6.3.3 Constructors*

The class `RoomBookingClient` has two constructors, one each for applets and applications.

**Constructor for applets.** The constructor for applets has a single parameter of type `java.applet.Applet`. It initializes the ORB in a way that is appropriate for applets.

```
/** constructor for applets */
RoomBookingClient( java.applet.Applet applet ) {
    try
    {
        // initialize the ORB
        orb = ORB.init( applet, null );
        ior = applet.getParameter("NameServer");
        root_context = NamingContextExtHelper.narrow(
                orb.string_to_object(ior));
        is_application = false;
    }
    catch(Exception system_exception ) {
        System.err.println( "constructor RoomBookingClient: " +
                          system_exception );
    }
}
```

**Constructor for applications.** The constructor for Java applications initializes the ORB in the default way.

```
/** constructor for applications */
RoomBookingClient() {
    try
    {
        // initialize the ORB
        orb = ORB.init((java.lang.String[])null, null);
```

```
        root_context = NamingContextExtHelper.narrow(
                orb.resolve_initial_references("NameService"));
    }
    catch(Exception system_exception ) {
        System.err.println( "constructor RoomBookingClient: " +
                                system_exception );
    }
}
```

### 8.6.3.4 init_GUI()

The method `init_GUI()` defines the principal layout of our graphical user interface. It takes one argument, which is of type `java.awt.Container`. Depending on from where we call the method, we supply either an object of type `Applet` or of type `Frame`, which are both extensions of the `Container` class. The relationships between these classes are shown in Figure 8.7.

After setting the background and creating some button objects, we create two panels, one for the title and another one where we display information from the Room Booking system. If the GUI was created from an application, we add an exit button to the title panel. For the layout we use the Java layout manager and a `BorderLayout`.

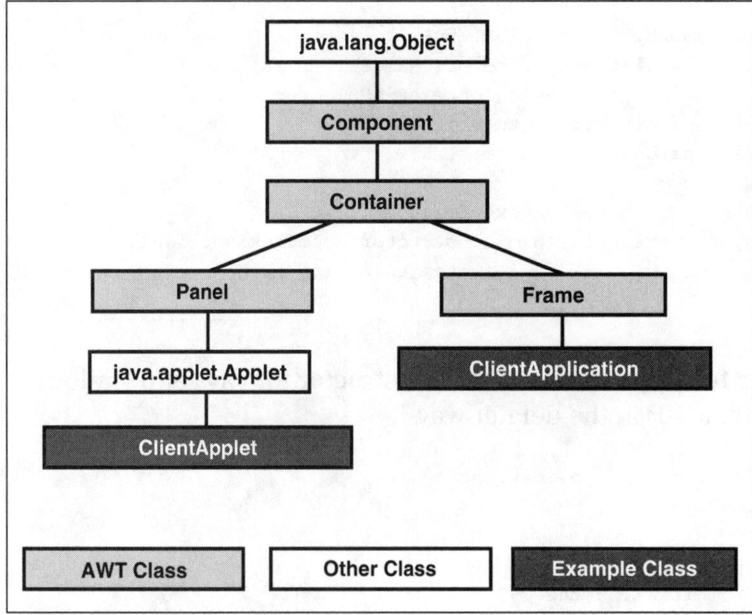


**Figure 8.7** GUI class relationships.

```
public void init_GUI( java.awt.Container gui ) {

    // initialize widgets
    gui.setBackground( Color.white );

    viewButton = new Button("Back");
    viewButton.setFont(new Font("Helvetica", Font.BOLD, 14));
    viewButton.setBackground( red );
    viewButton.setActionCommand("View");
    viewButton.addActionListener( (ActionListener) this );

    bookButton = new Button("Book");
    bookButton.setFont(new Font("Helvetica",Font.BOLD,14));
    bookButton.setBackground( red );
    bookButton.setActionCommand("Book");
    bookButton.addActionListener( (ActionListener) this );

    cancelButton = new Button("Cancel");
    cancelButton.setFont(new Font("Helvetica",Font.BOLD,14));
    cancelButton.setBackground( red );
    cancelButton.setActionCommand("Cancel");
    cancelButton.addActionListener( (ActionListener) this );

    exitButton = new Button("Exit");
    exitButton.setFont(new Font("Helvetica",Font.BOLD,14));
    exitButton.setBackground( red );
    exitButton.setActionCommand("Exit");
    exitButton.addActionListener( (ActionListener) this );

    mainPanel = new Panel();
    titlePanel = new Panel();

    titlePanel.setLayout( new GridLayout(2,3));
    titlePanel.setFont(new Font("Helvetica",Font.BOLD,20));
    titlePanel.setBackground( red );
    titlePanel.add( new Label("", Label.CENTER) );
    titlePanel.add( new Label("Room Booking System",
                    Label.CENTER) );
    titlePanel.add( new Label("", Label.CENTER) );
    if( is_application ) {
        titlePanel.add( new Label("", Label.CENTER) );
        titlePanel.add( exitButton );
        titlePanel.add( new Label("", Label.CENTER) );
    }

    gui.setLayout(new BorderLayout());
    gui.add( "North", titlePanel );
    gui.add( "Center", mainPanel );
    gui.setSize( 700, 300 );
    gui.validate();
}
```

### 8.6.3.5 init_from_ns()

We have decided on a naming convention for the room booking system illustrated in Figure 8.2. Room objects are bound to names in the context "/BuildingApplications/Rooms", and the Meeting Factory object is bound to the name "/BuildingApplications/MeetingFactory". The method init_from_ns() resolves the "Rooms" context and obtains an object reference to the Meeting Factory using methods from the NamingContextExt interface, which we introduced in Chapter 7.

```
public void init_from_ns() {
    try {
        // get room context
        room_context = NamingContextExtHelper.narrow(
                            root_context.resolve_str(
                                "BuildingApplications/Rooms"));

        if( room_context == null ) {
            System.err.println( "Room context is null," );
            System.err.println( "exiting ..." );
            System.exit( 1 );
        }

        // get MeetingFactory from Naming Service
        meeting_factory = MeetingFactoryHelper.narrow(
                root_context.resolve_str(
                    "BuildingApplications/MeetingFactory"));

        if( meeting_factory == null ) {
            System.err.println("No Meeting Factory registered
                                at Naming Service" );
            System.err.println( "exiting ..." );
            System.exit( 1 );
        }
    }
    catch(SystemException system_exception ) {
        System.err.println( "Initialize ORB: " +
                            system_exception );
    }
    catch(UserException naming_exception) {
        System.err.println( "Initialize ORB: " +
                            naming_exception );
    }
}
```

### 8.6.3.6 view()

The method view() displays information about the current availability of rooms. Therefore it has to find out about all existing rooms and call the view() operation on each of them.

Object references for the available rooms can be obtained from the Naming Service. We have already initialized a room context in which, according to our convention, room objects are bound.

We query the room context by using the operation list() defined in the interface CosNaming::NamingContext. As explained in Chapter 7, the operation list() has three parameters:

- in long length—the maximum length of the list returned by the second parameter, which is an int in Java.
- out CosNaming::BindingList—a sequence of names. Because it is an out parameter we use a Holder object in the Java language binding.
- out CosNaming::BindingIterator—a binding iterator, that is, an object from which further names can be obtained. It is also an out parameter, and so we use a holder object.

In our implementation, we demonstrate the use of the list as well as the iterator. We create a temporary `Vector` in which we store the room objects we obtain from the naming service. We obtain those references from the room context via the resolve() operation. We then narrow the resulting object to the right type. We go through the binding list as well as through the binding iterator. Once we have obtained all the rooms and temporarily stored them in the room vector, we convert the vector into an array of rooms.

```
public boolean view() {

    try {
        // list rooms
        // initialize binding list and binding iterator
        // Holder objects for out parameter
        BindingListHolder blHolder = new BindingListHolder();
        BindingIteratorHolder biHolder =
                                  new BindingIteratorHolder();
        BindingHolder bHolder = new BindingHolder();
        Vector roomVector = new Vector();
        Room aRoom;

        // we retrieve 2 rooms via the room list
        // more rooms are available from the binding iterator
        room_context.list( 2, blHolder, biHolder );

        // get rooms from Room context of the Naming Service
        // and put them into the roomVector
        for( int i = 0; i < blHolder.value.length; i++ ) {
            aRoom = RoomHelper.narrow(
                        room_context.resolve(
                            blHolder.value[i].binding_name ));
```

```
        roomVector.addElement( aRoom );
    }

    // get remaining rooms from the iterator
    if( biHolder.value != null ) {
        while( biHolder.value.next_one( bHolder ) ) {
            aRoom = RoomHelper.narrow(
                        room_context.resolve(
                            bHolder.value.binding_name ) );
            if( aRoom != null ) {
                roomVector.addElement( aRoom );
            }
        }
    }

    // convert the roomVector into a room array
    rooms = new Room[ roomVector.size() ];
    roomVector.copyInto( rooms );

    // be friendly with system resources
    if( biHolder.value != null )
        biHolder.value.destroy();
```

We create an array of labels, one for each room, that is eventually used to display the names of the rooms. We also create an array of type `boolean` for internal use, to store information about whether each slot is already booked.

```
    // create labels and slots according to the
    // number of rooms
    Label[] r_label = new Label[rooms.length];
    slotButton = new Button[rooms.length][Room.MaxSlots];
    booked = new boolean[rooms.length][Room.MaxSlots];
    mainPanel.removeAll();
```

Then we define the layout of the rest of the table.

```
    // define layout for the table
    GridBagLayout gridbag = new GridBagLayout();
    GridBagConstraints c = new GridBagConstraints();
    mainPanel.setLayout(gridbag);
    c.fill = GridBagConstraints.BOTH;
    c.gridwidth = 2;
    c.gridheight = 1;
    Label room_label = new Label("Rooms",
                                 Label.CENTER );
    room_label.setFont(new Font("Helvetica",
                       Font.BOLD, 14));
    gridbag.setConstraints( room_label, c);
```

```
mainPanel.add( room_label );
// and so on for the header of the table
```

Next we initialize the elements of the label array by creating objects of type `java.awt.Label`. The constructor we use takes a string argument, which we set to the name of a room. We obtain the name by invoking the accessor method for the attribute name of the interface Room.

```
// show the label with the room name
for( int i = 0; i < rooms.length; i++ ) {
    c.gridwidth = 2;
    c.gridheight = 1;
    r_label[i] = new Label( rooms[i].name() );
    r_label[i].setFont(new Font("Helvetica",
                       Font.BOLD, 14));
    gridbag.setConstraints( r_label[i], c);
    mainPanel.add( r_label[i] );
```

For each of the rooms we invoke the operation view(), which returns an array of Meeting objects. For such arrays a valid object reference identifies a Meeting object, which is booked into the indexed slot, while a nil object reference means an empty slot. We go through the array and create either a green or red button depending on whether the slot is empty or not.

```
    // call view operation on the i-th room object and
    // create book or free button
    meetings = rooms[i].View();
    c.gridheight = 1;
    for( int j = 0; j < meetings.length; j++ ) {
        if( j == meetings.length - 1 )
            c.gridwidth = GridBagConstraints.REMAINDER;
        else
            c.gridwidth = 1;
        if( meetings[j] == null ) {
            // slot is free
            slotButton[i][j] = new Button("Book");
            slotButton[i][j].setBackground( green );
            slotButton[i][j].setForeground(
                                 Color.white);
            slotButton[i][j].setFont(
                 new Font("Helvetica", Font.BOLD, 14));
            slotButton[i][j].setActionCommand(
                                        "Slot"+i+j);
            slotButton[i][j].addActionListener(
                             (ActionListener)this );
            booked[i][j] = false;
        }
        else {
            // slot is booked - view or cancel
```

```
                        slotButton[i][j] = new Button("View");
                        slotButton[i][j].setBackground( red );
                        slotButton[i][j].setFont(
                                    new Font( "Helvetica",
                                            Font.BOLD, 14));
                        slotButton[i][j].setActionCommand(
                                                "Slot"+i+j);
                        slotButton[i][j].addActionListener(
                                        (ActionListener)this );
                        booked[i][j] = true;
                    }
                    gridbag.setConstraints( slotButton[i][j], c);
                    mainPanel.add( slotButton[i][j] );
                }
            }
            // some more laying out
            mainPanel.validate();
        }
        catch(SystemException system_exception) {
            System.err.println("View: " + system_exception);
        }
        catch(UserException naming_exception) {
            System.err.println("View: " + naming_exception);
        }
        return true;
    }
```

### 8.6.3.7 cancel()

To cancel a meeting, the method `cancel()` invokes the operation cancelBooking() on the appropriate room object, providing the selected slot as an argument. If the selected slot does not contain a Meeting object reference the operation cancelBooking() raises an exception of type `NoMeetingInThisSlot`. This can happen only when there are multiple clients running that attempt to cancel the same meeting in overlapping time intervals. A more sophisticated approach would be to use the CORBA Transaction Service.

```
    public boolean cancel() {
        try {
            rooms[selected_room].cancelBooking(
                Slot.from_int(selected_slot) );
        }
        catch(NoMeetingInThisSlot no_meeting ) {
            System.err.println("Cancel :" + no_meeting );
        }
        catch(SystemException system_exception) {
            System.err.println("Cancel :" + system_exception);
```

```
        }
        // show bookings of all rooms
        return view();
    }
```

### 8.6.3.8 process_slot()

The method `process_slot()` sets state variables and determines whether a red or a green button has been pressed and how to proceed in each case. If a green button was pressed it invokes the method `booking_form()`, allowing the user to enter meeting details. If a red button was pressed it invokes the method `booking_details()`, which displays the meeting details of the selected meeting and provides buttons to cancel the meeting or to return to the main view. The implementation of both methods is omitted, but the complete code can be found on the Web site for this book.

```
    public boolean process_slot( int selected_room,
                                 int selected_slot ) {
        this.selected_room = selected_room;
        this.selected_slot = selected_slot;
        if( booked[selected_room][selected_slot] ) {
            // view the meeting details, potentially cancel
            meeting_details();
        }
        else {
            // get meeting details and book
            booking_form();
        }
        return true;
    }
```

### 8.6.3.9 book()

The booking of a meeting, managed by the method `book()`, involves two tasks: creation of the appropriate Meeting object and booking of the selected meeting. We create the Meeting object using the Meeting Factory. This is done by invoking the operation CreateMeeting(). Its two parameters are obtained from two text fields.

The newly created meeting is then booked by calling the operation book() on the selected room object. It is again possible that someone else has booked the slot in the meantime. If so, we catch an exception of type `SlotAlreadyTaken`.

```
    public boolean book() {
        try {
```

```
            Meeting meeting =
                meeting_factory.CreateMeeting(
                    purpose_tf.getText(),
                    participants_tf.getText() );
            System.out.println( "meeting created" );
            String p = meeting.purpose();
            System.out.println("Purpose: "+p);
            rooms[selected_room].Book(
                 Slot.from_int(selected_slot), meeting );
            System.out.println( "room is booked" );
        }
        catch(SlotAlreadyTaken already_taken ) {
            System.out.println( "book :" + already_taken );
        }
        catch(SystemException system_exception ) {
            System.out.println( "book :" + system_exception );
        }
        // show bookings of all rooms
        return view();
    }
```

### 8.6.3.10 actionPerformed()

The method `actionPerformed()` is defined in the interface `ActionListener`, which the class `RoomBookingClient` implements. We check if an event that occurred relates to one of the actions we have defined for the buttons we introduced in the GUI. If this is the case we invoke the appropriate method.

```
    // catch and process events
    public void actionPerformed( ActionEvent ev ) {
        if(ev.getActionCommand().equals("View"))
            view();
        if(ev.getActionCommand().equals("Book"))
            book();
        if(ev.getActionCommand().equals("Cancel"))
            cancel();
        if(ev.getActionCommand().equals("Exit"))
            exit();
        // look for free/book button pressed
        for( int i = 0; i < no_of_rooms(); i++ ) {
            for( int j = 0; j < Room.MaxSlots; j++ ) {
                if( ev.getActionCommand().equals("Slot"+i+j) ) {
                    process_slot( i, j );
                }
            }
        }
    }
```

## 8.7 Extensions to the Example Application

The example can also be extended to include various other CORBA services. We outline possible extensions. In Chapter 10, we extend the example to use persistent object references.

The Trading Service can be used as an alternative to the Naming Service for locating objects. The server classes would *register* objects with the Trading Service, and a client would *query* the Trading Service to search for Room and Meeting Factory objects.

The Transaction Service could be used to ensure ACID properties to booking and cancellation operations. In the current implementation we do not explicitly roll back the creation of a Meeting object when it cannot be booked into a particular slot.

The Security Service could be used to authenticate users and to authorize a user to execute certain operations. For example, only a user who booked a meeting originally should be allowed to cancel it. We explain approaches to authentication and authorization with CORBA in Chapter 12, "Security."

The Notification Service could be used to notify certain users that a meeting in which they are participating is now starting or if such a meeting is cancelled. The Notification Service is introduced and explained in Chapter 11, "Events."

We revisit the room booking application in Chapter 15 when we explain design approaches for scalability.

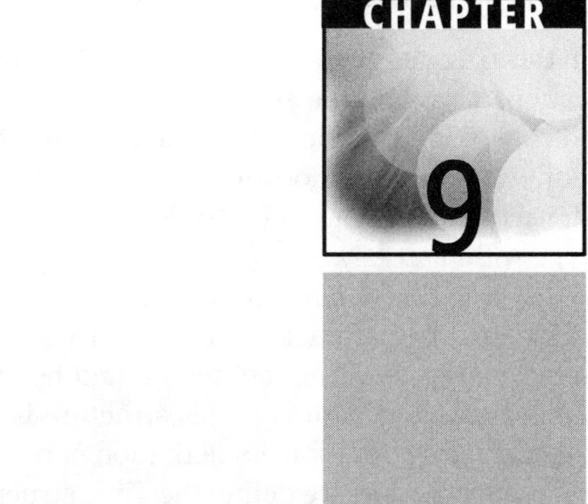


# Advanced Features

In this chapter we explain and give examples of how to use some advanced CORBA features. Mostly, the features explained in detail here have already been introduced in Chapter 5, "OMG IDL to Java Mapping," and Chapter 6, "ORB Run-Time System": TypeCodes, Anys, Interface Repository (IR), Dynamic Invocation Interface (DII), Dynamic Skeleton Interface (DSI), and the Tie approach. We also introduce Portable Interceptors and present a more complete example of applet servers.

To demonstrate these advanced features we will adapt the extended Hello World example from Chapter 4, "A First Java ORB Application." For the implementation of objects in applets we present a more appropriate example.

## 9.1 The Any Type and TypeCodes

In this section we demonstrate the use of Anys as parameters of IDL-defined operations. We use a variant of the extended Hello World example in Chapter 4.

## 9.1.1 Interface Specification

In this IDL, although we have changed the signature of the interface specification, we retain the semantics of the hello() operation. Both the result of the operation and the only parameter are of type Any. As before, the operation will return the location of the object implementation as a string, this time contained in an Any. This is an example of the use of a predefined data type within an Any.

The any_time parameter is an example of passing a user-defined data type in an Any. The parameter will contain a structure with two fields, both short integers, representing the minute and hour of the local time at the object implementation. Although this structure is not directly used in the specification of the operation, its definition needs to be available to the client and the server. Hence, we define the Time structure within the module.

```
module com {
...
module chapter9 {
    module helloWorld {
        struct Time {
            short hour;
            short minute;
        };
        interface GoodDay {
            any hello( out any any_time );
        };
    };
};...};
```

## 9.1.2 Object Implementation

The object implementation class `GoodDayImpl` extends the servant base class `GoodDayPOA`, which is generated by the IDL compiler. We also keep the same private variable `any_location` and the constructor.

```
package com.wiley.compbooks.brose.chapter9.any;

import java.util.Calendar;
import org.omg.CORBA.*;
import com.wiley.compbooks.brose.chapter9.helloWorld.*;

class GoodDayImpl extends GoodDayPOA {
    private String location;

    /** constructor */
```

```
GoodDayImpl( String location ) {
    this.location = location;
}
```

The signature of the method `hello()` corresponds to the IDL mapping for Anys, as explained in Chapter 5. We have an Any for the result and declare a variable of type `AnyHolder` for the `out` parameter.

We create a `date` object, as in the original example. In the next step we create an object of the class `Time`, which is the Java representation of the IDL type definition struct Time. We use the default constructor of this class, which takes two parameters corresponding to the fields of the structure. We provide values for the parameters by invoking methods on the object `date` to obtain the current time in hours and minutes. Again we have to cast the integer values to type `short`.

Objects of type Any are created by the ORB, by calling `create_any()` on the ORB object. From within servants, the ORB object the servant is associated with is available using the inherited method `_orb()`. Alternatively, we could have obtained a reference to the ORB Singleton object. The Singleton ORB is not a full ORB, so you cannot resolve initial references with it or convert between references and stringified IORs. It is intended to be used as a factory for Anys and TypeCodes only, which would be just what is needed here. In this example, we use the servant's ORB reference, however.

Now we have to insert the value of the time variable into the Any. We do this using the `insert()` methods that are generated in the helper class by the IDL compiler.

```
/** operation hello */
public Any hello( AnyHolder any_time)
    throws SystemException {

    // get location time of the server
    Calendar date = Calendar.getInstance();

    // create time-structure assign hour and minute to it
    Time struct_time = new Time(
        (short) date.get(Calendar.HOUR),
        (short) date.get(Calendar.MINUTE) );

    // create an any and shuffle structure into it
    any_time.value = _orb().create_any();
    TimeHelper.insert( any_time.value, struct_time );

    // create an any and shuffle location into it
    Any any_location = _orb().create_any();
```

```
        any_location.insert_string( location );
        return any_location;
    }
}
```

Now the Any object any_time contains the value of struct_time. Figure 9.1 illustrates the object any_time.

The operation result is stored in the variable any_location, an Any holding a string value. Once again we obtain an Any object from the ORB. Because string is a predefined IDL type, we insert the value of location by calling the method insert_string() on the Any object. There are similar methods defined in the class CORBA.Any for the other predefined data types, which are listed in Chapter 5. The last task of the implementation is to return the Any any_location.

The server class implementation is the same as in Chapter 4. It is *also* called Server, but it is defined in a different package.

## 9.1.3 Client Implementation

The client implementation follows the same structure that we used before.

### *9.1.3.1 Initialization and Invocation*

We declare two variables, any_location and any_time of type Any and AnyHolder, for the method's result and its parameter, respectively.

```
package com.wiley.compbooks.brose.chapter9.any;

import java.util.*;
import java.io.*;
import org.omg.CORBA.*;
import com.wiley.compbooks.brose.chapter9.helloWorld.*;

public class Client {
```

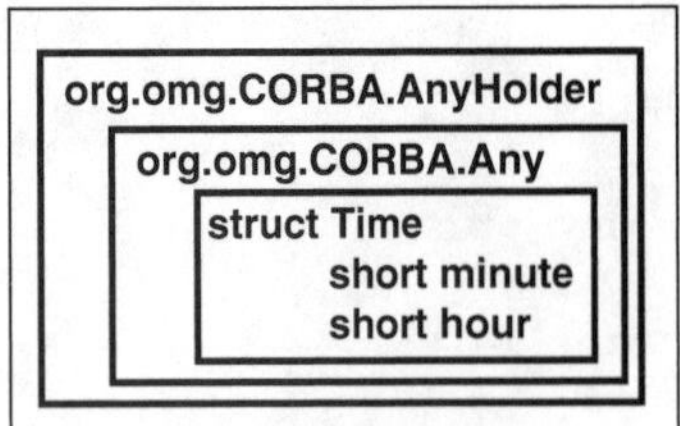


**Figure 9.1** AnyHolder object.

```
public static void main(String args[]) {

    AnyHolder any_time = new AnyHolder();
    Any any_locality;

    // get stringified IOR from command line
    String ior = new String( args[0] );

    try {
        // initialize the ORB.
        ORB orb = ORB.init( args, null );

        // get object reference ..
        org.omg.CORBA.Object obj = orb.string_to_object( ior );

        // and narrow it to GoodDay
        GoodDay goodDay = GoodDayHelper.narrow( obj );

        if( goodDay == null )
            System.exit( 1 );

        // invoke the operation
        any_locality = goodDay.hello( any_time );
```

We initialize the ORB, convert the command-line argument into an object reference, and narrow it to the right type. Then we invoke the method `hello()` with the argument `any_time` and assign the result to `any_location`.

### 9.1.3.2 Obtaining TypeCodes

TypeCodes are a run-time representation of IDL types. They are explained in detail in Chapter 6. In the following example, we obtain type information about the values contained in the Anys. First we declare a variable `tc` of type `TypeCode`. Then we obtain the TypeCode of the value held in the container variable `any_time`. The container object's public variable `value` stores the Any that was returned as an `out` parameter. The Any object referred to by `value` has a method `type()`, which returns the TypeCode of the stored value. In this example the value is a Java object representing an IDL struct.

A TypeCode represents an attributed type tree. It provides various methods to obtain the values of the attributes. For example, we query the Interface Repository identifier of the type by calling the method `id()` on the TypeCode object. Similarly we get the name of the type by invoking the method `name()`.

Because we are expecting the Any to contain an IDL structure, we need to traverse the type tree to obtain type information about the fields of the struct. The method member_count() returns the number of fields, and member_name() returns the name of the indexed field.

Because type definitions differ in their structure, operations on TypeCode objects are valid only for particular kinds of TypeCodes. If an inappropriate method is invoked, the exception BadKind is raised. The method member_name() raises the exception Bounds when the index is out of bounds.

```
// declare a type code object
TypeCode tc;

// get type of any_time.value and
// print type information
tc = any_time.value.type();
try {
    System.out.println("IfRepId of any_time: "
                       + tc.id() );
    System.out.println("Type code of any_time: "
                       + tc.name() );
    for( int i = 0; i < tc.member_count(); i++ )
        System.out.println("\tname: "
                           + tc.member_name(i) );
}
catch(org.omg.CORBA.TypeCodePackage.BadKind ex_bk) {
    System.err.println("any_time: " + ex_bk);
}
catch(org.omg.CORBA.TypeCodePackage.Bounds ex_b) {
    System.err.println("any_time: " + ex_b);
}
```

In the following code, we check if the value of any_location is of the expected kind, TCKind.tk_string, and if so we query for its length. Note that the length refers to the type definition and not the current value. The method length() returns the maximum size of a bounded string, sequence, or array. If the type is unbounded it returns zero. We must again catch the exception BadKind.

```
// get length any_locality.value
tc = any_locality.type();
try {
    if( tc.kind() == TCKind.tk_string )
        System.out.println( "length of any_locality: "
                            + tc.length() );
    else
        System.out.println(
            "any_locality does NOT contain a string.");
```

```
        }
        catch(org.omg.CORBA.TypeCodePackage.BadKind ex_bt){
            System.err.println("any_locality: " + ex_bt);
        }
```

When executing the client, the preceding code will produce the following result:

```
IfRepId of any_time:
  IDL:com/wiley/compbooks/brose/chapter9/helloWorld/Time:1.0
Type code of any_time: Time
        name: hour
        name: minute
length of any_location: 0
```

### *9.1.3.3 Unpacking the Results*

Now we proceed to the normal behavior of the client; that is, we obtain the results and print them. We can print the Anys directly by using their predefined `toString()` method, or we can obtain the contained value and print it in a customized manner. We show both possibilities.

First we obtain the string from `any_location` by invoking the `extract_string()` method. To get the time object from the Any `any_time.value` we then call the extract method provided by the helper class, which takes an Any as an argument. Once we have the values in variables of basic types we print the message in the same way as in the original example.

```
        // get String from any_locality
        String locality = any_locality.extract_string();

        // get struct from any_time
        Time time = TimeHelper.extract( any_time.value );

        // print results to stdout
        System.out.println("Hello World!");
        if( time.minute < 10 )
            System.out.println("The local time in " +
                                locality +" is " +
                                time.hour + ":0" +
                                time.minute + "." );
        else
            System.out.println("The local time in " +
                                locality + " is " +
                                time.hour + ":" +
                                time.minute + "." );
    }
```

```
        // catch CORBA system exceptions
        catch(SystemException ex) {
            System.err.println(ex);
        }
    }
}
```

When the client is invoked, it prints the results in the following form:

```
Hello World!
The local time in Berlin is 12:23.
```

## 9.2 Interface Repository and Dynamic Invocation Interface

In this section we present a client that is capable of invoking operations on an object whose type was unknown to the client at compile time. So far, clients have used stub code generated by an IDL compiler to create a proxy object on which they have invoked methods corresponding to each operation. The structure of the example is as follows:

- Initialize the ORB (section 9.2.1)
- Browse the Interface Repository (section 9.2.2)
- Unparse and print the type information obtained from the Interface Repository (section 9.2.3)
- Create a Request object (sections 9.2.4–9.2.6)
- Execute the client (section 9.2.7)

To make invocations on objects without having access to IDL-generated code we have to obtain information about the interface type of the object and invoke a method without an IDL-generated client-side proxy class. The first task is carried out using the Interface Repository, which contains type information about interfaces. Typically the Interface Repository is populated by an IDL parsing tool. Some ORB vendors use their IDL compilers for this purpose. Our client will query the Interface Repository using a standard method on the object reference, defined in CORBA::Object. This returns a reference to an Interface Repository object that represents the target object's interface type. The object is part of a type tree that the client can traverse.

The second task is carried out using the Dynamic Invocation Interface (DII). It provides a Request object that can be used for the invocation of methods on arbitrary objects. The DII's interface Request is defined in the

CORBA module using pseudo-IDL. It is the programmer's responsibility to initialize a Request pseudo-object with all the necessary information (a target object reference, an operation name, argument types, and values) in order to make an invocation.

Figure 9.2 illustrates the process by which interface information is obtained and used to invoke the object implementation. The IDL compiler creates the skeleton code for the server side as usual. Here, it also populates the Interface Repository with the types specified in the IDL file. The client can then query the Interface Repository about the type of Any object reference it obtains.

## 9.2.1 Initializing the ORB

The client obtains an object reference from, for example, a stringified object reference or from the Naming or Trading Service. For simplicity, we

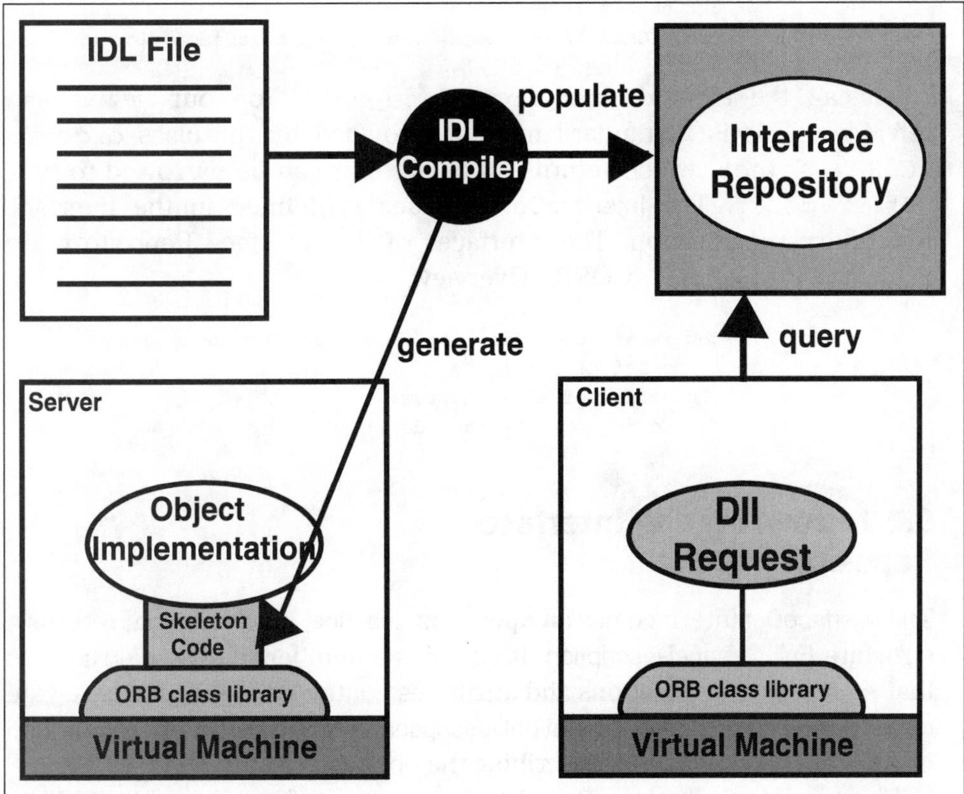


**Figure 9.2** DII client.

use stringified object references in our example. Note that we cannot narrow the object reference to its particular interface type because we do not know its type and do not have access to the narrow method, which is part of the code generated by the IDL compiler.

```
package com.wiley.compbooks.brose.chapter9.dii;

import java.io.*;
import org.omg.CORBA.*;
import org.omg.CORBA.InterfaceDefPackage.*;

public class DiiClient {
    public static void main(String args[]) {
        // get stringified IOR from command line
        String ior = new String( args[0] );

        try {
            // initialize the ORB
            ORB orb = ORB.init( args, null );

            // get object reference
            org.omg.CORBA.Object obj = orb.string_to_object( ior );
```

We call the method `_get_interface_def()` on our new object reference. This is a standard method, provided by the class `org.omg.CORBA.Object`, which returns an object that can be narrowed to type `InterfaceDef`. The InterfaceDef interface is defined in the Interface Repository specification. The interfaces of the Interface Repository are explained in Chapter 2, "CORBA Overview."

```
            // get interface definition from Interface Repository
            InterfaceDef if_def =
                InterfaceDefHelper.narrow(
                    obj._get_interface_def());
```

## 9.2.2 Browsing the Interface Repository

The InterfaceDef interface has an operation describe_interface() that returns a structure FullInterfaceDescription. It contains a number of nested structures that represent the operations and attributes contained in the interface. One of the nested structures, OperationDescription, describing an operation also contains nested structures describing the operation's parameters.

The structure FullInterfaceDescription represents a flattening of the objects in the Interface Repository to provide all the necessary type information in a single data structure without the need to make further calls to Interface Repository objects to query their types. Alternatively, traversal of the Interface Repository can be done by obtaining object references to OperationDef objects and AttributeDef objects that can be queried to discover their component definitions. This is more costly in terms of the number of remote invocations, however.

```
// using the Interface Repository
// get full interface description
FullInterfaceDescription full_if_desc =
    if_def.describe_interface();
```

In our client we store the interface description in a variable `full_if_desc`. The type is defined in IDL as the following struct. We show only the type definitions we use in the example.

```
typedef string Identifier;
typedef sequence <OperationDescription> OpDescriptionSeq;
struct FullInterfaceDescription {
    Identifier          name;
    RepositoryId        id;
    RepositoryId        defined_in;
    VersionSpec         version;
    OpDescriptionSeq    operations;
    AttrDescriptionSeq  attributes;
    RepositoryIdSeq     base_interfaces;
    TypeCode            type;
};
```

We use the members name and operations, which is a sequence of OperationDescription structs:

```
typedef sequence < ParameterDescription > ParDescriptionSeq;
typedef sequence < ExceptionDescription > ExcDescriptionSeq;
struct OperationDescription {
    Identifier          name;
    RepositoryId        id;
    RepositoryId        defined_in;
    VersionSpec         version;
    TypeCode            result;
    OperationMode       mode;
    ContextIdSeq        contexts;
    ParDescriptionSeq   parameters;
    ExcDescriptionSeq   exceptions;
};
```

In turn, parameters and exceptions that are part of an operation are described by structures.

## 9.2.3 A Simple Unparser

The following code traverses the nested structures and prints all operations of the interface in a simplified version of OMG IDL syntax. We go through all the operations defined in the interface, obtaining the result type in the form of a TypeCode, the operation name, which is a string, and the parameters. The method `toString()` is available on TypeCode objects and prints them in IDL syntax.

```
int no_of_parameters;

// print various information
System.out.println("Querying the Interface
                    Repository\n");
System.out.println("interface " +
                    full_if_desc.name + " {\n" );
for(int i=0; i < full_if_desc.operations.length; i++){
    no_of_parameters =
        full_if_desc.operations[i].parameters.length;

    // print the type code of the operation's result
    // and the name of the operation
    System.out.println("    " +
                    full_if_desc.operations[i].result +
                        " " +
                    full_if_desc.operations[i].name +
                        " (" );
```

The parameters are described by a sequence of structures of type ParamDescription:

```
enum ParameterMode { PARAM_IN, PARAM_OUT, PARAM_INOUT };
struct ParamDescription {
   Identifier       name;
   TypeCode         type;
   IDLType          type_def;
   ParameterMode    mode;
};
```

The parameter's type member is of type TypeCode, and its name is an Identifier, which is an alias of string. The parameter mode is an integer, and its values are defined in the enumerated type `ParameterMode`. We have to convert the mode value into strings.

```
// define and initialize text representations
// for parameter modes
String mode, in, inout, out;
in = new String("in");
inout = new String("inout");
out = new String("out");

char last_char = ',';

// print parameters of the operations
for( int j = 0; j < no_of_parameters; j++ ) {
    // set the right text for the parameter mode
    switch (full_if_desc.operations[i].
            parameters[j].mode.value() ) {
        case ParameterMode._PARAM_IN:
            mode = in; break;
        case ParameterMode._PARAM_INOUT:
            mode = inout; break;
        case ParameterMode._PARAM_OUT:
            mode = out; break;
        default:
            mode = new String("unknown mode");
    }

    // deal with separating commas
    if( j == no_of_parameters - 1 )
        last_char = ' ';

    // print mode, type, and name of the parameter
    System.out.println("          " +
                       mode + "  " +
                       full_if_desc.operations[i].
                         parameters[j].type + " " +
                       full_if_desc.operations[i].
                         parameters[j].name +
                       last_char );
}
System.out.println("    );\n};\n");
```

### 9.2.4 Creating Requests

Now that we have discovered the type of the object, we want to invoke an operation on it. We will need the DII to do this. This requires the creation of a Request object, as illustrated in Figure 9.3. A Request has three components:

- string—carries the name of the operation to be invoked
- NamedValue—carries the type and value of the operation's result
- NVList—carries the mode, type, and value of the operation's parameters

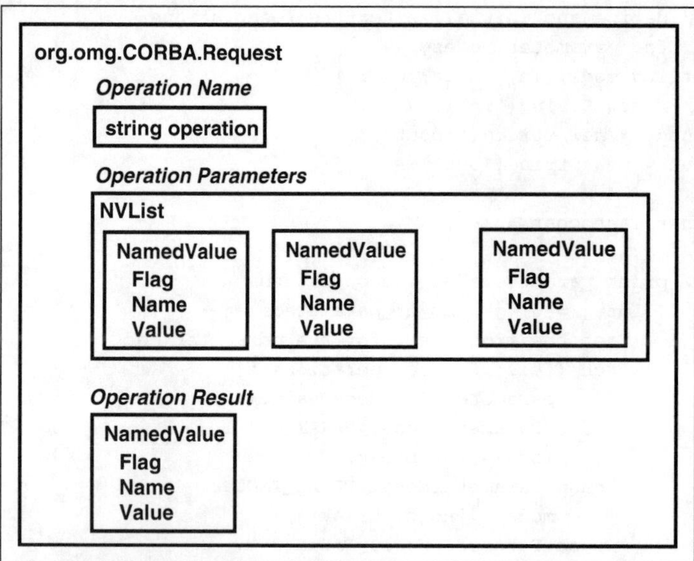


**Figure 9.3** Request object.

To create the request object, we call the operation `_request()` on the target object reference. This is a purely local call and does not involve the actual target object at all. As a parameter, we pass the operation name. For simplicity we have chosen to invoke the first operation of the interface specification we obtained when initializing the client, which is `full_if_desc.operations[0]`.

```
// create request
Request request =
    obj._request(full_if_desc.operations[0].name );
```

The resulting Request has only one of the three components shown in Figure 9.3 initialized, its operation name. It already contains an NVList for the operation arguments and a NamedValue to hold the result, but these need to be initialized before we can invoke the request.

## 9.2.5 Initializing the Request

We need to initialize the NamedValue for the result and the NVList containing the arguments to the operation. A NamedValue is a data type defined in pseudo-IDL in the module CORBA. It is a triple of a name of type `String`, a typed value of type `Any`, and a mode of type `int`. Appropriate constants are defined in the class `org.omg.CORBA.ParameterMode`. An NVList is an object containing a list of NamedValue objects. See Chapter 6 for details.

There are no operations to create and manage NamedValue objects directly. Instead we retrieve the empty argument NVList from the Request object.

```
// create and initialise arg_list
NVList arg_list = request.arguments();
```

We can now insert a single element using the method `add_value()`. This method has three parameters, one for each of the components of a NamedValue. The tricky part here is to create an Any that carries the type and the value of an argument. For out parameters we need to put only the type information into the Any. For in and inout parameters, the problem can be solved using output streams, which the portability layer defined in the IDL/Java mapping gives us.

If you look at the code generated for IDL-defined types you will find examples of the use of output streams. The following code shows the implementation of the method `insert()` defined in the class `TimeHelper`, which has been generated by the IDL compiler. It is the Helper class for the struct Time that we defined for the previous example.

```
public static void insert(
    org.omg.CORBA.Any any,
    com.wiley.compbooks.brose.chapter9.helloWorld.Time s ){

    any.type( type() );
    write( any.create_output_stream(),s);
}
```

The method `insert()` creates an output stream and writes the values into it. Before it does this, it provides the Any with a TypeCode to ensure the type safety of the insertion. The filling of the output stream is delegated to a method `write()`, which is shown here:

```
public static void write(
    org.omg.CORBA.portable.OutputStream out,
    com.wiley.compbooks.brose.chapter9.any.helloWorld.Time t){

    out.write_short(t.hour);
    out.write_short(t.minute);
}
```

The method takes the two fields of the struct and writes them into the output stream using methods of the output stream class. To write output streams for arbitrary data types you would need to traverse the type tree and write the leaves of this tree, which are values of predefined IDL types, to the stream using the corresponding methods provided by the output stream class.

We now continue to initialize the argument list. As described previously, we add NamedValues for each operation argument. The list is populated using the NVList method add_value().

```
no_of_parameters =
    full_if_desc.operations[0].parameters.length;

for( int i = 0; i < no_of_parameters; i++ ) {
    Any argumentAny = orb.create_any();
    argumentAny.type(
        full_if_desc.operations[0].parameters[i].type);

    // add empty value
    arg_list.add_value(
        full_if_desc.operations[0].parameters[i].name,
        argumentAny,
        full_if_desc.operations[0].parameters[i].
            mode.value() + 1 );
}
```

For the argument list we use a for loop over the parameter specifications from the interface description and add corresponding values for each argument with the add_value() method. The values are Any objects created by the ORB, which we set to the right type using TypeCodes from the OperationDescription. The argument list must contain values for in and inout arguments. Note that this method deals properly only with out parameters. To be able to provide usable in or inout argument values without any static knowledge of the target interface, user feedback would be required. An appropriate graphical user interface could be used to let users provide or select argument values.

Before we can finally invoke the request, we must also set the result type. This can be done by calling the Request object's set_return_type() operation. As an argument, we have to provide a TypeCode of the right kind. This TypeCode can also be found in the description of the operation that we retrieved from the Interface Repository.

```
// set the request's return type
request.set_return_type(
    full_if_desc.operations[0].result );
```

## 9.2.6 Invoking Requests and Getting Results

When the result type is set, we can finally invoke the request.

```
// invoke request
request.invoke();
```

Invoking the request results in an invocation on the object reference from which we obtained the Request. Once the call is completed, the Request object will place the result of the operation and the values for the inout and out parameters into the argument NVList and the NamedValue for the result.

Next we print the value of the result and the values of the out parameters of the operation. We use the `toString()` method on the Any objects provided by the VisiBroker implementation of Anys, which allows us to print the value of Any objects directly using `System.out.println()`, as shown here. Note that this is proprietary. For truly portable code, we would have to explicitly parse the resulting Any to be able to print it properly.

```
                // get result
                Any res_any = request.result().value();
                System.out.println("result:\n    " +
                                   res_any ); // VB-specific

                // get out parameters
                NVList nv_list = request.arguments();
                for( int i = 0; i < no_of_parameters; i++ ) {
                    System.out.println( nv_list.item( i ).name() +
                                        ":\n " +
                                        nv_list.item( i ).value() );
                }
            }
            // catch CORBA system exceptions
            catch(CORBA.SystemException ex) {
                System.err.println(ex);
            }
        }
    }
```

## 9.2.7 Executing the Client

When executing the DII client we can invoke operations on almost arbitrary objects, except that the code presented previously is not capable of providing valid in or inout arguments. In our example we invoke the first operation defined in the interface. The following output is produced when the object reference used refers to an object supporting the extended Hello World interface introduced in Chapter 4.

```
../dii>java com.wiley.compbooks.brose.chapter9.dii.DiiClient
      IOR:000000000000001e49444c3a48656c6c . . .

Quering the Interface Repository

interface GoodDay {
```

```
    string hello (
        out short hour,
        out short minute
    );
};

Make a DII call for operation: hello
result:
    "Berlin"
hour:
    16
minute:
    19
```

As another example we use the DII client program to invoke the Any HelloWorld object we implemented in section 9.1. Again the client queries the Interface Repository and prints the interface specification in OMG IDL syntax. As in the previous section, the interface GoodDay again provides an operation `hello()`. This time, though, the result and the *only* parameter are both of type `Any`, one of them containing the result string and the other a Time struct. The client creates the corresponding Request object and invokes it.

```
../dii>java com.wiley.compbooks.brose.chapter9.dii.DiiClient
        IOR:000000000000001b49444c3a48656c6c . . .

Quering the Interface Repository

interface GoodDay {

    any hello (
        out any any_time
    );
};

Make a DII call for operation: hello
result:
    "Berlin"
any_time:
    struct Time{short hour=2;short minute=0;}
```

It is possible to extend our implementation toward a completely generic CORBA client. One necessary extension would be to provide a graphical user interface for selecting operations and entering and displaying parameters. The combination of portability provided by Java and interoperability through IIOP would make such a tool almost universally usable.

## 9.3 Dynamic Skeleton Interface

Similar to the DII on the client side, the Dynamic Skeleton Interface (DSI) provides an interface on the server side that allows the invocation of methods on objects without compiler-generated skeletons. We introduced the CORBA specification of the DSI in Chapter 2 and explained its mapping to Java in Chapter 6. In this section we demonstrate how to program with the DSI. Once again, we use a modified Hello World example to illustrate it.

The implementation of the server class is the same as before, only we provide a different implementation of the GoodDay interface. The interface is implemented by a Java class called `GoodDayImpl`, but, of course, it is located in a separate package.

```
package com.wiley.compbooks.brose.chapter9.dsi;

import java.io.*;
import java.util.Calendar;
import org.omg.CORBA.*;
import org.omg.PortableServer.*;
import com.wiley.compbooks.brose.chapter9.helloWorld.*;

class GoodDayImpl
    extends org.omg.PortableServer.DynamicImplementation {
    private String location;

    /** constructor */
    GoodDayImpl( String location ) {
        this.location = location;
    }
```

The implementation class extends the class `DynamicImplementation`. This class, in turn, extends the servant base class `Servant`. As with the static implementation class we declare a private field `location`. This field is initialized from the class constructor's argument when creating `GoodDayImpl` objects.

The base class `Servant` has one abstract method that we need to implement. This method is called `_all_interfaces()` and is used to return type information about all the IDL interfaces this servant implements. This method is usually contained in the generated skeleton code, but here we have to provide it explicitly.

We describe the interface type in the form of an Interface Repository identifier. These identifiers are strings with the following syntax (in EBNF): "IDL:" {*module_name*"/"}* *interface_name*":" *major*"." *minor*. The major/minor pair are currently always 1 and 0, as the use of versioning in the Interface Repository is not well defined. In the implementation of the `_all_interfaces()` method, we return an array of these identifiers. In our example, the array contains just a single identifier:

```
public String[] _all_interfaces(POA poa, byte[] objectID){
    return new String[]{"IDL:com/.../helloWorld/GoodDay:1.0"};
}
```

Note that the IDL module and interface are identical to those implemented using the skeleton method; this is just another way of implementing the same interface type.

The class `DynamicImplementation` defines an abstract method `invoke()`. This method is called whenever an invocation is made on the dynamic implementation object. The method has one parameter that is of class `ServerRequest`, which is very similar to the corresponding class `Request` in the DII in structure, but different in signature. The class `ServerRequest` is defined in Java as

```
package org.omg.CORBA;

public abstract class ServerRequest {
    public java.lang.String operation ();
    public org.omg.CORBA.Context ctx();
    public void arguments(org.omg.CORBA.NVList);
    public void set_result(org.omg.CORBA.Any);
    public void set_exception(org.omg.CORBA.Any);
}
```

Within the implementation of the method `invoke()` we need to analyze the server request object to determine which operation has been invoked. The DSI is usually used to dynamically delegate incoming requests for operations that were not defined at the time the server was written. Of course, the server must be able to interpret the semantics of the request or forward the request somewhere where it is understood. Examples of this sort of behavior can be found in generic wrappers whose clients define IDL in a particular pattern that is understood by the server, which identifies the corresponding legacy functionality to perform the required task, and in bridges that simply pass on the request uninterpreted.

In our example we provide only one operation as a demonstration of dealing with the ServerRequest. This is implemented directly in the `invoke()` method. If the operation name of an incoming request is not "hello" we throw the CORBA system exception BAD_OPERATION.

```
// method
public void invoke( ServerRequest request ) {
```

```
if( !request.op_name().equals("hello") ) {
    throw new BAD_OPERATION();
}
```

Otherwise, we proceed with the implementation of the hello() operation by creating a Calendar object and getting the current time. To return the result and the out parameters we have to wrap the values in Any objects and put them into the Server Request object. This needs to be done earlier when we are expecting some arguments to our operation, as the ServerRequest requires us to pass an NVList with all the parameter names and types initialized, into which it places the values that came from the client. In our case, we are passing out only parameters, so we can create the NVList after the processing is done.

We create the Any objects in the usual way and insert our values using the appropriate insert methods on the Any object. For user-defined data types we would use output streams as described in the previous section. The one thing special with this example is that we have to wrap each of the Any objects in another Any. The reason is that the DSI passes all argument and result types in Anys, and here these are Anys themselves.

```
// get local time of the server
Calendar date = Calendar.getInstance();

// create anys for hour and minute and insert values

Time time = new Time( (short) date.get(Calendar.HOUR),
                      (short) date.get(Calendar.MINUTE));

Any time_any = _orb().create_any();
TimeHelper.insert( time_any, time );

// create an any for the out parameter and
// insert the time any
Any param_any = _orb().create_any();
param_any.insert_any( time_any );
```

We now create a Name Value list for the arguments to which we add the Any object we just created for the out parameter. Then we set the parameters. Finally, we create another Any object to hold the Any containing the location string and set it as the result of the ServerRequest object.

```
// create the list of named values and add our
// parameter any
NVList parameters = _orb().create_list(0);
parameters.add_value("any_time",
                      param_any,
                      ARG_OUT.value );
```

```
        // set our parameter list
        request.arguments( parameters );

        // create an any for the operation result and insert
        // the location any
        Any result_any = _orb().create_any();
        result_any.insert_any( location_any );

        // set the result and return
        request.set_result( result_any );
    }
}
```

When a client invokes methods on an object implemented with the DSI, it does not notice any difference to invoking an object implemented with an IDL-generated skeleton.

## 9.4 Tie Mechanism

So far we have constructed statically typed object implementations by inheritance of skeleton classes generated by the IDL compiler. These skeletons implement the network management, marshaling, and incoming request delegation of the CORBA object. They are then extended to provide methods that support the operations in the IDL interface. The inheritance approach, however, has the following shortcomings.

**Java single inheritance.** Because Java supports only single class inheritance, an object implementation cannot extend any application-specific class as it already extends the skeleton class.

**One implementation object for multiple interfaces.** There are occasions where it makes sense for one Java object to implement multiple IDL interfaces, for example, an application-specific interface and a general management interface. This cannot be achieved via Java extension because the implementation object needs to extend two or more skeletons.

A solution to these problems is to use delegation instead of inheritance. This is achieved by generating a *pseudo-implementation* or *Tie class* that inherits the skeleton. Rather than implementing the operations, this pseudo-implementation class calls methods on another object that actually implements the operation's semantics. Figure 9.4 compares the inheritance approach with the delegation approach. The delegation approach is also known as the Tie mechanism.

We use the Hello World example in this chapter to demonstrate the Tie approach. We have to modify both the server class and the object implementation class and introduce the pseudo-implementation class.

Let's start with the implementation class. The only difference to the inheritance approach is in the declaration of class `GoodDayImpl`.

```
package com.wiley.compbooks.brose.chapter9.tie;

import java.util.Calendar;
import org.omg.CORBA.*;
import com.wiley.compbooks.brose.chapter9.helloWorld.*;

public class GoodDayImpl implements GoodDayOperations {
// implementation as before
```

While the implementation class extends the skeleton class in the inheritance approach, in the Tie approach it implements the interface `GoodDayOperations`. This implementation class could inherit another, application-specific class.

The interface `GoodDayOperations` is the base interface for the interface `GoodDay`, but it does not extend `org.omg.CORBA.Object`. It simply declares the signature of the methods corresponding to the IDL operations, and because this class is generated it ensures a type-safe implementation class.

```
package com.wiley.compbooks.brose.chapter9.tie.helloWorld;

public interface GoodDayOperations {
    public org.omg.CORBA.Any hello(
```

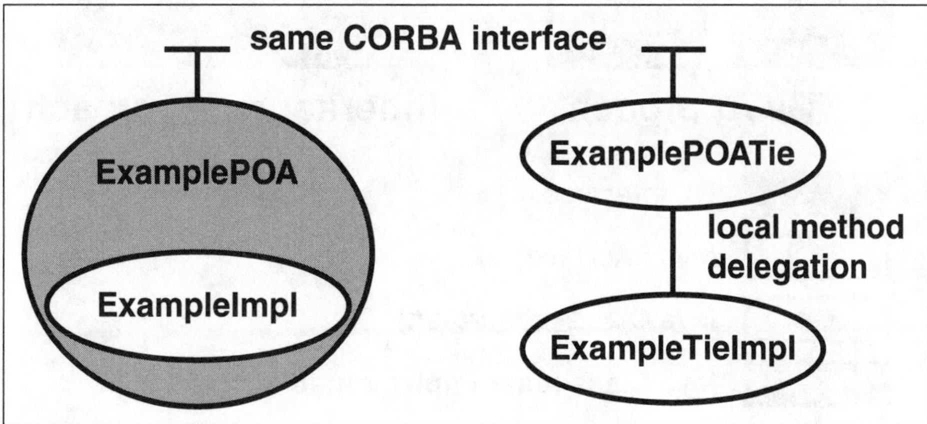


**Figure 9.4** Inheritance versus delegation.

```
        org.omg.CORBA.AnyHolder any_time
    );
  }
```

Within the server class, we initialize the ORB and the POA. Then we create the implementation object `goodDayImpl` and supply it as a parameter to the constructor of the Tie object `goodDayPseudoImpl`. Finally, we create an object reference from the servant object `goodDayPseudoImpl`. Figure 9.5 shows the various interfaces and classes of both approaches and illustrates their relationships.

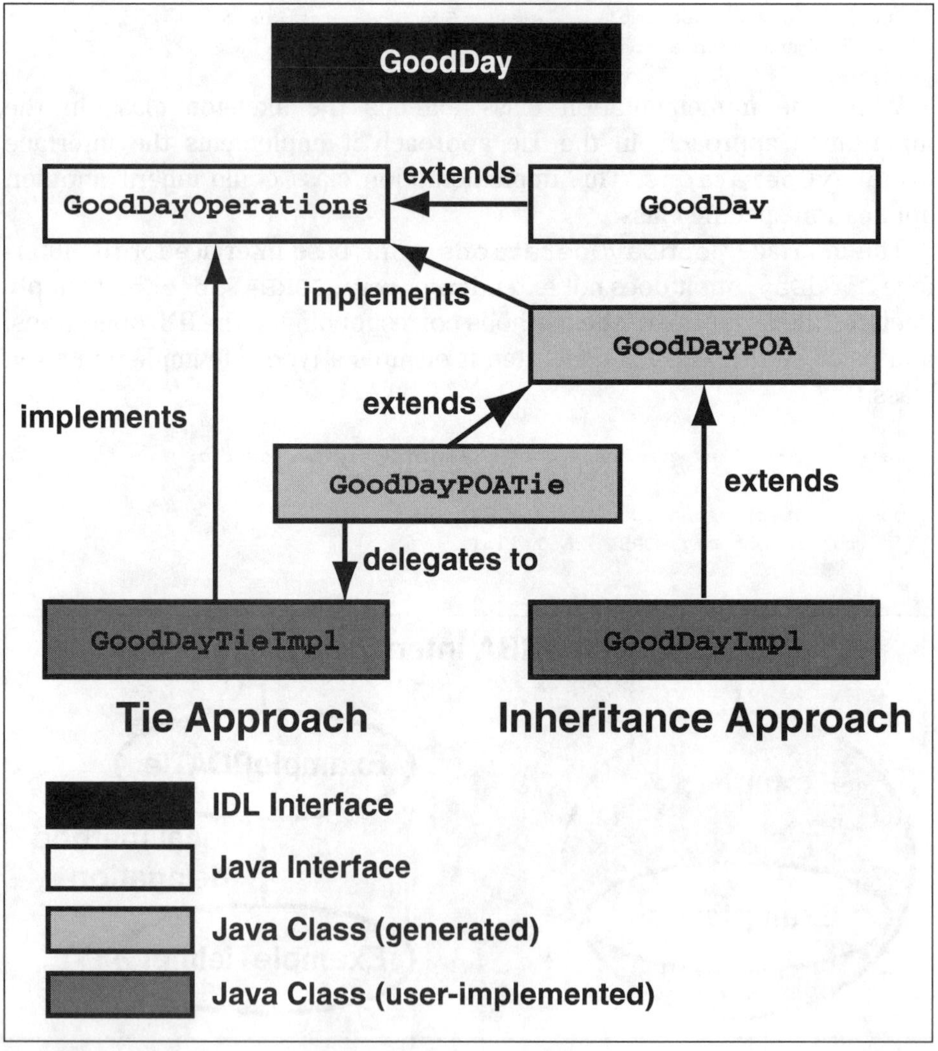


**Figure 9.5** Tie class dependencies.

```
package com.wiley.compbooks.brose.chapter9.tie;

import org.omg.CORBA.*;
import org.omg.PortableServer.*;
import com.wiley.compbooks.brose.chapter9.helloWorld.*;

public class Server {

    public static void main(String[] args) {

        try {
            //init orb
            ORB orb = ORB.init( args, null );

            //init object adapter
            POA poa = POAHelper.narrow(
                orb.resolve_initial_references("RootPOA"));

            // create an implementation object
            GoodDayImpl goodDayImpl = new GoodDayImpl( args[0] );

            // create a Tie object
            GoodDayPOATie goodDayPseudoImpl =
                new GoodDayPOATie( goodDayImpl );

            // export the object reference
            org.omg.CORBA.Object obj =
                poa.servant_to_reference( goodDayPseudoImpl );
            System.out.println( orb.object_to_string( obj ) );

            // wait for requests
            poa.the_POAManager().activate();
            orb.run();
        }
        catch(UserException u) {
            System.err.println(u);
        }
        catch(SystemException e) {
            System.err.println(e);
        }
    }
}
```

To understand what is happening behind the scenes, let's have a look at the class `GoodDayPOATie`. This is the Tie or pseudo-implementation class.

The Tie class extends the skeleton class, which connects it with the ORB run-time system and provides the marshaling and unmarshaling routines. The class has a private variable, an object reference of type `GoodDayOperations` called `_delegate`. This variable will be initialized by each of the constructors. As has already been shown in the server class, the implementation object is provided as a parameter to the constructor.

```
package com.wiley.compbooks.brose.chapter9.helloWorld;

import org.omg.PortableServer.POA;

public class GoodDayPOATie
    extends GoodDayPOA {

    private GoodDayOperations _delegate;
    private POA _poa;

    public GoodDayPOATie(GoodDayOperations delegate) {
        _delegate = delegate;
    }

    public GoodDayPOATie(GoodDayOperations delegate, POA poa) {
        _delegate = delegate;
        _poa = poa;
    }

    public GoodDay _this() {
        return GoodDayHelper.narrow(_this_object());
    }

    public GoodDay _this(org.omg.CORBA.ORB orb) {
        return GoodDayHelper.narrow(_this_object(orb));
    }

    public GoodDayOperations _delegate() {
       return _delegate;
    }

    public void _delegate(GoodDayOperations delegate) {
       _delegate = delegate;
    }

    public org.omg.CORBA.Any hello(
        org.omg.CORBA.AnyHolder any_time
    ) {
        return _delegate.hello(any_time);
    }
}
```

Once a method is invoked by a client, the tie object calls the method `hello()` on the real implementation object `_delegate` and returns the result from this invocation back to the client. Note that the out parameter is also set by the delegate.

# 9.5 Portable Interceptors

CORBA implementations have long had proprietary mechanisms that allowed users to insert their own code into the ORB's flow of execution. This code, which is sometimes known as "filters," "transformers," or "interceptors," is called at particular stages during the processing of requests and may directly inspect and even manipulate requests. For example, it is possible to monitor the requests mediated by the ORB. In addition, most proprietary implementations also allow you to modify request arguments, redirect requests to different target objects, or encrypt and decrypt message buffers before and after transport.

Because this message filtering mechanism is extremely flexible and powerful, the OMG made an attempt to standardize interceptors in CORBA 2.2 so that applications using interceptors would be portable between ORB implementations. The results of this first ad hoc attempt, however, were not satisfactory, and interceptors remained severely underspecified. A second attempt at specifying interceptors was carried out more carefully and resulted in a much more detailed document, the Portable Interceptor specification. At the time of this writing, the Portable Interceptor specification was not yet finally approved, but it had reached the status of a draft specification (OMG document ptc/2000-03-03).

One of the main requirements for an interceptor mechanism that was not met by either existing implementations or the first Interceptor specification in CORBA 2.2 was the provision of a portable interface for dealing with service context. Some advanced services, such as the Transaction Service or the Security Service, need access to client-side service context information when requests are received.

The problem with service context is that it typically cannot be expressed as additional, explicit request parameters. The reason is that CORBA services such as the Transaction or the Security Service do not add any application functionality at all. Rather, these services are used to meet nonfunctional requirements such as integrity, confidentiality, or transactional operation semantics. It is neither practical nor even possible to rewrite all application interfaces so that the necessary context information can be passed as operation arguments. Even in cases where the changes would be small, such as adding a single argument for a transactional context, modifying interfaces is undesirable because it hinders reuse in different environments.

To be able to pass service context data implicitly, service implementations had to rely on proprietary ORB interfaces because no standard way of passing this data existed. Applications using these services are thus tied to particular ORB implementations.

Portable Interceptors are intended to solve this problem. The idea is to define a standard interface to register and execute application-independent code that, among other things, takes care of passing service contexts. Ideally, this code would be provided by service implementors and distributed together with the service interfaces. Anyone could download and install this code locally and then use the service interfaces, independent of the actual ORB implementation used on the client side.

The definition of a context-passing framework in the Portable Interceptor specification is added value when compared to any existing interceptor mechanism. However, the specification does not support one popular Interceptor feature—network buffer access. Most proprietary interceptor implementations allowed user code to inspect or even modify network buffers directly before or after network transport so that, for example, a message's integrity or confidentiality could be protected by cryptographic means. This functionality is now provided by the Security Service, and so no low-level buffer access needs to be provided through the Interceptors API.

In the remainder of this section, we provide an overview of the specification (section 9.5.1) and a complete example of using interceptors to create a simple logging mechanism (section 9.5.2). We do not go into the details of creating, maintaining, and sending service contexts, however.

## 9.5.1 The Portable Interceptors Specification

Portable Interceptors are designed to allow the insertion of user-defined code into the ORB's flow of execution. All Portable Interceptors have purely local implementations and implement subtypes of the following IDL interface:

```
module PortableInterceptor {
    interface Interceptor { // locality-constrained
        readonly attribute string name;
    };
};
```

It is possible to register any number of anonymous Interceptors, that is, Interceptors with empty names; however, only a single Interceptor may be registered for any given name.

Two classes of Interceptors are defined: Request Interceptors and IOR Interceptors. Request Interceptors are called during request mediation. IOR Interceptors are called when new object references are created so that service-specific data can be added to the newly created IOR in the form of tagged components. We will explain both kinds of Interceptors in more detail. Figure 9.6. illustrates the interception points for both Request and IOR Interceptors.

### 9.5.1.1 Request Interceptors

The ORB calls Request Interceptors on the client and the server side. This is done for both outgoing and incoming requests and results. The main purpose of Request Interceptors is to manipulate service context information, but they can also carry out many other useful tasks.

In general, Interceptors are supposed to be transparent to clients, object implementations, and other Interceptors. They may raise exceptions or redirect requests to different targets, but they are not allowed to modify request parameters. The ClientRequestInterceptor interface provides operations that correspond to the five interception points shown in Figure 9.6.

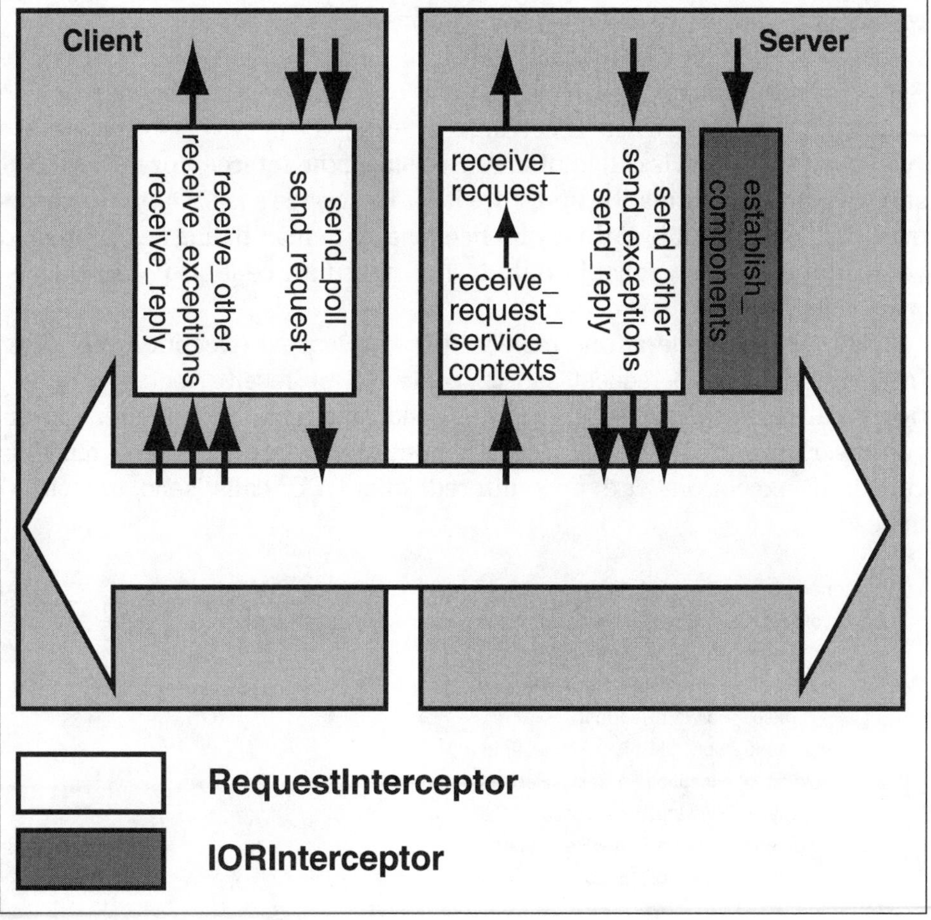


**Figure 9.6** Interception points.

```
interface ClientRequestInterceptor : Interceptor { // locality-constrained
    void send_request  (in ClientRequestInfo ri) raises (ForwardRequest);
    void send_poll (in ClientRequestInfo ri);
    void receive_reply (in ClientRequestInfo ri);
    void receive_exception (in ClientRequestInfo ri) raises (ForwardRequest);
    void receive_other (in ClientRequestInfo ri) raises (ForwardRequest);
};
```

The operation send_request is called for any ORB-mediated, outgoing request. The interceptor may raise a ForwardRequest exception to signal that the ORB should retry the operation with a new object reference that is provided in the body of the exception. In this case, no other Interceptor will see the request at this interception point. Rather, the receive_other() operation will be called to signal the ForwardRequest exception. If a system exception is raised, the receive_exception() operation of any remaining Interceptors is called instead. The send_poll() operation is called when clients poll for results of deferred synchronous invocations.

Like the ClientRequestInterceptor interface, the interface ServerRequestInterceptor provides operations that match the server-side interception points. When receiving requests, the receive_request_service _contexts() operation is called first. At this stage, the Interceptor may extract service context information and store it for its service's use. Operation arguments are not available at this point because no unmarshaling has happened yet. Arguments are available only at the next interception point, that is, when receive_request() is called.

If any of these operations raises a ForwardRequest exception, no other Interceptor's receive_request_service_contexts() or receive_request() operation is called. Rather, the ORB will call send_other() on any remaining Interceptors. For returning from successful operation processing, send_reply() is called. If exceptions are encountered, the ORB calls send_exception() instead.

```
interface ServerRequestInterceptor : Interceptor { // locality-constrained
    void receive_request_service_contexts (in ServerRequestInfo ri)
        raises (ForwardRequest);
    void receive_request (in ServerRequestInfo ri)
        raises (ForwardRequest);
    void send_reply (in ServerRequestInfo ri);
    void send_exception (in ServerRequestInfo ri)
        raises (ForwardRequest);
    void send_other (in ServerRequestInfo ri)
        raises (ForwardRequest);
};
```

The request information passed to client-side Interceptors is a locality-constrained object of type ClientRequestInfo while Server Request Interceptors receive ServerRequestInfo arguments. Both interfaces extend the base interface RequestInfo, which provides general information about the request, such as the request ID, the operation name, and lists of parameters, expected exceptions, and request context objects. All attributes in this interface are readonly, so Interceptors cannot change any aspect of the request itself, such as parameter values.

```
interface RequestInfo { // locality-constrained
    readonly attribute unsigned long request_id;
    readonly attribute string operation;
    readonly attribute Dynamic::ParameterList arguments;
    readonly attribute Dynamic::ExceptionList exceptions;
    readonly attribute Dynamic::ContextList contexts;
    readonly attribute Dynamic::RequestContext operation_context;
    readonly attribute any result;
    readonly attribute boolean response_expected;
    readonly attribute Messaging::SyncScope sync_scope;
    readonly attribute ReplyStatus reply_status;
    readonly attribute Object forward_reference;
    any get_slot (in SlotId id) raises (InvalidSlot);
    IOP::ServiceContext get_request_service_context (in IOP::ServiceId id);
    IOP::ServiceContext get_reply_service_context (in IOP::ServiceId id);
};
```

Note that not all of these attributes will be accessible at all interception points. For example, the result attribute is set only after a result has been sent by the server. Moreover, with the portable, stream-based Java language binding, most of the request information is already marshaled when Interceptors are called. Making it accessible to Interceptors would require the expensive extra work of unmarshaling the data again. The ORB is therefore allowed to raise the NO_RESOURCES exception when an Interceptor tries to access the arguments, exceptions, and contexts attributes of a RequestInfo object.

The response_expected attribute provides information about whether this request is a oneway request. If it is FALSE, the sync_scope attribute defines how far the request is passed on before control is returned to the invoking client. If response_expected is TRUE, this attribute is undefined. The SyncScope type definition is adopted from the CORBA Messaging specification and allows the following values:

```
module Messaging {
    typedef short SyncScope;
```

```
    const SyncScope SYNC_NONE = 0;
    const SyncScope SYNC_WITH_TRANSPORT = 1;
    const SyncScope SYNC_WITH_SERVER = 2;
    const SyncScope SYNC_WITH_TARGET = 3;
};
```

The reply_status attribute defines the outcome of the request. If its value is LOCATION_FORWARD or LOCATION_FORWARD_PERMANENT, the forward _reference attribute will contain the object reference to which the request will be forwarded. The possible values for reply_status are:

```
module PortableInterceptor {
    typedef short ReplyStatus;
    const ReplyStatus SUCCESSFUL = 0;
    const ReplyStatus SYSTEM_EXCEPTION = 1;
    const ReplyStatus USER_EXCEPTION = 2;
    const ReplyStatus LOCATION_FORWARD = 3;
    const ReplyStatus LOCATION_FORWARD_PERMANENT = 4;
    const ReplyStatus TRANSPORT_RETRY = 5;
};
```

The get_slot() operation is used by Interceptors to access a service-specific slot in the PortableInterceptor::Current object. This object, which is just a slot table, is used by service-specific Current objects to store service context data. Interceptors can extract this data using their service-specific slot IDs. They can also inspect the service context data that is already present in this request or reply using get_request_service_context() or get_reply_service_context().

In addition to the attributes in the common supertype RequestInfo, Client and Server Request Interceptors have access to specific information in objects of type ClientRequestInfo and ServerRequestInfo, respectively.

```
interface ClientRequestInfo : RequestInfo { // locality-constrained
    readonly attribute Object target;
    readonly attribute Object effective_target;
    readonly attribute IOP::TaggedProfile effective_profile;
    readonly attribute any received_exception;
    readonly attribute CORBA::RepositoryId received_exception_id;
    IOP::TaggedComponent get_effective_component (
        in IOP::ComponentId id
    );
    IOP_N::TaggedComponentSeq get_effective_components (
        in IOP::ComponentId id
    );
    CORBA::Policy get_request_policy (in CORBA::PolicyType type);
    void add_request_service_context (
```

```
        in IOP::ServiceContext service_context,
        in boolean replace
    );
};
```

The ClientRequestInfo interface provides information about the target object in the target attribute. The effective_target attribute may be set to a different object after a ForwardException has been received. For example, this happens when the original reference pointed to an Implementation Repository that responds to requests by sending a ForwardRequest containing a new reference. The remaining attributes and operations provide information about exceptions, the IOP profile used for the request, and specific, named components within that profile. It is also possible to retrieve the effective policy for the operation. Finally, Client Request Interceptors may add service context data to the request using the add_request_service_context() operation.

The ServerRequestInfo interface provides target object information in the form of the target's object ID and POA identifier. It also contains the RepositoryId of the target object's most derived interface and lets the Interceptor determine other target types using the target_is_a() operation. With the set_slot() operation, an Interceptor can set the contents of a slot in the PortableInterceptor::Current object and thus pass data from the request to the context of the operation execution, which will be performed by the servant. From within the servant implementation, this data is available using service-specific Current objects. Like the Client Request Interceptor, the Server Client Request Interceptor can add service context data using the add_reply_service_context() operation, but it is added to the reply rather than to the request.

```
interface ServerRequestInfo : RequestInfo { // locality-constrained
    readonly attribute any sending_exception;
    readonly attribute CORBA::OctetSeq object_id;
    readonly attribute CORBA::OctetSeq adapter_id;
    readonly attribute CORBA::RepositoryId target_most_derived_interface;
    CORBA::Policy get_server_policy (in CORBA::PolicyType type);
    void set_slot (in SlotId id, in any data)
        raises (InvalidSlot);
    boolean target_is_a (in CORBA::RepositoryId id);
    void add_reply_service_context (
        in IOP::ServiceContext service_context,
        in boolean replace
    );
};
```

### 9.5.1.2 IOR Interceptors

IOR Interceptors are not involved in request processing at all. They are defined so that services can add data to object references when the reference is created. This may be information that describes the server's or object's capabilities with regard to this service. For example, a Security Service implementation could use an IOR Interceptor to add an IOR component that contains information for using the Secure Socket Layer (SSL) transport protocol.

There is just one interception point for IOR Interceptors for which the IORInterceptor interface has a corresponding operation.

```
interface IORInterceptor : Interceptor {  // locality-constrained
    void establish_components (in IORInfo info);
};
```

The ORB calls establish_components() on all its registered IOR Interceptors when it is assembling the set of components to be included in the IOP profiles for a new object reference. Interceptors use the IORInfo object passed as the operation's argument to provide these components. Interceptors are not allowed to throw exceptions during the execution of this operation.

```
interface IORInfo { // locality-constrained
    CORBA::Policy get_effective_policy (in CORBA::PolicyType type);
    void add_ior_component (in IOP::TaggedComponent component);
    void add_ior_component_to_profile (
        in IOP::TaggedComponent component,
        in IOP::ProfileId profile_id
    );
};
```

An Interceptor can use the get_effective_policy() operation to find out about the effective, server-side policies for the object. This information may, in turn, determine which, if any, components an Interceptor adds to the reference's IOP Profile. If the add_ior_component() operation is used for this task, the component will be included in all profiles. If an Interceptor uses the add_ior_component_to_profile(), the component will be added only to the identified profile.

## 9.5.2 Programming with Interceptors

As an example, we will write a simple client-side logging mechanism using Request Interceptors. The mechanism records every remote invocation and also logs the round-trip time of the request. That is, the implementation stores the start time of every outgoing request and the time the response is returned by the server. It then records the difference in the log. The code was run on JacORB 1.1, which contains an implementation of the draft specification.

### 9.5.3.1 Writing the Interceptor

To implement a request interceptor, we provide a class `ClientLogInterceptor` that implements the `ClientRequestInterceptor` interface. To mimic the semantics of locality-constrained objects, this class extends a class `LocalityConstrainedObject` that provides dummy method implementations for all operations in `org.omg.CORBA.Object`. This is necessary here because the Java language mapping in its current form does not define a general mapping for locality-constrained interfaces.

The `ClientLogInterceptor` has three private fields: a date object, a table of requests, and a stream object to which the log is written. The class constructor initializes these fields:

```
package com.wiley.compbooks.brose.chapter9.interceptor;

import org.omg.PortableInterceptor.*;
import java.util.*;
import java.io.*;

public class ClientLogInterceptor
    extends LocalityConstrainedObject
    implements ClientRequestInterceptor{

    private Calendar date;
    private Hashtable tableTable;
    private PrintStream logStream;

    /** constructor */
    public ClientLogInterceptor() {
        date = Calendar.getInstance();
        tableTable = new Hashtable();
        logStream = System.out;
    }
```

To implement the interface, the class provides method implementations for the IDL attribute name inherited from interface Interceptor and for the five interception operations defined by the `ClientRequestInterceptor` interface.

```
    public String name() {
        return "ClientLogInterceptor";
    }
```

The logging functionality is implemented by the two methods, `send_request()` and `receive_reply()`; the remaining three methods are empty. The method `send_request()` is called for every outgoing request. If a response is expected from the server, we enter the current system time into a table indexed by the request's ID. Because request IDs are not guaranteed to be unique across different targets, we need to add a second layer of indexing. The implementation manages another table indexed by target objects to hold the tables with the requests' start times. A simpler solution would have been to convert the target object reference to a string and just tag the request ID onto this string. To do this, we would need a reference to the ORB, however. As explained in the text that follows, an Interceptor cannot get at a fully functional ORB reference, so we are left with only the two-level indexing scheme just described.

```
public void send_request(ClientRequestInfo ri)
    throws ForwardRequest {
    if( ri.response_expected()) {
        Integer id = new Integer(ri.request_id() );
        Hashtable table =
            (Hashtable)tableTable.get( ri.target());
        if( table == null ) {
            table = new Hashtable();
            tableTable.put( ri.target(), table );
        }
        table.put( id,
                   new Long( System.currentTimeMillis()));
    }
}
```

The method `receive_reply()` performs the actual logging. For every reply received, it looks up the target object's request table. From this table, it then retrieves the request's start time using the request ID as the key. Finally, it prints a log message containing the request ID, the operation name, and the difference between the current time and the request's start time:

```
public void receive_reply(ClientRequestInfo ri) {
    Hashtable table =
        (Hashtable)tableTable.get( ri.target());
    if( table == null ) {
        logStream.println(
            "error: no request table for object");
        return;
    }

    long t = System.currentTimeMillis();
    Long startTime  =
        (Long)table.remove( new Integer(ri.request_id() ));
```

```
        if( startTime != null ) {
            logStream.println( "id: " + ri.request_id() +
                               " operation: " + ri.operation() +
                               " roundtrip: " +
                               ( t - startTime.longValue()) +
                               " msecs. ");
        }
        else
            logStream.println("unexpected reply for request " +
                               ri.request_id() );
    }
    // empty methods
    public void send_poll(ClientRequestInfo ri){
    }

    public void receive_exception(ClientRequestInfo ri)
       throws ForwardRequest{
    }

    public void receive_other(ClientRequestInfo ri)
       throws ForwardRequest{
    }
}
```

### 9.5.3.2 Registering the Interceptor

To use the preceding code, we need to create an Interceptor object and tell the ORB about it. Interceptor registration is done at ORB initialization time and is performed by objects that provide the ORBInitializer interface defined in the PortableInterceptor module. The Initializer is passed an `ORBInitInfo` object that provides a subset of the functionality of the ORB. Because the Initializer is run at ORB initialization time, the ORB itself is not yet available, so only the `ORBInitInfo` object can be used to bootstrap into CORBA. This object is not capable of converting between object references and strings, so it would not solve our indexing problem to pass it to the newly created Interceptor instance.

```
package com.wiley.compbooks.brose.chapter9.interceptor;
import org.omg.PortableInterceptor.*;
import org.omg.PortableInterceptor.ORBInitInfoPackage.*;

public class ClientInitializer
    extends LocalityConstrainedObject
    implements ORBInitializer {

    public ClientInitializer(){}

    // Interceptor initialization and registration
```

```
    public void post_init(ORBInitInfo info) {
        try {
            info.add_client_request_interceptor(
                new ClientLogInterceptor());
        }
        catch (DuplicateName e) {
            e.printStackTrace();
        }
    }

    // unused
    public void pre_init(ORBInitInfo info) {
    }
}
```

When registering the Interceptor, we must be prepared to handle the `DuplicateName` exception that will be raised by the `ORBInitInfo` object if it finds that another Interceptor has already been registered under this name.

Our Log Interceptor can now be used with arbitrary CORBA client programs. The only thing we need to do is make the ORB use the preceding Initializer. This is achieved by setting a specific Java property. As an example, we run the Client program from this chapter's Any example:

```
> java -Dorg.omg.PortableInterceptor.ORBInitializerClass.LogInit=\
com.wiley.compbooks.brose.chapter9.interceptor.ClientInitializer\
com.wiley.compbooks.brose.chapter9.any.Client
id: 0 operation: hello roundtrip: 9 msecs.
IfRepId of any_time: IDL:com/wiley/.../helloWorld/Time:1.0
Type code of any_time: Time
        name: hour
        name: minute
length of any_locality: 6
Hello World!
The local time in Berlin is 4:28.
```

The output is the same as usual, but we get one additional line of output from the Log Interceptor, announcing that it took 9 milliseconds for the hello operation to return. The Java property name for the Initializer must begin with `"org.omg.PortableInterceptor.ORBInitializerClass."`; its value is the Initializer's Java class name

## 9.6 Applet Server

So far we have considered only cases where applets invoke objects but do not provide object implementations of their own. In this section we show how a CORBA server can be implemented as an applet:

- Introduction of the application and interface specification (sections 9.5.1 and 9.5.2)
- Overview of implementation classes (section 9.5.3)
- Object implementation (section 9.5.4)
- Applet implementation (section 9.5.5)

The main motivation to have CORBA objects hosted by applets is the ability to make callbacks into the applet, but there can also be cases where we might want to have interapplet communication, as in the following example.

## 9.6.1 The Application

Because none of the examples introduced previously fits this case, we will use a fresh one called AppletTalk. It is based on two applets that can interact with each other by sending messages. Figure 9.7 illustrates this.

For simplicity we consider only two-party talk, although the implementation is easily extensible to support multiparty talks. The talking applets are instances of the same class. This class acts as a speaker, a client sending some text by invoking an operation offered by an object reference. It also acts as a listener, offering an object to receive messages.

Although Figure 9.7 shows direct connections between the two applets, this would be the case only when using signed applets and setting the browser security level so that it allows requests to connect to and receive connection requests from arbitrary machines on the network. More likely, the communication would be routed via an IIOP gateway residing on the host from which the applets have been downloaded.

Applets register themselves with the CORBA Naming Service using the name context's bind() operation. Interested parties can establish connections by resolving the name of the potential partner to an object reference. Once a party decides to quit the system it simply deregisters its name from the Naming Service using the unbind() method.

## 9.6.2 The Interface Specification

As we see in the IDL specification, the interface Listener provides an operation message. The applet will host an object of this interface type. The operation has an in parameter that is a string. This is a message sent from the other party. The interface is defined inside a module, Talk.

```
module com {
...
module appletServer {
module Talk {
```

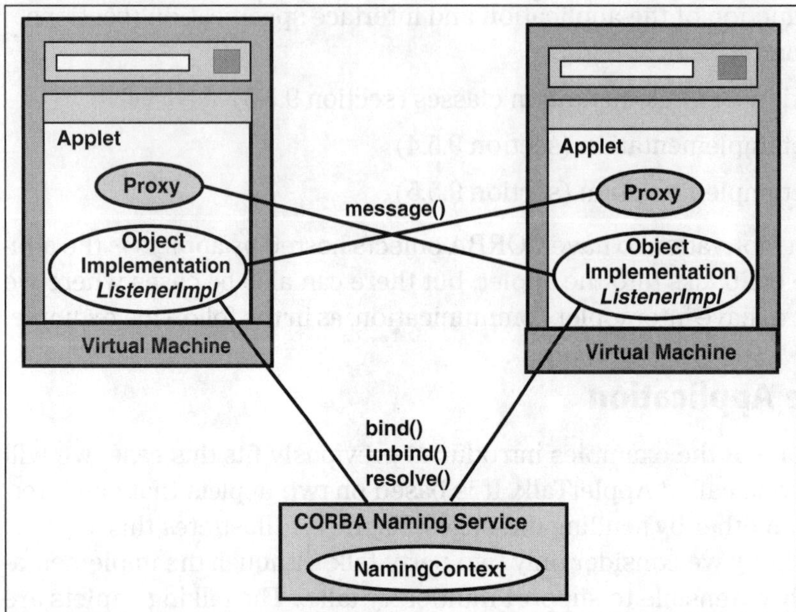


**Figure 9.7** AppletTalk.

```
    interface Listener {
        void message( in string msg );
    };
}; ... };
```

The IDL specification is rather simple, and so is the implementation. All the complexity is taken care of by the ORB. There seems to be the problem of handling two event loops: one for CORBA events, that is, incoming requests, and another one for GUI events from the user. Because Java ORBs are multithreaded, this is taken care of, however. The ORB has its own thread to listen for incoming requests. This thread does not interfere with the GUI event loop.

## 9.6.3 Structure of the Implementation

Let's go through the implementation. We have two implementation classes `ListenerImpl`, which contains the servant code that implements the IDL-defined interface, and `AppletServer`, which extends the Java applet class. The class `AppletServer` provides the following methods:

- `init()`—initializes the GUI and the ORB. It also instantiates the implementation objects.

- `actionPerformed()`—handles user-initiated events. We implement the Java interface `ActionListener` to catch events caused when the user clicks buttons in the GUI.
- `register()`—registers the object implementation with the Naming Service.
- `deregister()`—unbinds the object implementation from the Naming Service.
- `updateTalkers()`—retrieves a list of registered applets from the Naming Service.
- `connect()`—connects an applet (client) to another applet (server) by resolving a name into an object reference.
- `disconnect()`—disconnects an applet (client) from its current communication partner.
- `display()`—displays a string in a particular text field. This method is used by the implementation object `ListenerImpl` to display the message received through a method invocation.
- `clear()`—clears the text areas for reading and writing.

## 9.6.4 Object Implementation

The implementation of the interface Listener follows the same pattern we have used before. We define a class `ListenerImpl,` which extends the servant base class `ListenerPOA`. The constructor of the implementation class has a parameter of type `AppletServer`. We store this reference in a private variable `talkApplet`. This reference is used to eventually display incoming messages in a text area controlled by the applet.

```
package com.wiley.compbooks.brose.chapter9.appletServer;

import java.awt.*;
import java.awt.event.*;
import java.util.Vector;
import org.omg.CORBA.*;
import org.omg.PortableServer.*;
import org.omg.CosNaming.*;
import com.wiley.compbooks.brose.chapter9.appletServer.Talk.*;

class ListenerImpl
    extends ListenerPOA {
    private AppletServer talkApplet;

    /** constructor */
    ListenerImpl( AppletServer applet ) {
```

```
        talkApplet = applet;
    }

    /** operation */
    public void message( String msg ) {
        talkApplet.display( msg );
        return;
    }
}
```

The implementation of the method `message()` is quite simple. We invoke the method `display()` on the applet `talkApplet`, which, in turn, displays the message in a text area of the applet (see section 9.6.5).

## 9.6.5 Applet Implementation

The implementation of the applet `AppletServer` has the typical applet structure. First, we declare a number of private variables that determine the state of the applet. There are four variables for CORBA-related objects, `orb`, `myListener`, `remoteListener`, and one for the root naming context. The others are for various GUI elements.

```
public class AppletServer
    extends java.applet.Applet
    implements ActionListener {

    private ORB orb;
    private NamingContextExt naming;
    private Listener remoteListener;
    private ListenerImpl myListener;

    private Panel namePanel;
    private Panel buttonPanel;
    private Panel textPanel;
    private Panel talkersPanel;
    private Button registerButton;
    private Button connectButton;
    private Button sendButton;
    private Button updateButton;
    private Button clearButton;
    private Label nameLabel;
    private Label talkersLabel;
    private Label partnerLabel;
    private TextField nameField;
    private TextField talkersField;
    private TextField partnerField;
    private TextArea inArea;
    private TextArea outArea;

    private String myName;
```

The implementation of the init() method has two parts. The first part initializes the GUI components. The second part initializes the ORB and creates and connects the object.

### 9.6.5.1 Initializing the GUI

In the first part we initialize the various GUI components. We create text areas for the incoming messages inArea, and for outgoing messages outArea. Three text fields are created: nameField to enter the name string to register this applet as, talkersField to display the names of other applets currently registered, and partnerField to enter the string of an object/applet you want to talk to. There are also five buttons:

- registerButton—to register and deregister the applet's listener object with the Naming Service
- connectButton—to connect to and disconnect from another applet
- sendButton—to send a message to the listener object obtained from the Naming Service
- clearButton—to clear this applet's text areas
- updateButton—to retrieve the names of other listener objects from the Naming Service

```
public void init() {
   registerButton = new Button("register");
   registerButton.setFont(new Font("Helvetica", Font.BOLD, 20));
   registerButton.setActionCommand("register");
   registerButton.addActionListener( (ActionListener) this );

   connectButton = new Button("connect");
   connectButton.setFont(new Font("Helvetica", Font.BOLD, 20));
   connectButton.setActionCommand("connect");
   connectButton.addActionListener( (ActionListener) this );

   sendButton = new Button("send");
   sendButton.setFont(new Font("Helvetica", Font.BOLD, 20));
   sendButton.setActionCommand("send");
   sendButton.addActionListener( (ActionListener) this );

   updateButton = new Button("update");
   updateButton.setFont(new Font("Helvetica", Font.BOLD, 20));
   updateButton.setActionCommand("update");
   updateButton.addActionListener( (ActionListener) this );

   clearButton = new Button("clear");
   clearButton.setFont(new Font("Helvetica", Font.BOLD, 20));
```

```
clearButton.setActionCommand("clear");
clearButton.addActionListener( (ActionListener) this );

nameLabel = new Label("Enter name: ");
nameLabel.setFont(new Font("Helvetica", Font.BOLD, 14));
nameField = new TextField();
nameField.setFont(new Font("Helvetica", Font.BOLD, 14));

talkersField = new TextField();
talkersField.setFont(new Font("Helvetica", Font.BOLD, 14));
talkersLabel = new Label("Currently registered: ");
talkersLabel.setFont(new Font("Helvetica", Font.BOLD, 14));

partnerField = new TextField();
partnerField.setFont(new Font("Helvetica", Font.BOLD, 14));
partnerLabel = new Label("Talk to: ");
partnerLabel.setFont(new Font("Helvetica", Font.BOLD, 14));

namePanel = new Panel();
textPanel = new Panel();

namePanel.setLayout( new GridLayout(3,3));
namePanel.add( nameLabel );
namePanel.add( nameField );
namePanel.add( registerButton );
namePanel.add( talkersLabel );
namePanel.add( talkersField );
namePanel.add( updateButton );
namePanel.add( partnerLabel );
namePanel.add( partnerField );
namePanel.add( connectButton );

Panel inPanel = new Panel();
inPanel.setLayout(new BorderLayout());

Label inLabel = new Label("Write here:");
inLabel.setFont(new Font("Helvetica", Font.BOLD, 14));

inArea = new TextArea("", 40, 5 );
inArea.setFont(new Font("Helvetica", Font.BOLD, 14));

Panel buttonPanel = new Panel();
buttonPanel.setLayout( new FlowLayout());
buttonPanel.add( sendButton );
buttonPanel.add( clearButton );

inPanel.add("North", inLabel );
inPanel.add("Center", inArea );
inPanel.add("South", buttonPanel );

Panel outPanel = new Panel();
outPanel.setLayout(new BorderLayout());
```

```
Label outLabel = new Label("Read here:");
outLabel.setFont(new Font("Helvetica", Font.BOLD, 14));

outArea = new TextArea("", 40, 5 );
outArea.setEditable(false);
outArea.setFont(new Font("Helvetica", Font.BOLD, 14));

outPanel.add("North", outLabel );
outPanel.add("Center", outArea );

textPanel.setLayout( new GridLayout(2,1));
textPanel.add( inPanel );
textPanel.add( outPanel );

setLayout( new BorderLayout());
add( "North", namePanel );
add( "Center", textPanel );
```

We choose a layout for our GUI elements by using the layout manager class `BorderLayout` for the panels and `GridLayout` for the buttons, label and text fields, and text area. The effect is shown in the screen shots in Figures 9.8 and 9.9.

### 9.6.5.2 Initializing the ORB and Object Creation

In the second part of the implementation of the `init()` method we initialize the ORB. Then we create the implementation object `myListener` by calling its constructor `ListenerImpl()` and passing it to a reference to the applet (`this`). We also retrieve the initial reference to the Naming Service, as already explained in Chapter 7, "Discovering Services," and Chapter 8, "Building Applications."

```
try {
    //init ORB
    orb = ORB.init( this, null );
    POA poa = POAHelper.narrow(
        orb.resolve_initial_references("RootPOA") );
    // create a Listener object
    myListener = new ListenerImpl( this );
    naming = NamingContextExtHelper.narrow(
        orb.resolve_initial_references("NameService"));
```

Once the implementation object is created we activate it and its POA.

```
    // activate the object
    poa.activate_object( myListener );
```

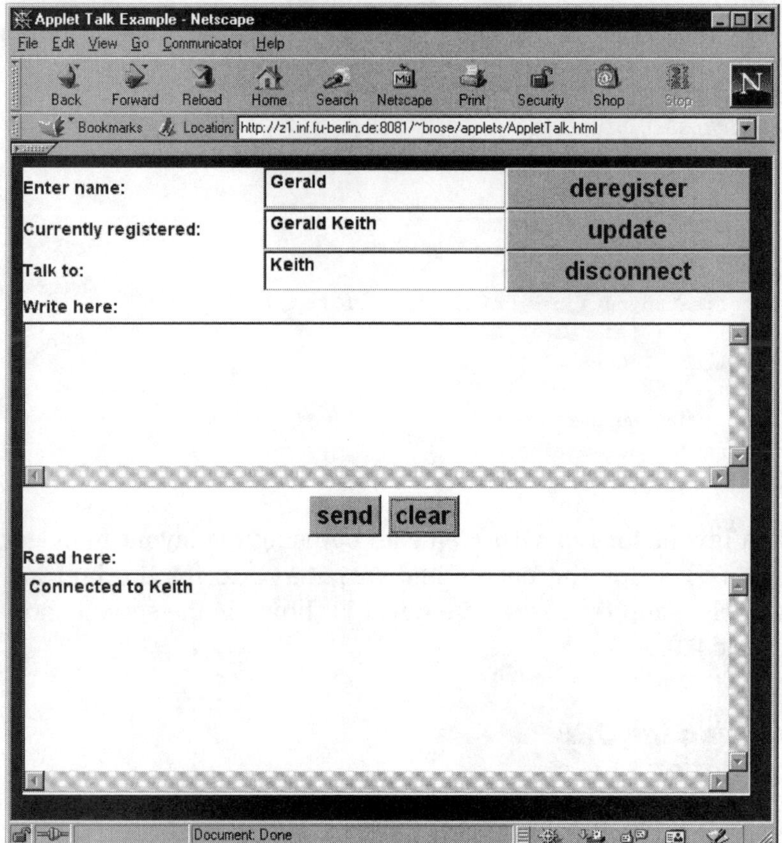


**Figure 9.8** AppletTalk: establishing a session.

```
            poa.the_POAManager().activate();
        }
        catch(UserException u) {
             u.printStackTrace();
        }
        catch(SystemException e) {
             e.printStackTrace();
        }
    }
```

In the other examples we have seen so far, the last statement in a server's main routine was an infinite loop such as orb.run(). There is, however, no need for a special loop. In this case the applet already provides its own event loop.

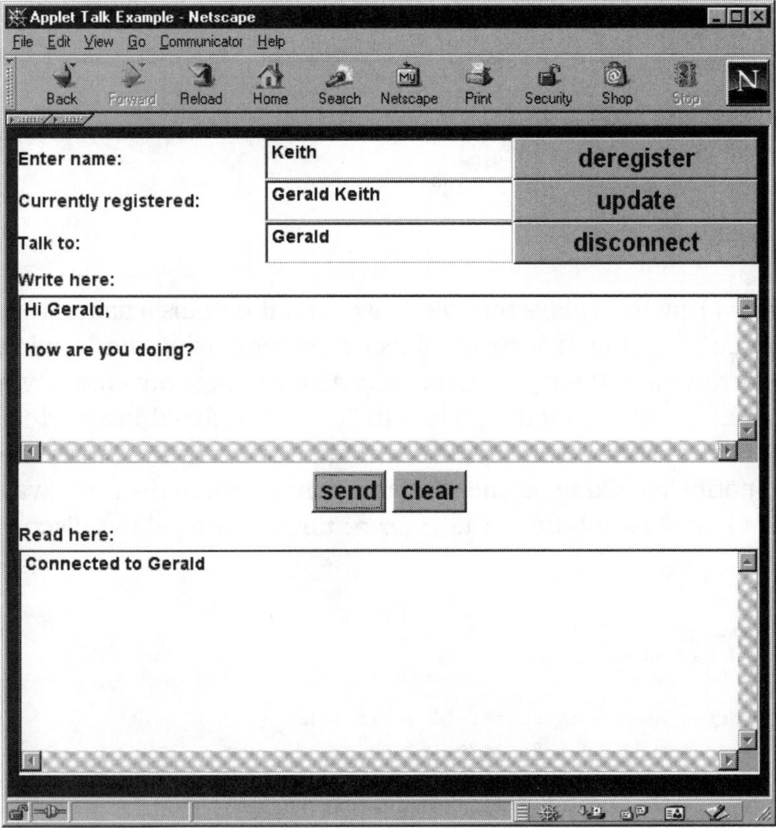


**Figure 9.9** AppletTalk: sending a message.

Now we have a look at the additional methods we have declared in the class. The method `register()` gets a name from the `nameField` and registers the object implementation `myListener` under this name with the Naming Service. If no exceptions occur, the `registerButton` is then relabeled and made to answer deregister events rather than register events.

```
public synchronized void register() {
    try {
        myName = nameField.getText();
        naming.bind( naming.to_name(myName + ".talker" ),
                     myListener._this() );
        registerButton.setLabel("deregister");
        registerButton.setActionCommand("deregister");
```

```
        }
        catch(UserException ue) {
            outArea.append( "register " + myName +
                            " failed: " + ue );
        }
        catch(SystemException se) {
            outArea.append( "Exception: " + se );
        }
    }
```

The `connect()` method plays the role of a client. It obtains a name from the `partnerField`, resolves it to an object reference using the Naming Service, and narrows it to the type `Listener`. As a naming convention, we set the kind attribute of the binding name to "talker" to avoid inadvertent name clashes. The method then invokes the method `message()` on the new object to notify its talking partner that it is connected. In the same way as `register()`, it then modifies the `connectButton` to allow disconnecting.

```
    public void connect() {
        // invoke the operation
        try {
            String name = partnerField.getText();
            if( name != null && name.length() > 0 ) {
                //resolve name and narrow it to Listener
                remoteListener = ListenerHelper.narrow(
                    naming.resolve(
                        naming.to_name( name + ".talker" )));
            // send initial message
            remoteListener.message( "Connected to " +
                                    myName + "\n" );
            connectButton.setLabel("disconnect");
            connectButton.setActionCommand("disconnect");
            }
        }
        // catch exceptions
        catch(UserException ue) {
            outArea.append( "resolve failed: " + ue );
        }
        catch(SystemException se) {
            outArea.append( "Exception: " + se );
        }
    }
```

The method `deregister()` deregisters a listener from the Naming Service and switches the `registerButton` back again. It also clears the `nameField`.

```
public void deregister() {
    try {
        if( myName != null ) {
            naming.unbind(
                naming.to_name( myName + ".talker" ));
        }

        registerButton.setLabel("register");
        registerButton.setActionCommand("register");
        myName = null;
        nameField.setText("");
    }
    catch(UserException ue) {
        System.err.println(ue);
    }
    catch(SystemException se) {
        System.err.println(se);
    }
}
```

To disconnect from the current communication partner, we implement the method `disconnect()`. It sends a farewell message to the `remoteListener` and then releases the reference. It then cleans the `partnerField` and resets the `connectButton` to accept connect events again.

```
public void disconnect() {
    // send last message
    remoteListener.message( myName + " is disconnecting . . . \n");
    remoteListener._release();
    remoteListener = null;
    partnerField.setText("");
    connectButton.setLabel("connect");
    connectButton.setActionCommand("connect");
}
```

The method `updateTalkers()` retrieves a list of potential communication partners from the Naming Service. It uses a private method `list()` that recursively appends the names of all bindings in a naming context and its subcontexts to its argument vector if the name's kind attribute is "talker." It also strips this kind attribute from the returned strings. The contents of the vector are displayed in the `talkersField`.

```
public void updateTalkers() {
    StringBuffer sb = new StringBuffer();
    Vector talkersList = new Vector();
```

```
        list( naming, talkersList );
        for( int i = 0; i < talkersList.size(); i++ ) {
            String s = (String)talkersList.elementAt(i);
            sb.append( s.substring(0,s.indexOf(".talker")) + " ");
        }
        talkersField.setText( sb.toString());
    }

    private void list( NamingContextExt n, Vector v ) {
        try {
            BindingListHolder blsoh =
                new BindingListHolder(new Binding[0]);
            BindingIteratorHolder bioh =
                new BindingIteratorHolder();

            n.list( 0, blsoh, bioh );
            BindingHolder bh = new BindingHolder();

            if( bioh.value == null )
                return;

            while( bioh.value.next_one( bh )) {
                String stringName =
                    n.to_string( bh.value.binding_name);
                if( stringName.endsWith(".talker"))
                    v.addElement(
                        stringName.substring(0,
                            stringName.indexOf(".talker"))
                );

                if( bh.value.binding_type.value() ==
                    BindingType._ncontext ) {

                    NameComponent [] name = n.to_name(stringName);
                    NamingContextExt sub_context =
                        NamingContextExtHelper.narrow(
                            n.resolve(name)
                        );
                    list(sub_context,v);
                }
            }
        }
        catch (Exception e) {
            e.printStackTrace();
        }
    }
```

The `display()` method displays a string in the applet's text field `outArea`. It is used by the `Listener` implementation object to display incoming messages. The `clean()` method simply clears the two text areas for reading and writing.

```
public void display( String msg ) {
    outArea.append( msg );
}
public void clear() {
    outArea.setText(null);
    inArea.setText(null);
}
```

Finally, we implement the method `actionPerformed()`. It watches for events caused by clicking one of the buttons we have declared and created earlier. For each of the buttons we invoke an appropriate method.

```
public void actionPerformed(ActionEvent ev) {

    // catch and process events
    if(ev.getActionCommand().equals("connect") ) {
        connect();
    }
    if(ev.getActionCommand().equals("disconnect") ) {
        disconnect();
    }
    if(ev.getActionCommand().equals("register") ) {
        register();
    }
    if(ev.getActionCommand().equals("update") )      {
        updateTalkers();
    }
    if(ev.getActionCommand().equals("clear") ) {
        clear();
    }
    if(ev.getActionCommand().equals("deregister") ) {
        deregister();
    }
    if(ev.getActionCommand().equals("send") ) {
        // invoke the operation
        try {
            remoteListener.message( inArea.getText() );
        }
        // catch exceptions
        catch(SystemException ex) {
            outArea.append( "Exception: " + ex );
        }
    }
}
}
```

## 9.6.6 Executing the Application

Once the classes are compiled, we can start our AppletTalk example. We have two instances of our class `AppletServer`. Figure 9.8 shows the applet after it has been registered with the Naming Service under the name "Gerald," and another party, under the name of "Keith," has established contact with it.

Figure 9.9 shows the applet server registered as "Keith" with a message that is ready to be sent, and Figure 9.10 shows the "Gerald" applet server once it has received the message and is about to return an answer. Finally, Figure 9.11 shows the other applet again after receiving the answer and a message that the applet registered as "Gerald" is disconnecting.

**Figure 9.10** AppletTalk: receiving a message.

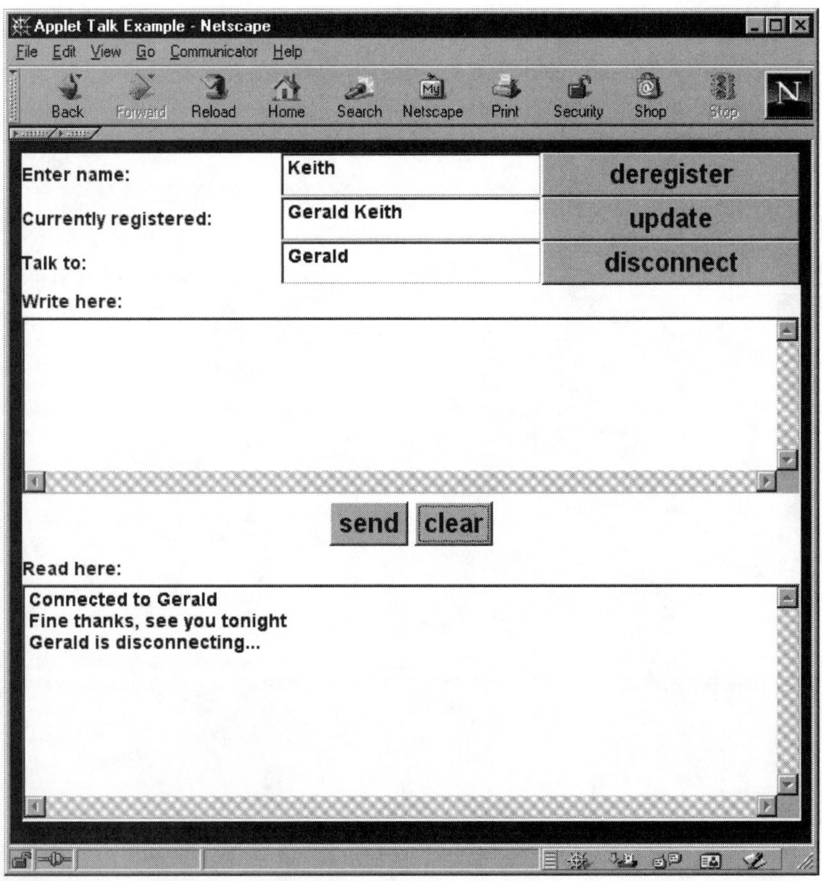


**Figure 9.11** AppletTalk: receiving a disconnect notice.

# Practical POA Programming

This chapter explains how to make more advanced use of the Portable Object Adapter. The POA and its policy configurations were introduced in section 2.3.6 of Chapter 2, "CORBA Overview." We discuss in more detail which POA policies are suitable for specific applications and environments, and we present a detailed example using some of the most important policy combinations. We also demonstrate the use of Java serialization as a simple persistence mechanism.

As a running example for this chapter, we revisit and considerably extend the Room Booking example from Chapter 8, "Building Applications," into a multiuser meeting application.

## 10.1 POA Policies Revisited

As explained in Chapter 2, individual POAs can be created with different combinations of policies. These policies determine how the POA manages objects and servants. They also determine how a POA uses its internal data structures. POA policies are a structured and extremely flexible way of configuring server applications. They also provide you with a high degree of control over the inner workings of your server. Without this degree of control, tuning your server applications to the real-world requirements and limitations of their actual environments would be much harder, if not impossible.

It is important to understand the implications of certain policy combinations for two reasons. First, the POA can be configured to use user-defined code for activating and deactivating objects and for managing Servants. This is particularly useful when persistent object state has to be managed. Second, the selected set of POA policies has fundamental consequences for both the performance and scalability of your applications.

To determine how the POA has to be configured in a given situation, the main design factors we need to take into account are the following:

- How many objects will the POA host?
- What is the expected request load?
- Do objects have persistent state?

The first two questions essentially define how critical scalability and performance are in a given setting. If memory is scarce and scalability is crucial, we might have to restrict the POA's memory usage. For example, we might have to set the SERVANT_RETENTION policy to NON_RETAIN so that the POA does not use its Active Object Map (AOM) to store the association between active objects and incarnating servants. For very large numbers of objects and servants, this table might otherwise consume too much space.

A POA that does not use an AOM has to find servants dynamically, and it will need to do so on every single request it receives. There are two options for this case. If the REQUEST_PROCESSING policy is set to USE_SERVANT_MANAGER, a Servant Manager has to provide servants for every request, which will have performance impacts, especially if the servant manager instantiates Java objects on every request or moves data from and to secondary memory, both of which are expensive operations. If a Default Servant is used, however, the time to look up servants can be minimal. The Meeting Service presented in section 10.2.5 of this chapter is an example of using a Default Servant.

If performance is of high priority we will probably use the AOM, that is, set the RETAIN policy. Request processing can thus be more efficient because finding Servants that are already active requires just a single table lookup. In fact, the choice of whether to use the AOM is just an example of the classical trade-off between time and space.

The number of objects that have to be handled is not only a scalability factor, however. It also has implications for the way objects can be activated. For a small number of objects, it is possible to perform all activations in advance and set the REQUEST_PROCESSING policy to USE_ACTIVE_OBJECT_MAP_ONLY. This policy requires that the RETAIN policy is also selected. This way, no dynamic activation overhead will be incurred. The Digital Secretary example presented in section 10.2.7 shows this policy in combination with a PERSISTENT life span policy.

If the expected number of objects is large or if the objects cannot be determined in advance, however, we might have to use a Default Servant or a Servant Manager to activate objects. Even for moderate numbers of objects it is usually more convenient to use a Servant Manager, especially if persistent state must be loaded and stored. For large numbers of essentially stateless objects, a Default Servant might be the best choice, as in the transient case. The extended Room Booking example presents combinations of the PERSISTENT Life Span and USE_SERVANT_MANAGER Request Processing policies with both RETAIN and NON_RETAIN policies.

Figure 10.1 gives an overview of the example POAs used in this chapter. It compares these to the policies used by the Root POA and a standard POA. A standard POA is created if the `create_POA()` operation is called with an empty list of policies. Note that a standard POA differs from the Root POA in its Activation policy. The figure omits all standard policy values for the example POAs and focuses on the differences between POAs.

So far, we have not paid much attention to either the Activation policy or the Thread policy. The reason for this neglect is that both policies can be seen as basically implementation details with only limited impact on application performance, scalability or coding convenience. For Java ORBs, which are multithreaded anyway, using the SINGLE_THREAD_MODEL does not make sense unless Servants are not thread-safe and need to be protected. In most cases, allowing concurrent access will achieve higher throughput although there might be cases where the additional overhead of thread management, in fact, outweighs these benefits.

Using the IMPLICIT_ACTIVATION policy basically just results in more convenient coding because objects can be activated by simply calling `_this()` on a Servant, but this does not have direct implications for an application's run-time behavior. It does have indirect implications, though, as IMPLICIT_ACTIVATION requires the SYSTEM_ID and RETAIN policies to be present. Usually, it is also used in conjunction with the UNIQUE_ID assignment policy and the TRANSIENT Life Span policy. None of the persistent POAs in this chapter uses an IMPLICIT_ACTIVATION policy.

## 10.2 Managing Objects with Persistent State

So far, the examples in this book have been restricted to CORBA objects with transient lifetimes, that is, objects that disappear together with their

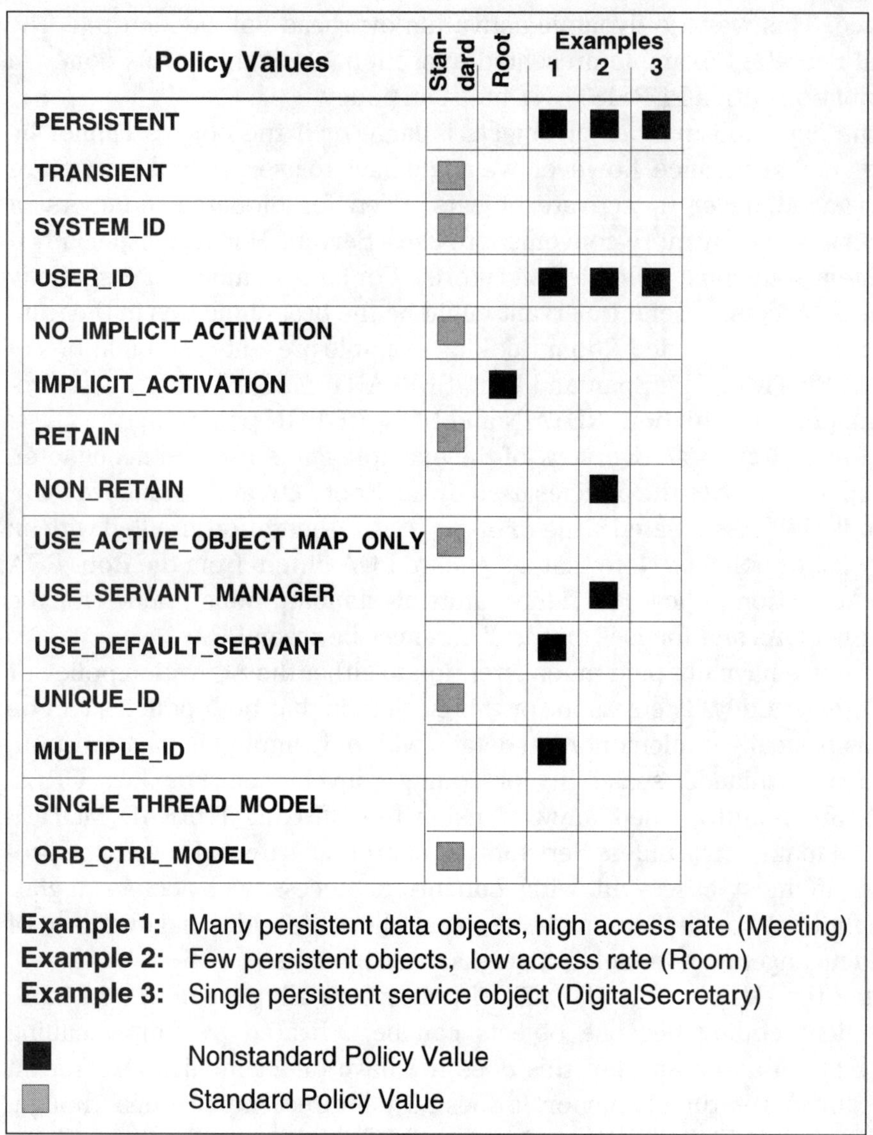

| Policy Values | Stan-dard | Root | Examples 1 | 2 | 3 |
|---|---|---|---|---|---|
| PERSISTENT | | | ■ | ■ | ■ |
| TRANSIENT | ▨ | | | | |
| SYSTEM_ID | ▨ | | | | |
| USER_ID | | | ■ | ■ | ■ |
| NO_IMPLICIT_ACTIVATION | ▨ | | | | |
| IMPLICIT_ACTIVATION | | ■ | | | |
| RETAIN | ▨ | | | | |
| NON_RETAIN | | | | ■ | |
| USE_ACTIVE_OBJECT_MAP_ONLY | ▨ | | | | |
| USE_SERVANT_MANAGER | | | | ■ | |
| USE_DEFAULT_SERVANT | | | ■ | | |
| UNIQUE_ID | ▨ | | | | |
| MULTIPLE_ID | | | ■ | | |
| SINGLE_THREAD_MODEL | | | | | |
| ORB_CTRL_MODEL | ▨ | | | | |

**Example 1:** Many persistent data objects, high access rate (Meeting)
**Example 2:** Few persistent objects, low access rate (Room)
**Example 3:** Single persistent service object (DigitalSecretary)

■ Nonstandard Policy Value
▨ Standard Policy Value

**Figure 10.1** Important POA policy combinations.

POAs and that do not maintain state beyond their own lifetime. Many applications do require objects that maintain persistent state and can be reactivated after their enclosing server processes have been shut down and restarted. This starting up of server processes might even take place on demand when a client request arrives and the target object's process is found to be inactive. The mechanism used by CORBA to start servers on demand is called the Implementation Repository. The precise functionality of the interface of the Implementation Repository is not defined in any of the OMG's specification, but most ORB vendors provide an implementation of this component. To set up servers for operation with an Implementation Repository, we refer you to your ORB vendor's documentation.

In this section we explain how the POA can be configured for applications with persistent state. We show how persistent object references are created and how Servant Managers and Default Servants can be used to load and store object state on object activation, and to decide when objects are to be deactivated so that resources can be reclaimed. To do this, we extend the room booking example of Chapter 8 to become a fully distributed, multiuser meeting service integrated with personal digital secretaries to manage individual diaries.

In the remainder of this section, we present the application example and explain its architecture (section 10.2.1), IDL interfaces (section 10.2.2), and common data structures (section 10.2.3). Java serialization as a simple persistence mechanism is presented in section 10.2.4. We then examine the individual server processes that cooperate in this application and explain how their POAs are configured (sections 10.2.5–10.2.7).

## 10.2.1 A Multiuser Meeting Application

The distributed application that we use as the main example in this chapter allows users to maintain a personal diary of appointments. Figure 10.2 shows the graphical front end to the Digital Secretary Service with which users can browse their personal diaries and create, edit, or delete meetings.

These appointments include meetings with other users at specific locations. Setting up such a meeting involves booking available rooms for the intended day and hour. For the selected day, a meeting can be set up by clicking the "New" button. The dialog window to select and enter meeting information is shown in Figure 10.3.

The Meeting Dialog offers three combo boxes provided by the Java Swing API to select the starting hour, the name of a person to meet, and the known rooms where the meeting could take place. The text field on the right allows the user to enter text describing the meeting's purpose. The names of the persons with whom it is possible to arrange meetings are retrieved at startup time from the CORBA Naming Service. Every user's Digital Secretary registers under its user's name so that others can find and contact it. The rooms offered in the combo box are retrieved using our own Building Service, which is the successor of the room booking service of Chapter 8.

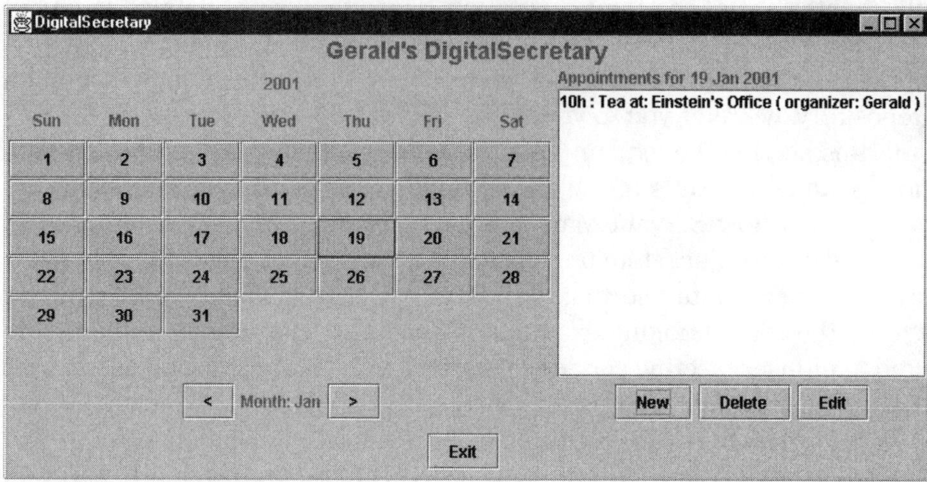


**Figure 10.2** The Digital Secretary GUI.

The Building Service is a separate server process that gives access to all rooms in one building, allows the addition of new rooms to the building, and enables viewing of each room's bookings. Each Building Server registers with the Naming Service under its building's name. Figure 10.4 shows the graphical interface to the Building Service. Clicking on a room in the room list displays its bookings for the current day.

The display is limited to show just the name of the organizer of a meeting, not its purpose. This limitation was introduced only to keep the graphical

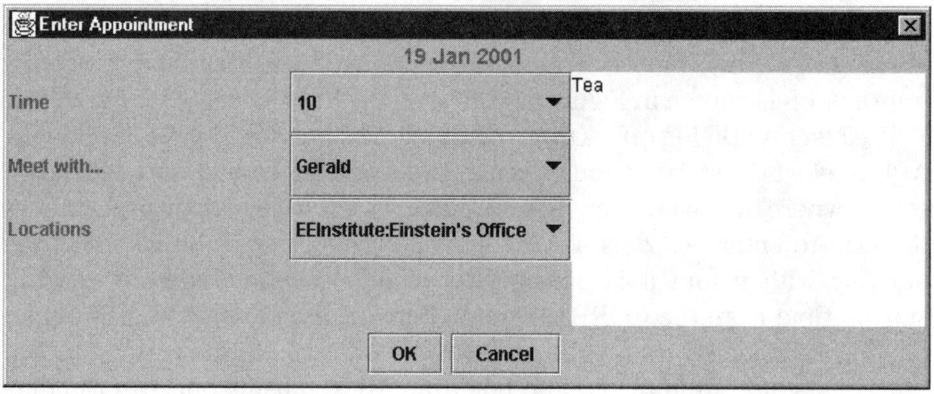

**Figure 10.3** The Meeting Dialog.

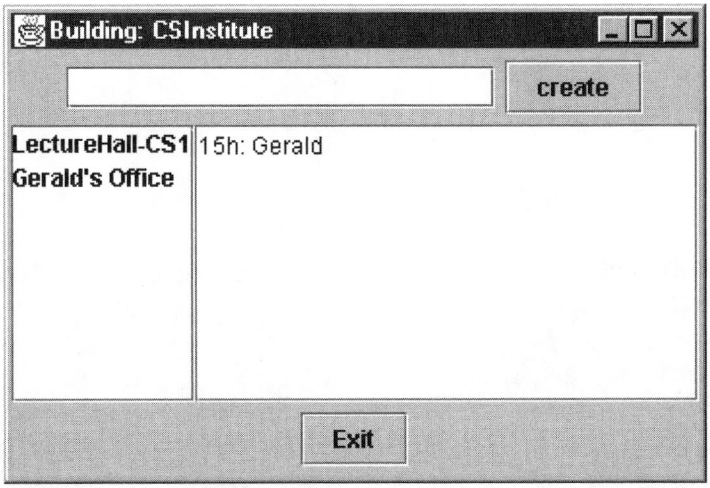

Building: CSInstitute

create

LectureHall-CS1 | 15h: Gerald
Gerald's Office

Exit

**Figure 10.4** The Building Service.

interface simple. We assume that meeting information is mainly accessed through the Digital Secretary rather than the Building Service, so the purpose is displayed in the Digital Secretary GUI only.

The last component in this application is the Meeting Service, which creates and stores all meeting information but does not have a graphical interface itself. Its operations are accessed through the Digital Secretary. Note that all the services described here will have to manage persistent state unless we assume that all processes run all the time. The Building Service keeps a list of rooms and their bookings, the Meeting service hosts the information about all meetings, and the Digital Secretary keeps a personal diary of user appointments.

In this chapter, we do not make the assumption that all processes run all the time, which is not realistic anyway. Rather, we show how the POA supports applications that need to store and load object state.

## 10.2.2 The IDL Interfaces

After the short overview of the application in the preceding section, we now present the IDL definitions necessary for this system. We first refine the date definitions from Chapter 9, "Advanced Features," to include years, months and days.

```
module com {
...
```

```
module chapter10 {
module office {

    // Basic type definitions for diaries

    typedef short Hour;
    typedef short Day;
    enum Month {
       jan, feb, mar, apr, may, jun,
       jul, aug, sep, oct, nov, dec };
    typedef long Year;

    struct Date {
        Year the_year;
        Month the_month;
        Day  the_day;
        Hour the_hour;
    };
```

The first interface necessary for the application is Meeting. To be able to define it, we need three exception declarations and two forward declarations for the interfaces DigitalSecretary and Room. These will be defined later in the file.

```
    exception IllegalDate {};
    exception AlreadyEngaged {};
    exception SlotAlreadyTaken {};

    // forward declaration
    interface DigitalSecretary;
    interface Room;

    typedef DigitalSecretary Participant;
    typedef sequence < Participant > ParticipantList;

    // the Meeting interface
    interface Meeting {

        // the purpose attribute describes the purpose of this meeting.
        readonly attribute string purpose;
        readonly attribute Participant organizer;
        readonly attribute Room location;
        readonly attribute Date when;

        exception MeetingCanceled {
            string reason;
        };
```

```
    // show the participants of the meeting
    ParticipantList getParticipants()
        raises ( MeetingCanceled ) ;

    // join the participants of this meeting
    void addParticipant( in Participant who )
        raises ( MeetingCanceled );

    // let the rest hold their meeting without me . . .
    void removeParticipant( in Participant who )
        raises ( MeetingCanceled );

    // cancel the meeting.
    void cancel( in string reason )
        raises ( MeetingCanceled ) ;

    // move to a different Room and/or time
    // Both arguments must be present.
    void relocate( in Room when, in Date when )
        raises ( MeetingCanceled, SlotAlreadyTaken );
};
```

The Meeting interface has attributes that represent its purpose, the person responsible for organizing it, its location, and the time for which it is scheduled. There are three operations to access the list of participants for this meeting. The first of these, getParticipants(), retrieves the list of participants. The other two operations, addParticipant() and removeParticipant(), allow clients to add or remove participants from the list.

All three operations raise the MeetingCanceled exception, which signals that the meeting has been canceled by calling the cancel() operation. This operation takes a string argument that explains the reason for canceling. This reason string will then be part of any subsequent MeetingCanceled exception.

The relocate() operation relocates a meeting in both time and space. The two arguments describe the new location and time. If the room the meeting is to be held in is not available at the desired time, the operation raises the SlotAlreadyTaken exception.

Meeting objects are created by MeetingFactories. In fact, we assume that only one such factory exists for any system because all meeting information is local to it. In effect, a MeetingFactory defines a domain for all its clients in the same way that the Naming Service defines a domain. The MeetingFactory interface has just one operation, create(), which takes as its argument all the information that is necessary to initialize a Meeting object.

```
interface MeetingFactory {

    Meeting create( in string purpose,
                    in Room location,
                    in Date time,
                    in Participant organizer,
                    in ParticipantList participants)
      raises( IllegalDate );
};
```

Now that the interfaces to set up meetings have been described, we continue with the IDL definitions needed by the Building Service. We have to forward-declare Building first to be able to describe the Room interface.

```
// A Room provides operations to view, make, and cancel bookings.
// Making a booking means associating a meeting with a time-slot
// (for this particular room).

interface Building; // forward declaration

interface Room {

    // the building this room belongs in
    readonly attribute Building site;

    // The attribute name names a room.
    readonly attribute string name;

    // the room does not keep references to meetings, just descriptive text
    typedef sequence< string > Bookings;

    // exceptions raised by Room operations
    exception NoMeetingAtThisTime {};
```

Rooms have two read-only attributes, one that represents their name and another that contains a reference to the Building they are in. The Room interface is not designed to give access to meetings directly; it just displays meeting information as strings, so we define the type Bookings to be just a sequence of strings.

```
    // viewBookings returns the bookings of a room.
    Bookings viewDayBookings(in Year a_year, in Month a_month, in Day a_day);

    // view today's bookings
    Bookings viewBookings();
```

```
        // book a room:
        // bookings can be made only in one-hour slots!
        void book( in Date slot, in string meeting_description )
            raises( SlotAlreadyTaken );

        void cancelBooking( in Date slot )
            raises( NoMeetingAtThisTime );
    };
```

Operations on rooms allow clients to view bookings on a particular day, using viewDayBookings(), or on the current day, using viewBookings(). To book a room for a given time slot, the operation book() is used. Canceling a booking for a particular time slot is possible with the operation cancelBooking(), which raises the NoMeetingAtThisTime exception if the slot is not booked.

Let's now look at the Building interface, which is both a factory and a container of rooms. The Building interface contains just two operations, one to create new rooms with a given name, the other to retrieve all the existing rooms in the building in a sequence. The building also has a name attribute. Within the entire application, all buildings must have distinct names. Also, all rooms in a building must be created with unique names.

```
typedef sequence< Room > RoomSeq;

    interface Building {
        readonly attribute string name;

        Room create(in string name);
        RoomSeq list();
    };
```

The final interface that we need to present here is that of a Digital Secretary, which represents users in the system. In the Meeting interface, the type Participant was used instead of DigitalSecretary to emphasize the user role in that particular context, but remember that Participant is typedef'd to DigitalSecretary.

```
    //  the interface of the secretary service
    interface DigitalSecretary {

        // user name this secretary works for
        readonly attribute string name;

        // send a message to user
        oneway void notify(in string message);
```

```
        // Propose to join a meeting. The receiver of this
        // invocation may or may not choose to join.
        void invite( in Meeting a_meeting )
            raises( AlreadyEngaged );
    };

}; // end module office
}; }; }; }; };
```

The DigitalSecretary interface has a name attribute to represent its user. Its notify() operation sends messages to the user. An implementation might, for example, forward that message to its human user by sending an e-mail, or it might pop up a window on the screen. The implementations of some of the operations in the Meeting interface might choose to notify users of events such as the cancellation or relocation of a meeting in which they intended to participate.

The final operation, invite(), is used to propose a user to join a meeting, which can be accomplished by the DigitalSecretary calling the addParticipant() operation in the meeting interface on behalf of the human user. We do not provide further detail on the implementation of either the notify() or the invite() operations in this chapter; they just serve to make the example more realistic.

## 10.2.3 Common Data Structures

Before we examine the implementation of each of the services in turn, we need to introduce the Java data structure used to hold diary entries. We implement this as a Java class `Diary`, which is used by both the implementation of rooms and the Secretary Service. It also shows how Java serialization can be used to store and retrieve CORBA object references.

```
package com.wiley.compbooks.brose.chapter10.office;

import java.util.*;
import java.io.*;
import org.omg.CORBA.*;

public class Diary
    extends java.util.TreeMap
    implements java.io.Externalizable {

    private static DateComparator comparator =
        new DateComparator();
```

```
private transient Calendar calendar;
private transient ORB orb;
```

The class `Diary` implements the Java interface `java.io.Externalizable` to allow instances to be serialized. In this case, we do not implement `java.io.Serializable` because `Diary` needs complete control over the serialization process even though all state is actually kept in its superclass. You will see other examples where we do implement `Serializable`, which is a little more convenient.

To manage diary entries sorted by date, `Diary` makes use of features inherited from `java.util.TreeMap`, one of JDK 1.2's sorted collection classes. Next, we initialize it with a custom comparison operator that maintains the desired order. We omit the code for this class, `DateComparator`, for brevity. As usual, you can find the implementation on the companion Web site at www.wiley.com/compbooks/brose.

Every time instances of this class are deserialized, they need to be given the current date by providing a new instance of the Java `Calendar` class. For this reason, the calendar field can be marked `transient`, which means that it is never considered in the serialization itself. As we shall see, the Diary also needs an ORB instance to convert between stringified IORs and live object references. This ORB instance is also transient and must be reset every time a Diary instance is deserialized.

```
/** this constructor is for use by deserialization only ! */
public Diary() {
    super( comparator );
}

public Diary(ORB orb) {
    super( comparator );
    this.orb = orb;
    calendar = Calendar.getInstance();
}
```

The second of the two constructors is the one that should be used by clients of this class; the first is provided only for use by the serialization mechanism. Before we will show how serialization is done, let's look at the functionality provided by the class `Diary`. As has been mentioned already, a `Diary` represents a collection sorted by dates, that is, by instances of the Java class `Date` that was generated from our definition of the Date struct in IDL.

```
public Date currentDate() {
    calendar.setTime( new java.util.Date());
    return new Date(
            calendar.get( Calendar.YEAR ),
            Month.from_int( calendar.get( Calendar.MONTH )),
```

```
                calendar.get( Calendar.DAY_OF_MONTH ),
                calendar.get( Calendar.HOUR_OF_DAY ));
    }

    void enter(Date when, java.lang.Object what)
        throws AlreadyEngaged {

        if( get( when ) != null )
            throw new AlreadyEngaged();
        put( when, what );
    }
```

Diary adds just a few simple convenience methods to the ones provided by TreeMap. The first of these is a factory method for Date instances with the current date and time. The enter() method just enters arbitrary data into the diary, but it throws the AlreadyEngaged exception when it finds that a time slot is already in use. The put() and get() methods used here are inherited from TreeMap.

The remaining three methods allow us to remove or retrieve all entries that are stored for a given day. The getToday() method is just a shortcut for calling getDay() with date parameters for the current day.

```
    public void clearDay( int year, Month month, int day) {
        Date date = new Date( year, month, day, 0);
        for( int i = 0; i < 24; i++ ) {
            date.the_hour = i;
            remove( date );
        }
    }

    public java.lang.Object[] getDay( int year,
                                      Month month,
                                      int day){

        Date fromDate = new Date( year, month, day, 0);
        Date toDate = new Date( year, month, day, 24);
        SortedMap submap = subMap(fromDate, toDate);
        java.lang.Object[] result = submap.values().toArray();
        return result;
    }

    /** get appointments for today
    */
    public java.lang.Object[] getToday() {
        Date current = currentDate();
        return getDay(current.the_year,
                      current.the_month,
                      current.the_day );
    }
```

## 10.2.4 Serializing Object References

The Diary class is a generic container in the sense that it does not restrict the types of objects that it can hold. In particular, we can use it to hold both CORBA object references and any other kind of information. In our application, we want to use Diary instances in two different servers. First, a Diary will be used within the Digital Secretary implementation to manage a user's personal appointment schedule. Second, every room will use a separate Diary to manage its bookings. In the latter case, it will be enough to store simple strings that describe meetings.

CORBA object references need special treatment when it to comes to serialization. In general, object references cannot be serialized using the standard Java serialization mechanism if your Java ORB implements the standard Java portability interface. The portability interface requires that all references extend org.omg.CORBA.portable.ObjectImpl, which is defined like this:

```
/****
  Copyright(c)1999 Object Management Group. Unlimited rights to
  duplicate and use this code are hereby granted provided that this
  copyright notice is included.
*****/

package org.omg.CORBA.portable;

abstract public class ObjectImpl implements org.omg.CORBA.Object {
    private transient Delegate __delegate;
    ...
}
```

The important thing here is that the vendor-specific Delegate implementation is marked transient. Consequently, it has to be reset after each deserialization; however, there is no portable way of doing this. You might not be surprised by this; after all, we know that the ORB interface provides the object_to_string() and string_to_object() operations to "serialize" object references as strings, and these work fine. The point to be noted here is that this does not automatically blend with the Java serialization mechanism: Serializing a hash table full of references is easy, but after deserialization the references won't be usable anymore.

What all this boils down to is that we need to hook some code into the serialization and deserialization process that ensures that all object references in a container are turned into strings on serialization, and that the reverse operation is carried out on deserialization. The only way to avoid writing this code would be not to store object references at all but their string representations—which would incur the run-time overhead of converting the reference on every container access rather than once at serialization time.

To make our Diaries serializable in such a setting, we provide implementations of the methods `readExternal()` and `writeExternal()` defined in Java's `Externalizable` interface.

```
public void writeExternal(java.io.ObjectOutput out)
    throws IOException {

    HashMap currentDiary = new HashMap();
    Set keySet = keySet();

    // iterate over all keys in the Map
    for( Iterator iter = keySet.iterator(); iter.hasNext();){
        java.lang.Object key = iter.next();
        java.lang.Object value = get( key );

        // remove any object reference and enter
        // its string representation in a separate map
        if( value instanceof org.omg.CORBA.Object ){
            iter.remove();
            currentDiary.put( key,
                                orb.object_to_string(
                                    (org.omg.CORBA.Object)value));
        }
    }
    // overwrite mappings in this map with
    // those from currentDiary
    putAll( currentDiary );

    // write the state onto the stream
    ((ObjectOutputStream)out).writeObject(
            (java.util.TreeMap)super.clone());
}
```

The `writeExternal()` method needs to iterate over all values in the Diary and convert references to strings. It can do so using the methods defined for collections in Java, which are available here because `Diary` extends `TreeMap`. The proper way of doing this is to collect all stringified IORs in a separate `HashMap` and to copy this map back into the Diary. The last statement finally serializes the Diary state, which is kept in the superclass part of this class.

```
public void readExternal(java.io.ObjectInput in)
    throws IOException {

    try {
```

```
            putAll((java.util.TreeMap)
                            ((ObjectInputStream)in).readObject());
        }
        catch( ClassNotFoundException c ) {
            throw new IOException( c.getMessage());
        }
        calendar = Calendar.getInstance();
    }
```

The `readExternal` method reads the externalized `TreeMap` contents from the input stream and creates a new calendar instance. It cannot, however, convert the stringified references back because it needs an ORB instance to do this—which is not available here. The `orb` field of the Diary class was marked transient because the ORB itself cannot be serialized.

At this stage, we must defer the reinitialization of the Diary until the client calls `init()` and passes an ORB argument. The `init()` method then performs the inverse operations with respect to serialization.

```
    void init(ORB orb) {
        this.orb = orb;
        Set keySet = keySet();
        HashMap currentDiary = new HashMap();
        keySet = keySet();

        for( Iterator iter = keySet.iterator(); iter.hasNext();){
            java.lang.Object key = iter.next();
            java.lang.Object value = get( key );
            if( value instanceof String &&
                ((String)value).startsWith("IOR:") ){

                iter.remove();
                currentDiary.put( key,
                                MeetingHelper.narrow(
                                    orb.string_to_object(
                                        (String) value)));
            }
        }
        putAll( currentDiary );
    }
```

## 10.2.5 Implementing the Building Service

The Building Service offers the interface Building, which provides a factory operation to create Rooms in the building and a list operation to retrieve the rooms in a building. Room objects maintain a diary of bookings and allow clients to view these bookings as well as to make new room reservations. In our example design, individual Room Servants are always local to the process that hosts their Building. To allow us to shut down and restart the server, object references to both Buildings and Rooms are persistent, and the implementations of both interfaces manage their own persistent state. This service provides an example of setting up a POA for use with a Servant Manager, in this case a Servant Locator.

### 10.2.5.1 Implementing the Interfaces

Before we discuss and explain the POA configuration for the Building server let us look at the implementations of the Building and Room interfaces. The Room interface is implemented in a Java class `RoomImpl.java` that extends the generated skeleton class `RoomPOA`. Our implementation class also implements the Java interface `java.io.Serializable`, which enables loading and storing instances in files.

```
package com.wiley.compbooks.brose.chapter10.office;

/**
 * RoomImpl.java
 */

import java.util.Vector;
import java.io.*;
import org.omg.CORBA.*;
import com.wiley.compbooks.brose.chapter10.office.RoomPackage.*;

public class RoomImpl
    extends RoomPOA
    implements java.io.Serializable {

    private String name;
    private String siteIOR;
    private Diary diary;

    transient Building site;
    public transient boolean dirty = false;
    public transient ORB orb;

    // constructor
    public RoomImpl( String name, Building building, ORB orb ) {
        this.orb = orb;
        this.name = name;
        this.site = building;
        diary = new Diary(orb);
    }
```

A Room has a name and a reference to its Building. It also keeps its own schedule of bookings, using the `Diary` class, which was explained in sections 10.2.3 and 10.2.4. For the same reasons that required the Diary to convert between object references and stringified IORs on serialization, the `RoomImpl` class uses an extra String field `siteIOR` to hold the stringified reference to its Building. The actual Building reference is kept in a transient field, so it is never serialized. The ORB reference, which is needed for the reference conversion, is likewise transient. Finally, we use a Boolean flag `dirty` to determine whether any state changes have occurred such that state must be written. This flag is also transient, which has the effect of automatically clearing it during serialization. The `RoomImpl` constructor initializes these fields.

```
public String name() {
    return name;
}
public Building site() {
    return site;
}
```

The read-only attributes of the IDL interface are mapped to the usual accessor methods. The operations also have straightforward implementations. Each method makes use of the booking information kept in the Diary.

```
public String[] viewDayBookings ( int year,
                                  Month month,
                                  int day) {
    java.lang.Object[] bookings =
        diary.getDay( year, month, day );
    String[] meetings =
        new String[bookings.length];
    System.arraycopy(bookings,0,meetings,0, bookings.length);
    return meetings;
}

public String[] viewBookings() {
    java.lang.Object[] bookings =
        diary.getToday();
    String[] meetings =
        new String[bookings.length];
    System.arraycopy(bookings,0,meetings,0, bookings.length);
    return meetings;
}
```

The first two operations simply retrieve booking information from the Diary and return it. Neither of them effects any state changes, so the `dirty` flag remains unset. The following two operations do set this flag, however.

```
public void book( Date slot, String meeting_description )
    throws SlotAlreadyTaken {

    try {
        diary.enter( slot, slot.the_hour +
                     "h: " +  meeting_description );
        dirty = true;
    }
    catch( AlreadyEngaged ae ) {
        throw new SlotAlreadyTaken();
    }
}

public void cancelBooking( Date slot )
    throws NoMeetingAtThisTime {

    java.lang.Object o = diary.remove( slot );
    if( o == null )
        throw new NoMeetingAtThisTime();
    dirty = true;
}
```

The `book()` method tries to enter descriptive text for a booking into the Diary. If this fails with an `AlreadyEngaged` exception, the exception is caught and a `SlotAlreadyTaken` exception is thrown instead. Note that the Room implementation does not enter any object references into the Diary, which would be perfectly legal because we explicitly prepared the Diary implementation for this case. We assume, however, that the Building Service will not be used to access actual meeting information. To directly contact the meeting organizer or even cancel a meeting, the Meeting Service has to be used. The `cancelBooking()` method tries to remove data from the Diary for a given date. Failing that, it throws a `NoMeetingAtThisTime` exception.

To load and store `RoomImpl` instances, we use Java serialization again. Serializing instances is easier than with Diary instances because there is no state in superclasses that we need to worry about. Thus, we can simply use the default mechanism. We need to convert only one object reference into a string and vice versa. This is done in the serialization method `writeObject()` and in a method `init()`, which must be called after deserialization. Again, the reason for having an additional `init()` method is that we need the ORB reference to be able to turn the stringified reference kept in `siteIOR` back into a live reference to a Building object.

```
private void writeObject(java.io.ObjectOutputStream out)
    throws IOException {
```

```
        siteIOR = orb.object_to_string((org.omg.CORBA.Object)site);
        out.defaultWriteObject();
    }

    public void init( ORB orb ) {
        this.orb = orb;
        diary.init(orb);
        this.site =
            BuildingHelper.narrow(orb.string_to_object(siteIOR));
    }
}
```

We can now turn to the implementation of the Building interface, which we implement in a class `BuildingImpl`.

```
package com.wiley.compbooks.brose.chapter10.office;

import java.io.*;
import java.util.Vector;
import org.omg.CORBA.*;
import org.omg.PortableServer.*;

public class BuildingImpl
    extends BuildingPOA
    implements java.io.Serializable {

    transient POA factoryPOA;
    transient ORB orb;

    Vector roomList;
    Vector roomImplList;
    String name;

    public BuildingImpl(POA poa, ORB orb, String name) {
        factoryPOA = poa;
        this.orb = orb;
        roomList = new Vector();
        roomImplList = new Vector();
        this.name = name;
    }
```

This class is also serializable, and like `RoomImpl`, it needs an ORB reference that is stored in a transient field. In addition, it keeps a reference to a POA that will be used for creating CORBA objects. Both these references are initialized using arguments passed to the constructor. Internally, a `BuildingImpl` instance keeps two Vectors to store references to the Java objects of type `RoomImpl` it has created and to store the corresponding CORBA object references.

Serialization of instances of this class is done following the same pattern that has already been described twice, namely converting object references to strings, and calling an additional `init()` method so that the necessary ORB reference for converting strings back into objects can be passed. Because `BuildingImpl` also needs a POA reference, this is also passed as an argument to `init()`.

The functionality offered by this class is mostly simple. The two operations `name()` and `list()` return the Building's name and an array of object references that have been created in this `BuildingImpl` instance. The most interesting method implementation in this class is that of `create()`.

```
    public String name(){
        return name;
    }
    public Room[] list() {
        Room[] result = new Room[ roomList.size() ];
        roomList.copyInto( result );
        return result;
    }

    public Room create( String name ) {

        try {
            // create new reference
            Room result = RoomHelper.narrow(
                             factoryPOA.create_reference_with_id(
                                 name.getBytes(),
                                 "IDL:com/wiley/compbooks/brose/
                                 chapter10/office/Room:1.0"
                             )
                         );

            // store reference
            roomList.addElement( result );

            try {
                // create a new Servant instance
                RoomImpl room = new RoomImpl( name, _this(), orb );
                roomImplList.addElement( room );

                // save initial object state
                File f = new File( RoomLocator.filePrefix + name );
                FileOutputStream fout = new FileOutputStream(f);
                ObjectOutputStream out =
                    new ObjectOutputStream(fout);
                out.writeObject( room );
```

```
            }
            catch( IOException io ) {
                System.err.println("Error opening output file "
                                    +name);
            }
            return result;
        }
        catch( Exception e ) {
            e.printStackTrace();
        }
        return null;
    }
```

The `create()` method is responsible for creating and returning CORBA object references. Of course, it must also ensure that Servants for these references can be found and that these Servants will be able to find the initial state. In this case, the state comprises just the name that was passed as an argument to the constructor.

To create references, the `BuildingImpl` instance uses the `create_reference_with_id()` method on the POA with which it was initialized. The parameters to this operation are a byte array that defines the new object's ID and a Repository Identifier that describes the object's type. The POA must have been set up with the USER_ID ID Assignment policy. If it has a SYSTEM_ID policy and the POA detects that the supplied ID was not previously generated by it, this operation will throw a BAD_PARAM exception. For the object ID, we take the Room's name and convert it to a byte array.

The `create()` method now stores the reference we just created so it can be returned later in the result of the `list()` method. It then creates an instance of the implementation class `RoomImpl` and stores this reference in the `roomImplList` vector. Note that there is no association between the newly created CORBA object and the Servant at this time; that is, the CORBA object is not activated. The task to provide the correct Servant for a given operation request is left to a Servant Locator, which we will show in the text that follows. At this stage, the only implicit relationship between the abstract CORBA object and the Servant is that both know about the CORBA object's ID.

Finally, we must ensure that the Servant's state can be found by the Servant Locator when it activates the CORBA object. To do this, we simply serialize the Servant using a convention that the Servant Locator will also use, which is to use the concatenation of a constant String prefix and the Room's name as a file name. The Servant is then serialized to this file. Once this is done, we can return the Room's object reference.

### 10.2.5.2 Configuring the POA

To be able to use references to Rooms for more than the server's lifetime (more precisely: the lifetime of the POA that created the objects), the PERSISTENT value for the Life Span policy is necessary. This decision is fundamental for the design of this service. Without it, we would not have needed to manage persistent state—unless perhaps scalability requirements dictated it. That is, unless we wanted to temporarily remove unused Servants from memory and reclaim their resources.

The second important decision we have to make is about using the AOM for maintaining the association between object references and Servants. Should those associations be kept and stored in the AOM (the RETAIN policy), or do we want objects to be associated with Servants only for the duration of the request (NON_RETAIN)? For the example, let us assume that Rooms usually receive only one request to retrieve their bookings and are left unused for a while after the request, so we don't want to keep the association around any longer and would rather minimize memory usage. We thus select the NON_RETAIN Servant Retention policy here. If we made different assumptions here, we would have to select different policy settings.

As a consequence of choosing the NON_RETAIN policy, we have to configure a way of determining Servants on demand, which will inevitably incur a certain run-time overhead. This is done by selecting a value for the Request Processing policy. Our choice here is restricted by the Servant Retention policy we just selected. It is not possible to combine NON_RETAIN with a value of USE_ACTIVE_OBJECT_MAP_ONLY. An attempt to create a POA with this combination will throw an INVALID_POLICY exception.

The first possible option is to use a Default Servant, which would receive all requests for objects not found in the AOM. While it is possible to use a USE_DEFAULT_SERVANT policy here, we decided to provide a Servant Locator instead and demonstrate the use of a POA with the USE_SERVANT_MANAGER policy.

Servant Managers come in two types, corresponding to the value of the Servant Retention policy. For a RETAIN policy, the Servant Manager has to be a Servant Activator. A Servant Activator returns a Servant for a given object ID, and the Servant and object ID will then be entered into the AOM and kept until the object is deactivated. In contrast, the NON_RETAIN policy requires a Servant Locator, which provides a Servant only for the current request and does not keep the association any longer. This is the Servant Manager we use in this example.

Before we show the implementation of the Servant Locator, let's complete our discussion of the POA policies selected for this service. With persistent object references and persistent state, it is usually straightforward to let our code assign object IDs rather than having the POA generate these IDs. The obvious reason is that we can choose object IDs that are also used as file names or primary database keys—which we want to do in our Servant Locator. Thus, we also select the USER_ID ID Assignment policy.

Here is the class `RoomLocator` that implements our Servant Locator.

```
package com.wiley.compbooks.brose.chapter10.office;

import java.io.*;
import org.omg.CORBA.*;
import org.omg.PortableServer.*;
import org.omg.PortableServer.ServantLocatorPackage.*;

class RoomLocator
    extends ServantLocatorPOA {

    public static String filePrefix = ".room_";
```

The `RoomLocator` class implements the skeleton class for Servant Locators, `ServantLocatorPOA`. The reason for this is that Servant Managers are CORBA objects themselves, even if they are locality-constrained and cannot be remotely invoked. Unlike the POA, but just like any other CORBA object, they need to be activated by a POA. You will see this activation in the implementation of the server's `main()` method.

The `preinvoke()` method is called by the POA for each operation. As its return value it delivers a Servant that is capable of processing the request for `operation` on behalf of the target object identified by its object ID. The `preinvoke()` method also receives the target object's POA as an argument. The last argument, `the_cookie`, is a holder object that allows the Servant Locator to pass values out of the `preinvoke()` method. The POA guarantees to pass this value to the `postinvoke()` method, which will be invoked after the actual operation processing in the Servant completes.

```
    public Servant preinvoke(byte[] oid,
                             POA adapter,
                             String operation,
                             CookieHolder the_cookie)
        throws ForwardRequest {

        String fileName = filePrefix + new String(oid);
        RoomImpl room = null;
        try {
            File f = new File( fileName );
```

```
            if( f.exists() ) {
                FileInputStream f_in = new FileInputStream(f);

                if( f_in.available() > 0 ) {

                    // deserialize a Servant
                    ObjectInputStream in =
                        new ObjectInputStream(f_in);
                    room = (RoomImpl)in.readObject();

                   // initialize it
                    room.init(_orb());
                    in.close();
                }
                f_in.close();
                return room;
            }
            else
                throw new org.omg.CORBA.OBJ_ADAPTER(
                                          "Failed to activate");
        }
        catch( IOException io ) {
            System.err.println("File seems corrupt");
            throw new org.omg.CORBA.OBJ_ADAPTER(
                                          "Failed to activate");
        }
        catch( java.lang.ClassNotFoundException c ) {
            System.err.println("Could not read object from file, class
not found!");
            throw new org.omg.CORBA.OBJ_ADAPTER(
                                          "Failed to activate");
        }
    }
```

Our implementation of `preinvoke()` simply uses the passed object ID to build the name for a file that is then opened. Using Java serialization, a `RoomImpl` object is read from the file and then initialized using its `init()` method. In the call to `init()`, we pass an ORB reference that is needed to call `string_to_object()`. Our Servant Locator is a Servant itself, so it can use the inherited method `_orb()` to retrieve the ORB to which it is connected. After `init()` completes, the Locator closes all streams and returns the `RoomImpl` instance.

The `postinvoke()` method is called by the POA after the Servant has finished processing the request. The POA passes the same arguments as in `preinvoke()`, plus the Servant itself. Before the Servant Locator uses Java serialization as usual to write the servant out to a file again, we check whether any state changes have occurred by testing the `RoomImpl` instance's `dirty` flag. If it has not been set, no serialization is necessary, and the call returns immediately. This will be the case for most operations, so there is no extra I/O involved.

```
    public void postinvoke( byte[] oid,
                            POA adapter,
                            String operation,
                            java.lang.Object the_cookie,
                            Servant the_servant)
        throws ForwardRequest {

        RoomImpl room  = (RoomImpl)the_servant;
        if( !room.dirty )
            return;

        // otherwise: serialize the Servant
        String fileName = filePrefix + new String(oid);
        try {
            File f = new File(fileName);
            FileOutputStream fout = new FileOutputStream(f);
            ObjectOutputStream out =
                new ObjectOutputStream(fout);
            out.writeObject( room );
        }
        catch( IOException io ) {
            io.printStackTrace();
            System.err.println("Error opening output file " +
                                fileName );
        }
    }
}
```

We are now ready to examine the class `BuildingServer`, which puts together all the pieces presented in this section.

```
package com.wiley.compbooks.brose.chapter10.office;

import java.io.*;
import org.omg.CORBA.*;
import org.omg.PortableServer.*;
import org.omg.CosNaming.*;
import org.omg.CosNaming.NamingContextPackage.*;

public class BuildingServer {

    static ORB orb;
    public static void shutdown() {
        orb.shutdown(false);
    }
```

The `BuildingServer` class needs a way to start regular shutdowns. This is achieved by providing a static method `shutdown()`, which calls the

ORB's `shutdown()` method. The graphical user interface shown in Figure 10.3 has an "Exit" button, and pressing this button results in the GUI calling back this `shutdown()` method. Shutting down the ORB will wake up the main thread blocked in `orb.run()`, as we will see in the Building Server's `main()` method.

```
public static void main(String[] args) {

    String str_name;
    String filename;
    String buildingName;
    BuildingImpl building = null;

    if( args.length != 1 ) {
        System.out.println("Usage: java BuildingServer name");
        System.exit( 1 );
    }

    buildingName = args[0];
    filename = "." + buildingName + "_rooms";

    try {
        //init
        orb = ORB.init( args, null );
        POA rootPOA = POAHelper.narrow(
            orb.resolve_initial_references( "RootPOA" ));
```

The Building Server initializes its ORB and Root POA as usual. It requires one command-line argument to determine which building it is serving. A Building object, like Rooms, has a PERSISTENT Life Span policy and manages persistent state, but it does not need either a Servant Manager or a Default Servant. Rather, it is activated once and kept in memory all the time. Therefore, we create a separate POA just for the Building object.

```
        // create a user defined poa for the building
        org.omg.CORBA.Policy [] policies =
            new org.omg.CORBA.Policy[3];
        policies[0] = rootPOA.create_id_assignment_policy(
                          IdAssignmentPolicyValue.USER_ID);
        policies[1] = rootPOA.create_lifespan_policy(
                          LifespanPolicyValue.PERSISTENT);
        policies[2] = rootPOA.create_servant_retention_policy(
                          ServantRetentionPolicyValue.RETAIN);

        POA buildingPOA = rootPOA.create_POA(
                              "BuildingPOA",
                              rootPOA.the_POAManager(),
                              policies);
```

```
for ( int i = 0; i < policies.length; i++ )
    policies[i].destroy();
```

When the `create_POA()` operation associates a set of policies with a new POA, it effectively copies the policy objects. The caller can then destroy the policy objects, which we do here to release resources.

Because we want to use the same mechanism for determining file names for objects, we set up the `buildingPOA` with a USER_ID policy. To keep the object activated until shut down, we select the RETAIN policy. Actually, this selection is redundant as all policies not explicitly specified assume their standard values, as illustrated in Figure 10.1 at the beginning of this chapter. Thus, it is not necessary to select other policy values like USE_ACTIVE_OBJECT_MAP_ONLY because this is the standard value for the Request Processing policy.

```
// create another poa for the room objects
policies = new org.omg.CORBA.Policy[4];
policies[0] = buildingPOA.create_id_assignment_policy(
    IdAssignmentPolicyValue.USER_ID);
policies[1] = buildingPOA.create_lifespan_policy(
    LifespanPolicyValue.PERSISTENT);
policies[2] =
    buildingPOA.create_request_processing_policy(
     RequestProcessingPolicyValue.USE_SERVANT_MANAGER);
policies[3] =
    buildingPOA.create_servant_retention_policy(
        ServantRetentionPolicyValue.NON_RETAIN);

POA roomPOA = buildingPOA.create_POA(
                            "RoomPOA",
                            rootPOA.the_POAManager(),
                            policies);

RoomLocator roomLocator = new RoomLocator();
roomPOA.set_servant_manager(roomLocator._this(orb));

for (int i = 0; i < policies.length; i++ )
    policies[i].destroy();
```

For managing Room objects, we create another POA with the desired policy combination, as discussed in this section, that is a PERSISTENT value for the Life Span policy, USER_ID for ID Assignment, USE_SERVANT _MANAGER for Request Processing, and NON_RETAIN for Servant Retention. We then create a `RoomLocator` and set it as the `roomPOA`'s Servant Manager by calling `set_servant_manager()` on the `roomPOA`. Note that the `RoomLocator` itself is implicitly activated on the Root POA by calling `_this()` on the Locator object. It would not be correct to activate it on the Building POA because the Servant Locator is not persistent.

```
// read persistent state from a file
try {
    File f = new File( filename );
    if( f.exists() ) {
        FileInputStream f_in = new FileInputStream(f);
        if( f_in.available() {
            ObjectInputStream in =
                new ObjectInputStream(f_in);
            building = (BuildingImpl)in.readObject();
            in.close();
        }
        f_in.close();
    }
}
catch( Exception e ) {
    e.printStackTrace();
}
if( building == null ){
    building =
        new BuildingImpl( roomPOA, orb, buildingName );
}
else
    building.init( roomPOA, orb );
```

After all POAs have been created and the Servant Locator activated, we read the Building object's state from a file, using the name argument passed from the command line as part of the file name. If an appropriate file was found, the object is deserialized from the file and initialized. Otherwise, a new `BuildingImpl` object is created. Both ways, the `BuildingImpl` is initialized with the `roomPOA`, which it uses internally to create Room objects.

```
buildingPOA.activate_object_with_id(
    "Building".getBytes(), building );
org.omg.CORBA.Object obj =
    buildingPOA.servant_to_reference( building );


rootPOA.the_POAManager().activate();
```

The Building is activated on the Building POA, and a Building reference is obtained from this POA. Finally, we enable request processing for all POAs by activating the Root POA's POA Manager, which is also the Manager of all other POAs in this server. We can now export the object reference using the Naming Service so that other components of the system may retrieve and use it.

```
            // register with naming service
            str_name = "BuildingService/" + buildingName;

            NamingContextExt root = NamingContextExtHelper.narrow(
                orb.resolve_initial_references("NameService"));
            try {
                // make sure the context is bound
                root.bind_new_context(
                    root.to_name("BuildingService" ));
            }
            catch( AlreadyBound ab ) { // does not matter
            }
            root.rebind( root.to_name( str_name), obj );
```

As a convention, all Building Service references are bound within a separate Naming Context. We ensure that this Naming Context exists and bind the Building reference using its string name. Finally, the server starts the graphical user interface and calls `orb.run()` to block waiting for requests.

```
            RoomGUI gui = new RoomGUI( building );

            // wait for requests
            orb.run();

            // this will be executed after the GUI
            // has called shutdown ()
            try {
                File f = new File(filename);
                FileOutputStream fout = new FileOutputStream(f);
                ObjectOutputStream out =
                    new ObjectOutputStream(fout);

                // save state
                out.writeObject((BuildingImpl)building);
            }
            catch( IOException io ) {
                io.printStackTrace();
                System.err.println("Error opening output file " +
                                        filename );
            }
            System.exit(0);
        }
        catch(UserException ue){
            System.err.println(ue);
        }
        catch(SystemException se) {
            System.err.println(se);
        }
    }
}
```

The GUI allows users to create new rooms interactively and to shut down the service by calling the static `shutdown()` method. We omit the GUI code here; it can be found on the companion Web site to this book (www.wiley.com/compbooks/brose). If the `shutdown()` method is called, the server's main thread continues after `orb.run()`. At this stage, all POAs have been destroyed and all Servants deactivated. In this example, the only activated Servants that could be deactivated are the `BuildingImpl` and the `RoomLocator` instances. Before exiting from the program, the server saves the Building state using Java serialization as usual. Figure 10.5. illustrates the relation between the POAs, the Servant Locator, and the Building and Room objects.

## 10.2.6 The Meeting Service

The Meeting Service presented in this section uses a different POA configuration than the Building Service. The service manages objects of type Meeting, which can be created by every user of the system. The number of these objects will constantly increase over time as the number of users of the system increases and more and more meetings are organized using the system. We keep all meeting information, even that of meetings that have already taken place, because providing historical information is an important part of the functionality offered by the application. Obviously, this constitutes a potential scalability problem. If we wanted to keep all objects activated the POA's AOM would soon take up a considerable amount of memory—and continue to ask for more.

Because we assume that meeting information will be accessed frequently during certain periods of time, we don't want it to be swapped out on disk all the time. To provide satisfactory interactive response time, we have to keep meeting objects activated after their creation and thus select the RETAIN policy. We also assume that these response times won't be necessary after the meeting has actually taken place. Consequently, meeting objects can be deactivated, their internal state saved to disk, and all resources reclaimed after the meeting date has passed. The objects still exist, of course, so the only thing users might notice when accessing older meeting objects is a small delay when the objects are reactivated.

Another requirement is that this behavior should be exhibited consistently over many lifetimes of the server process, so we need to manage persistent object references and persistent object state even before any deactivations occur.

What kind of hooks does the POA provide for situations like these? Servant Managers, it turns out, are not sufficient here. A Servant Locator, on

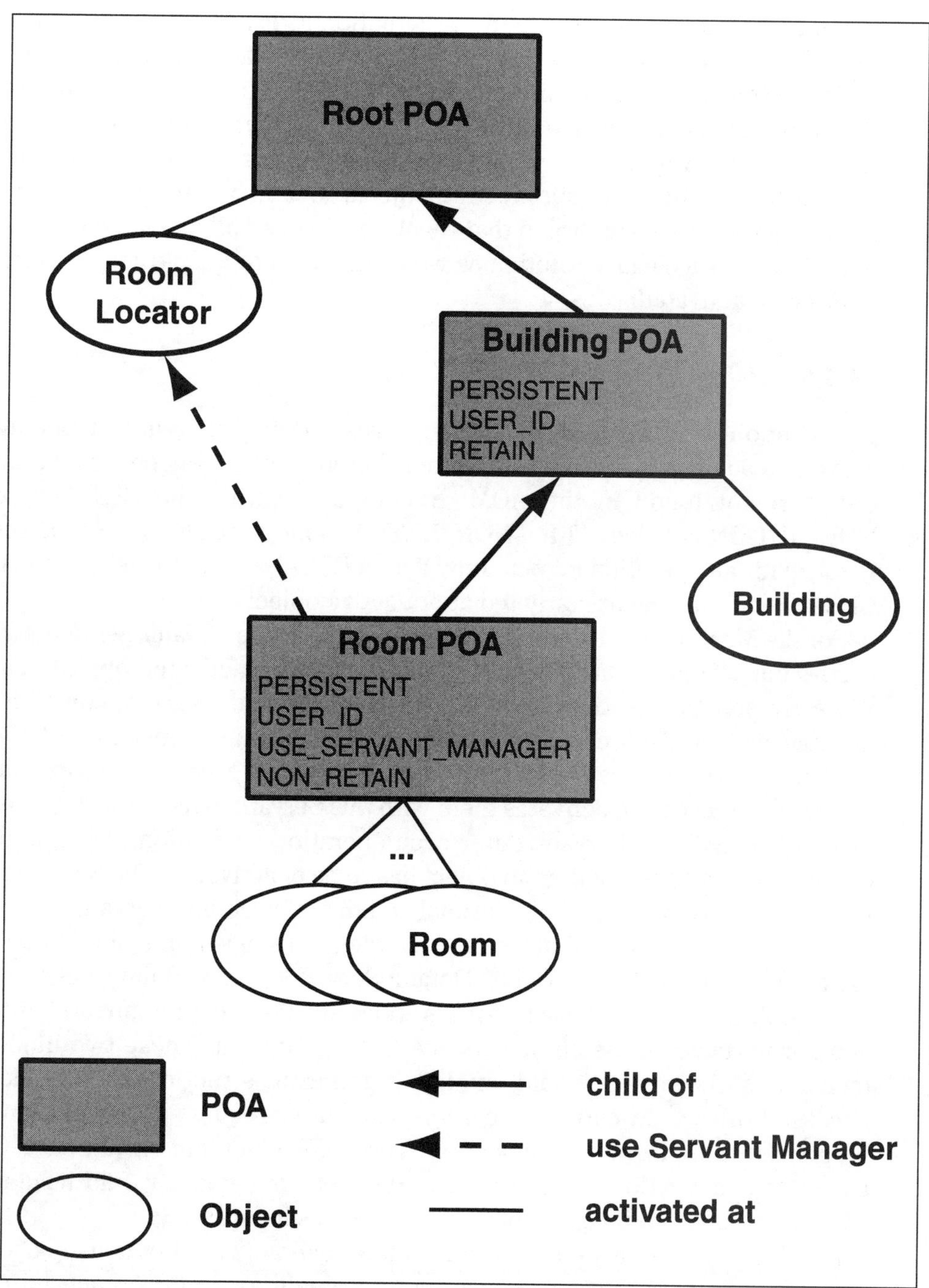


**Figure 10.5** POAs in the Building Service.

the one hand, is not applicable in this situation as it combines only with a NON_RETAIN policy, but we do want to keep objects activated for a certain period of time and thus require the RETAIN policy. A Servant Activator, on the other hand, is not called until etherealization, that is, until objects are explicitly deactivated. Thus, a Servant Activator does not provide us with any support for deactivating Meeting objects. Deactivation could be done by setting up a separate thread that regularly checked all activated objects, but this is not an elegant solution as we would need to keep track of which objects are activated.

#### 10.2.6.1 Using Default Servants

The solution we want to illustrate here uses a Default Servant. A Default Servant is a specially registered Servant that is invoked whenever a target object is not found in the AOM. It combines with either RETAIN or NON_RETAIN policies. With a NON_RETAIN policy, the Default Servant is invoked for all operation invocations. With a RETAIN policy, it receives just those operations that are targeted at nonactive objects.

For the Meeting Service example, we design a single Default Servant that carries out *all* operation processing itself, that is, for activated objects that represent pending meetings and for no-longer-activated ones that constitute meeting history. This can be achieved by registering an instance of the implementation as a Default Servant and also using a Meeting Factory that creates references and activates them with this Servant, which now behaves just like an ordinary Servant. After each operation invocation, the Default Servant then checks whether an object has to be deactivated. The Servant is thus used in two roles: that of a normal and that of a Default Servant.

We have chosen to combine these two roles in a single implementation to illustrate the flexibility offered by Default Servants. It would have been just as possible to separate these two roles and write a regular Servant and have another unrelated class implement the Default Servant. These two implementations, however, would exhibit significant structural similarities because both would carry out certain tasks after request processing and before returning from the invocation: The regular Servant would have to check its deactivation conditions, and the Default Servant would have to save any changes to the state of the object it was incarnating.

As a last note, let us point out that Default Servants are not usually used this way. The normal usage is for them to handle operation requests for objects that are essentially stateless and potentially transient, so the Default Servant does not have to look up the state for the target object it is incarnating and store it again after the request. In such a situation, using just a single Java object can save both look-up time and memory usage. As an example, consider an application-level proxy that receives requests for thousands of target objects and simply forwards these to the actual targets.

The Default Servant in this example, however, does have to store and restore object state for deactivated objects. It does this on every request, which does trigger a certain run-time overhead. In this case, this is the trade-off we are prepared to accept for the benefit of minimizing memory usage and thus allowing the server to scale to a very large number of objects. Other situations may demand higher performance while perhaps allowing more memory consumption. While this may sound as if using Default Servants (or Servant Managers, for that matter) with persistent objects imposes prohibitive performance penalties, please note that industrial-strength implementations would usually implement sophisticated caching strategies and thus be able to avoid having to access secondary storage most of the time.

### 10.2.6.2 Implementing the Default Servant

The Default Servant for the Meeting Server is implemented in the Java class `MeetingDefaultServant`. It extends the skeleton class for Meeting objects.

```
package com.wiley.compbooks.brose.chapter10.office;

import org.omg.CORBA.*;
import java.util.*;
import java.io.*;
import com.wiley.compbooks.brose.chapter10.office.MeetingPackage.*;
import org.omg.PortableServer.*;
import org.omg.PortableServer.POAPackage.*;

class MeetingDefaultServant
    extends MeetingPOA {

    private ORB orb;
    private POA poa;
    private Calendar calendar;
    private DateComparator dateComparator;

    MeetingDefaultServant(ORB orb, POA poa) {
        this.orb = orb;
        this.poa = poa;
        calendar = Calendar.getInstance();
        dateComparator = new DateComparator();
    }
```

The MeetingDefaultServant uses four private fields; two of these are for its ORB and POA references. The other two, a Calendar and a DateComparator, are needed to determine the time at which a particular object can be deactivated and its state written out to disk.

To manage object state, we define an inner class MeetingState:

```
public static class MeetingState
    implements java.io.Serializable {

    /* transient data */
    transient boolean dirty = false;
    transient DigitalSecretary[] participants;
    transient DigitalSecretary organizer;
    transient Room location;
    transient byte[] oid;

    /** the actual state */
    String purpose;
    String[] participantIORs;
    String organizerIOR;
    String locationIOR;
    Date when;
    boolean canceled = false;
    String cancelReason = null;
}
```

The inner class MeetingState has fields for all attributes in the IDL interface and also for the list of Participants, which can be manipulated using operations in the Meeting interface. As usual, we have to prepare for the object reference-to-string conversions on serialization, so the MeetingState class has additional string-typed fields for all object references. Fields that hold object references are marked transient, as is the dirty flag and the object ID field. The value of the object ID field could also be serialized, but we have to determine the object ID on each request anyway before we can restore the state, so saving it does not have any advantages.

The method implementations of class MeetingDefaultServant all follow the same pattern. First, the state for the current target object is restored. Then, the request is executed. Finally, state is released again and potential results are returned from the method.

```
public String purpose() {
    MeetingState state = restoreState();
    String result = state.purpose;
    releaseState(state);
    return result;
}
```

As another example of how Meeting operations are implemented, here is the code of the method `cancel()`. We omit the other method implementations here for brevity.

```
public void cancel(String reason)
    throws MeetingCanceled {

    MeetingState state = restoreState();
    if( state.canceled ) {
        releaseState(state);
        throw new MeetingCanceled(state.cancelReason);
    }
    state.canceled = true;
    state.cancelReason = reason;
    notifyParticipants("Meeting " + state.purpose +
                       " has been canceled.");
    state.dirty = true;
    releaseState(state);
}
```

The `cancel()` method first checks whether the meeting has already been canceled. In this case, state is released immediately and the `MeetingCanceled` exception is thrown, indicating the original reason for canceling the meeting. Otherwise, the method sets the `canceled` field to TRUE, stores the new reason string, notifies all participants, and sets the dirty flag. Finally, the state is released.

Let us now look at the way the `MeetingDefaultServant` stores and restores Meeting state.

```
private synchronized MeetingState restoreState() {
    try {
        // get this object's ID
        byte [] oid = _object_id();

        // deserialize state
        String filename = ".meeting_" + new String( oid );
        ObjectInputStream in =
            new ObjectInputStream(
                new FileInputStream ( filename ));
        MeetingState state = (MeetingState)in.readObject();

        // convert strings to references
        state.participants =
            new DigitalSecretary[state.participantIORs.length];

        for(int i = 0; i < state.participantIORs.length; i++){
            state.participants[i] =
                DigitalSecretaryHelper.narrow(
```

```
                    orb.string_to_object(
                        state.participantIORs[i]));
            }

            state.organizer = DigitalSecretaryHelper.narrow(
                    orb.string_to_object(state.organizerIOR));
            state.location = RoomHelper.narrow(
                    orb.string_to_object(state.locationIOR));
            state.oid = oid;
            in.close();
            return state;
        }
        catch( Exception e ) {
            throw new RuntimeException( e.getMessage());
        }
    }
```

To restore Meeting state, the Default Servant first needs to determine the object ID of the object it is currently incarnating. This ID can be retrieved from the invocation context using the method `_object_id()` that is inherited from the superclass `Servant`. Together with a constant string prefix, this object ID is used as a file name. From the file, a `MeetingState` object is deserialized. Before it can be returned and used, we need to convert stringified IORs back into object references as usual.

The `releaseState()` method is responsible for writing state to disk if any changes in the state have occurred. As usual, reference-to-string conversions have to be carried out.

```
    private synchronized void releaseState( MeetingState state ) {

        // check if we need to do anything
        if( doRelease( state )) {
            try {

                // do we have to do any I/O?
                if( state.dirty ) {

                    // deserialize
                    String filename =
                        ".meeting_" + new String( state.oid );
                    ObjectOutputStream out =
                        new ObjectOutputStream(
                            new FileOutputStream( filename ));

                    // convert references to strings
                    state.participantIORs =
                        new String[state.participants.length];
                    for( int i = 0;
```

```
                    i < state.participantIORs.length;
                    i++){
                   state.participantIORs[i] =
                       orb.object_to_string(
                           state.participants[i]);
               }
               state.organizerIOR =
                   orb.object_to_string(state.organizer );
               state.locationIOR =
                   orb.object_to_string(state.location );
               out.writeObject( state );
           }
           // schedule for deactivation
           try {
               poa.deactivate_object( state.oid );
           }
           catch( ObjectNotActive ona ) {
               // never mind . . .
           }
       }
       catch( Exception e ) {
           throw new RuntimeException( e.getMessage());
       }
   }
}
```

The `releaseState()` method writes state only for objects that are actually to be deactivated. Deactivation is a nonblocking call on the POA. The POA will wait until all current operations on the object have finished before beginning the deactivation process. If new requests arrive before deactivation begins, these are also executed first. Note that we catch and ignore the `ObjectNotActive` exception that is potentially thrown by the `deactivate_object()` method. This exception will be thrown by the POA whenever we try to deactivate objects that have been deactivated before and are now being incarnated by this Servant in its Default Servant role rather than its regular Servant role.

To find out whether it is actually time to deactivate an object, the `releaseState()` method calls `doRelease()`.

```
private boolean doRelease( MeetingState state ) {
    // update calendar time
    calendar.setTime( new java.util.Date());
    // compare current time to meeting time
    int i = dateComparator.compare( state.when,
        new Date( calendar.get( Calendar.YEAR ),
        Month.from_int( calendar.get( Calendar.MONTH )),
        calendar.get( Calendar.DAY_OF_MONTH ),
        calendar.get( Calendar.HOUR_OF_DAY ))
```

```
            );
        return ( i < 0 );
    }
```

This method implements the time check that was mentioned at the beginning of this section. It uses a `DateComparator` object to compare the current system time with the scheduled meeting time. If the meeting time has already passed, `doRelease()` returns true.

### 10.2.6.3 Implementing the Server

The Meeting Server, which configures the POA to use our Default Servant, is shown next. It also uses a Meeting Factory, which we will present after explaining the server's setup.

```
package com.wiley.compbooks.brose.chapter10.office;

import java.io.*;
import org.omg.CORBA.*;
import org.omg.PortableServer.*;
import org.omg.CosNaming.*;
import org.omg.CosNaming.NamingContextPackage.*;

public class MeetingServer {

    public static void main(String[] args) {

        MeetingFactoryImpl meetingFactory;

        try {
            //init
            ORB orb = ORB.init( args, null );
            POA rootPOA = POAHelper.narrow(
                orb.resolve_initial_references( "RootPOA"));

            // create policies and a poa
            org.omg.CORBA.Policy [] policies =
                new org.omg.CORBA.Policy[5];

            policies[0] = rootPOA.create_id_assignment_policy(
                IdAssignmentPolicyValue.USER_ID);
            policies[1] = rootPOA.create_lifespan_policy(
                LifespanPolicyValue.PERSISTENT);
            policies[2] = rootPOA.create_request_processing_policy(
                RequestProcessingPolicyValue.USE_DEFAULT_SERVANT);
            policies[3] = rootPOA.create_servant_retention_policy(
                ServantRetentionPolicyValue.RETAIN);
            policies[4] = rootPOA.create_id_uniqueness_policy(
```

```
        IdUniquenessPolicyValue.MULTIPLE_ID);
    POA meetingPOA = rootPOA.create_POA("MeetingPOA",
                            rootPOA.the_POAManager(),
                            policies);
```

The server first initializes the ORB and obtains a reference to the Root POA as usual. It then creates a number of policies for the POA with which Meeting objects will be created. As mentioned previously, the life span of meeting objects is persistent, and we want to assign object IDs using our own conventions again. The POA should also use a Default Servant and a RETAIN Retention policy, so all objects not explicitly activated by the Meeting Factory and kept in the AOM will be incarnated by the Default Servant. We must also select the MULTIPLE_ID policy to allow a single Servant to execute requests for multiple objects. Finally, a POA with this combination of policies is created as a child of the Root POA.

```
    // create and register the Default Servant
    MeetingDefaultServant mds =
        new MeetingDefaultServant( orb, meetingPOA );
    meetingPOA.set_servant( mds );

    for (int i=0; i<policies.length; i++)
        policies[i].destroy();
```

To register our Default Servant implementation, we create an instance of our implementation class and register it using the POA's `set_servant()` method. Finally, we need to export an object reference for the Meeting Service to the Naming Service. At this stage, there are no Meeting objects, and there is no way to create any. The server now creates a Meeting Factory and activates it. This activation is done implicitly during the call to `_this()` and uses the Root POA rather than the Meeting POA. This is appropriate as the Meeting Factory itself does not need to be persistent. After exporting the reference, request processing is enabled by activating the POA Manager.

```
    // register with naming service
    NamingContextExt root = NamingContextExtHelper.narrow(
       orb.resolve_initial_references("NameService"));

    meetingFactory = new MeetingFactoryImpl( meetingPOA );
    root.bind( root.to_name( "MeetingService" ),
               meetingFactory._this(orb) );

    rootPOA.the_POAManager().activate();
    // wait for requests
    orb.run();
}
```

```
            catch(UserException ue) {
                System.err.println(ue);
            }
            catch(SystemException se) {
                System.err.println(se);
            }
        }
    }
```

### 10.2.6.4 Implementing the Factory

The last missing piece in the Meeting Service is the implementation of the Meeting Factory. Its only tasks are to create new Meeting references and to activate the Default Servant under yet another object ID on the Meeting POA.

```
package com.wiley.compbooks.brose.chapter10.office;

import org.omg.CORBA.*;
import org.omg.PortableServer.*;
import java.util.Calendar;

class MeetingFactoryImpl
    extends MeetingFactoryPOA {

    private POA myPOA;
    private Calendar calendar;

    public MeetingFactoryImpl(POA myPOA) {
        this.myPOA = myPOA;
        calendar = Calendar.getInstance();
    }
```

Our implementation extends the skeleton class `MeetingFactoryPOA`. It has two instance variables that are initialized in the constructor. The POA argument is the POA the Factory instance uses for activating objects. The Calendar is used to decide whether a given meeting date is valid. This check is done in the implementation of the `create()` method.

```
    public Meeting create(String purpose,
                          Room location,
                          Date time,
                          DigitalSecretary organizer,
                          DigitalSecretary[] participants )
        throws IllegalDate {

        // update current time
        calendar.setTime( new java.util.Date());
```

```
        int year = calendar.get( Calendar.YEAR );
        int month = calendar.get( Calendar.MONTH );
        int day =  calendar.get( Calendar.DAY_OF_MONTH );

        // compare
        if( time.the_year < year ) {
            throw new IllegalDate();
        }
        else if( time.the_year == year) {
            if( time.the_month.value() < month ) {
                throw new IllegalDate();
            }
            else if( time.the_month.value() == month ) {
                if( time.the_day < day ) {
                    throw new IllegalDate();
                }
                else if( time.the_day == day ) {
                    if( time.the_hour <=
                        calendar.get( Calendar.HOUR_OF_DAY )) {
                        throw new IllegalDate();
                    }
                }
            }
        }
```

The `create()` method first checks for illegal dates. This ensures that only Meeting objects with future dates can be created. If the date is valid, a new object reference for a Meeting object is created. This is done without any reference to a Servant at this stage.

```
        try {
            String key = purpose +
                         time.the_year +
                         time.the_month.value() +
                         time.the_day +
                         time.the_hour;

            Meeting m = MeetingHelper.narrow(
                myPOA.create_reference_with_id( key.getBytes(),
"IDL:com/wiley/compbooks/brose/chapter10/office/Meeting:1.0"));
```

Before the object can be activated, however, we need to find a Servant for it. We already have one such Servant available, the Default Servant that is registered at the Meeting POA. It can be retrieved using the POA's `get_servant()` method. It is not sufficient just to nominate the Servant, though. We also need to make the Meeting object's initial state available to the Servant. This state is given by the arguments to the `create()` method. The `MeetingDefaultServant` class provides a `createState()` operation that creates and stores a `MeetingState` object, which is later used by the Default Servant to restore and store object state, as explained in section 10.2.6.2 of this chapter.

```
((MeetingDefaultServant)myPOA.get_servant()).createState(
                                key.getBytes(),
                                purpose,
                                location,
                                time,
                                organizer,
                                participants );

            myPOA.activate_object_with_id( key.getBytes(),
                                          myPOA.get_servant());

            location.book( time, organizer.name() );
            return m;
        }
        catch( SystemException se ) {
            se.printStackTrace();
        }
        catch( UserException ue ) {
            ue.printStackTrace();
        }
        return null;
    }
}
```

Before returning a reference to a newly created Meeting object, the Factory thus creates and stores the object's initial state using the `createState()` method provided by the Default Servant. It then activates the object by associating it with the Default Servant in the Meeting POA's AOM. Note that the Default Servant is used here in its role as an ordinary Servant. The only special thing here is that all Meeting objects are incarnated by the same Servant instance. The Meeting Factory now books the Meeting's location, that is, it calls `book()` on the Room passed to `create()` as the `location` argument. If any exceptions occur during this second part of the processing of `create()`, the returned Meeting object will be a nil CORBA reference.

Figure 10.6 illustrates the relation between the POAs, the Default Servant, and the Meeting objects.

## 10.2.7 The Digital Secretary Service

The last component of our distributed application is the Digital Secretary, which has two distinct functions. First, it provides a graphical user interface to a personal diary manager. This part is not remotely accessible. Second,

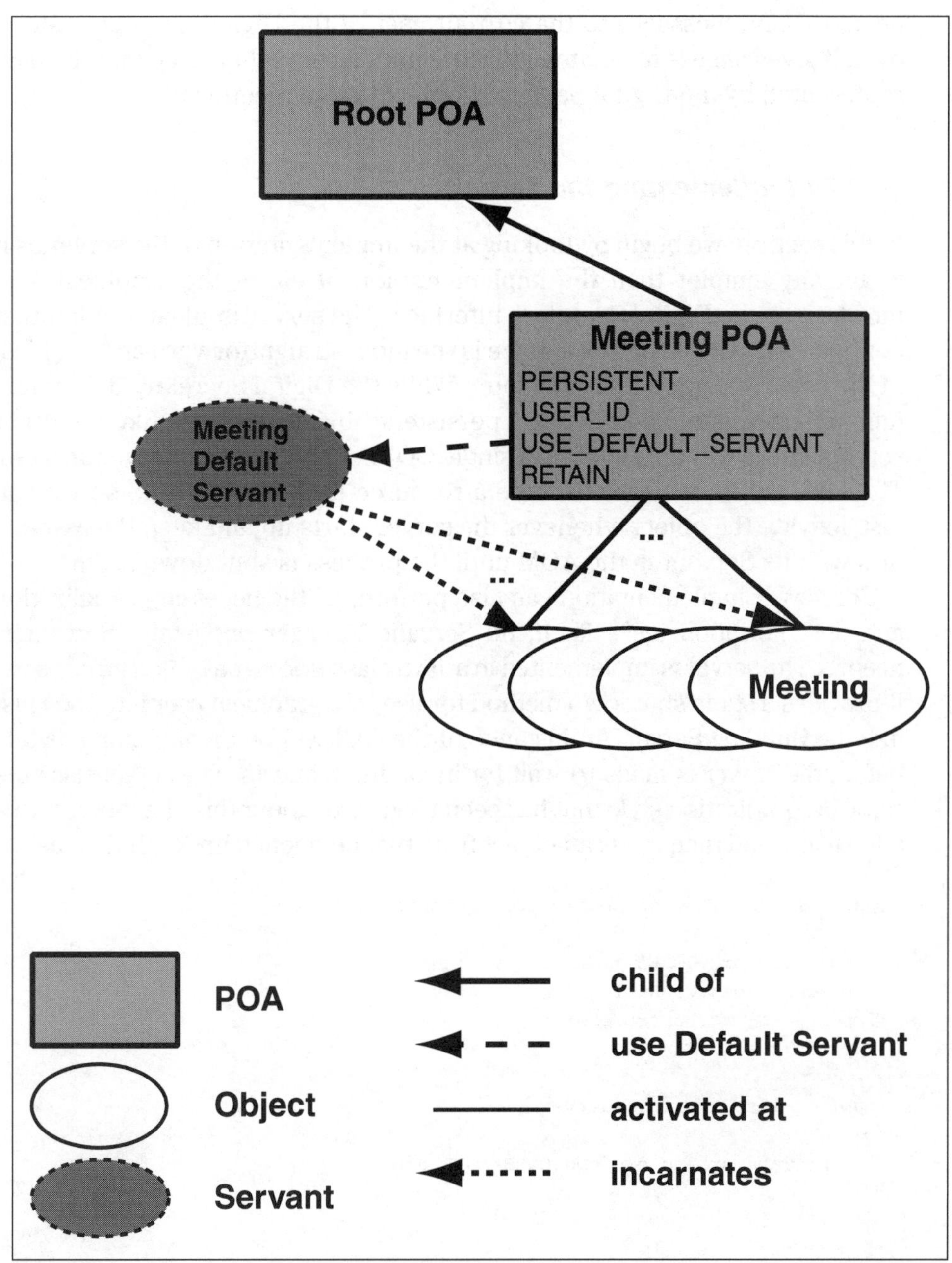


**Figure 10.6** The POAs for the Meeting Service.

the Digital Secretary provides a CORBA interface that allows other components to send messages to the current user of the Digital Secretary. Moreover, it gives access to a name attribute and allows others to invite the user represented by the Digital Secretary object to join meetings.

### 10.2.7.1 Implementing the Server

In this section, we begin by looking at the implementation of the server as it is actually simpler than the implementation of either the graphical user interface or the Digital Secretary interface. The server implementation that configures the POA for this service is the most straightforward and simplest of the ones presented in this chapter. While the Digital Secretary does maintain persistent state and needs a persistent object reference like the other servers, there will only ever be a single CORBA object in the server process. The POA will thus never become a resource usage bottleneck, so we can just activate the object whenever the server starts up and keep the association with its Servant in the AOM until the process is shut down again.

The server implementation can also perform all the necessary serialization and deserialization tasks itself; no Servant Manager or Default Servant is needed. The server is implemented in a Java class `SecretaryServer.java`. It provides a static shutdown method for use by a graphical user interface just like the Building Server. An instance of the GUI will be created immediately before the server is made to wait for incoming requests. The server uses the same deserialization style that has been used throughout this chapter. It forms a file name and then reads an object from the file opened under that name.

```
package com.wiley.compbooks.brose.chapter10.office;

import org.omg.CORBA.*;
import org.omg.CosNaming.*;
import org.omg.PortableServer.*;
import java.io.*;

public class SecretaryServer {

    private static org.omg.CORBA.ORB orb;

    /**
     * shutdown.
     */

    public static void shutdown() {
        orb.shutdown(false);
    }
```

```
public static void main( String args[] ) {

    if( args.length == 0 ) {
        System.err.println(
            "usage: java SecretaryServer <username>");
        System.exit(1);
    }

    // set up the file name to read state from
    String name = args[0];
    String filename = "." + name + "_pss";
    DigitalSecretaryImpl secretaryImpl = null;

    // deserialize DigitalSecretary state
    try {
        File f = new File( filename );
        if( f.exists() ) {
            FileInputStream f_in = new FileInputStream(f);

            if( f_in.available() > 0 ) {
                ObjectInputStream in =
                    new ObjectInputStream(f_in);
                secretaryImpl =
                    (DigitalSecretaryImpl)in.readObject();
                in.close();
            }
            f_in.close();
        }
    }
    catch( Exception e ) {
        e.printStackTrace();
    }



    try {
        // intialize the ORB and Root POA
        orb = org.omg.CORBA.ORB.init(args, null);
        org.omg.PortableServer.POA rootPOA =
            org.omg.PortableServer.POAHelper.narrow(
                orb.resolve_initial_references("RootPOA"));

        // retrieve Naming Service reference
        NamingContextExt nc = null;
        nc = NamingContextExtHelper.narrow(
            orb.resolve_initial_references("NameService"));
        if( nc == null ) {
            System.err.println("No Nameserver! Exiting . . . ");
            System.exit( 1 );
        }
```

```
// init the secretary implementation
if( secretaryImpl == null ) {
    secretaryImpl =
        new DigitalSecretaryImpl( name, orb );
}
```

After initializing the ORB and obtaining a reference to the Root POA, the server also tries to obtain a reference to the Naming Service. Because the Naming Service is essential for the internal workings of the Digital Secretary implementation, the server cannot continue without it. The server then checks to see if it successfully deserialized a `DigitalSecretaryImpl` object. If not, we assume that this is the first time the Secretary Service is started for that particular user, so we simply create a new implementation object.

```
// create policies for a new poa
org.omg.CORBA.Policy [] policies =
    new org.omg.CORBA.Policy[2];
policies[0] = rootPOA.create_id_assignment_policy(
    IdAssignmentPolicyValue.USER_ID);
policies[1] = rootPOA.create_lifespan_policy(
    LifespanPolicyValue.PERSISTENT);

// create the POA
POA secretaryPOA = rootPOA.create_POA("SecretaryPOA",
                                 rootPOA.the_POAManager(),
                                 policies);

// activate the Digital Servant object
secretaryPOA.activate_object_with_id(name.getBytes(),
                                        secretaryImpl );
// activate the POA Manager
secretaryPOA.the_POAManager().activate();

for (int i=0; i<policies.length; i++)
    policies[i].destroy();

// export the reference
nc.rebind( nc.to_name( name + ".secretary" ),
     secretaryPOA.servant_to_reference(secretaryImpl));

// initialize the implementation
secretaryImpl.init( secretaryPOA, nc, orb );

// start the GUI
SecretaryGUI gui = new SecretaryGUI( secretaryImpl );
// wait for requests until the ORB is shut down
orb.run();
```

As usual, we create policy objects as arguments for the `create_POA()` invocation. Here, all we need to do is to create the PERSISTENT Life Span policy and the USER_ID ID Assignment policy. The USE_ACTIVE_OBJECT_MAP_ONLY and RETAIN policies that we also want to use are the standard values for the Request Processing and the Servant Retention policies, so we need not explicitly set them.

After the POA is created, the server activates the Digital Secretary object using the `activate_object_with_id()` method, to which it supplies the user name as the object ID and the `DigitalSecretaryImpl` instance as a Servant. To enable request processing, we activate the POA Manager and export the object reference of this Digital Secretary Service. Finally, the implementation is initialized with references to its POA, Naming Service, and ORB, and the GUI is started up. The server then blocks in `orb.run()` to wait for incoming requests.

The only active threads in the application now are event handling threads in the GUI and, potentially, request processing threads for active requests in the ORB. When a user clicks on the GUI's "Exit" button, the GUI will eventually call back and invoke `shutdown()`. This will unblock the main thread after all POAs and Servants have been destroyed and etherealized. All that remains to be done now is to serialize the internal state of the `DigitalSecretaryImpl` instance by writing it to a file.

```
            try {
                File f = new File(filename);
                FileOutputStream fout = new FileOutputStream(f);
                ObjectOutputStream out =
                    new ObjectOutputStream(fout);

                out.writeObject(
                    (DigitalSecretaryImpl)secretaryImpl);
            }
            catch( IOException io ) {
                System.err.println("Error opening output file " +
                                    filename );
                System.exit(1);
            }
            System.exit(0);
        }
        catch( Exception e ) {
            e.printStackTrace();
            System.exit(1);
        }
    }
}
```

### 10.2.7.2 Implementing the Interface

The implementation of an accessor method for the IDL attribute name and methods for the operations notify and invite is straightforward. Note that we have to implement `_notify()` rather than `notify()` because IDL compilers will detect the name clash between the IDL operation name and the method in class `java.lang.Object` and therefore prepend an underscore in the generated code. For simplicity, we do not flesh out the invitation functionality of our meeting application here but simply turn an invitation into another notification.

```
package com.wiley.compbooks.brose.chapter10.office;

import java.util.*;
import org.omg.CORBA.*;
import org.omg.CosNaming.*;
import org.omg.CosNaming.NamingContextPackage.*;
import org.omg.PortableServer.*;

class DigitalSecretaryImpl
    extends DigitalSecretaryPOA
    implements java.io.Serializable {

    private String name;
    private Diary diary;

    private transient ORB orb;
    private transient NamingContextExt naming;

    private transient MeetingFactory meetingFactory;
    private transient String [] locations;
    private transient String [] buildingNames;
    private transient String [] secretaryNames;
    private transient Hashtable locationTable;
    private transient DigitalSecretary _this;

    public DigitalSecretaryImpl(String name, ORB orb) {
        this.name = name;
        this.orb = orb;
        diary = new Diary(orb);
    }

    public String name() {
        return name;
    }

    public void _notify(String msg) {
        System.out.println("Got notification: " + msg );
    }
```

```
public void invite(Meeting a_meeting)
     throws AlreadyEngaged {

    _notify("You have been invited to join a meeting " +
            a_meeting.purpose() );
}
```

The implementation class `DigitalSecretaryImpl` needs to be serializable, like all other implementations of objects with persistent state in this chapter. The state managed by this implementation consists only of the user name and the user's appointment diary; no object references are kept that would require conversions to strings and vice versa. It is thus not necessary to override the `writeObject()` method from `java.io.Serializable`.

The transient fields of this class hold references that are kept to provide easy access from the GUI, and other references that are needed to look these up. These include a reference to a Meeting Factory, an array of Buildings, and an array that holds all Rooms of all buildings that were found at initialization time. We also keep a hash table for quick lookup of Room objects by name. Another array stores the names of all other users currently registered at the Naming Service. The `_this` variable holds an object reference to the object incarnated by this Servant instance. Why this field is necessary will be explained in the text that follows in the implementation of the `scheduleMeeting()` method.

All transient references need to be re-initialized after deserialization, and the Diary also requires calling its `init()` method. To do all this, we provide an `init()` method for this class that must be called after creating or deserializing instances of this class:

```
public void init(POA myPOA, NamingContextExt naming, ORB orb)
    throws NotFound, CannotProceed {

    this.naming = naming;
    try {
        // get a reference to the object incarnated
        // by this Servant
        _this = DigitalSecretaryHelper.narrow(
            myPOA.servant_to_reference( this ));

        // retrieve the reference to the MeetingFactory
        // from the Naming Service
        meetingFactory = MeetingFactoryHelper.narrow(
            naming.resolve( naming.to_name("MeetingService")));

        // get a reference to the NamingContext for Buildings
        // and get all registered buildings
        NamingContextExt roomContext =
```

```
            NamingContextExtHelper.narrow(
                naming.resolve(naming.to_name("RoomService")));

        buildingNames = findBindings( roomContext, null );

        // look up other registered users
        secretaryNames = findBindings( naming, ".secretary" );

        // get all rooms from all buildings
        locationTable = new Hashtable();
        for( int i = 0; i < buildingNames.length; i++ ) {
            Building roomFactory = BuildingHelper.narrow(
                roomContext.resolve(
                    roomContext.to_name( buildingNames[i] )));

            // store rooms in hash table
            Room [] rooms = roomFactory.list();
            for( int j = 0; j < rooms.length; j++ ) {
                String locname = ( buildingNames[i] + ":" +
                                   rooms[j].name());
                locationTable.put( locname, rooms[j] );
            }
        }
        Enumeration locs = locationTable.keys();
        locations = new String[locationTable.size()];
        for( int i = 0; locs.hasMoreElements(); i++ ) {
            locations[i] = (String)locs.nextElement();
        }
        diary.init(orb);
    }
    catch( Exception in ) {
        in.printStackTrace();
    }
}
```

The `init()` method first sets the Naming Service and `_this` references. The `_this` reference is obtained from the POA by calling `servant_to_reference()` with this instance as the argument. The `init()` method retrieves other references from the Naming Service. The Meeting Factory reference is found this way. To retrieve lists of references from the Naming Service using specific naming conventions, `init()` calls a local method `findBindings()`, which recursively searches Naming Contexts for bindings with names that match a given string suffix.

To retrieve all Digital Secretaries, `findBindings()` is called with a suffix of `".secretary"`. To retrieve a list of Buildings, the search starts in a Naming Context bound to the name `"RoomContext"` in the root context. Building names in this context have no special suffixes, so this argument to `findBindings()` is null. The implementation of `findBindings()` is very similar to that of the `ContextLister.list()` method presented in Chapter 7, "Discovering Services." It is omitted here for brevity but is available on the companion Web site for this book.

After retrieving a list of Building references, we set up lists of all Rooms in each Building. All Rooms are then entered in a hash table, using a hash key that consists of their name concatenated to their Building's name. For easy GUI display in Java Swing Combo Boxes, we extract all Room names from the hash table and store them in a separate array. Finally, the Diary is initialized.

The remaining methods in this class are all simple accessors to the instance variables initialized in `init()`. They are used by the GUI exclusively. The only method that provides any additional functionality is `scheduleMeeting()`.

```
public String [] secretaryNames() {
    return secretaryNames;
}
public String [] buildingNames() {
    return buildingNames;
}
public String[] getLocations() {
    return locations;
}
public MeetingFactory getMeetingService() {
    return meetingFactory;
}
Diary getDiary() {
    return diary;
}

Meeting scheduleMeeting( String[] meetingData,
                         Date currentDate ) {

    Date when = new Date( currentDate.the_year,
                          currentDate.the_month,
                          currentDate.the_day,
                          Integer.parseInt( meetingData[2] ));
    Meeting m = null;
    try {
        m = meetingFactory.create(
                meetingData[0],
                (Room)locationTable.get( meetingData[1]),
                when,
                _this,
                new DigitalSecretary[] {
                    DigitalSecretaryHelper.narrow(
                        naming.resolve(
                                naming.to_name(
                      meetingData[3] + ".secretary" )))
```

```
                }
            );
        if( m != null )
            diary.enter(when, m );
    }
    catch( Exception e ) {
        e.printStackTrace();
    }
    return m;
}
```

The scheduleMeeting() method is called from within the GUI when the user wishes to create a new Meeting object. It is used to convert string arguments that the GUI provides after the user has selected values from lists and entered text into a text field to the proper formats expected by the Meeting Factory.

The currentDate argument is a Date instance that describes the day the user wishes to schedule a Meeting. The intended hour of the day is not set correctly in this argument but provided separately as a string in the argument array meetingData. Thus, the correct date for the Meeting is obtained by extracting the year, month, and day information from currentDate and converting the string at position 2 in the argument array to an integer value defining the hour of the day.

The first argument required by the Meeting Factory's create() method is a string describing the Meeting's purpose. This string is available directly from the argument array provided by the caller of scheduleMeeting(). The GUI extracts this string from a text field. The second argument to create() is a Room reference that we need to set up using another string. We expect the Room name at position 1 in the argument array. Using this string as a key, we can look up the reference to this Room in the locationTable that we prepared in init().

The create() method expects two more arguments that we need to fabricate from the argument strings to scheduleMeeting(). The first is a reference to the organizer of the meeting, and the second is an array of Participants. The organizer of the new Meeting is the Digital Secretary object incarnated by this Servant. The superclass of all Servants, org.omg.PortableServer.Servant, provides a method _this_object() that returns this reference, but it returns the correct result only when called from within the context of executing a CORBA request—which is not the case here. The call to scheduleMeeting() originated from within the GUI's event handling mechanism when the user clicked on a specific button, so there is no CORBA request context defined at this stage. For this reason, we stored the reference to the CORBA object incarnated by this Servant in the field _this during initialization.

Finally, we set up a Participant array of Digital Secretary references. For simplicity, this array consists of a single reference here. This reference is resolved from the Naming Service using another string argument provided by the GUI. We now create a new Meeting object using the Meeting Factory. If the `create()` call was successful and the returned Meeting is not null, it is entered in the Diary.

We conclude the presentation of the example application here. The implementation of the graphical user interface is beyond the scope of this chapter, but like all other code it is available from the companion Web site for this book at www.wiley.com/compbooks/brose.

# Events

In this chapter we explain events in the Java/CORBA world. Event-based communication provides an important alternative to the invocation-based, client/server paradigm that we have used exclusively until now. The CORBA notion of events is defined by the OMG Notification Service. This service specification was adopted in mid-1998 as the successor of the original Event Service. It fixes a number of shortcomings of the original service and extends it considerably.

Because the Notification Service is backward compatible with the Event Service, any existing clients of the Event Service will also operate with an implementation of the Notification Service. They will not, of course, be able to make use of the improvements introduced by the Notification Service. This backward compatibility has had considerable influence on the design of the Notification Service specification, so we first introduce the Event Service concepts and interfaces and then present the refinements and improvements introduced by the Notification Service. Finally, we compare the Notification Service with current Java notification systems.

This chapter covers the following:

- An introduction to Events (section 11.1)
- CORBA Event Service concepts (section 11.2)

- The main interfaces of the CORBA Event Service (section 11.3)
- An Event Service example (section 11.4)
- Notification Service concepts and main interfaces (section 11.5)
- A Notification Service example (section 11.6)
- An overview of Java event notification systems (section 11.7)

## 11.1 Events

The term "event" is widely used in programming, but unfortunately it is quite overloaded. Moreover, the features supported by existing event notification systems vary a lot. An event is an occurrence of some sort and as such is atomic. It should be stressed that an event and an event notification are not the same, and that the latter term refers to the actual data that is communicated. In this respect, the Notification Service is not only a technological, but also a terminological improvement over the Event Service. Unfortunately, you will find that the terms are used interchangeably in many systems. Event notifications are sometimes also referred to as *implicit invocations*, and it will become clear in this section what this means.

We first discuss a few central characteristics that can be observed in most event notification systems to provide a clear distinction between event-driven and invocation-based (client/server) communication. Note that existing systems may vary with respect to some of these characteristics. We then discuss at a more abstract level what we believe to be the main benefits of event-driven systems.

The first important characteristic of event-driven communication is that each notification is sent by a single supplier, but it is delivered to potentially multiple consumers. Standard operation invocations always have a single target only. From a more global perspective, we classify event communication as *many-to-many* because a supplier's notifications may reach multiple consumers, and notifications received by a consumer may come from multiple suppliers.

The second important point is that a supplier of event notifications does not know or reference its consumers, nor do consumers hold references to suppliers. A client, in contrast, must have an object reference to be able to make an invocation. This property is one reason for calling an event notification an implicit invocation—the receivers of the data are not explicitly addressed.

Another property of event systems is that sending notifications is non-blocking: A supplier does not block to wait until the message reaches all its consumers. A regular synchronous invocation, however, returns only when operation processing has ended, thus synchronizing client and server. (The send operation may still block, for example, until either the transport layer or an intermediary like a channel has received the event.) Note that notifications are not the only way for nonblocking interactions. CORBA also allows invoking operations asynchronously either using the DII, as explained in Chapter 6, "ORB Run-Time System," or using an ORB that implements the new CORBA Messaging Specification. Receiving a notification is usually an implicit operation. By *implicit*, we mean that consumers need not call an explicit receive operation but that data is delivered in push style. Many event notification platforms also allow a consumer to receive notifications explicitly, however.

The last property of event notifications we want to point out here is that they need to be self-describing. The reason is that the consumer entry point for notifications is generic, so all dispatching must be done explicitly by the consumer based on the event data. Another consequence of this genericity is that the syntactic correctness of notification messages is not guaranteed because they cannot be statically type-checked like invocations. Thus, notifications must be parsed and checked explicitly by consumers.

The most important aspect of event-driven communication when compared to client/server communication is *decoupling* or *autonomy*—suppliers and consumers of event notifications need to know much less about their communication partners and their contexts than clients and servers. Thus, it is much easier to configure or reconfigure event-based systems than client/server systems, which makes it attractive for integrating legacy systems where defining an invocation interface would be hard or even impossible. In the remainder of this section we further refine this notion of decoupling. This discussion is not required for understanding the rest of this chapter and may be skipped by the impatient reader.

We can describe decoupling at four different levels:

- Spatial
- Temporal
- Syntactic
- Semantic

First of all, suppliers do not know the identity of consumers and vice versa. Typically, this kind of insulation is achieved by inserting an intermediary ("channel," "queue," "router") into the communication, which forwards event notifications to consumers. Let's call this *spatial* decoupling because it relates to the logical extension of a distributed system in terms of its components.

*Temporal* decoupling is also accounted for by introducing intermediaries and means that sending a notification and receiving it can happen at completely arbitrary times—except, of course, that a notification can be consumed only after it was sent. In general, a supplier need not (and cannot) concern itself with if and when its event notification is consumed, nor should a consumer be concerned with when it was sent. While this discussion may appear a little artificial, the net result is that supplier and consumer code contains many fewer assumptions about the communication environment and is thus generally much easier to reuse in different environments.

To carry this yet a little further, we can say that a supplier is both syntactically and semantically decoupled from consumers of its event notifications. *Syntactic* decoupling here means that suppliers and consumers use a generic communication mechanism that is independent of the actual interfaces provided by these parties. The gist is that reassembling such a system requires no relinking of code. In its purest form, a supplier is even *semantically* independent of its environment. If notifications contain only data that describes an event in the supplier and absolutely no data that was included because of built-in assumptions about how consumers should best interpret the notification, then the supplier is absolutely autonomous.

This degree of autonomy is possible only for suppliers, however. Consumers must know how to interpret notifications to get any work done. Also, if suppliers provide only minimal event notifications, consumers might need a way to obtain more specific information that is necessary for processing the event data, such as querying a device's complete state via an invocation as a reaction to an event notification that signaled some state change in the device.

## 11.2 CORBA Event Service Concepts

The CORBA Event Service provides a way of distributing event notifications to any number of interested parties without requiring the originator of the event data to know the receivers and to make several calls to specific objects. The Event Service's *event channel* takes event data from a *supplier* and delivers that data to one or more *consumers*. The channel may act as a client to the supplier, *pulling* the event data from the supplier, or it may provide an object interface that allows the supplier to *push* the event data into the channel. When the data is to be delivered to consumers, the same options are available: The channel may push the event data to the consumer, or it may wait until the consumer pulls the event data from the channel. Channels may also use a combination of the push and pull approaches with different clients.

The specification defines the communication interfaces used to push and pull event data to and from suppliers and consumers. It then defines the Event Channel in terms of proxy suppliers and consumers. That is, the channel is an intermediary object between a supplier and a consumer, and it acts toward a supplier as a *proxy consumer* and toward a consumer as a *proxy supplier*.

The event channel provides administration interfaces that allow clients to choose whether to act as a supplier or consumer, then choose the appropriate interface for either push or pull model communication. The final step in beginning communications with an event channel is to connect to the channel, supplying any necessary callback object references (for example, to allow the channel to call a pull operation at an event supplier).

## 11.2.1 Push Model Communications

As we have already noted, the event service acts as a proxy that receives an event communication on behalf of consumers and then passes the event data to the consumers on the supplier's behalf. It is as if the supplier directly called an interface at the consumer to push some event notification by invoking a push() operation that the consumer supplies. See Figure 11.1 for a diagram representing this interaction.

The interface for this invocation when an event channel is involved in the interaction is the same, but the invocation happens twice, once by the supplier at the event channel, once by the channel at the consumer. This is shown in Figure 11.2.

## 11.2.2 Pull Model Communications

When a consumer wishes to be the active party in direct event data transmission, it must invoke a pull() operation on an object reference supplied by the event supplier. In some cases the consumer may not wish to make a

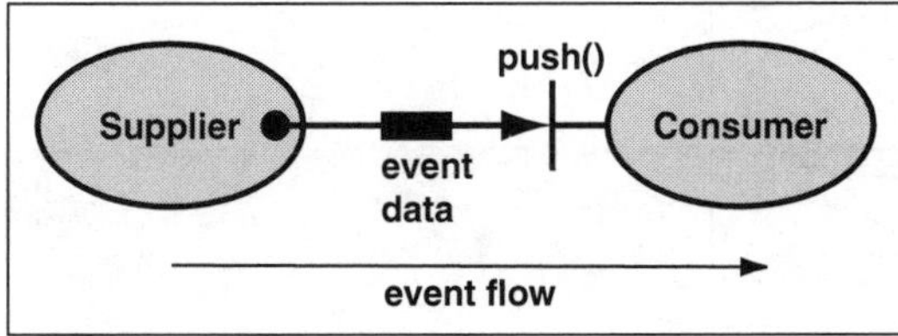


**Figure 11.1** Direct push.

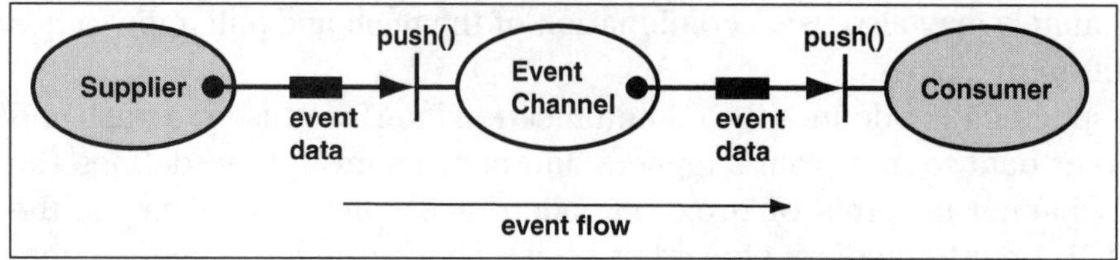


**Figure 11.2** Event channel push.

blocking operation invocation that must wait until an event notification is generated. In this case another operation, try_pull(), must be supported by the supplier. This operation returns immediately with an event notification, if one is available, or with no data if none is available. Figure 11.3 represents an interaction between a pull model consumer and supplier.

As with push model communications, an event channel can be interposed between the supplier and consumer. The channel will call pull() or try_pull() at the supplier's interface and then store the event data until the consumer calls pull() or try_pull() at the identical interface offered by the channel, as depicted in Figure 11.4.

## 11.2.3 Mixed-Mode Communications

When an event channel is used, not only can multiple suppliers place event notifications into the channel for transmission to multiple consumers, but the model chosen by the suppliers to deliver the event data can be either push or pull, regardless of the model chosen by the consumers. Figure 11.5 depicts a mixture of push and pull model suppliers and consumers.

The Event Service specification does not prescribe the semantics of event notification delivery to be implemented by event channels. An event channel could keep track of what event data has been transmitted to which consumers and store data until it is delivered to every consumer. On the other hand, the semantics might be that each notification supplied need only be forwarded to one of the consumers connected to the channel. Most imple-

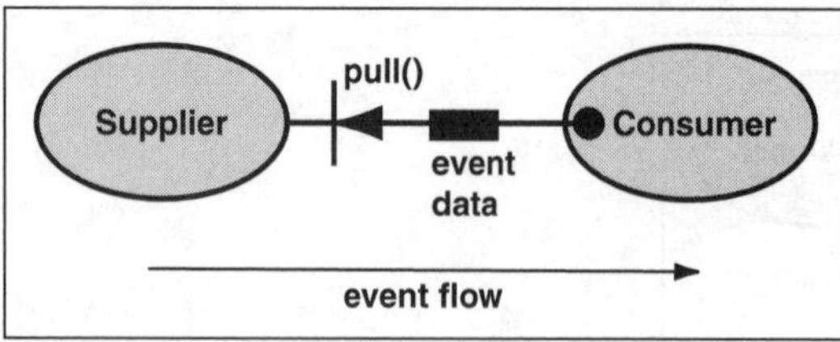


**Figure 11.3** Direct pull.

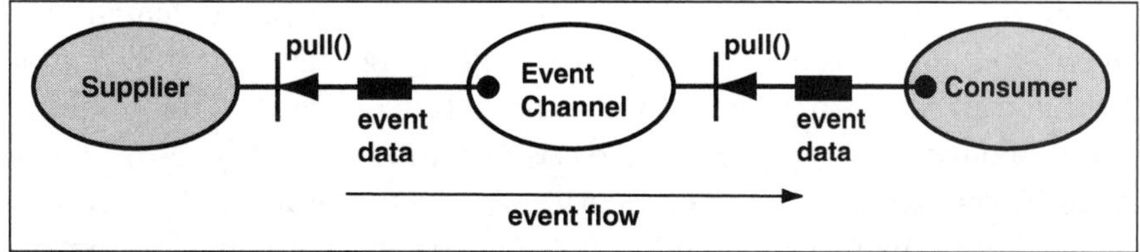


**Figure 11.4** Event channel pull.

mentations of the Event Service assume the former semantics, and some can be configured to provide different semantics or various qualities of service.

## 11.2.4 Federated Event Channels

Because event channels implement the same interfaces as the suppliers and consumers using them, it is possible to connect event channels simply by making one channel act as the supplier to another. This configuration can be used to provide alternative paths of delivery for fault tolerance by running different event channels on different hosts and connecting them in a federation. Then consumers can connect to more than one channel in case a host becomes unavailable, but they have to deal with multiple instances of the same data.

## 11.2.5 Event Types

So that we can define generic interfaces for event communications, the data transmitted by the push and pull operations must be wrapped in an Any. This means that there is an extra layer of unmarshaling before an event consumer can access the data it receives, and the TypeCode for the data must also be transmitted.

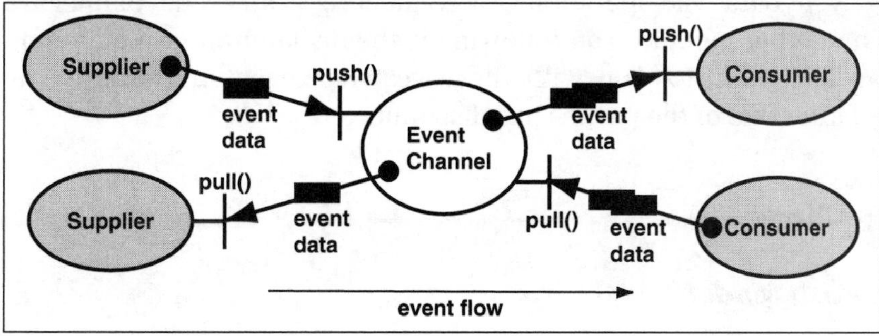

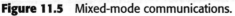

**Figure 11.5** Mixed-mode communications.

The Event Service accounts for this problem by defining a mechanism for typed event communication. That is, instead of using push and pull operations that have an Any as a parameter, we can define operations that include parameters of particular types. Because it is not known what types of applications we'll wish to use, the specification defines operations that return references of the type Object, which must be narrowed at run time to produce an agreed interface type that has an operation (or operations) with typed parameters.

Typed Event Services can be implemented to suit a particular application and recognize a limited number of typed communication interfaces. Alternatively, Event Service implementations that use the Dynamic Server Interface and the Interface Repository to accept any invocation could also implement this functionality. This would allow applications to use agreed interfaces for type-specific invocations for ease of programming.

## 11.3 Interface Specifications

Let's have a look at the interfaces that provide the Event Service functionality. First we will provide the definitions for the interfaces that facilitate the push and pull communications (section 11.3.1). Then the interfaces that the event channel offers to provide proxy consumers and proxy suppliers are shown in section 11.3.2. The Administration interfaces are given in section 11.3.3. Finally, we present the Typed Event Channel interfaces in section 11.3.4.

### 11.3.1 Module CosEventComm

The interfaces supporting the push and pull operations used to transmit event data are all defined in the CosEventComm module. These interfaces use a notion of being *connected* while event data is being transmitted and *disconnected* when either party decides not to continue transmitting or receiving event data. The operations for connecting to an event channel are defined in another module. The following is the declaration of the module and of an exception to deal with the case when event transmission is attempted after one of the parties has disconnected.

```
module CosEventComm {
  exception Disconnected{};
```

#### *11.3.1.1 Push Model*

Now let's look at the IDL for the first of two pairs of interfaces: PushConsumer and PushSupplier.

```
interface PushConsumer {
   void push (in any data) raises(Disconnected);
   void disconnect_push_consumer();
};
```

This interface is supported by the consumer of event data to allow suppliers (including an event channel) to push event data using the push() operation. The supplier may decide to terminate the connection by calling disconnect_push_consumer(). The push() operation will raise the Disconnected exception if its supplier client has already called disconnect_push_consumer(). It is assumed that the consumer has an object reference to a reciprocal interface supported by the supplier so that it may also disconnect. This interface is called PushSupplier.

```
interface PushSupplier {
   void disconnect_push_supplier();
};
```

Note that PushSupplier supports a disconnect operation but no communications operations. This is because the supplier is the active party in this model and calls the consumer, which supports the push() operation. In the next section we will show how the consumer and supplier become connected (swap object references to each other's interfaces).

### 11.3.1.2 Pull Model

In pull model communications it is the supplier that is passive, offering an interface that the consumer may call at any time. This interface is called PullSupplier.

```
interface PullSupplier {
   any pull () raises(Disconnected);
   any try_pull (out boolean has_event)
      raises(Disconnected);
   void disconnect_pull_supplier();
};
```

The pull consumer that calls these operations cannot be sure that any new event data will be waiting for it at the supplier, so it has a choice between two pull operations. A call to pull() will block until some data is ready. A call to try_pull() will return immediately with data if there is any, or with an undefined result if there is none. Its out parameter has_event will be TRUE if there is a valid result or FALSE otherwise. The disconnect_pull_consumer() operation allows the consumer to signal that it will no longer pull any event data.

Once again, there is a reciprocal interface that allows the supplier to disconnect. Its definition is as follows:

```
    interface PullConsumer {
        void disconnect_pull_consumer();
    };
};  // CosEventComm
```

## 11.3.2 Module CosEventChannelAdmin

The interfaces defined in CosEventComm can be implemented for use in any context as a pattern for transmitting event data, and they are inherited for use by event channels. The IDL for event channel interfaces is in the module CosEventChannelAdmin. This module facilitates the connection of suppliers and consumers to the proxy interfaces of an event channel. An exception, AlreadyConnected, is raised when a connection to a channel is attempted after one is already established.

```
module CosEventChannelAdmin {
    exception AlreadyConnected {};
    exception TypeError {};
```

The TypeError exception is used by the interfaces for typed event communication. Its use will be explained in section 11.3.4.

### *11.3.2.1 Proxy Interfaces*

The event channel supports proxy consumers that event suppliers connect to and communicate with using the push and pull operations inherited from the CosEventComm interfaces. They also support proxy suppliers that event consumers connect to in order to receive notifications via the same push and pull operations inherited into other interfaces. We describe all four combinations of push and pull models with consumer and supplier roles.

#### Proxy Push Consumer

The first interface defined is ProxyPushConsumer. It inherits from PushConsumer and supports one additional operation called connect_push_supplier(), which takes a PushSupplier object reference that the channel will use when it wishes to disconnect from the supplier.

```
interface ProxyPushConsumer: CosEventComm::PushConsumer {
    void connect_push_supplier(in CosEventComm::PushSupplier push_supplier)
        raises(AlreadyConnected);
};
```

Once the supplier has provided its callback interface to the connect_push_supplier() operation, it may begin calling the push() operation that the proxy interface inherits from PushConsumer. Any further calls to connect_push_supplier() will raise the AlreadyConnected exception. The PushSupplier interface provided by the supplier contains only a disconnect operation, and it is therefore not essential to transmitting event data. For this reason some event channels will accept a nil object reference as an argument to connect_push_supplier().

When the supplier is finished providing event data it will call the disconnect_push_consumer() operation, which is also inherited from PushConsumer. See Figure 11.6 for a graphical representation of the life cycle of a connection to an event channel.

Each of the other proxy interfaces works in essentially the same way, although the operations each inherits from its corresponding CosEventComm interfaces will be different.

### Proxy Pull Supplier

The ProxyPullSupplier interface is for use by pull model consumers. The inherited operations are pull(), try_pull(), and a disconnect operation.

```
interface ProxyPullSupplier: CosEventComm::PullSupplier {
    void connect_pull_consumer(in CosEventComm::PullConsumer pull_consumer)
        raises(AlreadyConnected);
};
```

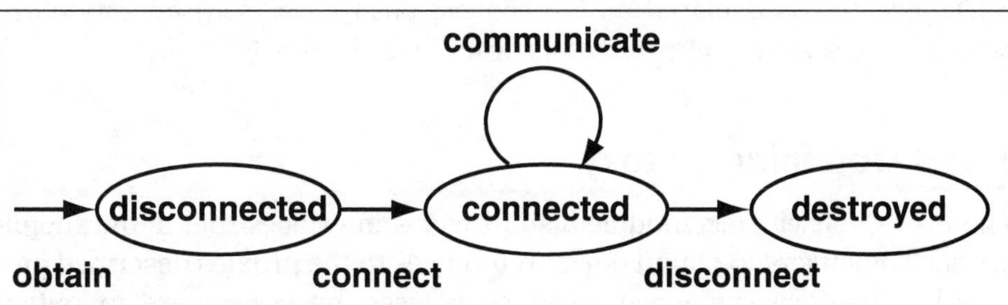

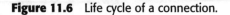

**Figure 11.6** Life cycle of a connection.

Once again, the PullConsumer interface type supplied as a parameter to the connect operation contains only a disconnect operation, and nil object references may be acceptable to some event channels.

### Proxy Pull Consumer

The ProxyPullConsumer interface supports the connect_pull_supplier() operation, which takes a callback object reference parameter of type PullSupplier. The event channel will use this callback to invoke the supplier's pull() and try_pull() operations.

```
interface ProxyPullConsumer: CosEventComm::PullConsumer {
  void connect_pull_supplier(in CosEventComm::PullSupplier pull_supplier)
    raises(AlreadyConnected,TypeError);
};
```

The connect_pull_supplier() operation may raise a TypeError exception as well as the usual AlreadyConnected. This is to allow typed event channels to narrow the argument they receive to a derived interface that supports extra operations. If the object reference passed will not narrow, then TypeError will be raised. See section 11.3.4 for the details of typed event channels.

### Proxy Push Supplier

The final proxy interface is ProxyPushSupplier, which is used by consumers that supply a PushConsumer callback object reference argument to the connect_push_consumer() operation so that the event channel can use the callback's push() operation to transmit event data to the consumer.

```
interface ProxyPushSupplier: CosEventComm::PushSupplier {
  void connect_push_consumer(in CosEventComm::PushConsumer push_consumer)
    raises(AlreadyConnected, TypeError);
};
```

The exceptions declared on the connect_push_consumer() operation are raised in the same circumstances as described previously.

## 11.3.3 Obtaining a Proxy

The EventChannelAdmin module also provides interfaces that allow suppliers and consumers to obtain object references to the proxies described previously. The ConsumerAdmin interface is used by consumers to obtain references to supplier proxies.

```
interface ConsumerAdmin {
      ProxyPushSupplier obtain_push_supplier();
      ProxyPullSupplier obtain_pull_supplier();
};
```

The SupplierAdmin interface allows suppliers to obtain references to the channel's consumer proxies.

```
interface SupplierAdmin {
   ProxyPushConsumer obtain_push_consumer();
   ProxyPullConsumer obtain_pull_consumer();
};
```

Finally, the EventChannel interface represents the "front door" to an Event Service implementation. Its operations for_consumers() and for_suppliers() give consumers and suppliers references to the Admin interfaces described previously.

```
interface EventChannel {
   ConsumerAdmin for_consumers();
   SupplierAdmin for_suppliers();
   void destroy();
};
```

The destroy() operation is provided to complete the life cycle of an event channel. There is no standard factory interface defined to create new event channels. Many implementations of the Event Service provide their own channel factory, but relying on vendor-specific extensions to OMG specifications has the usual drawbacks.

### 11.3.4 Typed Event Communication

The Event Service specification allows for the use of typed operations to transmit event data instead of the generic push and pull operations defined in CosEventComm. Two new interfaces that inherit from the CosEventComm interfaces supporting push and pull operations are defined in the module CosTypedEventComm. These interfaces are TypedPushConsumer and TypedPullSupplier.

Typed event communication reuses the ProxyPullConsumer and ProxyPushSupplier interfaces, but it expects that subtypes of the parameters to their connect operations will be passed by the channel's clients so that they can be narrowed to an agreed interface type that provides typed operations.

Hence, the declaration of the TypeError exception is to be raised by the connect operations in these interfaces.

```
module CosTypedEventComm {
    interface TypedPushConsumer : CosEventComm::PushConsumer {
        Object get_typed_consumer();
    };
```

The TypedPushConsumer interface supports all of the functionality of the generic PushConsumer interface, but implementations may use the generic operations by returning a NO_IMPLEMENT system exception. Instead of a connect operation, the typed push consumer interface supports the operation get_typed_consumer(). Its return type is Object, but the supplier must narrow the returned object reference to an agreed interface type. This narrowed interface type must support operations with only in parameters and no return values, as event data travels in only one direction. The mechanism for choosing this interface type is provided by the TypedSupplierAdmin and TypedConsumerAdmin interfaces explained in section 11.3.4.3.

The TypedPullSupplier interface works in the same manner as the TypedPushConsumer interface.

```
    interface TypedPullSupplier : CosEventComm::PullSupplier {
        Object get_typed_supplier();
    };
};
```

The interface returned from get_typed_supplier() can be made equivalent to a typed push model interface X by defining an interface PullX. The PullX interface must contain an operation pull_op() for each operation op in X. The parameters of pull_op() must be equivalent to those in op, but tagged as out parameters instead of in parameters. PullX should also support another operation for each op in X, called try_op(), each of which must return a Boolean. A return value of TRUE indicates that the values in the out parameters are valid event data—that is, there was an event notification waiting to be pulled.

### *11.3.4.1 Typed Event Types*

The typed event channel administration interfaces offer the same functionality as the generic event channel. That is, they offer interfaces to obtain appropriate proxies for supplier and consumer, for push and pull model communications. One extra feature is provided: the ability to specify which type of interface to use for typed communication. This will be the type of object reference returned from the get_typed_supplier() and get_typed _consumer() operations defined earlier.

```
module CosTypedEventChannelAdmin {
    exception InterfaceNotSupported {};
    exception NoSuchImplementation {};
    typedef string Key;
```

The CosTypedEventChannelAdmin module introduces two new exceptions to deal with two error cases:

- InterfaceNotSupported is raised when the event channel cannot support the typed interface required by its clients.
- NoSuchImplementation is raised when the event channel cannot make invocations on an interface type.

It also defines a string type, Key, that is used to nominate the interface type required, or offered, by the client.

### *11.3.4.2 The Typed Proxy Interfaces*

The TypedProxyPushConsumer interface has all of the operations of the equivalent generic proxy, as well as those of the new TypedPushConsumer interface we defined.

```
interface TypedProxyPushConsumer :
        CosEventChannelAdmin::ProxyPushConsumer,
        CosTypedEventComm::TypedPushConsumer {};
```

Likewise, the TypedProxyPullSupplier interface inherits from both the generic proxy and the new TypedPullSupplier interface.

```
interface TypedProxyPullSupplier:
        CosEventChannelAdmin::ProxyPullSupplier,
        CosTypedEventComm::TypedPullSupplier {};
```

Each object returned by a typed event channel will also implement the operations of an additional interface or be capable of calling the operations of an additional interface that is implemented at its client. The bootstrap operations described in the next section provide the mechanism for the channel and its client to agree on the type of that interface.

### 11.3.4.3 The Typed Admin Interfaces

The interface TypedSupplierAdmin is used by typed event suppliers to obtain proxies that support typed event transmission operations, while the TypedConsumerAdmin interface is used by typed event consumers to obtain proxies that support similar operations.

#### TypedSupplierAdmin

This interface is an extension of the untyped event channel's supplier administration interface and has operations for push and pull model event transmission.

```
interface TypedSupplierAdmin :
        CosEventChannelAdmin::SupplierAdmin {

        TypedProxyPushConsumer obtain_typed_push_consumer(
                in Key supported_interface )
            raises(InterfaceNotSupported);
```

The obtain_typed_push_consumer() operation takes a Key parameter that the supplier uses to specify which interface type it wishes to use for typed communications. The supplier will then call the get_typed_consumer() operation on the returned TypedProxyPushConsumer object reference. The resulting Object return type can then be narrowed to the type given as the Key parameter. If the channel cannot supply an object reference of this interface type it will raise an InterfaceNotSupported exception from obtain_typed_push_consumer().

```
        ProxyPullConsumer obtain_typed_pull_consumer (
                in Key uses_interface )
            raises( NoSuchImplementation );
}; //TypedSupplierAdmin
```

The obtain_typed_pull_consumer() operation returns an ordinary Proxy PullConsumer interface. If the channel cannot make calls to the interface type specified in the uses_interface parameter it will raise the NoSuch Implementation exception.

Once the ProxyPullConsumer is obtained, the supplier must use its connect_pull_supplier() operation, passing it an interface that supports PullSupplier (the argument type), as well as PullX, where X is the interface type specified in the uses_interface parameter of the previous operation. The connect_pull_supplier() operation will raise the TypeError exception if it cannot narrow the object reference supplied to type PullX.

### TypedConsumerAdmin

This interface behaves in a similar way to its supplier counterpart, and it is used by consumers to obtain typed proxy supplier object references.

```
interface TypedConsumerAdmin : CosEventChannelAdmin::ConsumerAdmin {
        TypedProxyPullSupplier obtain_typed_pull_supplier(
            in Key supported_interface)
        raises (InterfaceNotSupported);
```

The obtain_typed_pull_supplier() operation returns a TypedProxyPullSupplier object reference. The consumer will call the get_typed_supplier() operation on this reference, which will return an object reference that can be narrowed to the interface type specified in the supported_interface parameter. The channel raises the InterfaceNotSupported exception from the call to obtain_typed_pull_supplier() if it cannot supply a reference of the type specified in Key.

```
        ProxyPushSupplier obtain_typed_push_supplier(
            in Key uses_interface)
        raises(NoSuchImplementation);
};
```

The obtain_typed_push_supplier() operation returns an ordinary Proxy PushSupplier object reference, to which the consumer must connect. It does this by supplying a subtype of the PushConsumer interface that also supports the interface type the consumer specified in the uses_interface parameter. Like its supplier counterpart, the operation will raise the NoSuch Implementation exception if it cannot use this interface type. The returned ProxyPushSupplier's connect operation will raise the TypeError exception if the consumer's object reference does not support the interface type it specified.

### TypedEventChannel

The TypedEventChannel interface acts as a bootstrap for all kinds of typed Event Service clients. It offers similar operations to generic event channels to gain access to the Admin interfaces we described.

```
interface TypedEventChannel {
    TypedConsumerAdmin for_consumers();
    TypedSupplierAdmin for_suppliers();
    void destroy ();
};
}; // module TypedEventChannelAdmin
```

## 11.4 An Event Service Example

The example that we present in this section uses the Event Service as introduced in the previous sections. It will be extended to make use of Notification Service features in section 11.6.

Consider an office environment with a few centralized printers. As a user of a printer, you probably prefer being notified by the printer exactly when your job has finished printing and is ready to be collected rather than having to walk up to the printer, only to find that the printer has run out of paper, or your job has not even started printing because someone else is printing the complete set of OMG specifications.

In this example, we use mixed-mode communication between suppliers and consumers of event data. The printer acts as a push supplier and simply emits event notifications whenever its state changes, that is, when a job has been printed or canceled, paper runs out, or the printer jams. On the client side, we use a pull consumer that regularly checks for available event notifications. We do not provide a GUI for the example, but the rationale behind this design is that the client wants control over when it has to update windows on the screen and thus does not want to handle incoming notifications at all times.

The IDL that we use for the example is the following:

```
module com {
...
module chapter11 {
module office {

  typedef long JobID;
  typedef string UserID;

  struct Job {
       JobID job_id;
       UserID user_id;
  };

  enum Status { CANCELED, PRINTED, ONLINE, OFFLINE, JAMMED, OUT_OF_PAPER };

  union PrinterStatus switch( Status ) {
     case CANCELED:
     case PRINTED: Job the_job;
  };
```

We first define a few types that will later be used to hold event data. The printer state is defined to be a union of one of the elements of the Status enumeration and, for states like canceled or printed, the ID of the job that was printed or canceled.

```
    interface Printer {
      typedef string Document;
      exception OffLine {};
      exception AlreadyPrinted {};
      exception UnknownJobID {};

      JobID print(in Document text, in UserID uid)
        raises (OffLine);

      void cancel(in JobID id, in UserID uid)
        raises (AlreadyPrinted, UnknownJobID);

      void setOffLine(in boolean flag);
    };
  }; }; }; }; }; };
```

The Printer interface defines printable documents to be simple strings and also declares two exception types for printer operations. The print() operation returns the ID the printer assigns to the job it creates when a document is submitted for printing. Using this ID, clients can refer to the job when trying to cancel it using the cancel() operation. If the printer is offline, the operation raises the OffLine exception; otherwise the job is scheduled for printing.

The cancel() operation tries to remove the job with the given ID from the printer queue, but this operation may fail in various ways. First, the job might already have been printed. In this case, the AlreadyPrinted exception is raised. If the supplied job ID falls outside the range of valid job IDs, the operation raises the UnknownJobID exception. Finally, the job that is to be canceled might have been submitted by a different user than the one calling the cancel() operation. In this case, the NO_PERMISSION system exception is raised, which is not listed in the operation signature. Finally, the setOffLine() operation can be used to set the printer offline or online again, depending on the value of the argument flag.

All three operations in the printer interface effect internal state changes in the printer. As a result, the printer will send event notifications describing this state change after each operation. The IDL definitions do not give any indications of these events, as IDL has no concept to describe event notifications. The extended IDL introduced by the CORBA Component Specification in Chapter 14, "CORBA Components," does have language constructs that describe the event notifications supplied or consumed by a component, but at this stage we don't have any means to do so.

If a document is printed, the printer sends an event notification containing an Any holding the PrinterStatus union with a discriminator value of PRINTED and a Job member describing the printed job. A similar event notification is created as a result of the cancel operation. If the setOffLine() operation is called, the PrinterStatus union does not contain a Job structure.

## 11.4.1 Implementing the Supplier

The implementation of the Printer interface is straightforward, but using the Event Service requires some special initialization. The implementation class `PrinterImpl` is defined in a package `event`. The Java classes generated from the IDL reside in the `office` and `office.PrinterPackage` packages. To function as a Push Supplier, we need to implement the `PushSupplierOperations` interface here so we can create a Tie for this Servant later. If we did not have to extend the skeleton class `PrinterPOA`, we could have extended the Push Supplier skeleton class instead.

```
package com.wiley.compbooks.brose.chapter11.event;

import org.omg.CosEventChannelAdmin.*;
import org.omg.CosEventComm.*;
import org.omg.CosNaming.*;
import org.omg.CORBA.Any;
import org.omg.CORBA.ORB;
import org.omg.PortableServer.*;

import java.util.Hashtable;
import com.wiley.compbooks.brose.chapter11.office.*;
import com.wiley.compbooks.brose.chapter11.office.PrinterPackage.*;

class PrinterImpl
    extends PrinterPOA
    implements PushSupplierOperations {

    private EventChannel channel;
    private SupplierAdmin supplierAdmin ;
    private ProxyPushConsumer proxyPushConsumer;
    private ORB orb;
    private POA poa;

    private Hashtable queue;
    private int jobId;
    private int printIdx;
    private boolean offline;
    private boolean disconnected;
    private PrintThread printThread;
```

```
static class JobInfo {
    public int jobId;
    public String userId;
    public String text;

    public JobInfo(int jobId, String userId, String text) {
        this.jobId = jobId;
        this.userId = userId;
        this.text = text;
    }
}
```

We declare fields to hold references to the event channel and the Admin interface for suppliers. Using this interface, we will obtain a reference to a proxy push consumer, for which we also declare a field. Finally, we need to remember our ORB and POA, plus a couple of fields to hold the actual printer state. For this state, we use a hash table indexed by job IDs, a separate index that denotes the ID of the next job to be printed, and flags to represent offline and disconnected states. Finally, we store a reference to a separate thread that simulates the printing. The inner class `JobInfo` is used to store information about print jobs in the printer queue.

```
static public void main (String argv[]) {

    org.omg.CosEventChannelAdmin.EventChannel channel = null;
    org.omg.CORBA.ORB orb = org.omg.CORBA.ORB.init(argv, null);

    try {

        // initialize POA, get naming and event
        // service references
        POA poa = POAHelper.narrow(
            orb.resolve_initial_references("RootPOA") );

        NamingContextExt nc = NamingContextExtHelper.narrow(
            orb.resolve_initial_references("NameService"));

        channel = EventChannelHelper.narrow(
            nc.resolve(nc.to_name("office_event.channel")));
```

After initializing the ORB and Root POA and obtaining a reference to the Naming Service, we try to find an event channel bound to the name `"office_event.channel"` at the Naming Service. As the Event Service does not define a factory interface, we cannot create this event channel if it does not exist. We are now ready to create the printer implementation, connect it to the event channel, and finally export its reference to the Naming Service.

```
            // create the printer implementation
            PrinterImpl printer = new PrinterImpl( channel,
                                                   orb,
                                                   poa );

            // connect the implementation to the event channel
            printer.connect();

            // create an object reference, activate, and export it
            org.omg.CORBA.Object printerObj =
                poa.servant_to_reference( printer );
            nc.bind( nc.to_name("Printer"), printerObj);

            // wait for requests
            poa.the_POAManager().activate();
            orb.run();
        }
        catch (Exception ex) {
            ex.printStackTrace();
        }
    }
}
```

The actual initialization of the printer is done in its class constructor and in the `connect()` method.

```
    public PrinterImpl(EventChannel channel, ORB orb, POA poa) {
        // set the ORB and event channel
        this.orb = orb;
        this.poa = poa;
        this.channel = channel;
    }

    public void connect() {

        // create a PushSupplier Tie for this Servant
        PushSupplierPOATie thisTie =
            new PushSupplierPOATie( this );

        // get admin interface and proxy consumer
        supplierAdmin = channel.for_suppliers();
        proxyPushConsumer = supplierAdmin.obtain_push_consumer();

        // connect the push supplier
        try {
            proxyPushConsumer.connect_push_supplier(
                PushSupplierHelper.narrow(
                    poa.servant_to_reference( thisTie )));
        }
        catch( Exception e ) {
            e.printStackTrace();
```

```
        }
        // initialize "queue" and start printer thread
        queue = new Hashtable();
        printThread = new PrintThread();
    }
```

To be able to publish notifications in push style, the printer must obtain a reference to an object that supports the push() operation. This reference can be retrieved by calling `obtain_push_consumer()` on the admin interface for suppliers, which, in turn, can be obtained by calling `for_suppliers()` on the channel. We can then connect the printer's `PushSupplier` reference to the proxy push consumer by calling `connect_push_supplier()`.

The `cancel()` method implements one of the three printer operations that create notifications. We will look at this operation as an example and omit the other implementations for brevity as creating and sending notifications work exactly the same in all three cases. As usual, the complete code is available on the companion Web site (www.wiley.com/compbooks/brose).

```
    public void cancel(int id, String uid )
        throws UnknownJobID, AlreadyPrinted {

        if( id > jobId || id < 0)
            throw new UnknownJobID();

        if( id < printIdx )
            throw new AlreadyPrinted();

        JobInfo job = (JobInfo)queue.get( new Integer( id ));
        if( job != null ) {
            if( !job.userId.equals( uid ))
                throw new org.omg.CORBA.NO_PERMISSION();
            queue.remove( new Integer( id ));
```

After checking the operation preconditions for valid IDs, the job ID is used as an index into the hash table that represents the printer queue. We check that the job owner's user ID and the one provided as the `uid` argument are the same and then remove the job from the queue.

```
            System.out.println("-CANCELED JOB #" + id  + "-");
            Any cancelEvent = orb.create_any();
            PrinterStatus status = new PrinterStatus();
            status.the_job( Status.CANCELED,
                            new Job( id, job.userId ) );
            PrinterStatusHelper.insert( cancelEvent, status );
            try {
                proxyPushConsumer.push( cancelEvent );
            }
            catch( org.omg.CosEventComm.Disconnected d ) {
```

```
                    // ignore
                }
            }
        }
```

After removing the job from the queue, an event notification is created. We first create the Any that will hold the event data and then create an instance of the PrinterStatus class that represents the IDL union of the same name. The status object is initialized with the job and user IDs and inserted into the any. Finally, the notification is sent to the channel by calling push() on the ProxyPushConsumer.

## 11.4.2 Implementing the Consumer

The event consumer is also the client of the Printer interface. It is implemented in a class PrintClient.

```
package com.wiley.compbooks.brose.chapter11.event;

import org.omg.CosNaming.*;
import org.omg.CosEventChannelAdmin.*;
import org.omg.CosEventComm.*;
import org.omg.CORBA.Any;

import com.wiley.compbooks.brose.chapter11.office.*;
import com.wiley.compbooks.brose.chapter11.office.PrinterPackage.*;

import org.omg.PortableServer.*;

public class PrintClient
    extends PullConsumerPOA {

    /**
     * releases any resources, none in this case
     */
    public void disconnect_pull_consumer() {
    }
```

Our client extends the skeleton class for pull consumers. The only operation that it needs to implement is disconnect_pull_consumer(), which will be invoked by the event channel to disconnect the consumer. We don't do anything here because the client terminates anyway after just a few interactions with the channel. Let's continue and look at the client program's main method.

```
    static public void main  (String argv[]) {
        EventChannel channel = null;
```

```
ConsumerAdmin consumerAdmin;
ProxyPullSupplier  proxyPullSupplier = null;
PullConsumer pullConsumer;
Printer printer = null;
String userid = "MeMyselfAndI";

// check for user ID on the command line
if( argv.length > 0 )
    userid = argv[0];

// initialize ORB

org.omg.CORBA.ORB orb = org.omg.CORBA.ORB.init(argv, null);
POA poa = null;

try {
    // inititialize POA
    poa = POAHelper.narrow(
        orb.resolve_initial_references("RootPOA"));

    // get naming service reference
    NamingContextExt nc = NamingContextExtHelper.narrow(
        orb.resolve_initial_references("NameService"));

    // find the event channel reference and the Printer
    channel = EventChannelHelper.narrow(
        nc.resolve(nc.to_name("office_event.channel")));

    printer = PrinterHelper.narrow(
        nc.resolve(nc.to_name("Printer")));

    poa.the_POAManager().activate();
```

We initialize the ORB as usual, but because we have to provide a callback reference to the client as a pull supplier, we also need to initialize and later activate an Object Adapter. We use the Naming Service to retrieve the event channel and the Printer reference, so we first obtain a Naming Service reference as usual and then resolve the event channel name and the Printer name.

To connect to the event channel using the `connect_pull_consumer()` operation, we have to supply a callback reference to a Consumer object. It is legal to simply supply a nil CORBA Object here, which means that the supplier won't be able to call back. In our simple example, this would be sufficient, but we show how to do that nonetheless. Consequently, we have to create an object and activate the object. This is done using implicit activation:

```
    // create and implicitly activate the client
    pullConsumer =
(org.omg.CosEventComm.PullConsumer)new PrintClient()._this(orb);
```

Before we can connect to the event channel, we need references to the supplier admin object that let us select the appropriate supplier proxy for the event communication style that we want to use. Because we want to pull notifications from the channel ourselves, we have to obtain a proxy pull supplier reference. Finally, the client can be connected as a pull consumer.

```
        // get the admin interface and the supplier proxy
        consumerAdmin = channel.for_consumers();
        proxyPullSupplier = consumerAdmin.obtain_pull_supplier();

        // connect ourselves to the event channel
        proxyPullSupplier.connect_pull_consumer( pullConsumer );
    }
    catch (Exception e) {
        e.printStackTrace();
        System.exit(1);
    }
```

To make the Printer generate some event notifications, we call a couple of Printer operations. Let's print a few jobs and then try to cancel one of them again.

```
    // print a couple of jobs
    for( int i = 0; i < 5; i++ ) {
        try {
            System.out.println("Sending job, ID #" +
                printer.print("A test job", userid));
        }
        catch( OffLine ol ) {
            System.err.println("Printer found off line.");
            break;
        }
    }

    // wait a few seconds to give the printer a chance
    // to start printing
    try {
        Thread.sleep(7000);
    }
    catch( Exception e ) {}

    // try to cancel the last job
    int job = 4;
    try {
        System.out.println( "Canceling job ID #" + job );
        printer.cancel( job, userid );
    }
    catch( UnknownJobID uji ) {
        System.err.println( "Unknown job ID #" + job );
    }
```

```
catch( AlreadyPrinted ap ) {
    System.err.println( "Could not cancel, job #" +
                        job + " already printed" );
}
catch( org.omg.CORBA.NO_PERMISSION np ) {
     System.err.println( "Could not cancel, job #" +
                         job + ", no permission" );
}
```

After generating some printer activity, we can actually expect printer-generated notifications. Because we sent five jobs to the printer, let's see whether we can get a notification for each job. Note that we cannot rely on the exact number or the ordering of notifications without hard-coding assumptions about the Quality of Service (QoS) provided by the underlying Event Service implementation. The Event Service specification does not provide interfaces to determine or manage QoS features, so there is no portable way that an application can find out whether, for example, there is guaranteed 100% message delivery even in the presence of network errors and potentially failing suppliers or consumers. At the other extreme, the Event Service might provide only best-effort delivery and immediately give up on errors.

There is also no way to determine if and how long an event channel buffers event data. The length of a potential buffering interval is crucial for pull consumers, which need know how often they must check for available notifications. Obviously, the amount of buffer space allocated for a channel also has great impact on the scalability of an event channel—that is, how many messages and consumers it can handle before running out of resources. QoS properties like these are entirely up to implementations of the Event Service specification.

Our client does not depend on the exact number or the order of notifications that it receives and just tries to pull five notifications. After five attempts it simply disconnects from the channel and exits, regardless of how many notifications it actually received. To pull a notification from the channel without blocking if none is available, the client calls `try_pull()` on the proxy pull supplier. This call returns immediately, and the value of the Boolean out parameter indicates whether the result of the invocation contains valid event data.

```
for( int i = 0; i < 5; i++ ) {
    org.omg.CORBA.BooleanHolder bh =
        new org.omg.CORBA.BooleanHolder();

    try {
        // try to pull an event
        Any received = proxyPullSupplier.try_pull(bh);
        if( bh.value ) {
```

```
                // got an event, check if we know it
                if( received.type().id().equals("IDL:com/
wiley/compbooks/brose/chapter11/office/PrinterStatus:1.0"){

                    // extract the event data
                    PrinterStatus printerStatus =
                        PrinterStatusHelper.extract( received );
                    Status status = printerStatus.discriminator();
                    if( status == Status.PRINTED )
                        System.out.println("Printed job " +
                            printerStatus.the_job().job_id );
                    else if( status == Status.CANCELED )
                        System.out.println("Canceled job" +
                            printerStatus.the_job().job_id );
                }
                else
                    System.out.println("Unknown event.");
            }
            Thread.sleep(2000);
        }
        catch (Exception e) {
            e.printStackTrace();
        }
    }

    // disconnect and shutdown
    proxyPullSupplier.disconnect_pull_supplier();
    orb.shutdown(true);
}
```

To interpret the notification, the client must first check the type of the event data contained in the Any. If it was clear that only a single type of notifications can ever be transmitted via a certain channel this check could be omitted. After checking the event data type, the event data is extracted from the Any and printed to the screen. Before pulling the next notification, the client waits for two seconds.

## 11.5 The Notification Service

Event-based communication is an important alternative to invocation-based communication in CORBA. Its specification in the original Event Service has a number of shortcomings, however, which severely restrict its use and usefulness. These shortcomings are as follows:

**No filtering**. All notifications sent to an event channel will be forwarded to all consumers, with no chance to filter notifications before they are delivered. This can imply a considerable amount of useless traffic, if consumers want only certain notifications, and it is, in fact, a serious scalability limitation. The only way to limit the number of messages per channel is to set up different event channels. This means, however, that new channels must be created for every new kind of event in a system, and this poses a management problem if it is done in too fine-grained a fashion.

**No Quality of Service (QoS).** The Event Service does not define a concept of QoS. Neither does it provide the interfaces with which clients of the service could find out about the currently provided level of QoS or could configure channels for their specific requirements.

**No information about required or supplied notifications.** The Event Service does not allow consumers to find out about existing suppliers and the types of events they offer. Vice versa, suppliers cannot find out whether any consumers are connected to the channel that are interested in the event notifications the supplier offers. Again, network load could be reduced if suppliers sent only notifications that they know are required by consumers or if suppliers disconnected from a channel when they learn that interesting notifications are no longer offered.

**Unstructured event data.** Event data is wrapped into instances of the generic type Any, thus allowing arbitrary data to be passed easily. The lack of a standard notification format means that filtering notifications can be done only at the communication end-points and must be hard-coded into applications. Typed events as specified by the Event Service have proven to be too difficult to use and implement.

The Notification Service specification addresses all these problems and defines a much more flexible and scalable architecture for a notification infrastructure. In this section, we first give an architectural overview of the differences between the Event and Notification Services and explain some of the main interfaces. We then explain Structured Events, Filters, and Quality of Service administration in more detail.

## 11.5.1 Notification Service Architecture and Interfaces

The Notification Service architecture builds on the same concepts as the Event Service, but it both refines and extends them. The central concept, and the anchor point, is again the event channel. The Notification Service also supports the same push, pull, or mixed-mode communication styles. The overall architecture of the Notification Service is illustrated in Figure 11.7. All unlabeled interfaces to the event channel are proxy suppliers and consumers, as in the Event Service.

The first notable difference between the Event Service and the Notification Service is that the latter provides additional types of events. While it is still possible to send event data wrapped in Anys, the Notification Service allows you to transmit structured event messages and sequences of Structured Events. We will explain Structured Events and event sequences in more detail in the text that follows. Any-based communication is possible using either Event Service or Notification Service proxies. The Notification Service also supports Typed Events, which are not shown in Figure 11.7.

Another difference is that the Notification Service supports the flexible grouping of clients of its interfaces. As in the Event Service, an event channel allows you to choose whether you want to act as a supplier or a con-

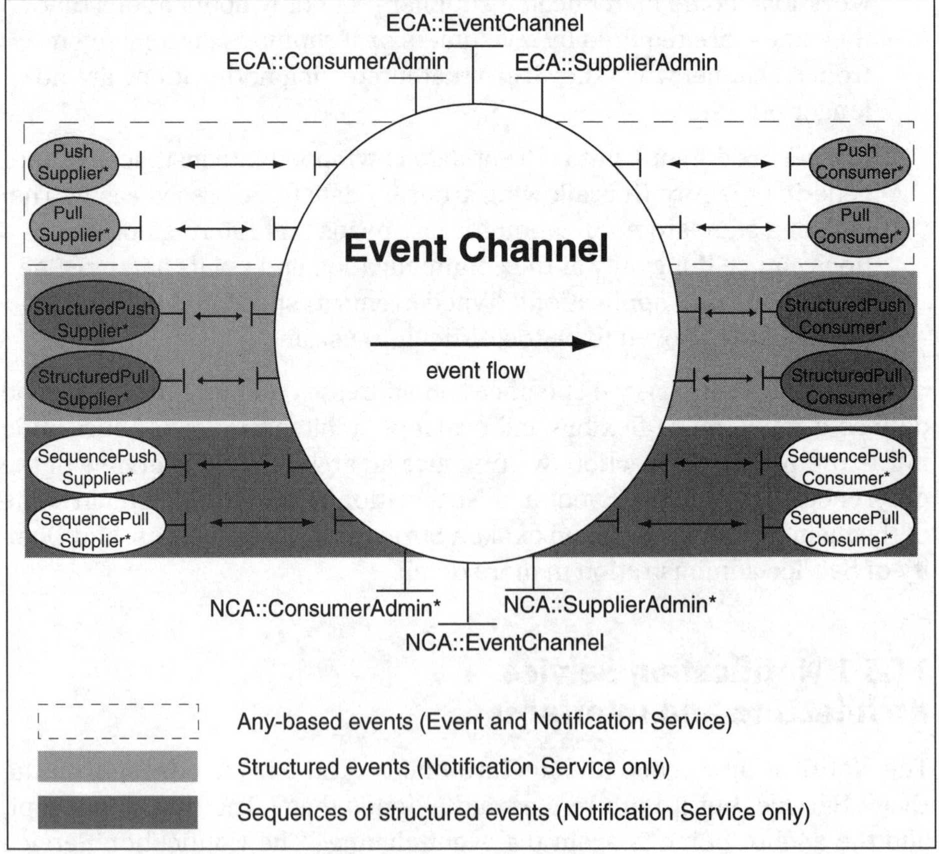


**Figure 11.7** Notification Service Architecture.

sumer of notifications, but unlike the Event Service it can manage more than just a single supplier or consumer admin interface. In Figure 11.7, this is denoted by an asterisk next to the Notification Service admin interface names.

The EventChannel interface is defined in module CosNotifyChannelAdmin and extends the original interface from CosEventChannelAdmin. Thus, existing Event Service clients can use the Notification Service event channel without noticing any difference.

```
module CosNotifyChannelAdmin {
    // Forward declarations
    interface ConsumerAdmin;
    interface SupplierAdmin;

    interface EventChannel :
            CosNotification::QoSAdmin,
            CosNotification::AdminPropertiesAdmin,
            CosEventChannelAdmin::EventChannel {

        readonly attribute EventChannelFactory MyFactory;
        readonly attribute CosNotifyChannelAdmin::ConsumerAdmin default_consumer_admin;
        readonly attribute CosNotifyChannelAdmin::SupplierAdmin default_supplier_admin;
        readonly attribute CosNotifyFilter::FilterFactory default_filter_factory;

        CosNotifyChannelAdmin::ConsumerAdmin new_for_consumers(
                            in InterFilterGroupOperator op,
                            out AdminID id );

        CosNotifyChannelAdmin::SupplierAdmin new_for_suppliers(
                            in InterFilterGroupOperator op,
                            out AdminID id );

        CosNotifyChannelAdmin::ConsumerAdmin get_consumeradmin ( in AdminID id )
            raises (AdminNotFound);

        CosNotifyChannelAdmin::SupplierAdmin get_supplieradmin ( in AdminID id )
            raises (AdminNotFound);

        AdminIDSeq get_all_consumeradmins();

        AdminIDSeq get_all_supplieradmins();

    }; // EventChannel
```

While every event channel has default supplier and consumer admin objects, any number of new admin objects can be created for every channel with the new_for_consumers() and new_for_suppliers() operations. Each of these operations returns an internal identifier for the new admin object. Existing admin objects can be retrieved from the channel using the get _consumeradmin() and get_supplieradmin() operations and providing the identifier as an argument.

In the same fashion, admin interfaces allow you to keep track of the proxies they create, and to retrieve individual proxies using these ProxyID identifiers, as shown in the ConsumerAdmin interface that follows. The parameter ctype required by the operations to obtain proxy references determines which kind of notifications, Any-based, Structured Events, or Sequence of Events, the proxy will be able to send or receive. The AdminLimitExceeded exception is raised if the number of proxies exceeds the administrative property MaxConsumers for this channel. The attributes MyOperator, priority_filter, and lifetime_filter will be explained in section 11.5.3.

```
interface ConsumerAdmin :
                    CosNotification::QoSAdmin,
                    CosNotifyComm::NotifySubscribe,
                    CosNotifyFilter::FilterAdmin,
                    CosEventChannelAdmin::ConsumerAdmin {

    readonly attribute AdminID MyID;
    readonly attribute EventChannel MyChannel;
    readonly attribute InterFilterGroupOperator MyOperator;
    attribute CosNotifyFilter::MappingFilter priority_filter;
    attribute CosNotifyFilter::MappingFilter lifetime_filter;
    readonly attribute ProxyIDSeq pull_suppliers;
    readonly attribute ProxyIDSeq push_suppliers;

    ProxySupplier get_proxy_supplier (
            in ProxyID proxy_id )
        raises ( ProxyNotFound );

    ProxySupplier obtain_notification_pull_supplier (
            in ClientType ctype,
            out ProxyID proxy_id)
        raises ( AdminLimitExceeded );

    ProxySupplier obtain_notification_push_supplier (
            in ClientType ctype,
            out ProxyID proxy_id)
        raises ( AdminLimitExceeded );

    void destroy();
}; // ConsumerAdmin
```

The Notification Service specification now defines a standard factory interface for event channels that uses the same identification scheme to allow clients to retrieve channels created by a factory.

```
    interface EventChannelFactory {

      EventChannel create_channel (
                       in CosNotification::QoSProperties initial_qos,
                       in CosNotification::AdminProperties initial_admin,
                       out ChannelID id)
        raises(CosNotification::UnsupportedQoS,
          CosNotification::UnsupportedAdmin );

      ChannelIDSeq get_all_channels();

      EventChannel get_event_channel ( in ChannelID id )
        raises (ChannelNotFound);

    }; // EventChannelFactory
  }; // CosNotifyChannelAdmin
```

The create_channel() operation accepts two sets of initial properties. The property types used in the specification are defined in the CosNotification module as sequences of name/value pairs.

```
  module CosNotification {
    typedef string Istring;
    typedef Istring PropertyName;
    typedef any PropertyValue;

    struct Property {
      PropertyName name;
      PropertyValue value;
    };
    typedef sequence<Property> PropertySeq;
    typedef PropertySeq QoSProperties;
    typedef PropertySeq AdminProperties;
    // ...
  };
```

The first argument of create_channel() defines a number of QoS properties for the entire channel, and the second argument defines initial administrative properties. The specification defines a number of standard property names and associated values that are understood by the Notification Service. Admin properties for event channels include the maximum number of suppliers and consumers that can be connected and the maximum event queue length. You will see some examples of QoS properties later in this section. It is possible to manage the QoS and Admin properties of a channel using operations in the CosNotification::QoSAdmin and the CosNotification::AdminPropertiesAdmin interface, respectively, both of which the EventChannel interface extends.

QoS properties that are managed at the channel level are effectively shared by all clients of the channel, both suppliers and consumers. Some situations may require setting properties for particular subsets of clients or even for individual clients. For this reason, the Notification Service also provides management operations for QoS properties at the level of admin objects and at the level of individual proxies. Consequently, the base interfaces for proxies, CosNotifyChannelAdmin::ProxyConsumer and CosNotifyChannelAdmin::ProxySupplier, and the base interfaces for admin objects, CosNotifyChannelAdmin::ConsumerAdmin and CosNotifyChannelAdmin::SupplierAdmin, all extend CosNotification::QoSAdmin.

This principle of grouping users of interfaces that share common properties is a major improvement over the original Event Service. It is also used when assigning filters. Filters are explained in detail in section 11.5.3. Like QoS properties, filters can be assigned to both proxies and admin objects, but not to the channel as a whole. The operations to set and remove filters are defined in the interface CosNotifyFilter::FilterAdmin.

```
module CosNotifyFilter {

  interface FilterAdmin {

    FilterID add_filter ( in Filter new_filter );

    void remove_filter ( in FilterID filter )
      raises ( FilterNotFound );

    Filter get_filter ( in FilterID filter )
      raises ( FilterNotFound );

    FilterIDSeq get_all_filters();

    void remove_all_filters();
  }; // FilterAdmin
}; // CosNotifyFilter
```

To make these operations available for proxies and admin objects, this interface is inherited by the proxy and admin interfaces in the same way as mentioned previously.

## 11.5.2. Structured Events

Structured Events were introduced to provide more strongly typed event messages that allow easier filtering. Because interfaces to process these notification structures and the Structured Event format are well defined and known to the Notification Channel, filtering and forwarding of notifications can be implemented more efficiently and without any need for user-defined interfaces as with Typed Events. Figure 11.8 depicts the format of Structured Events.

A Structured Event comprises a header and a body. The header is composed of a fixed and a variable portion and contains mandatory information about the event. The fixed portion of the event header is designed to be minimal so that lightweight notifications may be created that need not contain other information. It comprises the *domain_name* of a particular vertical industry domain, such as telecommunication or health care, the *type_name* for the type of event within the domain, such as ConnectionProblem or VitalSigns, and the *event_name* of the individual event instance. The IDL definition of a Structured Event is given in module CosNotification.

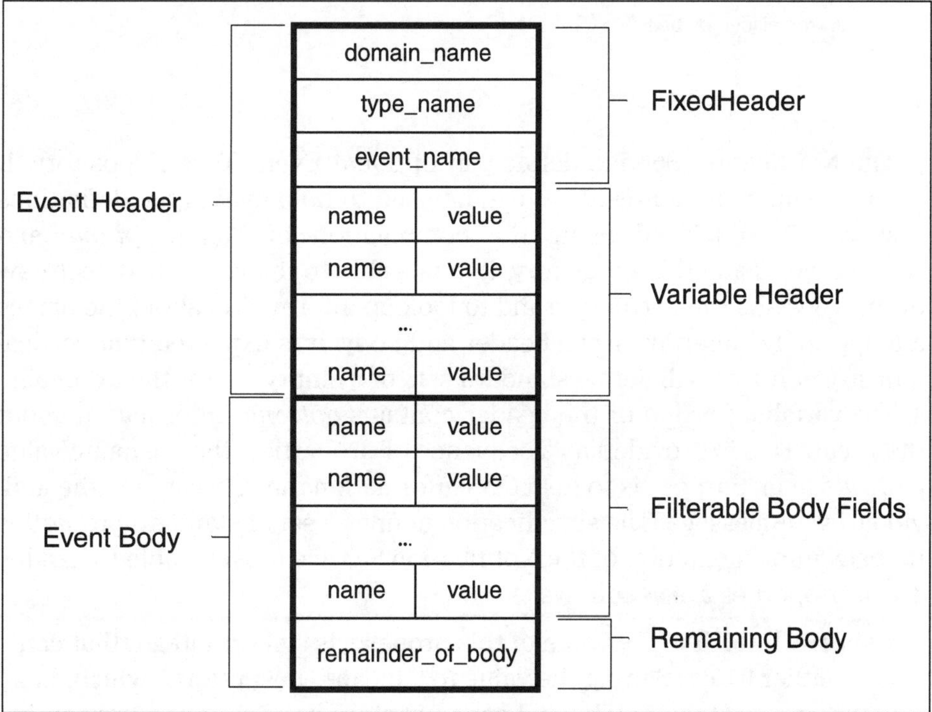


**Figure 11.8** Structured Event format.

```
module CosNotification {
   typedef PropertySeq OptionalHeaderFields;
   typedef PropertySeq FilterableEventBody;

   struct EventType {
      string domain_name;
      string type_name;
   };
   typedef sequence<EventType> EventTypeSeq;

   struct FixedEventHeader {
      EventType event_type;
      string event_name;
   };

   struct EventHeader {
      FixedEventHeader fixed_header;
      OptionalHeaderFields variable_header;
   };

   struct StructuredEvent {
      EventHeader header;
      FilterableEventBody filterable_data;
      any remainder_of_body;
   };
};
```

The Notification Service defines an optional Event Type Repository. If such a component is present, it can be used to hold event type definitions that can be retrieved using the combination of *domain_name* and *type_name*. Using this repository, it is possible to dynamically detect new event types and their structure and to look up information about the names and types of properties in the header and body. It is expected that vertical industry domains will define standard sets of event types for their domain.

The variable portion of the header contains *optional* information about the event. This is provided as a sequence of properties, that is, name/value pairs. Its main purpose is to hold QoS information that is related to the individual event message. The specification defines a set of standard properties that any implementation of the Notification Service must be able to handle. These properties are as follows:

**EventReliability.** The value of this property is a short integer that can be either 0 or 1. Setting the value to 0 means "best effort," which, in turn, means that the channel need not store notifications persistently to be able to retransmit them after failure. A value of 1 means "persistent" and causes the channel to store and retransmit the message after recovery, which is meaningful only if ConnectionReliability is also set to 1, as explained later.

**Priority.** The short integer value of this property indicates the relative priority of the event when compared to other events on the channel. Default is 0; both negative and positive values are possible.

**StartTime.** The associated value is of type TimeBase::UtcT and denotes the absolute time after which the notification may be delivered.

**StopTime.** The associated value is of type TimeBase::UtcT and denotes the absolute time after which the notification should be discarded.

**Timeout.** The TimeBase::UtcT value of this property denotes the relative time with respect to the time the channel received the notification, after which the notification should be discarded.

The body of a Structured Event is intended to contain the actual event contents. It is divided into a sequence of properties called *filterable data* and the *remaining body*. The filterable part of the notification should contain those fields of the notification on which consumers are most likely to base filter decisions. The rest of the event data is transmitted in the remaining body, which holds an Any.

Note that it is not required to use the fields of the notification structure in this way. It is perfectly legal to leave the filterable body of the notification structure empty and let filter decisions be based on the contents of the remaining body, even if that is likely to result in suboptimal throughput. Also, the complete contents of the notification could be inserted into optional header fields, leaving the body empty. The Structured Event layout was designed this way to make filtering straightforward and efficient, but it does not force you to use it that way.

### 11.5.3 Event Filtering

The main contribution of the Notification Service is the ability to filter event notifications. This allows consumers to subscribe to exactly those notifications they are interested in and to reduce message traffic. As pointed out in the previous section, filter objects can be assigned to proxies and/or admin objects. Filters come in two types.

The first kind of filters is of type CosNotifyFilter::Filter and affects the decision whether a notification is forwarded by a proxy. Filters of the second kind have the type CosNotifyFilter::MappingFilter and affect how the values of certain QoS properties are treated. We describe the first type of filters, which is the more important one, first.

### 11.5.3.1 Filters

Filter objects are added to a proxy or admin object using the add_filter() operation in the CosNotifyFilter::FilterAdmin. Here is the CosNotifyFilter::Filter interface.

```
module CosNotifyFilter {
   typedef long ConstraintID;

   struct ConstraintExp {
      CosNotification::EventTypeSeq event_types;
      string constraint_expr;
   };

   typedef sequence<ConstraintID> ConstraintIDSeq;
   typedef sequence<ConstraintExp> ConstraintExpSeq;

   struct ConstraintInfo {
      ConstraintExp constraint_expression;
      ConstraintID constraint_id;
   };

   typedef sequence<ConstraintInfo> ConstraintInfoSeq;

   interface Filter {

      readonly attribute string constraint_grammar;

      ConstraintInfoSeq add_constraints ( in ConstraintExpSeq constraint_list )
         raises (InvalidConstraint);

      ConstraintInfoSeq get_constraints( in ConstraintIDSeq id_list )
         raises (ConstraintNotFound);

      ConstraintInfoSeq get_all_constraints();

      void remove_all_constraints();

      void destroy();

      boolean match ( in any filterable_data )
         raises (UnsupportedFilterableData);

      boolean match_structured ( in CosNotification::StructuredEvent filterable_data )
         raises (UnsupportedFilterableData);
```

```
        boolean match_typed ( in CosNotification::PropertySeq filterable_data )
            raises (UnsupportedFilterableData);

        CallbackID attach_callback ( in CosNotifyComm::NotifySubscribe callback );

        void detach_callback ( in CallbackID callback)
            raises ( CallbackNotFound );

        CallbackIDSeq get_callbacks();
    }; // Filter
```

Each filter encapsulates a set of constraints on notifications. These constraints are specified in a declarative constraint language, which is denoted by the constraint_grammar attribute. A Notification Service implementation may provide arbitrary constraint languages, but it is required to provide at least the default filtering constraint language. We will give an impression of this language in a minute, but let's first look at how filters are created.

While it is possible to implement user-defined filters, the normal way of obtaining filters is from a filter factory. A reference to a filter factory can be obtained from the default_filter_factory attribute of an event channel. The create_filter() operation requires a string argument that defines for which constraint grammar the filter will accept constraints. The string name of the default constraint grammar is "EXTENDED_TCL", where TCL stands for "Trader Constraint Language" because the default constraint language is an extension of the constraint language defined in the Trading Service specification. If the filter factory does not support the required grammar, an InvalidGrammar exception is raised.

Mapping filters are created in a similar way but require an additional default value. The reason for this value will become clear when we explain mapping filters below.

```
    interface FilterFactory {

        Filter create_filter (in string constraint_grammar)
            raises (InvalidGrammar);

        MappingFilter create_mapping_filter (
                            in string constraint_grammar,
                            in any default_value)
            raises (InvalidGrammar);

    }; // FilterFactory
};
```

Once a filter is created, constraints can be added to it using the add_constraints() operation. Individual constraint expressions consist of a sequence of event types to which the constraint applies and a string in the constraint language that expresses the constraint on events of this type. The event type sequence for a constraint can be left empty, in which case it is applied to events of all types. Event types can also be specified using the wildcard symbol '*'.

A constraint is a predicate on a notification. Whenever a notification arrives at a proxy, the constraints of all filters that are associated with it or the admin object that is responsible for the proxy are evaluated. This evaluation is triggered by calling match() for Any-based events, match_structured() for Structured Events, or match_typed() for Typed Events on the filter object. Within a filter, individual constraints are combined using OR semantics, so the match operation returns TRUE if at least one filter constraint is satisfied.

The same semantics applies to the results of different filters associated with the same proxy. When multiple filters apply, their constraints will be evaluated until one of them is satisfied. If such a filter is found, the matching operation returns TRUE; otherwise, it returns FALSE. When the results of filters associated with a proxy and those of filters associated with its admin object are combined, the actual Boolean operator depends on the value of the MyOperator attribute in the admin object that is set on creation of the admin object. It is thus possible to use either AND or OR as the logical operator for the combination of results of filters from these different sets.

Constraints can refer to variables that are bound to parts of the event message. In the default constraint language, variable names can refer to all parts of the current notification, which is denoted by `$`. Variables within the constraint string are resolved by trying to match the variable name with a property name in either the *variable_header* or *filterable_data* portion if the notification is a Structured Event. As an example, the constraint `"$.priority > 3"` can be evaluated to TRUE if the notification contains a property of that name with an integer value that is larger than 3. This constraint is shorthand for either `"$.header.variable_header(priority)"` or `"$.header.filterable_data(priority)"`. Note how the syntax treats a sequence of name/value pairs as an associative array indexed by property names and thus allows it to conveniently specify constraints on individual properties in a sequence.

### 11.5.3.2 Mapping Filters

Unlike filters, mapping filters are not used to decide whether an event message is to be forwarded or discarded by a proxy. Rather, they help the receiver of a notification automatically "adjust" two specialized properties that, in turn, can influence the delivery policies of other filters. The two properties recognized by mapping filters are event priority and lifetime.

The reason for introducing mapping filters is that these properties are set by the sender of a notification, but the receiver might have different opinions on what would be appropriate priority and lifetime values for the event. Mapping filters give consumers control over these properties. The MappingFilter interface is structurally very similar to the Filter interface, so we don't reproduce it here. Unlike filters, mapping filters can be attached only to receiving proxies and admin objects, that is, to objects of subtypes of ConsumerAdmin or ProxySupplier. To this end, these interfaces both provide updatable attributes for mapping filters that will be applied to the priority or lifetime properties of notifications. You have already seen these attributes in the ConsumerAdmin interface in section 11.5.1.

When a notification is received by a proxy that has mapping filters associated with it or its managing admin object, the proxy calls the mapping filter's match() operation. The mapping filter then tries to apply its constraints to the notification. If one of these constraints matches, the proxy will use the default value of the mapping filter as the new value for the priority or lifetime property of the event. This default value was supplied when creating the mapping filter using a filter factory, as explained earlier.

## 11.5.4 Quality of Service

The original Event Service specification left QoS issues as an implementation choice, but the Notification Service provides standard interfaces to control the QoS characteristics of notification delivery. We have already seen that QoS properties are represented as name/value pairs and can be set at different levels or scopes. To summarize, the CosNotification::QoSAdmin interface and its subtypes let you define QoS properties at the channel scope, at the scope of admin objects for suppliers and consumers, and for individual proxy suppliers and consumers. Finally, as shown in section 11.5.2, it is possible to set QoS characteristics for individual Structured Event messages.

The QoS properties set at the different levels form a hierarchy that determines how properties can override other properties and which properties are actually applied. As you would expect, the more specific settings override more general ones in case of conflict. For example, the QoS characteristics of a proxy supplier may override those of the consumer admin that created the proxy, or a message-level property can override a channel-level one.

Note that there may be cases where overriding a QoS property may not work because, for example, the selection of best-effort delivery at the channel level may have resulted in the use of an implementation that is not capable of honoring a property setting that requires more reliable delivery in an individual event message. Also note that it is not possible to globally and reliably determine end-to-end QoS because notifications have to pass through proxies that may have user-defined QoS properties. Thus, end-to-end QoS cannot be guaranteed without user cooperation.

The Qos properties defined by the Notification Service are the following:

**EventReliability** and **ConnectionReliability.** The Notification Service treats the reliability of connections to clients and the reliability of notification delivery as separate issues. Both properties can take on the numeric values 0 ("BestEffort") or 1 ("Persistent"). If both properties are set to BestEffort, no delivery guarantees are made. If ConnectionReliability is set to Persistent, the Notification Service will maintain information about connected clients persistently and thus be able to reestablish connections after failure and recovery of client processes. It will not store and retransmit messages, however, unless EventReliability is also set to Persistent. The combination of EventReliability=Persistent and ConnectionReliability=BestEffort is meaningless and need not be supported by an implementation.

**Priority**. This is a numeric value indicating the relative priority of event messages on a channel, 0 by default. Ordering of notification messages can be based on priority.

**StartTime**, **StopTime**, and **Timeout**. As explained previously for Structured Events, these values determine the period an event notification is considered valid by a channel.

**MaxEventsPerConsumer**. This is an upper bound for the number of messages queued for a single consumer. The default value is 0, which means that no limit is imposed.

**OrderPolicy.** The value of this property defines in which order notifications are delivered. The following values are supported: AnyOrder, FifoOrder, PriorityOrder, DeadlineOrder. With DeadlineOrder, the Notification Service will try to deliver those messages first that will time out the soonest. PriorityOrder is the default value for this property.

**DiscardPolicy.** This property defines which notifications should be discarded in case internal resource limits are reached. Possible values are AnyOrder, FifoOrder, LifoOrder, PriorityOrder, and DeadlineOrder.

**MaximumBatchSize.** This property is meaningful only for consumers of sequences of Structured Events. It limits the number of notifications that will be delivered within each sequence. The default value is 1.

**PacingInterval.** Like MaximumBatchSize, this property applies only to consumers of sequences of Structured Events. Its value is of type TimeBase::TimeT and defines the maximum period of time that the channel will collect individual notifications into a sequence.

Not all the properties listed here are supported at all levels of QoS administration. Figure 11.9 summarizes the QoS properties defined by the Notification Service and the different levels at which these settings are supported.

| Property | Per-Message | Per-Proxy | Per-Admin | Per-Channel |
|---|---|---|---|---|
| EventReliability | X | | | X |
| ConnectionReliabilty | | X | X | X |
| Priority | X | X | X | X |
| StartTime | X | | | |
| StopTime | X | | | |
| Timeout | X | X | X | X |
| StartTimeSupported | | X | X | X |
| StopTimeSupported | | X | X | X |
| MaxEventsPerConsumer | | X | X | X |
| OrderPolicy | | X | X | X |
| DiscardPolicy | | X | X | X |
| MaximumBatchSize | | X | X | X |
| PacingInterval | | X | X | X |

**Figure 11.9** QoS properties.

# 11.6 A Notification Service Example

As an example of using the Notification Service, we modify the Event Service example from section 11.4. Imagine that the event channel used for printer events also carries event notifications created by the central coffee machine and your department's machine pool. The coffee machine emits notifications whenever it is switched on or off and whenever a cup of coffee is poured. While this does not directly tell you how much coffee is left, it does allow you to estimate your chances of finding some coffee left. The machine pool generates notifications whenever equipment like laptop computers or portable overhead beamers is taken from or returned to the pool.

Using the same event channel for even a limited variety of event types like this does create some traffic (even though it won't be that much for this scenario) and also means that consumers will have to sift through a lot of messages to find those in which they are really interested. In the example, we will refine our Print Client to illustrate using Structured Events. We will also show how to attach a filter to its supplier proxy such that only printer-type event notifications get delivered. In fact, we are interested only in notifications that signal that a job has finished printing or has been canceled.

The application logic remains the same as in the original example, but the initialization of and connection to the event channel and the generation of notifications differ. Let's first look at the supplier side.

## 11.6.1 Implementing a Structured Event Supplier

The `PrinterImpl` class for this example is implemented in package `notification`. The implementation class now imports classes from packages that implement Notification Service modules rather than their Event Service equivalents. Also, `PrinterImpl` now extends `StructuredPushSupplierOperations` rather than just `PushSupplierOperations`. This is necessary because we want to use Structured Events rather than notifications that are contained in Anys.

```
package com.wiley.compbooks.brose.chapter11.notification;

import org.omg.CosNotification.*;
import org.omg.CosNotifyComm.*;
import org.omg.CosNotifyChannelAdmin.*;

import org.omg.CosNaming.*;
```

```
import org.omg.CosNaming.NamingContextPackage.*;
import org.omg.CORBA.Any;
import org.omg.CORBA.ORB;
import org.omg.PortableServer.*;

import java.util.Hashtable;
import com.wiley.compbooks.brose.chapter11.office.*;
import com.wiley.compbooks.brose.chapter11.office.PrinterPackage.*;

class PrinterImpl
    extends PrinterPOA
    implements StructuredPushSupplierOperations {

    private NotificationChannel channel;
    private SupplierAdmin supplierAdmin ;
    private StructuredProxyPushConsumer pushConsumer;
    private ORB orb;
    private POA poa;

    private Hashtable queue;
    private int jobId;
    private int printIdx;
    private boolean offline;
    private boolean disconnected;
    private PrintThread printThread;
```

The inner class `JobInfo` is implemented just as in the first version and is omitted here. Again, the event channel is looked up using the Naming Service. If none is found, we create one. We did not do that in the original example because the Event Service did not have a standardized factory interface for event channels. Because the Notification Service provides this interface, we try to look up a factory and use it.

```
    static public void main (String argv[]) {

        EventChannel channel = null;
        org.omg.CORBA.ORB orb = org.omg.CORBA.ORB.init(argv, null);

        try {
            // initialize POA, get naming and event
            // service references
            POA poa = POAHelper.narrow(
                orb.resolve_initial_references("RootPOA") );

            NamingContextExt nc = NamingContextExtHelper.narrow(
                orb.resolve_initial_references("NameService"));

            try {
                // look up event channel
                channel = EventChannelHelper.narrow(
```

```
                nc.resolve(nc.to_name("office_event.channel"))
            );
        }
        catch( NotFound nf ){
            // if none is available, look up a factory . . .
            EventChannelFactory factory =
                EventChannelFactoryHelper.narrow(
                    nc.resolve(nc.to_name("CosNotification"))
                );

            // ...and create a channel
            org.omg.CORBA.IntHolder idHolder =
                new org.omg.CORBA.IntHolder();

            Property[] qos = new Property[0];
            Property[] adm = new Property[0];
            channel =
                factory.create_channel(qos, adm, idHolder);
            nc.bind( nc.to_name("office_event.channel"),
                channel);
        }
```

Using the reference to an event channel factory, we create a channel object. We do not specify any QoS or administrative properties at this level. The Printer object is created as before, and any remaining initializations are delegated to its `connect()` method.

```
        // create a Printer object, implicitly activate it,
        // and advertise its presence
        PrinterImpl printer =
            new PrinterImpl( channel, orb, poa );
        printer.connect();

        org.omg.CORBA.Object printerObj =
            poa.servant_to_reference( printer );
        nc.bind( nc.to_name("Printer"), printerObj);

        // wait for requests
        poa.the_POAManager().activate();
        orb.run();
    }
    catch (Exception ex) {
        ex.printStackTrace();
    }
}
```

The `connect()` method retrieves the supplier admin and obtains a proxy push consumer. Because we don't need any admin-specific settings, we just use the channel's default supplier admin object. To obtain a proxy push consumer, we need to provide an argument of type ClientType that determines for what kind of event communication the proxy is created. We want Structured Events, so we supply the corresponding client type value and an integer holder for the out argument. This argument will hold an identifier of the new proxy consumer. When the proxy reference is returned we create a CORBA object reference as a call-back reference to the printer and connect it to the proxy.

```
public void connect() {

    StructuredPushSupplierPOATie thisTie =
        new StructuredPushSupplierPOATie( this );

    // get admin interface and proxy consumer
    supplierAdmin = channel.default_supplier_admin();
    ClientType ctype = ClientType.STRUCTURED_EVENT;
    org.omg.CORBA.IntHolder proxyIdHolder =
        new org.omg.CORBA.IntHolder();

    try {
        pushConsumer =
            StructuredProxyPushConsumerHelper.narrow(
               supplierAdmin.obtain_notification_push_consumer(
                                                   ctype, proxyIdHolder)
            );
    }
    catch (AdminLimitExceeded ex) {
        System.err.println("Could not get consumer proxy,
                    maximum number of proxies exceeded!");
        System.exit(1);
    }

    // connect the push supplier
    try {
        pushConsumer.connect_structured_push_supplier(
            StructuredPushSupplierHelper.narrow(
                 poa.servant_to_reference( thisTie ))
            );
    }
    catch( Exception e ) {
        e.printStackTrace();
    }
    // initialize "queue" and start printer thread
    queue = new Hashtable();
    printThread = new PrintThread();
}
```

Now that the printer is prepared to send notifications, let's look at how Structured Events are created. Again, we look only at the printer's `cancel()` method as the creation of other printer event notifications works exactly the same. The first part of this method is identical to the same method in the original example.

```
public void cancel(int id, String uid )
    throws UnknownJobID, AlreadyPrinted {

    if( id > jobId || id < 0)
        throw new UnknownJobID();

    if( id < printIdx )
        throw new AlreadyPrinted();

    JobInfo job = (JobInfo)queue.get( new Integer( id ));
    if( job != null ) {
        if( !job.userId.equals( uid ))
            throw new org.omg.CORBA.NO_PERMISSION();
        queue.remove( new Integer( id ));
        System.out.println("-CANCELED JOB #" + id  + "-");

        if( generateEvents() ) {
            // create a structured event
            StructuredEvent cancelEvent =
                new StructuredEvent();

            // set the event type and name
            EventType type =
                new EventType("office", "printer");
            FixedEventHeader fixed =
                new FixedEventHeader(type, "canceled");

            // complete header date
            Property variable[] = new Property[0];
            cancelEvent.header =
                new EventHeader(fixed, variable);
```

To set up the Structured Event, we have to insert a proper header first. As explained in section 11.5.2, the header comprises a fixed and a variable part. The fixed part is initialized with the event type and name, whereas we leave the variable part empty.

To finish the event set-up, we now need to supply an event body, which is made up of the filterable data and the remaining body. For the cancel event, the relevant information is the job ID and the job's user ID, both of which can be used for filtering. We create corresponding properties and insert these into the `filterable_data` part of the event body. The remaining body contains just an empty Any.

```
                // set filterable event body data
                cancelEvent.filterable_data = new Property[2];
                Any jobAny = orb.create_any();
                jobAny.insert_long( job.jobId );
                cancelEvent.filterable_data[0] =
                    new Property("job_id ", jobAny );

                Any userAny = orb.create_any();
                userAny.insert_string( job.userId );
                cancelEvent.filterable_data[1] =
                    new Property("user_id ", userAny );

                cancelEvent.remainder_of_body = orb.create_any();

                try {
                   pushConsumer.push_structured_event(cancelEvent);
                }
                catch( org.omg.CosEventComm.Disconnected d ) {
                   // uncritical, ignore
                }
            }
        }
    }
```

## 11.6.2 Implementing a Structured Event Consumer

As before, the consumer is implemented in a class `PrintClient`, but like the printer implementation, this class now resides in the `notification` package and extends the skeleton class for pull consumers of Structured Events.

```
package com.wiley.compbooks.brose.chapter11.notification;

import org.omg.CosNotification.*;
import org.omg.CosNotifyComm.*;
import org.omg.CosNotifyFilter.*;
import org.omg.CosNotifyChannelAdmin.*;

import org.omg.CosNaming.*;
import org.omg.CORBA.Any;

import com.wiley.compbooks.brose.chapter11.office.*;
import com.wiley.compbooks.brose.chapter11.office.PrinterPackage.*;

import org.omg.PortableServer.*;

public class PrintClient
    extends StructuredPullConsumerPOA {
```

```
public void disconnect_structured_pull_consumer() {
    System.out.println("Disconnected!");
}

public void offer_change(EventType added[],
                         EventType removed[]){
}
```

The method `disconnect_structured_pull_consumer()` needs to be implemented by this class to allow the event channel to call back when it disconnects. The `offer_change()` method implements an operation of this name in the CosNotifyComm::NotifyPublish interface. It is called by the channel to inform consumers of changes in the event types offered on the channel so that a consumer may either prepare for new events or, if the notifications it is interested in are no longer offered, disconnect from the channel.

The only other method in this class is `main()`, which initializes the client, retrieves references, and associates a filter with its supplier proxy. Again, we use the structured variants of any consumer and supplier interfaces because we use Structured Events.

```
static public void main  (String argv[]) {

    EventChannel channel = null;
    FilterFactory filterFactory = null;
    Filter filter = null;
    ConsumerAdmin consumerAdmin;
    StructuredProxyPullSupplier  proxyPullSupplier = null;
    StructuredPullConsumer structuredPullConsumer;
    Printer printer = null;
    String userid = "MeMyselfAndI";

    if( argv.length > 0 )
        userid = argv[0];

    // initialize ORB
    org.omg.CORBA.ORB orb = org.omg.CORBA.ORB.init(argv, null);
    POA poa = null;

    try {
        // inititialize POA
        poa = POAHelper.narrow(
            orb.resolve_initial_references("RootPOA"));

        // get naming service reference
        NamingContextExt nc =
            NamingContextExtHelper.narrow(
                orb.resolve_initial_references("NameService"));
        // find the event channel reference and the Printer
```

```
channel = EventChannelHelper.narrow(
    nc.resolve(nc.to_name("office_event.channel")));

printer = PrinterHelper.narrow(
    nc.resolve(nc.to_name("Printer")));

poa.the_POAManager().activate();

// create and implicitly activate the client
structuredPullConsumer =
  (StructuredPullConsumer)new PrintClient()._this(orb);
```

So far, the only difference between the Event Service `PrintClient` and this one is that this implementation is a `StructuredPullConsumer` rather than just a `PullConsumer`. We now retrieve a consumer admin from the channel by calling the `default_consumer_admin()` method, which does not create a new admin but delivers the default admin object for consumers. Using this reference, we create a `StructuredProxyPullSupplier`. This works exactly the same as for the `StructuredProxyPullConsumer` that we created on the supplier side. Via the proxy, we connect the client's call-back reference to the channel.

```
// get the admin interface and the supplier proxy
consumerAdmin  = channel.default_consumer_admin();

proxyPullSupplier =
   StructuredProxyPullSupplierHelper.narrow(
       ConsumerAdmin.obtain_notification_pull_supplier(
           ClientType.STRUCTURED_EVENT,
           new org.omg.CORBA.IntHolder()
       )
   );

// connect ourselves to the event channel
proxyPullSupplier.connect_structured_pull_consumer(
    structuredPullConsumer );
```

We are now ready to create a filter and initialize it. To create a filter, we retrieve the channel's default filter factory and call `create_filter()` on it, asking for a filter that accepts constraints in the default constraint language.

```
// get the default filter factory
filterFactory = channel.default_filter_factory();
if( filterFactory == null ) {
    System.err.println("No default filter Factory!");
}
else {
```

```
            filter =
                filterFactory.create_filter("EXTENDED_TCL");
```

We then create an array of event types to which the filter should be applied, which in this case has just a single element that denotes printer events. A constraint expression consists of this set of event types and an expression string in the constraint language. Our simple constraint expression just requires the event name field in the event header's fixed portion to be the string `"printed"`. The constraint is then added to the filter by calling `add_constraints()`, which takes an array of constraints with just that single element. Finally, the filter can be added to our supplier proxy. Note that it would be just as possible to add the filter to our consumer admin, but this filter would then affect any consumer that uses this admin object to connect to the channel.

```
            // specify event types
            EventType [] eventTypes = new EventType[] {
                new EventType("office", "printer") };

            // create constrain expression
            ConstraintExp constraint =
                new ConstraintExp ( eventTypes,
                    "$.header.fixed_header.event_name == 'printed'"
                );

            // add constraint expression to filter
            filter.add_constraints(
                new ConstraintExp[]{ constraint } );

            // attach filter to the proxy
            proxyPullSupplier.add_filter(filter);
        }
    }
    catch (Exception e) {
        e.printStackTrace();
        System.exit(1);
    }
```

As in the original example, we call a few operations on the printer to make it generate some notifications.

```
    // print a couple of jobs
    for( int i = 0; i < 5; i++ ) {
        try {
            System.out.println("Sending job, ID #" +
                printer.print("A test job", userid));
```

```
        }
        catch( OffLine ol ) {
            System.err.println("Printer found off line.");
        }
    }

    // wait a sec . . .
    try {
        System.out.println("Sleep . . . ");
        Thread.sleep(7000);
    }
    catch( Exception e)
    {}

    // try to cancel the last job
    int job = 4;
    try {
        System.out.println("Cancelling job ID #" + job );
        printer.cancel( job, userid );
    }
    catch( UnknownJobID ol ) {
        System.err.println("Unknown job ID #" + job );
    }
    catch( AlreadyPrinted ap) {
        System.err.println("Could not cancel, job #" +
                                job + " already printed");
    }
    catch( org.omg.CORBA.NO_PERMISSION np) {
        System.err.println("Could not cancel, job #" +
                                    job + ", no permission");
    }

    int eventsReceived = 0;
    for( int i = 0; i < 5; i++ ) {
        org.omg.CORBA.BooleanHolder bh =
            new org.omg.CORBA.BooleanHolder();

        try {
            // try to pull an event
            StructuredEvent event =
              proxyPullSupplier.try_pull_structured_event(bh);

            if( bh.value ) {
                System.out.println("got structured event.");
                FixedEventHeader fixed_header =
                    event.header.fixed_header;
                System.out.println("\t\"" +
                    fixed_header.event_name + "\":" +
                    fixed_header.event_type.domain_name + "." +
                    fixed_header.event_type.type_name
```

```
                );

                Property properties [] = event.filterable_data;
                System.out.println("\t" + properties[0].name +
                   ":" + properties[0].value.extract_long());

                System.out.println("\t" + properties[1].name +
                   ":" + properties[1].value.extract_string());
            }
            Thread.currentThread().sleep(2000);
        }
        catch (Exception e) {
            e.printStackTrace();
        }
    }

    // disconnect and shut down
    proxyPullSupplier.disconnect_structured_pull_supplier();
    orb.shutdown(true);
    }
}
```

Again, we don't want to block the client if no event notifications are available, so we use a variant of `try_pull()` to pull notifications. For Structured Events, this operation is called `try_pull_structured_event()`. Because we know that only those printer event messages will pass our filter that signal that a job was printed, we need not perform any more checks on the received message. Rather, we directly access the relevant properties in the `filterable_data` part of the event body and print their values.

## 11.7 Java Events and CORBA

So far we have looked at events only from the CORBA perspective. Java also has events, as you will know if you have programmed with the Java AWT or Swing libraries or with JavaBeans. These Java events rely on Java method invocations. There is another, more generic Java event mechanism that is part of the Beans component model. This is known as InfoBus. InfoBus notifications are self-describing data objects. The delivery of an event notification is controlled by its type and value. Finally, the Java Message Service (JMS) specification defines a Java API to messaging infrastructures for the enterprise that also allows event communication. In this section we investigate how these concepts fit into the CORBA world and how they compare to the Notification Service.

## 11.7.1 Java Events

One of the core features of Java AWT, Swing, or JavaBeans are events. The event model is based on a subset of the package `java.util`. The relevant classes are `EventObject`, the interface `EventListener`, and the exception `TooManyListenersException`:

```
public class EventObject extends Object {

     // constructor - source is the object the event occurred in
     public EventObject( Object source );

     // getSource() returns the object the
     // event occurred initially upon
     public Object getSource()
}
```

Both GUI elements and JavaBeans use events as a convenient mechanism to propagate state change notifications from a source object to a set of listener objects. These notifications are mainly focused on but not limited to events occurring in the context of user interfaces, for example, mouse events and keyboard actions. They can also be used to signal changes in JavaBeans properties to interested listeners.

A source object creates and "fires" an event to a number of event listeners. The notification itself is an object, and its class should extend the class `EventObject`, which is the abstract base class for all Java event notifications. The listener objects implement the interface `EventListener`. Firing the event results in the source objects invoking a method on each of the listener objects.

The event object encapsulates the data associated with the event and provides methods to access it. The event targets implement a method that has an event object as its parameter. This method is invoked by an event source object on all the event targets it wants to notify. Figure 11.10 illustrates the firing of an event. Java events work only within the boundaries of a JVM.

We have used the Java event model in all the examples in this book that include GUI components. Typically, we have one class that implements the interface `ActionListener`, which is an extension of the interface `EventListener`. We have other objects such as buttons that are the event sources. We then invoke `addActionListener()` on the event source object to register the event listener. The implementations of the `ActionListener` interface contain the method `actionPerformed()`, which is invoked when one of the event sources fires an event. The events `ActionListeners` deal

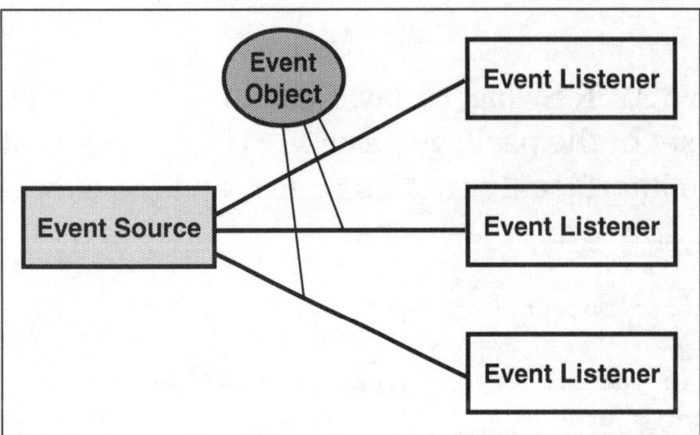


**Figure 11.10** Java events.

with are of the type `ActionEvent`, which is an extension of the class `EventObject` (indirectly via the class `AWTEvent`).

## 11.7.2 InfoBus

InfoBus is an extended Java event mechanism for JavaBeans. InfoBus enables components to exchange data asynchronously. It differs from the basic Java event model in two major ways:

- Producers and consumers of notifications are decoupled; they have to know only a common InfoBus.
- The delivery of a notification is determined by a name convention for data items.

Like plain Java events, InfoBus is designed only for communication between components running in the same JVM.

InfoBus was originally developed by Lotus and is now part of the JavaBeans component architecture. InfoBus has the following major activities: establishing membership of the InfoBus, listening for InfoBus notifications, rendezvousing with consumers, and providing access to data items.

### *11.7.2.1 Membership*

A Java component connects to the InfoBus. This requires the programmer to implement the Java interface `InfoBusMember`, obtain an instance of an `InfoBus` object, and associate the `InfoBusMember` with the `InfoBus`. The last step is also known as *joining*.

The `InfoBus` class has the following static methods to create an instance of the InfoBus:

```
public static synchronized InfoBus get( Component c );
public static synchronized InfoBus get( String busname );
```

Once you have implemented and created an `InfoBusMember` object, you call `join()` on the `InfoBus` object to associate the member with the bus. This is shown in Figure 11.11.

```
public synchronized void join( InfoBusMember member );
```

### *11.7.2.2 Listening for InfoBus Events*

Once an object that is an InfoBus member has joined an InfoBus, the member can listen to InfoBus notifications via the normal Java event model. There are two kinds of events, one for data consumers and one for data producers. Of course, a component can be a data producer as well as a data consumer. There are listener classes and methods to add those listeners for each kind of event. The interface `InfoBus` defines the following methods for adding and removing listeners:

```
public class InfoBus {
   public void addDataProducer( InfoBusDataProducer producer );
   public void addDataConsumer( InfoBusDataConsumer consumer );
   public void removeDataProducer( InfoBusDataProducer producer );
   public void removeDataConsumer( InfoBusDataConsumer consumer );
}
```

The two interfaces, `InfoBusDataProducer` and `InfoBusDataConsumer`, are extensions of the class `InfoBusEventListener`, which add methods specific to producers and consumers, respectively. We have a closer look at these interfaces next.

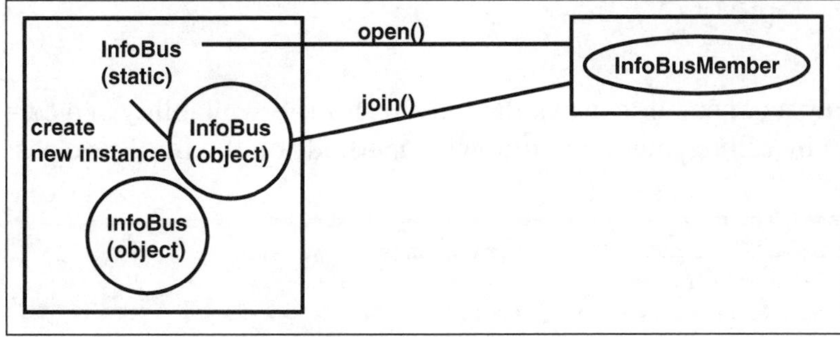


**Figure 11.11** Establish InfoBus connections.

### 11.7.2.3 Rendezvous

The rendezvous has three phases. A producer *announces* the availability of a data item. A consumer is sent this announcement. Alternatively, a consumer may ask about certain data, for example, when it has just started up and has not been able to listen to announcements. In either case, the consumer finds out about the availability of a data item and requests it. The code that follows demonstrates these three phases.

A producer calls the method `fireItemAvailable()` on the InfoBus:

```
public class InfoBus {
   public void fireItemAvailable( String dataItemName,
      InfoBusDataProducer producer );
}
```

This method creates an event of type `InfoBusItemAvailableEvent`, and the InfoBus sends it to all registered data consumers. Sending the event means that InfoBus invokes the method `dataItemAvailable()` on each registered `InfoBusDataConsumer`.

```
public interface InfoBusDataConsumer extends InfoBusEventListener {
   public void dataItemAvailable( InfoBusItemAvailableEvent e );
}
```

The `InfoBusDataConsumer` interface must be implemented by an application programmer. The implementation of the method `dataItemAvailable()` handles the event. Typically that would involve checking whether the announced data item is of interest to the consumer. If so, the consumer requests the data item by calling `requestDataItem()` on the object `InfoBusItemAvailableEvent`.

```
public interface InfoBusItemAvailableEvent extends InfoBusEvent {
   public DataItem requestDataItem( string itemName,
      InfoBusDataConsumer consumer );
   }
```

Alternatively, a consumer can ask the InfoBus for the availability of a certain data item by calling one of the following methods on the InfoBus class.

```
public class InfoBus {
    public DataItem findDataItem( String dataItemName,
        DataFlavor[] flavors,
        InfoBusDataConsumer consumer );
    public DataItem findDataItem( String dataItemName,
        DataFlavor[] flavors,
```

```
        InfoBusDataConsumer consumer,
        InfoBusDataProducer producer );
    public DataItem[] findMultipleDataItems( String dataItemName,
        DataFlavor[] flavors,
        InfoBusDataConsumer consumer );
  }
```

The InfoBus creates and fires an event object of type `InfoBusItem RequestEvent`.

```
  public interface InfoBusItemRequestEvent extends InfoBusEvent {
    InfoBusItemRequestEvent( string itemName,
      InfoBusDataConsumer consumer );
    public void setDataItem( DataItem item );
    public DateItem getDataItem();
}
```

Firing the event means invoking the method `dataItemRequested()` on all data producers registered with the InfoBus.

```
  public interface InfoBusDataProducer extends InfoBusEventListener {
    public void dataItemRequested( InfoBusItemRequestEvent e );
    ...
  }
```

Either way, at the end the consumer has obtained a data item it can now access, as shown in Figure 11.12.

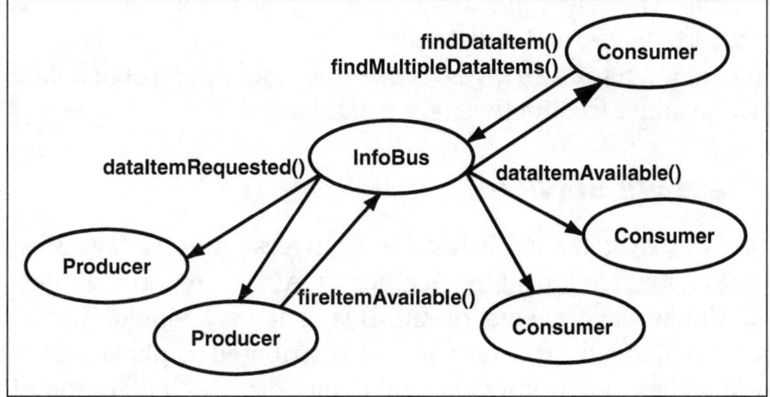


**Figure 11.12** InfoBus rendezvous.

#### 11.7.2.4 Access to Data Items

A data access object implements the interface `DataItem`. This interface is implemented by all data items. It provides some generic methods, for example, for firing events about changes to a data item. Methods to manipulate the data in a data item are provided by various subclasses and depend on the kind of data they contain.

The interface `ImmediateAccess` gives access to the item in the form of a string or an object. It also allows the programmer to set the value of the data item. The difference between `getValueAsString()` and `getPresentationString()` is that the former returns the raw data, while the latter returns the data in a formatted way; for example, a string representing currency data may include the characters "$", ".", and ",".

```
public interface ImmediateAccess extends DataItem {
   public String getValueAsString();
   public Object getValueAsObject();
   public String getPresentationString();
   public void setValue(ImmediateAccess newValue )
      throws InfoBusAccessException;
}
```

The interface `CollectionAccess` gives access to data that is a collection of items. This interface is extended by the interface `ArrayAccess` or `KeyedAccess` depending on the type of the collection. The interface `ArrayAccess` is intended for array-like collections, while the interface `KeyedAccess` is for hash tables and dictionaries.

The interface `RowSetAccess` is provided for data items corresponding to tables in relational databases. The interface provides methods for accessing meta-data, for example, to obtain the number of columns or the name and type of a column. There are also methods to access rows and columns and to retrieve, insert, delete, and update rows.

Finally, the interface `DbAccess` gives a consumer more control of a data item. It allows a consumer to directly query a database.

### 11.7.3 Java Message Service

In late 1998, Sun Microsystems published the first version of its Java Message Service (JMS) specification. JMS specifies an API for enterprise messaging systems. Unlike Java events or InfoBus, but very similar to the CORBA Notification Service, it is targeted at distributed applications in potentially heterogeneous environments, and it supports the integration of legacy software into loosely coupled event communication systems.

While a number of commercial implementations of the specification are available, it should be stressed that JMS specifies only a messaging model and the interface to a messaging system, but not the messaging system itself and its transport details. In particular, it does not define the wire protocol for messages, a message type repository, and administration APIs. JMS is also liberal about how much of its specification must be implemented to claim conformance. The reason is that JMS is intended to be used as the Java API for a number of existing, widely deployed message queueing systems, which should be easy to adapt to JMS. In this respect, JMS plays the same role for messaging systems that JDBC plays for databases.

JMS defines a number of message formats and two messaging styles, which are called *domains* in JMS parlance. Finally, it specifies a filtering mechanism called *selector*. We will provide only a high-level overview of JMS here and briefly look at each of these points in turn.

### 11.7.3.1 JMS Messages

The structure of JMS messages is similar to that of Structured Events. They consist of a fixed header, a number of optional properties that allow filtering, and a body. The main difference between Structured Events and JMS messages is that JMS headers contain 10 fields and not 3, and that JMS bodies have 1 of 5 predefined formats, whereas there is a single type of body for Structured Events, which is an Any. The different message body types define specific accessor and modifier methods for their contents data.

The fixed fields in the JMS message header contain information about the message destination, its delivery mode, a message ID, a time stamp, a correlation ID, a ReplyTo destination, a redelivered flag, a message type, an expiration time, and a priority.

The use of message properties to allow filtering is again very similar to the Notification Service, the main difference being that JMS does not recognize any QoS properties on messages and thus defines only one set of message properties, not two. Selecting QoS properties for the message is done via extra parameters in the `publish()` or `send()` methods with which suppliers can send notifications. Only two such properties are supported in this case, message priority and event reliability ("persistence").

The five message body types defined by JMS are as follows:

- **StreamMessage**—a message body containing a stream of primitive Java values

- **MapMessage**—a message body containing name/value pairs
- **TextMessage**—a String, supporting, for example, messages in XML
- **ObjectMessage**—a generic message body that consists of a Serializable Java object
- **BytesMessage**—an uninterpreted stream of bytes

### 11.7.3.2 Message Selectors

Message Selectors are strings containing selection expressions and work like Notification Service Filters in that only those messages that match are delivered. The main differences are the selector language, the fact that selectors cannot evaluate the message body, and the lack of an equivalent concept for mapping filters.

The JMS selector message is a subset of the SQL 92 conditional expression syntax, and in many respects it is similar to the Notification Service's default constraint language. The JMS specification does not, however, allow for other selector languages.

### 11.7.3.3 JMS Messaging Domains

JMS distinguishes two messaging styles called domains: the point-to-point domain and the publish/subscribe domain. The specification does not require an implementation to support both domains, but it must support at least one of them.

In the point-to-point domain, suppliers and consumers communicate via *queues*. As you would expect from a queue, messages are FIFO-ordered. A message can be received by only a single consumer and is then removed from the queue. It is possible, though, to browse the messages in the queue without removing them. The point-to-point domain model does not actually qualify as event communication according to our definition in section 11.1 because it is not many-to-many. This is the style of communication supported in traditional message queuing systems.

In the publish/subscribe domain, communication is one-to-many as in the Notification Service. Suppliers send messages to named *topics* rather than to queues. Topics may be assembled into hierarchies such that one topic becomes a subtopic of another. The intended effect is that all messages sent to a subtopic such as "Dickens" will also be received by consumers of the more general topic like "Novelist." The JMS specification does not define any interfaces for managing topics but leaves this to the implementations.

## 11.7.4 Comparison of the Various Event Models

The notification delivery mechanisms we have looked at so far can be categorized by various aspects of the communication model. The most important distinction is between purely local communication, as provided by the Java event approach or InfoBus, and distributed notification delivery, as supported by JMS and the Notification Service. We don't consider the basic Event Service here.

With respect to decoupling, Java events do not actually qualify as an event system because suppliers and consumers are, in fact, more tightly coupled than with regular invocations. Note that sending a notification blocks until all listeners have returned and that both event listeners and suppliers need to know each other.

Filtering of notifications is supported by all systems except Java events, as are certain QoS properties. The CORBA Notification Service provides more flexibility and control than any of the other systems and is also language independent. InfoBus requires both suppliers and consumers to be JavaBeans, while JMS implementations may provide limited language interoperability. JMS could even be used as a simplified and thus perhaps more convenient API to the Notification Service, but any non-Java clients would need to rely on a number of conventions if keeping the JMS communication model was desired.

## 11.7.5 Distributing Java Events with CORBA

The Java event model supports only local event communication, but in some cases your distributed application may need to address remote event listeners using this style, possibly because of the way JavaBeans are integrated or your GUI is designed. Therefore, the Java event approach is put on top of the CORBA communication model, allowing event data to cross JVM boundaries. The interfaces and conventions of the Java framework are kept wherever possible. Figure 11.13 illustrates this approach.

We define some IDL that corresponds to the Java classes and interfaces used for transmitting notifications. The Event IDL struct corresponds to the data part of the `EventObject` class. This struct is mapped to a Java interface by the IDL compiler. The IDL interface EventListener corresponds to the JavaBeans interface `EventListener`, and the IDL interface EventSource provides management operations corresponding to those of the class `EventObject`.

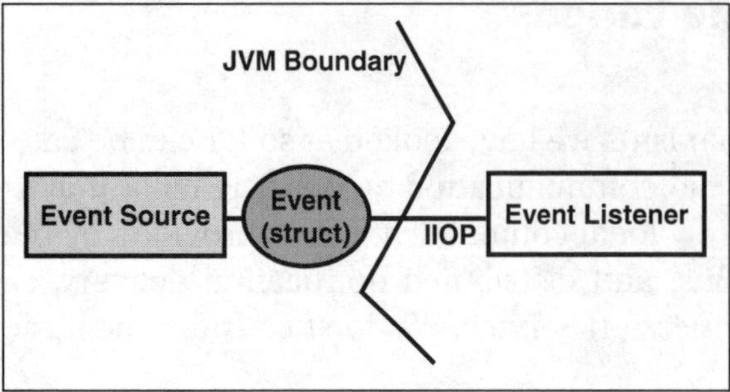


**Figure 11.13** Distributing Java events with CORBA.

```
module com {
...
module chapter11 {
module JavaEventType {

    exception ListenerAlreadyKnown{};
    exception UnknownListener{};

    struct Event {
        Object source;
        string str;
    };

    interface EventListener {
        oneway void handle_event( in Event event );
    };

    interface EventSource {
        void addEventListener( in EventListener listener )
            raises(ListenerAlreadyKnown);
        void removeEventListener( in EventListener listener )
            raises(UnknownListener);
};};};};};
```

Whenever the event source creates an event it notifies the registered listeners by invoking the IDL operation handle_event(). The object reference of the source is now a CORBA interoperable object reference instead of the Java object reference. Instead of remodeling the Java event class as a CORBA struct, you can directly deliver Java event objects using RMI/IIOP and the object-by-value feature.

# Security

Security is an important issue for most distributed applications, in particular when deployed over the Internet. Security is not a single, well-defined concept, however, but stands for a collection of issues with complex interrelations. In particular, there is no such thing as absolute security. Rather, security must be carefully defined in terms of concrete security requirements for applications and their environments. Security measures usually incur costs, in terms of increased complexity of administration or degraded performance or usability. Thus, planning security measures always has to include weighing these against their costs.

Securing resources is not a playground for homegrown approaches if you have real assets to protect. Even seemingly simple security protocols exhibit surprisingly subtle flaws, so we strongly recommend not to "roll your own" but to rely only on established security technology. This chapter does not show how security can be achieved in a given system in a comprehensive manner, but it does present the security technology that you will have to use in Java/CORBA environments. For a general introduction to security we refer you to Bruce Schneier, *Secrets and Lies* (Wiley 2000).

Some security measures are usually in effect in the environment even independent of the requirements of your applications. The security restrictions imposed by browsers on applets and those imposed by firewalls on network traffic represent obstacles that need to be accommodated to make CORBA applications work. We cover applet security issues in section 12.1 and firewalls in section 12.2. To meet security requirements within CORBA applications, IIOP can be secured using SSL (section 12.3). The CORBA Security Service (section 12.4) addresses more advanced security requirements.

## 12.1 Applet Security Issues

Java virtual machines included in Web browsers that execute applet byte code usually install security managers to restrict the capabilities of code compared with the full JVM specification. The restrictions are in access to local resources, in particular the local file system, but also printers and other devices as well as networking. Applets are allowed to open network connections only to the host from which they were downloaded. These restrictions are known as *applet sandboxing.*

From a CORBA point of view, these network restrictions create a major problem. CORBA provides location transparency, which means that as long as a client holds an IOR it can invoke operations on the object that it denotes, regardless of its location, but applets may open network connections only to the host from which they were downloaded. Applet sandboxing breaks CORBA location transparency.

A solution to this problem is to put a forwarder on the Web server, as shown in Figure 12.1. This forwarder program is also known as the IIOP gateway. The ORB will transparently send all operation invocations from CORBA-enabled applets loaded from this Web server to the IIOP gateway instead of to the actual object. The IIOP gateway acts as a proxy for the object, sending the invocation to the object and passing the reply back to the applet.

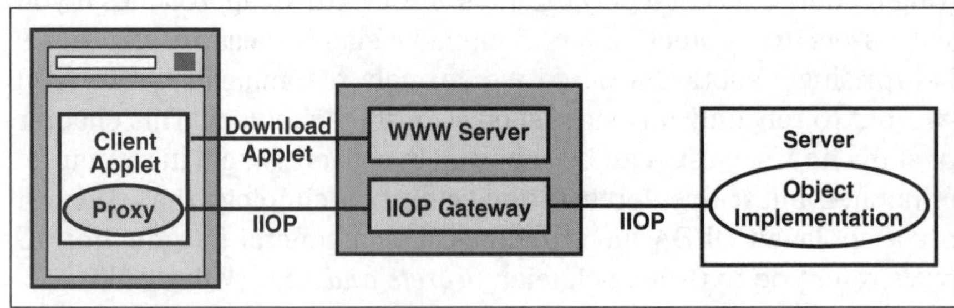


**Figure 12.1** Restoring CORBA location transparency using an IIOP gateway.

The concept of an IIOP gateway is implemented in a number of Java ORBs. Visigenic's Gatekeeper provides IIOP gateway functionality (among other things), as do Iona's Wonderwall and JacORB's Appligator. Without such a gateway, Java applets will not be able to use references to objects that do not reside on the Web server host.

An alternative approach to overcoming applet sandboxing is to use signed applets, that is, applets that are downloaded in Jar files with a trusted digital signature. If users agree to grant an applet the requested privileges, the applet can open direct connections to servers. Signed applets could also be granted privileges for printing and accessing the local file system. These privileges are granted based on the identity of the applet signer and require client-side policy files that determine which signature is granted which privileges. We do not explain applet signing in any more detail here. Please refer to your browser documentation and the documentation provided by Sun Microsystems for more information

## 12.2 Firewalls

Firewalls are components that protect a collection of resources, an *enclave*, by restricting network access. In a sense, they exercise access control at a coarse to medium granularity. Firewalls can impose restrictions based on the origin or destination of the traffic or the type of protocol, or the restrictions can be application-specific. Firewalls can provide some basic level of protection if they are properly administered, but they should not be exclusively relied on for comprehensive protection in high-risk environments. Rather, they should be used to complement more flexible mechanisms such as those provided by the CORBA Security Service.

Firewalls create a complex problem for CORBA applications deployed on the Internet. The most general scenario is illustrated in Figure 12.2. The server-side objects are protected by inbound firewalls and clients can be behind client-side, outbound firewalls. Note that larger organizations might employ multiple levels of nested firewalls on both sides.

The problem is complex because IIOP messages must pass both inbound and outbound firewalls. Standard firewall products are not well suited to IIOP because they are mostly configured statically based on host addresses and port numbers, but it is hard to predict in advance which hosts and ports will be involved in an invocation because port assignment is dynamic in CORBA.

The OMG has recognized the problem and adopted a CORBA Firewall Security Specification (OMG Document orbos/98-05-04) that is now part of

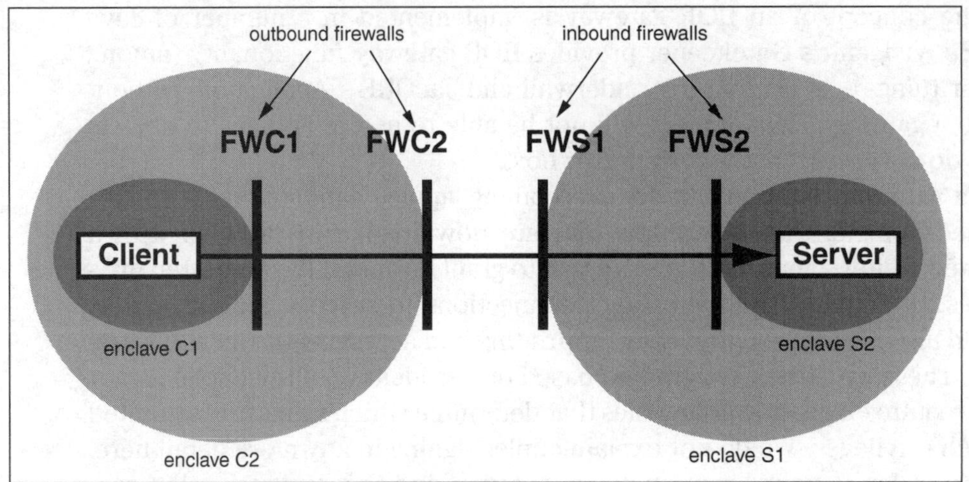


**Figure 12.2** Generic firewall scenario.

the CORBA 3 suite of specifications. We investigate this topic by looking into several aspects of the firewall problem. First we look at client-side and server-side firewalls and give an introduction to their different kinds of operation. We then present the approach taken in the Firewall Specification.

A client-side or *outbound* firewall is typically put in place by a company to restrict employee access to the Internet. One reason to do this is to prevent usage of insecure external services or to hide internal machine addresses. Internet service providers also have firewalls in place in some cases. These usually restrict the Internet access of their subscribers to certain protocols, for example, HTTP and NNTP. Some further restrictions may also apply, for example, an NNTP gateway that allows access only to selected news groups.

A server-side or *inbound* firewall is set up to restrict external accesses to internal resources. Inbound and outbound firewalls for an enclave can be combined to run on the same hardware or even in the same process, but they are functionally independent and can thus also be separated from each other.

## 12.2.1 Types of Firewalls

Firewalls operate using different mechanisms. The most common mechanisms are the filtering of packets based on transport-level data and filtering based on application data. The former does not require a firewall to understand a packet's contents while the latter does involve interpreting it. We explain each of these mechanisms in the following subsections. Note that firewall installations are typically combinations of these different types.

### 12.2.1.1 Packet Filtering

Packet filtering can be done at various levels in the protocol stack. Decisions are made based on data in the protocol header. In the simplest case, when filtering is done at the IP layer, firewalls base their decisions on the origin and destination addresses of IP packets and are closely coupled with routers. To implement a particular policy, the firewall sets restrictions on the router. Note that the networking restrictions imposed by browsers on applets are actually just an instance of a very simple outbound packet filter that disallows all accesses other than to the applet host.

Current firewalls mostly operate on the transport level, so origin and destination of packets can be described in terms of the IP addresses of individual hosts and/or subnets, the transport type (TCP, UDP) and the TCP or UDP port numbers. We refer to these firewalls as *packet filtering firewalls* or just *packet filters* for short. Sometimes they are also referred to as *chokes*. Figure 12.3 illustrates the mechanism of a packet filtering firewall. Typically such firewalls allow policies stated in rules such as these:

- Allow all kinds of packets, but only to this IP address and this port.
- Allow incoming traffic only from the specified IP subnets.

This scheme works for any protocol built on top of TCP and is thus also applicable to HTTP and IIOP. To enable cooperation between a CORBA application and both outbound and inbound filtering firewalls, CORBA servers must run on specific ports that are accepted by *all* packet filters. VisiBroker, for example, allows servers to start with the option `-DOAport`, which makes the server listen on the specified port. This forces all client connections to the server to use this port. This port, however, can be used only by CORBA objects residing in one process. If a second process hosting CORBA objects is started on the same machine it will find this port already in use.

It might be necessary to make packet filters permeable for the traffic related to a CORBA application. Destination IP addresses and port numbers can sometimes be enabled on filtering firewalls, especially when the clients of an application are in the same organization as the application provider. Then, the provider can negotiate a security policy for the client-side firewall with systems administrators. This can extend to situations where organizations have clients in multiple locations and use the Internet for communication between them. Other organizations providing a service to a finite set of

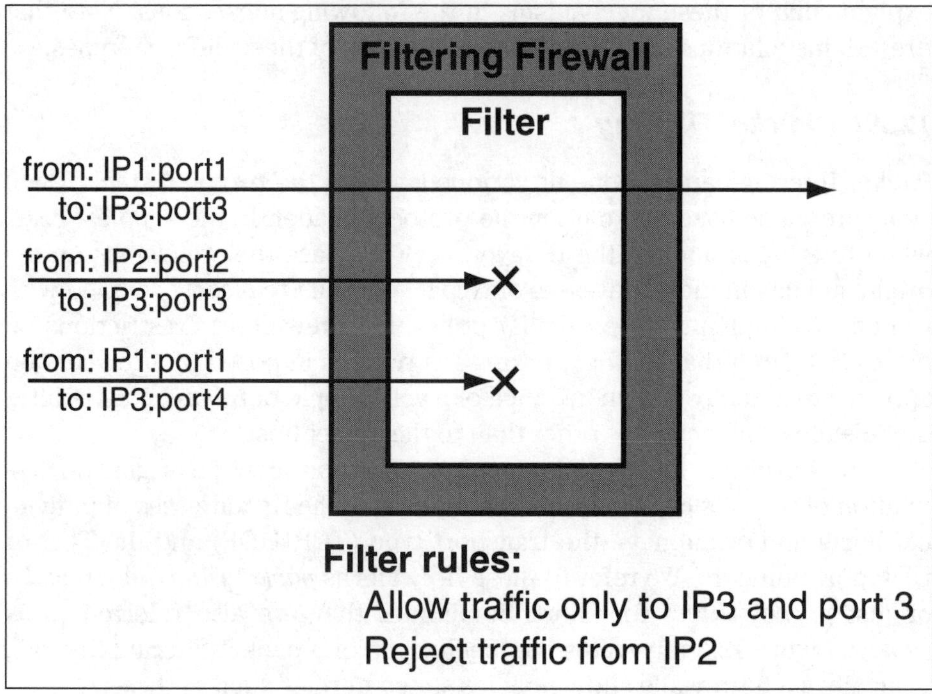


**Figure 12.3** Packet filtering firewalls.

known customers can require that these customers modify their client-side firewall policy.

In many situations it is not possible to configure all involved firewalls to allow IIOP traffic to pass to its intended target addresses, however. We present approaches to work around these restrictions after explaining the second type of firewalls.

The main reason why packet filtering firewalls should not be relied on exclusively for controlling access to resources is that the information on which they base filtering decisions is unreliable—packets and connections are usually not authenticated, and network addresses and port numbers in IP and TCP headers can be forged by skilled attackers. Allowing packets to pass based on their origin addresses thus can prevent only simple attacks.

The lack of authentication and encryption in the lower layers of the protocol stack has led to the definition of an Internet standard called IPSEC. It can be used both with today's version of the IP protocol and its potential successor, IPv6. It is not yet widely used on the Internet, though. Thus, the only way that firewalls can make *reliable* decisions today is by employing authentication in higher protocol layers themselves.

### 12.2.1.2 Application-Level Gateways

Simple packet filters leave the application contents of packets uninterpreted. Application-level gateway firewalls do interpret the contents and make decisions based on this interpretation. Thus, the software running on the gateway must understand individual protocols. Gateways can be installed on a single *bastion host* that handles all gateway functions, or they can be a set of computers and programs that divide this labor between them and handle different individual protocols on different machines.

Gateway firewalls are typically combined with packet filters such that the gateways are the only hosts in the protected domain that can be externally accessed. There are too many possible combinations for many different environments to explain them here, so we sketch just one such combination in Figure 12.4.

Figure 12.4 focuses on inbound traffic. External access to the enclave is limited by a dual-homed packet filter that blocks all incoming traffic except for packets addressed to the gateway G. In particular, host H is not directly reachable. In Figure 12.4, the gateway handles just a single protocol XY and rejects all messages for other protocols. To allow XY communication

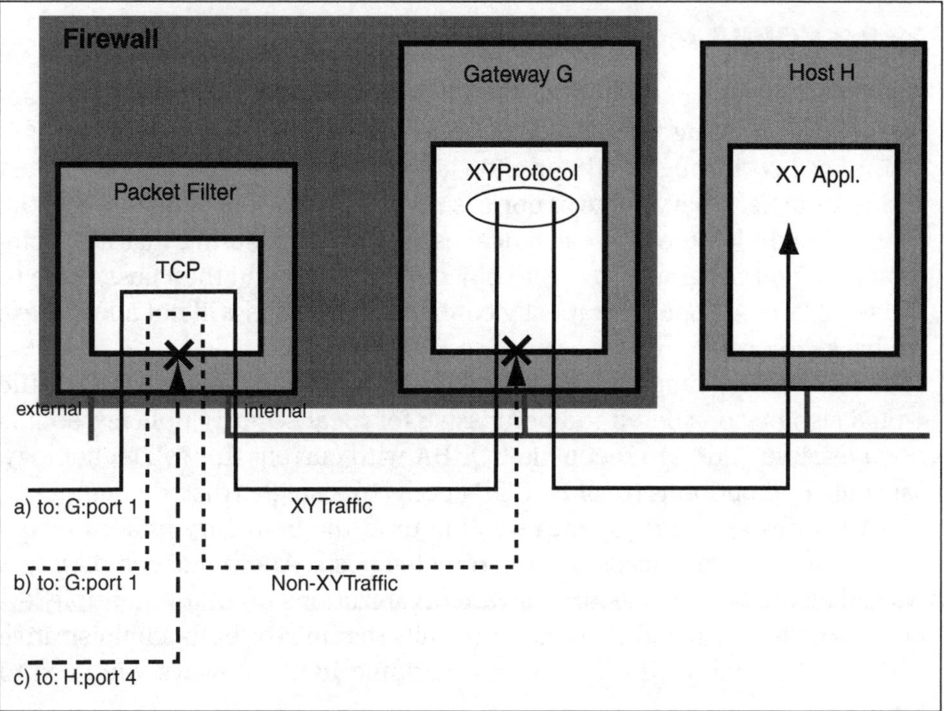


**Figure 12.4** Gateway firewalls.

between host H and the outside world, the gateway must be able to map incoming traffic to internal hosts, which depends on characteristics of the actual protocol.

Gateway firewalls are often configured to act as *proxies*, and sometimes the terms *proxy* and *gateway* are used interchangeably. A proxy is a gateway that acts as a client to a server and as a server to a client, thereby shielding each communication end-point from direct contact with the other and also hiding the real end-point addresses. Gateways can also sometimes be operated in a pass-through mode such that clients and servers appear to be communicating directly and are not aware of the gateway. Typically, proxy firewall products come with HTTP (Web), FTP (file transfer), NNTP (news), and SMTP (e-mail) gateways. A popular technology to build TCP proxy firewalls is NEC's SOCKS library, which can also be used to implement firewalls that authenticate connections.

There are also IIOP gateways including Inprise's Gatekeeper and Iona's Wonderwall, but these gateways are not yet integrated into firewall vendors' offerings, and it is unclear how quickly integrated IIOP gateways will become widely available. Currently, IIOP gateways must be used as supplements to other firewall products.

## 12.2.2 CORBA and Firewalls

Given the dynamic nature of IIOP, it is hard or impossible to configure standard packet filtering firewalls, both inbound and outbound, to allow IIOP traffic to flow through without allowing arbitrary network accesses. Just opening the necessary range of ports is usually not sufficient because not all of them might be known in advance, especially considering that it is common for client programs to create object references and then pass these to the server for call-backs. Statically configured firewalls will not allow these callbacks to occur.

In most cases, simply opening additional ports for inbound TCP traffic would also be considered too permissive for local security policies, so it is not a feasible option to reconcile CORBA with current firewall technology. The only real option is to allow IIOP access to a single trusted component, an IIOP gateway, which operates within or at the boundary of a protected enclave and forwards messages to protected hosts. Additional complexity is caused by the fact that security-aware organizations often use multiple levels of both inbound and outbound firewalls that mirror both administrative and trust boundaries. In these cases, multiple IIOP gateways will need to cooperate.

We first present a very simple approach to work around the problem,

HTTP tunneling. In general, HTTP tunneling is inadequate for a number of reasons, so the OMG Firewall Specification does not even consider it but describes an IIOP gateway component called GIOP proxy. We explain GIOP proxies and finally point out some problems with this approach.

### *12.2.2.1 HTTP Tunneling*

A common workaround for restrictions imposed by outbound firewalls is HTTP tunneling. Outbound firewalls are typically set up to prevent the use of external services that are considered insecure by local administrators, but they usually allow HTTP connections. HTTP tunneling means that an IIOP request is enclosed in an HTTP envelope and sent via the HTTP protocol. The receiving HTTP server must be able to understand these special HTTP requests. It takes the IIOP request out of the HTTP envelope and makes the real IIOP request on the target objects. Figure 12.5 illustrates the idea behind HTTP tunneling. In this way, any client that can load a CORBA applet using HTTP can make invocations using HTTP calls to the same machine.

VisiBroker and OrbixWeb support HTTP tunneling in the ORB's applet library. Their respective gateways, Gatekeeper and Wonderwall, act as special HTTP servers.

HTTP tunneling suffers all the shortcomings of HTTP, which we discussed in Chapter 1, "Benefits of Java Programming with CORBA." Also, HTTP tunneling disables callbacks into the applet because there is usually no HTTP/IIOP gateway installed on the client side that can respond to an HTTP request by extracting an IIOP request and forwarding it to the callback object. Moreover, HTTP tunneling is not readily usable for non-applet clients. For applets, *all* requests are redirected to the host from which the applet was downloaded, but for regular clients extra configuration is required to know which requests need to be redirected and to which HTTP server.

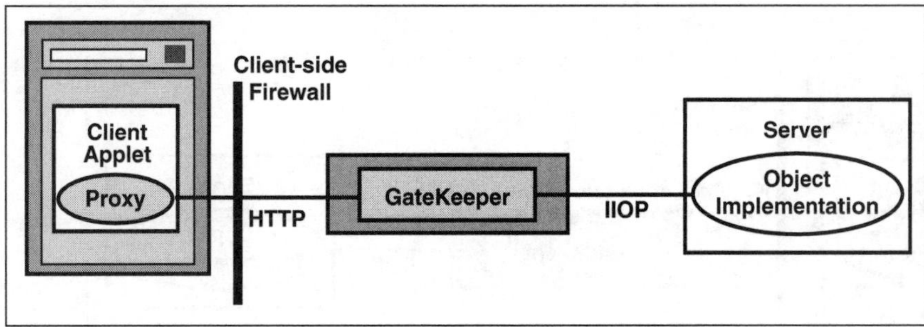


**Figure 12.5** HTTP tunneling with Gatekeeper.

One other attempt can be made to overcome client-side firewalls without using HTTP tunneling. If the firewall is blocking requests only to certain ports (for example, all ports but 80—the HTTP port—or 443—the SSL port), the gateway can be configured to listen on port 80. This prevents an ordinary HTTP server from running on the same machine. The applet, however, needs to be loaded from this machine.

Figure 12.6 shows a solution to this dilemma. There are two hosts. One provides normal Web services; the other machine hosts the VisiBroker Gatekeeper listening on port 80. Because the Gatekeeper is a functionally complete HTTP server, the applet can be loaded via the Gatekeeper. Similarly, port 443 could be used for IIOP traffic, in particular when using IIOP over SSL, as explained later in this chapter.

In the general case, both these approaches fall short of integrating CORBA with common firewalls and provide only a client-side workaround for the restrictions imposed by browsers and outbound firewalls.

### *12.2.2.2 GIOP Proxies*

We have repeatedly mentioned IIOP gateways that receive and forward IIOP messages and act as proxies. Because IIOP is just GIOP over TCP, the terms IIOP gateway and GIOP proxy actually refer to the same functionality. We use the term GIOP proxy to specifically refer to the OMG-specified functionality and the term IIOP gateway to refer to the general approach.

Figure 12.7 illustrates nested enclaves with multiple firewalls on the client and server side and a callback from the server to the client. All firewalls here are assumed to contain IIOP gateways and to function as both outbound and inbound firewalls.

When IIOP gateways are used, client ORBs must know how to contact the gateway. In particular, they need to know the first outbound firewall and the first inbound firewall on the server side. In Figure 12.7, the first outbound firewall is FWC1, and the first inbound firewall is FWS1. These firewalls may then

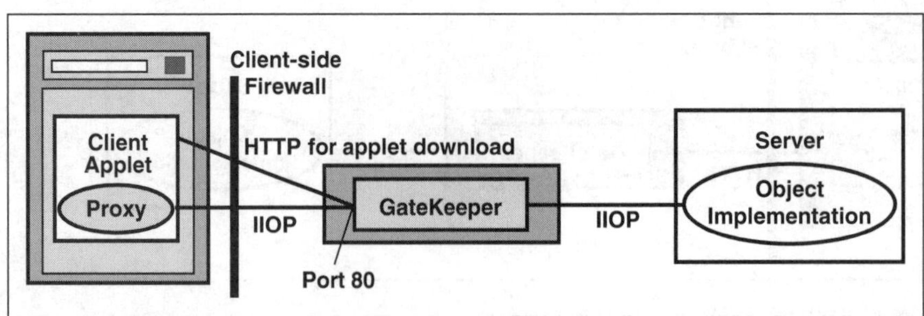


**Figure 12.6** IIOP via port 80.

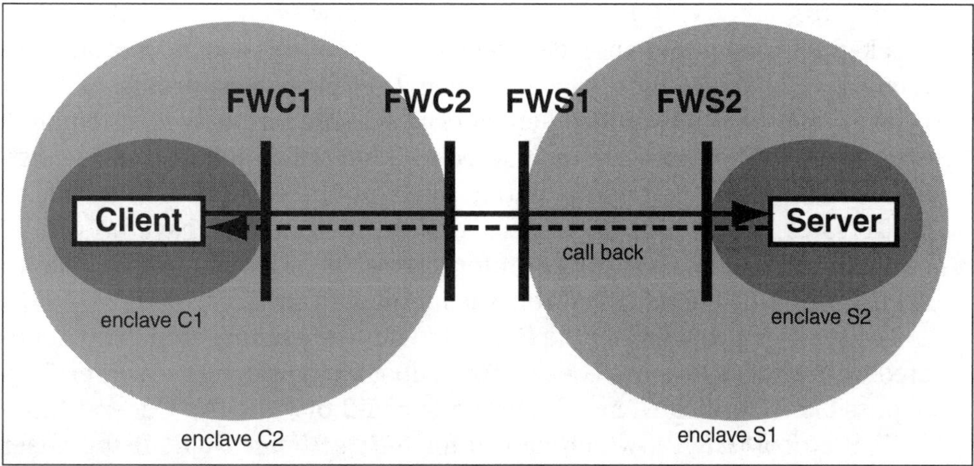


**Figure 12.7** Nested enclaves.

be configured to know any further firewalls in the chain, if any, so a client need not be aware of the entire chain of firewalls, which would not be practical.

The approach taken by the Firewall specification and by Gatekeeper is to require the client-side ORB run time to know about outbound gateways and to embed information about server-side inbound gateways in the object reference. The Firewall specification defines a new POA policy `FirewallPolicyValue` for this purpose. If a POA is configured with a value of EXPORT for this policy, the object references created by it will contain addressing information for server-side GIOP proxies in an additional IOR component. This requires the POA to know about the GIOP proxy at the server's enclave, however, so effectively the ORBs on both ends of the communication need to be firewall-aware.

An alternative to the static addition of IOR profiles containing firewall information at object creation time is the proxification of object references at run time. Proxifying an IOR means replacing the addressing information it contains with the address of a proxy that is capable of reaching the actual target. Iona's Wonderwall, for example, requires administrative operations to explicitly proxify IORs, but other products allow the transparent proxification of references and the creation of proxy objects on the firewall when references leave the enclave through the firewall. These techniques do not require ORB run times to be aware of the firewall configurations and are thus much more flexible and easier to use.

### Callbacks

An additional problem is posed by callbacks. If a client passes the reference of a callback object in its own address space to a server, it needs an inbound

GIOP proxy at the entrance to its enclave. Otherwise, any callbacks will be blocked by inbound client-side firewalls. Moreover, inbound proxies are required in all enclosing enclaves. In many settings, these proxies will not be available, especially if the client enclaves do not normally host remotely accessible CORBA services. In other cases where inbound proxies do exist, information about their configuration might not be accessible to the client that creates the callback reference. Applets, for example, have no way of obtaining the necessary firewall information and will also not be able to accept incoming connections from the inbound firewall.

The solution proposed by the OMG is to use the existing connection initiated by the client to send requests for callback requests by the server. This is possible if both sides implement version 1.2 of CORBA's General Inter-ORB Protocol (GIOP), which allows for *bidirectional* GIOP. If the client could contact the server and both parties agree on this protocol, callbacks can be sent by the server on the same connection without the need for further configuration of the firewall.

While this approach does allow callbacks, it has two serious security implications. First, because the existing transport and security context is reused, the client has no way of demanding additional server authentication on top of that carried out during connection establishment. Also, it cannot reject requests sent over this connection by refusing to connect because that would defeat the whole purpose of bidirectional GIOP.

Second, because of the way bidirectional GIOP is designed, a server has no way of verifying the protocol information supplied by the client that tells it where to send the message. This means that it would be possible for a malicious client to trick the server into sending its callback requests to any port on arbitrary hosts.

The Revision Task Force working on the joint revised submission for the Firewall specification was unable to resolve either the issues with bi-directional GIOP or the problems with call-backs. Consequently, the OMG issued a new RFP for CORBA Firewall Traversal in fall 2000, just as this book went to press. At this stage, it is unclear whether the Firewall Specification will become obsolete altogether, or whether new submissions will be able to suggest workable solutions that can be accommodated by the existing specification.

## 12.3 IIOP over Secure Socket Layer

Secure Socket Layer (SSL) is a security protocol that sits directly on top of the TCP/IP transport protocol. It has become popular in the context of the

Web for securing HTTP connections and is also widely used in other contexts because of its wide availability and relative ease of use. The OMG recognized this popularity and issued an RFP soliciting a specification for IIOP over SSL that was to be integrated into the CORBA Security specification as a simple mechanism to allow secure interoperation between ORBs from different vendors. The OMG adopted the specification resulting from the RFP process in mid-1997.

A number of vendors made implementations available that could also be used without the Security Service, of which no complete implementation existed at the time. We describe the Security Service in the next section. As you will see, it is extremely general and covers most security issues that can arise in distributed applications. A full-fledged Security Service is also very complex and not easy to install, configure, and manage, however. For this reason, separate implementations of IIOP over SSL are frequently used as a simpler alternative for applications that do not require the fine-grained administration of policies and the more advanced mechanisms provided by the Security Service. With a well-administered public key infrastructure (PKI), SSL is capable of providing reasonable levels of security by protecting the confidentiality and integrity of messages. In this section, we explain the main concepts of SSL.

We do not show any code that makes use of SSL in this section. The reason is that application code need not be aware of SSL at all when it is used through the Security Service, as explained in section 12.4. If SSL is used without the Security Service, the API to initialize SSL functionality is vendor-dependent, but generally contains only a few bootstrap operations, so we don't show any code to do this. The difficult part of using SSL is not in the application code, but in the necessary public key infrastructure that embodies the proper management procedures to create and distribute the digital certificates required by SSL.

### 12.3.1 SSL

SSL is a protocol on top of TCP/IP that adds security capabilities. The SSL API is an extension to the TCP/IP socket API. SSL's security capabilities include encryption of the messages sent through an SSL communication channel, authentication of the server based on digital certificates and signatures, and optional authentication of the client. Note that we use the terms *client* and *server* differently in this context. In SSL the client is the program that initiates an SSL connection, and the server is the program that accepts the connection. The client and server participating in an SSL connection are also known as *peers*.

SSL authentication is based on public key cryptography. Public key technology uses a pair of asymmetric keys for encryption and decryption. This means that a message encrypted with one key can be decrypted only by using the other key of the pair. If you keep the *private key* secret and distribute the *public key*, anyone can encrypt messages using the public key that only you can decrypt (using your private key). Furthermore, messages that are encrypted with the private key can be decrypted only with the corresponding public key. Assuming that the other party obtained your public key from a trusted place, this provides proof that the message was from you. If two parties exchange their public keys they can establish a two-way encrypted communication.

Authentication means verifying a party's claimed identity. In SSL this is based on digital certificates as defined in the ISO standard X.509. In general, a digital certificate can be regarded as a digitally signed statement made by someone about someone else. An X.509 certificate in particular is used to bind a public key to a name by the authoritative statement of the issuing and signing party. It contains the name of the signer, the name of the party who owns the certificate (the *subject* which is identified by it), the public key of this party, and time stamps.

The digital signature on a certificate can be checked mechanically by anybody in possession of the signer's public key. If the verification succeeds, the certificate was indeed signed by the owner of that key pair, and it was not tampered with during transmission. Whether the statement contained in a certificate is accepted depends not only on its authenticity and integrity, however, but also on the trust in the signer. You don't usually take just anybody's word for fact. If the signer is a known certification authority and considered trustworthy, that is, if you accept the signer's authority and trust in the correctness of its statement, you believe that the public key and the name in the certificate actually belong together.

Obtaining and verifying a certificate, however, is only the first step in establishing the identity of your peer. The only information that a certificate gives you is that a name and a public key belong together. Given that the name and the public key are public knowledge, anyone can obtain this information and fake an identity. What you need to prove is that whoever presents the certificate also has the private key corresponding to the public one contained in the certificate. Digital signatures are used to prove this. The mechanism behind the digital signature involves creating a random message and encrypting a cryptographic hash value of it with the private key.

If mutual authentication during the SSL connection setup is required, client and server each send a random message to the other party. This is also called a *challenge*. Both parties then create a cryptographic hash value of the challenge, sign this value with their private key, and return a response consisting of the signed random and their public key certificate. Both parties can then verify each other's signatures using the public key from the transmitted certificates.

Although asymmetric encryption technology can be used for encrypting the data once the SSL connection is established, a symmetric encryption mechanism is typically used. Symmetric algorithms are less computationally complex than asymmetric ones. Symmetric mechanisms work by having the two parties share a secret code that is used to encrypt and decrypt messages going in either direction. Once the server is authenticated, it can send the client a secret code encrypted with the client's public key, and at that point both parties use this secret code for encrypting messages.

When messages are encrypted, their integrity is automatically verified through the decryption process—if a message was tampered with it simply does not decrypt correctly. SSL also provides data integrity without encrypting the entire message by using a message authentication code (MAC). This allows you to detect if someone in the transmission path has corrupted the message, but it saves the computation necessary to fully encrypt messages. Instead, only the MAC generation requires cryptographic computation. MAC encryption is based on the private key and a part of the message itself. There are various options for the encryption mechanism and MAC algorithm. SSL contains a handshake protocol to establish the algorithms used for a particular session.

## 12.3.2 Public Key Infrastructures

Using SSL to secure your CORBA communications requires digital certificates, but the supporting infrastructure on the Internet is quite rudimentary. You can obtain certificates from certificate authorities (CAs) such as Verisign or Thawte, but there is little support for storing them and integrating them with directory servers.

In fact, the definition, operation, and maintenance of a secure and workable PKI require much thought and care because the entire security of the SSL protocol hinges on the proper administration of public key certificates. Especially if SSL is used as the security mechanism in the Security Service and, for example, access control decisions are made based on SSL credentials, certificates must be managed in a secure and flexible way.

Today, many large companies create and operate their own PKIs that follow internal policies and allow them to create certificate structures that are tailored to their organizational needs. These infrastructures are used, for example, to create keys and certificates that live on employee's smart cards and can be used for physical access control as well as for signing internal documents and for SSL. Within the organization, directory servers can be used to efficiently store and retrieve certificates. Only the top-level signing key might need external certification, which can be carried out by official or commercial certification authorities.

Interaction with CAs is typically offline; that is, obtaining a public key certificate is not a synchronous operation invocation. Rather, the CA will have to carefully check the application and the submitted data for correctness, which requires out-of-band communication and might take a few days. In many architectures, CAs are contacted only indirectly through local registration authorities (RAs), which forward the request after an initial check.

The OMG has issued an RFP for a Public Key Infrastructure in early 1999, and the corresponding specification was adopted by the OMG board in mid-2000. The PKI specification defines IDL interfaces for interacting with certification authorities.

## 12.4 Overview of the CORBA Security Service

The CORBA Security Service defines a framework for the use of many different underlying security technologies—such as Kerberos, DCE Security, or SESAME—to secure CORBA applications. It provides interfaces that are generic enough to allow the use of any of these technologies. This means, however, that not all of the functionality that the interfaces provide will be supported by all of the technologies that implement security.

Because of its generic approach and the inherent complexity of security issues, the Security Service is one of the longest and most complex service specifications available from the OMG. In this section, we merely introduce the service and do not provide any programming examples. A complete example of a security-aware application using the Security Service API would be beyond the scope of this book.

### 12.4.1 Overview of Security Goals and Terminology

In this subsection we provide an overview of the aims of a secure object system and a summary of the security features that are specified in the Security Service. Last, we discuss the levels of conformance to this specification.

#### *12.4.1.1 Security Requirements*

A distributed object system may need to fulfill several different security requirements. Security requirements are prime examples of nonfunctional requirements and are usually defined *negatively*, that is, as the absence of undesirable properties or occurrences rather than in terms of desired system functions. Often, security requirements are classified in the following broad categories:

- Confidentiality—Information is available only to those for whom it is intended.
- Integrity—Information is modified only by those authorized to do so and is transferred without interference or corruption.
- Accountability—Users' security actions are recorded so that they can be held accountable for them.
- Availability—Authorized users cannot be maliciously denied service.

### 12.4.1.2 Threats to Security

There are several ways in which security can be breached so that the preceding requirements are not met. The following list gives typical examples of security breaches that an adequate security system should be able to detect and stop or prevent:

- Otherwise authorized users gaining access to information or services they are not permitted to access
- A user pretending to be someone else and using this false identity to access information or services that he or she would otherwise not be able to access, or without being charged
- Monitoring communications channels for confidential messages intended for others
- Modifying, deleting, or replaying messages on communications channels
- A user performing untraceable malicious actions
- A user denying his or her participation in certain activities, for example, signing a contract

Any security service that is supposed to prevent breaches like these must not be bypassable, and it must also be able to monitor *all* security-related actions. To guarantee this, it is not sufficient to verify just the correctness and completeness of the service implementation itself and potentially the security mechanisms used by it. It is also necessary to justify the level of trust put into the underlying operating system and hardware.

The most elaborate security service will do no good if attackers are able to capture keystrokes from your keyboard before they reach the computer, can access persistent object state on an unprotected file system, directly read out information from memory—or grab a user's password from a Post-it attached to a monitor or from a slip of paper in the waste bin.

#### 12.4.1.3 Features of the Security Service

The CORBA Security specification defines the following functionality to provide safeguards against the possible breaches mentioned:

**Identification and authentication.** The provision of identities to principals (human users and objects that require their own identity) and the ability to verify that the principals are who they claim to be.

**Authorization and access control.** A way of deciding whether a principal is allowed to access an object. This includes the ways in which administrators can specify which principals (or groups of principals) may access particular objects and how applications may decide whether to grant access to a principal.

**Auditing.** Keeping records of which principals perform which invocations on secured objects. The specification also defines the means of deciding which actions to audit and which to ignore.

**Communications security.** This may include several actions: authentication of the client to its target object, authentication of the target object by the client, protecting the integrity of messages transmitted, and protecting the confidentiality of messages transmitted.

**Non-repudiation.** Creation, transmission, and storage of irrefutable evidence that a principal performed an action so that it can be retrieved later in case of a dispute. This may include evidence of creation of objects and the sending or receipt of messages.

**Administration of security policy.** Interfaces that apply security to a domain, including many objects and applications regardless of whether the applications are security aware.

#### 12.4.1.4 Security Conformance Levels

The Security Service can be implemented to conform to one of two levels of security, with a single optional facility: nonrepudiation. There are also ways of implementing ORBs to make them security-ready without actually providing a security mechanism underneath.

Security Level 1 is designed to allow ORB security to be applied to applications that are not security-aware. It provides for user authentication and for this authentication to be available to the applications run by the users. It will then apply the security policies specified to the objects in the secure ORB's domain. This includes provision of message integrity (and confidentiality where required), as well as access control as specified by administration policy. It will also allow for auditing of certain security events.

Security Level 2 provides all of the facilities of Level 1, as well as some enhanced integrity, trust, and auditing. It also provides interfaces to applications so that they can find out about the domain's policies and their own privileges and decide how to apply them.

The Security specification also defines three ways in which ORBs can implement security so that the mechanism they use can be replaced. These are of interest only to ORB implementers.

## 12.4.2 Security Model

The model of security in an ORB system uses the notions of clients, target objects, and operation invocations, as specified in CORBA. The processes of building a request, transmitting it to the target object over a network, and then executing an operation and sending a reply are all augmented by security procedures that ensure that the security policies of the domain are enforced. This model is very general, as it aims to include all of the possible security functions that may be required in any application, and it expresses them in generic terms that can describe the behavior of many different underlying security mechanisms.

Figure 12.8 illustrates the two main components of CORBA Security, Access Control and Secure Invocation, and the role of the Current and Credentials objects, which will be explained in more detail later. It does not show authentication, audit, or non-repudiation. It also illustrates the close relation between the ORB and this service. Because of this close relation, the CORBA Security Service cannot be regarded an independent Object Service like the Notification Service, but it is sometimes referred to as an ORB Service.

The subsections that follow explain principals and their security attributes, how a secure invocation is made, how security information can be delegated to other objects, how non-repudiation works, and what kinds of security domains the security specification defines.

### *12.4.2.1 Principals and Security Attributes*

In the security model the users and some of the applications are called principals, and they are given authenticated identities. Sometimes a principal

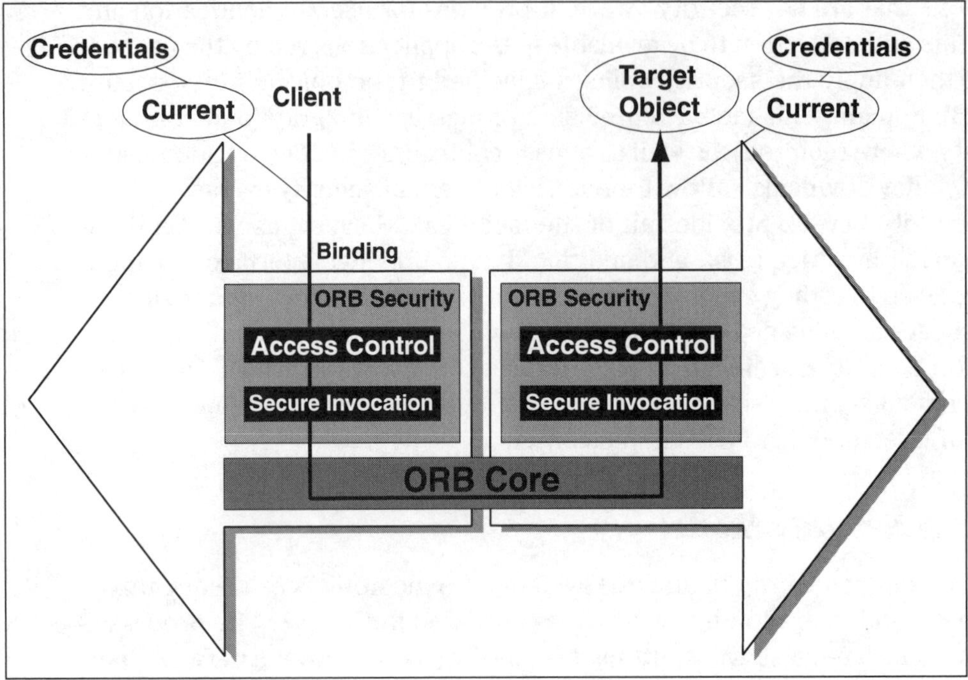


**Figure 12.8** Security model.

will have more than one identity. For example, a user may have an access identity that he or she uses to log on to a system, and an audit identity, which is known only to the system administrator and is associated with the principal at log-on time.

Authentication usually requires the principal to have a *security name*, which is then used along with some authentication information (such as a password, or on a smart card) to produce some *privilege attributes*. These are stored along with the principal's identity attributes and some public information in a *credential* (shown in Figure 12.9).

Without explaining the use of specific interfaces and operations, the Security specification explains the high-level concepts for making a secure operation invocation. Some of the actions explained may be performed by the application, if it is security-aware. If the application is not security-aware, then all of the actions are performed by the Security Service, using context information where necessary.

A secure invocation is made using the following steps:

Establish a *security association* between the client and target object. This means that a satisfactory level of trust in the identity of the other must be reached between the client and target object. Often the client

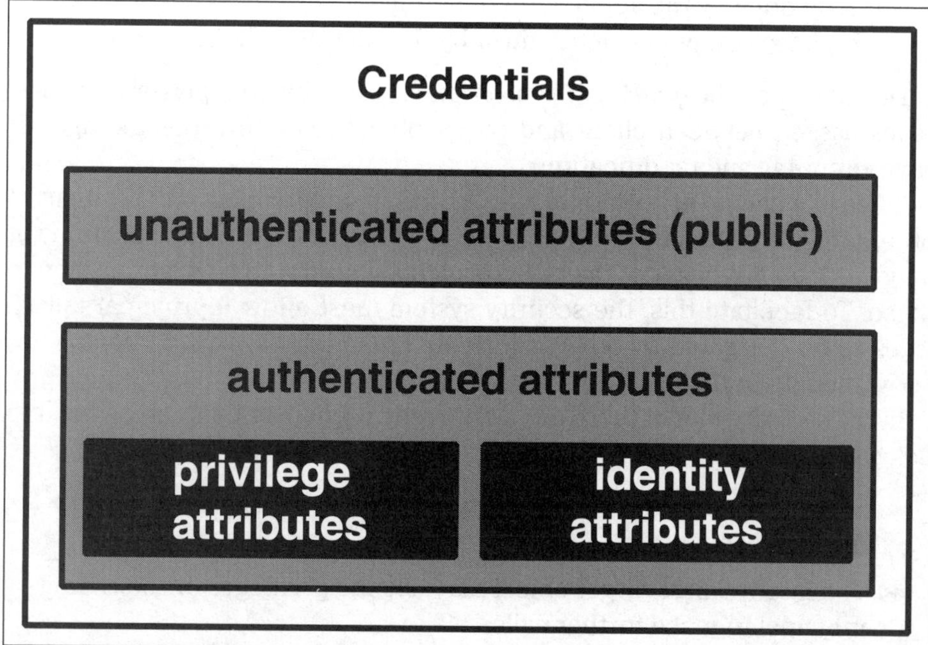


**Figure 12.9** Credentials.

trusts that it received a reliable object reference, and only the target object needs to perform an authentication of the client's identity. This is done by establishing a *binding* between the client and the target object. This allows them to share security information that the Security Service provides in the *current execution context.* This context is represented by an object called *Current,* which provides operations and attributes that allow client and target to set their own security attributes and access those of the other party.

Using the Current object, the target object (or the Security Service) decides whether, based on the authenticated identity and privileges of the client, the requested invocation is permitted. This can be done by looking at Access Control Lists or at policies about what group membership, role, security clearance, or the like the client principal must have in order to be granted access. It may be performed without any intervention from the application at all, as the security administrator can specify policy about access that is automatically enforced by the Security Service.

If security policy dictates that auditing is required, the appropriate information about the invocation must be sent to an *audit channel.* This can be done by the application or automatically by the Security Service, based on policy determined by the security administrator.

Depending on the *quality of protection* required by both parties, the messages passed between client and target object may be protected against eavesdropping and modification.

Often in a client/server model like CORBA, a target object will be client to other target objects in the application. If a target is to make invocations, it may need the privileges of the client principal in order to have permission to do so. To facilitate this, the security system must allow a principal's privileges to be delegated to other principals (called *intermediate objects*) to allow them to perform a task.

In the security model there are a number of schemes that can be used to delegate privileges:

- The intermediate target object may use its own privileges to make further calls.
- The intermediate target object may use the privileges of the calling principal to make further calls.
- The privileges of the caller and the intermediate target object may be combined to make calls in two ways: The two sets of privileges may both be used, or they may be combined into a single new set of credentials.

The scheme that is used may be limited by the capabilities of the security mechanism. The style of delegation used by particular objects will be determined by the security administrator, who will set delegation policies.

### 12.4.2.2 Non-repudiation Services

When clients perform particularly sensitive or irrevocable actions with, for example, financial, safety, or confidentiality consequences, then it may be important to create and store irrefutable evidence of these actions. Non-repudiation services allow this evidence to be generated and later verified when proof of an action is requested so that a client principal (or target object) may be held responsible for its actions.

It may be necessary to generate and store evidence of various sorts of actions. These actions might include the creation of a new object, the creation of a request, or the receipt of a request or a reply. As shown in Figure 12.10, non-repudiation services support interfaces to service components that perform evidence generation and verification and evidence storage and retrieval.

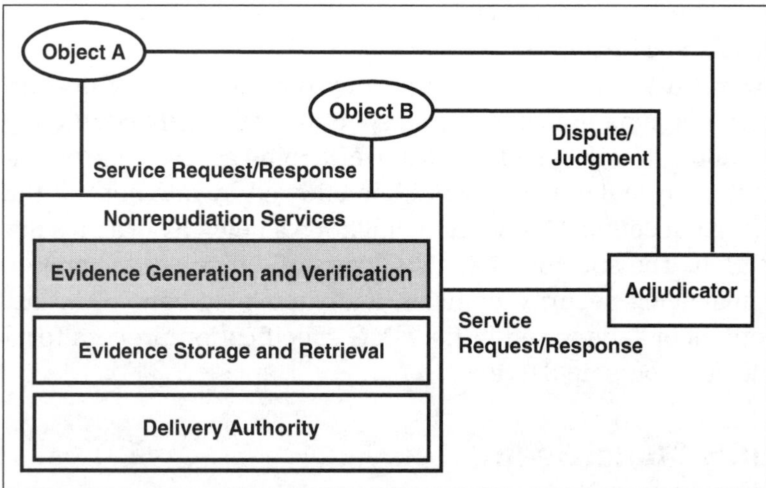


**Figure 12.10** Non-repudiation service.

There may be two other independent agents involved in a non-repudiation service. A *delivery authority* is responsible for the delivery of evidence between the objects taking part in the application. It also delivers evidence to an independent *adjudicator* that is consulted when there is a dispute about the actions that have taken place in the system.

### 12.4.2.3 Security Domains

A domain is a scope within which common characteristics are exhibited and common rules can be applied. In terms of security, there can be several types of domains. A *security technology domain* is the scope within which a single security technology is applied.

In a secure distributed object environment, only some applications are aware of security, even though all applications may take advantage of security services. Security-unaware applications are secured by placing the application within one or more *security policy domains*. Access to the applications is then mediated by the security policies of the domains that enclose them.

Policy domains can be organized in hierarchies, with the inner subdomains overriding policies or providing additional policies to their parent domains. An application's objects are subject to the policies of the innermost subdomain that encloses them. Domains may simply overlap, however, and policies relating to different aspects of security (for example, auditing and access control) may have different scopes. Often the use of a particular security technology means that a particular arrangement of security policy domains must be used.

The CORBA Security Service does not specify the semantics of domain hierarchies or overlapping domains with respect to potentially conflicting policies. For example, if an object is in two overlapping access control policy domains and a particular access would be allowed by one but not the other, whose decision counts? While there might be a quick answer, it's not in the specification. The specification also does not define administrative interfaces for managing security domains and their members. This last point is currently being addressed in the OMG specification process for a Security Domain Membership Service.

## 12.4.3 Security Model Seen by Applications

The Security Service specification explains the interfaces to be used by application developers, ORB implementers, Security Service implementers, and security administrators. In this section we present the interfaces to security components that application developers may use to develop security-aware applications. The specification is written to allow the use of any underlying security mechanism, and thus not all interfaces will be applicable to all mechanisms.

### *12.4.3.1 Finding the Security Features of an ORB*

The ORB interface has been extended to add a new operation to the ORB pseudo-object. It is called `get_service_information()` and returns service information for a given service type. If called with an argument denoting the Security Service, it returns details of the security facilities and mechanisms available within this ORB.

### *12.4.3.2 Authentication of a User Principal*

Often a user will be authenticated outside the ORB security system, for example, by a security log-on. In this case the credentials that the user is given are available through the Current object. The Current object is associated with a client's binding to a target object that the client will use to make a secure invocation on the target object. The user may use Current to choose which privileges to associate with the secure invocation.

If the user is not authenticated by an external mechanism, then it must use a PrincipalAuthenticator object to authenticate itself and acquire credentials for use in secure invocations. Both interfaces will be explained in more detail in the text that follows.

#### 12.4.3.3 Selecting Privileges

A client can use the Credentials object that it obtains through either the Current object or directly from a PrincipalAuthenticator to select from the privileges available to it. It may also obtain information about the security features that are implemented in the system and about the security policies that apply to it in the current domain.

The Credentials object supports an operation called set_privileges() that allows the client to select the types of security and the privileges that will be used for secure invocations from the client. Clients can also make copies of the credentials using the copy() operation on their Credentials object so that they can customize the copies for use with different targets.

The Current object has two operations, get_credentials() and set_credentials(), that allow the default credentials object used for invocations to be inspected and changed.

#### 12.4.3.4 Making a Secure Invocation

A binding must be established between the client and the target object so that they can share security information. The binding conveys the user principal's credentials to the target object, where they can be used to determine whether the principal is allowed access to the target object or to particular operations on the object. Audit and non-repudiation policies may also be applied using information about the client's credentials obtained via the Current object at the target. This is done using the operation get_attributes() supported by both the Current object and the Credentials object to which it refers.

When a target object must make other invocations in order to complete the current request, it must apply the delegation policy that is set by the security administrator. This may allow it to use the client's credentials that it has received or to combine its own credentials with the client's. It creates or selects appropriate credentials by using the same operations on the Current and Credentials objects that the client used in order to select the privileges for the initial invocation.

When the target object processes the incoming request, it must decide whether to allow the access. This is done by querying the current access control policy that is effective at the target. To do this, the target (or the

Security Service) retrieves a local Access_Decision object from the Current object. The Access_Decision object provides the access_allowed() operation, which returns TRUE if the access control policy for the target object permits the access. In this case, the request may be processed; otherwise, the access must be rejected.

The target must also decide whether to audit the invocation. It does this by first checking the policy for auditing that it inherits from the security domain by supplying an audit policy argument to the get_policy() operation on the Current object. It may also decide autonomously to do its own auditing, and for this it uses an AuditDecision object, which has an operation called audit_needed(). If an audit is required then the AuditDecision object will return an appropriate audit channel from its audit_channel() operation.

#### *12.4.3.5 Non-repudiation*

If non-repudiation is supported by the security service then the user can obtain an NRCredentials object from its Current object and set this as its default Credentials object using set_credentials(). The NRCredentials object has operations called get_NR_features() and set_NR_features()that allow the user to choose the type of evidence generation and select other non-repudiation features.

A number of calls to the NRCredentials object are required to generate evidence of an invocation. Which of these are required depends on the implementation of the non-repudiation service.

- generate_token()—creates an unforgeable token to be used in the evidence
- verify_evidence()—can be used to check if evidence is valid

Some non-repudiation services require evidence generation to be done in multiple steps and so another operation is provided:

- form_complete_evidence()—uses the original token to generate further evidence, such as time stamps

### 12.4.4 Overview of Application Security Interfaces

A number of the security interfaces defined in the Security Service are designed to provide a layer of abstraction for ORB security implementers so that they can replace underlying security mechanisms with a minimum of effort. We will look only at the interfaces designed for use by security-aware applications. Note that applications need not have any awareness of security in order to be protected by the Security Service. These applications can be made secure by the security administrator, which sets security policy to be enforced by the ORB without the need for the application developer to do any security programming.

### 12.4.4.1 Common Security Types

The Security module defines the data types and constants that are used within the modules SecurityLevel1 and SecurityLevel2. The definitions in the Security module depend on the Time Service module, Time because reliable distributed time stamps are needed to avoid several kinds of attacks on secure systems, as well as for the creation of evidence for non-repudiation and logs for auditing.

The types defined here include a number of integers and opaque types because the data types to be used by the underlying security service are unknown to the specifiers of this service. The use of *family* identifiers is also widespread. A family is a unique identifier representing a concept in the Security Service, for example, identity or privilege. All features of security services, known as *security attributes*, are qualified by the family to which they belong.

```
typedef sequence<octet> Opaque;
struct ExtensibleFamily {
        unsigned short family_definer;
        unsigned short family;
};
typedef unsigned long SecurityAttributeType;
struct AttributeType {
        ExtensibleFamily attribute_family;
        SecurityAttributeType attribute_type;
};
typedefsequence<AttributeType> AttributeTypeList;
struct SecAttribute{
        AttributeType attribute_type;
        Opaque defining_authority;
        Opaque value;
};
typedef sequence <SecAttribute> AttributeList;
```

This module also defines a number of standard SecurityAttributeTypes, which are given as constants relative to a family; for example,

```
// identity attributes; family=0
const SecurityAttributeType AuditId = 1;
const SecurityAttributeType AccountingId = 2;
const SecurityAttributeType NonRepudiationId = 3;
```

These are used in Attribute structures along with a family identifier. The type is named ExtensibleFamily because it is anticipated that new families and corresponding attribute types will be defined when new kinds of underlying security services are used with these interfaces.

Many other types are defined for use in all of the other security interfaces. We have provided only enough definitions to show the flavor of the specification and to show the single signature needed for Security Level 1 in the following section.

### 12.4.4.2 Security Level 1

The first level of conformance to the Security Service does not allow principals in applications to choose the privileges they will apply or allow objects to enforce their own security policies. The Current object defined in the module SecurityLevel1 allows an application to find out which security attributes are defined in the domains within which it operates.

```
interface Current:CORBA::Current { // PIDL
    Security::AttributeList get_attributes(
        in Security::AttributeTypeList attributes
    );
};
```

The get_attributes() operation returns the values associated with all of the attribute types provided in the list argument.

### 12.4.4.3 Security Level 2

The second conformance level defines all the interfaces that are used in security-aware applications, as well as the interfaces used by ORB security implementers to allow replaceability of security mechanisms. The applications use the interfaces called Current, RequiredRights, PrincipalAuthenticator, Credentials, and Object. We will provide a brief explanation of the operations supported by these interfaces, but the signatures of the operations will not be shown because they contain too much detail for an introduction to security.

### 12.4.4.4 Current

The Current interface specifies operations and attributes that are available to both clients and target objects. The attributes are references to other objects specified in the Security Service. The operations are all applicable to both client and target unless otherwise stated.

In the SecurityLevel2 module, the Current interface inherits the Current interface from SecurityLevel1. It extends this functionality with read-only attributes that return object references to the following objects: RequiredRights, AccessDecision, AuditDecision, and PrincipalAuthenticator.

It also gives access to Credentials objects that have been initialized outside of the ORB (i.e., by some means other than using a PrincipalAuthenticator object). The respective attributes are received_credentials for credentials that were received from a calling client and own_credentials. The Current interface also defines operations to set and get the credentials objects used for invocations in a client context. They are the following:

- get_credentials()—returns the current default Credentials object
- set_credentials()—allows modified Credentials to be used for invocations
- remove_own_credentials()—removes a Credentials object from the list of own credentials

Clients that want to find out about the available security mechanisms at a target can invoke the get_security_mechanism() operation, passing the target object reference as a parameter. The Current object also supports the get_policy() operation with which policies of a given type can be retrieved at both the server and the client side.

### 12.4.4.5 RequiredRights

The RequiredRights interface offers two operations, one for use by a client principal to discover what rights it needs in order to make an invocation on a particular operation on a particular object reference, and the other for use by a target object to set the rights required on its operations. The use of this interface assumes that access to operations on objects is granted on the basis of policy specified in terms of principal groups given the rights to perform certain kinds of actions. This is much like file modification privileges under UNIX.

- get_required_rights()—returns the set of rights that a client principal must have in order to use an operation. It can be thought of as "ls -l" in UNIX file terms, which reveals read, write, and execute permissions on files.
- set_required_rights()—used to set the rights required to invoke an operation. It is much like the "chmod" command used to change permissions on files in UNIX.

### 12.4.4.6 PrincipalAuthenticator

This interface provides only three operations: get_supported_authen_methods(), authenticate(), and continue_authentication(). The first operation can be used to find out about the authentication methods for a given security mechanism that are supported by the authenticator.

The other operations are used by a principal to obtain a reference to a Credentials object for later use in making secure invocations. Some underlying authentication services will allow the user to provide its security name and authentication data (such as a password) and will return the credentials required in one step using the authenticate() operation. Other authentication services, however, require more than one interaction. Rather than returning a reference to a Credentials object, they will return some *continuation data* that must be supplied to the continue_authentication() operation with some *response data* in order to obtain either credentials or additional continuation data. Eventually, assuming that the responses are satisfactory to the authenticator, the principal will have obtained some valid credentials.

### 12.4.4.7 Credentials

The Credentials interface allows a principal to choose from the security features and privileges available to it after authentication. This interface is used by both clients and object implementations awaiting invocations. The Credentials pseudo-object can be copied so that different available features and privileges can be set on different object references (on the client side) or for use with different incoming requests (on the target object side).

- copy()—provides a duplicate set of Credentials.
- destroy()—destroys the Credentials object.
- get_security_feature()—allows a principal to find out which security features are available. The return value is a sequence of security features such as authentication of the other party, confidentiality, auditing, and non-repudiation.
- get_attributes()—allows a principal to discover a set of security attributes, such as its identity or privileges.
- set_privileges()—to update the set of privileges that a client wishes to use. The client passes a sequence of attributes belonging to a privileges family as a parameter.

There are two other operations on Credentials that relate to the expiration of credentials after a time limit within some security mechanisms.

- is_valid()—returns a Boolean indicating whether the credentials are still valid, as well as a time when they are expected to expire.
- refresh()—allows the application to update the credentials in the Credentials object that have expired. It returns a Boolean to indicate whether the update was successful.

In addition to these operations, the Credentials interface provides a read-only attribute mechanism that represents the security mechanism for which the credentials are valid, and two pairs of attributes that can be used to set options for secure associations. These options express policies about what the client or target is prepared to support or requires when accepting a security association or making an invocation, for example, whether mutual authentication is required. The attributes are called accepting_options_supported and accepting_options_required, invocation_options_supported, and invocation_options_required, respectively.

#### 12.4.4.8 Object

The Object pseudo-IDL interface provided by the CORBA module incorporates a set of operations that were provided to allow security information to be accessed. We have already described these operations in section 6.1 of Chapter 6, "ORB Run-Time System," so we simply list these operations again.

- get_policy()—returns the *effective* policy of a given type for the object
- get_domain_managers()—returns a list of DomainManager objects for the domains to which the object immediately belongs
- set_policy_overrides()—used to associate new policies with an object reference by either adding to or overriding existing policies

### 12.4.5 Common Secure Interoperability (CSI)

The Security Service Specification also addresses the problem of secure interoperability between different ORBs with security implementations. These ORBs would, of course, need to use the same security mechanisms. The Security Service defines interoperability protocols that allow compliant implementations of the Security Service to negotiate and establish *security associations*. The two interoperable protocols defined by the Security Service are the *Secure Inter-ORB Protocol* (SECIOP) and IIOP over SSL (SSLIOP).

In order to be able to establish a security association with a server, a client needs to know about the security technology supported by the server. IORs that support SECIOP contain extra information, known as tags, to indicate the protocol and security mechanisms the object's server supports. They also contain the security identity of the target object, so that it can be authenticated by the client during a connection, and some security policy attributes so that the client can determine if the security policy in its domain is compatible.

The rest of the SECIOP specification provides details of additional security message types that need to be transmitted to share the security context between client and target. This is how the Current object can contain the same information on both sides. There are also tags defined for object references to objects that support the DCE interoperability protocol so that different vendors can use one another's objects.

SECIOP internally consists of two layers. The Sequencing Layer protects messages against replay, dropping, or reordering, and the Context Management Layer defines the message types to set up security associations and transmit integrity or confidentiality-protected messages.

SECIOP can be used by any of the following established security mechanisms: the Simple Public-Key GSS-API (SPKM), Kerberos V5, and ECMA's SESAME (CSI ECMA). SSLIOP is used when SSL is employed as the security mechanism. Figure 12.11 illustrates the relationship between the protocols and their related security mechanisms.

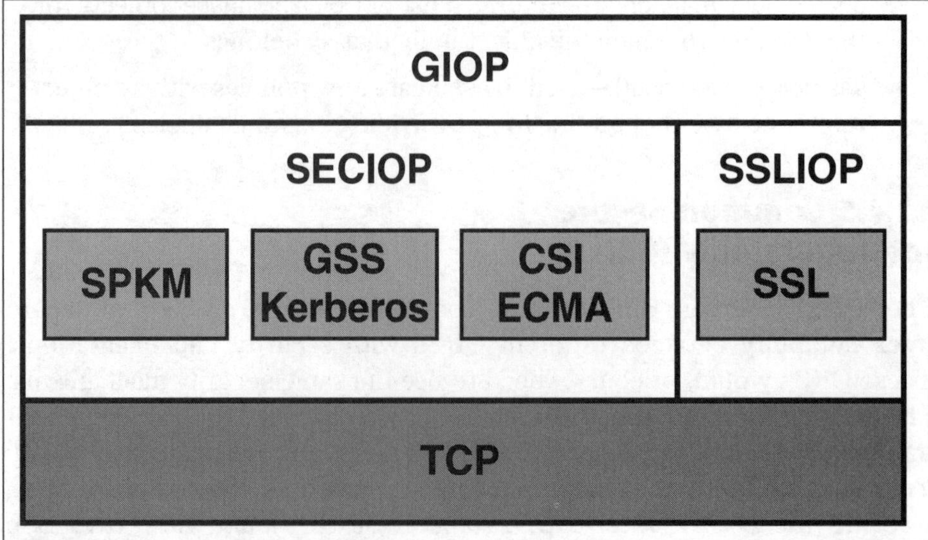


**Figure 12.11** Secure interoperability protocols and mechanisms.

The Security Service defines three levels of secure interoperability, which differ in the delegation models they support and the kind of security information about the principal that is provided at the target.

- **CSI Level 0.** Supports identity-based policies only, so no additional security attributes are available. No delegation is possible, so any delegated calls must be made using the intermediate object's credentials.
- **CSI Level 1.** Supports identity-based policies like Level 0. It also supports unrestricted delegation, which means that the initiating principal has no control over delegation, so intermediate objects can impersonate the principal.
- **CSI Level 2.** Supports identity- and privilege-based policies and controlled delegation. All the principal's security attributes can be made available at the target, and the principal has control over the delegation model used.

The different security mechanisms that can be used with SECIOP and SSLIOP provide different CSI levels. SPKM and SSL provide only CSI Level 0, GSS Kerberos provides Level 0 or Level 1, and CSI ECMA can provide any of the three CSI levels.

The OMG is currently revising the CSI part of the Security Service because CSI in its current form has a number of limitations that restrict full interoperability. In particular, there is no standard format for credentials that would allow higher-level, mechanism-independent authorization or delegation. The OMG has issued an RFP for a second version of CSI that should address these points and define standardized *privilege attribute certificates* (PACs). The RFP mandates a layered approach with separate authentication, message protection, and authorization layers.

CHAPTER

13

# The Persistent State Service

Most real-word applications require persistence in one form or another. We have already discussed persistent object *references* in this book; in this chapter we deal with persistent object *state*. To understand the difference, remember that when a POA creates persistent references, this means that objects are reachable through these references independent of how long its hosting process and POA live. Making an object's state persistent means that this state outlives individual object incarnations, that is, it is available to the object regardless of how often server processes, POAs, and individual servants are created and destroyed. It might even outlive the CORBA object itself and later be accessible by means outside of CORBA, but that is of no concern to us here. Persistent references and persistent state are not necessarily used together, although most often they are. It is just as possible, however, to have persistent references to objects with transient state, or even to have transient objects that work with persistent state.

In Chapter 10, "Practical POA Programming," we discussed examples that show how Java serialization can be used as a simple mechanism to make the state of individual objects persistent. In many cases more elaborate and more efficient means of storing state are required. The OMG has specified the Persistent State Service (PSS) to deal with persistent state. It is a service for servant developers who have to define ways of persisting state; clients of the object will never see the PSS. The PSS replaces its unsuccessful predecessor, the Persistent Object Service (POS), which was never widely accepted or implemented.

The PSS is not an interface to a complete, object-oriented database management system (OODBMS). While it does provide persistent storage of objects, it deliberately leaves out two main features that are commonly found in relational or object-oriented DBMSs: queries and transactions. The reason for this omission is simple: separation of concerns. The OMG always had separate service specifications for persistence, transactions, and queries because these three services, while intimately related, are each useful in its own right. Separate specifications allow for simpler and more lightweight specifications and implementations. We do not cover either transactions or queries in any detail here. For an introduction to the Object Transaction Service (OTS) we refer you to Jon Siegel, *CORBA 3 Fundamentals and Programming*, second edition (Wiley 2000). Programming the OTS is explained in Andreas Vogel and Madhavan Rangarao, *Programming with Enterprise JavaBeans, JTS, and OTS* (Wiley 1999).

The PSS defines language concepts and an API to make object state persistent, but such an API already exists for Java. Java programs can access SQL databases through the JDBC API, so how does this API compare to the PSS? First of all, JDBC offers *more functionality* than the PSS because it provides access to an underlying DBMS's query and transaction capabilities in addition to mere storage management. Second, it provides *less abstraction* than the PSS because its data definition language (DDL) is limited to SQL. The PSS, in contrast, offers an object-oriented data definition language called PSDL (Persistent State Definition Language) that is much more appropriate for persisting object state than SQL. At the same time, it is designed to allow mappings to SQL databases, OODBMS, and even plain files. Thus, you can implement the PSS using JDBC, and it is likely that we will see Java implementations of the PSS that use JDBC to connect to existing database products.

In this chapter we cover the following topics:

- Introduction to PSS concepts (section 13.1)
- A Persistent State example (section 13.2)
- The PSDL language (section 13.3)
- PSS main interfaces (section 13.4)

## 13.1 PSS Concepts

The PSS is different from any other OMG service because it addresses features of the implementation of objects, namely the object's internal state and how it is made persistent. CORBA has always avoided referring to implementation details in IDL, so why does the PSS violate this policy?

The first part of the answer has to do with the importance of persistence in general and its role in the new CORBA Component Model (CCM). We explore the CCM in Chapter 14, "CORBA Components," but it should be noted here that persistence is one of the key services provided by the Component Container, so the interface to this service required standardization.

The second part of the answer is that no persistence features are actually exposed in object interfaces. Rather, the PSS defines a new description language, the Persistent State Definition Language (PSDL). This language is a superset of IDL, and while it does define persistence-related details that are part of your data model, it does this in a declarative way and without implementation language-specific features. Effectively, it creates a second layer of abstraction between entirely abstract CORBA interfaces and concrete implementations.

PSDL definitions are interpreted by PSDL compilers and mapped to implementation constructs for particular persistence mechanisms, such as object-oriented or relational databases or simply file systems. Specific PSDL compilers are supplied by the vendors of PSS implementations and can be thought of as roughly equivalent to database schema generators for particular programming languages. They do not, however, operate on programming language constructs such as Java classes but on the more abstract PSDL definitions.

The main concepts introduced by the PSS are Datastores, Storage Homes, Storage Objects, and Catalogs. These concepts are illustrated in Figure 13.1 and explained below.

Let's examine a Datastore and its contents first. A *Datastore* is the actual storage mechanism that manages the data. This can be, for example, a database or a set of files. A Datastore contains Storage Homes, which in turn contain Storage Objects. These are depicted in the right half of Figure 13.1. On the left side are process-local representations of Storage Homes and Storage Objects through which the actual data that is kept in the Datastore is accessed.

Persistent data is stored in the form of individual *Storage Objects*. If you are familiar with relational databases, you might think of these Storage Objects as tuples or rows. Storage Objects have a storagetype, which is

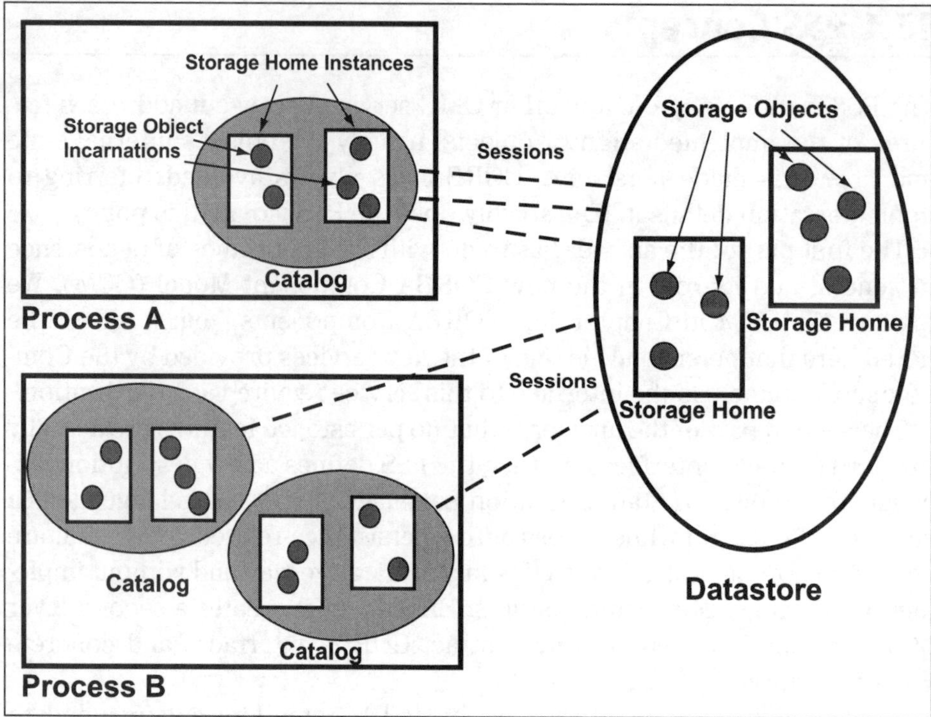


**Figure 13.1** PSS concepts.

declared statically in PSDL and defines the state members of the Storage Objects and the operations that can be invoked on them. These operations are sometimes also called *stored methods*.

Storage Objects have individual identities and are globally accessible via unique identifiers, their pids; however, they are not CORBA objects. Storage Objects have no object reference and cannot be accessed using CORBA invocations. Rather, they represent the persistent state of individual CORBA objects, with which they are associated. We will show how this is done in an example. Storage Objects can also be identified using their short-pid rather than the globally unique pid, but the short-pid identifies a Storage Object relative only to its containing Storage Home.

Storage Objects reside in *Storage Homes* within the Datastore. If the Datastore is a relational database, for example, Storage Homes would be mapped to database tables. Like Storage Objects, Storage Homes have types that are also declared statically in PSDL. There are three important restrictions for Storage Homes. First, there can only be a single Storage Home of any given type within a Datastore. Second, Storage Homes contain Storage Objects of one type only. Third, for any given storagetype, there can only be a single Storage Home in a Datastore.

Storage Objects and Storage Homes live in Datastores. Clients of the PSS need local representations in their own address spaces to be able to access data in a Datastore. The representative of a Storage Object is a *Storage Object Instance.* Because we are concerned with Java only, Storage Object Instances are just Java objects that are instances of those Java classes that represent a Storage Object's type.

Storage Object Instances can be in one of two states. Either they can be connected to a Storage Object in the Datastore, or they can be disconnected. A connected Storage Object Instance is called *Storage Object Incarnation*, and changes on it will propagate into the Datastore. The difference between a Storage Object Instance and a Storage Object Incarnation might seem subtle at first, but it really is analogous to the way servants are referred to—Java objects of servant classes are always servants, but they need not incarnate a CORBA object all the time.

Like Storage Objects, Storage Homes also have their representatives on the client side, that is, the object implementation that uses the PSS. These are called *Storage Home Instances.* To retrieve a Storage Object and obtain a Storage Object Incarnation, a PSS client first needs to get hold of a Storage Home. Storage Home Instances, in turn, can be obtained only in the context of *Sessions.* Sessions are logical connections between the client process and the Datastore and are represented by *Catalogs* on the client side. Catalogs can also be defined in PSDL and thus be used as scopes for Storage Homes, but this is not required. It is also possible to retrieve Storage Homes using generic sessions. The Persistent State Service defines interfaces to create both transactional and nontransactional sessions, and these sessions can be managed explicitly or automatically.

## 13.2 A PSS Example

Let's look at a simple example to clarify the concepts introduced in the previous section. The example is taken from the Meeting Service example in Chapter 10. Please note that, unlike any other example in previous chapters of this book, the code presented here could not be tested because no Java implementation of the Persistent State Service was available at the time of writing.

For the example in Chapter 10, we had to make the state of individual Meeting objects persistent using Java serialization. The code that did this was part of the implementation of our default servant. We pointed out that the example design would not perform very well because of the amount of I/O that was involved for every single access and that efficient caching was required to make the approach feasible in real-world settings.

Efficient caching is something that databases are usually good at, so by delegating the responsibility for managing the persistent state to a PSS implementation of a database vendor, we can combine ease of development with efficient access to persistent object state. To take advantage of the PSS, we have to do two things:

- Write PSDL definitions for Storage Homes and storagetypes and implement any operations on Storage Objects or Storage Homes, if necessary
- Modify the implementation of our server and default servant to initialize and use the PSS.

## 13.2.1 PSDL Definitions

In this section we explain how state members and operations for Storage Objects are defined. This section is meant to give a short impression of how the PSS is used to make CORBA object state persistent, so we leave many of the PSDL details unexplained here. PSDL is explained in greater detail in section 13.3. Before we write any PSDL, let's look at the Meeting interface again:

```
interface Meeting {
    readonly attribute string purpose;
    readonly attribute Participant organizer;
    readonly attribute Room location;
    readonly attribute Date when;

    exception MeetingCanceled {
        string reason;
    };

    ParticipantList getParticipants()
        raises ( MeetingCanceled ) ;

    void addParticipant(in Participant who)
        raises ( MeetingCanceled );

    void removeParticipant(in Participant who)
        raises ( MeetingCanceled );

    oneway void cancel(in string reason)
        raises ( MeetingCanceled ) ;

    void relocate( in Room where, in Date when )
        raises ( MeetingCanceled, SlotAlreadyTaken );
};
```

In the implementation of the example in Chapter 10 we defined a separate Java class that represented the state of a Meeting object and could be serialized to disk. Using PSDL, we can now define a storagetype that represents this class. From our PSDL definition, a PSDL compiler can generate Java code specifically for the PSS implementation we are using. To find out which state members we need to define, let's look at the `MeetingState` class we used in Chapter 10.

```
public static class MeetingState
    implements java.io.Serializable {

    /* transient data */
    // ...

    /** the actual state */
    String purpose;
    String[] participantIORs;
    String organizerIOR;
    String locationIOR;
    Date when;
    boolean canceled = false;
    String cancelReason = null;
}
```

In addition to representations for the four attributes defined in the interface, the class `MeetingState` defines two variables to deal with cancellations of meetings, `canceled` and `cancelReason`, and a representation for the list of participants. For simplicity, we use the same approach here and define an abstract storagetype for Meeting objects as follows. Note that we use a string representation for object references again.

```
// file: Meeting.psdl
#include "Office.idl"
module com {
...
module chapter13 {

    abstract storagetype MeetingState {
        state string purpose;
        readonly state string organizer;
        state string location;
        state Date when;
        state boolean canceled;
        state string cancelReason;
        state CORBA::StringSeq participants;
    };
```

```
        abstract storagehome MeetingStateHome of MeetingState {
            factory create(in string purp,
                           in string org,
                           in string loc
                           in Date when,
                           in boolean cancld,
                           in string cncl_reason,
                           in CORBA::StringSeq participants
                           );
    };

    storagetype MeetingStateImpl
        implements MeetingState {};

    storagehome MeetingStateHomeImpl of MeetingStateImpl
        implements MeetingStateHome {};
};
```

Note that the only read-only state member is organizer. The definition of the factory operation create() in the abstract Storage Home MeetingState-Home is effectively a constructor definition. The PSDL compiler is now able to generate all the required implementation code for the target language and PSS implementation from these definitions. It maps abstract storagetypes and abstract Storage Homes to Java interfaces of the same name. Non-abstract definitions are mapped to Java classes. The differences between abstract and concrete storagetypes and Storage Homes are explained in more detail in section 13.3. For now, just remember that the abstract definitions define the types of Storage Objects and Homes and that the nonabstract ones define the Java class names for the generated implementations.

## 13.2.2 Servant and Server Implementation

Because we did not define any operations on `MeetingState`, we don't have to provide method implementations but can use the generated class `MeetingStateImpl` directly in the servant implementation. Here is the modified servant:

```
package com.wiley.compbooks.brose.chapter13;

import java.util.*;
import java.io.*;
import com.wiley.compbooks.brose.chapter10.office.*;
import com.wiley.compbooks.brose.chapter10.office.MeetingPackage.*;
import org.omg.CORBA.*;
```

```
import org.omg.PortableServer.*;
import org.omg.PortableServer.POAPackage.*;

class MeetingDefaultServant
    extends MeetingPOA {

    private ORB orb;
    private POA poa;
    private Calendar calendar;
    private DateComparator dateComparator;
    private MeetingStateHomeImpl myHome;

    MeetingDefaultServant(ORB orb, POA poa, MeetingStateHomeImpl myHome) {
        this.orb = orb;
        this.poa = poa;
        this.myHome = myHome;
        calendar = Calendar.getInstance();
        dateComparator = new DateComparator();
    }
```

The constructor for this version of the default servant implementation takes a Storage Home Instance as an additional argument. Whenever a request is received, the default servant retrieves a Storage Object Incarnation for the target object from the Storage Home Instance. This is done in the following method `myState()`, which uses the target object's ID as the short-pid for the Storage Object.

```
    MeetingStateImpl myState() {
        return (MeetingStateImpl)myHome.find_by_short_pid(_object_id());
    }

    public String purpose() {
        return myState().purpose();
    }

    public DigitalSecretary organizer(){
        return DigitalSecretaryHelper.narrow(
            orb.string_to_object( myState().organizer()));
    }
    // ...
}
```

The implementation of the servant is now much simpler than with direct file access, as in the original version. In particular, the responsibility for efficiently ensuring consistency in the presence of potentially concurrent accesses is delegated to the PSS implementation.

Finally, we have to modify the implementation of the Meeting Server such that it creates a session with a Datastore and retrieves a Storage Home instance, which it then passes to the default servant.

```
package com.wiley.compbooks.brose.chapter13;

import com.wiley.compbooks.brose.chapter10.office.*;

import java.io.*;
import org.omg.CORBA.*;
import org.omg.PortableServer.*;
import org.omg.CosNaming.*;
import org.omg.CosNaming.NamingContextPackage.*;
import org.omg.CosPersistentState.*;

public class MeetingServer {

    public static void main(String[] args) {

        MeetingFactoryImpl meetingFactory;
        try {
            //init
            ORB orb = ORB.init( args, null );

            // get connector registry
            ConnectorRegistry registry =
                ConnectorRegistryHelper.narrow(
                    orb.resolve_initial_registry("PSS"));

            // get connector
            Connector connector =
                registry.find_connector("my_vendor:implementation-id");

            // create session
            Session session =
                connector.create_basic_session(
                    org.omg.CosPersistentState.READ_WRITE,
                      "",
                    new Parameter[0]);

            // get storage home
            MeetingStateHome home =
                (MeetingStateHome)session.find_storage_home(
         "PSDL:com/wiley/compbooks/brose/chapter13/MeetingStateHomeImpl
         :1.0");
```

After initializing the ORB, we obtain a reference to its Connector Registry that, in turn, lets us retrieve a Connector. Connectors are the entry points to particular PSS implementations and allow us to create sessions. They are explained in more detail in section 13.4 of this chapter. Using the session object, we can retrieve a Storage Home Instance of a given PSDL type. The rest of the server implementation is the same as in the original version; the only difference is that the Storage Home Instance is passed to the default servant constructor.

```
        // get root POA
        POA rootPOA =
            POAHelper.narrow( orb.resolve_initial_references(
            "RootPOA"));

        // create a user defined poa
        org.omg.CORBA.Policy [] policies =
            new org.omg.CORBA.Policy[5];
        policies[0] = rootPOA.create_id_assignment_policy(
            IdAssignmentPolicyValue.USER_ID);
        policies[1] = rootPOA.create_lifespan_policy(
            LifespanPolicyValue.PERSISTENT);
        policies[2] = rootPOA.create_request_processing_policy(
            RequestProcessingPolicyValue.USE_DEFAULT_SERVANT);
        policies[3] = rootPOA.create_servant_retention_policy(
            ServantRetentionPolicyValue.RETAIN);
        policies[4] = rootPOA.create_id_uniqueness_policy(
            IdUniquenessPolicyValue.MULTIPLE_ID);

        POA meetingPOA = rootPOA.create_POA("MeetingPOA",
            rootPOA.the_POAManager(),
            policies);

        MeetingDefaultServant mds =
            new MeetingDefaultServant( orb, meetingPOA, home );

        meetingPOA.set_servant( mds );

        for (int i=0; i<policies.length; i++)
            policies[i].destroy();

        // register with naming service
        NamingContextExt root =
           NamingContextExtHelper.narrow(
               orb.resolve_initial_references("NameService"));

        meetingFactory = new MeetingFactoryImpl( meetingPOA );
        root.bind(
            root.to_name( "MeetingService" ),
            meetingFactory._this(orb) );

        rootPOA.the_POAManager().activate();
        // wait for requests
        orb.run();
    }
    catch(UserException ue) {
        ue.printStackTrace();
        System.err.println(ue);
    }
    catch(SystemException se) {
        se.printStackTrace();
```

```
                System.err.println(se);
            }
        }
    }
```

There is one last piece missing that we have omitted here for brevity. The implementation of the Meeting Factory originally used the default servant to create Meeting objects and to create files with the initial state. This factory would now have to use the Storage Home's factory operation create() to set up new Storage Objects in the Datastore.

## 13.3 The Persistent State Definition Language

The PSS specification introduces a declarative language for the definition of stateful, non-CORBA objects. This language, the *Persistent State Definition Language* (PSDL), is a superset of IDL. This means that it extends IDL with concepts to define Storage Objects and Storage Homes. IDL already has concepts to define stateful objects that are not remotely accessible through operation invocations, namely, value types. The authors of the PSS specification, however, chose to introduce different language constructs that are more focused on database technology. We treat PSDL in detail in this section because it is also used in the CORBA Component Model that we cover in Chapter 14.

PSDL is designed to let application developers specify in a language-independent way what state members should be stored by the persistence mechanism and which operations are supported by Storage Objects and Storage Homes. Also, it lets developers define certain persistence-related characteristics like keys and the lifetime dependencies of aggregations and aggregates. This is possible using *abstract* storagetypes and abstract Storage Homes. This abstract specification expresses everything a servant programmer needs to know about the persistent data model. To make the state of CORBA objects persistent, a servant programmer uses the Java interfaces generated by a PSDL compiler from these abstract specifications and the interfaces to the Datastore defined by the PSS.

Abstract definitions are sufficient for a PSDL compiler to generate mechanism-dependent, default implementation code. In many cases, however, these definitions are too general to provide efficient access to persistent storage because they do not make direct use of features provided by the persistence mechanism, such as marking a key as primary or defining the representation of a reference for a storagetype. Also, most PSS implementations will provide their own set of structured and collection types that can be used to efficiently implement the behavior of Storage Objects. These implementation details can be expressed in separate, nonabstract definitions of storagetypes and Storage Homes so that servant developers can be insulated from them.

## 13.3.1 Abstract Storagetypes

PSDL definitions are written in `.psdl` files. An abstract storagetype can be defined as in the following example:

```
// file: employee.psdl
abstract storagetype Person {
    state string full_name;
    readonly state long social_security_number;
    readonly state ref<Person> spouse;
    void marry(in ref<Person> the_spouse);
};
abstract storagetype Employee: Person {
    state string phone_number;
    state string office;
};
```

Storage Objects can have operations or state members. The state members of Storage Objects are defined in state clauses. Like attributes in interfaces, state members can be declared to be read-only. The types of state members can be IDL base types, string types, structured types, local or abstract interfaces. State member types can also be previously defined abstract storagetypes or references to a storagetype.

If the type of a state member is a storagetype, a Storage Object of the state member type will be *embedded* in the Storage Object. An embedded object's lifetime is limited by the lifetime of the enclosing object. It has no identity of its own and cannot be referenced directly, that is, without navigating through the aggregate Storage Object.

Aggregation relations between Storage Objects are important, but in many cases relations are a little less close. Even a relation like marriage (which *is* a close relation), for example, is usually not an aggregation—none of the two persons involved properly "contains" the other so that he or she does not have an identity of his or her own, and the two don't necessarily die at the same time.

To allow a Storage Object to reference another that is not embedded, PSDL has *reference types*. To define a state member type that is a reference to another Storage Type T, the state member is defined to have type ref<T>.

In the example storagetype Person, we defined the state member spouse to be a reference to another Person.

Operations declared in an abstract storagetype follow the same rule as the operations in IDL interfaces. The only difference is that they allow abstract storagetypes as their arguments. The operation marry() declared in the storagetype Person takes a reference to another Storage Object of type Person, the new spouse, as its argument.

Storagetypes can inherit from each other, much like IDL interfaces. Storagetype inheritance follows the same rules as IDL interface inheritance, so storagetypes can inherit from multiple base types. All storagetypes inherit directly or indirectly from the base type StorageObject, which is defined in the module CosPersistentState:

```
module CosPersistentState {
    typedef CORBA::OctetSeq Pid;
    typedef CORBA::OctetSeq ShortPid;

    abstract storagetype StorageObject {
        void destroy_object();

        boolean object_exists();

        Pid get_pid();
        ShortPid get_short_pid();

        StorageHomeBase get_storage_home();
    };
};
```

If the operation destroy_object() is called on a Storage Object Incarnation, the associated Storage Object is destroyed, but not the Incarnation. Calling object_exists() on an incarnation yields TRUE if it represents an actual Storage Object. The two operations get_pid() and get_short_pid() return the pid and the short-pid of the associated Storage Object. The short-pid is an identifier that identifies only a Storage Object relative to its containing Storage Home, whereas the pid is a global identifier. Finally, get_storage_home() returns the Storage Home for this Storage Object.

### 13.3.2 Abstract Storage Homes

We can define the abstract Storage Homes for the preceding storagetypes as follows:

```
abstract storagehome PersonHome of Person {
    factory create_person(in string name, in long ssn );
    key ssn_key social_security_number;
};
abstract storagehome EmployeeHome of Employee: PersonHome {
    factory create_employee(in string name, in long ssn, in string phone, in string offc);
};
```

The type of the Storage Objects managed by a Storage Home is defined after the keyword of. The definition of an abstract Storage Home can introduce factory operations to create Storage Objects of the type managed by a Storage Home. Like Java constructors, there can be multiple factory operations in a Storage Home. Unlike constructors, factory operations have names, all of which must be unique within the Storage Home.

Abstract Storage Homes can define keys for the Storage Objects they manage. A key is a value that uniquely identifies a Storage Object. In the example, the Storage Home PersonHome defines the state member social_security_number of storagetype Person as the key ssn_key. There can be multiple keys for the Storage Home, and keys can be defined as a combination of state members. The state members that together constitute a key must all have types that are *comparable*, that is, they must be one of the following IDL types: integral, narrow or wide char or string, fixed, sequence of octet, struct with only comparable members, or valuetype with only public and comparable state members.

Storage Home definitions like storagetypes can also list operations, but they do not have state of their own. The preceding example definitions do not contain operations on Storage Homes. Finally, abstract Storage Homes support multiple inheritance. The abstract Storage Home EmployeeHome inherits operations, factories, and key declarations from its base type PersonHome.

## 13.3.3 Catalogs

Catalogs are the units of session management in the PSS. Applications access Datastores through sessions, and a Catalog defines the scope of a session in terms of the Storage Homes that can be accessed. The catalog for EmployeeHomes and PersonHomes is declared like this:

```
catalog HumanResources {
    provides PersonHome persons;
    provides EmployeeHome employees;
};
```

Additionally, Catalogs can define local operations, but we don't show any of this here.

### 13.3.4 Implementing Storage Objects

Abstract storagetypes contain all the type information that is necessary for a PSDL compiler to generate implementation code in a target language for a specific PSS implementation. To allow the generation of more efficient code for a target platform, it is possible to give the compiler a few implementation hints in the form of nonabstract storagetypes.

```
storagehome PersonHomeImpl of Person implements PersonHome;
storagetype PersonImpl implements Person {
    ref social_security_number;
};
storagetype EmployeeImpl: PersonImpl implements Employee {
    store spouse as PersonImpl scope PersonHomeImpl
};
```

Just like Java classes, storagetypes are declared as implementations of those abstract storagetypes that are listed after the keyword implements. Storagetypes can implement multiple abstract storagetypes, but they can inherit from only a single nonabstract storagetype. The storagetype EmployeeImpl inherits from PersonImpl.

If any of the abstract storagetypes implemented by a storagetype contains operations, the PSDL compiler maps the storagetype to an abstract Java class, so developers have to provide implementations of the operations in subclasses. In our example, the abstract storagetype Person declared the marry() operation, so the Java classes PersonImpl and EmployeeImpl that are generated by the PSDL compiler are both abstract.

The implementation hints that can be dropped in storagetypes are *reference representations* and *store directives*. Many relational databases, for example, do not provide separate object identifiers. Instead of a reference, a foreign key must be given that identifies the referenced record. For these systems, the storagetype can define the representation of a reference to this type in terms of values of its state members, that is, as a key. This is done in a ref clause, as shown previously, which is similar to a key declaration. The identifier or identifiers in this clause must refer to previously defined state members, just as in a key declaration.

Store directives define how state members are stored. A store directive is required in a storagetype definition if the abstract storagetype that is implemented has state members of an abstract storagetype. In this case, it is necessary to define the implementation storagetypes that should be used for storing these members. If the state member's type is an abstract storagetype *reference*, the store directive is optional. If it is given, it is possible to specify in which Storage Home the referenced Storage Object should be stored. In the example above, we have forward declared a Storage Home for Persons so that it can be used in the scope expression of the store directive in EmployeeImpl.

### 13.3.5 Implementing Storage Homes

Like abstract storagetypes, abstract Storage Homes can have concrete implementations that allow more efficient code to be generated. In fact, the main use of nonabstract Storage Homes is to mark one of the keys declared by an abstract Storage Home as the primary key. Knowing which key is used as the primary key allows the underlying persistence mechanism to set up more efficient access paths for this key. Here is an example:

```
storagehome PersonHomeImpl of PersonImpl implements PersonHome {
    primary key ssn_key;
};
```

The Storage Home PersonHomeImpl implements the abstract Storage Home PersonHome. It is defined as the Storage Home for Storage Objects of type PersonImpl and defines the key ssn_key, which was declared in the definition of PersonHome, as the primary key for this Storage Home.

## 13.4 PSS Interfaces

The Persistent State Service defines an API for a persistence mechanism that can be used across different persistence implementations. As a consequence, changing the persistence mechanism by, for example, using a database system instead of flat files for storage or updating from a relational to an object-relational database system is possible without changes in the application code. Even if the implementations of Storage Objects and Storage Homes rely on nonportable features of a particular PSS product, porting requires only changing and recompiling the PSDL definition and modifying these implementations, but the application code itself is insulated from these changes.

The entry point that represents a PSS implementation is a *Connector*. To retrieve the Connector for a specific PSS implementation the client has to look it up in a *Connector Registry*. The Connector Registry is provided by the ORB as another initial reference. It can be obtained by calling orb.resolve_initial_references("PSS"). The Connector Registry is necessary because a PSS client could be using multiple PSS implementations at the same time.

All interfaces to the Persistent State Service are defined in module CosPersistentState, and all interfaces are declared local.

```
module CosPersistentState {

    native StorageObjectBase;
    native StorageObjectFactory;
    native StorageHomeFactory;
    native SessionFactory;
    native SessionPoolFactory;

    local interface Connector;
    exception NotFound {};

    local interface ConnectorRegistry {
        Connector find_connector( in string implementation_id )
            raises( NotFound );

        void register_connector( in Connector c );

        void unregister_connector( in string implementation_id )
            raises( NotFound );
    };
```

A Connector can be looked up in a registry under an implementation ID using the find_connector() operation. The implementation identifier consists of an OMG-assigned vendor ID and an implementation-dependent string. The other operations of a Connector Registry allow clients to register new Connectors or to unregister them again.

Once a Connector is obtained, it can be used to create Catalogs that represent sessions or session pools and provide access to a Datastore. The difference between individual sessions and session pools is that if they are associated with transactions, then individual sessions give programmers explicit control over the transaction association. Session pools manage transactional sessions implicitly. A full discussion of transactions is beyond the scope of this chapter, however.

Both Session and SessionPool inherit from the interface CatalogBase:

```
typedef short AccessMode;
const AccessMode READ_ONLY = 0;
const AccessMode READ_WRITE = 1;
```

```
local interface CatalogBase {
        readonly attribute AccessMode access_mode;

        StorageHomeBase find_storage_home(in string storage_home_id)
          raises (NotFound);

        StorageObjectBase find_by_pid(in Pid the_pid)
          raises (NotFound);

        void flush();
        void refresh();
        void free_all();
        void close();
};

local interface Session: CatalogBase {}; // empty interface

local interface TransactionalSession: Session {
    // omitted ...
};

local interface SessionPool: CatalogBase {
    // omitted ...
};
```

Catalogs can be created with read-only or read/write access modes. The attribute access_mode indicates which of these modes of access is valid for the current Catalog. If the access_mode is read-only, then all Storage Object Incarnations obtained from the Catalog are read-only.

Using Catalogs, Storage Home instances can be retrieved with the find_storage_home() operation. The argument identifier for a Storage Home can either be the identifier declared in the provides clause of a Catalog definition in PSDL, or it can be a repository-style type ID such as `"PSDL:com/wiley/compbooks/brose/chapter13/StoreAllImpl:1.0"`. Finally, the identifier can have the format `":datastore_name"`. In this case, the operation returns a generic Storage Home instance for `java.lang.Object` in the named Datastore. If no matching Storage Home is found, the NotFound exception is raised.

The find_by_pid() operation locates a Storage Object with the given pid and returns a Storage Object Incarnation for this object. If it cannot find a Storage Object for the give pid, the operation raises the NotFound exception.

The flush() and refresh() operations deal with caching. If the PSS implementation uses caching, calling flush() will write out any cached data, whereas refresh() will refresh locally cached data. The free_all() operation deals with garbage collection for languages that do not have built-in garbage collection. It sets the reference count for all Storage Object instances obtained through this Catalog to 0. Finally, close() terminates the Catalog and the associated session and flushes the Catalog.

Now that we have looked at Catalogs, we can return to the Connector interface with which we can create these Catalogs.

```
typedef short TransactionPolicy;
const TransactionPolicy NON_TRANSACTIONAL = 0;
const TransactionPolicy TRANSACTIONAL = 1;

typedef short IsolationLevel;
const IsolationLevel READ_UNCOMMITTED = 0;
const IsolationLevel READ_COMMITTED = 1;
const IsolationLevel REPEATABLE_READ = 2;
const IsolationLevel SERIALIZABLE = 3;

struct Parameter {
    string name;
    any val;
};
typedef sequence<Parameter> ParameterList;
typedef sequence<TransactionalSession> TransactionalSessionList;

local interface Connector {
    readonly attribute string implementation_id;

    Pid get_pid(in StorageObjectBase obj);
    ShortPid get_short_pid(in StorageObjectBase obj);
```

The Connector interface defines an attribute for its implementation ID, which is the one that was used to look up the Connector in the Connector Registry. The two operations get_pid() and get_short_pid() return the pid and short-pid for a StorageObject. The next group of operations in the Connector interface deals with sessions.

```
Session create_basic_session(
        in AccessMode access_mode,
        in TypeId catalog_type_name,
        in ParameterList additional_parameters );

TransactionalSession create_transactional_session(
        in AccessMode access_mode,
        in IsolationLevel default_isolation_level,
        in EndOfAssociationCallback callback,
```

```
        in TypeId catalog_type_name,
        in ParameterList additional_parameters );

    SessionPool create_session_pool(
        in AccessMode access_mode,
        in TransactionPolicy tx_policy,
        in TypeId catalog_type_name,
        in ParameterList additional_parameters );

    TransactionalSession current_session();

    TransactionalSessionList sessions(
        in CosTransactions::Coordinator transaction);
```

The create_basic_session() operation creates and returns a nontransactional, basic session with the given access mode. The catalog_type_name parameter is an empty string, or it contains the PSDL type ID of the catalog, as in "PSDL:com/wiley/compbooks/brose/chapter13/StoreAllImpl:1.0". The additional_parameters argument will typically contain implementation-dependent parameters such as file or database names. If a session with the desired access mode cannot be created, the system exception PERSIST_STORE is raised.

To create a transactional session, the Connector interface provides the create_transactional_session() operation. Three of its parameters are the same as in create_basic_session(). The additional parameter default_isolation_level describes the desired level of isolation for the transactional session. The callback parameter is a reference that can be passed to the implementation in order to be notified when a session is released by the implementation. Again, PERSIST_STORE is raised if a session with the desired access mode cannot be created.

Session pools can be created with the create_session_pool() operation. The parameter tx_policy determines whether the session pool manages transactional or nontransactional sessions. The operation current_session() returns the transactional session that is associated with the calling thread. To retrieve more than one session that is associated with a given transactional resource, the sessions() operation can be used.

```
    StorageObjectFactory register_storage_object_factory(
        in TypeId storage_type_name,
        in StorageObjectFactory _factory );

    StorageHomeFactory register_storage_home_factory(
        in TypeId storage_home_type_name,
        in StorageHomeFactory _factory );
```

```
            SessionFactory register_session_factory(
                  in TypeId catalog_type_name,
                  in SessionFactory _factory );

            SessionPoolFactory register_session_pool_factory(
                  in TypeId catalog_type_name,
                  in SessionPoolFactory _factory );
      }; // end Connector
}; // end CosPersistentState
```

The last four operations in the Connector interface all register factory objects and return the previously registered factory of the given kind, if any. These factory objects are needed by the PSS implementation to be able to create implementation objects of user-defined classes that implement abstract storagetypes, abstract Storage Homes, or Catalogs.

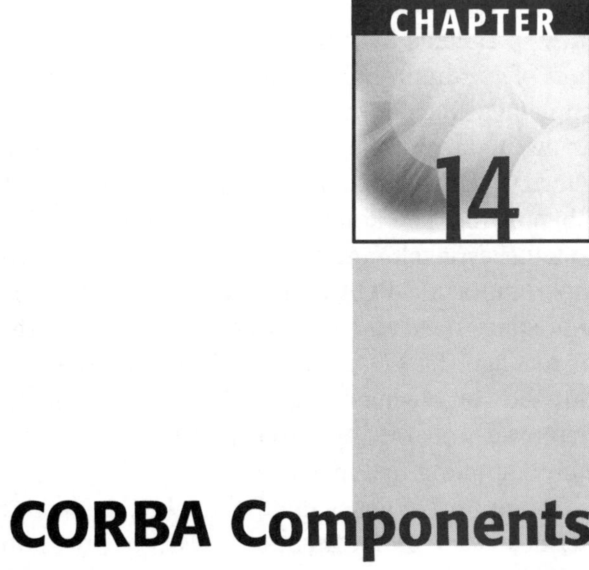


# CORBA Components

CORBA provides a flexible programming paradigm for developing distributed applications and a set of advanced and powerful object services. This flexibility and comprehensive functionality, however, come at the price of a certain complexity: Developing enterprise applications that make use of the more advanced features of the ORB and rely on services such as Security, Notification, Persistent State, and Transactions requires a substantial development effort.

Large-scale CORBA applications are not only hard to develop, they can also be hard to deploy, configure, and maintain. Consider a simple configuration example with a few server processes hosting objects that require other objects to exist at creation time. To start up the application, the individual processes must be started in the right order and probably rely on a Naming Service and a set of naming conventions so that dependent servers can retrieve the required references. This is easy to get wrong with a couple of dozens servers. It usually also results in an overall system architecture where the individual system components are tightly coupled because both mechanisms and policies to look up and retrieve the required objects are built into the application. Reusing just part of the application in different contexts then requires rewriting some of the configuration code.

The specification of the CORBA Component Model (CCM) addresses these problems by introducing the concept of *components* and the definition of a comprehensive set of interfaces and techniques for specifying, implementing, packaging, and deploying components. The CCM introduces a new declarative language, the Component Implementation Definition Language (CIDL). This language is a superset of PSDL, which we introduced in Chapter 13, "The Persistent State Service." CIDL is used by code generators to relieve developers from the burden of writing repetitive code for the most important POA and service usage patterns and for managing persistent state. Basically, developers need not write server main lines anymore or manage the POA. Instead, they can concentrate on providing the functionality, or business logic, of their components. These will eventually be deployed to *containers* that provide the server-side run-time environment for component instances.

To support component packaging, installation, and deployment, CCM defines *descriptor* formats in XML that describe software packages, individual components, component assemblies, and their dependencies. Implementations of the Components specification will come with code generators and visual tools that automatically generate these descriptors and allow them to be modified through visual interaction with users.

This chapter is an introduction to Components and provides you with an overview of the CCM specification. At the time of this writing, the CCM is still in finalization at the OMG, and no implementations are available, so we do not provide a comprehensive and fully tested example in this chapter. In particular we cover the following:

- The Component model (section 14.1)
- Container programming model (section 14.2)
- Component implementation framework (section 14.3)
- Component packaging and deployment (section 14.4)
- A comparison of the CCM with Enterprise Java Beans (section 14.5)

## 14.1 The Component Model

IDL interface definitions define a named set of features, namely, operations and attributes. These features are accessible to clients through object references. The CCM extends IDL with new language constructs to describe component types in IDL. Component types support the definition of features not available in interface definitions. The CCM, however, does not define a new kind of reference to component instances. Component instances are accessed through regular CORBA object references. The type of these references is an IDL interface that is implicitly defined through the component definition and is called the component's *equivalent interface*. The definition of the equivalent interfaces is generated automatically from the component definition. We will frequently refer to this interface as many component model concepts are directly mapped to definitions in this interface.

The features supported by component type definitions are collectively called *ports* and can be broadly classified into two categories. The first category of ports is called *facets* (section 14.1.1) and specifies a component's functionality as a set of interfaces rather than as a single interface as with simple IDL interface definitions. The second category could be called "configuration ports" (section 14.1.2) and expresses how a component can be connected to other components that communicate either through invocations or event notifications. We explain these sets of features in the following two subsections. Note, however, that the CCM distinguishes between *basic* and *extended* components and that basic components may not provide any of the new component features. Basic components are a simple way to turn a regular CORBA object into a component and are similar in functionality to an Enterprise Java Bean. In fact, basic components can be mapped to Enterprise Beans by bridges, thus allowing Java clients to access basic components as if they were Enterprise Beans.

Finally, we describe the concept of component *homes* (section 14.1.3). Component homes are generalizations of the factory design pattern and facilitate the creation and location of component instances.

### 14.1.1 Facets

Multiple interfaces are important for objects that have various uses and can be used in different contexts. In simple cases, you might simply want to distinguish between a service and a management interface for an object. In other cases an object might encapsulate an elaborate protocol, such as a workflow, so providing different interfaces for the individual stages of the protocol is a natural choice.

To express that the functionality of a set of interfaces actually belongs to a single object, you would have to define a new interface that inherits from all the interfaces that are to be combined. The resulting interface is usually long and complicated. The only alternative is to define an entry point interface with operations that allow navigation between the other interfaces of the object. This design nicely mirrors the different uses in different contexts, but it requires some well-written prose explanations because the relationships between these interfaces are not clear simply from their IDL definitions.

An example for this second design is the Event Service, which we presented in Chapter 11, "Events." The central interface CosEventChannelAdmin::EventChannel consists of just two operations to navigate to the entry points for consumers or suppliers of events, the interfaces ConsumerAdmin and SupplierAdmin. Each of these, in turn, provides two operations to obtain references to proxy consumers or suppliers for push or pull mode communication, respectively. All that these operations in any of these interfaces do is to provide clients with an interface to the event channel for their particular usage type.

The OMG recognized the need for Multiple Interfaces and issued a corresponding RFP in 1996. The specification process was terminated by the OMG in 1999 without a resulting document being adopted and published. The CCM can be regarded as the legitimate fulfillment of these requirements as it defines all the necessary concepts even without formally aligning them to the original RFP. The only requirement of the Multiple Interfaces RFP that is not met by the Component specification is the ability to provide multiple interfaces of the same type at the same port.

Component types allow the combination of different interfaces that are not related by inheritance. In the terms of the CCM, the interfaces provided by a component are called the component's *facets*. A hypothetical event channel component, for example, could be defined as follows:

```
#include <CosEventChannelAdmin.idl>
module ComponentEventChannel {

  interface ManagedObject {
     // management operations
  };

  component EventChannelComp supports ManagedObject {
     // facets
     provides ProxyPushCosumer proxy_push_consumer;
     provides ProxyPushSupplier proxy_push_supplier;
     provides ProxyPullCosumer proxy_pull_consumer;
     provides ProxyPullSupplier proxy_pull_supplier;
  };
```

A component type name is defined after the keyword component. The component's own interface, its equivalent interface, is defined implicitly through the component definition. The equivalent interface for the EventChannelComp component inherits from the user-defined interface

ManagedObject. This relationship is expressed using the supports keyword. Component definitions cannot introduce new operations, so the only way to define operations in the component interface is by declaring supported interfaces.

Component facets are defined with the keyword provides. Each facet has a name and a type, which must be an interface type. Facet names are used to navigate between the component's own interface and its individual facets. Figure 14.1 shows the EventChannelComp component and its four facets.

Navigation from the component to its facets is possible through operations in the component's equivalent interface. The equivalent interface for the EventChannelComp component would look like this:

```
interface EventChannelComp : Components::CCMObject, ManagedObject {
    ProxyPushCosumer provide_proxy_push_consumer();
    ProxyPushSupplier provide_proxy_push_supplier();
    ProxyPullCosumer provide_proxy_pull_consumer();
    ProxyPullSupplier provide_proxy_pull_supplier();
};
```

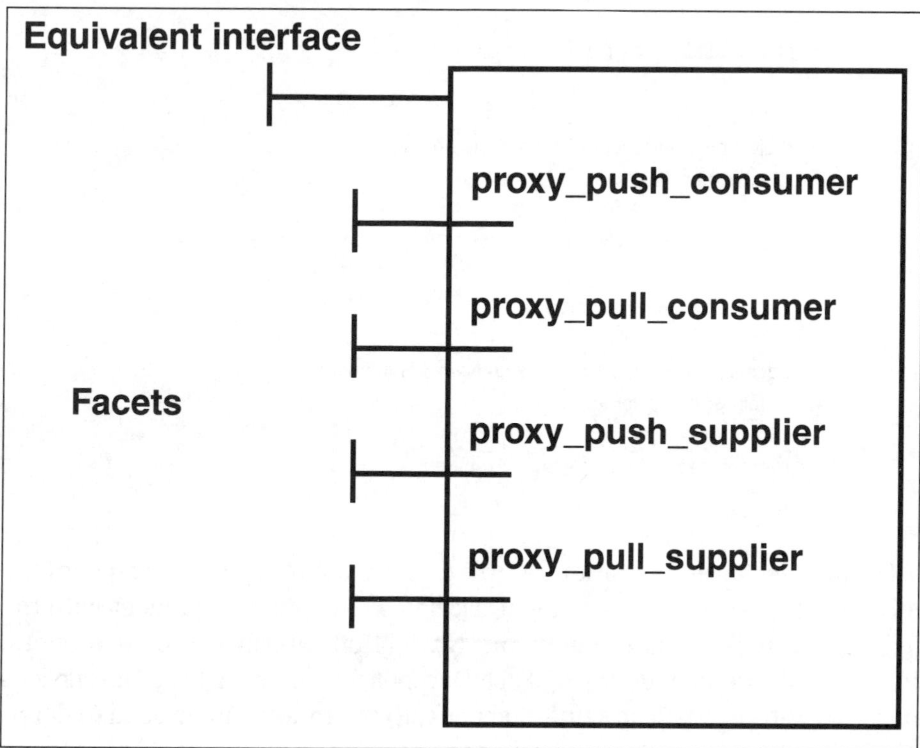


**Figure 14.1** The EventChannelComp component and its facets.

The operations in the equivalent interface allow clients of the component to retrieve references to any of its facets. The equivalent interface inherits additional, generic navigation operations through the Components::Navigation interface, which is inherited by the Component base interface CCMObject from which all component interfaces inherit. The Navigation interface is defined as follows:

```
module Components {
    typedef string FeatureName;
    valuetype FacetDescription {
        public CORBA::RepositoryId InterfaceID;
        public FeatureName Name;
    };

    valuetype Facet : FacetDescription {
        public Object ref;
    };

    typedef sequence <Facet> Facets;
    typedef sequence <FacetDescription> FacetDescriptions;

    exception InvalidName {};

    interface Navigation {
        Object provide_facet(in FeatureName name)
          raises(InvalidName);

        FacetDescriptions describe_facets();

        Facets provide_all_facets();

        Facets provide_named_facets (in NameList names)
          raises(InvalidName);

        boolean same_component(in Object ref);
    };
```

The provide_facet() operation returns a reference to the named facet of the current component or raises the InvalidName exception if no facet with the given name exists. Additionally, the Navigation interface provides operations to retrieve sequences of FacetDescriptions or even FacetDescriptions plus facet references. The same_component() operation can be used to determine whether two references belong to the same component.

The operations described so far all support navigation from the component to its facets. To navigate the other way, from a facet to its component, the CCM adds the operation get_component() to the CORBA::Object interface. If the target of this operation is a facet, the operation returns a reference to its component. If the target is a component itself, the same reference is returned. Otherwise, a nil reference is returned.

## 14.1.2 Configuration and Composition Ports

The functionality of a component is provided through its supported interfaces and its facets. The component definition may not introduce new operations. The component ports explained in this subsection do not describe functionality but are designed to support the configuration of individual components and the composition of assemblies of interacting components. We explain *attribute*, *receptacle*, *emitter*, *publisher*, and *consumer* ports in the following subsections.

### *14.1.2.1 Attributes and Inheritance*

The configuration of individual components is supported by its *attribute* ports. Attributes are declared in a component definition exactly like attributes in interfaces, but the intention is that they should be used only for configuration purposes, although nothing prevents their use for arbitrary other purposes. The components specification extends the IDL syntax for attribute declarations such that attributes can be declared to raise exceptions, which is not possible in standard IDL.

To add a few attributes to our component examples, we can use component inheritance:

```
component ConfigurableEventChannel : EventChannelComp {
    readonly attribute string description;
    attribute long timeout;
};
```

The derived component type ConfigurableEventChannel extends its base type by adding two attributes, one of which is a read-only attribute. Component inheritance results in an inheritance relationship between the two equivalent interfaces:

```
interface ConfigurableEventChannel: EventChannelComp { // ... };
```

Note that inheritance between component types, unlike interface inheritance, is restricted to single inheritance.

### 14.1.2.2 Receptacles

The composition of a system of components is supported by the declaration of receptacles and event sources and sinks. Often, individual components require specific references to other objects or components because they rely on services provided by these to be able to provide their own functionality. As you have seen in the examples throughout this book, server processes are often written to retrieve these references from files or from Naming or Trading Services and to initialize servants with these references. The dependency between the services provided by the objects in this server and the retrieved references is never made explicit and is visible only in the source code of the implementation. This information, however, is essential to be able to deploy an application that uses this implementation or to successfully reuse the implementation code in other contexts.

While it would have been possible to express a component's relationships to specific foreign interfaces using attributes and descriptive texts, the CCM introduces *receptacles* as a more explicit language concept. A receptacle is a named connection point that accepts interfaces and connects these to the component for future use. For example, we can extend the definition of our event channel component to use the OMG's Telecom Log Service and express this usage relation by defining a logger receptacle.

```
#include <DsEventLogAdmin.idl>
component SimplexLoggingEventChannel : ConfigurableEventChannel {
    // receptacle
    uses EventLog logger;
};
```

Figure 14.2 illustrates the ports of a LoggingEventChannel component.

The preceding definition of a receptacle results in the following equivalent interface, which provides operations to manage the connection between a receptacle and an object of the declared type:

```
interface SimplexLoggingEventChannel : ConfigurableEventChannel {

    // connection operations for receptacle logger
    void connect_logger(in EventLog conxn)
      raises(Components::AlreadyConnected, Components::InvalidConnection);

    EventLog disconnect_logger()
      raises(Components::NoConnection);

    EventLog get_connection_logger();
};
```

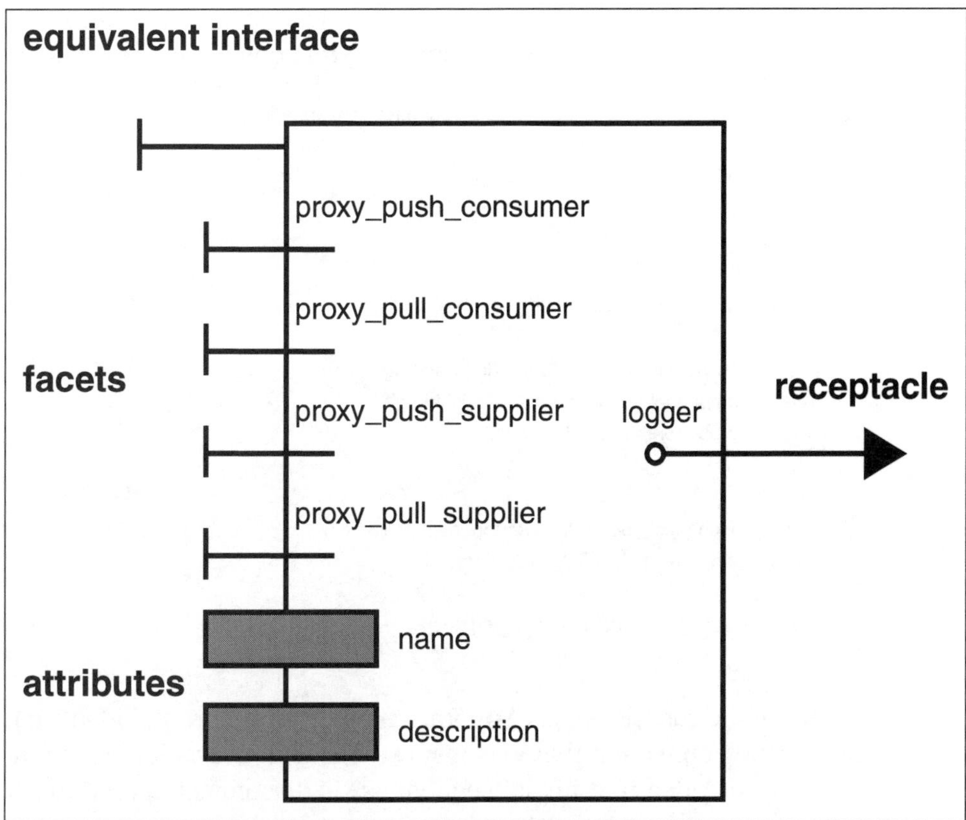


**Figure 14.2** Facets, receptacles, and attributes.

At any time, a receptacle defined in this way can be connected only to a single object reference. If the operation connect_logger() was called when the receptacle is already connected it would raise the AlreadyConnected exception. The receptacle is called a *simplex* receptacle in such a case. The relationships between a component and other objects that can be expressed using receptacles are not restricted to one-to-one relations, however. The uses clause, unlike the provides clause, has an optional keyword multiple that allows the definition of *multiplex* receptacles. We can thus define an alternative component type MultiplexLoggingEventChannel that uses multiple EventLogs:

```
component MultiplexLoggingEventChannel : ConfigurableEventChannel {
    // receptacle
    uses multiple EventLog logger;
};
```

To support multiple connections between a receptacle and object references, the equivalent interface now provides different connection operations:

```
interface MultiplexLoggingEventChannel : ConfigurableEventChannel {

    struct loggerConnection {
        EventLog objref;
        Components::Cookie ck;
    };
    sequence <loggerConnection> loggerConnections;

    Components::Cookie connect_logger(in EventLog conxn)
      raises(Components::ExceededConnectionLimit,
            Components::InvalidConnection
            );

    EventLog disconnect_logger(in Components::Cookie ck)
      raises(Components::InvalidConnection);

    loggerConnections get_connections_logger();
};
```

The caller of the connect_logger() operation receives an internal identifier, a Cookie, for the connection that was just established. The caller is responsible for saving the identifier for subsequent use in disconnect operations. If the component implementation has defined an upper limit for the number of connections for a receptacle and the limit is exceeded, it may raise the ExceededConnectionLimit exception on new connection attempts.

### 14.1.2.3 Event Sources and Sinks

As explained in Chapter 11, event-driven communication is an important alternative to invocation-based communication and particularly useful to decouple an object from its environment. For the same composition reasons as with invocation interfaces, it is necessary to be able to describe a component's "event interfaces," that is, the types of event notifications it produces or consumes at its ports. In fact, event sources and sinks are special types of facets and receptacles because event communication is ultimately mapped to the invocation of operations in interfaces.

The extended IDL for components can be used to define notification-related ports. In addition to supporting the composition of components that communicate via notifications, these static declarations are used to automatically generate IDL and event implementation code for using the Notification Service, which relieves developers from writing much of the code responsible for using the service.

The event model and the service implementation provided by the component run time are those of the Notification Service, which was explained in Chapter 11. We explain the component run-time environment, the container, in detail in section 14.2. Compared with the Notification Service, the event model used by components is restricted in a number of ways so that the definition of notification sources and sinks in component type definitions can be kept simple. Of course, this does not in any way limit the event communication in component implementations that use independently managed event channels.

The first restriction is on the event notifications that can be used. All notification values must be instances of valuetypes derived from the abstract valuetype Components::EventBase. These values will be inserted into an Any and then transmitted in the body of the Notification Service's Structured Events. This typing of notifications is necessary in order to match event sources with compatible event sinks. The second restriction is that event communication through IDL-defined ports uses the push model only. Here is a simple example:

```
module Sensors {

  valuetype SensorEvent : Components::EventBase {
      public long sensor_value;
  };
  component TemperatureSensor {
      publishes SensorEvent sensor_source;
  };
  component HighTemperatureAlarm {
      consumes SensorEvent sensor_sink;
  };
```

In the example, all notifications are of type SensorEvent, which is derived from Components::EventBase. The component type TemperatureSensor is defined to publish sensor events through its sensor_source port, and component type HighTemperatureAlarm defines a port sensor_sink to receive sensor event notifications.

The equivalent interface generated for the event consumer, the HighTemperatureAlarm component in the example, would look like this:

```
  module HighTemperatureAlarmEventConsumers {
      interface SensorEventConsumer : Components::EventConsumerBase {
          void push(in SensorEvent evt);
      };
  };
```

```
interface HighTemperatureAlarm : Components::CCMObject {
    HighTemperatureAlarmEventConsumers::SensorEventConsumer
    get_consumer_sensor_sink();
};
```

The component definition HighTemperatureAlarm generates a separate module with an interface that defines a push() operation with the appropriate event type parameter. The equivalent interface itself has a generated operation to navigate to the component's event consumer interface. This illustrates the fact that an event sink is actually a special-purpose facet.

Suppliers of event notifications are not like facets, however. Rather, they are very similar to receptacles in that they allow consumers to connect to them. This is illustrated by the IDL generated for the TemperatureSensor definition:

```
module TemperatureSensorEventConsumers {
    interface SensorEventConsumer : Components::EventConsumerBase {
        void push(in SensorEvent evt);
    };
};
interface TemperatureSensor : Components::CCMObject {
    Components::Cookie subscribe_sensor_source(
        in SensorEventConsumer  consumer
      )
      raises(Components::ExceededConnectionLimit);

    TemperatureSensorEventConsumers::SensorEventConsumer
      unsubscribe_sensor_source(in Components::Cookie ck)
        raises (Components::InvalidConnection);
};
```

The subscribe operation is the equivalent of the connect operation for a receptacle and returns a Cookie to identify the consumer for subsequent unsubscribe operations. The unsubscribe operation behaves exactly like the disconnect operation for receptacles.

There is yet another similarity between event sources and receptacles. An event source declared with the publish keyword, a publisher, is similar to a multiplex receptacle because it allows multiple consumers to be subscribed. At run time, the publisher is the only supplier of events on the event channel, so we get 1-to-*n* communication style. But what about a simplex event source? In fact, the CCM allows the definition of event sources that accept only a single consumer. These event sources are called emitters, and the IDL keyword to define an emitter port in a component type is emits instead of publishes. Unlike with publishers, the event channel used for emitters allows multiple event sources, so communication can be $n$-to-1. Emitters are intended to be used for configuration purposes only. Figure 14.3 illustrates all port types covered in this section.

### 14.1.3 Component Homes

The CORBA object model does not have classes like object-oriented programming languages. Thus, there is no other way for clients to create new CORBA objects than the factory design pattern. Wherever it is necessary to let clients create objects, factory operations have to be provided in some interface, often in dedicated factory interfaces for particular object types. You have seen examples of this in Chapter 10, "Practical POA Programming," where we defined a factory interface for Meeting objects.

The OMG Life Cycle Service defined standard interfaces for factories with which objects can be moved or copied between factories and also destroyed again. The Life Cycle Service did not add any language constructs for the definition of factories to IDL, however, so designers were still left with only a pattern, but no specific tool or run-time support for life cycle operations.

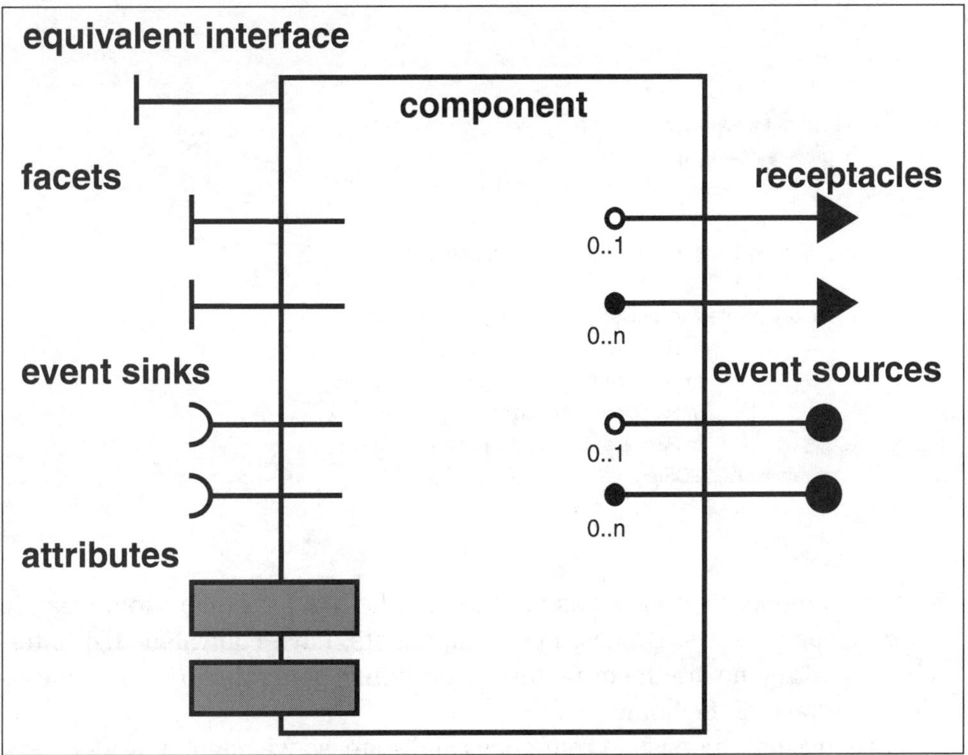


**Figure 14.3** Component ports.

The CORBA Components specification now extends IDL to support the definition of Component Homes. Homes can be regarded as type managers for component types and can provide an arbitrary set of operations, but they always provide at least one no-argument factory operation for components of the type they manage. Additionally, they can provide more factory operations and "finder" operations to retrieve individual, preexisting component instances. If a component home is defined to have a primary key, this home will have an implicit lookup operation that uses this primary key to retrieve instances. Homes are the primary entry point for clients into the world of components.

As an example, we could define a Meeting component that supported the Meeting interface as defined in Chapter 10 and a Meeting home for it:

```
#include "../chapter10/office.idl"

module com {
module wiley {
module compbooks {
module brose {
module chapter14 {

module office {

  component MeetingComponent {
        provides Meeting;
  };

  home MeetingHome manages MeetingComponent {

        factory createMeetingComponent ( in string purpose,
                        in Room location,
                        in Date time,
                        in Participant organizer,
                        in ParticipantList participants)
            raises( IllegalDate );
  };
};
```

The home MeetingHome has another, implicit factory operation, create(), without parameters. Homes, like components, have equivalent IDL interfaces, and the no-argument factory operation is generated into the equivalent interface of the home.

Meetings have persistent references and state, so we might consider associating Meetings with a primary key through the home. This would result in finder operations being generated in the equivalent interface that use this primary key. In our design of the application in Chapter 10, however, no such lookup operations were required. Moreover, we would have to redesign some of the data types to come up with a valid primary key. This would be necessary as the obvious choice for the primary key for a Meeting, the combination of the Room and the Date the meeting is scheduled, is not encapsulated into a single valuetype and therefore cannot be used as a primary key. The CCM restricts primary keys to be instance of valuetypes derived from the abstract valuetype Components::PrimaryKeyBase. It excludes valuetypes with members whose type is an object reference, which would be the case here.

## 14.2 The Component Container

In the previous section we focused on features of the component model that allowed the description of composable and configurable component types. An implementation of the CCM provides much more, however, than just an extended IDL. In this section, we describe the run-time environment for component instances: the component container. Containers do the following:

- Create and manage component instances (section 14.2.1)
- Provide a simplified standard API to the CORBA services Transactions, Security, Persistence, and Notification (section 14.2.2)

For a set of central usage patterns called *component categories*, the container provides a convenient environment and hides much of the complexity of programming the POA and managing Transactions, Notifications, and Persistence. For example, the component may rely on the container to provide persistence and use *container-managed* persistence. In this case, the component developer defines the state that is to be persisted using the Persistent State Service's PSDL. These declarations are then associated with the component using CIDL. Storing and restoring are done automatically by the container, which uses generated code for this task.

Alternatively, persistence can be managed by the component itself. This is called *self-managed persistence*. To use self-managed persistence, the component developer uses CIDL to define state, as explained in section 14.3, and implements specific callback interfaces. Persisting or restoring state is triggered by the container by invoking operations in the callback interfaces.

The interactions between the container and component implementations happen through two sets of local interfaces. The first set of interfaces is called the *internal* API and consists of the interfaces provided by the container to component implementations. The second set of interfaces are *call-*

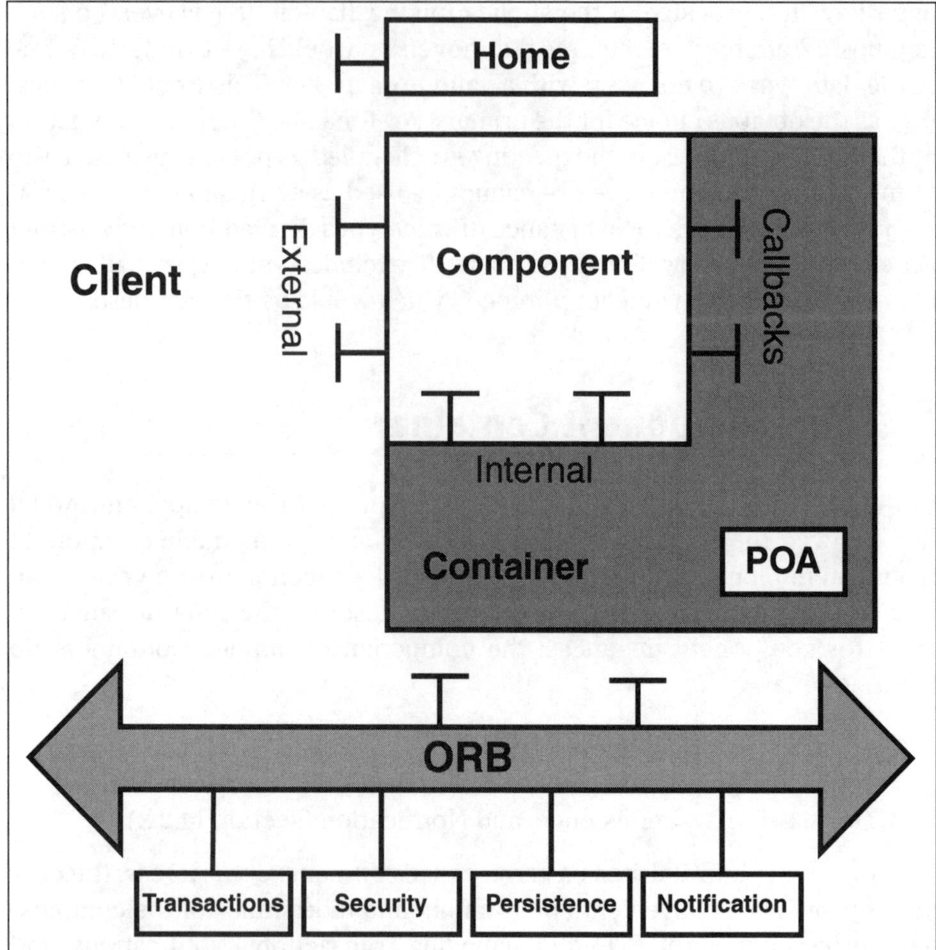


**Figure 14.4** The component container.

*back* interfaces provided by component implementations to the container. Figure 14.4 illustrates the component container and the interfaces provided and used by it.

The container programming model defines two API types for containers and component implementations. Which one gets used depends on the component category of the implementation in the container. We first describe component categories and then the container API types.

## 14.2.1 Component Categories

The CCM defines four standard component categories that determine how the component implementation and the container interact. Every compo-

| Component Category | Container API type | Primary Key | EJB Type |
|---|---|---|---|
| Service | session | — | — |
| Session | session | — | Session |
| Process | entity | — | — |
| Entity | entity | yes | Entity |

**Figure 14.5** Component categories and container API types.

nent category corresponds to a frequently used pattern for a component. The CCM also defines an empty category that you can use if you want to define the interaction with the container yourself. A container for the empty category exposes all CORBA functions directly to the component. Finally, CCM defines two additional categories for EJB Session and Entity Beans, respectively. The rationale behind this is that CORBA component containers are designed also to provide run-time environments for EJB components.

Component categories are not defined in IDL and are not properties of component types. Rather, you select the component category using the Component Implementation Definition Language (CIDL), as explained in section 14.3 of this chapter. Figure 14.5 summarizes the component categories and their relation to the container API.

Component categories differ in a number of respects. One of the differences between categories is the way the lifetime of instances of component implementations or servants is managed by the container. The CCM defines four different lifetime policy options for servants. Possible values for this policy are *method*, *transaction*, *component*, and *container*.

A servant lifetime of *method* means that the container will activate and passivate a servant before and after every single request such that no resources are permanently associated with a servant. Obviously, this incurs extra run-time overhead. A lifetime policy of *transaction* causes the container to activate the servant at the first request within a transaction. The servant will be passivated when the transaction completes. If a lifetime policy of *component* is selected, the component implementation will be activated on the first request and passivated only when explicitly requested by the component implementation itself. In a similar vein, a lifetime value of *container* causes the container to activate the implementation on the first request. It is kept activated until the container decides to deactivate it again.

The component categories defined for the container programming model are the following:

**Service.** If a component implementation's category is defined as *service*, then the component instance has only transient lifetime. Unlike any other component category, the lifetime of service components is restricted to the lifetime of a single operation; that is, its servant lifetime policy is *method*. Service components cannot be associated with persistent state and primary keys, and not even transient state is visible to clients. Consequently, a home for service components provides only factory operations but no finder operations.

Service components can be thought of as functions or command objects that require no further client interaction and are useful for wrapping procedural legacy applications. A computation that just returned a result would be an example of such a component. A service component is equivalent to a stateless EJB session bean. While service components are accessed using standard object references, these references do not represent any kind of identity.

**Session**. A CORBA session component, like a service component, has only transient lifetime and no persistent state. Its lifetime policy may be set to any value and is thus not a priori as limited as that of a service component. Typically, a session component will have the lifetime of a client interaction, hence the name. An example could be an online shopping session at an Internet book store. Session components are equivalent to a stateful EJB session bean.

**Process**. A process component has both a persistent reference and persistent state and is used to model business processes, usually tasks with a well-defined lifetime. The component home provides factory operations, but no finder operations for components of this category. The rationale here is that it does not make sense to assign a primary key—a persistent identity—to a process component because the task that it models will be complete at some stage and then will cease to exist. The reference to the component instance can be stored for later use, but it is valid only until the task has finished. A component that modeled a business process consisting of ordering, delivering, and billing items would be an example of a process component.

**Entity**. The entity component category is used for modeling persistent entities. The important difference to any other component category is that entities expose their persistent identity, that is, a primary key. This key may be used to retrieve a reference to the associated component instance through finder operations on the component home.

## 14.2.2 Container API Types

A container API type is both a library (the internal interfaces) and a framework (the callback interfaces) for component developers. The two API types defined in the Components specification are called *session* and *entity*. The session API type is used for components with transient lifetime, and the entity API type is used for persistent components. We examine a few of the central interfaces defined in the CCM for the container APIs in this section, but we do not cover them all.

Before looking at the differences between the internal and callback interfaces associated with the two types, let's briefly look at some of the interfaces common to both API types. A common *internal* interface is CCMContext, which is the bootstrap interface used by component instances to access the various services provided by the container. A reference to the CCMContext is passed to a component after the component instance is created, and each component gets its own reference to the context.

```
typedef SecurityLevel2::Credentials Principal;
exception IllegalState { };

local interface CCMContext {
    Principal get_caller_principal();
    CCMHome get_CCM_home();
    boolean get_rollback_only()
      raises (IllegalState);
    Transaction::UserTransaction get_user_transaction()
      raises (IllegalState);
    boolean is_caller_in_role (in string role);
    void set_rollback_only()
      raises (IllegalState);
};

typedef CosPersistentState::CatalogBase CatalogBase;
typedef CosPersistentState::TypeId TypeId;
exception PolicyMismatch { };
exception PersistenceNotAvailable { };

local interface CCM2Context : CCMContext {
    HomeRegistration get_home_registration ();
    Events::Event get_event();
    void req_passivate ()
      raises (PolicyMismatch);
    CatalogBase get_persistence (in TypeId catalog_type_id)
      raises (PersistenceNotAvailable);
};
```

All components can access container functionality through the local CCMContext interface. Basic components are limited to CCMContext, but extended components can also use the operations provided in the CCM2Context interface. The get_caller_principal() operation gives access to the caller's security credentials, and the get_CCM_Home() operation returns the home for the component. To find out if the current caller is a member of a given role, the is_caller_in_role() operation can be used.

The other three operations are concerned with transactions and raise an IllegalState exception if no transaction is currently active. The get_user _transaction() operation is used to implement self-managed transactions and returns a reference to UserTransaction. The remaining two operations, set_rollback_only() and get_rollback_only(), are used to mark the current transaction for rollback and test for this condition, respectively. The CCM2Context interface adds operations to CCMContext that are unique to extended components, such as accessors to persistence and event services and support for passivating the servant.

### 14.2.2.1 The API Type Session

The session container API type is designed for use with transient object references to components from either the service or session component category. It refines the context interfaces for both basic and extended components and also contains an optional callback interface SessionSynchronization, which we omit here. It can be implemented by session components to be notified of transaction boundaries.

The internal interfaces provided by the container are SessionContext for basic components and Session2Context for extended components. SessionContext adds a single operation get_CCM_object(), which returns the reference to the component. If this operation is invoked for an extended component, it returns a specific facet reference. If called outside of a callback operation, it raises the IllegalState operation. The Session2Context can be used by extended session components to create object references.

```
local interface SessionContext : CCMContext {
    Object get_CCM_object() raises (IllegalState);
};

enum BadComponentReferenceReason {
    NON_LOCAL_REFERENCE,
    NON_COMPONENT_REFERENCE,
    WRONG_CONTAINER
};
```

```
exception BadComponentReference {
      BadComponentReferenceReason reason;
};
exception IllegalState { };

local interface Session2Context : SessionContext, CCM2Context {
      Object create_ref (in CORBA::RepositoryId repid);
      Object create_ref_from_oid (
            in PortableServer::ObjectId oid,
            in CORBA::RepositoryId repid);
      PortableServer::ObjectId get_oid_from_ref (in Object ref)
        raises (IllegalState, BadComponentReference);
};
```

Session components must implement the SessionComponent callback interface. It provides the operation set_session_context() for associating a context with the component. The operations ccm_activate(), ccm_passivate(), and ccm_remove() are called by the container after activating, after passivating, and before destroying the component instance. The component implementation can use these operations to manage servant lifetimes. All operations may raise the following exception.

```
enum CCMExceptionReason {
      SYSTEM_ERROR,
      CREATE_ERROR,
      REMOVE_ERROR,
      DUPLICATE_KEY,
      FIND_ERROR,
      OBJECT_NOT_FOUND,
      NO_SUCH_ENTITY
};

exception CCMException {
      CCMExceptionReason reason;
};

local interface SessionComponent : EnterpriseComponent {
      void set_session_context (in SessionContext ctx)
        raises (CCMException);
      void ccm_activate()
        raises (CCMException);
      void ccm_passivate()
        raises (CCMException);
      void ccm_remove ()
        raises (CCMException);
};
```

### 14.2.2.2 The Entity Container API Type

This container API type is designed for use with persistent references, that is, for either process or entity component categories. The internal interfaces we examine are the context interfaces for basic and extended components and the callback interface for components, EntityComponent.

```
local interface EntityContext : CCMContext {
      Object get_CCM_object ()
        raises (IllegalState);
      PrimaryKeyBase get_primary_key ()
        raises (IllegalState);
};

exception BadComponentReference {
      BadComponentReferenceReason reason
};

local interface Entity2Context : EntityContext, CCM2Context {
      ComponentId get_component_id ()
        raises (IllegalState);
      ComponentId create_component_id (
            in FacetId target_facet,
            in SegmentId target_segment,
            in SegmentDescrSeq seq_descrs);
      ComponentId create_monolithic_component_id (
            in FacetId target_facet,
            in StateIdValue sid);
      Object create_ref_from_cid (
            in CORBA::RepositoryId repid,
            in ComponentId cid);
      ComponentId get_cid_from_ref (
            in Object ref) raises (BadComponentReference);
      };
```

The context interface for basic components provides the same get_CCM _object() operation as the context interface in the session API type. The additional operation get_primary_key() can be used only by components of entity category because these are the only components that have primary keys.

```
exception CCMException {
      CCMExceptionReason reason
};

local interface EntityComponent : EnterpriseComponent {
      void set_entity_context (in EntityContext ctx)
```

```
            raises (CCMException);
        void unset_entity_context ()
            raises (CCMException);

        void ccm_activate ()
            raises (CCMException);
        void ccm_passivate ()
            raises (CCMException);
        void ccm_remove ()
            raises (CCMException);

        void ccm_load ()
            raises (CCMException);
        void ccm_store ()
            raises (CCMException);
};
```

The EntityComponent interface is the callback interface implemented by components that use the entity API type. It is basically equivalent to the SessionComponent interface explained previously. In addition to the operations in SessionComponent, it provides the unset_entity_context() operation to remove the context. The operations ccm_load() and ccm_store() are called by the container to allow the component to implement the management of its persistent state (self-managed persistence). If the component uses container-managed persistence, these operations can be implemented using generated code.

## 14.3 Component Implementation

The component concepts described in the preceding sections might seem to add a considerable amount of complexity to application development. In fact, however, this complexity has always been there. Persistence, transactions, and security are issues that simply have to be dealt with in the context of distributed enterprise applications. The contribution of the CORBA component specification is that it provides you with means to describe these issues at higher language levels and to have most of the code generated for you.

In this chapter, we have looked at both the most abstract concepts and parts of the least abstract features of the CCM. At the most abstract level, components are new entities in the CORBA object model. This model manifests itself in IDL, which had to be extended to accommodate the new concepts. At the lowest level, implementers must use and implement the interfaces defined by the component container, which manages the instances of component implementations. In this section, we look at the Component

Implementation Definition Language (CIDL) that fills the gap between the component model and its supporting infrastructure.

The IDL extensions introduced by the CCM describe externally visible characteristics of components like interfaces and event behavior. CIDL, in contrast, describes aspects of a component's implementation that are irrelevant to clients of the component but essential for code generation and deployment of implementations in containers—for example, a component's category or persistent state. In the rest of this section, we examine the concepts provided by CIDL.

## 14.3.1 Compositions

The top-level language construct to define the implementation of IDL-defined component types is a *composition.* A composition describes the category of a component implementation as well as the names of *executors* for the component home and the component itself. These executors are the target language implementations of the component and its home. Because we are concerned with Java only, an executor is simply a Java class. The term executor was introduced by the specification to avoid confusion with servants. Servants and executors both serve the same purpose of providing implementation code. They do this at different levels in different frameworks, however, so using different terminology helps to avoid confusion.

As an example, we define a composition that implements the MeetingComponent defined in section 14.1.3. The following example is not yet complete, but we will add the missing pieces in the following sections.

```
// CIDL
composition process MeetingImpl {
    home executor MeetingHomeImpl {
        implements MeetingHome;
        manages MeetingProcessImpl;
    };
};
```

The composition uses process as the component category for the component implementation. This means that the entity container API type will be used and that both the reference and the state of the component are persistent. In our example in Chapter 10, meetings were actually something in between processes and entities because they represented both the process of setting up, managing, and holding the meeting and the persistent entity "meeting data." Our example design in Chapter 10 made the conceptual transition from process to entity at the time the meeting finished and turned meeting information into a persistent entity. In CIDL, we have to settle for one category, so we implement meetings as processes. In fact, the only difference this makes is that we cannot associate the MeetingHome with a primary key. The decision for this component category does not limit a MeetingComponent's lifetime, so we can still keep the component around as long as we like.

The preceding composition does not explicitly refer to the type MeetingComponent anywhere. This is not necessary because it is implicitly referenced by the home type MeetingHome. The names of the executors MeetingHomeImpl and MeetingProcessImpl will be used as the Java class names for the code generated from this CIDL definition. These classes will be abstract, so component developers need to provide subclasses for them.

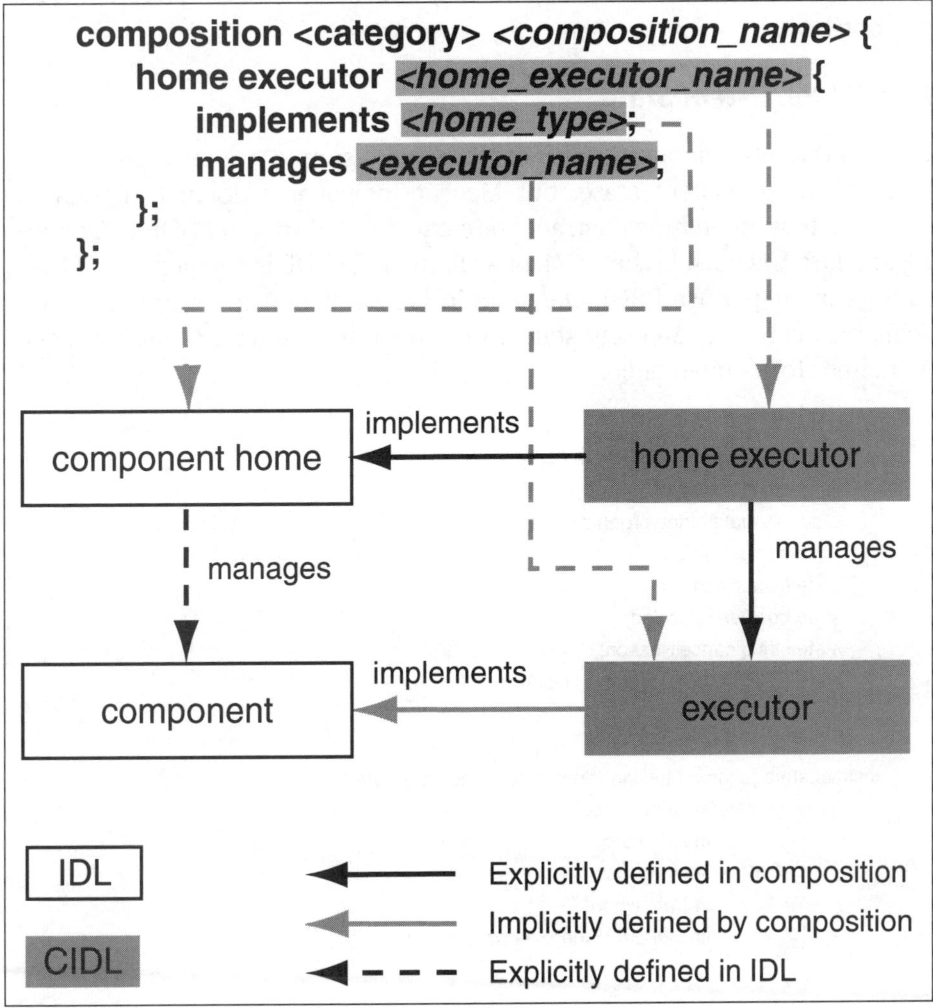


**Figure 14.6** Composition relationships.

The relationship between the component type, its home, and their executors are illustrated in Figure 14.6, which is taken from the specification.

Only a few parts of the component implementation are missing at this stage; the rest is automatically generated by the CCM development environment. The first missing piece is the implementation of the component's business logic in the component executor. A component developer will have to write a subclass of the generated component executor class `MeetingProcessImpl` with implementations of the operations in the Meeting interface, which is provided by the MeetingComponent.

The last missing piece that must be provided by the component developer is a subclass of the home executor `MeetingHomeImpl`. This class needs to provide two static methods to create instances of the home executor and the component executor. These two methods are the entry points into the composition.

#### 14.3.1.1 Persistent State

To keep the first encounter with compositions simple, we omitted any declarations of persistent state, but MeetingComponents do have persistent state. We have seen how abstract state can be declared in PSDL in Chapter 13, and PSDL is used in the CCM as well. In fact, CIDL is a superset of PSDL, so we can simply use PSDL elements in our CIDL specification. The PSDL declarations for the Meeting state were given in Chapter 13, but we repeat them here for convenience.

```
// CIDL/PSDL
abstract storagetype MeetingState {
    state string purpose;
    readonly state string organizer;
    state string location;
    state Date when;
    state boolean canceled;
    state string cancelReason;
    state CORBA::StringSeq participants;
};

abstract storagehome MeetingStateHome of MeetingState {
    factory create(in string purp,
                   in string org,
                   in string loc
                   in Date when,
                   in CORBA::StringSeq participants
                   );
};
```

What is missing now is the link between storage types and Storage Homes on the one side and the composition on the other. This missing link is provided by two additional clauses in the definition of a composition. The first clause links the composition to a PSDL-defined catalog, and the second clause connects a home executor to an abstract Storage Home. This Storage Home is referenced after the keyword bindsTo.

```
// catalog definition (not given in chapter 13)
catalog MeetingCatalog {
    provides MeetingStateHome meeting_state_home;
};

// second version of MeetingImpl
composition process MeetingImpl {
    uses catalog {
        MeetingCatalog meeting_catalog;
    };

    home executor MeetingHomeImpl {
        implements MeetingHome;
        bindsTo meeting_catalog.meeting_state_home;
        manages MeetingProcessImpl;
    };
};
```

The relationships between the parts of the composition and the abstract storagetype and Storage Home is illustrated in Figure 14.7. This diagram is more complex than the previous one, but it helps to identify the implicit relationships between the elements of the definitions.

Our second version of the composition definition still lacks one thing. The component home MeetingComponent defined previously has a createMeetingComponent() operation that we could directly delegate to the create() operation in the abstract Storage Home, which is responsible for creating storage objects. CIDL allows us to declare this delegation using the following syntax:

```
home MeetingHome manages MeetingComponent {
    factory createMeetingComponent ( in string purpose,
                in string organizer,
                in string location,
                in Date time,
                in CORBA::StringSeq participants)
      raises( IllegalDate );
};
```

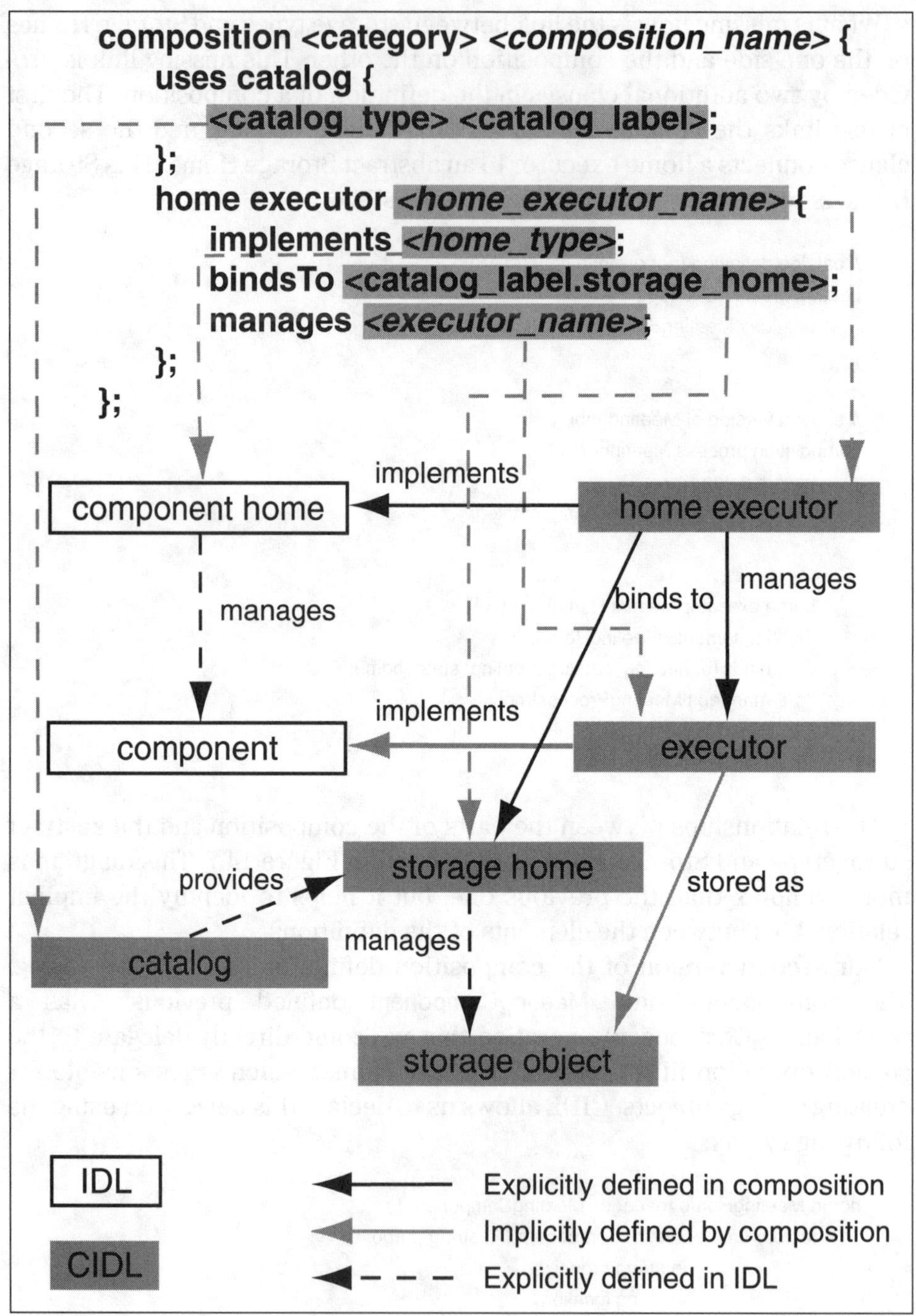


**Figure 14.7** Composition with persistent state management.

```
// third version of MeetingImpl
composition process MeetingImpl {
      uses catalog {
            MeetingCatalog meeting_catalog;
      };

      home executor MeetingHomeImpl {
            implements MeetingHome;
            bindsTo meeting_catalog.meeting_state_home;
            manages MeetingProcessImpl;
            delegatesTo abstract storagehome {
               createMeetingComponent : create;
            };
      };
};
```

With this last definition of the composition, a CCM environment can generate almost the entire implementation of MeetingComponents as well as the necessary code to deal with the management of persistent state. Developers need to write hardly any code on top of what is required to implement the business logic.

CIDL offers some more features to define delegation from operations on the home to the home executor instead of to the abstract Storage Home. Moreover, it allows the definition of *segmented executors* for better resource usage. The rationale for segmented executors is that the number of operations that need to be implemented for components with more than one facet can grow quickly. If implementations have to deal with storage objects, memory consumption can be decreased if only those storage objects that are currently required are kept incarnated. For this purpose, developers can split the implementation of entity or process components into *segments*. Each segment is assigned one or more of the component's facets and is thus associated with a different subset of all Storage Homes used by the component. The container can now activate the different segments of the component separately as they are needed. This way, only those Storage Objects need to be managed that are actually required. We don't show any examples of using segments here, however.

## 14.4 Component Packaging and Deployment

In the preceding sections we have explained how components are declared and implemented by a component developer and how the component container manages them. In this section, we describe how component implementations can be packaged and deployed. Both packaging and deployment will be supported by sophisticated tools, similar to the ones delivered with current Application Servers. Because these are by definition vendor-specific we concentrate only on the logical steps that have to performed.

The term *deployment* in this context covers the following activities:

- Selecting target containers for component implementations
- Installing component homes and instances from packages
- Configuring component properties
- Connecting components via interface and event ports

All these tasks are usually carried out with the help of deployment tools for the target CCM product. To understand why deployment includes installing *instances*, remember that containers are dynamic entities that are hosted by running processes and that a process may potentially provide multiple containers. Component deployment thus covers more than just statically installing code on a machine.

Component implementations come in *packages*. Packages are the unit of distribution and deployment and are contained in archive files. Archives, in turn, contain code as well as files with descriptive text written in the Extensible Markup Language (XML). These XML files are called *descriptors* and guide the deployment process. The CCM defines four different descriptors:

- Software Package Descriptors
- Component Descriptors
- Component Assembly Descriptors
- Property File Descriptors

The second and third descriptors are used to provide information about the two kinds of packages defined by the CCM, the *Component Package* and the *Component Assembly Package*. A Component Package contains implementations of a single component, whereas a Component Assembly contains a collection of component packages. An assembly's descriptor describes how components are connected. In the remainder of this section, we explain all four descriptor types and how they are created and used.

### 14.4.1 Software Package Descriptor

The concept for distributing and deploying software that is defined by the CCM is the Component Package. Its descriptor is called *Software Package Descriptor* rather than Component Package Descriptor, however. The descriptor is an XML file with a ".csd" extension that is located in a special directory "meta-inf" in the archive containing the package. Software package descriptors can be created and modified manually using standard text editors, but in most cases these descriptors will be generated by tools provided by the software development environment for your CCM product.

The CCM specification defines an XML Document Type Definition (DTD) for each descriptor type to define its syntax. The DTD for the Component Package Descriptor is called `softpkg`. Here is its root element:

```
<!ELEMENT softpkg
( title
| pkgtype
| author
| description?
| license
| idl
| propertyfile
| dependency
| descriptor
| implementation
| extension
)* >
```

We are not going to explain every single XML element of this or any of the other descriptors, but just examine the main elements of each description. The Software Package Descriptor has two main parts. The first part describes the package itself and some properties that are shared by all the implementations in the package. This part of the descriptor contains general package information such as the package title and author and references to licenses. It also contains information about the IDL that describes the component that is implemented in this package and, in this example, a dependency of all implementations in the package on a particular ORB product. Finally, a separate property file is referenced. This property file contains attribute settings for the component or home and is used to configure the component.

The second main part of the descriptor is a list of XML elements of type `implementation` and their children, most importantly a Component Descriptor, which we describe separately in the text that follows. In addition to the component descriptor, implementation descriptions may specify for which operating system and processor type the implementation was built and which programming language and compiler were used for building. The `code` element describes the location and type of the implementation and optionally gives an entry point to the code. It is also possible to specify dependencies on the environment in terms of required files in the `dependency` child element of implementation.

Here is an example of a descriptor for a component package:

```
<?xml version="1.0"?>
<softpkg name="Meeting" version="1,0,1,0">

    <pkgtype>CORBA Component</pkgtype>
    <title>Meeting</title>

    <author>
        <company>Wiley Inc.</company>
        <webpage href="http://www.wiley.com/compbooks/brose/>
    </author>

    <description>
        The MeetingComponent from Chapter 14
    </description>

    <license href=
        "http://www.wiley.com/imaginary/some-license.html" />

    <dependency type="ORB">
        <name>SomeCCMEnabledORB</name>
    </dependency>

    <idl id="IDL:M1/Bank:1.0" >
        <link href=
            "ftp:/ftp.wiley.com/imaginary/idl/Office.idl"/>
    </idl>

    <propertyfile>
        <fileinarchive name="meeting_props.cpf"/>
    </propertyfile>

    <implementation id="DCE:600dc527-0110-11ae-ac3d-0200090a4e1e">
        <os name="WinNT" version="4,0,0,0" />
        <os name="Win95" />
        <processor name="x86" />
        <compiler name="Sun javac" />
        <programminglanguage name="Java" />

        <descriptor type="CORBA Component">
            <fileinarchive>processcontainer.ccd</fileinarchive>
        </descriptor>

        <code type="Java Class">
            <fileinarchive name="MeetingImpl.class"/>
            <entrypoint>createMeetingHome</entrypoint>
        </code>

        <dependency type="Java Class">
            <localfile name="SomeRequiredUtility.class"/>
```

```
      </dependency>
  </implementation>

<implementation>
    <!— another example implementation —>
</implementation>

</softpkg>
```

## 14.4.2 Component Descriptor

The CORBA Component Descriptor is an XML file with a ".ccd" extension. It describes two kinds of component characteristics and is automatically generated by the CIDL compiler that processes the component's CIDL definition. The DTD for this descriptor type is called `corbacomponent`. Again, we reproduce only its root element here:

```
<!ELEMENT corbacomponent
( corbaversion
, componentrepid
, homerepid
, componentkind
, interop?
, transaction?
, security?
, threading
, configurationcomplete
, extendedpoapolicy*
, repository?
, segment*
, componentproperties?
, homeproperties?
, homefeatures+
, componentfeatures+
, interface*
, extension*
)>
```

The first kind of component characteristics are general component features, as expressed in a component's IDL definition. This includes the interfaces supported by the component, its facets, receptacles, event sources, and sinks. This information can be displayed in design tools and used to connect components, for example, by connecting a facet to another component's receptacle. These component features are defined in XML in `componentfeature` elements.

The second kind of characteristics includes information from the CIDL definition such as the component category and segmented executors. It also includes information not present in any other static description that may have to be edited by the developer or packager. This includes information about transactional characteristics, threading policies, Quality of Service information for event ports, the required rights for accessing particular operations, and information about Storage Homes. The complete list of XML elements is too long to describe in detail here. In general, these XML descriptions will be hidden by tools in your CCM environment that display the information in the descriptor and allow you to modify it.

The following example gives a good impression of the descriptiveness of Component Descriptors. It describes the categories, features, service usage, and policies for a component BookStore and its home BookStoreHome. This example descriptor is an abbreviated version of an example in the CCM specification.

```
<?xml version="1.0"?>
<!DOCTYPE corbacomponent SYSTEM "corbacomponent.dtd">
<corbacomponent>
    <corbaversion> 3.0 </corbaversion>
    <componentrepid repid="IDL:BookStore:1.0" />
    <homerepid repid="IDL:BookStoreHome:1.0" />

    <componentkind>
        <entity>
            <servant lifetime="process" />
        </entity>
    </componentkind>

    <security rightsfamily="corba" />
    <threading policy="multithread" />
    <configurationcomplete set="true" />

    &lt;segment name="bookseg" segmenttag="1">
        <segmentmember facettag="1" />
        <segmentmember facettag="2" />
        <containermanagedpersistence>
            <storagehome id="PSDL:BookHome:1.0" />
            <pssimplementation id="ACME-PSS" />
            <catalog type="PSDL:BookCatalog:1.0" />
            <accessmode mode="READ_ONLY" />
            <psstransaction policy="TRANSACTIONAL" >
                <psstransactionisolationlevel level=
                    "SERIALIZABLE"/>
            </psstransaction>
            <params>
                <param name="x" value="1" />
            </params>
```

```
        </containermanagedpersistence>
    &lt;/segment&gt;

    <homefeatures name="BookStoreHome"
        repid="IDL:BookStoreHome:1.0">
        <operationpolicies>
            <operation name="*">
                <transaction use="never" />
            </operation>
        </operationpolicies>
    </homefeatures>

    <componentfeatures name="BookStore" repid="IDL:BookStore:1.0">
        <ports>
            <provides
                providesname="book_search"
                repid="IDL:BookSearch:1.0"
                facettag="1">
                <operationpolicies>
                    <operation name="getByAuthor">
                        <requiredrights>
                            <right name="get"/>
                        </requiredrights>
                    </operation>
                    <operation name="getByTitle">
                        <requiredrights>
                            <right name="get"/>
                        </requiredrights>
                    </operation>
                </operationpolicies>
            </provides>

            <provides
                 providesname="shopping_cart"
                 repid="IDL:CartFactory:1.0"
                 facettag="2" />
            <uses
                 usesname="fedex_rates"
                 repid="IDL:ShippingRates:1.0" />
            <emits
                 emitsname="low_stock"
                 eventtype="StockRecord">
                 <eventpolicy policy="normal" />
            </emits>
            <publishes
                publishesname="offer_alert"
                eventtype="SpecialOffer">
                <eventpolicy policy="normal" />
            </publishes>
        </ports>
    </componentfeatures>
</corbacomponent>
```

## 14.4.3 Component Assembly Descriptor

Using the two descriptors introduced so far, we can package implementations of a single component in a component package. In most situations—certainly in the more interesting cases—components are deployed in groups or *assemblies* that must be correctly set up to allow component interactions. The unit of deployment for assemblies is the component assembly package. A component assembly package is a ZIP archive containing a set of component packages and property files and an assembly descriptor. The extension for assembly package archives is ".aar".

The assembly descriptor describes the components in the assembly, how components are partitioned and connected to each other. The descriptor thus has the role of a template for instantiating components and their homes. Like the component descriptor, an assembly descriptor will be created using special visual tools. The XML file containing the descriptor has a ".cad" extension and is placed into the "meta-inf" directory of the containing archive. The DTD for the assembly descriptor is called `componentassembly` and has the following root element:

```
<!ELEMENT componentassembly
( description?
, componentfiles
, partitioning
, connections?
, extension*
)>
<!ATTLIST componentassembly
id ID #REQUIRED
derivedfrom CDATA #IMPLIED >
```

The components that make up the assembly are simply listed by their component files, that is, their component packages. An important concept for the instantiation of components is their *placement*. A placement is the term used by the CCM to describe a deployed home, which, in turn, determines the location of component instances because component instantiations are always relative to their homes.

For this purpose, the XML document type for component assembly descriptors defines an XML element `homeplacement` that is a child of the `partitioning` element. The definition of a placement in the descriptor has a number of important child elements that define how components are instantiated by this home. Additionally, it is possible to determine a property file for the home and its components. Moreover, the installer of the assembly can be instructed to register the home with a Naming Service, a Trading Service, or a special home finder service.

The `componentinstantiation` child of the `homeplacement` element describes a specific instantiation instantiated relative to the home. It contains a number of instructions that determine how this instantiation has to be performed. In particular, it is possible to reference a property file for initial configuration of the instantiated component with a set of properties. Moreover, it is possible to specify that the component should be registered with a Naming or Trading Service by the installer. For registration with a Trader, a set of trader properties needs to be given that describes the service offer.

For specific component homes, it is possible to express colocation constraints such that these homes will be deployed to the same process or host, which implies that component instantiations from these homes are likewise colocated. The XML for component assembly descriptors uses the elements `processcollocation` and `hostcollocation` to group the placement of homes as shown in the example that follows. A deployer can then decide on which particular host and process to install the homes.

Finally, the assembly descriptor defines the initial connections between components that should be performed at deployment time. The corresponding XML elements instruct the deployer or the deployment tool which receptacles have to be connected to which facets, and which event sources should be connected to which event sinks.

The following example assembly descriptor uses most of the features described in this section. It is also an abbreviated example from the CCM specification.

```
<!DOCTYPE componentassembly SYSTEM "componentassembly.dtd">
<componentassembly id="ZZZ123">

    <description>Example assembly"</description>

    <componentfiles>
        <componentfile id="A">
            <fileinarchive name="ca.ccd"/>
        </componentfile>
        <componentfile id="B">
            <fileinarchive name="cb.ccd"/>
        </componentfile>
        <componentfile id="C">
            <fileinarchive name="cc.ccd">
                <link href="ftp://www.xyz.com/car/cc.car"/>
            </fileinarchive>
        </componentfile>
        <componentfile id="D">
            <fileinarchive name="cd.ccd"/>
        </componentfile>
        <componentfile id="E">
            <fileinarchive name="ce.ccd"/>
```

```
        </componentfile>
    </componentfiles>

    <partitioning>
        <homeplacement id="AHome">
            <usagename>Example home for A components</usagename>
            <componentfileref idref="A"/>
            <componentimplref idref="an A impl"/>
            <homeproperties>
                <fileinarchive name="AHomeProperties.cpf"/>
            </homeproperties>
            <componentproperties>
                <fileinarchive name="defaultAProperties.cpf"/>
            </componentproperties>
            <registerwithhomefinder name="AHome"/>
            <componentinstantiation id="Aa">
                <usagename>
                     Example component instantiation
                </usagename>
                <componentproperties>
                    <fileinarchive name="AaaProperties.cpf"/>
                </componentproperties>
                <registercomponent>
                    <registerwithnaming name="sink"/>
                    <registerwithtrader>
                        <traderproperties>
                            <traderproperty>
                                <traderpropertyname>
                                    ppm
                                </traderpropertyname>
                                <traderpropertyvalue>
                                    10
                                </traderpropertyvalue>
                            </traderproperty>
                        </traderproperties>
                    </registerwithtrader>
                </registercomponent>
            </componentinstantiation>
        </homeplacement>


        <processcollocation cardinality="*">
            <usagename>Example process collocation</usagename>
            <impltype language="C++" /> <!— optional —>

            <homeplacement id="BHome">
                <componentfileref idref="B"/>
                <componentinstantiation id="Bb"/>
            </homeplacement>

            <homeplacement id="CcHome">
```

```
                <componentfileref idref="C"/>
                <componentinstantiation id="Cc"/>
            </homeplacement>
        </processcollocation>

        <hostcollocation cardinality="1">
            <usagename>Example host collocation</usagename>

            <homeplacement id="DHome">
                <componentfileref idref="D"/>
                <componentinstantiation id="Dd"/>
            </homeplacement>
            <homeplacement id="EHome">
                <componentfileref idref="E"/>
                <componentinstantiation id="Ee"/>
            </homeplacement>
        </hostcollocation>

    </partitioning>

    <connections>
        <connectinterface>
            <usesport>
                <usesidentifier>abc</usesidentifier>
                <componentinstantiationref idref="Aa"/>
            </usesport>

            <providesport>
                <providesidentifier>abc</providesidentifier>
                <componentinstantiationref idref="Bb"/>
            </providesport>
        </connectinterface>

        <connectevent>
            <consumesport>
                <consumesidentifier>pqr</consumesidentifier>
                <componentinstantiationref idref="Aaa"/>
            </consumesport>
            <emitsport>
                <emitsidentifier>mno</emitsidentifier>
                <componentinstantiationref idref="Ee"/>
            </emitsport>
        </connectevent>
    </connections>
</componentassembly>
```

## 14.4.4 Property File Descriptor

Property files are used to specify sets of properties for the initial configuration of components or homes. These properties are described in XML, so the terms *property file* and *Property File Descriptor* are really synonyms. The file extension for property files is ".cpf".

The properties that can be expressed in XML are named values of IDL base types, structs, sequences, and object references. The value of an object reference is a stringified object reference that will be converted back into a live reference before it is assigned. As an example, consider the following descriptor, which defines property `queueLen` of type long, a string sequence `documentNames`, and a struct `prerequisites` of type requirementStruct.

```
<properties>
    <simple name=queueLen type="long">
        <description>Size of queue</description>
        <value>4096</value>
        <defaultvalue>256</defaultvalue>
    </simple>

    <sequence name="documentNames" type="sequence<string>">
        <simple type="string"><value>Readme</value>
        </simple>
        <simple type="string"><value>User's Guide</value>
        </simple>
        <simple type="string"><value>Install Guide</value>
        </simple>
        <simple type="string"><value>Reference Manual</value>
        </simple>
        <simple type="string"><value>Examples</value>
      </simple>
    </sequence>

    <struct name="prerequisites" type="requirementStruct">
        <description>Installation Requirements</description>
        <simple name="disk" type="short"><value> 48 </value>
        </simple>
        <simple name="RAM" type="short"><value> 128 </value>
        </simple>
        <simple name="CPU" type="string"><value> Pentium </value>
        </simple>
    </struct>

</properties>
```

## 14.5 CORBA Components versus EJB

If you are familiar with Enterprise JavaBeans (EJB), you will note many similarities and close correspondences between the concepts of EJB and CCM. Both are designed for essentially the same purpose, that is, supporting the development of enterprise-level applications. Both offer a component concept, containers as run-time environments, a set of APIs specifically designed for enterprise applications, and a deployment infrastructure. Moreover, both the EJB and the CCM specifications define mappings to the other component technology so that EJB clients can access CCM components as if they were EJB components and vice versa.

EJB and CCM are not equivalent, however. This section gives an overview of the differences between the two server-side component technologies. We do not give an overview of EJB here or explain how to program it. There are plenty of other books that describe EJB. If you are not familiar with EJB, the remainder of this chapter might still give you an impression of some of its capabilities through the differences to CCM.

Because of the current lack of CCM implementations and because the EJB specification is still evolving as well, we concentrate on the fundamental concepts of EJB and CCM rather than compare actual products. The specification documents we are referring to are the EJB 1.1 specification, the EJB 2.0 public draft issued by Sun Microsystems in mid-2000, and the OMG documents ptc/99-10-04 and orbos/99-02-05. In the remainder of this section, we compare CCM with EJB for interoperability and outline differences in their container and component models.

## 14.5.1 Interoperability

Generally, the main reason for using CORBA-based technology instead of language or platform-specific solutions is the level of interoperability that CORBA provides between heterogeneous system components and between implementations from different vendors. If interoperability is an important requirement in a component project, the question arises whether EJB provides the same level of interoperability. The answer is: "basically, yes." For a more detailed picture, let's examine interoperability between products from different vendors and language interoperability separately.

### *14.5.1.1 Vendor Interoperability*

The authoritative answer to the question of whether products from different EJB vendors interoperate as well as CORBA implementations have proved to do cannot be given yet because of the lack of experience with existing products at this stage. There are no implementations of the EJB 2.0 specification, which clarifies a number of interoperability issues with EJB 1.1. From a conceptual point of view, however, product interoperability is possible because EJB relies on an established technology to reach this goal—

CORBA. EJB uses CORBA both for standardized communication between distributed components and for standard service APIs.

By having the two main interfaces for Enterprise JavaBeans, `javax.ejb.EJBHome` and `javax.ejb.EJBObject`, extend `java.rmi.Remote`, EJB natively uses RMI for communication. Because Sun has now defined RMI-IIOP as a conceptual bridge between RMI and IIOP, it is possible to remotely invoke enterprise beans using IIOP. The EJB specification prescribes IIOP as a mandatory requirement for interoperability between EJB implementations and also constrains the Java RMI types that can be used by enterprise beans to the subset of legal RMI-IIOP types.

In a similar vein, compliant EJB implementations are required to use the CORBA Naming and Transaction Service APIs. For secure interoperability, EJB relies on CORBA's Common Secure Interoperability (CSI) using SSL/IIOP. In all of these areas EJB does not compete with CORBA but simply uses it.

#### 14.5.1.2 Language Interoperability

The other kind of interoperability that we need to check is between component implementations and clients written in different languages. With CORBA, a client written in any language can invoke objects implemented in any other language using an IDL language mapping, standardized GIOP request messages, and the IIOP transport. From a more Java-centric perspective, a Java/CORBA client can thus invoke operations on non-Java servers, and Java implementations can be accessed from CORBA clients in any other language.

With EJB, we get *almost* the same level of language interoperability. Java clients can use RMI-IIOP to invoke methods on arbitrary implementations, essentially using CORBA without having to use IDL. This is possible if the target interface relies only on the RMI-IIOP subset of IDL as defined for EJB; otherwise, code generated from an IDL/Java compiler must be used.

On the server side, language interoperability is more restricted because EJB targets only Java components, that is, Java classes that implement `javax.ejb.EJBObject` and are deployed in an EJB container. There are no mappings of EJB interfaces to other languages and thus no containers that would accept EJB components written in, for example, COBOL. The only possibility to create enterprise beans not written in Java is to provide Java wrappers around implementations written in other languages. The "language mapping" from Java that must be used in this case is the Java Native Interface (JNI), which defines how Java can call native C code.

Of course, individual implementations of the CORBA component specification would also be limited to a single implementation language, but at least theoretically it would be possible to buy different products that would host components implemented in other languages.

## 14.5.2 Component Models and Containers

We have already pointed out the conceptual and terminological similarities between CCM and EJB. Both technologies center around components that run in containers and define high-level interfaces to services like naming, transaction, security and persistence. Both provide XML descriptors to aid in deploying components. A few conceptual differences are worth pointing out, however.

The most obvious difference between EJB and CCM is that EJB does not define any definition languages that are separate from Java. CCM, in contrast, makes extensive use of IDL and CIDL constructs to define components and their implementations, and it uses these definitions as input to code generators. As we have seen in section 14.4 of this chapter, much of the information expressed in IDL and CIDL is eventually mapped to XML descriptions in the various descriptors. The absence of a declarative language like IDL/CIDL does not imply that EJB is necessarily less expressive than CCM, however. EJB also makes extensive use of XML descriptors, and in principle, any concept that cannot be conveniently modeled in Java could be mapped to some XML construct.

Having said that, it should be pointed out that EJB does not have equivalents for all of the concepts offered by IDL/CIDL. In particular, EJB has no concept of facets, receptacles, event sources, or event sinks. In fact, EJB 1.1 does not define an event notification service at all. Because of this conceptual restriction, CCM distinguishes between basic and extended CORBA components. Basic components have only a supported interface but no ports and can be mapped to enterprise beans and vice versa, thus allowing pure Java clients to access basic components as if they were enterprise beans.

The component categories defined by CCM are a superset of the types of enterprise beans defined by EJB 1.1. As illustrated in Figure 14.5, CCM has equivalents for EJB's session and entity beans and also defines a process component that has no counterpart in EJB. Because CCM also prescribes that any Java implementation of the specification must implement the complete EJB 1.1 specification as well as RMI-IIOP, the CCM is a superset of EJB 1.1.

The EJB 2.0 specification, however, adds both an event service API and a new type of beans to EJB. The event service API is the Java Message Service (JMS), and the new type of beans are called *message-driven beans*, which have no direct counterpart category in CCM. Message-driven beans are simply JMS message listeners implemented as enterprise beans. They are completely managed by the container and are never directly exposed to clients. Clients interact with message-driven beans only indirectly by sending messages to JMS topics or queues. With the addition of message-driven beans we cannot regard CCM as a superset of EJB anymore, although this relationship might be reestablished by future versions of the CCM.

# Performance, Scalability, and Management

So far in this book we have explained Java ORB technology, but we have paid little attention to how to go about using it effectively. In this chapter we explain more generally how to use the technology successfully. When CORBA is used the wrong way, the implemented applications, although they are functionally complete, can have performance and scalability problems. Performance and scalability, however, are key factors in the successful deployment of an application. One important aspect of achieving performance and scalability was covered in Chapter 10, "Practical POA Programming," where we explained how the POA can be configured for space-time trade-offs. In section 15.1 of this chapter we look at several other important techniques and design patterns for gaining high performance in CORBA applications and ensuring that the performance remains acceptable when the number of clients or objects participating in an application increases dramatically.

Another important issue for distributed applications is their management. In a centralized application there is one machine running a program or set of programs that can be controlled by an administrator using that machine. In distributed applications, especially those that support location transparency, as CORBA applications do, the objects that take part in the application may be running in many servers on many machines, some of them unknown to the administrator. Some planning is required to ensure that clients that suddenly withdraw from an application don't leave unused objects behind. Coping with this situation can be called distributed garbage collection. Another consideration is how to shut down an application gracefully. We look at these management issues in section 15.2. Section 15.3 is a brief summary of this chapter and the material covered in this book.

## 15.1 Scalability Issues

In this section we show a few techniques for enhancing the performance and scalability of a Java/CORBA application:

**Refining the object model (section 15.1.1).** The design of an application's objects may not translate into an efficient implementation when the objects are implemented and distributed. This is usually due to the extra cost of making distributed invocations. When decisions about the implementation and location of objects are made, some redesign may be necessary to optimize the communication between them. In this section we look at the object model of the room booking example from Chapter 8, "Building Applications," and optimize it for distribution.

**Threading models (section 15.1.2).** The use of threads to allow parallel processing can be employed to reduce the impact of the delays caused by remote invocations. When servers have many clients they can also employ threads to more evenly process the requests from all clients. Java builds threads into the language, and so threads are easy to use. We look at the use of threads in clients and servers and explain the threading models used by ORBs for delivering invocation requests.

**Distributed callbacks (section 15.1.3).** When a client makes a call to a remote object that may take some time to return, it is sometimes better to allow the object to respond asynchronously. The client can supply a callback reference for the server to invoke when it has results for the request. This allows the client's main thread to continue and delegate the task of dealing with the response to a CORBA object that it implements. We show an example of the use of callbacks.

**Iterators (section 15.1.4).** When a result of an invocation is very large it can be delivered in smaller pieces by using an iterator. This has the advantage that clients can use a small set of results at a time and need not keep the whole set. It also allows the server to generate further results as they are required and avoids the need to generate the entire response if the client decides not to retrieve the entire result set. We explain two models for the design and implementation of iterators, one driven by the client and the other by the server.

**Client-side caching (section 15.1.5).** Sometimes the cost of a remote call can be avoided altogether. If a particular operation is called multiple times and always returns the same result, this result can be cached by the client and returned later instead of making a remote call. We show a simple technique for implementing caching in a client.

**Monitoring performance (section 15.1.6).** Decisions about which parts of a distributed application to tune for performance should be based on the results of testing. Identifying the bottlenecks in an application may allow these parts to be improved and provide better performance for the whole application. We show some performance monitoring code using interceptors.

## 15.1.1 Refining the Object Model

In this section we look at the implications of distributing object-oriented designs with CORBA. We then redesign the object model introduced in Chapter 8, "Building Applications," to improve the communication between clients and objects.

When we design and implement an object-oriented application with CORBA we use two models that mirror one another:

**Functional model**—specifies the application or system in terms of classes and objects. Those objects represent the logical composition of functionality and are independent of the actual distribution of the various objects and of the infrastructure.

**Implementation model or design**—implements the specification of the application or system in terms of objects associated with various run-time entities such as machines, processes, JVMs, and threads.

Typically we start with a functional model, defined in terms of OMG IDL or perhaps the Unified Modeling Language (UML). Then as we implement the specification, we refine the UML classes or IDL interfaces and transform the specification into implementations of classes that must be instantiated in server programs running on machines in our distributed system. Sometimes, however, the more concrete considerations of the implementation model have an impact on the functional model. This section looks at the considerations of implementation and deployment, and their impact on the IDL specification.

The transformation of a functional model into a deployed application is a critical factor for the scalability of the system. The most important reason not to naively implement a functional model as if it were a nondistributed application is the very nature of distributed systems. A remote operation call is functionally equivalent to a local one, but it differs dramatically in its performance. Experience shows that a local invocation is in the order of microseconds, whereas a remote invocation is in the order of milliseconds, or even worse, depending on the quality of the network connection. To control the overall system performance it is important to carefully design a deployment model for distribution performance. In fact, it is not sufficient to simply distinguish between local and remote calls. In many cases, remote calls run over different networks with various performance parameters. As Java/CORBA applications are often deployed on the Internet, you could, for example, distinguish between remote invocations over modem connections (0.5–7 Kbyte/sec), corporate Internet connections (10–100 Kbyte/sec), intranets (100–1000 Kbyte/sec), or FDDI, high-speed Ethernet, and ATM (> 1 Mbyte/sec). To illustrate the problem and introduce some approaches to transforming a functional model into a deployment model, we revisit the room booking application introduced in Chapter 8.

The interface specification of the room booking application we presented in Chapter 8 is a purely functional object model. Even very fine-grain objects such as the Meeting objects are defined as CORBA objects, each with an OMG IDL interface. In that chapter, we took this model as a design and naively implemented it. Certain performance overheads are introduced by the design; this is a problem for scalability. For example, meetings are represented as objects. The access of each of a Meeting's attributes potentially results in a costly remote invocation.

Let us revisit the specification and implementation of the room booking application, taking scalability into account. The specification of the Room interface below keeps the signatures of the operations, but it changes the specification of a meeting. Here we specify a meeting as an IDL struct. The attributes of the Meeting interface become fields in the Meeting struct. We also add an extra field to indicate whether the meeting is booked.

```
module com {
...
module chapter15 {
module modeling {
module roomBooking {

    interface Room {

        struct Meeting {
            boolean booked;
            string purpose;
            string participants;
        };
```

```
        enum Slot { am9, am10, am11, pm12, pm1, pm2, pm3, pm4 };

        const short MaxSlots = 8;

        typedef Meeting Meetings[ MaxSlots ];

        exception NoMeetingInThisSlot {};
        exception SlotAlreadyTaken {};

        readonly attribute string name;

        Meetings view();

        void book( in Slot a_slot, in Meeting  a_meeting )
            raises(SlotAlreadyTaken);

        void cancel( in Slot  a_slot )
            raises(NoMeetingInThisSlot);
    };
};
};};};};};};
```

Now the Java `Meeting` class generated by the IDL compiler no longer extends the CORBA Object base class. In some language mappings, the meeting would be represented by an even more lightweight construct; for example, the mapping to C++ would generate a struct. This is the code generated by a Java IDL compiler:

```
package com.wiley.compbooks. . . . brose.chapter15.modeling.roomBooking
.RoomPackage;

public final class Meeting implements
    org.omg.CORBA.portable.IDLEntity {

    public boolean booked;
    public java.lang.String purpose;
    public java.lang.String participants;

    public Meeting () {}

    public Meeting (final boolean booked,
                    final java.lang.String purpose,
                    final java.lang.String participants) {

        this.booked = booked;
        this.purpose = purpose;
        this.participants = participants;
    }
}
```

In the implementation in Chapter 8, we obtained an IOR for a CORBA meeting object, on which we invoked remote operations. Now we obtain a struct (by value) and access the fields of the local Java object implementing it.

Figure 15.1 illustrates the two different specifications and their implementation configurations. The figures show the two applications after the `view()` operation has been invoked on a room object. We have omitted the Naming Service because it is used to locate Room objects in the same way in both approaches.

Let's go through the interactions step by step.

## *Viewing a Room's Bookings*

**Chapter 8 specification**—The view() operation returns an array of CORBA object references. The size of a CORBA object reference is in the order of 100 to 600 bytes. The client now has an array of IORs to remote meeting objects.

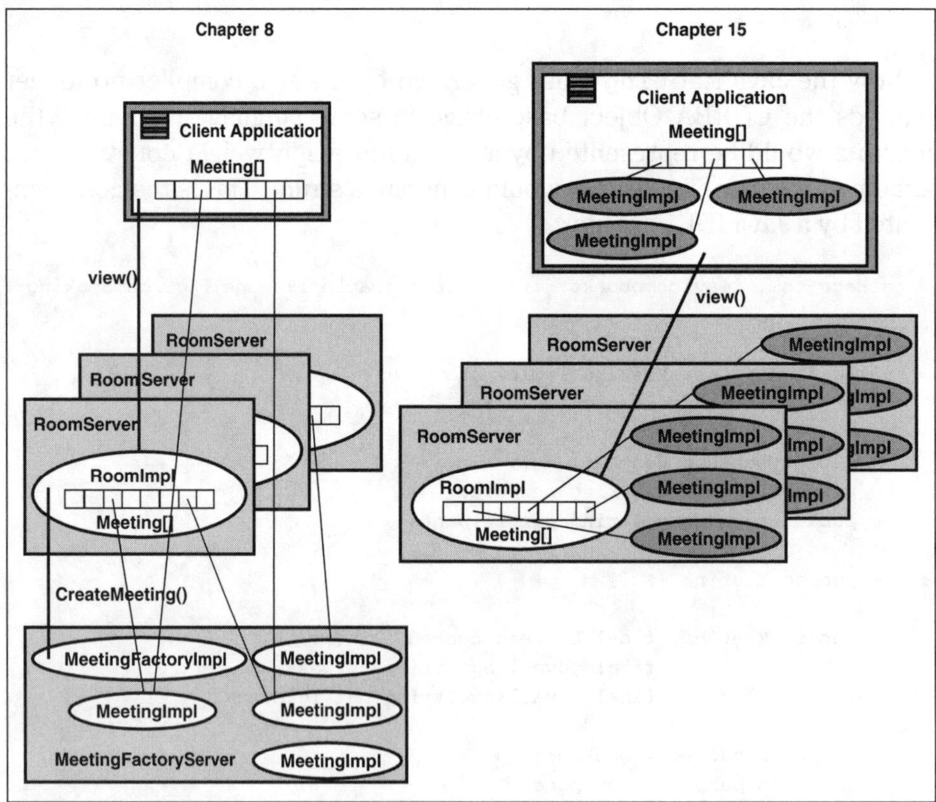


**Figure 15.1** Comparing the two approaches to the room booking application.

**Chapter 15 specification**—The view() operation returns an array of IDL structs represented by Java objects. The size of the Java objects is about 100 bytes, unless you have very long strings for the purpose and/or the participant fields. The client now has an array of references to local Java meeting objects.

### *Accessing Details of a Meeting*

**Chapter 8 specification**—The client makes two CORBA invocations on a remote Meeting object.

**Chapter 15 specification**—The client accesses fields of a local Java object.

### *Booking a Meeting*

**Chapter 8 specification**—The client makes a CORBA invocation on the remote MeetingFactory object, which creates a CORBA object and returns its IOR to the client. The client now makes a CORBA invocation on the remote Meeting object. The creation of a CORBA object with a transient object reference is slightly slower than the creation of a comparable Java object. Objects with persistent IORs may need much more time to be created.

**Chapter 15 specification**—The client instantiates a local `Meeting` Java object, initializes its contents locally, and passes it as an argument to a CORBA invocation on the remote Room object.

### *Canceling a Meeting*

**Chapter 8 specification**—The client makes a CORBA invocation on a remote Booking object, which makes another CORBA invocation on the Meeting object to deactivate it. The actual invocation is likely to be quick, as the Booking and the Meeting objects are probably colocated, but the deactivation of a persistent IOR could involve a remote call to an ORB agent.

**Chapter 15 specification**—The client makes a CORBA invocation on a remote Booking object, which sets the booked field of its local `Meeting` Java object to FALSE.

In summary, the Chapter 15 specification leads to far better performance than the Chapter 8 approach; however, the performance gain doesn't come for free. One reason for the performance improvement is an implicit client-side caching by bringing all data about meetings to the client when calling the view() operation. This could lead to outdated information at the client side. If the client refreshes its cache by calling view() frequently it can lose much of the performance gain, or performance could even be worse than it was originally.

There are no magic solutions for implementing the functional model; however, some rules of thumb can be applied. As we have seen, pros and cons of a specification depend on the usage of the objects. Your functional model should be analyzed by looking at the way in which the objects it specifies are used. You need to identify what data is exchanged, how much of it there is, and how often it is transferred between particular objects. This analysis should feed back into the design of the interfaces to optimize the data exchange, and it often results in respecifying your objects.

Sometimes the analysis must take the form of testing an application under load, looking for bottlenecks. We will look at this in section 15.1.6.

## 15.1.2 Threading Models

In this section we consider the execution of code in a single Java virtual machine. We start with a motivation for threading that is based on the user's perception of performance in an application: the reaction of the user interface to input. Improvements are demonstrated by an example of a multithreaded client. Then we look at the way in which servers can use threads to improve their performance.

### *15.1.2.1 Threading in Clients*

A major factor determining the success of an application is the quality of the user interface. Possibly the most annoying thing that can happen to a user is that the GUI blocks while waiting for a response. The synchronous nature of CORBA operation invocations and the relatively long duration of remote calls make CORBA-based distributed applications particularly vulnerable to the threat of a blocking GUI.

Figure 13.2 illustrates the behavior of a CORBA client making a simple operation call on a CORBA object. The client is blocked for the duration of the call. The duration can range from microseconds, when the client and the invoked object are colocated, to seconds when a remote invocation is made over a modem. The processing performed by the method implementing the operation may also lead to delays.

The approach to avoiding a blocked user interface that we look at here is to use threading in client code. We will look at two other proven design pat-

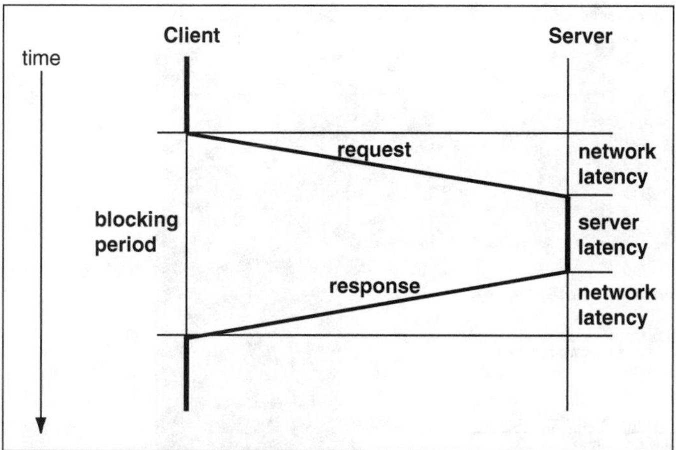


**Figure 15.2** Behavior of a naive interaction.

terns to address this problem in the next two sections, which address distributed callbacks and iterators.

### *15.1.2.2 Multithreaded Clients*

We will modify the Hello World applet client we introduced in Chapter 4, "A First Java ORB Application," as shown in Figure 15.3. We will substitute the text field with a text area to show more information on the screen. We will also add a second text area to the GUI just to demonstrate the nonblocking behavior that we can achieve using threads. The result is that you can type in the upper window while the client is busy interacting with an object.

```
package com.wiley.compbooks.brose.chapter15.mtClient.hello;

import java.awt.*;
import java.awt.event.*;
import java.io.*;
import java.net.*;
import org.omg.CORBA.*;

public class Applet
    extends java.applet.Applet
    implements ActionListener  {

    private ORB orb;
    private GoodDay goodDay;
    private Button helloWorldButton;
    private TextArea inArea;
    private TextArea outArea;
```

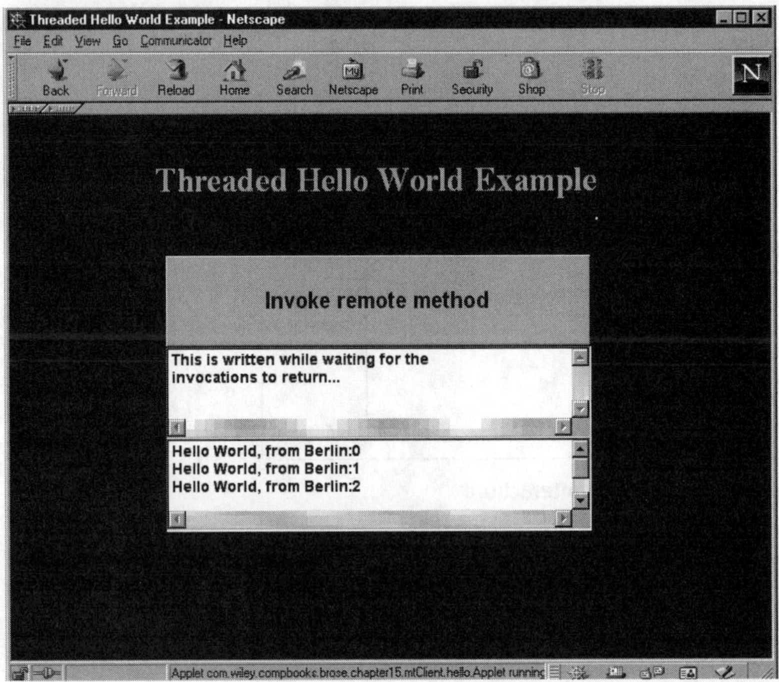


**Figure 15.3** Modified applet GUI.

```
public void init() {

    helloWorldButton = new Button("Invoke remote method");
    helloWorldButton.setFont(new Font("Helvetica",
                                      Font.BOLD, 20));
    helloWorldButton.setActionCommand("invoke");
    helloWorldButton.addActionListener( (ActionListener) this );

    inArea = new TextArea();
    inArea.setFont(new Font("Helvetica", Font.BOLD, 14));

    outArea = new TextArea();
    outArea.setEditable(false);
    outArea.setFont(new Font("Helvetica", Font.BOLD, 14));

    setLayout( new GridLayout(3,1));
    add( helloWorldButton );
    add( inArea );
    add( outArea );
```

As in Chapter 4, we use the applet's `readIOR()` method to obtain an object reference to a `GoodDay` object by reading a stringified object reference from a file on the Web server from which the applet is downloaded.

```
        try {
            // initialize the ORB (using this applet)
            orb = ORB.init( this, null );

            // bind to object
            goodDay = GoodDayHelper.narrow(
                orb.string_to_object( readIOR() ));
        }
        // catch exceptions
        catch(SystemException ex) {
            System.err.println("ORB is not initialized");
            System.err.println(ex);
        }
    }
```

Multithreaded clients spawn separate threads for each activity associated with a certain user event. In our case we create a new thread when the `hello world` button is pushed. Within this thread we will make the invocation, return the results back to the applet, and display them. The thread then terminates. As Figure 15.4 shows, the GUI will be blocked only while the new thread is created and started.

We have to add two things to the applet: a method that can be called by the thread to return the results of the operation and the code for creating and starting a new thread. The method `setResult()` displays a string in the output area.

```
    public void setResult( String str ) {
        outArea.append( str );
    }
```

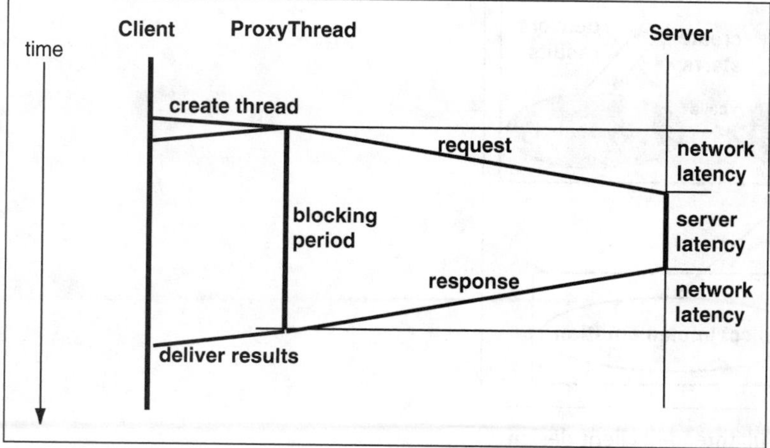


**Figure 15.4** Multithreaded client-threading behavior.

When the hello world button is pushed we create a new object of class ThreadedProxy, which extends java.lang.Thread. We initialize the new object with the reference to our applet and the reference to the CORBA object goodDay. Once the object is created, we start it by calling the method start(), which is defined in the class java.lang.Thread.

```
public void actionPerformed( ActionEvent e ) {

    if( e.getActionCommand().equals("invoke") ) {
        // invoke the operation via threaded proxy
        try {
            ThreadedProxy threadedProxy =
                new ThreadedProxy( this, goodDay );
            threadedProxy.start();
        }
        // catch CORBA system exceptions
        catch(SystemException ex) {
            System.err.println(ex);
        }
    }
}
```

Figure 15.5 shows the various objects in the multithreaded client and how they interact. The new object is an instance of the class ThreadedProxy.

The class ThreadedProxy extends the thread class of the Java class library. In its constructor we initialize the private fields goodDay and applet with references to the applet and a GoodDay object.

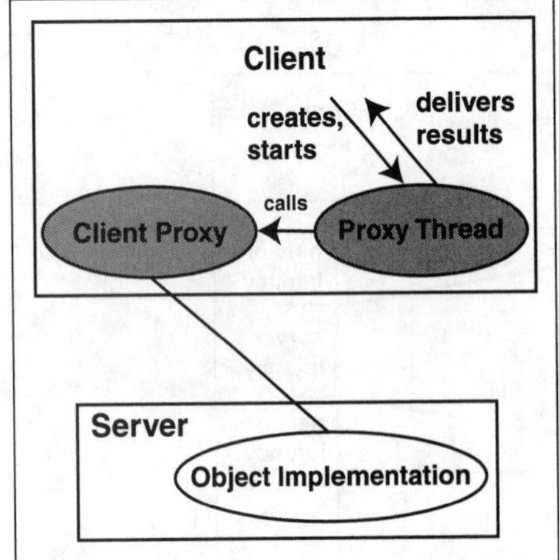


**Figure 15.5** Multithreaded client design.

```
package com.wiley.compbooks.brose.chapter15.mtClient.hello;

import org.omg.CORBA.*;

public class ThreadedProxy
    extends Thread {

    private GoodDay goodDay;
    private Applet applet;

    public ThreadedProxy( Applet applet, GoodDay goodDay ) {
        this.applet = applet;
        this.goodDay = goodDay;
    }
```

The functionality of a thread is in the implementation of the method `run()` defined by the Java thread class. We invoke the hello() operation on the CORBA object `goodDay` and display the result of the operation in the applet's output area by a calling `setResult()` on the applet.

```
    public void run() {
        // invoke the operation
        try {
            applet.setResult( goodDay.hello() );
        }
        // catch CORBA system exceptions
        catch(SystemException ex) {
            System.err.println(ex);
        }
    }
}
```

As an alternative to threading, the application can make deferred operation calls using the DII. The IDL/Java mapping defines the following methods on the class `Request`:

- `public void send_deferred();`—sends an invocation request and returns immediately
- `public void get_response();`—obtains an invocation response
- `public boolean poll_response();`—polls the `Request` object to find out if the response has arrived

As we saw in Chapter 9, the DII is more complex to use than generated stubs. There is also no compile-time type checking for DII invocations. Because threads are a language feature in Java and are easy to use, they are usually a better way to do other processing while waiting for an operation invocation to complete.

You can improve the performance of threaded clients by avoiding the creation of a new thread every time a CORBA call is made. Instead of just letting a used thread go out of scope, it can be returned to a thread pool. It is then available for further use. The added complexity of implementing your own thread pool manager needs to be weighed against the performance gain.

The overall performance of a multithreaded client also depends on the behavior of the server and, if the client is an applet, on the performance of the IIOP gateway. In the next section we explain different server-side threading models.

#### *15.1.2.3 Threading in Servers*

In the previous section our main purpose was to make the client responsive to the user by optimizing the communication between the client and the server. On the server side there is another problem, namely, how can a server handle hundreds or thousands of concurrent clients? Fortunately, application programmers do not have to deal with this problem explicitly because most Java ORB implementations already provide automatic mechanisms for multithreaded servers.

ORBs usually provide three threading models for server implementations: single-threaded servers, thread per connection, and thread pools or thread per request. Single-threaded servers (see Figure 15.6) place incoming requests in a queue and process only one invocation at a time. The problems are obvious. This leads to poor performance, as clients making apparently quick invocations must wait until all requests in the queue have been processed, even if they require much more processing. There is also the potential of deadlocks, which can occur when an object tries to make a callback to a single-threaded client program. Typically Java ORBs (unlike C or C++ ORBs) do not use single-threaded request processing because threads are a native concept in Java. It is possible to select single-threaded processing, however, by configuring the POA to use a thread policy with a value of SINGLE_THREAD_MODEL.

The thread-per-connection model uses one worker thread for each network connection, as shown in Figure 15.7. Typically all invocations originating from a single JVM to target objects that reside in the same server are multiplexed over the same connection. Invocations from this JVM are queued and processed sequentially by the worker thread.

Finally, the thread-per-request model creates a new worker thread for each incoming request, as illustrated in Figure 15.8. Typically there is a max-

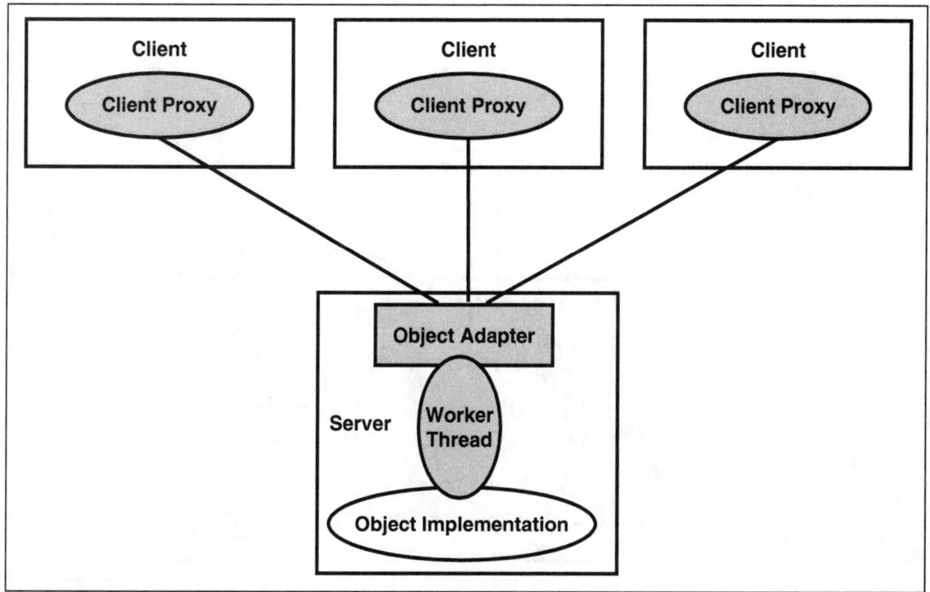


**Figure 15.6** Single-threaded servers.

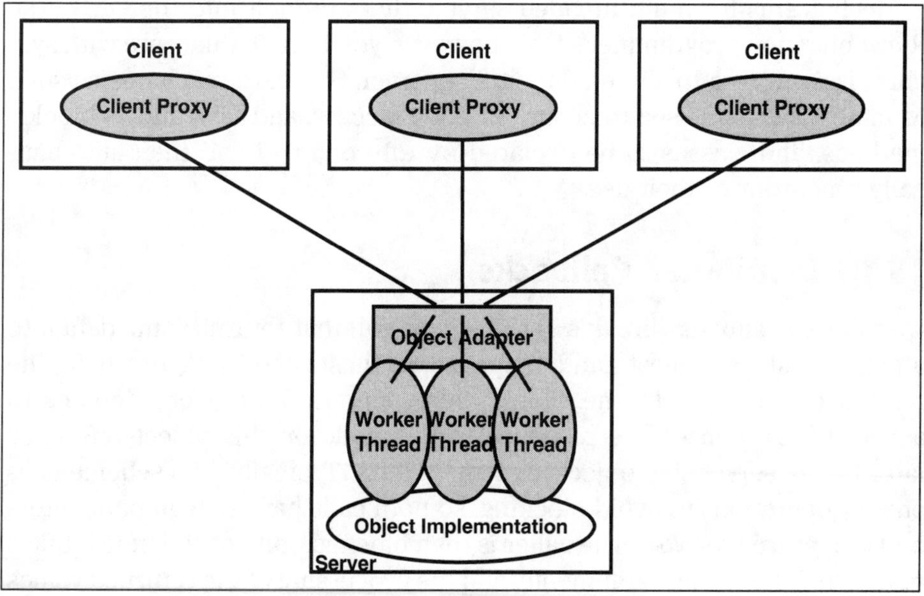


**Figure 15.7** Thread–per-connection.

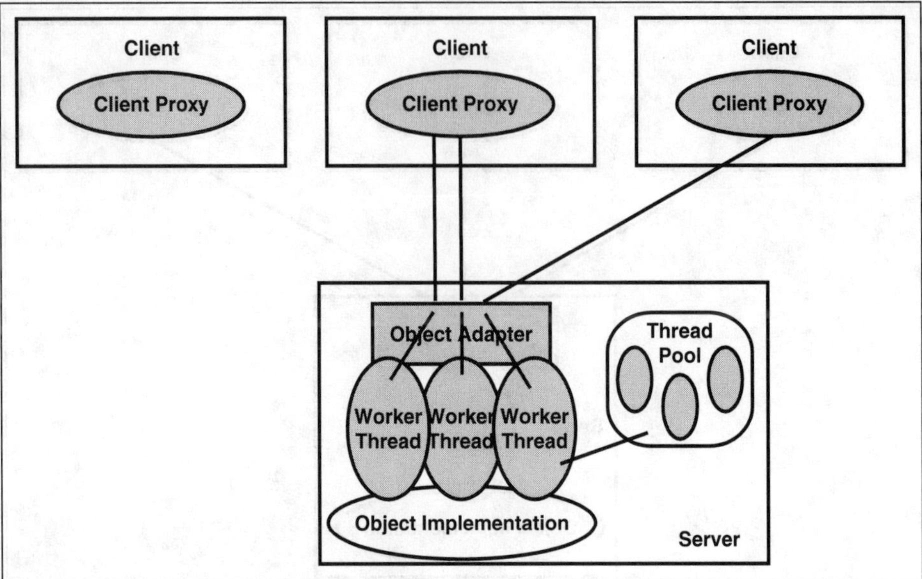


**Figure 15.8** Thread–per-request.

imum number of threads for use in the server, and threads that have finished processing a request are returned to a thread pool. This minimizes the cost associated with creating new threads. The default threading model of most Java ORBs is thread per request with thread pooling.

Mechanisms for multithreaded servers that are built into the ORB ease the application programmer's task; however, you have to take care with synchronizing access to shared data in the server. Standard mechanisms such as mutexes can be used to ensure safety of access, and Java allows blocks, methods, and classes to be declared `synchronized` and then automatically synchronizes their use.

## 15.1.3 Distributed Callbacks

Distributed callbacks break a synchronous call that returns some data into a pair of calls, a request and a response, as illustrated by Figure 15.9. The request call is made by the client, which supplies an object reference to accept the response. The response call is made on this object reference later by the server-side object implementation. Typically, this scheme uses oneway operations to avoid blocking, so both calls have only in parameters and the return type void. The caller is then blocked only for the time it takes to marshal the request arguments, and the processing of the returned values is delegated to another object.

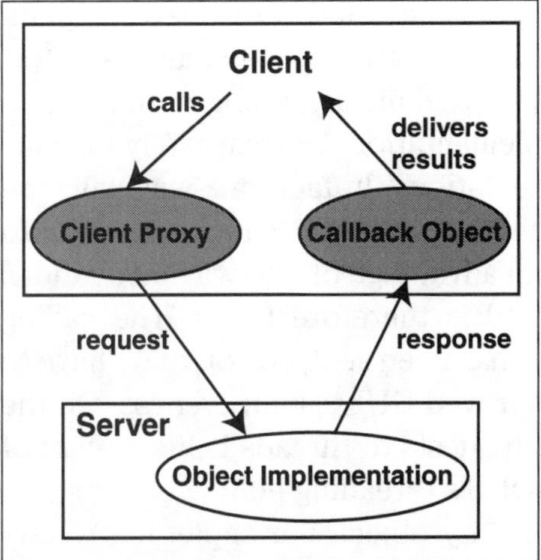


**Figure 15.9** Distributed callback design.

To allow the server-side object to call the client back, the client must host an object that implements an IDL-defined interface. The reference of this client-side object is provided as an in parameter of the request operation. As an example, we introduce a new interface in the hello IDL module and modify the hello() operation to fit the callback paradigm.

The hello module now contains two interfaces: GoodDay and Callback. The interface GoodDay now contains the operation requestHello(), which has an interface of type Callback as its in parameter. The interface Callback contains the operation responseHello(). It has one in parameter of type string that corresponds to the return value of the hello() operation as it was originally specified.

```
module com {
...
module chapter15 {
module callback {
module hello {

    interface Callback {
        oneway void responseHello( in string str );
    };

    interface GoodDay {
        oneway void requestHello( in Callback cb );
    };
};

}; ... };
```

Both operations are declared oneway. The semantics of oneway operations defined in CORBA is quite vague: It states that the call has best-effort semantics and is delivered at most once. Technically, doing nothing for a one-way call is a CORBA-compliant implementation. You can safely assume, though, that ORBs have better implementations. In fact, one-way calls are quite reliable because they are implemented with IIOP, which uses TCP to ensure that delivery is reliable. The main advantage of one-way invocations is that the call returns immediately and is therefore faster. The calling thread is blocked only until the message has been sent, so you don't have to create your own threads to achieve improved GUI responsiveness. On the server side, the allocation of incoming requests to threads is taken care of by the object adapter according to the ORB's threading policy.

To receive the callback from the `GoodDay` object, our applet has to create an object that implements the interface Callback. This can be done globally for the applet (one callback object that receives all callbacks), or a separate callback object can be instantiated for each invocation. Here we have chosen to create one object in the `init()` method of the applet. We initialize the POA and create the object in the usual manner.

```
// create callback object
poa = POAHelper.narrow(
    orb.resolve_initial_references( "RootPOA"));

org.omg.CORBA.Object obj =
    poa.servant_to_reference(new CallbackImpl( this ));

callback = CallbackHelper.narrow( obj );
poa.the_POAManager().activate();
```

When the `hello world` button is pushed we invoke the `requestHello()` method on the `GoodDay` object. We provide the object reference of the callback object created previously as the argument to the operation.

```
public void actionPerformed( ActionEvent e ) {
    if( e.getActionCommand().equals("invoke") ) {
        // invoke the operation
        try {
            goodDay.requestHello( callback );
        }
        // catch CORBA system exceptions
        catch(SystemException ex) {
            System.err.println(ex);
        }
    }
}
```

The implementation of the callback object is no different from any other object implementation. The implementation class extends the servant base class. We provide a reference to the applet to the constructor so that the result can be displayed. The implementation of `responseHello()` takes the string argument provided by the remote object implementation and calls the `setResult()` method on the applet that displays the result in the output area.

```
package com.wiley.compbooks.brose.chapter15.callback.hello;

import org.omg.CORBA.*;

public class CallbackImpl
    extends CallbackPOA {

    private Applet applet;

    CallbackImpl( Applet applet ) {
        this.applet = applet;
    }

    public void responseHello( String str ) {
        applet.setResult( str );
    }
}
```

The implementation of the `requestHello()` method on the server side does not return a value. First we simulate delay of the method execution by putting the thread to sleep for 10 seconds. Then we make the callback to the applet by invoking the `responseHello()` method on the callback object to deliver the result.

```
    // method
    public void requestHello( Callback callback) {
        try {
            // sleep for 10 seconds
            Thread.sleep(10000);
        }
        catch(InterruptedException e) { }

        callback.responseHello( "Hello World, from " +
                                location + ":" +
                                counter++ + "\n");
    }
```

Figure 15.10 shows the thread behavior of a distributed callback. Using callbacks also makes the client implicitly multithreaded, as the ORB creates a new thread to process the requests for the client-side callback object.

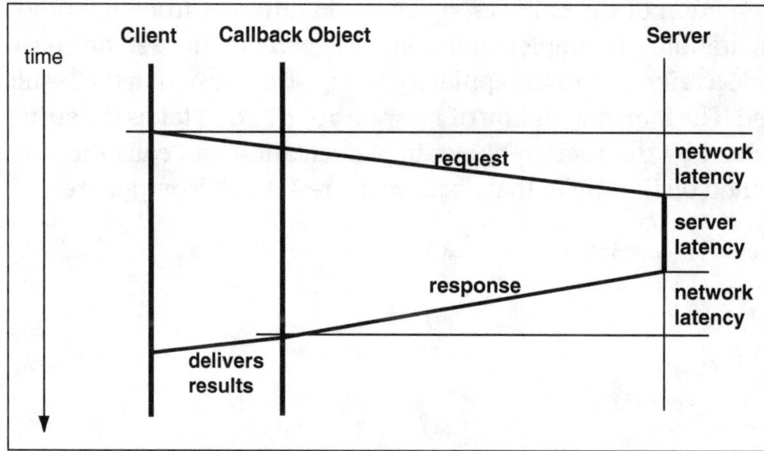


**Figure 15.10** Distributed callbacks' threading behavior.

If you want to use callbacks with applets, make sure that you never rely on HTTP tunneling for the communication, as this prevents callbacks. You also need to make sure that the IIOP gateway supports callbacks. VisiBroker's Gatekeeper, for example, enables callbacks into applets when using IIOP.

## 15.1.4 Iterators

Iterators are a commonly used design pattern to handle the transmission of large amounts of data. They allow access to large amounts of data in multiple smaller packages rather than in one big chunk. Another motivation is support for the *lazy evaluation* paradigm. This means that additional values are produced only on demand. This approach can avoid allocating large amounts of memory on both the client and the server sides. Clients can process a portion of the results and discard them before requesting more. They may also decide that they do not require the rest of the results and destroy the iterator. Servers using lazy evaluation can produce a small part of the total result at a time, either ready for the next call to the iterator or when the call is made on the iterator. When clients do not require all the results, the server can avoid the unnecessary processing required to produce the entire set.

The iterator pattern has been adopted in several CORBA specifications. We have already seen iterators in specifications of the CORBA Naming and Trading Services. The mechanism employed to implement iterators comes in various flavors. We present two kinds of iterators: pull and push. A client is in control when using a pull iterator and the server is in control when using a push iterator.

### 15.1.4.1 Pull Iterators

A pull iterator is a short-lived object created on the server side from which data can be obtained by a client as required. Figure 15.11 illustrates the interactions between a CORBA client, a CORBA object, and a pull iterator.

We again modify the Hello World example to demonstrate iterators. We introduce a new data type ResultSet, which is an unbounded sequence of strings. In a real application we would probably use a sequence of some other type to represent, for example, a row in a database table. The iterator would then serve as a way of accessing the results of a query that matched a large number of rows.

```
module com {
...
module pullIterator {
module hello {
    typedef sequence<string>ResultSet;

    interface PullIterator {
        boolean nextN( in long n, out ResultSet result_set);
        void destroy();
    };

    interface GoodDay {
        ResultSet hello( in long how_many, out PullIterator pull_iterator);
    };
};};};};};};
```

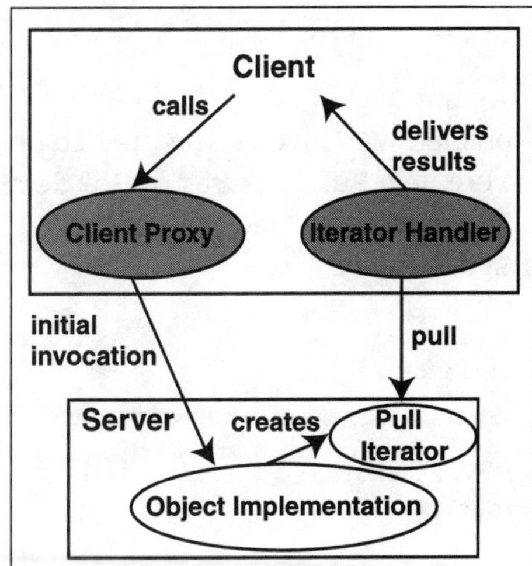


**Figure 15.11** Pull iterator.

The hello() operation of the GoodDay object has a new signature. It now returns a result of type ResultSet. The in parameter how_many allows the client to control the maximum length of the returned sequence. The out parameter pull_iterator is an object reference to a PullIterator that is created by the GoodDay object. After a client has made the hello() call on a GoodDay object it can query the PullIterator object for more data by calling its nextN() operation.

The Boolean result of the nextN() operation indicates whether there is any data left in the iterator. A client can again control the maximum length of the ResultSet, which is returned to the client via the out parameter result_set.

The destroy() operation is important for managing system resources. Although an iterator could destroy itself after it delivers all its data, a client could decide that it doesn't want to query the iterator any further, even if there is still data available. If this happened the iterator would never know that it has been abandoned by the client. Well-behaved clients will always call destroy() when they no longer want the iterator, but the iterator should have some time-out mechanism, as there is nothing but the programmer's discipline to ensure that the destroy() operation is actually invoked. In section 15.2 of this chapter we discuss the problem of distributed garbage collection in a more general manner.

Let's have a look at an applet that uses a pull iterator to access a large amount of data. First we declare and implement a new method on the applet. The method `setResult()` displays a `ResultSet` in the output area. The initialization of the applet is the same.

```
public void setResult( String[] resultSet ) {
    for( int i = 0; i < resultSet.length; i++ )
        outArea.append( resultSet[i] );
}
```

When the `hello world` button is pushed we invoke the `hello()` method. Before we can do this we have to create a `PullIteratorHolder` object for the out parameter of the `hello()` method. Once the `hello()` operation has returned we display the first result set.

```
public void actionPerformed( ActionEvent e ) {
    if( e.getActionCommand().equals("invoke") ) {
        // invoke the operation
        try {
            PullIteratorHolder pullIteratorHolder =
                new PullIteratorHolder();
            String[] resultSet =
                goodDay.hello( 5, pullIteratorHolder );
            outArea.append( resultSet );
            IteratorHandler iteratorHandler =
```

```
                    new IteratorHandler(
                        this, pullIteratorHolder.value );
                iteratorHandler.start();
            }
            // catch CORBA system exceptions
            catch(SystemException ex) {
                System.err.println(ex);
            }
        }
    }
```

We create a new object of type `IteratorHandler` that handles the further querying of the iterator in a separate thread. We initialize the `IteratorHandler` with references to the applet and the pull iterator. The key functionality of the class `IteratorHandler` is in the implementation of the method `run()`.

```
public class IteratorHandler
    extends Thread {

    public void run() {
        ResultSetHolder resultSetHolder = new ResultSetHolder();
        try {
            while( pullIterator.nextN( 5, resultSetHolder ) ) {
                applet.setResult( resultSetHolder.value );
            }
            pullIterator.destroy();
        }
        // ...
}
```

In the implementation of `run()` we create a new `ResultSetHolder` object. Then we call the `nextN()` method on the iterator and display the result set obtained in the applet by calling its `setResult()` method. We continue querying the iterator as long as it returns true, indicating that it contains more data. Finally, we destroy the iterator.

On the server side we have a new implementation of the `hello()` method provided by the `GoodDayImpl` class. We simulate a large amount of data by creating result sets on the fly. Many iterator implementations that use lazy evaluation do the same thing, although the new result sets are a meaningful response to the original call. Our response contains our standard string plus a counter so that we can watch the progress at the client side.

```
package com.wiley.compbooks.brose.chapter15.pullIterator.hello;

import org.omg.CORBA.*;

public class GoodDayImpl
    extends GoodDayPOA
```

```
{
    // ...

    public String[] hello( int howMany,
                           PullIteratorHolder pullIteratorHolder ){

        String[] resultSet = new String[ howMany ];
        for( int i = 0; i < howMany; i++ ) {
            resultSet[i] = new String(
                "Hello World, from " + location + ":" + i + "\n" );
        }

        PullIteratorImpl pullIteratorImpl =
            new PullIteratorImpl( howMany, 100, location );

        try {
            pullIteratorHolder.value = PullIteratorHelper.narrow(
                _poa().servant_to_reference( pullIteratorImpl ));
        }
        catch( Exception e ) {
            e.printStackTrace();
        }
        return resultSet;
    }
}
```

We create a result set of size `howMany` and fill it with our strings. Next we create an object of type `PullIteratorImpl`, which we initialize with the value of the counter, the maximum number of these sets (100), and the location string. The `GoodDayImpl` object acts as a `PullIterator` factory. Finally, we assign the object reference of the pull iterator to the value field of the holder object and return the result set created earlier.

The class `PullIteratorImpl` is a normal CORBA object implementation. It extends the servant base class `PullIteratorPOA`. In the implementation of the method `nextN()` we check first if the counter is beyond the maximum. This would mean that the iterator has done its job and delivered all the data to the client. If so, we return `false`.

```
public boolean nextN( int howMany,
                      ResultSetHolder resultSetHolder) {

    if( counter >= max ) {
        resultSetHolder.value = new String[0];
        return false;
    }

    try {
        // sleep for 4 seconds
        Thread.currentThread().sleep(4000);
```

```
            }
            catch(InterruptedException e) {
            }

            int diff = ( max - counter > howMany ?
                         howMany : max - counter );

            String[] resultSet = new String[ diff ];

            for( int i = 0; i < diff; i++, counter++ ) {

                resultSet[i] = new String(
                    "Hello World, from " + location + ":" +
                    counter + "\n" );
                System.out.println( resultSet[i] );
            }

            resultSetHolder.value = resultSet;
            return true;
        }
    }
```

If we have not exceeded the maximum, we simulate a processing delay by putting the thread to sleep for four seconds. Once the thread comes back to life we prepare the next result set to be returned to client in the same way as in the implementation of the `hello()` method shown previously. We then assign the result to the value field of the Holder object `resultSetHolder` and return TRUE.

```
        public void destroy(){
            try {
                _poa().deactivate_object( _object_id());
            }
            catch( Exception e ){
                e.printStackTrace();
            }
        }
```

The `destroy()` method releases any resources associated with the iterator in the POA by calling `deactivate_object()`.

### *15.1.4.2 Push Iterators*

Push iterators have the same basic characteristics as pull iterators, but they differ in the delivery mechanism. Pull iterators are queried by the client; push iterators are controlled by the server. Push iterators can be understood as a combination of iterators with callbacks. The iterator controls the delivery of the remaining data by making a series of callbacks.

We will adapt our GoodDay object to use a push iterator. Figure 15.12 illustrates the behavior of a CORBA client, a GoodDay object, and a client object receiving callbacks from a push iterator. Again we have two interfaces defined in an IDL file. There is the GoodDay interface that provides a hello() operation, as before; however, this time the client provides an interface on which the iterator can call. This interface is called Receiver. It provides one operation, nextN(), that takes a value of type ResultSet as an in parameter. Note that the interface Receiver is not the iterator itself but the interface the iterator calls to deliver data sets.

```
module com {
...
module chapter15 {
module pushIterator {
module hello {
    typedef sequence< string > ResultSet;
    interface Receiver {
        void nextN( in ResultSet result_set);
    };
    interface GoodDay {
        ResultSet hello( in long how_many, in Receiver receiver);
    };
};};};};};
```

We have not included a destroy() operation in the Receiver interface. Whether you do this depends on where the control of the application is. Typ-

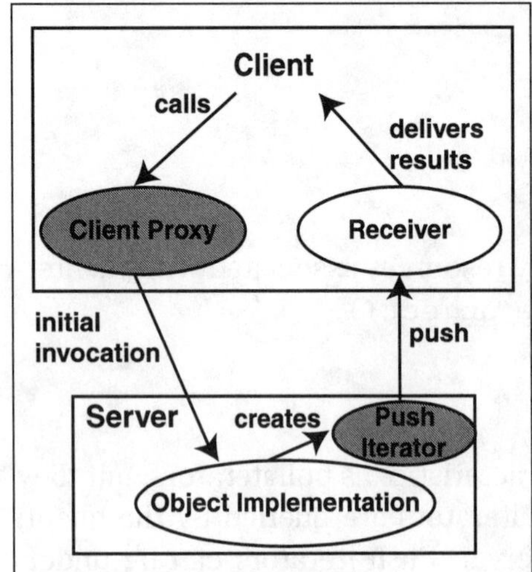


**Figure 15.12** Push iterator.

ically a client that initiates an action will destroy its own receiver object if it doesn't wish to receive any further results. Sometimes the design will give the server responsibility for cleaning up receivers, in which case you need a destroy() operation. An alternative is an operation that lets the server notify the client that the delivery is finished.

On the client side, when the `hello world` button is pushed, the applet creates the callback object for the push iterator, `receiver`, and obtains an object reference from the POA. Then we invoke the `hello()` method on the `goodDay` object and supply the reference to `receiver` as an argument. The other argument specifies an initial result set size of 5. The enclosing `setResult()` call will display the returned result set in the applet's output area.

```
    public void actionPerformed( ActionEvent e ) {
        if( e.getActionCommand().equals("invoke") ) {
            // invoke the operation
            try {
                Receiver receiver = ReceiverHelper.narrow(
                    poa.servant_to_reference(
                        new ReceiverImpl( this )));

                setResult( goodDay.hello( 5, receiver ));
            }

            // catch CORBA system exceptions
            catch( Exception ex) {
                System.err.println(ex);
            }
        }
    }
}
```

The class `ReceiverImpl` is again a normal object implementation, extending the servant base class. The implementation of the method is straightforward. We call the method `setResult()` on the applet and supply the `resultSet` we get from the iterator as its argument.

```
public class ReceiverImpl
    extends ReceiverPOA {
...
    public void nextN( String[] resultSet ) {
        applet.setResult( resultSet );
    }
}
```

On the server side the class `GoodDayImpl` implements the `hello()` method by preparing a result set of size `howMany` in the usual manner. Then we create a new object called `pushIterator` and start the thread associated with it.

```
public class GoodDayImpl
    extends GoodDayPOA {
...
    // method
    public String[] hello( int howMany, Receiver receiver ) {

        String[] resultSet = new String[ howMany ];

        for( int i = 0; i < howMany; i++ ) {
            resultSet[i] = new String(
                "Hello World, from " + location + ":" + i + "\n" );
        }
        PushIterator pushIterator =
            new PushIterator( receiver, howMany, 100, location );
        PushIterator.start();
        return resultSet;
    }
}
```

The push iterator is implemented in the class `PushIterator` by its `run()` method using a while loop. As long as the counter is less than the maximum, the iterator keeps pushing data sets to the applet. First we simulate some processing delay by putting the thread to sleep for five seconds. Then we prepare the result set and invoke the `nextN()` operation on the `receiver` object.

```
...
public class PushIterator
    extends Thread {
...
    public void run() {
        try {
            while( counter < max ) {
                try {
                    // sleep for 5 seconds
                    Thread.currentThread().sleep(5000);
                }
                catch(InterruptedException e) {
                }
                String[] resultSet = new String[ 5 ];
                for( int i = 0;
                     i < 5 && counter < max;
                     i++, counter++ ) {

                    resultSet[i] = new String( "Hello World, from "
                        + location + ":" + counter + "\n" );
```

```
                }
                receiver.nextN( resultSet );
            }
        }
        // catch CORBA system exceptions
        catch(SystemException ex) {
            System.err.println(ex);
        }
    }
}
```

Again, it is an alternative to declare the nextN() operation oneway, which has the same implications as discussed for callbacks.

## 15.1.5 Client-Side Caching

Another way to optimize communication is to cache data at the client side. The result of a remote invocation is kept in the client and further calls to the operation return the cached value without making a remote call. This approach is particularly useful when an attribute or operation that requires a remote call returns the same result repeatedly. There are two approaches to elegantly achieve client-side caching. The two approaches perform caching in the same way but on different abstraction levels, as shown in Figure 15.13.

You can explicitly encapsulate the IDL-generated client proxy object in a caching object. The caching object implements the Java interface that represents the IDL interface type. This is also the Java interface that the client-side proxy object implements. Your implementation of the methods of this interface will make a call to access the data from the remote object and keep the values in the local cache, or it will simply return the cached values without making a call. The condition for refreshing the cached values must be implemented according to some caching policy. This can be combined with callbacks indicating that the cache is invalid.

Alternatively, you can achieve the same effect by using extensions provided by some ORB implementations. Examples are VisiBroker's Smart

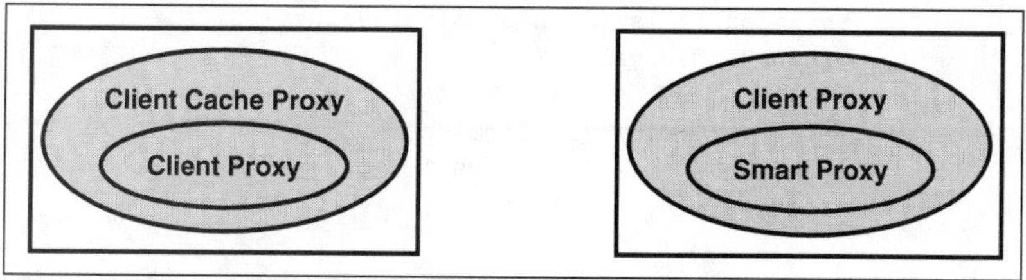


**Figure 15.13** Client-side caching.

Stubs and OrbixWeb's Smart Proxies. The idea is that the application programmer has access to an additional API through which the request is passed after the client calls the object reference proxy. Smart Stubs and Smart Proxies are particularly useful for accessing cached data.

We have implemented a caching example using the explicit approach. As an example we again extend the Hello World example from Chapter 4. We must implement a new client that talks to the same server. The client class becomes leaner than the original class, as we delegate most of the CORBA-related activities to the client cache class `GoodDayCache`.

We create an instance of the holder classes as in the original example. Then we create an instance of the caching proxy, of class `GoodDayCache`, which we will explain. We invoke the `hello()` method on the caching proxy instead of on the CORBA client proxy. Finally, we print the results as in the original example.

```
package com.wiley.compbooks.brose.chapter15.caching.hello;

import org.omg.CORBA.*;

public class Client {
    public static void main(String args[]) {

        // create Holder objects for out parameters
        ShortHolder minuteHolder = new ShortHolder();
        ShortHolder hourHolder = new ShortHolder();

        // create client caching proxy
        GoodDayCache goodDayCache = new GoodDayCache( args[0] );

        for( int i = 0; i < 20; i++ ) {
            // invoke the operation
            String location = goodDayCache.hello(
                hourHolder, minuteHolder );

            // print results to stdout
            System.out.println("Hello World!");
            if( minuteHolder.value < 10 )
                System.out.println("The local time in " +
                    location +" is " + hourHolder.value + ":0" +
                    minuteHolder.value + "." );
            else
                System.out.println("The local time in " +
                    location + " is " + hourHolder.value + ":" +
                    minuteHolder.value + "." );


            try {
                    Thread.sleep( 15000 );
```

```
            }
            catch( java.lang.InterruptedException ex ) {
                System.err.println(ex);
            }
        }
    }
}
```

As a test we make 20 invocations with a pause of 15 seconds between them so that we can see when the invocation on the caching proxy results in a remote call and when it returns locally cached data.

The caching proxy class has the same signature as the CORBA client proxy. We ensure this by implementing the Java interface `GoodDayOperations` generated by the IDL compiler. This class is generated for use by the Tie object implementation approach, but it fits our purpose as well.

```
package com.wiley.compbooks.brose.chapter15.caching.hello;

import java.io.*;
import org.omg.CORBA.*;

public class GoodDayCache
    implements GoodDayOperations {

    private GoodDay goodDay;
    private String location;
    private long lastTime;
    private long currentTime;
    private short hour;
    private short minute;
```

The major parts of the class are the constructor and the method implementation. In the constructor we initialize the ORB and obtain a reference to the object implementation.

```
    public GoodDayCache(String arg) {
        lastTime = 0;
        try {
            // initialize the ORB
            ORB orb = ORB.init(new String[0], null);

            // get object reference from command-line argument
            org.omg.CORBA.Object obj = orb.string_to_object( arg );

            // and narrow it to GoodDay
            goodDay = GoodDayHelper.narrow( obj );
        }
        catch(SystemException ex) {
```

```
            System.err.println(ex);
        }
    }
```

In the method implementation we implement the following caching policy: If the previous invocation was made within the last minute we return cached values; otherwise, we make a remote call. This makes sense for the example as the granularity of the time value returned by the server-side object is on the order of minutes.

```
    public String hello( ShortHolder hourHolder,
                         ShortHolder minuteHolder ) {

        currentTime = System.currentTimeMillis();

        if( currentTime - lastTime < 60000 ) {
            System.out.println("use cached data");
            hourHolder.value = hour;
            minuteHolder.value = minute;
        }
        else {
            System.out.println("make remote invocation");
            try {
                location = goodDay.hello( hourHolder, minuteHolder );
                hour = hourHolder.value;
                minute = minuteHolder.value;
                lastTime = currentTime;
            }
            catch(SystemException ex) {
                System.err.println(ex);
            }
        }
        return location;
    }
}
```

To run the example we first start the server, which is the same as in Chapter 4, and then our new client. Our output trace demonstrates that three out of four invocations are handled by returning cached data.

```
$ java com.wiley.compbooks.brose.chapter15.caching.hello.Server Montreal
> /tmp/ior
$ java com.wiley.compbooks.brose.chapter15.caching.hello.Client
cat /tmp/ior
make remote invocation
Hello World!
The local time in Montreal is 17:05.
use cached data
Hello World!
The local time in Montreal is 17:05.
```

```
use cached data
Hello World!
The local time in Montreal is 17:05.
use cached data
Hello World!
The local time in Montreal is 17:05.
make remote invocation
Hello World!
The local time in Montreal is 17:06.
```

## 15.1.6 Monitoring Performance

Now that we have investigated a number of ways of improving performance in clients, we still need to instrument the application to measure the performance results and find out where these techniques actually need to be applied. If a requirements specification states that the time for a certain user-initiated action should not exceed a certain number of milliseconds or seconds, you need to instrument each component of your application to isolate any performance bottlenecks. You have to find out exactly where your application introduces delays that break the requirements.

A simple way to instrument your application is to wrap each invocation on the client and server sides into a pair of statements that take the time, calculate the difference, and log the data. This approach, however, has multiple disadvantages. First, you litter the application with code that is designed to be used only during testing. Furthermore, you must be able to easily switch the performance measurement on and off; this means making all of your performance measurement code conditional. This clutters the application code even more.

CORBA's Portable Interceptors framework, which we introduced in Chapter 9, is a generic mechanism for instrumenting applications. It can also be used to decouple application logic from performance measurement code. In Chapter 9 we explained a simple client-side round-trip measurement example. In this section, the client interceptor is complemented with a corresponding server interceptor that measures how long the processing of individual operations takes. This is achieved by taking the system time when the request is received by the server and again when the response is sent back. This is mostly straightforward because server interceptors are called at these points by the ORB anyway. The code follows and is explained.

```
package com.wiley.compbooks.brose.chapter15.performanceMeasurement;

import java.io.*;
import org.omg.CORBA.*;
import org.omg.CORBA.portable.*;
import org.omg.PortableInterceptor.*;
```

```
public class TimerServerInterceptor
    extends LocalityConstrainedObject
    implements ServerRequestInterceptor {

    private int slotId;
    private PrintStream logStream;

    //...
    public void receive_request_service_contexts(
        ServerRequestInfo ri )
        throws org.omg.PortableInterceptor.ForwardRequest {

        try {
            Any timeAny = ri.get_slot( slotId );
            timeAny.insert_longlong( System.currentTimeMillis() );
            ri.set_slot( slotId, timeAny );
        }
        catch( Exception e ) {
            e.printStackTrace();
        }
    }
```

The two methods in the interceptor that we are interested in are `receive_request_service_contexts()` and `send_reply()`. The ORB calls these when the request arrives at the server and before the reply is sent back. In `receive_request_service_contexts()`, we need to record the system time. We also need to find a way of communicating this start time to the `send_reply()` method so that it can be subtracted from the end time. This can be done by wrapping the time in an Any and storing it in a slot of the `ServerRequestInfo` object that is passed as an argument to both methods. The Portable Interceptor specification defines how this object is passed around, how slot IDs are assigned, and how slots are accessed using slot IDs. The slot ID must be reserved for the use of this interceptor at system startup. This is done in a specific initializer object for the interceptor, which we explain below. For now it is sufficient to remember that both methods can find a shared slot in the info object using the slot ID field in this class and that the slot holds an Any. The `send_reply()` method can simply extract the longlong value that represents a system time in milliseconds from the slot's Any.

```
    public void send_reply(
        org.omg.PortableInterceptor.ServerRequestInfo ri ) {

        try {
            long now = System.currentTimeMillis();
            Any timeAny = ri.get_slot( slotId );
```

```
            logStream.println( " operation: " + ri.operation() +
                               " duration: " +
                               ( now - timeAny.extract_longlong())
                               + " msecs. ");

        }
        catch( Exception e ) {
            e.printStackTrace();
        }
    }
```

To complete the server-side example, here is an initializer that reserves the slot ID and creates the interceptor. This is done in the `post_init()` method, which is called by the ORB during ORB initialization.

```
package com.wiley.compbooks.brose.chapter15.performanceMeasurement;

import org.omg.PortableInterceptor.*;
import org.omg.PortableInterceptor.ORBInitInfoPackage.*;

public class ServerInitializer
    extends LocalityConstrainedObject
    implements ORBInitializer {

    public ServerInitializer() {
    }

    /** This method registers the interceptor. */

    public void post_init( ORBInitInfo info ) {

        try {
            int slotId = info.allocate_slot_id();
            info.add_server_request_interceptor(
                new TimerServerInterceptor( slotId ));
        }
        catch (DuplicateName e) {
            e.printStackTrace();
        }
    }

    public void pre_init( ORBInitInfo info ) {
    }
}
```

To instrument an application using the performance measurement interceptors we need to make the initializer known to the ORB. This is done by registering its class name using a special ORB property, as shown in Chapter 9:

```
$ java -Dorg.omg.PortableInterceptor.ORBInitializerClass.PerfInit=\
com.wiley.compbooks.brose.chapter15.performanceMeasurement.\
ServerInitializer  TestedServer
```

If a server is started with the interceptor initializer, you will see the following output for every invocation processed be the server:

```
operation: hello duration: 2 msecs.
```

In combination with the client-side interceptor from Chapter 9, you are now in a position to identify potential performance bottlenecks in your distributed application. By looking at the differences between the total duration of the call as measured on the client and the server side you can also infer the amount of communication involved versus the computation that took place at the server. The interceptor approach outlined previously relies only on Portable Interceptors and thus works for any ORB that complies with CORBA 2.3, but the output of the measurements is not presented in a particularly sophisticated fashion. The example could be extended to present results graphically and perhaps assemble certain kinds of statistics. Some Application Server products come with their own set of tools for performance monitoring and provide GUI clients to view the data in various forms, for example, the AppCenter management extension to the Inprise Application Server.

#### *15.1.6.1 A Test Client to Drive the Application*

Typically the GUI client driving your application is not useful for stress testing because it relies on human interactions and cannot simulate different loads. We suggest that you implement a stress-test client that uses the following pattern:

```
class TestClient {
    int noOfCycles;
    public static void main( String args ) {
        // get a number of cycles from the command line
        noOfCycles = ...
        // obtain IOR to an initial application object
        initialApplicationObject = ...
           for( int i =0; i < noOfCycles; i++ ) {
                // simulate typical client behavior
                // could be derived from use cases
           }
        }
    }
```

An implementation following this pattern can simulate various load levels. A more sophisticated implementation could be multithreaded. Alternatively, you could simulate different loads with single-threaded clients by starting multiple clients in their own JVMs. When using a multithreaded test client implementation you need to take the server-side threading model into account.

The implementation of a cycle in the test client depends on scenarios you would consider to be typical. It could be derived from use cases that may have developed as part of your analysis and design phase. This is another motivation to spend some time on the development and formalization of use cases after the design phase.

Because the test client is a command-line-driven Java application, it can be used from test scripts written in UNIX shells, in Perl, or as batch files. This will help to create an automated and repeatable test process. You may also consider commercial Java test tools. Their general approach is that they can capture activity on your client program and replay the captured sequences in different scenarios, simulating different loads.

#### 15.1.6.2 Analysis of the Performance Data

Once we have measured the performance of our application in the manner described previously, we can analyze it. The detailed measurements allow us to locate performance bottlenecks. Typically performance problems fall into one of the following categories. We also give you some hints on where to look for performance improvements.

- **Delay problem at light load.**
  - *Delay in the communication leg.* Make sure that the amount of data shipped between client and server is optimized using the techniques described in the previous sections.
  - *Delay in the computation leg.* Double-check your code for potential performance problems, in particular your POA configuration. Do performance measurements for non-ORB components, for example, databases. Try to cache data in the server-side CORBA objects.
- **Delay problem at heavy load.**
  - *Delay in the communication leg.* Make sure that you use the most appropriate threading model: thread-per-request.
  - *Delay in the computation leg.* Make sure that enough resources are available to your objects. Resources include those provided by

the operating systems such as threads, memory, CPU cycles, file descriptors, socket connections, and third-party resources, for example, available database connections. Reconfiguring and redistributing your servers is the only solution here.

## 15.2 Management

Managing distributed applications is a complex task and involves a wide range of activities that includes both monitoring the state of the application and performing the required administrative actions. The main areas of management can be described with the acronym FCAPS, which stands for Fault, Configuration, Accounting, Performance, and Security. Management is often performed by an administrator using a set of sophisticated GUI tools at his or her console that communicates with management agents colocated with the managed resources.

The interceptors presented in the previous section were mainly introduced as a tool for developing efficient applications, but because they allow performance monitoring they can also be regarded as part of a management agent. Other management facilities that you are likely to come across are tools for configuration management included in CCM implementations and tools that interface to the Security Service for managing security. There is no comprehensive approach or facility that would allow managing all these aspects of CORBA applications using just a single tool or framework, however.

Although it is beyond the scope of this book to present a comprehensive approach here, we have selected two specific management issues for discussion. These issues are related to managing the life cycle of objects and servers:

- **Distributed garbage collection**—cleaning up objects that are no longer required by their remote clients
- **Graceful shutdown**—the ability to safely shut down an application without needing to be aware of where all the servers and their objects are executing

The management approach that we take complements the use of factory objects for starting a distributed application. Factories provide a way of easily creating new objects with the characteristics that we require, as they are needed. We need to consider what to do when individual objects are no longer required, especially when their client programs shut down without indicating that they no longer require the objects they are using. We also need an approach to shutting down an entire application that ensures that the current objects can terminate cleanly. They may need to save their state or to clean up other objects they are using. We will show an implementation of a simple tool that monitors the objects created and allows them to be gracefully shut down. Section 15.2 has the following structure:

- Distributed garbage collection (section 15.2.1)
- Design of a management interface for graceful shutdown of a distributed application (section 15.2.2)
- Implementing a management tool (section 15.2.3)
- Implementing managed objects (section 15.2.4)
- Using the management tool (section 15.2.5)

## 15.2.1 Distributed Garbage Collection

Distributed garbage collection means that a distributed object will be destroyed once no (remote) client holds a reference to the object. CORBA does not address this problem except in the form of explicit operations to release objects, as specified in the Life Cycle Service. The problem of cleaning up when clients just discard object references is still unsolved. This is a common occurrence in applications deployed on the Internet because applet clients are not under the application's control.

CORBA does address the memory management of client proxies and server objects. We explained the general mechanism in Chapter 2, "CORBA Overview." The Java case is simpler because it allows the delegation of memory management to the Java garbage collection mechanism. This means that client proxies are garbage collected once all Java object references to the proxy go out of scope. The same applies to the server side, but here the object adapter holds a reference to the servant it obtained when the object was activated. To release this reference you must deactivate the object by calling `poa.deactivate_object()` or by destroying its object adapter. If the POA uses a Servant Locator you need to deactivate and destroy the Locator object.

In order to safely deactivate an object, you should be sure that there is no client out there holding an IOR to the object. Generally the ORB cannot determine this and hence cannot automate distributed garbage collection. For example, a client passes an object reference to a third-party object that stores it without making a connection to the server. Because the server does not know about the other reference it might just deactivate the object once the original client is done with it. This, however, does not mean that you cannot solve the problem of distributed garbage collection in your application because your application can keep information about the copying or passing of references to which the ORB does not have access.

First of all, clients that request an object to be created for their exclusive use should release the object once they are done with it by calling an explicit destroy operation. The implementation of this operation will release any references to itself, including the one held by the object adapter, and so prepare the object for garbage collection by Java. You have to declare this destroy operation in the IDL interface of the object. You can declare your own destroy operation or the object can inherit the CORBA LifeCycleObject interface and implement its remove() operation (see Figure 15.14).

```
exception NotRemovable { string reason; };
interface LifeCycleObject {
    ...
    void remove() raises( NotRemovable );
};
```

Note that the Life Cycle Service is a set of IDL interfaces intended as a design pattern you have to implement rather than as an off-the-shelf service such as the Naming or Event Services.

Another way of disposing of objects is to implement your factories as managers that control the complete life cycle of the objects they create. A client will create an object using a factory's create operations, use the object, and once a client is done it will call a destroy operation on the manager, passing the object's reference as an argument. The manager then releases the object reference held by the object adapter and removes its own reference to the object. Then, if there are no other references to the object, it is ready for disposal by the Java garbage collector. See Figure 15.15.

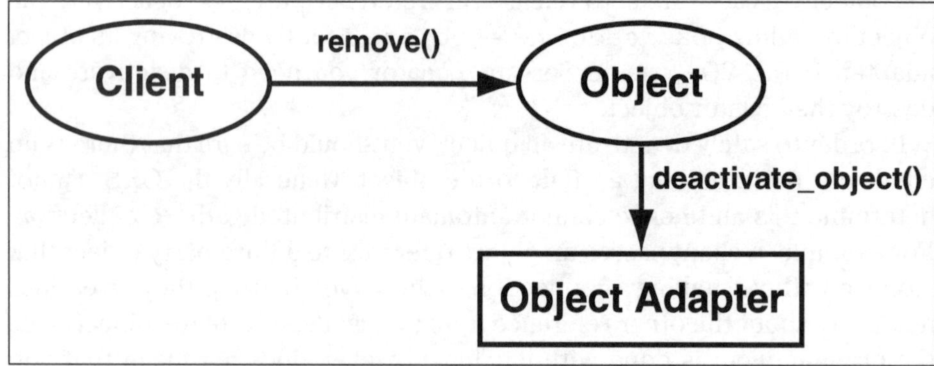


**Figure 15.14** Explicitly destroying objects.

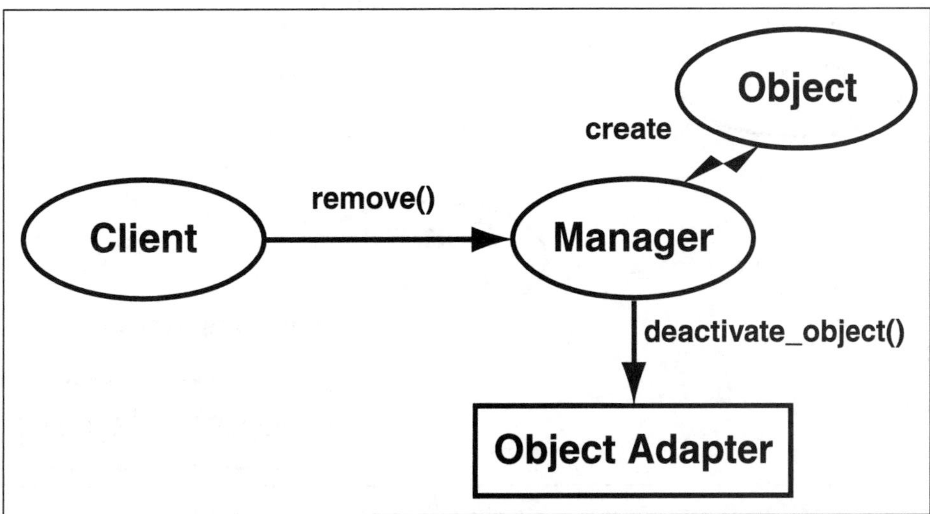


**Figure 15.15** Destroying objects via a manager.

This leaves us with two problems. First, what happens if multiple clients use the same transient object? Second, what needs to be done if a client terminates a connection abnormally, for example, due to a network failure?

A simple but robust approach is to give a transient object a certain lifetime. Once the lifetime has expired, the object is deactivated and made ready for Java garbage collection. The lifetime can be absolute or relative to the last invocation of the object. This mechanism can be easily implemented by a thread that is notified by the factory when the object is created. When using a relative lifetime, the thread must be notified when the object is invoked, for example, by an interceptor or a similar mechanism. The thread will check the elapsed time every so often, and once it passes the predetermined lifetime it will deactivate the object, as shown in Figure 15.16.

This approach has two advantages in addition to those of other garbage collection mechanisms. It aids resource management in the server, cleaning up objects created for clients that have been inactive for a while, for example, while the user is on lunch break. Also, it can assist in implementing security policies that require the time out of a user session after a given time.

## 15.2.2 Design of Management Interfaces

When managing a distributed system, we need to be able to use a client that invokes administrative operations on management interfaces supported by all the important objects in the application. The objects we need to admin-

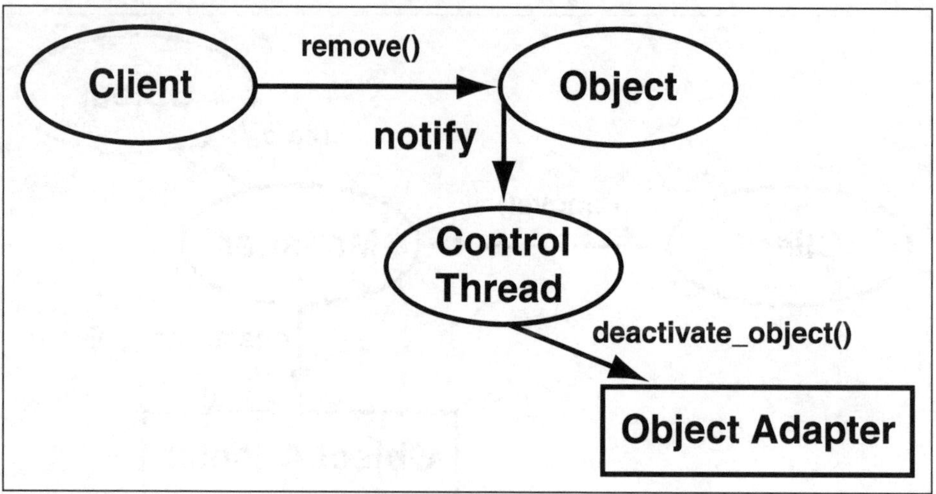


**Figure 15.16** Transient objects with a limited lifetime.

ister must register object references to their management interfaces, for example, in a Naming Service or a Trader. They may also hold references to objects they administer. In particular, factories may keep references to the objects they create. A hierarchy of administration can be set up to allow an administrator to delegate management functions. In the remainder of this section we show this principle by implementing the graceful shutdown of an application by adding some management interfaces to objects and creating a tool that maintains these objects.

We specify an interface called ManagedServer to be implemented by all objects you need to gracefully shut down. These are typically factories and manager objects, for example, session managers. Additionally there is a callback interface Manager that is implemented by a tool that you or a system operator would use to control the shutdown. Figure 15.17 illustrates the interfaces and their interactions.

As is shown in the following IDL, the interface ManagedServer has an operation prepareShutdown() that is called by the Manager object in the management tool we implement in section 15.2.3. It provides the IOR of a Manager object as an argument. Once the prepareShutdown() method has been called, the receiving object prepares its graceful shutdown, which typically includes the following:

- The object makes itself invisible; for example, it deregisters itself from the Naming Service, Trading Service, or a proprietary directory service. Now potential clients can't find the object anymore.

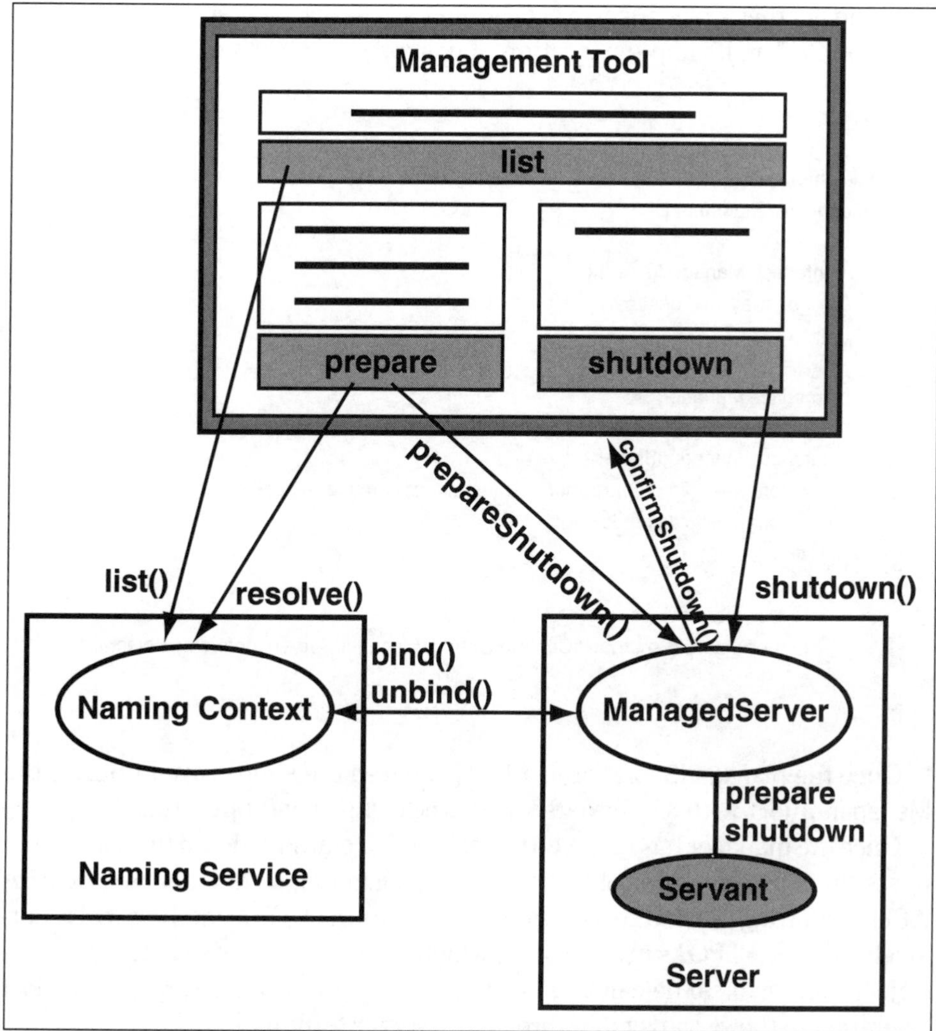


**Figure 15.17** Life cycle management.

- The object recursively shuts down the objects it controls in a graceful manner. The meaning of graceful here is a bit vague because it depends very much on the application. We have defined a separate interface ManagedObject that provides a destroy() operation for this purpose. If, for example, the initial object is a session manager, it makes all the session objects gracefully shut down by calling destroy(). This could mean that a session continues to be active until its client terminates the session or the session times out. All the objects controlled by the ManagedServer object should be deactivated. This means that a ManagedObject should call `deactivate_object()` on the POA in its implementation of destroy().

```
module com {
...
module chapter15 {
    module management {

        interface ManagedObject {
            oneway void destroy();
        };

        interface Manager;

        interface ManagedServer {
            oneway void prepareShutdown( in Manager managementTool );
            oneway void shutdown();
        };

        interface Manager {
            oneway void shutdownConfirmation( in ManagedServer confirmingObject );
        };
}; ... };
```

Once the ManagedServer object has prepared the shutdown it notifies the Manager object with a call to its shutdownConfirmation() operation.

Once the manager has received the callback it can shut down the server that hosts the ManagedServer object by calling shutdown(). The standard CORBA API for shutting down a server is `orb.shutdown()`. This method will recursively destroy all POAs in the server, which in turn deactivate all their CORBA objects, and makes the call to `orb.run()` return. If `orb.run()` is the last operation in the server's main thread, the server terminates.

Special care needs to be taken when a server hosts a number of independent objects. If the `shutdown()` method is invoked on just one of those objects it shuts down the entire server. Some other objects hosted by this server might not have a chance to prepare themselves for a shutdown. To avoid this problem, there should be a primary object per server that directly or indirectly controls all the other objects on the server. This object should be the only one implementing the ManagedServer interface.

## 15.2.3 Implementing a Management Tool

In order to monitor the objects supporting the ManagedServer interface, we need to have a management client that is run by an administrator when the application needs to be shut down. In this section we present the implementation of such a management tool.

Our tool is a client of the interface ManagedServer and an implementation of the interface Manager. We adopt a convention that ManagedServer objects from a particular application register themselves in the same context in the Naming Service. We see this registration in section 15.2.4. The tool allows users to nominate the Naming Context used by the objects they want to manage. It creates a list of all the managed objects bound in that context and allows the user to select objects to prepare for shutdown. When the objects call back to indicate that they are ready, it will shut down the server. The tool is composed of two classes:

- `ManagementTool`—extends the Java `Frame` class and creates and initializes instances of the other class
- `ManagerImpl`—implements the Manager interface and deals with all the GUI coordination

The class `ManagementTool` extends the class `Frame` and implements the interface `WindowListener`. Our implementation of the `WindowListener` interface is trivial, and we have omitted it here because it has no relevance to CORBA.

```
package com.wiley.compbooks.brose.chapter15.management;

import java.awt.*;
import java.awt.event.*;
import org.omg.CORBA.*;
import org.omg.PortableServer.*;

public class ManagementTool
    extends Frame
    implements WindowListener {

    public ManagementTool() {
        super( "CORBA Management Tool" );
        addWindowListener(this);
        setSize( 450, 275 );
    }

    // default implementation of the interface WindowListener

    public static void main( String[] args ) {
        ORB orb;
        POA poa;
        try {
            orb = ORB.init(args, null);
            poa = POAHelper.narrow(
                orb.resolve_initial_references("RootPOA"));
```

```
            ManagementTool managementTool = new ManagementTool();
            managementTool.setVisible(true);
            ManagerImpl manager =
                new ManagerImpl( managementTool );

            poa.servant_to_reference( manager );
            poa.the_POAManager().activate();
        }
        catch( Exception ex ) {
            System.err.println(ex);
        }
    }
}
```

In the static `main()` method of the class `ManagementTool` we create an instance of the class itself and make it visible on the screen. Then we create an instance `manager` of class `ManagerImpl`, passing a reference to the `ManagementTool` to its constructor. Finally, we create a CORBA object from `manager` and activate it so that it can pass its reference to the `prepareShutdown()` method of the managed objects and receive callbacks.

The class `ManagerImpl` is the core of the maintenance tool. It is an implementation of the callback interface, keeps the state of the managed objects, and controls the GUI. Its implementation performs the following actions to shut down an application:

- Look up objects in a specified naming context
- Select objects for shutdown
- Call `prepareShutdown()` on selected objects
- Wait for the callbacks that confirm the shutdown preparation
- Call `shutdown()` on prepared objects

Figure 15.18 shows a screen shot of the management tool GUI. This helps in understanding the implementation of the `ManagerImpl` class. The class implements the `ActionListener` interface according to the JDK event model. It declares a number of GUI components and three vectors to contain state information. The vector `candidateObjects` contains all objects found in a particular context that implement the ManagedServer interface. The vector `selectedObjects` contains the objects on which the operation `prepareShutdown()` has been invoked, and the vector `confirmedObjects` contains the objects that made the callback `shutdownConfirmation()`. The hash table `prepared ObjectNames` is used to store the names of prepared objects so that these names can be displayed as ready for shutdown when the objects call back.

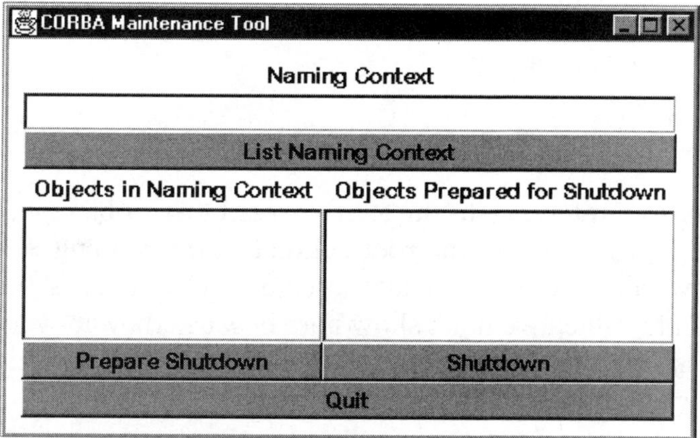


**Figure 15.18** Management tool GUI.

```
package com.wiley.compbooks.brose.chapter15.management;

import java.util.Vector;
import java.util.Hashtable;
import java.awt.*;
import java.awt.event.*;
import org.omg.CORBA.*;
import org.omg.CosNaming.*;

public class ManagerImpl
    extends ManagerPOA
    implements ActionListener {

    private Button prepareButton;
    private Button shutdownButton;
    private Button getContextButton;
    private Button quitButton;

    private TextField ncTextField;
    private TextField cbTextField;

    private Panel mainPanel;

    private java.awt.Container managementTool;
    private Manager manager;
    private ManagedServer managed;

    private Vector candidateObjects;
    private Vector selectedObjects;
    private Vector confirmedObjects;
    private Hashtable preparedObjectNames;
```

```
private org.omg.CORBA.Object obj;
private NamingContextExt root;
private NamingContextExt context;

private List candidateList;
private List confirmedList;
```

The constructor stores a reference to the `ManagementTool` object, initializes the ORB and the reference to the root context of the Naming Service, and creates new vector objects. It also creates and initializes the various GUI components, which we don't show here because they are very lengthy and do not assist in understanding CORBA concepts. The full code is on the Web site at www.wiley.com/compbooks/brose.

```
public ManagerImpl( java.awt.Container managementTool ) {

    this.managementTool = managementTool;

    ORB orb = ORB.init( (String[])null, null);
    try {
        root = NamingContextExtHelper.narrow(
            orb.resolve_initial_references("NameService"));
    }
    catch( org.omg.CORBA.ORBPackage.InvalidName in ) {}

    selectedObjects = new Vector();
    confirmedObjects = new Vector();
    preparedObjectNames = new Hashtable();
    // lots of code to create and initialize the GUI
}
```

The implementation of the method `actionsPerformed()` (defined in the Java interface `ActionListener`) controls the behavior of the class. The tool is driven by events from the GUI. In this application these are action events caused by pressing one of the four buttons we have created in the `Frame`.

If the button labeled `List Naming Context` is pressed, we get the value of the text field `ncTextField`, which is expected to contain a string describing a naming context. Then we obtain and display all objects bound in this naming context, as long as they are of the interface type ManagedServer. This behavior is encapsulated by the method `getContext()`.

The button labeled `Prepare Shutdown` leads to the invocation of the method `prepare()`, which invokes the prepareShutdown() operation on a selected object. The button labeled `Shutdown` invokes the method `shutdown()`, which in turn invokes the operation shutdown() on a selected object. The `Quit` button causes the application to exit.

```
public void actionPerformed( ActionEvent ev ) {

    if(ev.getActionCommand().equals("getContext"))
        getContext( ncTextField.getText() );
    if(ev.getActionCommand().equals("prepare"))
        prepare();
    if(ev.getActionCommand().equals("shutdown"))
        shutdown();
    if(ev.getActionCommand().equals("quit"))
        System.exit(0);
}
```

The method `getContext()` gets a string from the text field, which is expected to be a string name for a naming context of type CosNaming::NamingContextExt. This means that we expect an implementation of the Interoperable Naming Service so that we can easily convert between internal names and their string representations using the conventions introduced in Chapter 7, "Discovering Services." We try to resolve the string to a naming context object. If this doesn't succeed, we print a message in the text field and return.

If a naming context is resolved, we remove all entries from the candidate list and create a new vector for candidate objects. Now we invoke the list() operation on the naming context object. Since the operation has two out parameters we have to create the appropriate Holder objects, `BindingListHolder` and `BindingIteratorHolder`.

```
public void getContext( String contextString ) {

    if( contextString == null )
        return;

    try {
        // get context
        context = NamingContextExtHelper.narrow(
            root.resolve_str( contextString ) );

        candidateList.removeAll();
        candidateObjects = new Vector();

        // list bindings in context
        BindingListHolder blHolder = new BindingListHolder();
        BindingIteratorHolder biHolder =
            new BindingIteratorHolder();
        BindingHolder bHolder = new BindingHolder();
        ManagedServer m;

        context.list( 2, blHolder, biHolder );
```

We invoke the list() operation with the how_many parameter set to 2. This is done only to demonstrate the use of the binding iterator, even when there is a small number of objects. A production implementation would set the value far higher because the binding list is more effective than the iterator, using one remote call rather than many. The binding iterator would be seen as an overflow mechanism.

```
for( int i = 0; i < blHolder.value.length; i++ ) {
    m = ManagedServerHelper.narrow( context.resolve(
        blHolder.value[i].binding_name ) );
    if( m != null ) {
        candidateList.add(
            blHolder.value[i].binding_name[0].id );
        candidateObjects.addElement( m );
    }
}
```

We process the list and then the iterator, resolving all the names they contain. Because the resolve() operation returns object references of type CORBA::Object, we try to narrow these references to objects of type ManagedServer. Only if we succeed and `narrow()` returns a nonnull reference do we add the reference to the vector and its name to the candidate list.

```
if( biHolder.value != null ) {
    while( biHolder.value.next_one( bHolder ) ) {
        m = ManagedServerHelper.narrow(
            context.resolve(
                bHolder.value.binding_name ) );
        if( m != null ) {
            candidateList.add(
                bHolder.value.binding_name[0].id );
            candidateObjects.addElement( m );
        }
    }
}
```

When we are done with the binding iterator we call its destroy() operation. This notifies the iterator that it can clean up its resources and deactivate itself. Finally, we close the `try` block and catch exceptions.

```
if( biHolder.value != null )
    biHolder.value.destroy();
}
catch( SystemException system_exception ) {
    System.err.println( system_exception.toString() );
}
catch( UserException naming_exception ) {
```

```
            ncTextField.setText( "context "+contextString+
                                 " not found, try again" );
        }
        managementTool.validate();
}
```

The `prepare()` method starts by getting the index of the selected item from the list. If no selection has been a made, we just return. Otherwise we remove the item from the candidate list and the candidate vector. To be able to add the object's name to the list of prepared objects when it calls back later, we store its name in a hash table. Finally, we invoke `prepareShutdown()` on the selected object. If a CORBA system exception is thrown, we don't do anything because it is likely that we obtained a stale entry from the Naming Service.

```
public void prepare() {

    int selectedIndex = candidateList.getSelectedIndex();
    if( selectedIndex == -1 ) // no selection
        return;

    String name = candidateList.getItem( selectedIndex );
    candidateList.remove( selectedIndex );
    managed = (ManagedServer)candidateObjects.elementAt(
        selectedIndex );
    preparedObjectNames.put( managed, name );

    candidateObjects.removeElementAt( selectedIndex );
    selectedObjects.addElement( managed );

    try {
        managed.prepareShutdown( _this() );
    }
    catch(SystemException system_exception ) {
        // don't do anything, it's likely to be a stale entry
        // just remove name from the list which we do anyway
    }
    managementTool.validate();
}
```

The method `confirm()` is invoked by the implementation of the Manager interface when it receives a callback from a managed object. We add the object's name, which we retrieve from the hash table where we stored it, to the confirmed list. We also remove the object reference from the selected vector and add it to the confirmed vector.

```
public void confirm( org.omg.CORBA.Object confirmedObject ) {
    confirmedList.add(
```

```
            (String)preparedObjects.remove( confirmedObject ));
        selectedObjects.removeElement(
            (ManagedServer)confirmedObject );
        confirmedObjects.addElement( confirmedObject );
        managementTool.validate();
    }
```

The last method is `shutdown()`. Again we get the index of the selected list item and check if an item has actually been selected. We get the object that corresponds to the selected item and invoke `shutdown()` on it. If a CORBA system exception is thrown, it is most likely that the object has already been deactivated, for example, by calling `shutdown()` on another object in the same server. Anyway, because the object isn't there, we have achieved the shutdown and don't do anything.

```
    public void shutdown() {
        int selectedIndex = confirmedList.getSelectedIndex();
        if( selectedIndex == -1 ) // no selection
            return;

        try {
            ((ManagedServer)confirmedObjects.elementAt(
                selectedIndex )).shutdown();
        }
        catch(SystemException system_exception ) {
            // don't do anything, object is already gone ...
        }

        confirmedList.remove( selectedIndex );
        confirmedObjects.removeElementAt( selectedIndex );

        managementTool.validate();
    }
```

Finally, we remove the object's name from the list and its reference from the vector and update the GUI.

## 15.2.4 Implementing Managed Objects

To make the whole management approach work we also have to implement the ManagedServer interface at selected objects for the shutdown of their host server. As an example, we have selected the Room object from the application we introduced in Chapter 8. We create an interface called ManagedRoom that inherits the Room interface as well as the ManagedServer interface:

```
#include "../../chapter8/RoomBooking.idl"
#include "Management.idl"

module com {
...
module chapter15 {
module management {
module example {

    interface ManagedRoom :
        com::wiley::compbooks::brose::chapter8::roomBooking::Room,
        management::ManagedServer
    {};

}; .. };
```

The implementation of the interface is very similar to the original Room implementation. We have modified only the constructor and added methods for the implementation of the operations of the management interfaces. Besides the room name, the constructor also has a reference to a NamingContext object. We create this NamingContext object in the server and pass its reference to the constructor.

```
package com.wiley.compbooks.brose.chapter15.management.example;

import org.omg.CORBA.*;
import org.omg.CosNaming.*;
import com.wiley.compbooks.brose.chapter8.roomBooking.*;
import com.wiley.compbooks.brose.chapter8.roomBooking.RoomPackage.*;
import com.wiley.compbooks.brose.chapter15.management.*;

class ManagedRoomImpl
    extends ManagedRoomPOA {

    private String name;
    private Meeting[] meetings;
    private Manager mt;
    private NamingContextExt context;

    private Shutter shutter;
    private boolean shutdown = false;

    // constructor
    ManagedRoomImpl( String name, NamingContextExt context ) {
        this.name = name;
        this.context = context;
        meetings = new Meeting[ Room.MaxSlots ];
        shutter = new Shutter();
    }
```

An interesting addition is the field `shutter`, which references a separate thread used for shutting down the ORB. The constructor creates this thread and initializes the `shutter` field. This separate thread is required because it is not possible to call `orb.shutdown()` from within an operation context, for example, a thread executing the implementation of `shutdown()`. An attempt to do so would result in an BAD_INV_ORDER exception. The only way to achieve the desired effect is to let the method `shutdown()` wake up a blocked thread that can then make the call to `orb.shutdown()`.

The inner class Shutter does this for us when woken up by a notification:

```
public class Shutter
    extends Thread {

    public Shutter() {
        start();
    }

    public synchronized void run(){
        try {
            while( ! shutdown )
                wait();
            _orb().shutdown(true);
        }
        catch( Exception e) {
            e.printStackTrace();
        }
    }
}
```

In the implementation of the `prepareShutdown()` method, we unbind the object from the Naming Service so that it becomes invisible to potential new clients. Because of the simplicity of the room server, we don't have to do any other preparation to shut down, so we immediately make the call-back to the manager object.

```
public void prepareShutdown( Manager mt ) {

    this.mt = mt;
    try {
        context.unbind( context.to_name(
            "BuildingApplications/Rooms/" + name ) );
    }
    catch(UserException ue) {
        System.err.println(ue);
    }
    mt.shutdownConfirmation(
        ManagedServerHelper.narrow( _this() ) );
}
```

The Managed Room's `shutdown()` notifies the shutter thread, which in turn invokes the `shutdown()` method on the ORB, which makes `orb.run()` return, allowing the server to clean up and exit.

```
public void shutdown() {
    shutdown = true;
    synchronized( shutter ) {
        shutter.notify();
    }
}
// Room attribute and operations
...
```

The implementation of the Room interface's attribute and operations is the same as before. If we had used the Tie approach in the application in Chapter 8 we could have simply extended the Room implementation class because we wouldn't need to extend the skeleton class. We will also use the inheritance approach for the Room object, which prevents us from inheriting the existing Room implementation class.

The server implementation is nearly the same as in Chapter 8; it just instantiates ManagedRoom objects instead of Room objects and prints a message after `orb.run()` saying that the server is exiting.

## 15.2.5 Using the Management Tool

When you use the management tool to shut down Room servers you see the GUI populated, as shown in Figures 15.19 and 15.20. Once you have started the Naming Service and a number of managed rooms—Training Room, Meeting Room, and Board Room—you can shut down their servers.

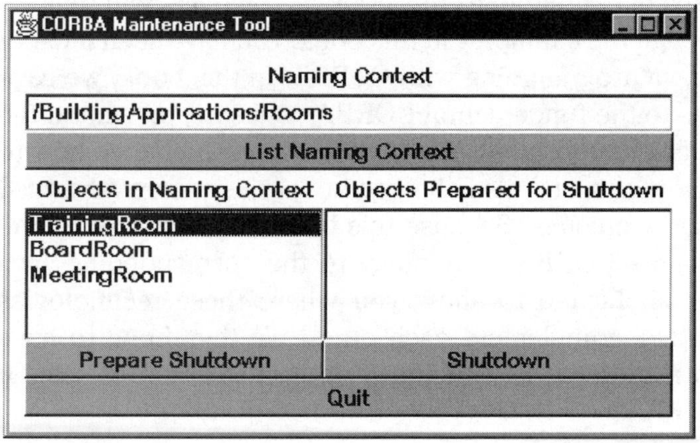

**Figure 15.19** Objects selected for preparing to shut down.

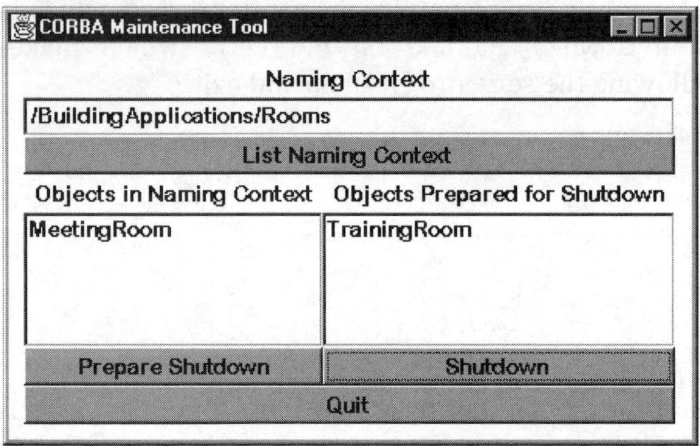


**Figure 15.20** Objects selected for shut down.

Figure 15.19 shows the three managed rooms with the Training Room selected for shutdown preparation. Figure 15.20 shows the situation where we have called `prepareShutdown()` on the Training Room, and the Board Room has already exited.

## 15.3 Summary

In this chapter, we presented a number of design patterns and implementation techniques that, together with the advanced POA configurations presented in Chapter 10, "Practical POA Programming," enable you to design your applications for both performance and scalability. Moreover, this chapter explained a few simple approaches to managing your CORBA applications.

The material covered here completes this book. If you have read thus far and have worked through the examples in this book, you have seen most of what's important in Java programming with CORBA. In this book, we gave detailed introductions to the fundamental CORBA concepts, presented the latest versions of the most important OMG specifications, explained how to program the central services, and also showed how to use more advanced CORBA programming techniques. Because this book is for Java programmers, we have compared CORBA technology to the corresponding Java technology wherever applicable to show you where these technologies compete and where they complement each other. We thus hope to have given you all the information to make the most of this ideal combination of worlds—Java and CORBA.

# Glossary

## Acronyms

**AB:** Architecture Board.
**AOM:** Active Object Map.
**API:** Application Programming Interface.
**BOA:** Basic Object Adapter.
**CCM:** CORBA Component Model.
**CGI:** Common Gateway Interface.
**CIDL:** Component Implementation Definition Language.
**CORBA:** Common Object Request Broker Architecture.
**DCE:** Distributed Computing Environment.
**DCE-CIOP:** DCE Common Inter-ORB Protocol.
**DII:** Dynamic Invocation Interface.
**DIS:** Draft International Standard.
**DSI:** Dynamic Skeleton Interface.
**DTC:** Domain Technology Committee.
**DTD:** Document Type Definition.
**EJB:** Enterprise Java Beans.
**ESIOP:** Environment-Specific Inter-ORB Protocols.
**EUSIG:** End User Special Interest Group.
**FDTF:** Financial Domain Task Force.
**FTF:** Finalization Task Force.
**GIOP:** General Inter-ORB Protocol.
**IDL:** Interface Definition Language.
**IIOP:** Internet Inter-ORB Protocol.
**IMCDTF:** Interactive Multimedia and Electronic Commerce Domain Task Force.
**INS:** Interoperable Naming Service.
**IOR:** Interoperable Object Reference.
**IR:** Interface Repository.
**ISIG:** Internet Special Interest Group.
**ISO:** International Standards Organization.
**J2EE:** Java 2 Enterprise Edition.
**J2SE:** Java 2 Standard Edition.
**JMS:** Java Message Service.
**JNDI:** Java Naming and Directory Interface.
**JRMP:** Java Remote Method Protocol.

**JSIG:** Japan Special Interest Group.
**JSP:** Java Server Pages.
**LDAP:** Light-weight Directory Access Protocol.
**MDTF:** Manufacturing Domain Task Force.
**OBV:** Objects-By-Value.
**ODP:** Open Distributed Processing.
**OMA:** Object Management Architecture.
**OMG:** Object Management Group.
**ORB:** Object Request Broker.
**PIDL:** Pseudo-IDL.
**PKI:** Public Key Infrastructure.
**POA:** Portable Object Adapter.
**PSDL:** Persistent State Definition Language.
**PSS:** Persistent State Service.
**PTC:** Platform Technology Committee.
**RFI:** Request For Information.
**RFP:** Request For Proposal.
**RMI:** Remote Method Invocation.
**RTSIG:** Real Time Special Interest Group.
**SIG:** Special Interest Group.
**SSL:** Secure Socket Layer.
**TSIG:** Transportation Special Interest Group.
**URL:** Uniform Resource Locator.
**UUID:** Universal Unique Identifier.
**XML:** Extensible Markup Language.

# Terms

**Access Control:** Verifying a caller's authorization to access objects.
**Activation:** *See* Object Activation.
**Any:** Predefined data type in OMG IDL that can contain self-describing values of *any* type.
**Architecture Board:** An OMG board that reviews proposals and technology for conformance to the OMA.
**Auditing:** Keeping records of which principals perform which invocations on secured objects.
**Authentication:** Verifying that principals are who they claim to be.
**Basic Object Adapter:** The first specification of an object adapter in the CORBA standard. Its interface is considered incomplete, and ORB vendors have used divergent implementations to complete its functionality. Now deprecated and replaced by the Portable Object Adapter.

**Byte-code:** Intermediate representation of programming language code. The Java byte-code is very popular, and virtual machines that can execute Java byte-code are available for most hardware platforms and operating systems.

**Certificate:** A digitally signed data structure. Usually binds a public key to a name (X.509 certificate).

**Common Facilities:** *See* CORBAfacilities.

**Common Gateway Interface:** Interface at HTTP servers that allows access to resources, e.g., databases or programs outside the server.

**Common Object Request Broker Architecture:** Architecture for distributed object systems defined by the OMG.

**Common Object Services:** *See* CORBAservices.

**Container:** Run-time environment for CORBA Components. The same term is used for the run-time environment of Enterprise Java Beans.

**CORBAfacilities:** A set of published specifications for application-level object services that are applicable across industry domains, e.g., Printing Facility, Systems Management Facility.

**CORBAnet:** Permanent showcase to demonstrate IIOP-based ORB interoperability sponsored by the OMG and most ORB vendors. CORBAnet is hosted by the Distributed Systems Technology Centre in Brisbane, Australia. CORBAnet can be accessed at http://www.corba.net.

**CORBAservices:** Set of published specifications for fundamental services assisting all object implementations, e.g., Naming Service, Event Service, Object Trading Service.

**Core Object Model:** The fundamental object-oriented model in the OMA that defines the basic concepts on which CORBA is based.

**Credential:** An encapsulation of a principal's identity and security attributes.

**DCE Common Inter-ORB Protocol:** Environment Specific Interoperability Protocol based on DCE. The first ESIOP adopted by the OMG.

**Distributed Computing Environment:** Distributed middleware developed under the control of the Open Group, formerly Open Software Foundation (OSF).

**Domain Task Force:** Group in the OMG responsible for specifying technologies relevant to a particular industry sector. It reports to the Domain Technical Committee.

**Domain Technology Committee:** OMG Committee that supervises several Domain Task Forces concerned with technology specification for particular domains.

**Draft International Standard:** ISO defines phases through which a potential International Standard must pass. Draft International Standard is the penultimate phase.

**Dynamic Invocation Interface:** Interface defined in CORBA that allows the invocation of operations on object references without compile-time knowledge of the objects' interface types.

**Dynamic Skeleton Interface:** Interface defined in CORBA that allows servers to dynamically interpret incoming invocation requests of arbitrary operations.

**Environment-Specific Inter-ORB Protocols:** CORBA interoperability protocols that use data formats other than the ones specified in the GIOP. *See also* DCE Common Inter-ORB Protocol.

**Firewall:** Networking software that prevents certain types of network connections and traffic for security reasons.

**General Inter-ORB Protocol:** Protocol that belongs to the mandatory CORBA Interoperability protocol specifications. It defines the format of the protocol data units that can be sent via any transport. Currently there is only one transport protocol defined, namely, IIOP.

**Implementation Repository:** Vendor-specific mechanism to start up CORBA server processes on demand.

**Interceptor:** Object called by the ORB at specific times during request processing. Used to manipulate Service Context.

**Interface Definition Language:** Language to specify interfaces of objects independent of particular programming language representations. OMG has defined OMG IDL.

**Interface Repository:** Component of CORBA that stores type information and makes it available through standard interfaces at run time. Typically, an Interface Repository is populated by an IDL compiler when processing IDL specifications.

**Interoperable Object Reference:** Object reference that identifies objects independent of the ORB environment in which they have been created.

**JavaBean:** A Java class that supports certain conventions to allow it to be inspected and used as a component by visual application builder environments.

**Language Mapping:** A Mapping of OMG IDL to a target programming language.

**Marshal:** Conversion of data into a programming-language and architecture-independent format.

**Nonrepudiation:** Creation, transmission, and storage of irrefutable evidence that a principal performed an action.

**Notification:** A message that informs about the occurrence of an event.

**Object Activation:** Performed by the POA. Associates an Object ID with a Servant.

**Object Adapter:** The ORB component that at invocation time locates the correct method in the correct programming language object based on an object reference. It is also informed by servers when objects are ready to be invoked.

**Object Deactivation:** Performed by the POA. Destroys the association of an Object ID with a Servant.

**Object Management Architecture:** The overall architecture and roadmap of the OMG, of which CORBA forms a part.

**Object Management Group:** An international industry consortium with over 800 members that specifies an object-oriented framework for distributed computing, including CORBA.

**Object Reference:** Opaque data structure that identifies a single CORBA object and enables clients to invoke operations on it, regardless of the object's location. Objects can have multiple object references.

**Object Request Broker:** The central component of the OMA that transmits operation invocation requests to distributed objects and returns the results to the requester.

**Object Services:** *See* CORBAservices.

**OMA Reference Model:** The structural model defining roles for the various components taking part in the OMA. It identifies five groups of objects to be specified: Object Request Broker, Object Services, Common Facilities, Domain Objects, and Application Objects.

**Open Distributed Processing:** Group within ISO that is concerned with the standardization of open distributed systems.

**Platform Technology Committee:** OMG Committee that supervises several Task Forces concerned with specifying the ORB platform infrastructure.

**Portable Object Adapter:** An object adapter with standard interfaces to associate CORBA object references to programming language object instances. The replacement for the Basic Object Adapter.

**Principal:** A user or system component with a verifiable identity.

**Private Key:** Private part of a key pair. Can be used to sign messages and to decrypt messages that were encrypted with the holder's public key.

**Pseudo-IDL:** IDL Interface definitions for components of ORB infrastructure that will not be implemented as CORBA objects.

**Public Key:** Public part of a key pair. Can be widely distributed to allow the verification of signatures made with the corresponding private key or to encrypt messages sent to the holder of the private key.

**Request For Information:** A formal request from an OMG body for submissions of information relating to a specific technology area.

**Request For Proposal:** A formal request from an OMG body for a submission of a technology specification in IDL with English semantics.

**Secure Socket Layer:** A protocol that extends TCP/IP sockets by providing authentication and encryption of communications.

**Servant:** Programming Language construct that implements IDL operations. A Java object.

**Servant Activator:** A Servant Manager that is used by a POA when activating CORBA objects. Only used with the RETAIN policy.

**Servant Locator:** A Servant Manager that is used in conjunction with the NON_RETAIN policy. Returns a Servant.

**Servant Manager:** An object associated with a POA that is used to activate or locate a Servant.

**Service Context:** Opaque data delivered with requests. Used to provide service-specific client context to the Servant, for example, Transactional Contexts.

**Special Interest Group:** Member group in the OMG that has a topic of interest in common. These groups report findings to Committees within the OMG or to the Architecture Board.

**TypeCode:** A run-time representation of an IDL type.

**Universal Unique Identifier:** Used in DCE to identify an entity.

**Unmarshal:** The inverse of marshaling.

# Index

*Page references followed by italic* t *indicate material in tables.*

**F**

## S